P9-DBK-600

Basic Bankruptcy Law
for Paralegals

EDITORIAL ADVISORS

Deborah E. Bouchoux, Esq.
Georgetown University

Therese A. Cannon
Executive Vice President
Western Association of Schools and College Accrediting Commission
for Senior Colleges and Universities

Katherine A. Currier
Chair, Department of Paralegal and Legal Studies
Elms College

Susan M. Sullivan
Director, Graduate Career Programs
University of San Diego

Laurel A. Vietzen
Professor and Instructional Coordinator
Elgin Community College

LIBRARY OF ROWAN COLLEGE
AT BURLINGTON COUNTY

ASPEN COLLEGE SERIES

Basic Bankruptcy Law for Paralegals

Eighth Edition

David L. Buchbinder

Member, California, Pennsylvania,
and New Jersey Bars

Wolters Kluwer
Law & Business

Copyright © 2011 David L. Buchbinder.
Published by Wolters Kluwer Law & Business in New York.

Wolters Kluwer Law & Business serves customers worldwide
with CCH, Aspen Publishers, and Kluwer Law International
products. (www.wolterskluwerlb.com)

No part of this publication may be reproduced or transmitted
in any form or by any means, electronic or mechanical, including photocopy, recording, or utilized by any information storage or retrieval system, without written permission from the
publisher. For information about permissions or to request
permissions online, visit us at www.wolterskluwerlb.com, or
a written request may be faxed to our permissions department
at 212-771-0803.

To contact Customer Service, e-mail customer.service@
wolterskluwer.com, call 1-800-234-1660, fax 1-800-901-9075,
or mail correspondence to:

> Wolters Kluwer Law & Business
> Attn: Order Department
> PO Box 990
> Frederick, MD 21705

Printed in the United States of America.

1 2 3 4 5 6 7 8 9 0

ISBN 978-0-7355-0786-9

Library of Congress Cataloging-in-Publication Data

Buchbinder, David L.
   Basic bankruptcy law for paralegals / David L. Buchbinder. — 8th ed.
     p. cm.
   Includes bibliographical references and index.
   ISBN 978-0-7355-0786-9
   1. Bankruptcy — United States. 2. Legal assistants — United
States — Handbooks, manuals, etc. I. Title.
   KF1524.85.B758 2011
   346.7307'8 — dc22
                               2011013972

About Wolters Kluwer Law & Business

Wolters Kluwer Law & Business is a leading global provider of intelligent information and digital solutions for legal and business professionals in key specialty areas, and respected educational resources for professors and law students. Wolters Kluwer Law & Business connects legal and business professionals as well as those in the education market with timely, specialized authoritative content and information-enabled solutions to support success through productivity, accuracy and mobility.

Serving customers worldwide, Wolters Kluwer Law & Business products include those under the Aspen Publishers, CCH, Kluwer Law International, Loislaw, Best Case, ftwilliam.com and MediRegs family of products.

CCH products have been a trusted resource since 1913, and are highly regarded resources for legal, securities, antitrust and trade regulation, government contracting, banking, pension, payroll, employment and labor, and healthcare reimbursement and compliance professionals.

Aspen Publishers products provide essential information to attorneys, business professionals and law students. Written by preeminent authorities, the product line offers analytical and practical information in a range of specialty practice areas from securities law and intellectual property to mergers and acquisitions and pension/benefits. Aspen's trusted legal education resources provide professors and students with high-quality, up-to-date and effective resources for successful instruction and study in all areas of the law.

Kluwer Law International products provide the global business community with reliable international legal information in English. Legal practitioners, corporate counsel and business executives around the world rely on Kluwer Law journals, looseleafs, books, and electronic products for comprehensive information in many areas of international legal practice.

Loislaw is a comprehensive online legal research product providing legal content to law firm practitioners of various specializations. Loislaw provides attorneys with the ability to quickly and efficiently find the necessary legal information they need, when and where they need it, by facilitating access to primary law as well as state-specific law, records, forms and treatises.

Best Case Solutions is the leading bankruptcy software product to the bankruptcy industry. It provides software and workflow tools to flawlessly streamline petition preparation and the electronic filing process, while timely incorporating ever-changing court requirements.

ftwilliam.com offers employee benefits professionals the highest quality plan documents (retirement, welfare and non-qualified) and government forms (5500/PBGC, 1099 and IRS) software at highly competitive prices.

MediRegs products provide integrated health care compliance content and software solutions for professionals in healthcare, higher education and life sciences, including professionals in accounting, law and consulting.

Wolters Kluwer Law & Business, a division of Wolters Kluwer, is headquartered in New York. Wolters Kluwer is a market-leading global information services company focused on professionals.

To my beloved father, Ralph

Summary of Contents

Contents

Preface

This book has evolved from a need to develop a nuts-and-bolts description of the bankruptcy system written to be understood by nonlawyers.

My primary intent has been to design this text as a basic primer for legal assistants or paralegal students to help them grasp the practical aspects of representing debtors or creditors within the bankruptcy system. To meet this challenge, I have explained practice and theory together in as concise a format as possible. I have chosen this approach because practice is almost always dictated by the underlying theory, and it is easier to learn a practice when one has been provided with the basic theory behind the practice.

In subsequent editions I have listened to the many thoughtful comments of paralegal instructors and students from all over the country, some of whom have gone to exceptional effort to hunt me down, to enhance the practical nature of the text, and to further simplify the subtleties and nuances of the Bankruptcy Code and system. Each new edition updates and revises the text to keep abreast of all statutory, case law, and rule changes that regularly take place.

Paralegals are invaluable in the bankruptcy system. Under proper legal supervision, paralegals can efficiently perform various tasks for clients at a substantial savings. Because much of bankruptcy practice is routine, presenting these routines and the reasons for them will help a paralegal be properly prepared to assist in a debtor or creditor bankruptcy practice. The introduction describes the role of paralegals in the bankruptcy system. The student should read the introduction twice, once at the beginning of the course and again at the end. In this way, the material will act as both an introduction and final review of the course.

It has not been my intent to analyze the complex subtleties of the Bankruptcy Code and its attendant case law interpretation, but rather to describe the routine events that occur in all bankruptcy proceedings, events that normally occur without dispute or litigation. These events account for a majority of bankruptcy practice, much of which is not problematic. Thus, law students and nonbankruptcy attorneys may also find this text a useful reference tool for finding the answers to common bankruptcy questions.

For example, by reading chapter 4 of the text and the forms accompanying chapter 4 in the forms disk, any student or practitioner can quickly learn the basic principles of providing notices to creditors or parties in interest in bankruptcy proceedings, and learn about the documents and timing involved.

My philosophical goal in undertaking this work has been to describe the Bankruptcy Code as a comprehensive system of debtor relief and debt collection, as well as the organization and practical functioning of this system. I am honored to have been given the opportunity to evolve the original work from the laboratory of time and use.

Upon completing this undertaking I have reached the inescapable conclusion that the Bankruptcy Code exists first and foremost as a tool of debt collection and not of debtor relief. Conversely, the debtor relief provided by the Bankruptcy Code is among the most liberal relief that has existed in the evolution of bankruptcy laws through Western history. The 2005 legislation will be perceived by many to restrict debtor relief while enhancing the debt collection aspects of the Code, particularly in consumer bankruptcy cases.

This book has also been prepared with the secondary purpose of aiding creditor representatives in understanding how the bankruptcy system may be properly utilized as a debt collection device to increase overall recovery rates.

Finally, I am optimistic that having described the Bankruptcy Code in this manner I may aid, however slightly, in enhancing the efficiency of the system.

David L. Buchbinder

April 2011

Acknowledgments

Acknowledgments to the First Edition

In early 1987, my associate Lauren Austin made a wild suggestion that I tape record my legal-assistant bankruptcy course at the University of San Diego and then transform the spoken word into a written text. After some thought, I decided to give it a whirl. My legal assistant at the time, Vicki Johnson, assisted me in the recording of my class during the spring of 1987.

Some 3,000 hours, 28 months, and five drafts later I take pleasure in gratefully acknowledging the encouragement and assistance of the many people who have aided me in this project.

My loyal long-distance typist, Joan Jackson, has been invaluable from the beginning of this project. She has been ably assisted by Lynn Williamson, Julie Rasmussen, and Mary Lou Staight, particularly in connection with the final manuscript draft. Numerous members of my staff have offered aid and sustenance with the footnotes and citation checking. Among them are Flora Calem, Beth Sandler, Adam Nach, and my friend and colleague, Mark R. Nims. Mr. Nims's comments were particularly instructive in helping me prepare a teacher's manual to accompany the text.

Susan Sullivan of the University of San Diego Legal Assistant Program has been a positive and encouraging force throughout. Indeed, but for her giving me an initial opportunity to teach, this book would never have been written.

Many of my colleagues, too numerous to mention individually, have also offered helpful advice and suggestions. I would particularly like to thank Kathryn Infante and Ted Simmons, Estate Administrators for the United States Bankruptcy Court for the Southern District of California, for their assistance. Ms. Infante provided me with the address of every Bankruptcy Court in the United States so the data resulting in the appendices could be obtained. Mr. Simmons regularly provided me with the statistical data contained in the footnotes regarding the numbers of annual bankruptcy filings nationwide. Mr. Larry Ramey of the United States Trustee Office provided me with this data for 1988. (In 2008, anyone can access all of this data on the Internet 24 hours a day, but that's not how it was in the "old days.")

The appendices turned out to be a project within a project. Ms. Austin rendered services above and beyond the call of duty in obtaining local rules from throughout the United States. Then she prepared preliminary tables from her own review of every set of rules. The effort involved has been considerable and the appendices would likely not exist but for her important contributions. Judge Keith M. Lundin of the Middle District of Tennessee gave me considerable encouragement when he caused an early draft of chapter 1, A Short History of Bankruptcy, to be published in the November 1988 issue of the Norton Bankruptcy Advisor.

The editorial staff at Little, Brown and Company has been most pleasant to work with. Richard Heuser, Elizabeth Kenny, Cathryn Capra, and Alistair Nevius have ably guided me through the actual publication preparation and process.

Finally, my thanks and love to my wife Deborah and my son Rafe for tolerating the many evening and weekend hours that have been devoted to this book

Acknowledgments to the Second, Third, Fourth, and Fifth Editions

I would like to thank those whose continuing support and encouragement have helped me bring to fruition the subsequent editions of Practical Guide, now known as Basic Bankruptcy Law for Paralegals.

Lynn Williamson, Julie Rasmussen, and Catherine Forrest provided many skillful services in the manuscript preparation and updating of the appendices for the second edition. Kristen DiPaolo was invaluable in helping me redraft the tutorial for the third edition.

Carolyn O'Sullivan, Betsy Kenny, Carol McGeehan, Jessica Barmack, Anne Starr, and Pat Wakeley of Little, Brown and Company have always been a pleasure to work with.

For the fourth edition, I would like to thank Betsy Kenny for her continuing supervision, and Curt Berkowitz and Barbara Rappaport for their time and care in bringing this edition to press on an expedited basis.

For the fifth edition, I have continued to be ably supervised by Betsy Kenny, Cathi Reinfelder, and Elsie Starbecker in the production process. I have also received invaluable editorial assistance from my friends Mark Gallagher, and William Hanafee III.

I am also grateful for the many constructive comments from instructors and students throughout the country who have kindly taken time to provide me with their thoughts on improving the text. I have made my best efforts to incorporate your suggestions into these latter editions.

Finally, my thanks and love to Deborah and Rafe for their continuing patience for the time it takes to keep these materials up to date.

Acknowledgments to the Sixth Edition

The sixth edition has been daunting. Hard on the heels of the publication of the fifth edition in November 2004, Congress passed the Bankruptcy Abuse Prevention and Consumer Protection Act of 2005, the most radical and sweeping modifications to the Bankruptcy Code since its adoption in 1978. This has required the most thorough revision of this text in record time. I have been most ably assisted in this process through these many months by Betsy Kenny. In the final production, I have been further ably assisted in this rush process by Carmen Corral-Reid. Finally, my thanks and love to Rafe for putting up with me.

Acknowledgments to the Seventh Edition

The seventh edition incorporates the evolution of the BAPCPA statute in case law and actual practice. This is particularly the case in the new area of "means testing," in which case law evolution would be necessary to flesh out the words in the statute. In addition, the means testing form has evolved, along with attendant case law, which now permits a meaningful means testing tutorial chapter.

The seventh edition also incorporates innovations made to the text in development of an abridged edition. The Practice Pointers and Practice Exercises are the invaluable contribution of the abridged edition co-author Robert Cooper. Thank you Robert so very much. Robert also contributed extensively to many of the text revisions.

Betsy Kenny and I have been working on this material together for almost 20 years. That speaks for itself. Thank you Betsy.

Acknowledgments to the Eighth Edition

I would like to thank Betsy Kenny at Aspen Publishing for her eternal editorial assistance. I would also like to thank Robert Cooper for his contributions to the work through the Abridged Edition. I would like to thank Jay Harward at Newgen for his tutelage during the production stage of this edition. Finally, I would like to thank the many instructors and students who think highly enough of this work to give me the continuing honor and privilege to say, "Thank you." I hope that in the process I have made a valuable contribution to the bankruptcy system.

Basic Bankruptcy Law
for Paralegals

Introduction

Paralegals and the Bankruptcy System

The use of paralegals to assist counsel engaged in bankruptcy practice has grown commensurate with the growth and acceptance of paralegals within the legal system in general. As in other areas of legal practice, bankruptcy paralegals can provide competent assistance to counsel in the areas of legal research, document preparation, fact investigation, and litigation support.

The Bankruptcy Courts that have examined the use of paralegals in bankruptcy practice overwhelmingly favor the concept. Many basic services can be provided to clients at a substantial cost savings because of the low hourly billing rates of paralegals compared to associate or partner attorneys. The services of paralegals can normally be compensated for under the bankruptcy system's fee application process described in chapter 7 infra. The Bankruptcy Courts' view of paralegal activity is best summed up in the following quotation:

> In effect, the goal of the paralegal is to perform a supervised legal function for a client at considerably less expense to the client. The concept is an efficient idea in today's legal market where attorney costs are escalating beyond the approach of clients in need of legal assistance.[1]

This is not to suggest, however, that a paralegal may operate independently of counsel in providing bankruptcy-related services to clients. The Bankruptcy Courts examining this issue have invariably and correctly found such independent activities to constitute the unauthorized practice of law.[2] In many states the unauthorized practice of law can be prosecuted as a misdemeanor. The paralegal must always tread cautiously in the face

---

1. In re Bonds Lucky Foods, Inc., No. 1, 76 B.R. 664, 671 (Bankr. E.D. Ark. 1986).
2. In re Caise, 359 B.R. 152, 155 (Bankr. E.D. Ky. 2006) ("the paralegal must work under the supervision and direction of a licensed lawyer"). See chapters 7 and 9 infra.

of clients who will invariably seek to pressure the paralegal to provide legal advice.

This text focuses on the theory, practice, and substantive law used by any member of the legal profession engaged in activity within the bankruptcy system, emphasizing the perspective of a paralegal working under the supervision of counsel. This introduction to the Full Edition will clarify the role and most useful functions that paralegals can provide to counsel in consumer bankruptcy practice. The authors suggest that students read this introduction both at the beginning and at the end of the course. The second reading will serve as a concise review of the course.

A. ROLE OF THE PARALEGAL

The role of paralegals in bankruptcy practice is similar to that of paralegals in other areas of legal practice. Research assistance, document preparation, and litigation support comprise the core of activity performed by paralegals in bankruptcy practice.

In the area of legal research, paralegals will be required to research specific legal issues based on counsel's factual analysis of a matter. The research activity may be as simple as verifying the existence and amount of a particular exemption, as described in chapter 9 of this text, or the research assignment may involve complex issues of adequate protection in relief from stay motions in chapter 11 of this text. Exemptions are items of property that individual debtors may keep after filing bankruptcy. Relief from stay motions typically concern an effort by a secured creditor to repossess or foreclose the debtor's property, such as a car or a home. All of these issues are critical to the rights of debtors and creditors in bankruptcy proceedings. Paralegals can participate in many aspects of these activities. This course will illustrate and amplify these activities. Nonetheless, regardless of the simplicity or complexity of a research assignment, the basic research methodology presented in chapter 23 will allow many issues to be competently researched in minimal time.

In the area of document preparation, paralegals aiding in bankruptcy practice will often provide substantial assistance to counsel in preparing Statements and Schedules and the Statement of Current Monthly Income for a debtor or proofs of claim for a creditor. In these two areas, bankruptcy paralegals will likely render a majority of their services. Chapters 21 and 22 of this text are tutorials about the preparation of a debtor's schedules and Statement of Current Monthly Income.

In smaller firms, paralegals may also be asked to prepare preliminary drafts of motions for relief from stay (see chapter 11 infra), complaints objecting to the dischargeability of a debt or the discharge of a debtor (see chapter 12 infra), and motions to sell property (see chapter 15 infra). In addition, paralegals may assist in preparing preliminary drafts of all or a portion of briefs or memoranda in support of or in opposition to motions in any area of bankruptcy law.

In the realm of bankruptcy litigation, a paralegal will provide litigation support services similar to those performed in other areas of legal practice. Preparing digests of depositions, assembling and marking exhibits for a trial or evidentiary hearing, compiling factual data for counsel to prepare or respond to discovery requests, and making charts or other demonstrative aids are all activities that occur in bankruptcy practice.

B. COMMON ACTIVITIES

A summary of the activities most commonly performed by paralegals in bankruptcy practice will help the student to synthesize many of the materials found later in this text. This summary may also serve as a useful guide to practitioners, particularly those who do not regularly practice bankruptcy law.

When representing debtors, the most common activity performed by a paralegal is assisting counsel in the preparation of the basic documents required to be filed in a bankruptcy proceeding as described in chapters 4 and 7 of this text with regard to Chapter 7 proceedings, or as described in chapter 17 of this text with regard to a Chapter 13 proceeding, respectively. The checklists and forms accompanying these text chapters will serve as useful practice aids for students in class and for practicing paralegals.

The most important basic documents in any proceeding, the Statements and Schedules and the Statement of Current Monthly Income, are very often prepared by paralegals in draft form from data provided by counsel. The tutorials in chapters 21 and 22 have been designed to educate and assist students in the effective preparation and reading of these materials as well as to explain the reason or reasons for the required data and its organization.

When representing creditors, paralegals will perform a number of basic tasks. Preparing a proof of claim, as described in chapter 15 infra, is by far the most common. Providing support to counsel in the preparation and prosecution of a motion for relief from the automatic stay, as described in chapter 11 infra, is another common activity performed by paralegals for creditor clients.

Obtaining a copy and providing a preliminary report to counsel concerning the information contained in a debtor's Statements and Schedules is a task that is also regularly performed by paralegals for creditor clients. The analysis provided in chapter 21 has also been designed to assist paralegals in performing this preliminary review. Because this analysis will always help a creditor's counsel or a trustee to determine the initial likelihood of a recovery for the creditors, the importance of this review cannot be overemphasized. Any creditor client will need to know this information in order to determine how much effort to expend in attempting to recover a dividend from a bankruptcy estate.

Regardless of the party represented, a paralegal will always provide invaluable litigation support. This support may involve the performing of services in connection with any of the various motions or adversary proceedings described throughout this text. Other than legal issues involving specific application of the Bankruptcy Code or Federal Rules of Bankruptcy Procedure, the types of activity conducted will not vary from those in any other litigation: facts and documents have to be investigated and organized, discovery may take place, depositions will have to be digested, briefs and motions may have to be written, and finally, the matter may have to be prepared for trial and actually tried. The value of paralegals to counsel in assisting with these services is well proven.

PART I

History and
Introduction

1

A Short History
of Bankruptcy

A. ORIGINS OF BANKRUPTCY SYSTEMS

Throughout history, financial crisis has affected the lives and relationships of individuals and businesses. Regardless of the era, unemployment, illness, unforeseen disaster, and technological advance have all caused financial failure. The methods developed by societies to resolve the effects of financial crisis are known as **bankruptcy systems**. Bankruptcy systems exist in any society where there are debtors (those who owe) and creditors (those who are owed). Bankruptcy systems have existed in some form from the first moment that a tribal chieftain or village elder ordered the seizure of a debtor's possessions and their distribution to multiple creditors in full or partial satisfaction of the creditors' claims.

Creditors have always sought to collect debts and debtors have always sought relief from debt. These contrasting concepts of debt collection and debtor relief are the foundation of any bankruptcy system. The primary focus of the **debt collection** features of bankruptcy systems has always been to formulate a body of rules ". . . to provide for the collection of assets of a debtor and the equitable distribution of the proceeds of those assets among . . . multiple creditors."[1] The primary focus of the **debtor relief** features of bankruptcy systems has vacillated throughout history from one extreme to another, from punishment to forgiveness. Bankruptcy systems that have contained liberal debtor relief provisions have existed primarily in sophisticated economies, where a continual

---

1. Merrick, A Thumbnail Sketch of Bankruptcy History, ABI Newsletter (July/Aug./Sept. 1987).

reconciliation of accounts has been an economic necessity. Simpler economies have tended to contain more conservative debtor relief concepts, the mere sparing of life sometimes being considered revolutionary. The one exception to this pattern appears to be ancient Israel, in which liberal debtor relief concepts prevailed in a simple agricultural economy.

While the historical trend of debtor relief has favored punishment rather than forgiveness, our present United States Bankruptcy Code departs from this trend in its liberal treatment of debtor relief. In many respects the U.S. Bankruptcy Code is perhaps the most liberal debtor relief bankruptcy system to come into existence since the jubilee year of the Old Testament.[2]

The jubilee year occurred every 50 years. (Every seventh year was a sabbatical year in which some limited form of debtor relief was afforded.[3]) The essence of the jubilee year is contained in the biblical verse: "And ye shall hallow the fiftieth year, and proclaim liberty throughout the land unto all the inhabitants thereof; it shall be a jubilee unto you; and ye shall return every man unto his possession, and ye shall return every man unto his family."[4] In the jubilee year, all debts would be discharged, some mortgages released, and all indentured servants or slaves freed (the concept of **discharge**, legal relief from debt, is the basic element of debtor relief). During the intervening years any family member had the right to redeem, by payment, any property or persons that had been seized or given in satisfaction of a debt.[5]

The debtor relief provided for in the Old Testament most likely derived from even earlier regulations that existed in ancient Mesopotamia, from where the early Hebrews migrated to the region that became Israel. In the seventeenth century B.C., King Ammi-Saduqa of Babylonia issued decrees releasing private debts in barley and silver and releasing people from debt slavery in an effort to resolve economic difficulties in his kingdom. This is the earliest recorded evidence of some form of debtor relief from which bankruptcy systems have evolved.[6]

---

2. 11 U.S.C. The Bankruptcy Abuse Prevention and Consumer Protection Act of 2005 ("BAPCPA"), Pub. L. No. 109-8, 119 Stat. 23 (2005), limits and restricts the scope of debtor relief as it has existed in American Bankruptcy practice from 1979 through 2005. BAPCPA demonstrates the pendulum-like nature of the treatment of debtor relief throughout history.

3. Leviticus 25:1-8.

4. Leviticus 25:10. If a portion of this verse seems familiar, it is because the phrase "proclaim liberty throughout the land unto all the inhabitants thereof" is the inscription on the Liberty Bell in Philadelphia.

5. Leviticus 25:11-55. The purpose of the jubilee year was to give debtors a second chance or fresh start. The "fresh start" concept is an essential feature of the United States Bankruptcy Code.

6. Gwendolyn Leick, Mesopotamia: The Invention of the City (Penguin Books 2001), at page 187.

Unlike in ancient Israel, second chances were not generally given to debtors in the other ancient civilizations of the Mediterranean basin. Early Greek law did not seek to discharge debtors or reconcile accounts: A debt was always collectible. In the fifth century B.C., the Twelve Tables regulated only the procedures for selling an individual into slavery to satisfy a debt.[7]

The commentators concur that death, slavery, mutilation, imprisonment, or exile were the lot of debtors in ancient Greece and also in republican Rome.[8] Roman republican law also provided that multiple creditors could, upon exhibiting a debtor in the forum for three days, divide the debtor up into pieces in satisfaction of the debts. Evidence exists suggesting that multiple creditors could also seize a deceased debtor's corpse and hold it for ransom from the debtor's heirs until the debts were satisfied.[9] This practice would make sense in Roman culture since the body had to remain whole if it were to commence a successful journey into the afterlife. The religious significance given to the satisfaction of a debt thus acted as an incentive to repayment. This appears to have been the state of insolvency law, as such, during the Roman Republic.

During the Empire, Roman debtor relief and collection law tended toward a greater liberality.[10] By approximately the second century A.D., debtor slavery had been abolished. Debtor imprisonment continued to exist, but this was distinguishable from slavery in that creditors could not use the services of an imprisoned debtor. The debtor could be held for ransom only until friends or family of the debtor paid the debt.[11] (Debtor imprisonment has existed throughout history, including the twentieth century.)

The Roman Empire encompassed much of present-day Europe, North Africa, and the Middle East. This vast area, comparable in size to the United States, developed a sophisticated commercial economy permitting free trade throughout its territories. All this in a civilization without motor vehicles, aircraft, computers, or any form of instant long-distance communication. In this environment, Rome developed an insolvency system that permitted exemptions (an **exemption** is property that a debtor may

---

7. Vern Countryman, Bankruptcy and the Individual Debtor — and a Modest Proposal to Return to the Seventeenth Century, 32 Cath. U. L. Rev. 809 (1983). Under the Twelve Tables a creditor had to provide a 60-day redemption period before a debtor could be sold into slavery. Payment of the debt within this period would prevent sale into slavery.

8. Id. See also Radin, Debt, 5 Ency. Soc. Sci. 33-34 (1931); Ford, Imprisonment for Debt, 25 Mich. L. Rev. 24 (1926).

9. Countryman, supra n.7; Radin, supra n.8; Ford, supra n.8.

10. Merrick, supra n.1; Radin, supra n.8; Ford, supra n.8.

11. Radin, supra n.8.

protect from seizure by creditors) and restrained personal execution.[12] This restraint took the form of a debtor's ceding all assets for distribution to creditors. Although this act would not discharge the debts, it did act to prohibit creditors from killing, mutilating, or selling the debtor into bondage. This procedure was known as *cessio bonorum*.[13] The assets so surrendered were distributed according to statutory priorities similar to modern United States bankruptcy law.[14] To a modern American observer this procedure would appear similar to a Chapter 7 liquidation proceeding. A form of composition agreement in which a discharge could be granted also came into use as the economy grew in sophistication.[15] A **composition agreement** is an agreement between a debtor and multiple creditors for the repayment of debt. These procedures would be recognizable today as the reorganization proceedings known as Chapter 11 and Chapter 13.

When the Western Roman Empire dissolved in the fifth century A.D., the then-existing economy of Western Europe also collapsed. Whereas for approximately five centuries it had been possible to trade between London and Constantinople (modern Istanbul) with identical currency, trade practices, laws, and language, this commonality ceased to exist. The rise of the Dark Ages caused a corresponding devolution of bankruptcy laws.

B.   BANKRUPTCY IN THE MIDDLE AGES

During the Dark Ages the financial system of Western Europe receded as an important factor of daily life. Debtor imprisonment returned to vogue, prevailing throughout the period.[16] The Church proclaimed debt and insolvency sinful. Debtors were subject to excommunication while alive or denial of a Christian burial upon death.[17] As had been the case in early

---

12. Radin, supra n.8 at 34, 37.
13. Merrick, supra n.1.
14. Riesenfeld, Evolution of Modern Bankruptcy Law, 31 Minn. L. Rev. 401, 432 (1947).
15. Id. at 439, citing Code of Justinian VII.71.8. Justinian reigned as emperor of the Eastern Empire during the sixth century A.D. Although after the final collapse of the Western Empire, which most historians date at A.D. 476, the Code of Justinian is generally accepted to be a codification of law as it existed during the Empire period. Justinian's Codes, therefore, demonstrate the evolution of bankruptcy law from the Republic to the Empire.

    A *composition* is an agreement between a debtor and two or more creditors that satisfies the debts for less than payment in full. See chapters 2, 24-28 infra.
16. Ford, supra n.8 at 25; Radin, supra n.8 at 34.
17. Ford, supra n.8 at 25.

Rome, religious sanctions were once again utilized as an incentive to debt repayment.

The debtor punishments of the Dark Ages were not radically different from the earlier practices of the Roman Republic. They were consistent with a simpler society in which there once again existed few entities with multiple creditors. In the Dark Ages, a serf would generally be beholden to only two creditors: the feudal lord and the Church. Certainly neither would tolerate an unsatisfied debt from a subservient soul.

The punishment of debtors was necessary to assist the land-owning and religious ruling classes to maintain their power. Forgiveness became a radical idea in this stratified economic structure. The lack of a commercial economy also eliminated any practical need for a reconciliation of accounts or balancing of books after an extended period of time.

International commerce and trade began its resurgence in the tenth century. As trade recommenced, the credit system resumed.[18] As the number of debtors with multiple creditors increased, the bankruptcy system began its renaissance.

The first bankruptcy laws that arose in the late Middle Ages were to a large degree reenactments of the *cessio bonorum* of the Roman Empire.[19] The focus of such statutes was twofold: the prevention of fraud upon creditors stemming from an inequitable distribution of assets and the protection of the debtor from imprisonment. If all assets were surrendered for distribution to creditors there would be no imprisonment. A discharge was not given or contemplated. These statutes were limited to use only by merchants. Loss of a trading place or bench (*banca*) in the local market would befall a debtor who fraudulently concealed or transferred assets while not paying his or her just debts. In Italy this was known as *banca rotta* and in France as *banquerotte*. This is the etymology of the English word *bankrupt*.[20] The composition agreement began to reappear in Western European law as early as 1256 in Spain.[21] A composition agreement provided some form of debtor relief in that a debtor could be released from the debts due those creditors who agreed to the composition. By the seventeenth century, the composition agreement existed throughout Western Europe with the exception of England, where such statutes did not come into regular existence until after 1705.[22]

---

18. Radin, supra n.8 at 34.
19. Merrick, supra n.1.
20. Countryman, supra n.7 at 810.
21. Riesenfeld, supra n.14 at 439-440.
22. Countryman, supra n.7 at 811-812. See infra this chapter.

C. EARLY ENGLISH INSOLVENCY LAWS

The emphasis of early English insolvency law was on punishment. For-giveness was rarely known to English debtors prior to 1705. This is an important point to recognize in any study of American bankruptcy law because the law of England as it existed in 1776 is the direct legal antecedent of American bankruptcy law.

Anglo-Saxon England practiced debtor imprisonment, although the sale of a debtor into slavery or debtor dissection was probably not per-mitted.[23] The first statute akin to a bankruptcy statute was enacted in 1283. The Statute of Acton Burnell authorized the seizure of a debtor's assets to satisfy debt. If the assets seized were insufficient to satisfy the debt then the debtor would be imprisoned until the debt was paid.[24] We rec-ognize at least part of this procedure today as a "writ of attachment," a common state law collection device.

From the thirteenth to fifteenth centuries, debtor imprisonment in England evolved under two related writs, *capias ad respondendum* and *capias ad satisfaciendum*. The former allowed a creditor to "attach" a debtor to ensure appearance at trial. The latter allowed a creditor to imprison a debtor in satisfaction of a judgment until the debt was actually paid.[25] Some form of debtor imprisonment existed in England until the twentieth century.[26] The first true insolvency law in England was not enacted until 1543.[27] This delay, in contrast to the rest of Western Europe, is attributable to England's lack of substantial involvement in international trade until the sixteenth century.[28] The statute of 1543 permitted the seizure and distribution of a debtor's assets to creditors and imprison-ment of the debtor if the debts remained unsatisfied. The proceeding applied only to merchants and was initiated by creditors. There was no discharge for the debtor.[29] To the extent that this proceeding was

---

23. Id. at 810-811. Ford, supra n.8 at 26.
24. 11 Edw. (1283). Countryman, supra n.7 at 811.
25. Countryman, supra n.7 at 811; Ford, supra n.8 at 27-28. A writ of *capias ad satisfaciendum* was used in 1989 in New Jersey to place a debtor into custody. A Bankruptcy Court refused to abrogate the writ. See 76 A.B.A. J. 28 (Feb. 1990); In re Bona, 110 B.R. 1012 (Bankr. S.D.N.Y. 1990). The use of a writ of *capias ad satisfaciendum* was affirmed by the New Jersey state courts as recently as 2000 in Marshall v. Matthei, 744 A.2d 209 (N.J. App. Div. 2000).
26. Ford, supra n.8 at 31. Ford points out that in 1921, 424 contract debtors were held im-prisoned in England.
27. 34 & 35 Henry VII, ch. 4 (1543).
28. Merrick, supra n.1 at 12.
29. Countryman, supra n.7 at 811-812; Merrick, supra n.1 at 13.

creditor initiated, it was similar to the present-day American involuntary petition.[30] In 1571 the Statute of Elizabeth further refined the system of asset distribution to creditors. This statute defined fraudulent transfers as acts of bankruptcy. Transactions deemed fraudulent that occurred within a fixed time prior to the bankruptcy filing were considered void. For instance, concealing property from creditors would be one such act.[31] This statute is a likely basis of today's concept of an avoidable transfer, which is a major feature of our Bankruptcy Code.[32] Composition agreements made their appearance in England rather late in comparison to the rest of Western Europe. When they did, compositions were permitted only in the Chancery Courts and only during a relatively short period of time (approximately 1583-1621). Another statute authorizing compositions existed for only one year, 1697-1698.[33] Because a discharge, legal relief from debt, could occur only as a result of a composition, punishment prevailed over forgiveness in early English bankruptcy law.

In 1705 England enacted a statute in which a composition with creditors could effectuate a full discharge of all debt.[34] The Statute of Anne appears to be the first law to recognize a full discharge or legal relief of debt by a debtor since the jubilee year of the Old Testament. Otherwise, the Statute of Anne is remarkably similar in appearance to the bankruptcy system as it existed at the height of the Roman Empire.

Under the Statute of Anne a debtor would receive a full discharge and be able to retain exempt property provided that certain conditions were complied with. The conditions were that a minimum dividend of eight shillings per pound be paid to creditors and that no act in fraud of creditors had taken place prior to the bankruptcy. If a lesser dividend were to be paid, a commissioner would determine the debtor's exemptions.[35] In 1732, the Statute of George added the consent by four-fifths of the creditor body as a requirement of the debtor receiving a discharge.[36] These statutes compose the formal roots of American bankruptcy law.

---

30. See chapter 3 infra.
31. 13 Eliz., ch. 7 (1571); Riesenfeld, supra n.14 at 422.
32. See chapters 16-18 infra.
33. Riesenfeld, supra n.14 at 442-443.
34. 4 Anne, ch. 17 (1705).
35. Countryman, supra n.7 at 812.
36. 5 Geo. II, ch. 30 (1732); Countryman, supra n.7 at 812.

LIBRARY OF ROWAN COLLEGE
AT BURLINGTON COUNTY

D. BANKRUPTCY IN THE UNITED STATES

America is a nation of debtors: "[I]t is stated that nearly half our total white immigration came over under indenture."[37] Indentured servitude acted as an alternative to debtor prison in some colonies.[38] Georgia was originally settled by indentured servants. In general, colonial bankruptcy law corresponded to that of England in the eighteenth century.[39] One goal of the Constitutional Convention was to establish the free flow of trade and commerce between the various states. In an effort to achieve this goal, the framers reserved for Congress the power "to establish . . . uniform laws on the subject of Bankruptcies throughout the United States."[40] By virtue of the Supremacy Clause, which provides that federal law is the supreme law of the land, the enactment of a federal bankruptcy law preempts the states from so acting and acts as the supreme law of the land.[41]

The power granted Congress to enact federal law on the various subjects, including bankruptcy, that are described in Article I, Section 8, of the Constitution, does not, however, require congressional action within a described area. Thus, although Congress has the power to enact bankruptcy laws, it is not required to do so. Accordingly, there is no constitutional requirement that there be a federal bankruptcy law. Bankruptcy laws were only in effect in the United States for short periods of time during the nineteenth century. However, a federal bankruptcy law has been continuously in effect since 1898.

Debtor imprisonment continued to be a prevalent practice in the United States until after 1830. After this date a movement toward debtor relief began and individual state constitutions began to abolish debtor imprisonment.[42] While debtor imprisonment lasted, however, there were periods of time during which substantially more debtors occupied prisons than convicted criminals.[43]

---

37. Countryman, supra n.7 at 813.
38. Countryman, supra n.7 at 813.
39. Ford, supra n.8 at 28. See also, Central Virginia Community College v. Katz, 546 U.S. 356 (2006), in which the Supreme Court discusses the evolution of American Bankruptcy Law from the early English Statutes.
40. U.S. Const., Art. I, §8.
41. U.S. Const., Art. VI.
42. Ford, supra n.8 at 32-33.
43. Ford, supra n.8 at 29, reports that in Pennsylvania, New York, Massachusetts, and Maryland there were three to five times as many persons imprisoned for debt as for crime. Countryman, supra n.7 at 814, cites statistics indicating that debtors constituted approximately 20% of all prisoners in Boston during the 1820s.

The first United States Bankruptcy Act was in effect from 1800 to 1803. This statute was virtually identical in its features to the law in England as it existed after 1732 as described above.[44]

The second United States Bankruptcy Act was enacted in 1841, effective in 1842, and repealed in 1843. This statute permitted voluntary proceedings and applied to nonmerchants as well as merchants. A voluntary proceeding was one initiated by a debtor seeking relief. Exemptions were expanded to include "necessaries of life" in addition to clothing. A discharge was granted with creditor consent. Certain transactions were void in fraud of creditors and some debts would not be affected by a discharge.[45]

The third Bankruptcy Act was in effect during the Reconstruction, 1867 to 1878.[46] This act expanded upon the scope of debtor relief provided for in the 1841 law by permitting state exemptions to be claimed by a debtor and by permitting, for the first time in a bankruptcy law since the Old Testament, a full discharge without creditor consent or payment of a dividend. Additionally, the 1867 Bankruptcy Act contained provisions permitting an "arrangement," or composition. Arrangements included elements similar to those of the present-day reorganization proceedings of Chapter 11 or 13.[47]

A fourth Bankruptcy Act was enacted in 1898 and remained in effect, with amendments, until October 1, 1979, when the present Bankruptcy Code became law.[48] The 1898 Act contained all of the basic elements that are present in today's Bankruptcy Code. An amendment enacted in 1938 contained provisions creating Chapters XI and XIII, the reorganization proceedings that still exist under the Bankruptcy Code.[49] The Supreme Court described the Act's liberal debtor relief provisions as providing a "fresh start" to debtors in their financial affairs.[50] In 1970 Congress authorized a commission to determine the desirability of reforming the Bankruptcy Act. In 1973 the Commission reported that modernization and recodification of the Bankruptcy Act was in order.[51] The report was accepted, and the Bankruptcy Code of 1978 was the result. An analysis

---

44. 2 Stat. 19 (1800). Countryman, supra n.7 at 813; Riesenfeld, supra n.14 at 407. See also notes 34-36 supra.
45. 5 Stat. 440 (1841); 5 Stat. 614 (1843); Countryman, supra n.7 at 814-815; Riesenfeld, supra n.14 at 407, 423.
46. 14 Stat. 517 (1867); 20 Stat. 99 (1878).
47. Countryman, supra n.7 at 815-816; Riesenfeld, supra n.14 at 409, 423, 446-447.
48. 30 Stat. 541 (1898). See chapter 2 infra.
49. 52 Stat. 541 (1938). Countryman, supra n.7 at 817; Riesenfeld, supra n.14 at 408. See chapters 23-27 infra.
50. Local Loan Co. v. Hunt, 292 U.S. 234 (1934).
51. Countryman, supra n.7 at 818; Report of the Commission on the Bankruptcy Laws of the United States, H.R. Doc. No. 137, 82d Cong., 1st Sess., pt. I, ch. 17 (1973).

of this Code in its present form, along with practical descriptions to aid in conducting many routine bankruptcy procedures, is the subject matter of this text.

Thus, the substantive foundations of our current United States Bankruptcy Code are rooted deep within the history of Western civilization. For individual debtors, the Bankruptcy Code emphasizes the discharge of debt and the allowance of exemptions, thus giving a fresh start to the debtor. Such liberal treatment of debtor relief has not existed since the jubilee and sabbatical years of ancient Israel. For creditors, the Bankruptcy Code emphasizes the orderly and consistent liquidation of assets and distribution of dividends. In various forms, this collection process has existed in sophisticated commercial economies since the Roman Empire.[52] Finally, the formal and stylistic aspects of the United States Bankruptcy Code began their evolution with the 1705 English Statute of Anne.

Summary

Bankruptcy systems exist in any society where there are debtors (those who owe) and creditors (those who are owed). The practice of the jubilee year in ancient Israel provided debtors a discharge or legal relief from debt.

In other ancient Mediterranean civilizations, debtors were punished and not legally forgiven from debt. During the later Roman Empire, a bankruptcy system developed in a sophisticated commercial economy. In this system, debtors were allowed to protect property from creditors. This concept was and is known as exemptions.

The United States Bankruptcy Code evolved from eighteenth-century English bankruptcy law. Our Bankruptcy Code provides for debtor relief in the form of a discharge and also permits debtors to protect exempt property. The Bankruptcy Code provides creditors with an orderly

---

52. Globalization has spawned a corresponding growth of bankruptcy statutes throughout the world bearing many similarities to Chapter 11 of the United States Bankruptcy Code. China recently revised a statute originally enacted in 1986. The original and the revised Enterprise Bankruptcy Law permits liquidations and reorganizations of business entities. See The Enterprise Bankruptcy Law of the People's Republic of China, Bankruptcy Strategist, Volume 25, Number 9 (July 2008). In 1991 Hungary became the first former Warsaw Pact country to enact a bankruptcy law. See ABI Newsletter (November/December 1991). A law permitting business bankruptcies became effective in Russia in 1993. See ABI Journal, April 1993. Poland became the most recent country to update its bankruptcy laws with a statute similar to Chapter 11. See Bankruptcy Court Decisions Newsletter, June 10, 2003, LRP Publications: "Poland to enact new insolvency law to aid economy."

process to liquidate the debtor's nonexempt assets and to distribute the proceeds as dividends. An analysis of the Code, in its present form, along with practical descriptions to aid in conducting many routine bankruptcy procedures is the subject of this text.

KEY TERMS

bankruptcy systems
composition agreement
debt collection

debtor relief
discharge
exemptions

DISCUSSION QUESTIONS

1. Why do individuals or businesses seek bankruptcy relief?

2. What distinguishes debtor relief from debt collection in a bankruptcy system?

3. How does the concept of debtor relief in modern American bankruptcy law compare with debtor relief found in England before the American Revolution? The Roman Empire? Medieval Europe?

4. Where does the term *bankruptcy* come from? What is the etymology of the term *bankruptcy*?

2

Introduction to the
Bankruptcy Code

A. ORGANIZATION OF THE BANKRUPTCY CODE AND A NOTE ON THE TEXT

The Bankruptcy Code was enacted into law in 1978 and became effective on October 1, 1979.[1] It has since been significantly amended four times, in 1984, 1986, 1994, and 2005.[2] The bankruptcy law is now properly known as the Bankruptcy Code. The law prior to 1979 was known as the Bankruptcy Act. Any reference to the present law as the Bankruptcy Act is therefore incorrect. Although the Bankruptcy Act used Roman numerals to identify its Chapters, the Bankruptcy Code uses Arabic numerals. This will explain references in older cases, for example, to Chapter XIII of the Bankruptcy Act.

---

1. Pub. L. No. 95-598, (92 Stat. 2549 1978).
2. The 1984 amendments are commonly known as BAFJA (the Bankruptcy Amendments and Federal Judgeship Act of 1984), Pub. L. No. 98-353 (July 10, 1984). The 1986 amendments are known as the Bankruptcy Judges, United States Trustees, and Family Farmer Bankruptcy Act of 1986, Pub. L. No. 99-554 (Oct. 27, 1986). The 1994 amendments are known as the Bankruptcy Reform Act of 1994, Pub. L. No. 103-394 (Oct. 26, 1994). The National Bankruptcy Review Commission, created in the 1994 amendments, delivered an 1,100-page report to Congress in late 1997. The document made 170 recommendations for changes or additions to the Code. The Bankruptcy Abuse Prevention and Consumer Protection Act of 2005, Pub. L. 109-8, 119 Stat. 23 (April 20, 2005) has its genesis in pro-credit-industry legislation introduced in reaction to the Commission Report. Throughout this text these amendments shall be referred to as BAPCPA.

The Bankruptcy Code is divided into nine Chapters.[3] In essence, it is primarily a self-contained system designed to resolve the financial affairs of a debtor. The Code's basic structure can be easily illustrated and briefly described in the form of a flow chart. This description also serves as a useful guide to understanding the organization of this text. Since the Bankruptcy Code is a system, it is best analyzed and described in a similar format, as in the nearby chart. We have attempted to use a "building block" approach, working from the simpler to the more complex concepts as the text progresses. This may necessitate some reference in earlier chapters of this text to concepts not discussed in detail until a later chapter. Where this occurs, an effort has been made to briefly define the concept that will be described in greater detail later. Reference back to the chart or to the glossary at the end of the text may help simplify this initial learning process. This same chart will also serve as an instant review of the entire text when it has been completed.

Code Chapters 1, 3, and 5 contain the rules that apply in all bankruptcy proceedings. These three Code Chapters contain the rules dealing with the fundamental debtor relief features of discharge, exemptions, and the automatic stay. These Chapters also contain the general rules regulating the debt collection features of claims and their priority of distribution.[4] These are the basic issues affecting debtors and creditors in a bankruptcy proceeding.

The remaining Code Chapters (7, 9, 11, 12, 13, and 15) comprise the specific types of bankruptcy proceedings that are available to debtors. The most common proceedings are Chapters 7, 11, and 13.[5] These three proceedings comprise in excess of 95 percent of all bankruptcies filed. Normally, the provisions contained in each of these Code Chapters will apply only to the specific Chapter proceeding that has actually been filed.[6]

---

3. All Chapters enacted in 1978 bore odd numbers (1, 3, 5, 7, 9, 11, and 13). Although apocryphal, it is believed Congress adopted this format so it could fill in other chapters later. In 1986, Congress did enact Chapter 12, the family farmer reorganization proceeding. A second reason for only enacting odd-numbered chapters may have been so that the various types of bankruptcy proceedings would still retain their common identities of Chapter 7 (VII), Chapter 11 (XI), and Chapter 13 (XIII). Chapter 15 was added to the Code in 2005 by BAPCPA.

4. See chapters 7, 9, 11, 12, and 16 infra.

5. For the fiscal year ending September 30, 2010, 1,596,355 bankruptcies were filed nationwide and 71.8% or 1,146,511 cases were under Chapter 7, less than 1% or 14,191 were Chapter 11, 707 were Chapter 12, and 27.2% or 434,839 were under Chapter 13. During this period, there were also 12 Chapter 9 filings and 95 Chapter 15 filings. Altogether this is almost double the number of filings for the fiscal year ending September 30, 2007. The annual number of filings is rapidly approaching the pre-BAPCPA numbers for the 2005 calendar year, which included a record 2,078,415 filings, of which 80% or 1,659,017 were under Chapter 7, <1% or 6,800 were under Chapter 11, 380 were under Chapter 12, and approximately 20% or 412,130 were under Chapter 13. See Bankruptcy Statistics at www.uscourts.gov.

6. 11 U.S.C. §103.

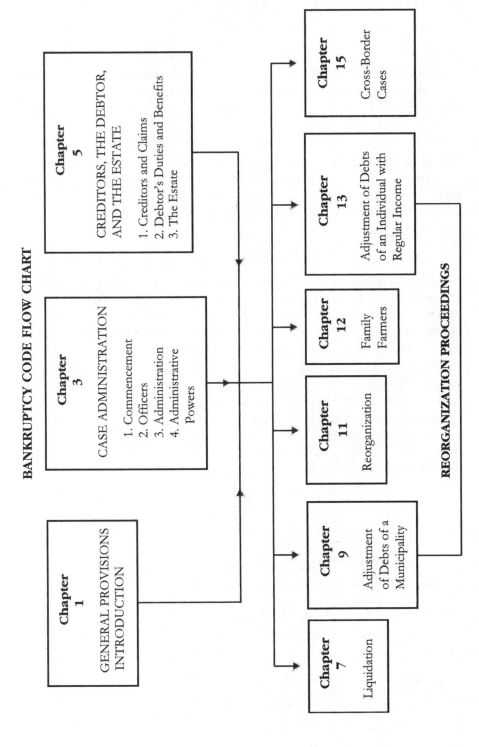

BANKRUPTCY CODE FLOW CHART

Chapter 1
GENERAL PROVISIONS
INTRODUCTION

Chapter 3
CASE ADMINISTRATION

1. Commencement
2. Officers
3. Administration
4. Administrative Powers

Chapter 5
CREDITORS, THE DEBTOR, AND THE ESTATE

1. Creditors and Claims
2. Debtor's Duties and Benefits
3. The Estate

Chapter 7
Liquidation

Chapter 9
Adjustment of Debts of a Municipality

Chapter 11
Reorganization

Chapter 12
Family Farmers

Chapter 13
Adjustment of Debts of an Individual with Regular Income

Chapter 15
Cross-Border Cases

REORGANIZATION PROCEEDINGS

21

B. OVERVIEW OF THE BANKRUPTCY CODE

Chapter 1 is the first Chapter of the Bankruptcy Code. It contains definitions and general procedural rules governing all bankruptcy proceedings.

This Chapter can also be referred to as the "Introduction" to the bankruptcy process. The provisions of Code Chapter 1 are described in chapters 4 and 6 of this text.

Code Chapter 3 contains various rules pertaining to the administration of bankruptcy estates, including rules relating to professionals and to such issues as the regulation of professional fees in bankruptcy proceedings.[7] This is part of the subject of chapter 7 of this text. Among the other rules of Chapter 3 are rules relating to the automatic stay and executory contracts.[8]

Code Chapter 5 contains rules governing creditors and claims, the debtor, and the estate. The core of the debtor relief and debt collection provisions is contained in this Code Chapter. The primary debtor relief features of exemptions and discharge are included here. These concepts are the subjects of chapters 9 and 12 infra. The debt collection features of claims and their priorities and the trustee's so-called avoiding powers are also contained in Code Chapter 5.[9]

The general Code Chapters 1, 3, and 5 are applicable to each of the various Chapter proceedings that a debtor may file under the Bankruptcy Code, but the provisions of Chapters 7, 9, 11, 12, 13, or 15 will normally apply only to that particular Chapter, unless it is made specifically applicable by another Code section.[10] For example, if a debtor files a Chapter 7 proceeding, the provisions of Chapters 1, 3, 5, and 7 will apply to the proceeding. The provisions of Chapter 11 (another "proceeding") will not.

Practice Pointer

To the extent that a specific provision of Chapters 7, 11, 12, or 13 conflicts with a general provision in Chapters 1, 3, and 5, the specific provision will generally control over the general provision.

---

7. 11 U.S.C. §§326, 327, 330, 331. See chapter 7 infra.
8. 11 U.S.C. §§362, 365. See chapters 11 and 15 infra.
9. 11 U.S.C. §§501-510, 522, 523-524, 541-559. See chapters 9, 14-17, and 21-22 infra.
10. 11 U.S.C. §103.

Chapter 7 is the most common type of bankruptcy proceeding. It may be described in one word: liquidation. The majority of all bankruptcies filed are Chapter 7 proceedings.[11] In a **liquidation** proceeding, all the debtor's nonexempt assets are sold. The proceeds are then distributed to the creditors according to their priority. The basic details of Chapter 7 proceedings are the specific subjects of chapters 7, 8, 10, and 18 through 22 of this text.

Chapter 13 is the second most common proceeding filed under the code. Chapter 13 is a reorganization proceeding for individuals with regular income where a qualified individual seeks expedited and summary approval of a repayment plan for a small consumer estate. Approximately 27 percent of all cases filed are Chapter 13 proceedings.[12] Chapter 13 is the subject of chapter 23 of this text.

A third type of proceeding is Chapter 11, which is commonly known as the "Reorganization" Chapter. Approximately 0.9 percent of all proceedings filed are filed under Chapter 11.[13] Chapter 11 is the most complex, time-consuming, and expensive type of bankruptcy proceeding. In a **reorganization** proceeding, a debtor seeks to avoid liquidation by proposing a viable plan of reorganization to the creditors that can be successfully confirmed and performed. Chapter 11 is described later in this text in chapters 24-26.

Both Chapter 11 and Chapter 13 are reorganization proceedings and, as a result, have many similarities. In a Chapter 11 case, a business or individual debtor proposes a plan to reorganize its business and avoid liquidation. The business may be Joe's Donut Shop down at the corner or it may be Texaco, Inc. Similarly, in a Chapter 13 case, an individual debtor proposes a plan to repay debt over a period of time, thus reorganizing the individual's affairs. To this extent, the goals of a Chapter 11 and Chapter 13 are identical.

There are three other Chapter proceedings that some debtors may file. They are Chapter 9, Chapter 12, and Chapter 15. These three proceedings comprise the remaining available bankruptcy proceedings. Chapter 9 is a reorganization proceeding for a municipal corporation—a city. Municipal corporations seeking reorganization have been provided with a special reorganization proceeding because in addition to being

---

11. Chapter 7 cases comprised approximately 72% of the filings for the 2010 fiscal year, 70% for fiscal 2009, 65% for fiscal 2008, 60% for fiscal 2007, 75% for fiscal 2006, and 75.5% for fiscal 2005.
12. Chapter 13 cases comprised approximately 27% of the filings for the 2010 fiscal year, 28% for fiscal 2009, 34% for fiscal 2008, 39% for fiscal 2007, 24.5% for fiscal 2006, and 24% for fiscal 2005.
13. Chapter 11 cases comprised approximately 0.9% of the filings for the 2010 fiscal year, 1.1% for 2009, 0.8% for 2008, 0.7% for 2007, 0.8% for 2006, 0.3% for 2005, and 0.6% for 2004.

business entities, a Chapter 9 debtor may also be a political entity. The provisions of Chapter 9 attempt to account for the special considerations that can arise when a political entity is also a debtor. Chapter 9 filings are rare. For example, in 1994, Orange County, California, filed a widely publicized Chapter 9 to avoid losses it incurred in speculative bond investments. In the last 12 months ending on September 30, 2010, there have only been a dozen Chapter 9 cases filed.

Chapter 12 was added to the Code in November 1986.[14] Chapter 12 is entitled the "Adjustment of Debts of a Family Farmer." It is a hybrid of Chapters 11 and 13. It was enacted as an experiment to assist financially distressed family farmers who desire to reorganize their affairs. Chapter 12 provides family farmers the essential benefits and cost savings of a Chapter 13 in what would otherwise have to be a Chapter 11 proceeding. Code Chapter 12 is described in chapter 27 of this text.

Chapter 15 was added to the Code in 2005. Entitled "Ancillary and Cross-Border Cases," it was intended "to incorporate the Model Law on Cross-Border Insolvency."[15] Chapter 15 exists to help resolve insolvency issues arising from the advent of the so-called Global Economy in the 1990s.

C.   THE BANKRUPTCY SYSTEM

The Bankruptcy Code is designed to function as a system. This point cannot be overemphasized. It is the key to understanding how the Bankruptcy Code works to resolve the financial affairs of a debtor. This understanding will aid the paralegal in providing realistic and practical results for either debtor or creditor clients. For unlike many other areas of the law, a specific provision of the Bankruptcy Code is often best understood in the context of its role within the entire system and not as an isolated statute. When approached in this manner, many aspects of the Code that may at first appear illogical will become logical, rational, and understandable.

The systems approach also helps in understanding the practical nature of the Code. In this context, the **Bankruptcy Code** is a largely self-contained legal, economic, and accounting system designed to

---

14. Pub. L. 99-554. Section 1001 of BAPCPA made Chapter 12 a permanent addition to the Bankruptcy Code.
15. 11 U.S.C. §1501(a).

reconcile all financial affairs of a debtor as they exist at the time of filing. All assets and liabilities are disclosed. Assets that are not exempt are available for liquidation and distribution to creditors according to a list of priorities designated by the Code. Most debts will be subject to the debtor's discharge. This is the most basic description of a bankruptcy proceeding. The specific details of this basic process, the documents involved and how to prepare them, are the subject matter of chapters 7, 29, and 30 of the text.

Bankruptcy proceedings appear and feel different than traditional litigation. For example, a Chapter filing of any type is best referred to as a proceeding. This distinguishes the bankruptcy proceeding itself from the various types of litigation or motions that may take place within the proceeding. For instance, a Chapter 7 proceeding may have activity occurring within it that constitutes independent litigation or other activity that will occur only by way of a motion. This semantic distinction will also help the reader to understand bankruptcy jurisdiction in simple terms.[16] The text will describe some suggested methods for presenting issues to the Bankruptcy Court either by way of motion or through litigation.

There are normally no plaintiffs or defendants in a bankruptcy proceeding. There is a debtor, a trustee, and creditors. Sometimes a debtor may have only one or two creditors, and sometimes a debtor may have several hundred or thousands of creditors. But the major players will always be the debtor, a trustee, and the creditors. The **debtor** is the entity that is bankrupt and owes the debts. The **creditors** are the entities to whom the debts are owed. The **trustee** is an independent third party who liquidates the estate's assets and distributes the dividends to the creditors. Trustees are described in chapter 10 of this text.

The traditional adversarial approach is not necessarily the most practical way to approach a bankruptcy problem. The bankruptcy system generally functions most efficiently when the debtor, creditors, and trustee cooperate. All of the major players, particularly in a reorganization proceeding, share a similar goal: satisfaction of debts while preserving the business. Litigation will not necessarily resolve a debtor's problems or even define their solutions. In bankruptcy practice, one must always be aware of the likely ultimate result and act on the basis of prudent economics. This philosophy will always aid in giving a reorganization proceeding the greatest chance for success. This philosophy also assists in the Chapter 7 effort to generate the greatest realistic dividend to unsecured

16. See chapter 28 infra.

creditors. This is the practical goal of Chapter 7, to "squeeze blood out of a turnip," at least from the collection standpoint.

If there is any other area of law that is comparable to the bankruptcy system, it is the probate system.[17] In probate, an estate is liquidated and the proceeds distributed first to creditors and then to the beneficiaries of the estate according to distributive priorities set by state law. Similarly, in bankruptcy an estate is liquidated, the proceeds are distributed to creditors by federal statutory priorities, and then any remaining proceeds are returned to the debtor's shareholders or to the debtor.

D.   COMPOSITION AGREEMENTS — A BANKRUPTCY ALTERNATIVE

A possible alternative to a bankruptcy proceeding in consumer bankruptcy cases is the common law concept of the composition agreement. Any transaction in which an individual and a creditor agree to a revision of their legal obligations to one another is a form of composition. Picking up the telephone and getting an extra month to pay a bill is a form of composition. Debt consolidations are a form of composition. A formal **composition agreement** comes into being when an individual and multiple creditors agree to a revision of existing obligations.

When an individual has a number of unpaid creditors, there is no prohibition against the person entering into a joint repayment plan simultaneously with multiple creditors. A composition agreement is therefore an agreement between a person and two or more creditors to extend repayment terms or to accept less than full payment in discharge of debts. An accepted composition agreement becomes a new contract between the person and the consenting creditors. A written document, defining all of the terms of repayment and signed by all the involved parties, is sufficient to be a valid composition agreement.

BAPCPA adds two provisions to the Bankruptcy Code that encourage the use of composition agreements in consumer bankruptcy cases. First, a debtor can object to a creditor's claim and reduce it by 20 percent if a

---

17. In In re Pacific Forest Industries, Inc., 95 B.R. 740, 744 (Bankr. C.D. Cal. 1989), the court said: "There is no other practice of law which is identical in nature to bankruptcy practice, but the Court believes that probate practice has some of the same elements. The attorney is dealing with a fiduciary, who he must advise. The decisions made by the Court may affect creditors who are not even yet known. There is a limited 'res' that will be dealt with and distributed."

debtor can show by clear and convincing evidence that the debtor made, at least 60 days prior to the bankruptcy filing, an offer to repay at least 60 percent of a debt over a period "not to exceed the repayment period of the loan, or a reasonable extension thereof" and the debt is otherwise dischargeable.[18] Second, any creditor receiving payments pursuant to such a payment plan, so long as the plan is created by an approved credit counseling agency, will not be subject to having to return the payment to a bankruptcy trustee as a preference.[19] These provisions are intended to encourage composition agreements in consumer cases. In the first instance, debtors are given an incentive to propose out of court 60 percent repayment plans, and creditors are subject to penalties in Bankruptcy Court for unreasonably refusing acceptance. The clear import of the provision is to encourage debtors to propose 60 percent or more composition agreements and for creditors to accept them. In the second instance, insulating approved composition agreement payments received by creditors from the trustee's preference powers acts as a further incentive for creditors to accept consumer composition proposals.

Summary

The United States Bankruptcy Code is primarily a self-contained system designed to resolve the financial affairs of a debtor. The Bankruptcy Code is organized into Chapters. There are nine such Chapters at the present time. Three Chapters (1, 3, and 5) contain rules that apply in all of the various Chapter proceedings. The rules in these three Chapters include the basic features of debtor relief, discharge, exemptions, and the automatic stay, as well as the basic features of debt collection, claims, and their priority of distribution.

The remaining six Chapters of the Bankruptcy Code (7, 9, 11, 12, 13, and 15) comprise the various types of bankruptcy proceedings available to debtors. The different proceedings may be categorized as either "liquidation" or "reorganization" proceedings.

In a liquidation, a debtor's nonexempt assets are sold by a trustee and the proceeds are distributed to the creditors. In a reorganization, the debtor will seek approval of a repayment plan that will avoid liquidation.

Chapter 7 is a liquidation proceeding. Chapters 9, 11, 12, and 13 are reorganization proceedings that apply to specific types of debtors. Chapters 11 and 13 are the most common reorganization proceedings.

---

18. 11 U.S.C. §502(k). See chapter 21 infra.
19. 11 U.S.C. §547(h). See chapter 16 infra.

A Chapter 11 is a business reorganization. A Chapter 13 is a consumer reorganization. Chapter 9 applies only to Municipal Corporations. Chapter 12 is a reorganization proceeding for family farmers.

Chapter 15 applies only to cross-border bankruptcies and may be either liquidations or reorganizations.

A composition agreement is an agreement between a person and one or more creditors for the repayment of existing debt. Two provisions of BAPCPA are intended to encourage individual consumers in proposing debt repayment plans.

KEY TERMS

Bankruptcy Code   **liquidation**
composition agreement   **reorganization**
creditor   **trustee**
debtor

DISCUSSION QUESTIONS

1. What is a liquidation proceeding?

2. What is a reorganization proceeding?

3. Identify:

    (a) Those Chapters of the Bankruptcy Code applicable to all bankruptcy proceedings;

    (b) Those Chapters of the Bankruptcy Code applicable to liquidation proceedings;

    (c) Those Chapters of the Bankruptcy Code applicable to reorganization proceedings.

4. Identify the major parties in a bankruptcy proceeding.

5. How can a consumer debtor negotiate a composition agreement with creditors? What are the advantages of doing this? Should counsel for a consumer debtor attempt to negotiate the composition agreement?

3

Filing a Petition

The first step in initiating any bankruptcy proceeding is to file a petition. If it is filed by the debtor, the petition is called a **voluntary petition**.[1] If the petition is filed by the debtor's creditors (to place the debtor into bankruptcy), it is referred to as an **involuntary petition**.[2] The debtor in an involuntary proceeding is known as an **alleged debtor** and is not generally considered to be bankrupt in a practical or legal sense until the court enters an order for relief.[3] Generally speaking, each person or entity in bankruptcy must file their own separate bankruptcy petition. A married couple, however, may be joint debtors in either a voluntary or an involuntary proceeding.[4] Other related debtors must have separate petitions filed by or against them, although the Federal Rules of Bankruptcy Procedure do permit procedural or substantive consolidation of proceedings in appropriate circumstances.[5]

A. GATEKEEPER PROVISIONS IN INDIVIDUAL BANKRUPTCIES

1. Prepetition Credit Counseling

BAPCPA added a number of provisions to the Bankruptcy Code that an individual debtor, or the debtor's legal representative, must actually

---

1. 11 U.S.C. §301; Bankruptcy Rule 1002.
2. 11 U.S.C. §303.
3. 11 U.S.C. §303(f), (h).
4. 11 U.S.C. §302. 1 U.S.C. §7.
5. Bankruptcy Rule 1015. See infra this chapter for a more detailed description.

comply with prior to filing a bankruptcy petition. These provisions may best be understood as gatekeeper provisions or prerequisites to an individual bankruptcy filing, because if they are not complied with, a filing may not take place, may be subject to dismissal, or the legal representative may be subject to sanctions or penalties.

Section 109(h) of the Bankruptcy Code requires **prepetition credit counseling** as a prerequisite to an individual debtor seeking bankruptcy relief. Corporations and partnerships are not subject to this requirement. An individual seeking bankruptcy relief must participate in an individual or group credit counseling session provided by an approved credit counseling agency within the 180 days prior to the debtor filing his or her petition.[6] The debtor must also provide proof of participation in the program by filing with the court, at the time the petition is filed, a certificate from the credit counseling agency that provided the services along with a copy of any debt repayment plan developed by the agency.[7] If the debtor fails to comply with these provisions, it may result in the dismissal of the case.[8] There are three exceptions to the prepetition credit counseling requirement. First, the Code provides that the United States Trustee may exempt a district from the requirement if the United States Trustee determines that approved credit counseling services in a district are not reasonably able to provide counseling services to individuals.[9] For example, the United States Trustee could determine that certain large rural districts are exempt from this requirement. However, with the availability of credit counseling services over the telephone and through the Internet, such exemptions are virtually nonexistent.

Second, a debtor may file a certification with the court at the time of filing stating that "exigent circumstances" merit a waiver of the rule, provided that the debtor made a request for counseling services and could not obtain them within five days of making a request from a counseling agency. A debtor seeking a waiver for exigent circumstances must still obtain the required credit counseling within 30 days from filing the petition, except that the court, for cause, may allow an additional 15 days.[10] Ultimately, failure of a debtor to comply with the requirement to obtain prepetition counseling and to file the certificate with the

---

6. 11 U.S.C. §109(h); 11 U.S.C. §111. The United States Trustee, a division of the Department of Justice, designates approved credit counseling agencies. The role and function of the United States Trustee is discussed at chapter 10 infra.
7. 11 U.S.C. §521(b).
8. 11 U.S.C. §109(h)(3)(B).
9. 11 U.S.C. §109(h)(2)(A).
10. 11 U.S.C. §109(h)(3)(B).

Bankruptcy Court will be sufficient grounds for dismissal of the case if the documents are not filed within the time periods provided for under the statute.

> ### *Practice Pointer*
> It is important to check the local rules for your jurisdiction. Some courts will dismiss the case automatically without a hearing if the certification seeking a waiver is not filed with the petition.

The third exception to the prepetition credit counseling requirement arises if, after notice and a hearing, the court finds that a debtor is not able to comply with the requirement due to mental incapacity, physical disability, or active military service in a military combat zone.[11]

Requiring individual debtors to obtain approved credit counseling as a prerequisite to file a petition is an entirely new concept in bankruptcy practice, raising questions and concerns that will have to be resolved by the courts. For example, what is an "exigent circumstance"? Is an imminent repossession, foreclosure, sheriff's sale, eviction, or termination of utility service an exigent circumstance? In any event, the five-day waiting period appears to be mandatory if the exigent circumstances exception is to apply. Since many debtors wait until the last minute to consult with a professional about their financial affairs, the five-day waiting period may increase foreclosures and repossessions, thereby depriving some debtors of the ability to save their homes or cars by seeking bankruptcy relief.[12]

New Code Section 111 provides the guidelines necessary for the approval of the budget and credit counseling agencies required under BAPCPA to provide both the prepetition credit counseling mandated by Section 109(h) and the financial management course now required as a condition to receive a Chapter 7 discharge (§727(a)(11)) or a Chapter 13 discharge (§1328(g)). (See chapters 7 and 23 infra.) The United States Trustee is charged with establishing the requirements to approve these agencies and to evaluate them on a regular basis. Although the agencies

---

11. 11 U.S.C. §109(h)(4).
12. Opinions are diverse. Some courts find imminent foreclosure to be an exigent circumstance. See, e.g., In re Giambrone, 365 B.R. 386 (Bankr. W.D.N.Y. 2007). Some find that imminent foreclosure is not an exigent circumstance. See, e.g., In re Hedquist, 342 B.R. 295 (8th Cir. BAP 2006). Some cases have found that obtaining credit counseling on the filing date is not sufficient. See, e.g., In re Francisco, 390 B.R. 700 (Bankr. D.N.M. 2008).

may charge a fee, the services are required to be provided without consideration of the ability to pay the fee. Prepetition credit counseling focuses upon the ability to qualify for bankruptcy relief, the types of chapters available, and whether or not the debtor has the ability to propose a reasonable nonbankruptcy repayment plan to creditors. In this regard, if a debtor proposes to repay at least 60 percent over the loan repayment period, and the creditor unreasonably refuses, this may constitute a ground to object to at least 20 percent of the claim in a bankruptcy case pursuant to new Section 502(k). Additionally, payments made to creditors pursuant to such a repayment plan are not considered preferential pursuant to new Section 547(h).

2. Debt Relief Agency Provisions

A second group of gatekeeper provisions added to the Code by BAPCPA establishes additional responsibilities for any "**debt relief agency**" providing "**bankruptcy assistance**" to an "assisted person." A debt relief agency, as defined under Section 101(12A), is any person, including a bankruptcy petition preparer, providing "bankruptcy assistance," as defined under Section 101(4A) to an "**assisted person**," defined under Section 101(3) as a person whose debts are primarily consumer debts and whose nonexempt property has a value of less than $150,000.

Practice Pointer

The Supreme Court has ruled that a bankruptcy attorney qualifies as a "debt relief agency" for purposes of Section 101(12A). Milavetz, Gallop & Milavetz, P.A. v. United States, _____ U.S. _____, 130 S. Ct. 1324 (2010).

Section 527 requires a debt relief agency to provide written notice to the debtor, as provided for in Section 342(b), describing the various chapters available to individual debtors along with a brief description of bankruptcy in general. Form 7.7 on the forms disk is a sample form. This notice is to be given within three days of offering to provide assistance to the assisted person, along with an additional notice advising the assisted person that they have a duty to be truthful, to accurately disclose all assets and liabilities, and to provide current monthly income. The notice will also state that their petition is subject to random audit. Section 527(b) requires that a statement be given to assisted persons about the obligations of the debt relief agency. This section sets forth the specific terms that must be included in this statement.

Section 528 requires written retainer agreements between debtors and all debt relief agencies within five days of first rendering services to an assisted person. The written retainer agreement must clearly and conspicuously explain the services to be rendered, the fees to be charged, and any payment terms to be assigned. Section 528 further requires that any advertising must make clear that any services being advertised are for bankruptcy services and clearly and conspicuously state: "We are a debt relief agency. We help people file for bankruptcy relief under the Bankruptcy Code," or a substantially similar statement. The purpose of these new provisions is to ensure that potential debtors will understand that the assistance they are receiving involves bankruptcy relief and not simply debt counseling or some other form of debt relief.

Section 526 enforces compliance with Sections 527 and 528. Section 526 requires a debt relief agency to perform all the services they promise to provide to an assisted person. These provisions of Sections 527 and 528 may not be waived. Failure to comply with any of the provisions in Section 526, 527, or 528 will make the debt relief agency liable for all damages and a refund of any fees paid. Additionally, state attorneys general, the court, and the United States Trustee are given authority to enforce these provisions, including the authority to seek an injunction against a debt relief agency that repeatedly violates these provisions.

In Milavetz, Gallop & Milavetz, P.A. v. United States, _____ U.S. _____, 130 S. Ct. 1324 (2010), a law firm challenged the constitutionality of the definition of "debt relief agency" at 11 U.S.C. §101(12A) and contended it should not apply to attorneys. The plaintiffs asserted that 11 U.S.C. §526(a)(4), barring advice to assisted persons to ". . . incur more debt in contemplation of such person filing . . ." bankruptcy, violates the First Amendment, and claimed that 11 U.S.C. §528, requiring disclosure as a debt relief agency in advertising, violates the First Amendment. The Supreme Court held that a law firm is a debt relief agency and that the regulation of speech contained in the debt relief agency provisions is otherwise constitutional.

With respect to the first point, the Court held the plain meaning of the Code to foreclose a ". . . reading of 'debt relief agency' excluding attorneys. A law firm representing consumer bankruptcy debtors is a debt relief agency." The Court then turned to the constitutionality of the remaining provisions. As to Section 526(a)(4), the Court found the phrase ". . . in contemplation of . . ." means advice ". . . most naturally read to forbid only advice to undertake actions to abuse the bankruptcy system." Incurring of debt for a "valid purpose" will not violate the provision. The lower courts will be left to determine a valid purpose. Since Section 528 requires disclosure that a debt relief agency helps people file for bankruptcy relief under the Bankruptcy Code, disclosures directed at misleading commercial speech will pass scrutiny if they are reasonably related to the State's interest in preventing deception of consumers. The Court found Section 528 to be just such a provision.

B. VOLUNTARY PETITIONS

A debtor initiates a voluntary proceeding by filing a petition conforming to Official Form 1.[13] The form is for the most part self-explanatory. The purpose of the various representations contained within the petition is to establish that the debtor is qualified to be a debtor under the particular Chapter commenced and that the proceeding has been filed in the district with the proper venue.[14] The debtor's involvement in related or prior bankruptcy proceedings must also be disclosed in the petition.

Venue is the proper Bankruptcy Court (federal judicial district) in which to commence a proceeding. A proceeding may be commenced in any district meeting one of the following qualifications: (1) the district in which the petitioner is domiciled, resides, or has its principal place of business; (2) the district in which the debtor's principal United States assets are located; or (3) the district in which the debtor has complied with either of the above for the greatest portion of the 180 days preceding the petition's filing.[15] As a practical matter, this means that venue is appropriate if either requirement 1 or 2 is met for at least 91 days preceding the filing of the petition. If a debtor has been in existence for less than 91 days, it will still qualify under either basic requirement because there will be no other location possible for establishing venue. Improper venue does not invalidate the effect of filing a petition.[16]

---

13. 11 U.S.C. §301; Bankruptcy Rule 1002; Official Form No. 1. See forms disk, Form 3.1.
14. See chapters 5 and 7 infra.
15. 28 U.S.C. §1408, 11 U.S.C. §109(a).
16. 28 U.S.C. §1412.

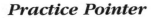

> ## *Practice Pointer*
>
> It is also important to not lose sight of the impact that the debtor's length of domicile will independently have on his/her ability to claim certain exemptions under Section 522. See chapter 9 infra.

Venue may be changed if a party in interest moves before the court to have the case transferred because the proceeding was initiated in an improper district or if the transfer is for the convenience of the parties and witnesses and in the interest of justice. Alternatively, the court may dismiss a case that has been filed in an improper venue.[17] For instance, it may be more convenient for a business debtor's proceeding to take place in the district where the principal assets are located when this is different from the principal (or headquarters) business address. On the other hand, it may be more convenient and logical for the proceeding to take place in the district where the corporate headquarters is located when the debtor has multiple locations, such as the parent entity of a franchise business, or a chain of retail stores. Because most proceedings are initiated by consumers, venue is infrequently a problematic issue.

The Federal Rules of Bankruptcy Procedure require a number of documents be filed along with the petition at the commencement of a voluntary proceeding or within certain limited time periods thereafter. Some of the required documents will vary depending upon the type of Chapter proceeding filed. Some of the documents may further vary according to the local rules of the district where the proceeding is filed.

In addition to the petition, a debtor must file certain other documents when a Chapter 7 petition is filed or the petition may not be accepted for filing by the court. In a situation where the debtor is filing to avoid an imminent foreclosure, repossession, or levy, a failure to file the minimum documents necessary for the clerk to accept the petition may be tantamount to legal malpractice. First, the filing fee must be paid when the case is filed. Debtors may also seek approval of the Bankruptcy Court to pay the filing fee in installments or to have the filing fee waived.[18] Second, every individual debtor must file a statement under penalty of perjury setting

---

17. 28 U.S.C. §1412; Bankruptcy Rule 1014.
18. Bankruptcy Rule 1006. 28 U.S.C. §1930(f) permits qualified indigent debtors to apply for a waiver of filing fees. This permits *in forma pauperis* petitions in appropriate circumstances. A qualified debtor is a debtor whose income is less than 150% of the official federal poverty line.

forth his/her Social Security number or a statement that the debtor has no Social Security number. This is because Federal Rule of Bankruptcy Procedure 1005 requires that all petitions contain only the last four digits of a debtor's Social Security number to protect privacy.[19] Third, a list containing the name and address of each creditor must be filed with the petition unless the Schedules of Assets and Liabilities are filed at the same time.[20] Fourth, the debtor's attorney must also file a declaration that there has been a disclosure to the debtor of the various types of Chapter proceedings available.[21] This last item has been incorporated in the petition in Official Form 1. Finally, 11 U.S.C. §521(b) requires a consumer debtor to file a prepetition credit counseling certificate showing compliance with Bankruptcy Code Section 109(h) as discussed in Section A, supra, or a certification explaining the "exigent circumstances" necessary to request 30 additional days to comply with the requirement.

Within ten days of filing, a "bankruptcy petition preparer" shall file a declaration under penalty of perjury disclosing any fee received from or on behalf of the debtor within 12 months preceding the filing, and any unpaid fee charged to the debtor pursuant to Section 110 (see chapter 7 infra). An unsupervised paralegal may be a bankruptcy petition preparer as defined in the Code.[22]

These minimum requirements will generally be used by regular bankruptcy practitioners only in an emergency, such as avoiding an immediate foreclosure, repossession, or attachment. Otherwise, it is recommended to file all of the documents described in this chapter required to be filed in connection with the proceeding at the time of filing. A filing that complies with only the minimum requirements is sometimes colloquially referred to as a "quickie" or "short form" filing.

If the debtor files a short form filing, within 15 days of filing a petition, the debtor must file a Statement of Financial Affairs, a Schedule of Assets and Liabilities, a Schedule of Current Income and Expenditures, and a Schedule of Executory Contracts and Unexpired Leases.[23] The Statement of Financial Affairs must conform to Official Form 7. An individual debtor's required claim of exemptions must also be included in the schedules.[24] All of the documents described in this paragraph are commonly referred to by bankruptcy practitioners as the debtor's **Statements and Schedules**.

---

19. Bankruptcy Rule 1005; Bankruptcy Rule 1007(f).
20. Bankruptcy Rule 1007(a)(1).
21. 11 U.S.C. §342(b); Pub. L. No. 98-353 §322; 11 U.S.C. §521(a)(1); 11 U.S.C. §527; Bankruptcy Rule 2016(b). See Section A, supra.
22. Bankruptcy Rule 2016(c).
23. 11 U.S.C. §521(a)(1); Bankruptcy Rule 1007(b)(1).
24. Bankruptcy Rule 4003(a).

Debtors must file copies of any evidence of payments received from any employer of the debtor within 60 days of filing; a statement of the amount of net monthly income and disclosure of any change of income reasonably anticipated over the 12 months succeeding the filing of the petition; the calculations necessary to determine compliance with Means Testing (see chapter 5 infra); a statement of current monthly income and expenditures; and a record of interests in educational IRA accounts or similar programs. Failure to file a required document by the 45th day from the filing of the petition will result in automatic dismissal on day 46, although an extension of up to 45 days may be sought for "justification." The court may also decline to dismiss the case for failure to comply if the debtor has made a good faith effort to comply and the court finds that administration of the case would be in the best interests of the creditors.[25]

Practice Pointer

Always make it a habit to check the applicability of the court's local rules. For example, some courts want the copies of the pay statements filed with the trustee and not with the court.

Not later than seven days prior to the meeting of creditors, individual debtors must provide to the trustee a copy of the debtor's federal income tax return for the tax year ending immediately prior to the filing of the petition. Failure to do so may result in dismissal of the case. Failure by a debtor to file any postpetition tax return or to provide copies of any returns requested can also result in dismissal of the case.[26]

The **Statement of Financial Affairs** is a questionnaire designed to elicit information sufficient to determine whether the debtor should receive a discharge or to reveal the existence of preferences or other avoidable transactions. The **Schedules** are an extended form of an accrual-based financial statement disclosing all liabilities and all assets of the debtor. The Schedule of Current Income and Expenditures discloses the existence or lack of surplus income after the payment of basic monthly expenses. It is relevant in Chapter 7 and Chapter 13

---

25. 11 U.S.C. §521(a)(1); 11 U.S.C. §521(f); 11 U.S.C. §521(i).
26. 11 U.S.C. §521(e).

proceedings.[27] Chapters 29 and 30 infra are devoted to an analysis of these documents. These documents comprise the core materials from which the trustee or the creditors may examine a debtor's financial affairs in any proceeding. They are the central "pleadings" of any bankruptcy. Whether the debtor is John Smith or a major corporation, the requirements are identical. The existence of nonexempt assets from which a distribution to creditors may occur is initially determined by analyzing the Statements and Schedules. The basic distributive rights of creditors to the assets can also be determined from a review of these documents.

Within 30 days of the filing, a consumer debtor must also file a statement of intention regarding disposition of secured collateral.[28] At the behest of consumer credit organizations, this provision was added to the Code in 1984 to expedite notification to secured creditors regarding a debtor's intent to retain and pay for, or to surrender, the collateral securing a secured debt. This requirement has helped to reduce relief from stay motions described in chapter 12 infra while assisting debtors and creditors alike in reducing the expenses and frustrations sometimes encountered in resolving a consumer's secured claim within the bankruptcy system. Chapters 12 and 21 of this text describe in more detail the automatic stay, the rights of a secured creditor, and the statement of intention.

Debtor's counsel must file a statement disclosing the compensation paid or to be paid in connection with the proceeding.[29] Form 4.5 on the forms disk is a sample. This document normally is to be filed within 15 days of the petition's filing.[30]

In a Chapter 13 proceeding, a debtor must also file his/her proposed Chapter 13 plan within 15 days of the petition's filing.[31] A number of additional documents must be filed in connection with a Chapter 11 or 12 proceeding. These materials are described in greater detail in chapters 24 and 27 infra.

Although it is permissible to file all of the required documents at various times, as noted above, it is generally more efficient and prudent to file them all together when the petition is filed. This will ensure that all necessary actions have been taken to protect the debtor's rights from the start of the proceeding. This will also eliminate any need to remember what must be done next and within what time limit. These documents, although numerous, are not generally so extensive or complex that they cannot all be filed with the petition except in an emergency. Many

---

27. 11 U.S.C. §521(a)(1); Bankruptcy Rule 1007(b). See chapter 23 infra.
28. 11 U.S.C. §521(a)(2). See forms disk, Form 21.3.
29. 11 U.S.C. §329.
30. Bankruptcy Rule 2016(b).
31. 11 U.S.C. §1321; Bankruptcy Rule 3015. See chapter 23 infra.

districts, particularly those in urban areas, have approved forms available for use, which helps make this task even easier to perform. Samples of all of these forms appear on the forms disk accompanying this text.

In appropriate circumstances, such as a proceeding with numerous creditors, or a debtor with complex financial transactions to be described in the Statement of Affairs, the court has discretion to grant an extension of time for the filing of the Statements and Schedules.[32] Not filing the documents in a timely manner, however, can result in a dismissal of the proceeding because the failure evidences a lack of prosecution.[33]

Section 302 of the Code permits the filing of **joint cases**. A joint case is filed by an individual and the individual's spouse. No other related entities may file a joint case.[34] However, there are provisions allowing the consolidation of two or more pending and related cases.[35] This is the only way two or more debtors who are not spouses may have a proceeding administered as one case.

For instance, if one spouse files a proceeding and then the other spouse files (assume they are separated so they each file a separate case), it is possible to obtain a court order consolidating the cases into one proceeding.

As another example, assume that a corporation files a bankruptcy proceeding and the owner of the corporation has guaranteed all of the corporation's debts and is subsequently forced to file an individual bankruptcy proceeding. Because many of the debts are identical (due to the guarantees), it is possible under the Bankruptcy Rules of Procedure to seek consolidation of the two proceedings into one.

As a third example, assume that a corporation and an individual file two separate and superficially distinct proceedings. Investigation discloses a distinct relationship between the debtors. Consolidation may also be appropriate in this instance.

Finally, assume that a group of related partnerships or corporations file proceedings. The partnerships may have a common general partner or partners. The corporations may be subsidiaries or affiliates of one another. (Subsidiaries and affiliates are described in more detail in chapter 6 infra.) Investigation may disclose substantial interrelationships between the various debtors that would make all proceedings more

---

32. Bankruptcy Rule 1007(c).
33. 11 U.S.C. §707(a); Bankruptcy Rule 1017; 11 U.S.C. §521(1).
34. 11 U.S.C. §302(a). Although rarely tested, at least one court has determined that the spouses have to be of opposite sexes. See In re Kandu, 315 B.R. 123 (Bankr. W.D. Wash. 2004). In another case, the court allowed a same-sex couple to claim a joint homestead exemption under state law. See In re Rabin, 359 B.R. 242 (9th Cir. BAP 2007).
35. 11 U.S.C. §302(b); Bankruptcy Rule 1015.

efficient and result in a more equitable distribution to all creditors if consolidation took place.

In each of the above examples, consolidation may be appropriate, although only spouses may initiate a joint case. (A joint case could be commenced in the first example.) There are two standard forms of consolidation. The court may consolidate two or more proceedings for all purposes. This is known as **substantive consolidation**. Substantively consolidated proceedings are treated as one case. Alternatively, the court may consolidate two or more proceedings for less than all purposes. This lesser form of consolidation is sometimes known as **administrative consolidation**.[36] Administrative consolidation may often save substantial time and expense in the administration of multiple related estates, although their assets and liabilities will remain segregated. It is a common occurrence in large corporate cases commonly filed in New York or Delaware that all the filing entities are administratively consolidated at the beginning of the case as a **first-day order**. See chapter 24 infra.

C. INVOLUNTARY PETITIONS

An entity is placed into bankruptcy against its will by the filing of an involuntary petition. There are different instances in which creditors, shareholders, or partners may force an entity into bankruptcy. A petition filed by an entity other than the debtor is called an involuntary petition. Section 303 of the Code contains the rules governing involuntary proceedings.[37] Section 303 is designed to equitably resolve the rights of an entity and its creditors while the issue of the involuntary bankruptcy is pending.

As discussed in chapter 1 supra, until the Bankruptcy Act of 1898, most bankruptcies were initiated as involuntary proceedings initiated by creditors against an alleged debtor. Until the twentieth century, involuntary bankruptcy was the traditional method of placing an entity debtor into bankruptcy. This is no longer the case in the United States. Almost all proceedings now filed today are voluntary; involuntary proceedings are rare.

Under the Bankruptcy Act and its many predecessors, a debtor became legally bankrupt only when the court entered an order adjudicating the

---

36. Bankruptcy Rule 1015.
37. 11 U.S.C. §303.

debtor bankrupt.[38] The Code has adopted the phrase "order for relief" to replace the prior language of "adjudicated as a bankrupt." Under the Bankruptcy Code, an order for relief arises automatically when a voluntary petition is filed.[39] In an involuntary proceeding, an order for relief will only issue upon a default by the debtor or upon the court's finding that cause exists to enter an order for relief in a contested proceeding.

The best way to consider the practical effect of an involuntary proceeding is to think of it in terms of a traditional lawsuit. The creditors who file the petition are the equivalent of plaintiffs, although they are generally referred to as **petitioning creditors**. Until an order for relief is entered, the debtor is usually referred to as an alleged debtor. The alleged debtor is the equivalent of a defendant. The specific relief or judgment sought by the petitioning creditors is the entry of an **order for relief**.

An involuntary petition is filed and served in a manner identical to a summons and complaint in a traditional lawsuit. A debtor may or may not contest the petition. If there is no opposition, the debtor will have an order for relief entered against it by default. If an alleged debtor contests the petition, the court will hold a trial to determine whether an order for relief should be entered. Discovery techniques and pretrial procedures may take place prior to the trial. The initiation of an involuntary petition thus constitutes the commencement of a lawsuit where the "plaintiffs" seek the entry of an "order for relief" as the judgment.[40] The time period between the filing of an involuntary petition and the entry of an order for relief can perhaps best be described as the period of time during which the creditors believe an alleged debtor is bankrupt while the alleged debtor believes it is not bankrupt. This period of time is often referred to as the "gap" or "limbo" period. Other provisions of the Bankruptcy Code help to establish the distributive rights of any creditors whose claims arise during this period.[41] These provisions are described in detail in chapter 21 infra.

Creditors may initiate involuntary proceedings for a number of reasons. First, a proceeding may be filed to prevent a debtor from continuing to commit known fraudulent transfers by wrongful dissipation of assets, thus improperly removing those assets from the reach of creditors.

Second, there might be a potential debtor who needs to file bankruptcy but who refuses. Perhaps the debtor owns a piece of property

---

38. 11 U.S.C. §41(f). This, of course, is a reference to 11 U.S.C. as it existed prior to October 1, 1978.
39. 11 U.S.C. §301.
40. 11 U.S.C. §303(h); Bankruptcy Rule 1018.
41. 11 U.S.C. §502(f); 11 U.S.C. §507(a)(2). See chapter 21 infra.

with enough equity to pay all creditors in full, but the property is about to be foreclosed upon. The potential debtor insists that no bankruptcy will be filed. Creditors in this instance might initiate an involuntary bankruptcy to gain the benefits of the automatic stay thereby preventing the immediate foreclosure. This will protect any equity in the property for payment of the creditor claims.[42]

A third common reason for filing an involuntary proceeding involves partnerships. As discussed above, a voluntary partnership filing must normally be accompanied by an authorization showing consent to the filing by all of the general partners or evidencing appropriate authority to file on behalf of all general partners.[43] Simply put, all general partners to a voluntary filing must sign the petition or the court must be provided with evidence that all general partners consent, such as a general management clause in favor of a managing partner or some other form of acceptable proxy. If one or more general partners refuse to consent to a voluntary filing, or if a debtor has a number of general partners and within the time limits for action it is not physically possible to obtain their written consent, the Code permits one general partner to file an involuntary proceeding.[44] Thus, one general partner may force a bankruptcy of the partnership over the objection of the remaining general partners.

An involuntary petition may only seek to place a debtor into Chapter 7 or Chapter 11 proceedings. An involuntary Chapter 12 or 13 proceeding cannot be initiated. Further, an involuntary proceeding may only be initiated against an entity that would also in the normal course qualify as a debtor under Chapter 7 or Chapter 11.[45]

Three specific types of entities may not have involuntary proceedings initiated against them: certain charitable and nonprofit organizations, such as churches, schools, or charitable foundations, and family farmers. Farmers are exempt from involuntary proceedings because Congress has determined that one lean year should not permit a farmer to be forced into bankruptcy by its creditors. It is for this same reason that involuntary Chapter 12 proceedings may not be initiated, as they are proceedings for family farmers. Finally, because Chapter 13 is an effort by a consumer to repay debt, Congress has found that to permit involuntary Chapter 13 filings would be akin to creating a form of involuntary servitude, because

---

42. 11 U.S.C. §362. See chapter 12 infra.
43. Bankruptcy Rule 1004(a).
44. 11 U.S.C. §303(b)(3).
45. 11 U.S.C. §303(a). See also chapter 4 infra.

it would force a debtor to repay debt.[46] Involuntary servitude is of course unconstitutional under the Thirteenth Amendment.[47]

The format of an involuntary petition is contained in Official Form 5.[48] Because the filing of an involuntary petition initiates a lawsuit or assumes the status of a lawsuit, a summons must be issued and served on the alleged debtor. Once served with the summons, the alleged debtor has 20 days to respond to the petition.[49] If the alleged debtor does nothing, the creditors can have an order for relief entered by default. This activity is equivalent to obtaining a default judgment in traditional nonbankruptcy litigation.[50]

Section 303(b) identifies the creditors who may file an involuntary proceeding. If the debtor has 12 or more creditors, three unsecured creditors with undisputed aggregate claims of at least $14,425 are required to file a proceeding.[51] The three creditors join together and file the involuntary petition. If an alleged debtor has 11 or fewer undisputed unsecured creditors, then any one such creditor may file the petition as long as the petitioning creditor is owed at least $14,425.[52] For example, if a potential debtor has 11 unsecured creditors owed in the aggregate less than $14,425, it will be impossible for the creditors to file an involuntary proceeding against the debtor because there is less than $14,425 in total debt and no single creditor is owed at least $14,425.

If the alleged debtor is a partnership, an involuntary petition may be filed by one or more of the general partners. This allows a partnership, where there is disagreement between the partners, to file a proceeding without the consent of all general partners. If a general partner has filed a bankruptcy proceeding, the partner's bankruptcy trustee has the authority to initiate the involuntary proceeding against the partnership.[53] For instance, assume a general partnership composed of three general partners, Moe, Curly, and Larry. The partnership owns a valuable piece of property that is about to be foreclosed upon. Moe and Larry want the partnership to file a bankruptcy immediately to gain the protections of the automatic stay. Curly opposes this. Moe and Larry file an involuntary

---

46. 11 U.S.C. §303(a). See also Historical and Revision Notes to Section 303.
47. U.S. Const. amend. XIII. In re Clemente, 409 B.R. 288 (Bankr. N.J. 2009).
48. See forms disk, Form 3.6.
49. Bankruptcy Rule 1010; Bankruptcy Rule 1011(b).
50. 11 U.S.C. §303(b).
51. 11 U.S.C. §303(b)(1). The 1994 Amendments added Section 104(b) to the Code. This provision acts to tri-annually adjust a number of the amounts set forth in various provisions of the Bankruptcy Code, such as Section 303(b)(1). The first adjustment took place on April 1, 1998. The text reflects the 2010 adjustments.
52. 11 U.S.C. §303(b)(2).
53. 11 U.S.C. §303(b)(3).

petition against the partnership seeking the entry of an order for relief over the objection of Curly. If either Moe or Larry were themselves debtors in a bankruptcy proceeding, their bankruptcy trustee would also have a right to file the involuntary petition. Once an involuntary petition is filed, additional qualified creditors may join in the filing of the petition simply by filing a one-page pleading with the court joining in the petition. This has the same effect as if the creditor had originally joined in the petition.[54] Significantly more than three creditors may therefore ultimately join in an involuntary petition.

There are benefits to be gained by the petitioning creditors in seeking the joinder of as many creditors as possible to an involuntary proceeding. For instance, a debtor may be able to show that one or more of the three originally petitioning creditors does not really have a proper claim, or that the total of the three claims is less than $14,425, or that one or more of the claims is actually in dispute. In each of these circumstances, a debtor may defeat an otherwise proper petition on this sort of technicality. The joinder of additional creditors provides for creditor unity and prevents a debtor from successfully contesting a petition on a procedural technicality. Joinder helps strengthen the case for the petitioning creditors.

The Code provides the alleged debtor an opportunity to contest the allegations of the petition.[55] The ability of an alleged debtor to do this makes the alleged debtor the functional equivalent of a defendant. If the allegations are contested, then the court will hold a trial to determine whether an order for relief should be entered. Due to the unique financial status that the involuntary filing creates for an alleged debtor, the Federal Rules of Bankruptcy Procedure direct the court to give preference to the matter on its calendar.[56] The Federal Rules of Bankruptcy Procedure applicable to adversary proceedings, which are essentially the Federal Rules of Civil Procedure, apply in contested involuntary proceedings.[57]

The petitioning creditors must prove the existence of one of two circumstances to obtain an order for relief. The first circumstance is that the debtor is generally not paying its debts as they become due.[58] This is not the same as being insolvent. Ironically, the debtor's solvency is technically irrelevant to the determination of whether to enter an order for relief in an involuntary proceeding. A debtor who is not paying its bills on time may or may not be insolvent.

---

54. 11 U.S.C. §303(c).
55. Bankruptcy Rule 1011(a).
56. Bankruptcy Rule 1013(a).
57. Bankruptcy Rule 1018. See Part VII of the Federal Rules of Bankruptcy Procedure. See also chapter 12 infra describing adversary proceedings.
58. 11 U.S.C. §303(h)(1).

Practice Pointer

Under the Code, "insolvent" means a financial situation in which the debtor's debts are greater than the fair valuation of all of his/her assets, exclusive of any exempt property or property improperly transferred or concealed. See 11 U.S.C. §101(32).

For example, a senior citizen with Alzheimer's disease may simply forget to pay bills or may throw them in the wastebasket. The person may be fabulously rich, but the person is not generally paying debts as they become due. An order for relief could be entered against this potential debtor. It is therefore important to recognize that the solvency of a debtor is not a conclusive issue to determine in connection with an involuntary proceeding except as insolvency may or may not relate to the debtor not generally paying its debts as they become due. Of course, presenting evidence of insolvency may be a relevant fact for the court to consider as evidence to assist it in making its determination.

The second circumstance that can result in the entry of an order for relief in an involuntary proceeding is that within 120 days prior to the filing of the petition, a custodian took possession of some portion of the estate's assets. For instance, the appointment of a receiver or an assignment for the benefit of creditors will cause this situation to arise.[59] This situation rarely arises in individual bankruptcy proceedings.

If the court can find that one of the two circumstances described above exists, then an order for relief will be entered. Once an order for relief is entered, the petition will then proceed exactly as if it had been initiated by the filing of a voluntary petition. All the documents previously described in this chapter will have to be filed, but the time limits will be counted from the date of the entry of the order for relief.[60] When the debtor is not available or does not file the required documents after the entry of an order for relief in an involuntary proceeding, it becomes the responsibility of the petitioning creditors to file the required documents to the best of their ability.[61]

The filing of an involuntary petition is a rather extreme creditor remedy. It has obvious and immediate adverse effects on an alleged debtor. For instance, a business may suffer immediate loss of business

---

59. 11 U.S.C. §303(h)(2).
60. Bankruptcy Rule 1007(c).
61. Bankruptcy Rule 1007(k).

merely due to the announcement of the filing. Although the creditors require ample protection in appropriate cases, a debtor who may not be found bankrupt requires protection to preserve the estate without the burden or stigma of a pending Title 11 proceeding. An improperly filed petition or a contested petition that takes too long to resolve can sometimes be fatal to what may have previously been a successful individual or business and become a self-fulfilling prophecy. Because of the diametrically opposed concerns of the creditors and the alleged debtor in these circumstances, certain provisions contained in Section 303 protect an alleged debtor while the issue of the petition is pending. Other provisions are designed to protect the creditors during the "gap" or "limbo" period. Once again, this is the period of time between the initiation of the petition and either the entry of an order for relief or a dismissal of the petition. This limbo period can also be described as that period of time during which creditors consider the entity bankrupt, but the alleged debtor considers itself as not bankrupt.

Where a debtor may be attempting to dissipate assets of an estate to the detriment of his/her creditors while contesting a petition, the creditors can seek the immediate appointment of an interim trustee prior to the entry of an order for relief. The court has further discretion to enter any appropriate order necessary to preserve the estate.[62] This provision affords the creditors protection in an appropriate case.

On the other hand, the court also has discretion to enter appropriate orders that protect the debtor. Under Section 303(e), the court can require petitioning creditors to post a bond to satisfy any damages that may be sustained by the debtor in the event the debtor is successful in contesting the petition.[63] The imposition of a significant bond acts as a deterrent to abusive creditors and a protection for debtors who do not properly belong in the bankruptcy system.

An alleged debtor may conduct business as usual. Consistent with the foregoing, however, the court may enter any appropriate order to protect the creditors or the alleged debtor.[64] This may sometimes result in the imposition of some controls and disclosure to the creditors regarding an alleged debtor's financial affairs while the involuntary petition remains pending.

If the court dismisses an involuntary petition, other than on agreement of the parties, the court has effectively rendered a judgment in favor of the alleged debtor. In this event, the court may order the petitioning

---

62. 11 U.S.C. §303(g).
63. 11 U.S.C. §303(e).
64. 11 U.S.C. §303(f).

creditors to pay the debtor's expenses, costs, attorneys' fees, and any actual damages caused by the petition. If the court further finds that the petitioners acted in bad faith, the court can also award a debtor punitive damages.[65] The bond referred to above should be based on an estimate of damages an alleged debtor may incur.[66] These burdens act as a deterrent to prevent creditors from abusing the system by wrongfully forcing entities into bankruptcy. If the court dismisses an involuntary petition against an individual and it determines that the petition was false or contained materially false statements, the court will seal all of the court records.[67] It may also enter an order preventing all consumer reporting agencies from reporting the bankruptcy and adversely affecting the debtor's credit.

Summary

A bankruptcy proceeding is initiated by the filing of a petition. The petition may be filed voluntarily or involuntarily: When a debtor files the petition, it is called a voluntary petition; when creditors file the petition, it is called an involuntary petition. The voluntary petition is the most frequently used method of initiating a bankruptcy proceeding. Consumer debtors must obtain a credit counseling certificate from an approved credit counseling service within 180 days prior to filing, absent exigent circumstances. A debt relief agency must provide disclosures to debtors and obtain written retainer agreements.

A debtor is not legally bankrupt until the court enters an order for relief. This order is automatic when a voluntary petition is filed, and it is the judgment that the petitioning creditors seek in an involuntary petition.

A debtor and his/her spouse may initiate a joint proceeding. No other combination of multiple debtors may initiate a proceeding together. However, two or more debtors may have their proceedings consolidated by motion for either substantive or administrative purposes.

The procedure of an involuntary petition can be compared to a non-bankruptcy lawsuit. The petitioning creditors are essentially plaintiffs who seek the entry of an order for relief against an alleged debtor who is essentially a defendant. An order for relief is entered upon either the debtor's default or after the court holds a trial upon a contested petition.

---

65. 11 U.S.C. §303(i).
66. 11 U.S.C. §303(e).
67. 11 U.S.C. §303(l).

When an involuntary petition is contested, the court must be able to make one of two findings to enter an order for relief. The first of these is that the debtor is not generally paying its debts as they become due. The second is that within 120 days prior to the filing, a custodian has been appointed to administer assets of the debtor. A custodian could be an assignee for the benefit of creditors or a state court receiver.

The period of time between the filing of an involuntary petition and the entry of an order for relief or dismissal of the petition is known as the "limbo" or "gap" period. During this period, the court may enter appropriate equitable orders to protect the rights of either the creditors or debtor. If the petition is dismissed, other than on agreement of the parties, the court may award the debtor costs, attorneys' fees, and actual damages. In an appropriate case, the court is empowered to award punitive damages.

When an order for relief is entered in an involuntary petition, the proceeding will thereafter continue as if it were a voluntary proceeding.

KEY TERMS

administrative consolidation
alleged debtor
assisted person
bankruptcy assistance
debt relief agency
first-day order
involuntary petition
joint case
order for relief
petitioning creditors

prepetition credit
   counseling
Schedules
Statement of Financial
   Affairs
Statements and Schedules
substantive consolidation
venue
voluntary petition

CHAPTER 3 CHECKLIST

3.1   VOLUNTARY PETITION DOCUMENT   *Authority*
      CHECKLIST
      3.1.1   To Be Filed with Petition:
           1.   Petition   Official Form 1
           2.   Filing fee   Bankruptcy
                                             Rule 1006

Filing fees effective
January 1, 2007:
    Chapter 7 — $299
    Chapter 11 — $1,039
    Chapter 12 — $239
    Chapter 13 — $274
Filing fees may be paid in install-
ments or waived for indigent debtors

3.	Statement of Social Security number	Bankruptcy Rule 1007(f)
4.	Corporate resolution or partnership consent	Bankruptcy Rule 1004; local rule
5.	List of creditors	Bankruptcy Rule 1007(a)(1)
6.	Prepetition credit counseling certificate	§109(h)
3.1.2	To Be Filed Within 10 Days of Petition — Bankruptcy Petition Preparer Statement of Compensation	§110 (h)
3.1.3	To Be Filed Within 15 Days of Petition — Statements and Schedules:	
1.	Schedules of Assets and Liabilities	11 U.S.C. §521(a)(1)(B)(i); Bankruptcy Rule 1007(b); Official Form 7
2.	Schedule of Current Income and Expenditures; Schedule of Executory Contracts and Unexpired Leases	11 U.S.C. §521(a)(1)(B)(ii); Bankruptcy Rule 1007(b); Official Form 6
3.	Statement of Financial Affairs	11 U.S.C. §521(a)(1)(B)(iii); Bankruptcy Rule 1007(b); Official Form 7
4.	Claims of exemptions	11 U.S.C. §522(1); Bankruptcy Rule 4003(a)
5.	Attorney statement of compensation paid or promised	11 U.S.C. §329; Bankruptcy Rule 2016(b)

3.1.4   To Be Filed Within 30 Days of Petition: 11 U.S.C.
         Statement of Intent re Secured   §521(a)(2)
         Collateral

3.1.5   To Be Filed Within 45 Days of Petition[68]

         1.   Attorney compliance with §342(b)   11 U.S.C.
                                                   §521(a)(1)(B)(iii)

         2.   Evidence of wages paid within 60   11 U.S.C.
              days of filing   §521(a)(1)(B)(iv)

         3.   Calculation of current monthly   11 U.S.C.
              income   §521(a)(1)(B)(v)

         4.   Disclosure of any increases in   11 U.S.C.
              income or expenses anticipated   §521(a)(1)(B)(vi)
              over the next 12 months

3.1.6   Within 7 Days of Creditor Meeting   11 U.S.C.
         Provide Trustee Tax Return for Year   §521(e)(2)(A)(i)
         Preceding the Filing

3.1.7   Failure to File Any Required Document   11 U.S.C. §521(i)
         Within 45 Days of Filing Results in
         Automatic Dismissal on 46th Day.
         One 45-Day Extension May Be Obtained.

3.2   SPECIAL CHAPTER 13 REQUIREMENTS
      3.2.1   Chapter 13 Plan (Within 15 Days)   11 U.S.C. §1321;
                                                   Bankruptcy
                                                   Rule 3015

3.3   INVOLUNTARY PETITION CHECKLIST
      3.3.1   Summons and Involuntary Petition   11 U.S.C. §303;
               Official   Form 5
      3.3.2   Qualifying Creditors

         1.   Three undisputed unsecured cred-   11 U.S.C.
              itors owed at least $14,425 in   §303(b)(1)
              aggregate

         2.   One undisputed unsecured   11 U.S.C.
              creditor owed at least $14,425   §303(b)(2)
              where there are 11 creditors or
              fewer

---

68. BAPCPA imposes these new requirements but does not state their deadline for filing except as
    set forth in 11 U.S.C. §521(i) requiring automatic dismissal on the 46th day if the required
    documents are not filed. The Bankruptcy Rules will undoubtedly be revised to account for
    these new requirements and should be consulted.

3.	One or more general partners where less than all consent to filing	11 U.S.C. §303(b)(3)
3.3.3	Obtaining an Order for Relief	
	1. Default	11 U.S.C. §303(b)
	2. Grounds for entering order in contested petition	
	a. debtor is not generally paying debts as they become due	11 U.S.C. §303(h)(1)
	b. appointment of custodian within 120 days of filing	11 U.S.C. §303(h)(2)

DISCUSSION QUESTIONS

1. How is a voluntary bankruptcy proceeding commenced?

2. What is a joint case?

3. How can multiple bankruptcy proceedings be consolidated? What is the difference between administrative and substantive consolidation?

4. Describe the basic documents filed by any debtor in a bankruptcy proceeding.

5. What are some of the reasons for initiating an involuntary bankruptcy against a debtor?

6. What are the grounds that petitioning creditors must prove to obtain an order for relief in an involuntary bankruptcy proceeding?

7. What provisions of the Bankruptcy Code protect the rights of creditors or the alleged debtor while an involuntary bankruptcy petition is pending?

8. What purposes might the prepetition credit counseling requirement serve? What drawbacks, if any, might the requirement have?

PRACTICE EXERCISES

Exercise 3.1

Draft a letter for your firm's prospective clients, the Bottomlines, explaining to them what information they should bring to a first meeting with your supervising attorney to discuss their financial affairs.

Exercise 3.2

Draft a letter to the Bottomlines, explaining to them the prepetition credit counseling requirement, including what they can expect, when the counseling must be completed, and where the services may be obtained.

Exercise 3.3

Draft a letter to the Bottomlines, satisfying the Section 527 Debt Relief Agency notice requirements.

Exercise 3.4

Prepare a draft Chapter 7 bankruptcy petition for the Bottomlines. You do not need to prepare any other pleadings to complete this exercise.

4

Chapter 1—General Provisions

Chapter 1 of the Code, 11 U.S.C. §101 et seq., contains a number of definitions and other general provisions. The provisions of Chapter 1 apply in all bankruptcy proceedings.[1] Many of the provisions of Chapter 1 are so broad and basic that their location and existence are sometimes forgotten when conducting bankruptcy research. Chapter 1 should not be overlooked. Substantial research time can be saved by seeking the meaning of a term or phrase within Chapter 1 rather than trying to find the answer by implication through use of another section or case law. Many items that are implicit in other Code sections or are not discussed in the case law are in fact explicitly set forth in Chapter 1.[2]

 Practice Pointer

Key definitions found in Section 101 include: "claim," "current monthly income," "debt relief agency," "domestic support obligation," "insider," "person," "security," and "transfer."

Section 102 contains several basic rules of construction. The phrases defined in Section 102 will always have the same meaning whenever used in another section of the Bankruptcy Code unless a specific provision states otherwise.

---

1. 11 U.S.C. §103(a). See chapter 2 supra.
2. See, e.g., 11 U.S.C. §101 Definitions.

A. NOTICE AND A HEARING

The first provision of Section 102 describes the phrase "*after notice and a hearing.*" This phrase, wherever used, signifies that due process must be given to the various parties involved in the proceeding before a court order authorizing the action that is sought to be performed can be obtained. In the context of the Bankruptcy Code, **due process** often means that the affected parties must merely be given notice and an *opportunity* to be heard. A hearing may not always be required.

When the phrase "after notice and a hearing" is used in a specific Code section, there are two basic ways to proceed: a **noticed motion** or an **ex parte** application. Many routine matters can be determined with a minimum of time and expense to all parties and prevent court calendars from becoming impossibly congested. Essentially, these are the general procedures governing motion practice in the Bankruptcy Courts.

The motion procedure set forth in Federal Rules of Bankruptcy Procedure (FRBP) Rule 9013 is the most common way of filing motions in the Bankruptcy Courts. Most matters coming through the Bankruptcy Court for decision will come before the court through this process.[3] The motion should state with particularity the relief sought, contain a proof of service, a notice of hearing, a proposed order for the relief requested, and be accompanied by one or more supporting affidavits unless the debtor is an individual consumer debtor.[4] When the value of an asset is in issue, as will commonly be the case in a **motion for relief from the automatic stay** (see chapter 11 infra), a valuation report must be filed with the motion.[5]

> ### *Practice Pointer*
>
> Additional motion practice requirements may also be imposed by local court rule. Local court rules frequently specify the time and place of filing as well as rules regarding schedules, use of briefs, and certifications of service.

---

3. FRBP 9013.
4. See FRBP 9006(d); FRBP 9013.
5. The local bankruptcy rules for your district will often include specific requirements for motions such as these.

A motion typically must be served at least 21 days prior to the hearing date, although local rules may vary this period in some situations.[6] Since FRBP 9006(f) requires that three additional days be added to any required notice period when the notice is given by mail, and since most notices are mailed in everyday practice, three days should be added to all notice periods. Notice periods, as described throughout the text, do not include this additional three-day period. Notice of the motion must be given to any entity against whom relief is sought, including the debtor, the debtor's attorney, the trustee, any creditor committee in the case (see chapter 10 infra), any entity having a lien on any property that may be affected by the motion's outcome, and any other entity that may be entitled to notice, such as the United States Trustee.

Any response to a motion should be filed and served within any time periods set by the court's local rules. Any party or entity served with the original motion must be served with any response filed by any party responding to the motion. It is possible that there may be multiple responses.[7] For example, where a trustee seeks to sell a piece of real property subject to two mortgages, a tax lien, a judgment lien, and the debtor's claim of exemption, all five of these parties could conceivably file a response to the motion.

Unless the debtor is an individual consumer debtor, any response must be accompanied by a proof of service, a proposed order for the relief requested, one or more supporting affidavits if there is a factual dispute, and a report of value if the value of a property is an issue in the motion, such as in a motion for relief from the automatic stay (see chapter 11 infra).[8]

Section 342(c) provides that any notice to a creditor contain the last four digits of the debtor's taxpayer identification number. Notices are to be sent to the address specified by the creditor, which the creditor may designate in at least two notices sent to the debtor within 90 days prior to the filing pursuant to new Section 342(c)(2) (as a practical matter, this information will likely come to be found in monthly statements). Creditors will also be able to file notices with a Bankruptcy Court designating an address to which bankruptcy notices are to be sent in Chapter 7 and 13 cases. Notices sent to a different address will not be effective until brought to the creditor's attention, pursuant to new Section 342(g).[9] This

---

6. FRBP 2002(a). There are some exceptions to this general rule. For example, FRBP 2002(b) requires 28 days' notice of a Chapter 11 disclosure statement hearing (see chapter 18 infra). The exceptions are noted in the text and are summarized in the Appendix.
7. FRBP 9014.
8. FRBP 9014.
9. If the creditor violates the automatic stay as a result of not receiving such notice of the debtor's filing, monetary sanctions may not be imposed per Section 342(g)(2).

provision thus has a potentially dramatic effect upon the automatic stay, the consequences of which will be left for case law to evolve.

Sometimes a matter coming before the Bankruptcy Court by way of a motion may contain disputed issues of fact that require further hearing by the court before a ruling can be made. In these instances, the court may conduct one or more preliminary hearings, often known as status conferences; may permit the parties to conduct discovery as in a traditional lawsuit; and may ultimately conduct the equivalent of a trial, commonly known as an **evidentiary hearing**, when the trial arises from a motion.

For example, Fran Fine objects to the claim of a store, Looks Like Jewelry, in her Chapter 13 case. Fran claims that the creditor store defrauded her into believing that the cubic zirconia she bought was really a big diamond. To resolve the matter, the court permits the parties to conduct discovery and ultimately holds an evidentiary hearing to rule on the objection. If Fran were suing Looks Like Jewelry in a traditional lawsuit, the evidentiary hearing would be the trial.

Some matters may be applied for without a noticed motion, on an ex parte basis (without notice in certain limited circumstances). A matter that comes before the court in this manner is generally called an ex parte application. Some examples of matters that may be brought before the court on an ex parte application include conversion of a case (see chapter 8 infra), dismissal of a Chapter 13 case (see chapter 17 infra), and requests for Rule 2004 examinations (see chapter 7 infra).[10]

An ex parte application should set forth with particularity the relief sought and be accompanied by a proof of service and a proposed order.[11] All ex parte applications must be served on the debtor's attorney, the trustee, and the creditors' committee in a case where there is a creditors' committee and any other entity required by federal law or by the FRBP, including the United States Trustee. No response is required, and the court will generally enter the order requested if there is no response. The FRBPs do not set forth a response time. Typically, local rules require any response to be filed five to seven days prior to the hearing.[12]

Sometimes emergencies arise that may require court orders in less time than the rules permit. For example, a trustee is appointed the interim trustee of a restaurant or store that sells perishable goods. The trustee

---

10. FRBP 9013. See appendix 1 for a list of matters that may be the subject of an application for an order.
11. FRBP 9013.
12. See, e.g., Local Rule 9014-3(i) of the Eastern District of Pennsylvania (answer due 14 days after service of motion) and Local Rule 9013-1(d) of the District of New Jersey (answer due seven days prior to hearing). Each of these rules permits the court to enter an order if no response is filed within the response period.

cannot wait 21 days or more to obtain court approval to sell the inventory. The tomatoes will get soft. The milk and eggs will spoil. The rules contemplate this sort of emergency and permit an order to be entered on less than 21 days' notice. In local procedure, such a practice may also be known as an *order shortening time*. Section 102(1)(B)(ii) specifically permits this sort of relief in appropriate circumstances.

The appendix summarizes matters that may be filed as noticed motions and matters that may be filed as ex parte applications, along with a summary of the parties to be served in each instance.

In understanding the due process provisions of the Code described in Section 102, it is helpful to identify the types of activities requiring some form of due process. It is also helpful to explore the practical implications of the imposition of due process upon both the courts and parties involved with the bankruptcy system. Affording parties due process is one of the most important and overriding features of the Bankruptcy Code.

Because virtually all of a debtor's financial affairs are placed under the jurisdiction of the court in a bankruptcy proceeding, many of a debtor's financial activities will require prior court approval. For instance, in a Chapter 11 case, a debtor will require court approval to liquidate assets, to assume or reject existing leases, and even to approve the officers' salaries.[13] The trustee in a Chapter 7 case will require court approval to liquidate or abandon assets, among other things.[14]

Most matters affecting the administration of an estate will require notice to all creditors by the party seeking permission to take a specific action. Matters affecting the rights of particular parties or assets, such as a motion for relief from the automatic stay, will require notice only to affected parties. Court orders in some ex parte matters may limit the notice period and may limit the number of parties who will actually receive the notice.[15]

Court action takes time. This "legal time" is often not consistent with the logic or pace of the business world. The time involved in making business decisions is often shorter than the bankruptcy system's decision-making process. Knowing how to use the system effectively can help to synchronize these two disparate and inconsistent decision-making processes as much as possible without requiring substantial

---

13. 11 U.S.C. §363; 11 U.S.C. §365; 11 U.S.C. §327; 11 U.S.C. §1107(b); Bankruptcy Rule 2014. See chapters 15 and 18 infra.
14. 11 U.S.C. §363; 11 U.S.C. §554. See chapter 18 infra.
15. Bankruptcy Rule 2002.

compromise. Besides, the minimum legal notice requirements cannot be compromised; they must be complied with.

B.   RULES OF GRAMMATICAL CONSTRUCTION

The remainder of Section 102 deals with various statements of grammatical or semantic construction. For example, use of the singular includes the plural.[16] This is self-explanatory. The word "or" is not exclusive.[17] This means that when the word "or" appears, its use means that any listed choice available in the affected section may apply. Proof of one given alternative will normally result in the application of the appropriate Code section in issue. Often more than one alternative may apply. For example, Section 363(f) provides five alternative means of selling a property "free and clear of liens." The existence of at least one alternative must be found to exist with regard to each lien upon the property.[18]

The words "include" and "including" are deemed to not be limiting.[19] This means that if a given Code section makes use of the words "includes" or "including," any following list provides examples of actions that may be taken or proven to allow application of a particular section. If, however, actions or facts not within the given list are shown to be within the intent of the Code section involved, the additional action or facts may be considered by the court.[20]

Conspicuously absent from Section 102 is a provision stating that the masculine includes the feminine. This is because the Bankruptcy Code has been written in a gender-neutral format.

C.   POWERS OF THE COURT

Section 105 concerns the court's powers. The Bankruptcy Courts have traditionally been considered courts of equity. Recall from chapter 1 of

---

16. 11 U.S.C. §102(7).
17. 11 U.S.C. §102(5).
18. See chapter 18 infra.
19. 11 U.S.C. §102(3).
20. For example, Section 1307(c) provides a list of situations that justify conversion of a Chapter 13 reorganization to a Chapter 7 liquidation. 11 U.S.C. §1307(a)(1). See chapter 23 infra.

the text that composition agreements in seventeenth-century England were within the jurisdiction of the Chancery, or equity, courts. Courts of equity have always had much discretion to formulate rulings and orders to give practical effect to the matters before them. Section 105 specifically gives the Bankruptcy Court equitable authority to enact any orders that are necessary to carry out the provisions of the Bankruptcy Code.[21] Some would suggest that an argument to the court based upon Section 105 is weak, signifying no authority elsewhere in the Code to support a proposed action. In fact, a Section 105 issue may involve a request for the court to rule against a specific provision in the Code where it does not make logical sense to apply it, such application not being in the best interests of the estate or creditors in a unique situation. This section is specifically designed to deal with those unique circumstances that may arise from time to time where no Code provision governs the conduct of the parties in a particular transaction, or where the court's equitable powers are necessary to enable the bankruptcy system to properly perform its intended purpose as a debt collection device.[22] Thus, when formulating an argument under Section 105, the most practical method of analysis is to apply the traditional nonbankruptcy concepts of equity balancing to the problem at hand. Reaching out to the court's inherent equitable powers is the essence of Section 105.

Practice Pointer

It is important to remember that Section 105 supplements powers already provided for under the Code. It does not create new substantive rights otherwise unavailable under the Code.[23]

Section 105(d) authorizes the court, on its own motion or at the request of a party in interest, and after notice to the parties in interest, to hold a status conference in any case and to issue any order deemed appropriate to ensure the expeditious and economic handling of a case. This provision was added to the Code in 1994 and simply codifies what

---

21. 11 U.S.C. §105.
22. Section 105 represents "the broad authority granted to bankruptcy judges to take any action that is necessary or appropriate 'to prevent an abuse of process.' " Marrama v. Citizens Bank of Mass., 549 U.S. 365, 375, 127 S. Ct. 1105, 1112, 166 L. Ed. 2d 956 (2007).
23. Section 105 also does not serve as "an independent source of subject matter jurisdiction." In re W.R. Grace & Co., 591 F.3d 164, 170 (3d Cir. 2009).

had been the existing practice of many Bankruptcy Courts. Under this provision, for example, the court may monitor the status of an adversary proceeding.

D. STATUTES OF LIMITATIONS

Section 108 concerns the effect of a bankruptcy proceeding upon non-bankruptcy statutes of limitation for any rights exercisable by the debtor or the bankruptcy estate. Section 108(a) effectively extends nonbankruptcy statutes of limitation for the protection of creditors and trustee. The reason for this is that the assets of a bankruptcy estate may include claims that a debtor has against third parties, such as personal injury claims or breach of contract claims. Sometimes, when a trustee is appointed in a proceeding, the debtor has not exercised its rights or a trustee does not immediately learn of the claim's existence. Section 108(a) therefore serves to extend any underlying nonbankruptcy statutes of limitation.

A trustee may select one of two defined limitations periods within which to proceed. The longer of the two periods may be utilized by the trustee to commence an action. Under Section 108(a), the limitations period will be the later of the original expiration date of the underlying statute of limitations, or two years after the entry of the order for relief.

For example, in California the statute of limitations to commence an action for breach of a written contract is four years.[24] Assume that a bankruptcy is filed three years after a claim arises. The trustee would actually have a total of five years from the date the claim arose to bring an action on behalf of the estate, because the two-year extension provided for under Section 108(a) is later than the four-year period provided for under California law. If three years and 364 days had expired prior to the filing of the bankruptcy proceeding, the trustee would have two years and one day to bring the claim. On the other hand, if only one year has elapsed prior to the bankruptcy filing, the original four-year limitation period of nonbankruptcy law will apply because it is longer than two years after the entry of the order for relief. Finally, if the statute of limitations has expired prior to the bankruptcy filing, Section 108(a) does not revive the claim for the trustee.

---

24. Cal. Code Civ. Proc. §337.

In some cases, an order may have already been entered prepetition in a nonbankruptcy proceeding fixing the period to file a response, cure a default, or take some other specified action. If the period within which to take action has not already expired at the time of the debtor's bankruptcy filing, the trustee will be given until the end of that period within which to respond, or 60 days from the date of the petition, whichever is later.[25]

 Practice Pointer

For example, Section 108(b) is frequently used to extend the state law period of redemption.

E.   WHO MAY BE A DEBTOR

Section 109 defines the entities that may be debtors in the various types of bankruptcy proceedings. Only *persons* may be debtors.[26] An individual is a person. A corporation can be a person. A partnership can also be a person.[27] A person has to reside or be domiciled in the United States or have a place of business or property in the United States. United States citizenship, however, is not required for a person to be a debtor in bankruptcy proceedings.[28]

 Practice Pointer

A "person" is defined under the Code to include individuals, corporations, and partnerships, but not governmental units.

Any person may file a bankruptcy proceeding under Chapter 7 except for railroads, insurance companies, banks, or savings and loan

---

25. 11 U.S.C. §108(b).
26. 11 U.S.C. §109(a). See chapter 6 infra.
27. 11 U.S.C. §101(41). See chapter 6 infra.
28. 11 U.S.C. §109(a).

institutions.[29] The insurance company prohibition does not bar insurance agents from filing—only the companies actually writing the insurance policies. There are separate regulatory agencies that deal with insolvent insurance companies because there are myriad issues arising that are too complex and unusual to be considered within the purview of the bankruptcy system. For example, there are the rights of the policy holders, the rights of the claim holders, and the rights of the shareholders and other general creditors. Separate regulation pays more careful attention to these precise relationships. Similarly, banks and savings and loans are regulated when they become insolvent either by state agencies or, in the case of federally insured financial institutions, by either the Federal Savings and Loan Insurance Corporation (FSLIC), the Federal Deposit Insurance Corporation (FDIC), or their successor, the Resolution Trust Corporation (RTC). When a financial institution is taken over by a regulatory agency, it means that the institution is effectively bankrupt.

Only municipalities may file under Chapter 9, if and only if state law permits the municipality to file a Chapter 9 bankruptcy case. States may bar municipalities from seeking Chapter 9 relief.[30]

Anyone who may be a debtor under Chapter 7 may also be a debtor under Chapter 11 except for stock brokers or commodity brokers.[31] A separate subchapter of Chapter 7 deals specifically with the issues arising when stock or commodity brokers file bankruptcy proceedings.[32] Filings of this type are most likely to occur only in those districts that are national financial centers, such as the Southern District of New York (New York City) and the Northern District of Illinois (Chicago). As a result, they are beyond the scope of this work. Railroads may file Chapter 11s. This is the only type of proceeding that railroads may file.[33]

In 1991, in Toibb v. Radloff, the U.S. Supreme Court examined whether or not an individual could qualify for Chapter 11 relief. In that case, an individual debtor not engaged in business sought Chapter 11 relief. The lower courts held that a nonbusiness debtor did not qualify for Chapter 11 relief. The Supreme Court disagreed, applying the literal language of the Code and concluding that individuals may seek Chapter 11 relief, because: "Under certain circumstances a consumer debtor's estate will be worth more if reorganized under Chapter 11 than if liquidated under Chapter 7."[34]

---

29. 11 U.S.C. §109(b).
30. 11 U.S.C. §109(c).
31. 11 U.S.C. §109(d).
32. 11 U.S.C. §§741-766.
33. 11 U.S.C. §109(d).
34. Toibb v. Radloff, 501 U.S. 157 (1991).

The 2005 BAPCPA legislation added Section 109(h) to the Code. This provision requires individual debtors to obtain a credit counseling certificate within the 180-day period prior to the petition filing as a prerequisite to filing, or to obtain a certificate within 30 days of filing when exigent circumstances are present. See chapter 3A supra.

The definition of who may be a debtor under Chapter 12 is described in chapter 27 infra.

There are four requirements that must be met to qualify for Chapter 13 relief. First the debtor must be an individual. *Individual* means a human being, not a partnership or corporation. Second, the debtor must have regular income. Under the Bankruptcy Act, a debtor had to be a wage earner to qualify for Chapter XIII. Under the Bankruptcy Code, a debtor need only be an individual with regular income. The following sorts of individuals can qualify to be Chapter 13 debtors: wage earners, individuals whose regular income sources are Social Security, disability, or other sorts of pensions, and individuals whose source of regular income may be dividends from trusts or stocks. Regular income can be many things. Sooner or later there is certain to be a reported proceeding where a state lottery jackpot winner will file a Chapter 13. If the jackpot to the debtor is paid over a period of time, the payments should meet the regular income requirements of Section 109.

Regular income does not mean that the income must be the same amount whenever received. It means that the income should be received at regular intervals: once a week, once a month, once in a while. A real estate agent receiving sporadic commissions will qualify as long as the amounts earned from the commissions can be predicted with some regularity.

Third, a Chapter 13 debtor must have unsecured debts of less than $360,475. Fourth, and finally, a Chapter 13 debtor must have secured debts of less than $1,081,400. If a Chapter 13 debtor has unsecured debts of $360,475 or more or secured debts of $1,081,400 or more, the individual may not file a Chapter 13 but instead will be required to file a Chapter 11 if repayment to creditors over time is desired. Further, Section 104(b) triannually adjusts the dollar limits contained in specified Code sections, including Section 109(e), to account for the effects of inflation. The limits stated in the text reflect the adjustment period for the three-year period beginning in 2010, which raised the respective limits from $336,900 to $360,475 and from $1,010,650 to $1,081,400 effective on April 1, 2010.[35]

---

35. 11 U.S.C. §109(e); 11 U.S.C. §101(30); 11 U.S.C. §104(b). See n.32 supra.

> ### *Practice Pointer*
> To recap:
>   Chapter 7 debtors can be individuals, cor-
>   porations, or partnerships, but not railroads,
> banks, or insurance companies.
>   Chapter 9 debtors are municipalities.
>   Chapter 11 debtors include anyone who could have
> filed under Chapter 7 plus railroads and certain banks.
>   Chapter 12 debtors are family farmers or family
> fishermen.
>   Chapter 13 debtors can only be individuals with regular
> income with less than a certain specified debt.

Section 109(g), added to the Code in 1984, exists to prevent an abuse to the system most commonly known as serial filing. A **serial filing** exists when a debtor files a bankruptcy and has it dismissed by the court (usually when the real estate is about to be foreclosed or when the repossession is about to occur after the automatic stay has been relieved). The same debtor immediately files another bankruptcy proceeding, requiring the creditor to return to court and seek relief from the automatic stay a second time. In this instance, the debtor may be attempting to abuse the system. Under Section 109(g), if the court dismisses a case because a debtor has willfully failed to abide by court orders or if a debtor dismisses a case voluntarily after a creditor obtains relief from the automatic stay, then the debtor will not qualify to file a new proceeding for 180 days.[36] In some situations, a Chapter 13 filed after receiving a Chapter 7 discharge will be permissible. (See chapter 23 infra.)

Summary

Chapter 1 of the Bankruptcy Code sets forth basic rules of construction and definitions that apply throughout the Code.

The most important provision of Chapter 1 pertains to the due process requirements in Code practice. Most actions that require court approval will require notice to creditors and an opportunity for them to be

---

36. 11 U.S.C. §109(g). Serial filing concerns are also addressed by Section 362(c)(3) and (c)(4) where automatic stay limitations are imposed. See chapter 11 infra.

heard either by way of a notice of intent or a formal properly noticed motion. As a result of Bankruptcy Rule 9006, the effective notice period by mail is 24 days. In exceptional circumstances, the court may approve an action without notice of a hearing or upon limited notice. An order obtained in such a manner is known as an ex parte order.

Section 105 provides Bankruptcy Courts with broad equitable powers to implement the purposes of the Bankruptcy Code.

Section 108 describes the effect of a bankruptcy proceeding on state statutes of limitation where the debtor is or may be a plaintiff.

Section 109 describes the entities that may be debtors in the various Chapter proceedings.

KEY TERMS

due process	notice and a hearing
evidentiary hearing	noticed motion
ex parte	regular income
motion for relief from the automatic stay	serial filing

CHAPTER 4 CHECKLIST

		Authority
4.1	MOTIONS	
4.1.1	Notice and an Opportunity to Be Heard	11 U.S.C. §102(1)
4.1.2	Twenty-Four-Day Notice Requirement	Bankruptcy Rules 2002(a), 9006(f)
4.1.2.1	Include debtor's name, address, and taxpayer identification number in any notice given	§342(c)
4.1.3	Noticed Motions	FRBP 9013
4.1.3.1	State relief sought includes proof of service, proposed order, affidavits	FRBP 9013

4.1.3.2	Notice of hearing	Consult local rule
4.1.3.3	Valuation report if value in issue	Consult local rule
4.1.3.4	Serve any entity against whom relief sought or with interest in property, trustee, debtor, and U.S. Trustee where required	FRBP 9013
4.1.3.5	Response due no later than five days prior to hearing date and served on parties serving or served with motion	Consult local rule
4.1.3.6	Response to include proposed order, report of value if in issue, affidavits	Consult local rule
4.1.3.7	Court may enter order if no response filed	Consult local rule
4.1.4	Application for an Order	FRBP 9013
4.1.4.1	Set forth relief, proof of service, and proposed order	FRBP 9013
4.1.4.2	Order may be entered if no response filed	Consult local rule

4.2   WHO MAY BE A DEBTOR

Chapter		Permitted Debtor	Exceptions	Authority
4.2.1	7	Any person[37]	Railroads, insurance companies, federally insured financial institutions	11 U.S.C. §109(b)
4.2.2	9	Municipality		11 U.S.C. §109(c)

---

37. A debtor must always be a person. Persons are individuals, partnerships, or corporations. 11 U.S.C. §§101(41), 109(a).

4.2.3	11	Any person qualified to be a Chapter 7 debtor	Stockbrokers, commodity brokers, railroads[38]	11 U.S.C. §109(d)
4.2.4	12	Family farmer with regular income		11 U.S.C. §101(18), §109(f)
4.2.5	13	Individual with regular income	Unsecured debts >$360,475; secured debts >$1,081,400	11 U.S.C. §101(30), §109(e)

DISCUSSION QUESTIONS

1. Describe who may be a debtor in:

   (a) Chapter 7,

   (b) Chapter 11,

   (c) Chapter 13.

2. Why are certain industries (banking, insurance, and railroads) not permitted to file Chapter 7 proceedings?

3. What are the procedures for filing or opposing a motion?

4. What distinguishes a noticed motion from an ex parte application?

5. When may a notice period be shortened?

---

38. Stockbroker and commodity broker liquidations have special subchapters in Chapter 7. Subchapter III of Chapter 7 (§§741-752) applies to the former. Subchapter IV of Chapter 7 (§§761-766) applies to the latter. Subchapter IV of Chapter 11 (§§1161-1174) applies to railroad proceedings.

5

Needs Based Bankruptcy or "Means Testing"

A. INTRODUCTION

Needs based bankruptcy or **means testing** is the centerpiece of the 2005 BAPCPA legislation. Means testing has fundamentally altered practice in consumer bankruptcy cases. The essence of means testing is that if an individual debtor can repay at least 25 percent of general unsecured debt over a 60-month period with minimum monthly payments of $117.08 ($7,025), or if a debtor can pay $11,725 or more over 60 months without regard to the percentage repaid, then a Chapter 7 petition is subject to dismissal for abuse unless the debtor consents to or voluntarily converts the case to a Chapter 13.[1] Means testing may only apply if the debtor's current monthly income is greater than the applicable state median income for a household of the debtor's size.[2] However, in such an event, the court and United States Trustee may nonetheless seek dismissal of a case for abuse under 11 U.S.C. §707(b)(1), which is procedurally identical to the law as it existed prior to the 2005 legislation.[3]

Because debtors and their attorneys are subject to penalties for improperly filing a Chapter 7 that should have been filed as a Chapter 13, means testing is a threshold issue. Its nuances will determine a debtor's

---

1. 11 U.S.C. §707(b)(2)(A). The amounts are subject to adjustment for inflation as per 11 U.S.C. §104(b). The amounts used in the text are those that became effective on November 1, 2010.
2. 11 U.S.C. §707(b)(7).
3. See chapter 7 infra. Perlin v. Hitachi Capital America Corp, 497 F.3d 264 (3d Cir. 2007); In re Paret, 347 B.R. 12 (Bankr. D. Del. 2007).

decision as to which Chapter to file and will greatly affect recommendations as to a client's options in seeking bankruptcy relief.

To determine a debtor's ability to repay a portion of unsecured debt under Chapter 13, means testing supplies a formula. If a debtor falls within the formula's parameters, it is presumed that the debtor's Chapter 7 filing is an abuse of Chapter 7, and a motion will be brought before the court to dismiss the petition. If the debtor does not fall within the formula's parameters, then no presumption of abuse arises, but the court or United States Trustee may still seek dismissal for abuse without the benefit of the presumption.[4] Prior to the enactment of means testing, a Chapter 7 petition was subject to dismissal pursuant to 11 U.S.C. §707(b) only for a "substantial abuse" of Chapter 7. BAPCPA eliminated the word "substantial" from the statute in what is now 11 U.S.C. §707(b)(1). The existence of the means testing formula makes this determinant of abuse a brightline test.

B. CURRENT MONTHLY INCOME

11 U.S.C. §707(b)(2)(A) contains the formula that determines when a Chapter 7 debtor's filing will be presumed an abuse of Chapter 7. The first element in the formula is the debtor's **current monthly income** as defined by Section 101(10A). This provision generally defines current monthly income as a debtor's average monthly income received from all sources in the 180 days prior to filing, without regard to whether or not the income is taxable. Current monthly income also includes amounts regularly paid by an entity other than the debtor for the household expenses of the debtor or a dependent of the debtor, but does not include Social Security benefits or payments to victims of terrorism.[5]

For example, June Cleaver earned $6,500 per month before being laid off three months prior to filing. She currently receives $1,400 every month in unemployment compensation and has received $4,200 since her layoff. She is also entitled to receive $800 per month in spousal support, but has only received $2,400 in the past six months, and nothing in the past three months. Her father who lives in the household regularly contributes his

---

4. Ibid. A statutory presumption functions as a rule of evidence. When a statute creates a presumption, this generally means that if facts giving rise to the presumption exist, then the burden of proof shifts to the opposition. See, for example, Federal Rule of Evidence 301.
5. 11 U.S.C. §101(10A).

$1,000 per month of Social Security benefits and his paycheck of $800 from Wal-Mart toward payment of the monthly household expenses. June's current monthly income is $5,150, consisting of a monthly average of $3,250 in compensation ($6,500 × 3 ÷ 6), $700 in unemployment ($1,400 × 3 ÷ 6), $400 in spousal support ($800 × 3 ÷ 6), and $800 from her father's paycheck. Remember that Social Security benefits are excluded from the definition of current monthly income. However, her actual monthly income is only $3,200, consisting of her $1,400 unemployment compensation, her father's Social Security benefit of $1,000, and her father's $800 paycheck. The fact that June does not actually receive some of her "current monthly income" may or may not constitute "special circumstances" described below. Under means testing, "current monthly income" and actual income are often not identical.

June's current monthly income multiplied by 12 is $61,800. If this amount exceeds the median income of her state for a household of two, then in a Chapter 7 June must completely fill out Official Form 22A. If her current monthly income is equal to or less than the median income for her state, then her Chapter 7 is not subject to dismissal for abuse under means testing.[6] A debtor's current monthly income and other necessary means testing calculations are performed and shown by use of Official Form 22. Chapter 30 below is a means testing tutorial.

"**Median family income**" is defined as income calculated and reported by the Census Bureau for a family of similar size for the most recent year available, adjusted by the Consumer Price Index.[7] These amounts are adjusted frequently. The amounts currently applicable may be found on the United States Trustee Program Internet website: www.justice.gov/ust. Links may also be found on many local bankruptcy court websites.

Practice Pointer

Information important to means testing that changes on a regular basis, such as household median income and allowable expenses as calculated by various IRS collection standards, can be found on the United States Trustee Program website: www.justice.gov/ust.

---

6. 11 U.S.C. §707(b)(7).
7. 11 U.S.C. §101(39A).

C. DEDUCTIONS

The second step in the formula is to deduct three groups of expenses from the current monthly income. The first group of deductions is the debtor's monthly expenses as calculated according to Internal Revenue Service collection guidelines, excluding payments for debts. Some of these standards are national, and some are local. There are national standards for day-to-day expenses, health care expenses, local expenses for housing and utilities, local expenses for transportation ownership and operation, and other necessary expenses.[8] Currently applicable amounts may be found on the United States Trustee Program website. Links may also be found on many local bankruptcy court websites. The forms disk includes links.

In Ransom v. FIA Card Services, _____ U.S. _____ (2011), the Supreme Court held that an expense deduction may not be taken as part of the debtor's means test if the debtor has no such costs: "Expenses that are wholly fictional are not easily thought of as reasonably necessary." When he filed Chapter 13, Ransom owned his car free and clear. He claimed a vehicle ownership expense deduction even though the IRS collection guidelines only permit one if the debtor is making a loan or lease payment. Resolving a conflict in the circuits, the Court explained: "Because Congress intended the means test to approximate the debtor's reasonable expenditures on essential items, a debtor should be required to qualify for a deduction by actually incurring an expense in the relevant category."

The following additional amounts are also included in this group of expenses: an additional utility allowance if in excess of IRS allowances and documentation is provided; actual expenses paid for the care and support of an elderly or disabled household member or immediate family member; the actual expense of a dependent child, up to $1,775 per year for private school tuition; and the amount of expense incurred to pay a Chapter 13 trustee in a Chapter 13, up to 10 percent of Plan payments (depending on the judicial district).[9]

The second group of deductions is the debtor's average monthly payments contractually due to secured creditors during the 60-month period following the petition. The payments to be made are totaled and then divided by 60. Thus, even if a car loan will be paid off in 24 months, the formula treats the total being paid over 60 months. For example,

---

8. 11 U.S.C. §707(b)(2)(A)(ii)(I).
9. 11 U.S.C. §707(b)(2)(A)(ii)(II)-(V).

if the monthly payment is $300 and 24 payments remain when the bankruptcy is filed, then the formula treats the monthly payment as $120 ($300 × 24 ÷ 60 = $120). Additionally, cure payments for arrearages that would be made in a Chapter 13 for loans secured by the debtor's primary residence, and secured loans necessary for the support of a debtor or dependent are aggregated and divided by 60.[10]

The third group of deductions is the debtor's expenses for payment of priority claims (claims payable pursuant to 11 U.S.C. §507(a)), such as priority taxes or unpaid support or alimony. These expenses are totaled and divided by 60. The quotient is deducted from current monthly income.[11]

If the amount of **surplus monthly income** available to a debtor after subtracting allowable deductions, multiplied by 60, would permit general unsecured creditors to be paid at least 25 percent of their claims or $7,025, or $11,725 or more over a 60-month period, without regard to the percentage repaid, then the Chapter 7 filing is presumed an abuse of Chapter 7. Stated another way, if a debtor can repay at least 25 percent over a 60-month period with minimum monthly payments of $117.08 ($7,025), or if a debtor can pay $11,725 or more over 60 months without regard to the percentage repaid, then abuse is presumed.[12] This means that if a motion is brought to dismiss the case as an abuse and the formula triggers the presumption of abuse, then the burden of proof shifts to the debtor to show that the filing is not an abuse.

For example, assume in the above example that June Cleaver is a family of two (herself and her father) living in New Castle County, Delaware. Since her annualized current monthly income of $61,800 exceeds the allowable median income of $61,424 for two people living in Delaware, June must fully complete Form 22. She owes her unsecured creditors $20,000. Her monthly mortgage is $1,200. She is two payments behind. She has a $250 per month car payment. The loan has 36 payments remaining. She is two payments behind. Based upon the IRS standards in effect as of November 1, 2010, June is allowed a National Standards allowance of $985, health care expenses of $204, a non-mortgage allowance of $452 and a housing allowance of $1,138, a transportation allowance of $299, and an ownership allowance of $496, for a total of $3,574. Her monthly mortgage payment is $1,200. She will use this amount instead of the mortgage allowance because it is the higher of

---

10. 11 U.S.C. §707(b)(2)(A)(iii).
11. 11 U.S.C. §707(b)(2)(A)(iv).
12. 11 U.S.C. §707(b)(2)(A)(i). The amounts are subject to adjustment for inflation as per 11 U.S.C. §104(b). The amounts in the text are the amounts that became effective on November 1, 2010.

the two amounts, and she may not deduct the same expense twice. The mortgage cure amount of $2,400 is divided by 60 and is $40 per month. Similarly, the car ownership expense of $496 is greater than her average monthly payment of $150, so the higher of the two expenses is used. The car payment cure amount of $500 is divided by 60 and is $8.33. This increases her allowable monthly expenses to $3,684.33. Subtracting this amount from her current monthly income of $5,150 results in monthly disposable income of $1,465.67. To this amount would be added an additional nominal deduction represented to be a hypothetical payment to a Chapter 13 trustee. According to the formula, June must either dismiss her case or convert it to a Chapter 13.

D. SPECIAL CIRCUMSTANCES

A debtor may rebut the presumption that a case is an abuse of Chapter 7 only by demonstrating the existence of "special circumstances" requiring an adjustment to current monthly income. To establish "special circumstances," a debtor must itemize each additional expense, provide documentation for each expense, and provide a detailed explanation of the special circumstances making the expense reasonable. The standard set forth in the statute is that the special circumstance must be like ". . . a serious medical condition or call to active duty military service." In the example, for instance, if June's unemployment runs out and she does not have a job, she will not have sufficient income to fund a plan. Deciding whether or not actually being broke is a special circumstance will be up to the courts. The debtor must attest to the accuracy of the information provided. The presumption of abuse is only rebutted if, after explaining and accounting for all the special circumstances, the debtor is unable to make the minimum payment required by the means testing formula. If she can still make the minimum payment the presumption is not rebutted.[13]

E. "TOTALITY OF CIRCUMSTANCES"

Even if a debtor successfully rebuts the presumption created by the means testing formula, the statute still permits dismissal as an abuse of Chapter 7

---

13. 11 U.S.C. §707(b)(2)(B).

if, for example, the debtor has filed the petition in bad faith or, if under the totality of circumstances, the filing is an abuse of Chapter 7. In practice, if the debtor's actual monthly income less the debtor's actual monthly expenses leaves disposable monthly income that would permit repayment of a substantial portion of unsecured debt over a 60-month period, under the "totality of the circumstances," abuse is more likely to be found. A below-median-income debtor's case is subject to dismissal for abuse under this provision.[14]

F.   PROCEDURE

The court, the United States Trustee, the trustee, or any party in interest may bring a motion to dismiss a case as an abuse of Chapter 7, if the debtor's current monthly income exceeds the applicable state median income for a particular debtor. If the debtor's income is less than the applicable state median, then no party in interest or the court may bring a motion to dismiss under means testing.[15] The United States Trustee is to review the debtor's schedules and file a statement within ten days after the meeting of creditors indicating whether the case should be presumed an abuse of Chapter 7. Typically, this notification is entered into the court docket electronically. If the notification indicates that the case is presumed to be an abuse of Chapter 7, then the United States Trustee must either file an appropriate motion within 30 days or a further report indicating the reasons why such a motion would not be appropriate.[16]

If a motion to dismiss for abuse of Chapter 7 is granted, and the court finds that the debtor was not substantially justified in filing Chapter 7, then the court may award the trustee attorneys' fees and costs. The debtor's attorney is subject to FRBP 9011 and sanctions for failing to properly investigate a debtor's financial affairs and in not assessing the case as an abuse of Chapter 7.[17] Alternatively, the court may also award a debtor attorneys' fees and costs if the court finds that a motion brought by a party in interest other than the United States Trustee or trustee was not substantially justified or that the motion was brought solely to coerce a

---

14. 11 U.S.C. §707(b)(3). See Perlin v. Hitachi Capital America Corp., 497 F.3d 264 (3d Cir. 2007); In re Paret, 347 B.R. 12 (Bankr. D. Del. 2006).
15. 11 U.S.C. §707(b)(6)(7). The case still remains subject to dismissal under the totality of circumstances as discussed above.
16. 11 U.S.C. §704(b). FRBP 1017(e) requires the motion to be filed within 60 days of the date first set for the meeting of creditors.
17. 11 U.S.C. §707(b)(4).

debtor into waiving a right guaranteed by the Bankruptcy Code. This latter provision, however, will not apply to small businesses (businesses with 25 or fewer employees) with claims of less than $1,175.[18]

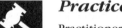

> ### *Practice Pointer*
>
> Practitioners should carefully maintain all the source material used to compute the various means testing calculations, so they can quickly corroborate how a particular item was calculated.

Means testing is an entirely new concept and raises many issues. The scope of the inquiry that counsel must conduct to avoid sanctions is problematic. To the extent that means testing requires bankruptcy practitioners to resort, on a regular basis, to materials outside of the bankruptcy system (IRS regulations and Census Bureau data), the bankruptcy system is no longer entirely self-contained.

G. NEEDS BASED BANKRUPTCY EXAMPLES

> ### *Practice Pointer*
>
> The reader should locate the applicable median income and IRS expense allowance deductions on the United States Trustee website, www.justice.gov/ust, and refer to them when reading the examples below.

Example 1

Lemuel Gulliver, of Montgomery County, Pennsylvania, lost his $120,000 per year job at an engineering firm two months ago. He has since been collecting $2,200 per month in unemployment. The unemployment runs out in two months. His spouse does not work.

---

18. 11 U.S.C. §707(b)(5).

They have two children, Bill and Ted, ages 10 and 12. Since Gulliver was laid off, the Gullivers have missed one $1,600 payment on their mortgage in favor of the Lilliput Mortgage Co. Lilliput is threatening foreclosure of their home. They own a 2008 Chevrolet Blazer for which they make monthly payments of $500 to the Bank of Laputa. They are current on their car payments. They have 20 more payments to make. They owe the Internal Revenue Service $1,500 for unpaid 2009 taxes, which they could not pay after Lemuel was laid off. They have $20,000 in credit card debt.

The first step is to determine Gulliver's current monthly income. Gulliver worked for four of the past six months receiving $10,000 per month, earning $40,000. He has collected two months of unemployment benefits at $2,000 per month, receiving $4,000. Since current monthly income is the average of income from all sources during the six-month period preceding the petition, both figures need to be added together and divided by six, resulting in current monthly income of $7,400. Assuming a median income of $78,626 for a household of four in Pennsylvania, since Gulliver's annual income of $88,800 exceeds the median allowable income, then Gulliver must fully complete the version of Official Form 22 applicable to the Chapter filed.[19]

The next step is to deduct allowable expenses from Gulliver's current monthly income. Looking up the IRS national standards for living expenses permits Gulliver to deduct $1,371, health care expenses of $240, non-mortgage housing and utility expenses of $689, mortgage expenses of $1,562, $299 in motor vehicle operating expenses for one car, and $496 for an ownership expense, equaling deductions of $4,657 per month. However, since the statute excludes payments for debts, Gulliver may not use the IRS mortgage/rent expense allowances because his mortgage payment is higher; and to allow two deductions otherwise would create duplication.[20] Similarly, from the $489 ownership allowance, deduct the average monthly payment of $166.67. The total allowable expenses in this group are now $4,528.33. Gulliver may also deduct other necessary expenses, which minimally includes all of the taxes that were withheld from his paycheck. For purposes of this example, assume that this amount is $2,500 per month.

---

19. In Chapter 7 cases, Official Form 22A applies; in Chapter 11, Form 22B applies; and in Chapter 13, Form 22C applies. All consumer debtors must complete the applicable form to the extent applicable. Since most debtors are under median, they will only need to complete those portions applicable to determining current monthly income. The income and expense figures used in the text are those in effect for the period commencing November 1, 2010.

20. In re Hardacre, 338 B.R. 718 (Bankr. N.D. Tex. 2006).

Pursuant to 11 U.S.C. §707(b)(2)(A)(iii), the Gullivers must average their secured debt repayments for the next 60 months. Their average mortgage payment is $1,600.00. Twenty payments of $500 remaining on the car total $10,000. Dividing this by 60 results in an average car payment of $166.67. The payments necessary to cure the mortgage default may also be accounted for, resulting in an additional monthly expense of $26.67 ($1,600/60 = $26.67).

Payments on any priority debt that Gulliver would have to repay in a Chapter 13 represent a final allowable deduction from current monthly income pursuant to 11 U.S.C. §707(b)(2)(A)(iv). The tax liability for 2009 fits in this category. $1,500 divided by 60 is $25.

According to the formula, then, Gulliver has current monthly income of $7,400, from which is deducted ($4,528.33 + $2,500 + $166.67 + $26.67 + $25), leaving a monthly surplus of $153.33. From this amount, Gulliver would be able to deduct an administrative expense multiplier representing fees that would be paid to a hypothetical Chapter 13 trustee, based on a monthly payment of $153.33. The administrative expense multiplier for the Eastern District of Pennsylvania is 10 percent, or $15.33. This lowers the monthly surplus income to $138.

Since Gulliver can pay his general unsecured creditors at least $117.08 per month for 60 months ($114 × 60 = $6,840), and since the total of $8,280 that can be paid exceeds $7,025 and would pay the Gullivers' unsecured creditors at least 25 percent, the presumption of abuse exists pursuant to the means testing formula. The court, the United States Trustee, panel trustee, or any party in interest may bring a motion to dismiss for abuse because Gulliver's current monthly income exceeds the state median for a household of four. Gulliver may attempt to rebut the presumption of abuse by explaining to the court the special circumstances that his unemployment of $2,200 per month runs out in two months and his actual income will then be zero. If the court does not consider this a special circumstance, Gulliver must either dismiss his case or convert it to a Chapter 13.

Example 2

Yossarian earns $80,000 per year at Catch-22 Software in Santa Clara County, California. He recently had a personal injury judgment entered against him for $100,000. The judgment is not covered by any insurance. Yossarian owes $50,000 in credit cards and $20,000 in unpaid child support for a child who does not live with him. He has a spouse and one child, Milo. His mortgage payments of $4,000 per month are current. His car payment of $700 per month is current. There are 60 payments left. Yossarian wants to file Chapter 7 to discharge the judgment and credit card debt.

First, calculate Yossarian's current monthly income. $80,000 divided by 12 is $6,666.67. Since $80,000 exceeds the median California income for a household of three of $67,562, Yossarian must complete Form 22A.

Second, deduct the Monthly National Standards for a family of three of $1,152, health care expenses of $180, a non-mortgage rent expense of $697, plus a vehicle operating expense allowance of $306. Since Yossarian's monthly mortgage payment of $4,000 is greater than the allowable housing expense deduction of $2,083, Yossarian will deduct the greater of the two. Similarly, he will not be entitled to an ownership expense deduction for his car payment, because the average payment of $700 exceeds the ownership allowance of $496, for a total living expense deduction of $2,335.

Assume that $2,000 per month is deducted from his paycheck for various taxes and other mandatory deductions. The average monthly payments for 60 months to secured creditors are $4,700 ($4,000 + $700). The child support claim would be a priority claim in Chapter 13. $20,000 divided by 60 is $333.33.

Yossarian's allowable deductions total $9,368.33, substantially exceeding his current monthly income of $6,666.67. Thus, no presumption of abuse will arise if Yossarian seeks Chapter 7 relief. Keep in mind also that there are additional deductions from current monthly income that have not been included in these examples.

Summary

Means testing places limitations on the choice of Chapter under which individual consumer debtors may file by essentially requiring conversion to a Chapter 13 or dismissal of the case if application of the means testing formula creates a presumption of abuse by the filing of a Chapter 7. The essence of means testing is that if an individual debtor can repay at least 25 percent of general unsecured debt over a 60-month period with minimum monthly payments of $117.08 ($7,025) or if a debtor can pay $11,725 or more over 60 months without regard to the percentage repaid, then a Chapter 7 petition is subject to dismissal for abuse unless the debtor consents to or voluntarily converts the case to a Chapter 13.

The complete means testing formula must be completed if a debtor's current monthly income exceeds the state median family income for a household of similar size. Deductions are made from current monthly income for basic monthly living expenses according to the Internal Revenue standards for collecting taxes from delinquent taxpayers. Additional deductions for payment of secured debts and for various other expenses permitted by the statute will determine if a debtor has sufficient surplus monthly income to trigger the presumption of abuse. A debtor may attempt to rebut the presumption of abuse upon a showing of "special circumstances."

Even if a debtor "passes" the means test, the case may remain subject to dismissal for abuse under the "totality of circumstances," or if the petition is filed in "bad faith."

A motion to dismiss for abuse, whether presumed abuse or the totality of the circumstances, must be brought within 60 days from the date first set for the meeting of creditors. Debtor's counsel is subject to potential sanctions if a motion is brought and granted, and counsel did not adequately confirm the debtor's representations. Alternatively, a moving party in interest that is a creditor is subject to sanctions for bringing an unsuccessful motion to dismiss or convert that is not well founded.

KEY TERMS

current monthly income   needs based bankruptcy
means testing   surplus monthly income
median family income

CHAPTER 5 CHECKLIST

		Authority
5.1	NEEDS BASED BANKRUPTCY	11 U.S.C. §707(b)(2)
5.1.1	Calculate debtor's current monthly income	§707(b)(2)(A)(i)
5.1.2	Deduct IRS expense allowance	§707(b)(2)(A)(ii)
5.1.3	Deduct average 60-month debt service	§707(b)(2)(A)(iii)
5.1.4	Deduct priority claims paid over 60 months	§707(b)(2)(A)(iv)
5.1.5	Subtract the sum of 5.1.2-5.1.4 from 5.1.1	

5.1.6   Abuse is presumed if surplus monthly income permits repayment of 25 percent over 60 months with minimum payments of $117.08, or if debtor can repay $11,725 or more without regard to percent repaid   §707(b)(2)(A)(i)

5.1.7   Special circumstances may permit deviation   §707(b)(2)(B)

DISCUSSION QUESTIONS

1. What is meant by the phrase "needs based bankruptcy" or "means testing"?

2. What is "current monthly income"?

3. What purpose or purposes does the concept of means testing serve?

4. Does means testing foster debtor relief or debt collection?

5. What is dismissal for abuse based on the totality of circumstances?

PRACTICE EXERCISES

Exercise 5.1
Complete the Form 22A Chapter 7 Means Test Calculations for the Bottomlines.

Exercise 5.2
Complete Schedules I & J for the Bottomlines.

6

Useful Definitions — Section 101

Section 101 is often overlooked when conducting bankruptcy research. This is probably because many practitioners do not normally use Section 101 on a regular basis since it does not contain familiar substantive rules of bankruptcy law. Nevertheless, Section 101 is critical because it contains definitions of many terms that are used frequently throughout the Code. Reference to a Section 101 definition will sometimes save substantial research time and will help to explicitly resolve questions only answered implicitly by other Code provisions. This chapter is an analysis of the definitions used most frequently in all aspects of bankruptcy practice. This knowledge also helps in acquiring a basic understanding of the Bankruptcy Code and system.

A. AFFILIATES

Section 101(2) defines *affiliates*. Affiliates are (1) nondebtor entities that own or control a 20 percent or more interest in a debtor, (2) nondebtor entities in which a debtor owns or controls 20 percent or more of the ownership interest, and (3) nondebtor entities that control or operate substantially all of a debtor's assets.[1] Affiliates may or may not be debtors. Affiliates may or may not also be insiders of a debtor. The distinction

---

1. 11 U.S.C. §101(2).

between affiliates and insiders acquires significance in the area of a trustee's avoiding powers and in the Code's distributive provisions.[2]

For example, Engulf and Devour, Inc., is the owner of more than
20 percent each of ten smaller entities. If Engulf and Devour files a Chapter 11, all of the smaller entities are affiliates. If one of the smaller entities
itself files a proceeding, Engulf and Devour would be a nondebtor affiliate.

B. CLAIM

Section 101(5) defines *claim*. Because a primary function of the bankruptcy system is to determine and pay dividends upon claims, it is germane to know when a transaction is considered to be a claim. Although
the Code definition appears lengthy and complex, it may be translated
into two simple sentences. First, a claim is a right to payment of any kind,
whether or not the amount has been previously determined or liquidated.[3] Second, a claim may also be a right to performance if the debtor's
breach can be compensated by monetary damages, whether or not the
amount has been previously determined.[4] A claim is considered liquidated when it has been reduced to a fixed sum.

Practice Pointer
Courts commonly turn to state law to determine the point at which an underlying cause of
action accrues.

C. COMMUNITY CLAIM

Section 101(7) defines *community claim* to mean: a claim against the
debtor that would be enforceable against community property under

---

2. See chapters 15-17 and 21 infra.
3. Most courts consider as a prerequisite that the claimant's "exposure" to the product or inci-
dent occur prepetition to qualify as a claim for bankruptcy purposes. See In re Grossman's Inc.,
607 F.3d 114, 125 (3d Cir. 2010).
4. 11 U.S.C. §101(5).

nonbankruptcy law.[5] This is of importance in those states utilizing community property law.[6] A debtor's discharge will normally effectuate a discharge on all of the debtor's community property, even if one member of the community has not filed a proceeding.[7]

D. CORPORATION

Section 101(9) defines *corporation*. A corporation is a business organized and registered according to nonbankruptcy or state law. The definition also includes associations that have all the powers of corporations under state law but are not incorporated under state law, such as unincorporated associations or business trusts.[8] For example, an unincorporated labor union is considered a corporation under the Bankruptcy Code.

E. CREDITOR

Section 101(10) defines *creditor*. The definition of *creditor* is a corollary to the definition of *claim*. A creditor is normally an entity with a claim that arises before the petition is filed.[9] This is known, more simply, as a prepetition claim. Entities whose claims arise after filing are not generally considered creditors for purposes of payment through the bankruptcy estate and are not affected by the bankruptcy proceeding except in several specific instances described elsewhere in this text.[10] A creditor not affected by a filing generally does not have its claim discharged and is generally not entitled to participate in any distribution of dividends.

---

5. 11 U.S.C. §101(7).
6. California, Arizona, New Mexico, Texas, Louisiana, Idaho, Nevada, and Washington.
7. See chapter 7 infra.
8. 11 U.S.C. §101(9).
9. 11 U.S.C. §101(10).
10. See chapters 8 and 21 infra. See also 11 U.S.C. §348(d); 11 U.S.C. §502(f), (g), (h), (i); 11 U.S.C. §503.

F.   CURRENT MONTHLY INCOME

An individual debtor's *current monthly income* is defined to include the debtor's average monthly income, from all sources received, in the six months preceding the filing of a bankruptcy petition as set forth in 11 U.S.C. §101(10A). This includes any amount received on a regular basis from any household member for payment of household expenses excluding Social Security payments and payments to war crimes victims. Current monthly income is utilized to determine the applicability of means testing for an individual debtor. See chapter 5 supra.

For example, Robert Goodwin lives with his spouse and three children. Two of the children are his wife's children from a former marriage. Robert receives $700 per month in SSI income. His wife, Zephorah, receives $3,000 wages that started three months ago. The family received food stamp assistance in the amount of $300 per month, but this ended two months ago. Zephorah is also entitled to receive $250 per month in child support, but she hasn't received any payments in three months. To determine Robert's current monthly income, each of the above amounts must be averaged for six months. Multiply each amount by the number of months actually received, divide by six, and then total the results. In the example, the Goodwin's current monthly income is $1,825, calculated as follows: (($3,000 × 3) + (300 × 4) + ($250 × 3) = $10,950) ÷ 6 = $1,825. Note that Robert's SSI income is not included.

G.   CUSTODIAN

Section 101(11) defines *custodian*: a third party appointed to administer assets of a debtor outside of the bankruptcy system. *Custodian* is a term of art used in the Bankruptcy Code to distinguish state court receivers, and others similarly situated, from bankruptcy trustees. A state court receiver appointed before the filing or an assignee for the benefit of creditors are the most common custodians encountered in bankruptcy practice. The trustees of a business trust are also custodians.[11]

---

11. 11 U.S.C. §101(11).

H.   DEBT

Section 101(12) defines *debt* as a liability on a claim.[12] That is, a debt is the inverse of a claim. A claim is what a creditor says it is owed; a debt is what a debtor says it owes. Ultimately, the two definitions are no more than two perspectives regarding an identical transaction or event.

I.   DEBT RELIEF AGENCY

A **debt relief agency**, as defined under 11 U.S.C. §101(12A), is essentially an individual consumer debtor's bankruptcy attorney or bankruptcy petition preparer (see chapter 7 infra).[13] Debt relief agencies are required to provide individual consumer debtors with written retainer agreements and the various prepetition notices described at chapter 3A supra.

Practice Pointer

In 2010, the Supreme Court in Milavetz, Gallop & Milavetz, P.A. v. U.S., 130 S. Ct. 1324, 1333 (2010), resolved a circuit split by holding that "attorneys who provide bankruptcy assistance to assisted persons are debt relief agencies within the meaning of the BAPCPA."

J.   DOMESTIC SUPPORT OBLIGATIONS

A "domestic support obligation," 11 U.S.C. §101(14A), is an obligation owed for the payment of spousal support, child support, or maintenance,

---

12. 11 U.S.C. §101(12).

13. Additionally, §101(3A) defines most individual consumer debtors as "assisted persons." An assisted person is an individual consumer debtor with less than $175,750 in nonexempt assets. This definition includes most consumer debtors. The amount is subject to triannual adjustment pursuant to 11 U.S.C. §104(b). Section 101(4A) defines "bankruptcy assistance" as goods or services provided to an assisted person for the purpose of providing advice or representation with respect to a bankruptcy case.

whether or not the unpaid amount accrued before or after the filing of the bankruptcy petition.

K. EQUITY SECURITY HOLDER

Section 101(17) defines *equity security holder*: an entity owning an interest in a debtor.[14] The shareholders of a corporation are its equity security holders. The partners of a partnership are its equity security holders. Equity security holders normally receive dividends from a bankruptcy estate only after all other creditors are paid in full.[15]

L. INDIVIDUAL WITH REGULAR INCOME

Section 101(30) defines *individual with regular income*. The meaning of this phrase has been previously described in chapter 4 supra. It includes individuals who have "regular" income that is "sufficiently stable" to make monthly payments to the trustee under a Chapter 13 plan.

M. INSIDERS

Section 101(31) defines *insiders*. Insiders are generally those entities in control of a debtor, or the debtor's relatives. The exact definition of an *insider* varies depending upon whether the debtor is an individual, a corporation, or a partnership. However, the basic principle is the same throughout. Those who are in control of, or who are related to, a debtor (in a family or business sense) are normally considered insiders.[16] Thus, the officers and directors of a bankrupt corporation are insiders of the corporation. The corporation is also an insider of any officer or director who files a proceeding. Partners are insiders of one another. For example,

---

14. 11 U.S.C. §101(16), (17).
15. See chapter 22 infra.
16. 11 U.S.C. §101(31).

David Addison and Madeleine Hayes are insiders to one another because they are partners of the Blue Moon Detective Agency. If they are married they would also be insiders because they would then be relatives.

An insider relationship between a debtor and creditor can affect the priority of dividend distribution to the insider creditor.[17] Insider status will also affect the time limits for certain transactions that may be avoidable by a trustee.[18] It is erroneous to believe that insiders and equity security holders are synonymous. They are not. An insider may or may not be an equity security holder. An equity security holder may or may not be an insider. For example, Ma Kettle owns one share of IBM. She is an equity security holder of IBM but not an insider. On the other hand, President Smith of IBM owns no stock. He is considered an insider of IBM but not an equity security holder.

N. INSOLVENCY

Section 101(32) defines *insolvent*. An entity is normally insolvent when the entity's liabilities (debts) exceed the value of its assets (property). This is a common accountancy definition of *insolvent* and is also commonly known as "balance sheet insolvency." This definition will suffice for most bankruptcy purposes. However, for purposes of the Code, the value of exempt and fraudulently transferred property is specifically excluded when performing this calculation.[19]

A partnership is insolvent if its debts are greater than the value of the partnership assets, excluding any fraudulently transferred assets, plus the net worth of each general partner, determined independently of the partnership in issue.[20] This method of calculation is consistent with the common law principle that a general partner is personally liable for partnership debts. For example, the Huey, Dewey, and Louie partnership has assets with a value of 25. The partnership has liabilities of 20. It is solvent. The partners fraudulently transfer assets with a value of 15 to Uncle Scrooge. The partnership is now insolvent, without considering the partners' net worth. Each partner, exclusive of the partnership, has a net worth of 1. The total asset value is now 13 (the total value of the

---

17. See chapter 22 infra.
18. See chapters 15-17 infra.
19. 11 U.S.C. §101(32)(A).
20. 11 U.S.C. §101(32)(B).

partnership assets and each partner's net worth). The value of the fraudulently transferred asset is not included in the computation. Because the debt owed is still 20, the partnership's liabilities (20) exceed its assets (13), and the partnership is deemed insolvent under the Code.

Historically, a debtor had to be insolvent to be bankrupt. However, the Code does not require that a debtor be insolvent to file a petition.[21] Insolvency is absent from the Section 109 requirements of who may be a debtor.[22] Nor is insolvency an element of proof required to obtain the entry of an order for relief against a debtor in an involuntary proceeding. Proving that a debtor is not generally paying its debts as they become due does not necessarily imply that a debtor is insolvent. As described in chapter 3 supra, situations may arise where a solvent entity can have an order for relief entered against it in an involuntary proceeding. It is therefore erroneous to believe that a debtor must be insolvent to be bankrupt. Under the Code, the insolvency of a debtor is normally only a specific issue to determine in connection with the application of certain of the trustee's avoiding powers.[23]

O.   JUDICIAL LIEN

Section 101(36) defines a *judicial lien*: a lien obtained by virtue of a court order or judgment. It can be a judgment, a prejudgment writ of attachment, or a postjudgment writ of execution.[24]

P.   LIEN

Section 101(37) defines a *lien* to mean: a charge against or a right to property to secure repayment of a debt or the performance of an obligation.[25] A lien in this sense may be either a judicial, consensual, or statutory lien. A trust deed or mortgage on real estate or a bank's security interest in

---

21. The exception to this rule is in the context of municipalities filing for bankruptcy under Chapter 9. 11 U.S.C. §109(c).
22. See chapter 3 supra.
23. See chapters 15-17 infra.
24. 11 U.S.C. §101(36).
25. 11 U.S.C. §101(37).

a vehicle is a consensual lien. A mechanic's or landlord's lien is a statutory lien. A judicial lien has just been described above. The common factor of these various rights is that they all create liens, legally enforceable interests in property to secure repayment or performance of an obligation. The Code also contains some fine distinctions between the various types of liens.

Q. MEDIAN FAMILY INCOME

Section 101(39A) defines *median family income* as the median income most recently calculated and reported by the Bureau of the Census, or if not currently calculated and reported, the most recently calculated and reported amount, adjusted upward by the Consumer Price Index.

R. PERSON

Section 101(41) defines a *person* to include: any kind of entity, individual, partnership, or corporation, except a governmental unit.[26] However, a governmental unit is considered a person when it has acquired rights in connection with a loan guaranty agreement and seeks placement on a Chapter 11 creditors' committee.[27] This definition, however, should not be construed to mean that governmental units are unaffected by operation of the Bankruptcy Code. Governmental units that are creditors are affected as much by the Bankruptcy Code as private creditors. Section 106 specifically waives any sovereign immunity of a governmental unit when the governmental unit is a claimant.[28]

---

26. 11 U.S.C. §101(41).
27. 11 U.S.C. §101(41); 11 U.S.C. §1102.
28. 11 U.S.C. §106. In United States v. Nordic Village, Inc., 503 U.S. 30 (1992), the Supreme Court held that 11 U.S.C. §106 does not act to waive the sovereign immunity of the federal government to permit the recovery of money claims. A similar ruling was applied to the states in Hoffman v. Connecticut Dept. of Income Maint., 492 U.S. 96 (1989). Section 106 was completely rewritten in 1994 to overrule these holdings. The revised Section 106 constitutes, for all practical purposes, an effective waiver of sovereign immunity in bankruptcy cases. Pub. L. No. 103-394 §113 (1994). However, as a result of the Supreme Court's ruling in Seminole Tribe of Florida v. Florida, 517 U.S. 44 (1996) (a nonbankruptcy case), numerous courts have held that Section 106, even as rewritten, remains in violation of the Eleventh Amendment. See, e.g., Sacred Heart Hospital of Norristown v. Commonwealth of Pa. Dept. of Pub. Welfare,

> ### *Practice Pointer*
> Note that there is a distinction between a "person" and an "individual." An "individual" can only be a "person," but a "person" encompasses more than just an "individual."

S.   SECURITY

Section 101(49) defines *security*. Several definitions within the Bankruptcy Code use the term *security*. Each definition is separate. The definition of the word *security* in Section 101(49) includes the various commercial documents commonly used to evidence an ownership interest in an entity or in certain sorts of financial assets, such as bonds or certificates of deposit.[29] Use of the word *includes* in the definition means that the court has discretion to interpret a document not included on the list as also being a security.[30] For purposes of a basic understanding, any document that evidences an intangible financial right will generally be considered a security under the Code. However, currency, checks, and certain specialized options or commodities are specifically not considered security.[31] Although these items may evidence the existence of an asset or claim, they do not constitute security within the Code.

T.   SECURITY AGREEMENT

Section 101(50) defines *security agreement*: an agreement that creates or provides for a security interest.[32] A security interest is an agreement that creates a lien.[33] A bank loan to finance a new car purchase usually creates a

---

133 F.3d 237 (1998). In Central Virginia Community College v. Katz, 546 U.S. 356 (2006), the Supreme Court held that 11 U.S.C. §106 is constitutional.
29. 11 U.S.C. §101(49).
30. See chapter 4 supra.
31. 11 U.S.C. §101(49)(B).
32. 11 U.S.C. §101(50).
33. 11 U.S.C. §101(51).

security interest in the car. A home loan is an agreement that usually creates a security interest in the real property by way of a mortgage or deed of trust. A security interest is generally considered perfected when the trust deed or mortgage is properly recorded or when a "UCC-1" is properly filed in a secured commercial transaction.

U. SINGLE ASSET REAL ESTATE

Section 101(51B) defines *single asset real estate*. Single asset real estate is real property that generates substantially all the gross income of a debtor who is not a family farmer and on which no substantial business is conducted other than the operation of the property and activities incidental thereto. Residential real property with three or fewer units is excluded from the definition. The purpose of this definition was to codify, for the sake of consistency, the many disparate conceptions of single asset real estate that had arisen in the case law.

For example, an apartment building with five units and secured debt of $500,000 (and whose only income is rental receipts) is single asset real estate. A golf course, restaurant, and subdivision project with secured debt of $20 million may or may not be a single asset real estate case. An office building with secured debt of $100 million is typically a single asset real estate case. Undeveloped land generating no income but with secured debt is single asset real estate.[34] This provision is most relevant in connection with the automatic stay (see chapter 12 infra).

V. STATUTORY LIEN

Section 101(53) defines *statutory lien* as: a lien created by operation of law and not by court order (a judicial lien) or agreement (consensual lien). A statutory lien cannot, however, include a judicial or consensual lien that may be created by statute. In this event, the lien would either be

---

34. 11 U.S.C. §101 (51B). See In re Oceanside Mission Assocs., 192 Bankr. 232, 234 (S.D. Cal. 1996), where the court stated: "If the debtor has no income, then substantially all of its income could be said to be generated by the property; i.e., substantially all of nothing is nothing."

a judicial or consensual lien but not a statutory lien.[35] Mechanic's liens or landlord's liens are common examples of liens that are created by statute or statutory liens.

W. TRANSFER

Section 101(54) defines a *transfer*. The definition is intentionally broad. A transfer is any type of means that human beings might devise to dispose of property or interests in property. Additionally, the creation of a lien, the creation of a security interest, and the foreclosure of a debtor's equity of redemption of property are all expressly noted as transfers.[36] This is an intentionally broad definition, because as technology develops there become more and more ways of creating means of transferring property or an interest in property.

Identifying precisely when a transaction takes place will determine the application of many substantive provisions of the Code, including determining when a preference or fraudulent transfer has occurred. Many of the following chapters will have occasion to discuss the effect of a transfer upon the operation of the Code section in issue.

Summary

Section 101 of the Code specifically defines many terms that are frequently used in other Code sections. This Section should not be overlooked when conducting bankruptcy research.

A claim is generally a right to payment or performance. A debt is the inverse of a claim.

Insiders are given special treatment in various Code sections. Whether the debtor is an individual, partnership, or corporation will determine who is an insider in relation to the debtor. Generally, family members or persons in control of a debtor's financial affairs will be insiders within the bankruptcy system.

The word *security* is contained within four different Section 101 definitions. Each of these definitions is different. This chart may assist in distinguishing between them:

---

35. 11 U.S.C. §101(53).
36. 11 U.S.C. §101(54).

Definition	Description	Authority
equity security holder	holder of an ownership interest in debtor (e.g., stock)	11 U.S.C. §101(17)
security	evidence of ownership (e.g., stock certificate)	11 U.S.C. §101(49)
security agreement	agreement creating a security interest	11 U.S.C. §101(50)
security interest	a consensual lien	11 U.S.C. §101(51)

Similarly, Section 101 contains four definitions of liens. These definitions are summarized as follows:

Definition	Description	Authority
lien	an interest in property to secure repayment or performance	11 U.S.C. §101(37)
judicial lien	a lien created by court order (e.g., writ of execution)	11 U.S.C. §101(36)
statutory lien	a lien created by statute	11 U.S.C. §101(53)
consensual lien	a lien created by a security agreement	11 U.S.C. §101(50), (51)

DISCUSSION QUESTIONS

1. What is the relationship between a claim and a debt?

2. What is an insider? Identify some possible reasons why the Bankruptcy Code may want to distinguish insiders from other parties to the proceeding?

3. What is a lien?

4. Identify the types of liens defined by the Bankruptcy Code.

5. What is the difference between *security* and *security agreement* as the Bankruptcy Code defines these terms?

6. Why is an equity security holder not defined as an insider by the Bankruptcy Code?

PART II

Debtor Relief

7

Overview of Chapter 7

A **consumer no asset bankruptcy** Chapter 7 case is a proceeding filed by an individual debtor or joint debtors in which there will normally be no assets available for the trustee to administer for distribution of dividends to unsecured creditors. Any assets owned by the debtor will be either secured or exempt. Consumer no asset proceedings comprise a majority of all of the proceedings that are filed. The basic outline of a consumer no asset Chapter 7 proceeding is equally applicable to all other types of bankruptcy proceedings. This is because the practical process of a consumer no asset proceeding, including documents to be filed and appearances to make, forms the core of all activity occurring in any bankruptcy proceeding.

A no asset Chapter 7 proceeding is filed by one person or by joint debtors. A husband and wife can file as joint debtors.[1]

> ### Practice Pointer
> The Bankruptcy Code describes "joint debtors" as an individual debtor "and such individual's spouse." The Code recognizes married couples but no other joint filings.

In a consumer no asset Chapter 7, all debtors seek the basic goals of debtor relief. One goal is to be able to claim all, or substantially all, of the debtor's assets as **exempt** and therefore free from the reach of the creditors or the trustee.[2] In plain English, the debtor gets to keep exempt

---

1. 11 U.S.C. §§301, 302. See chapter 3 supra.
2. See chapter 9 infra.

property. Second, debtors seek to obtain a discharge of their debt and the creditors' claims subject to the proceeding. A **discharge** is the term used to describe the release from debt that a debtor receives in a bankruptcy proceeding.[3] A debtor achieving the two goals of exempting property and obtaining a discharge receives the fundamental debtor relief provided for by the Bankruptcy Code. The protections of the **automatic stay** comprise the final element of debtor relief. These elements of debtor relief permit a debtor to obtain a fresh start in managing their financial affairs.

The **fresh start** is the primary reason for a consumer debtor to seek bankruptcy relief. Describing how to accomplish this objective is the subject of the next three chapters of this text. The initiation of a proceeding, the entry of an order for relief, and the documents that must be filed in connection with a Chapter 7 proceeding have already been identified in chapter 4 supra. This chapter concerns the basic activities that occur after the filing of a petition in a typical proceeding. Focusing on a consumer no asset proceeding will provide us with the basic model of the essential activities that occur in all bankruptcies.

A.   EMPLOYMENT AND COMPENSATION OF PROFESSIONALS

The Bankruptcy Code regulates the employment and compensation of professionals rendering services in any bankruptcy proceeding. Attorneys, accountants, appraisers, brokers, and the trustee are the most common such professionals. The provisions regulating professional employment and compensation are contained in Sections 326-331 of the Code.

Prior to filing a petition for an individual debtor, a debt relief agency, bankruptcy attorney, or petition preparer (see chapters 3 and 6 supra) must provide the disclosures required by Section 527. These notices must be given within three business days of first rendering services to a debtor. Additionally, a bankruptcy attorney or petition preparer must enter into a written retainer agreement within five business days of first rendering services to a debtor pursuant to Section 528. Section 526 provides penalties for noncompliance with these provisions. See chapter 3A supra.

In addition, all attorneys representing debtors must file a Statement of Compensation with the Bankruptcy Court. This Statement describes the

---

3. 11 U.S.C. §524.

fee that an attorney has received or is going to receive in connection with the proceeding. This requirement is mandated by Section 329(a) and is implemented by Bankruptcy Rule 2016(b). All fees paid to attorneys by the debtor within the one year period prior to the filing of the petition are also subject to disclosure.[4] Section 110 imposes a similar requirement on non-attorneys who are considered bankruptcy petition preparers (paralegals, see chapter 7B infra).

 Practice Pointer
A standardized form for the disclosure of attorney compensation can be found on the forms disk at Form 4.5.

Generally, a debtor or trustee may employ professionals. Attorneys, accountants, appraisers, and auctioneers are all professionals. A professional must be disinterested. The phrase **disinterested person** is defined in Bankruptcy Code Section 101(14). Most commonly, creditors, equity security holders, insiders, and persons who have an interest materially adverse to an estate are not disinterested. That is, the professional cannot normally have a potential or actual conflict of interest with the estate.[5] An attorney who is representing the debtor in a case therefore cannot represent the trustee in the same proceeding. Their interests are generally adverse to one another. Note, however, that the statute does not bar a nondisinterested person from representing a Chapter 7 debtor.[6] This is the one exception to the general rule. Thus, in-house counsel for a corporate debtor may represent the debtor in the corporation's Chapter 7 proceeding even if counsel is a creditor in the proceeding.

 Practice Pointer
Note also that it is not a conflict of interest for an attorney to serve as both the Chapter 7 trustee and as counsel for the trustee (i.e., as counsel for him or herself).

---

4. 11 U.S.C. §329(a); Bankruptcy Rule 2016(b). See chapter 3 supra.
5. 11 U.S.C. §§101(14), 327(a).
6. 11 U.S.C. §327(a).

A professional is not disqualified from employment solely due to representation of a creditor, unless another creditor objects. If an objection is raised by another creditor, there will be no disqualification unless the court finds an actual conflict of interest.[7] This provision permits counsel for a single creditor to be approved as counsel for a creditors' committee in a Chapter 11 case.[8] In such cases, counsel will normally be required to cease representing other parties in interest in connection with the bankruptcy proceeding.

A nondisinterested professional may also be employed for a special purpose provided that the professional is not adverse to the estate on the subject matter of the retention.[9] For instance, an attorney's knowledge and background of a debtor's activities may be so important that time and expense can be saved if the attorney/creditor continues to represent the debtor or trustee for limited purposes in the bankruptcy proceeding. Similarly, a debtor may have a personal injury claim as an asset and the trustee may wish to hire the debtor's personal injury attorney as special counsel for the estate to continue to prosecute the personal injury claim. The court will normally approve such applications to be retained for a special purpose.

To become properly retained by the estate or trustee, other than in a no asset proceeding, which merely involves the filing of the Statement of Compensation referred to above, a professional must file an application with the court and have the court approve the professional's retention by the estate or by the trustee.[10] This is the most important rule in connection with professional retention, namely that there be disclosure and prior court approval. If the professional does not obtain court approval for the retention, the court may deny the award of any compensation to the unapproved professional, regardless of the quality or quantity of the services.[11] A law firm performing services in a bankruptcy estate must therefore be certain to obtain prompt court approval of its retention, or counsel risks not being paid for the services rendered prior to approval of the retention.

A professional becomes approved to render services to a trustee, debtor-in-possession, or Official Creditors' Committee by filing a motion for an order authorizing employment.[12] The motion must include facts showing the necessity of employment, the name of the person to be employed, and reasons for the selection. The motion must describe the services to be rendered, disclose compensation arrangements, state that

---

7. 11 U.S.C. §327(c).
8. 11 U.S.C. §327(c); 11 U.S.C. §1103(b).
9. 11 U.S.C. §327(e).
10. 11 U.S.C. §327(a); Bankruptcy Rule 2014.
11. See, e.g., Palmer v. Statewide Group, 134 F.3d 378 (9th Cir. 1998) (nunc pro tunc retention is only approved in "exceptional circumstances").
12. 11 U.S.C. §327(a); 11 U.S.C. §1103(b); 11 U.S.C. §1107(b).

the professional is qualified to be retained within the meaning of Section 327, and disclose any interest that may be adverse to the estate. The motion must also be accompanied by a statement of the professional that the professional is a disinterested person. Any issue reflecting upon disinterestedness must be disclosed, and this remains a continuing duty throughout the course of employment. The court may also approve the professional on an interim basis, for the period of time prior to the hearing, as an ex parte matter. Failure to proceed promptly to become properly retained can result in a denial of payment, as described above.[13]

Section 328 provides that professional fees are to be reasonable. This Section also provides for the payment of contingent fees in appropriate matters. Although contingent fee arrangements were not permitted in practice under the Bankruptcy Act, the Bankruptcy Code specifically allows them in appropriate instances.[14] A contingent fee agreement will not be used in representing a debtor for general purposes of the proceeding itself. A contingent fee arrangement might, however, be acceptable to collect accounts receivable or to continue to prosecute personal injury claims. These are areas of legal practice in which contingent fees are ordinary and customary.

In Chapter 7, 12, and 13 proceedings, prefiling retainers paid to counsel are acceptable although the reasonableness of the retainer may be examined by the court. Local custom should be ascertained to determine the generally accepted fees permitted for Chapter 7 or 13 proceedings in a given district. Although prefiling retainers are permitted in Chapter 9 and Chapter 11 proceedings, local rule or practice may require compliance with the fee application process described below before any fees may be paid. Whether a retainer may be applied to the payment of fees prior to compliance with the fee application process is a matter of debate in the reported cases.[15]

 Practice Pointer
The debtor's obligation to pay for prepetition bankruptcy services is generally not dischargeable and the retainer paid is not considered to be a preference.

---

13. Bankruptcy Rule 2014; Bankruptcy Rule 2002; 11 U.S.C. §102. Representative forms are included on the forms disk accompanying this text. As to the duty of full disclosure and the risks of nondisclosure, see In re Leslie Fay Co., 175 B.R. 525 (Bankr. S.D.N.Y. 1993).
14. 11 U.S.C. §328(a).
15. See In re Printcrafters, Inc., 208 B.R. 968 (Bankr. D. Colo. 1997) for a representative example.

Professionals approved to render services to a bankruptcy estate or trustee are not paid for their services every month. Most law firms and other businesses customarily send bills to clients or customers every month and there is an expectation of prompt payment. In bankruptcy practice this is not the case. The Bankruptcy Code does not allow professionals to apply for compensation more than once every 120 days. A fee application brought during the pendency of a proceeding is commonly known as an **interim fee application**. In an exceptionally large proceeding the court may approve more frequent periods for the bringing of interim fee applications, but this is a rare practice.[16] Frequently, a period of time significantly longer than 120 days will pass before an application for compensation is brought, for the simple reason that to pay compensation the estate has to have funds available. If there are no available means for paying, it will be pointless to bring an application for compensation. Applications for interim compensation should be brought only upon giving due consideration to the needs of the estate and the ability of the professional to render competent services with or without receiving compensation until the close of the case. An application to approve compensation is always required at either the close of the proceeding or when all services to be rendered are complete. Such an application is known as a **final fee application**.

Interim and final fee applications are brought before the bankruptcy court as noticed motions pursuant to FRBP 2016 and 9013. (See chapter 4 supra.) FRBP 2016(a) requires a fee application to detail all time and charges and describe the services rendered and expenses incurred. Any payments previously made must be disclosed. A description in summary form of all services rendered, broken down by amounts and percentage of time spent, should also be included and is required in many local rules.[17] A sample application is included on the forms disk accompanying this text.

 Practice Pointer

Remember to always check local court rules and forms for the appropriate procedures to follow in seeking compensation. Courts frequently have rules governing the allowability of certain expenses and the manner in which application may be sought. Some courts have also adopted short form or standard order fee applications for certain routine services such as relief from stay motions and appearances in court.

---

16. 11 U.S.C. §331.
17. 11 U.S.C. §§330, 331; Bankruptcy Rule 2016(a).

In Lamie v. United States Trustee, 540 U.S. 526 (2004), the Supreme Court held that the precise wording of Bankruptcy Code Section 330(a)(1) does not permit a professional not employed by the estate to seek compensation therefrom. Thus, debtor's counsel in a case converted from Chapter 11 to Chapter 7 and in a Chapter 7 may not seek compensation from the bankruptcy estate.

The court will hold a hearing on an interim or final application for compensation. While a proceeding remains pending, the court will typically award only a percentage of the current charges for which compensation is sought. A typical award is 70-80 percent of the current charges. This percentage may vary from district to district in accordance with local practice. At the end of the proceeding, there will be a final hearing to approve all compensation earned in the proceeding. At this time, any withheld portions of prior applications may or may not be approved for payment.

The bankruptcy system makes a serious effort to control and limit the compensation paid to professionals. If counsel performs less than competently, the court has the discretion to "reward" such behavior when an application for compensation is brought. The "reward" may be a denial or reduction in the amount of compensation actually approved for payment. The Bankruptcy Courts scrutinize fee applications carefully. The United States Trustees have been specifically directed to review and comment upon applications for compensation brought in bankruptcy proceedings. The guidelines of the local United States Trustee will also need to be complied with. The Bankruptcy Court may, on its own motion, award less compensation than is requested. Among the factors the court will consider are the time spent, whether the services were necessary or beneficial to the estate, the complexity of the services, and the rates charged.[18]

A trustee's compensation is governed solely by Section 326. The trustee's maximum compensation is determined by an arithmetical formula based upon the percentage of an estate's assets that a trustee actually administers. The maximum compensation permitted a trustee is 3 percent of the value of the assets administered where the value of the assets administered is greater than $1 million. The percentage is higher for estates with a value of less than $1 million, but the maximum dollar compensation permitted at this level is $53,250.[19] This maximum compensation to a trustee is subject to review based on the same factors applicable to other professionals. Typically, a Bankruptcy Court will base a trustee's compensation on an equivalent hourly rate for legal or accounting services multiplied by the time a trustee has spent on a case, up to the

---

18. 11 U.S.C. §330, 28 U.S.C. §586(a)(3)(A). See chapter 10 infra.
19. 11 U.S.C. §326(a). 11 U.S.C. §330(a)(7) provides that a trustee's compensation awarded pursuant to Section 326 be considered as a commission.

maximum compensation permitted. In addition, a trustee is entitled to receive $60 from the debtor's initial filing fee.[20] Sometimes a trustee may put in ten minutes of work for the $60. Sometimes a trustee will work for many hours on a proceeding and still earn only the same $60. Further, a trustee does not receive compensation immediately, but normally receives the statutory percentage compensation at the close of a proceeding. The fee from the debtor's filing fee is usually received some time after a proceeding is closed. In a large case with many assets and a lot of work, a trustee may apply for interim compensation, although the maximum compensation must remain within the limits permitted by Section 326.[21] A trustee's application for interim or final compensation is brought before the court as a noticed motion pursuant to FRBP 2016 and 9013. (See chapter 4 supra.)

All professional compensation is considered an expense of administration and does not normally create a claim as described in this chapter supra. Administrative expenses are further described in chapter 21 infra.

B.   BANKRUPTCY PETITION PREPARERS

Section 110 of the Bankruptcy Code applies to bankruptcy petition preparers. Section 110(a) defines a **bankruptcy petition preparer** as a person other than the debtor's attorney or the attorney's employee under that attorney's direct supervision who prepares for compensation a document for filing with the Bankruptcy Court. An unsupervised paralegal may be a bankruptcy petition preparer. A *document for filing* is any document prepared for filing by a debtor in a bankruptcy case.

Section 110 is directed specifically at unsupervised paralegals preparing documents for filing by debtors with the Bankruptcy Court. This Section does not, however, authorize unsupervised paralegals to prepare or file documents with the Bankruptcy Court unless applicable state law permits such activities by paralegals. Thus, Section 110 does not affect state laws concerning the unlawful practice of law. Such laws remain expressly in effect (§110(k); see chapter 9C infra and the cases cited therein). A paralegal must therefore ascertain local law before acting independently to prepare bankruptcy documents for filing with the Bankruptcy Court.

Section 110 sets forth eight basic requirements for bankruptcy petition preparers to comply with. They are as follows:

---

20. 11 U.S.C. §330(b).
21. 11 U.S.C. §331.

1. The preparer must sign the document and include the preparer's name and address (§110(b)).
2. Provide a notice to the debtor, prior to the preparation of any document, stating that a petition preparer may not give legal advice (§110(b)(2)).
3. The preparer shall include the preparer's Social Security number on the document (§110 (c)).
4. The preparer shall furnish the debtor with a copy of the document not later than the time the document is presented to the debtor for signature (§110(d)).
5. The preparer shall not execute any document on behalf of a debtor nor provide legal advice to the debtor (§110 (e)).
6. The preparer shall not use the word *legal* or any other similar term in advertisements or advertise under any "legal" category (§110(f)).
7. The preparer may not receive or collect payment for court fees (§110(g)).
8. The preparer shall, at the filing of the petition, file a declaration under penalty of perjury disclosing any fees paid or promised by or on behalf of the debtor (§110(h); FRBP 2016(c)).

Violations of any of the foregoing requirements are subject to a discretionary fine of $500 (§110(1)(1)). Under §110(h), the court shall also disallow and order turned over to the trustee any fee found to be excessive. Acceptable fees will invariably vary from district to district; however, the 2005 legislation permits the adoption of rules that would set the fees bankruptcy petition preparers may charge.

Section 110(i) creates a civil remedy for damages against a bankruptcy petition preparer who violates Section 110 or commits any fraudulent, unfair, or deceptive act. The debtor, trustee, or the United States Trustee may move and seek recovery of the debtor's actual damages, the greater of $2,000 or twice the amount paid by the debtor to the preparer, plus reasonable costs and attorneys' fees for bringing the motion.

Section 110(j) provides yet a further check on a bankruptcy petition preparer's conduct by authorizing a party in interest, including the United States Trustee, to seek to enjoin a bankruptcy petition preparer from continuing to act as such where the preparer has engaged in fraudulent or deceptive conduct, has misrepresented the preparer's experience or education, or has violated Section 110 on a continuing basis. Like Section 110(i), Section 110(j) authorizes the court to award reasonable attorneys' fees and costs to the successful moving party.[22]

---

22. See In re Clarke, 426 B.R. 443 (Bankr. E.D.N.Y. 2009), aff'd in part, rev'd in part, 426 B.R. 457 (E.D.N.Y. 2010) (tailoring an injunction); In re Kangarloo, 250 B.R. 115 (Bankr. C.D. Cal. 2000) (calculating damages); In re Bernales, 345 B.R. 206 (Bankr. C.D. Cal. 2006)

A bankruptcy petition preparer also falls within the definition of a debt relief agency and is therefore also required to provide the notices set forth in Sections 342(b), 526, and 527 as described in chapters 4 and 7A supra.

The effect of Section 110 is to impose a heavy burden of compliance upon unsupervised paralegals who can prepare bankruptcy documents for debtors in a jurisdiction that has authorized such activities as not constituting the unlawful practice of law. However, although the requirements are numerous, any qualified and properly trained paralegal will not find compliance to be difficult.

C. THE CHAPTER 7 PROCESS

Although the Chapter 7 process is not set in motion in business cases until the debtor files a petition, in consumer cases, BAPCPA has created new requirements that effectively commence the Chapter 7 process before a petition is even filed. Recall that a consumer debtor must obtain a pre-petition credit counseling certificate as a prerequisite to filing a petition absent a showing of exigent circumstances. Even if exigent circumstances are shown, the certificate must be obtained within 30 days of filing, or the case is subject to dismissal on the forty-sixth day after filing. See chapter 4A supra. Also, recall that a debt relief agency must provide various notices to the debtor and enter into a written retainer agreement, within short intervals of time after first meeting a debtor. All of these provisions ought to be complied with at the initial conference with a client. See chapters 4A and 7A supra.

Once a debtor files a petition, a clear process is set in motion. The first event that occurs is the appointment of an interim trustee by the United States Trustee pursuant to Section 701. The **interim trustee** will serve as the trustee until the meeting of creditors.[23] In all judicial districts, there exist panels of private trustees. Private panel trustees are persons who act as trustees on a regular basis.

Under the United States Trustee system, which went into effect nationwide in 1988, the United States Trustee has been given the responsibility to appoint interim trustees.[24]

(permanently enjoining petition preparer). Section 110(l)(2), added by BAPCPA, permits the court to triple the fines assessed against a bankruptcy petition preparer who advises a debtor to exclude assets or use a false Social Security number, who fails to advise a debtor that the debtor is in fact filing a bankruptcy petition, or who files documents that do not disclose the bankruptcy petition preparer's identity.

23. 11 U.S.C. §701.
24. 11 U.S.C. §701(a); 28 U.S.C. §586(a)(1). See chapter 10 infra.

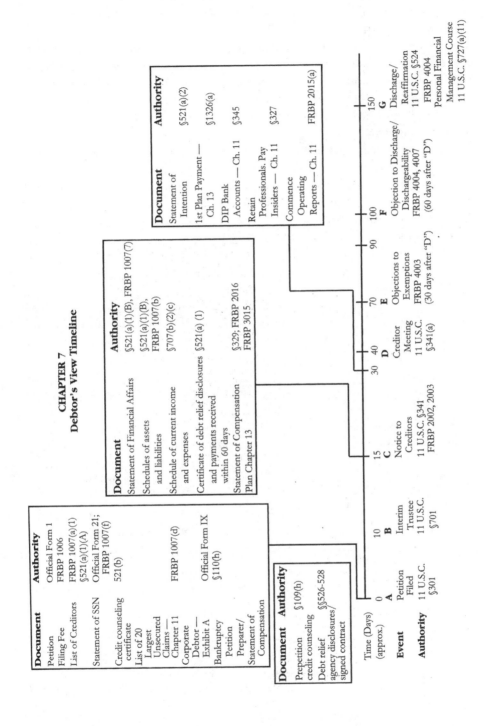

CHAPTER 7
Debtor's View Timeline

Document	Authority
Petition	Official Form 1
Filing Fee	FRBP 1006
List of Creditors	FRBP 1007(a)(1) §521(a)(1)(A)
Statement of SSN	Official Form 21; FRBP 1007(f)
Credit counseling certificate	521(b)
List of 20 Largest Unsecured Claims — Chapter 11	FRBP 1007(d)
Corporate Debtor — Exhibit A	Official Form IX
Bankruptcy Petition Preparer/ Statement of Compensation	§110(h)

Document	Authority
Prepetition credit counseling	§109(h)
Debt relief agency disclosures/ signed contract	§§526-528

Document	Authority
Statement of Financial Affairs	§521(a)(1)(B), FRBP 1007(7)
Schedules of assets and liabilities	§521(a)(1)(B), FRBP 1007(b)
Schedule of current income and expenses	§707(b)(2)(c)
Certificate of debt relief disclosures and payments received within 60 days	§521(a) (1)
Statement of Compensation	§329; FRBP 2016
Plan Chapter 13	FRBP 3015

Document	Authority
Statement of Intention	§521(a)(2)
1st Plan Payment — Ch. 13	§1326(a)
DIP Bank Accounts — Ch. 11	§345
Retain Professionals. Pay Insiders — Ch. 11	§327
Commence Operating Reports — Ch. 11	FRBP 2015(a)

Time (Days) (approx.)

0	10	15	30 40	70	90	100	150
A	B	C	D	E		F	G

Event	Petition Filed	Interim Trustee	Notice to Creditors	Creditor Meeting	Objections to Exemptions	Objection to Discharge/ Dischargeability	Discharge/ Reaffirmation
Authority	11 U.S.C. §301	11 U.S.C. §701	11 U.S.C. §341 FRBP 2002, 2003	11 U.S.C. §341(a)	FRBP 4003 (30 days after "D")	FRBP 4004, 4007 (60 days after "D")	11 U.S.C. §524 FRBP 4004 Personal Financial Management Course 11 U.S.C. §727(a)(11)

Next, the United States Trustee will send a notice to the creditors, to the debtor, and to the interim trustee advising all parties of the entry of an order for relief (the filing) and the appointment of the interim trustee.[25] This notice is usually given about five days after a proceeding is filed. Next, the United States Trustee will provide notice to the creditors advising them of the time and place of the **creditors' meeting** to be held pursuant to Section 341.[26] The form of the notice shall be substantially in the manner of Official Form 16. A sample is included on the forms disk accompanying this text.

Section 342(c) of the Bankruptcy Code, added by BAPCPA, requires that a debtor include the last four digits of the debtor's Social Security number and provide notice to a creditor at the address specified by the creditor in either communications to the debtor or in a registry maintained by the court. Creditors are given an opportunity to advise the Bankruptcy Court of the address to send notices in Chapter 7 and 13 cases. Notices to creditors not given in compliance with this provision are not effective until brought to the creditor's attention.[27]

The creditors' meeting is often erroneously called a "first meeting of creditors," even though under the Code there is only one required meeting of creditors. This misnomer has arisen because under the Bankruptcy Act there was a first meeting of creditors and a last meeting of creditors. The word "first" is now superfluous. Federal Rule of Bankruptcy Procedure 2003 requires that the meeting of creditors take place not less than 21 (because 21 days' notice is required under Bankruptcy Rule 2002(a)) and not more than 40 days after the order for relief is entered.[28] Because this timing is based upon the entry of an order for relief, the same time limit applies in both voluntary and involuntary proceedings. Remember, once an order for relief is entered in an involuntary proceeding, the matter proceeds in a manner identical to a voluntary proceeding.[29]

The meeting of creditors is the most visible aspect of many bankruptcy proceedings. In a no asset proceeding, it is normally the only appearance a debtor is required to make.[30] There is no judge present at the meeting of

---

25. 11 U.S.C. §342(a); Bankruptcy Rule 2002(a); Bankruptcy Rule 2008.
26. 11 U.S.C. §§341, 342(a); Bankruptcy Rule 2002(a); Bankruptcy Rule 2003.
27. 11 U.S.C. §342(c); 11 U.S.C. §342(g). The consequences of noncompliance for debtors and creditors alike will have to evolve in the case law. For example, the automatic stay is generally effective without notice (see chapter 12 infra). For a detailed analysis of the operation of Section 342(g), see In re Harvey, 388 B.R. 440 (Bankr. D. Me. 2008).
28. 11 U.S.C. §342(a); Bankruptcy Rule 2003. In a Chapter 13 case, the meeting of creditors may take place within 50 days of filing.
29. See chapter 3 supra.
30. 11 U.S.C. §343; Bankruptcy Rule 4002.

creditors, only a representative of the United States Trustee.[31] The representative administers the oath to the debtor and recites the debtor's duties under the Code as well as the discharge and reaffirmation process. The United States Trustee has been given the responsibility of conducting creditors' meetings under the United States Trustee program.[32]

At the meeting of creditors, the creditors are given an opportunity to elect a trustee. Elections for a specific trustee are infrequent. Section 702 contains the procedure for conducting such an election. The interim trustee will become the permanent trustee unless the creditors elect another trustee.[33]

The trustee and creditors may examine the debtor or debtors at the creditors' meeting. The trustee will ask questions based upon the trustee's review of the Statements and Schedules. In the typical no asset consumer proceeding, a trustee will normally ask ten basic questions. These questions are:

(1) State your name, Social Security number, and current address for the record. The Trustee will also request proof of the same, such as a Social Security card and a driver's license or other similar document.[34]

(2) Have you read the Bankruptcy Information Sheet provided by the United States Trustee?[35]

(3) Did you sign the petition, schedules, statements, and related documents you filed with the court?

(4) Did you read the petition, schedules, statements, and related documents before you signed them?

(5) Are you personally familiar with the information contained in the petition, schedules, statements, and related documents?

(6) To the best of your knowledge, is the information contained in the petition, schedules, statements, and related documents true and correct?

(7) Are there any errors or omissions to bring to my, or the court's, attention at this time?

(8) Are all of your assets identified on the schedules?

(9) Have you listed all of your creditors on the schedules?

---

31. 11 U.S.C. §341(c); Bankruptcy Rule 2003(b).
32. 11 U.S.C. §341(a); 28 U.S.C. §586(a)(5); Bankruptcy Rule 2003.
33. 11 U.S.C. §702(d).
34. 11 U.S.C. §521(h).
35. A sample Bankruptcy Information Sheet is contained at Form 7.7 on the forms disk. The information contained in the notice is similar to the notice required to be provided by a debt relief agency pursuant to 11 U.S.C. §342(b) within three days of providing bankruptcy assistance pursuant to 11 U.S.C. §527(a). See chapters 3A and 7A supra.

(10)   Have you filed bankruptcy before? (If so, the trustee must obtain the case number and the discharge information to determine the discharge eligibility of the debtor(s).)[36]

Many trustees will also ask the debtor: "What caused your financial difficulties?" The reason for this question is to comply with one of the requirements for a discharge — namely, that a debtor be able to describe satisfactorily a lack of assets to satisfy liabilities. See chapter 12E infra.

Section 341(d) to the Code requires the trustee to examine the debtor further to make sure the debtor is aware of:

1.   the consequences of seeking a discharge, including the effects on credit history;
2.   the debtor's right to file a petition under a different Chapter of the Code;
3.   the effect of receiving a discharge of debts; and
4.   the effect of reaffirmation (see section E infra).

If there are specific assets in the estate or issues involving the estate that the trustee is concerned about, additional questions will likely be asked. For example, if the debtor owns a home, the trustee will probably ask a series of questions to determine whether there may be any equity in the home that may be used to pay a dividend to unsecured creditors. If the debtor owns a vehicle, the trustee may ask similar questions pertaining to it. If the debtor is a plaintiff in any lawsuit or if the debtor has previously been involved in a business, the trustee will ask questions about each of these activities. However, in a typical no asset consumer proceeding, the average debtor may not own real estate, and there is little or no realizable equity in vehicles in most instances. So the basic questions will be asked and no others. Because creditors' meetings are usually scheduled in groups of ten or more, all to take place within an hour, there is not much time for extended examination. However, if the Statements and Schedules are complete and understandable and if the trustee is prepared, it is possible to successfully complete a series of examinations within a relatively short period of time.

After the trustee completes the examination, creditors are given an opportunity to further examine the debtor. A nonattorney may appear on behalf of creditors in consumer bankruptcy cases. For example, a para-legal working in the collection department of a department store could

---

36. A debtor may only receive a discharge once every eight years. 11 U.S.C. §727(a)(8). See chapter 12 infra.

appear and question debtors.[37] Sometimes creditors or their counsel will advise the trustee and demonstrate that a debtor may not be disclosing all pertinent information. Sometimes creditors or their counsel waste everybody's time asking irrelevant questions unrelated to a debtor's financial affairs. Sometimes a representative of a bank or finance company simply wants to know where a secured asset is and if it is currently insured. Creditors do have a right to come to the creditors' meeting and make inquiry of the debtor's assets and liabilities, but in actual practice, creditors rarely appear at these hearings.

D.   RULE 2004 EXAMINATIONS

Sometimes, creditors or a trustee will want to examine a debtor for more time than is available at the creditors meeting. Alternatively, a trustee or creditor may desire to examine a third party, not the debtor, regarding the debtor's financial affairs. The Federal Rules of Bankruptcy Procedure provide a method that allows any party in interest to take the examination of any person concerning a debtor's financial affairs. This method is called a **Rule 2004 Examination**.[38] Under the Bankruptcy Act, this was known as a Rule 205 Examination. The prior and present rules are virtually identical. It has been stated of Rule 205, the predecessor to Rule 2004, that it is "in the nature of an inquisition."[39] Objections on grounds of relevancy are not normally acceptable during one of these examinations. In fact, most objections will not be appropriate in a Rule 2004 Examination and any matter relevant to the proceeding is fair game.[40] Rule 2004 exists for the benefit of creditors or for the benefit of the trustee who desires to conduct an extensive examination of the debtor or a third party beyond the time limitations of the creditors' meeting.

 Practice Pointer
A Rule 2004 Examination is simply another form of a "deposition."

---

37. 11 U.S.C. §341(c). This provision was added by the 2005 legislation.
38. Bankruptcy Rule 2004.
39. 12 Collier on Bankruptcy §705.15 at 2-93 (14th ed. 1973).
40. Bankruptcy Rule 2004(b).

An order for a Rule 2004 Examination is obtained when the party seeking to conduct the examination files an application for an order with the court.[41] The order must be served personally, in a manner identical to service of a subpoena.[42] Nondebtor examinees and debtors, when required to travel more than 100 miles, one way, are entitled to compensation for mileage in reaching the place of examination.[43]

A Rule 2004 Examination, when appropriate, has several benefits in addition to the time factors described above. It is a form of discovery that permits a trustee or party in interest to determine the existence of assets or claims and the rights of the parties without incurring the additional expenses of commencing an adversary proceeding. In short, the Rule 2004 Examination is a method for conducting what are essentially depositions without having to file a lawsuit first. Rule 2004 Examinations are used extensively in motion practice under the Code. For example, a party may wish to take an appraiser's Rule 2004 Examination in connection with a motion for relief from the automatic stay. A creditors' committee may take Rule 2004 Examinations in connection with a motion to appoint a trustee in a Chapter 11 proceeding.

E.   DISCHARGE AND REAFFIRMATION

After the creditors' meeting, the next and final event that occurs in a typical no asset consumer proceeding is that an individual debtor or joint debtors will receive a discharge.[44] Up until 1986, debtors were also required to appear in court, before a judge, to receive their discharge.[45] The discharge hearing was typically held between 60 and 90 days after the meeting of creditors. The 1986 amendments to the Code made the requirement of discharge hearings discretionary with the court unless there is a **reaffirmation agreement** to approve.[46] Under the 2005 amendments, there will be a hearing if the debtor does not have an attorney or if the reaffirmation agreement is presumed an undue hardship within the meaning of 11 U.S.C. §524(m)(1). Receipt of a discharge will be automatic unless an objection to the discharge itself is filed. Pursuant to the 2005 legislation, a debtor will not receive a Chapter 7

---

41. Bankruptcy Rule 2004(a).
42. Bankruptcy Rule 2004(c).
43. Bankruptcy Rule 2004(e).
44. 11 U.S.C. §524; 11 U.S.C. §727. See chapter 13 infra.
45. See 11 U.S.C. §521(5) as it existed prior to November 1986.
46. 11 U.S.C. §524(d).

discharge unless the debtor also completes a course in personal financial management approved by the United States Trustee.[47]

The discharge legally relieves a debtor of all dischargeable obligations.[48] Section 524 concerns the effect of a discharge. Generally, a discharge voids any existing judgment and permanently enjoins the collection of any debt subject to the discharge. Certain debts are specifically not dischargeable. These debts are analyzed in chapter 12 infra. Secured debts are effectively not dischargeable if the debtor wants to keep the collateral.[49] The right to receive a discharge may not be waived.[50] In community property states, the community property of a nonfiling spouse is entitled to a discharge unless the nonfiling spouse would not be entitled to receive a discharge in a proceeding under the Code.[51] This would be the case if the nonfiling spouse would be unable to receive a discharge for any of the reasons enumerated in Section 727 as described in chapter 13 infra. Only a debtor's legal obligation to repay a discharged debt is relieved by a bankruptcy discharge; the underlying moral obligation to repay one's just debts is not affected by a bankruptcy discharge. Section 524(f) specifically states: "Nothing contained in . . . this section prevents a debtor from voluntarily repaying any debt."[52] So if a discharged debtor wants to voluntarily repay the neighborhood doctor, the law permits performance of the moral obligation. The reason for specific inclusion of this principle into the Code is historical.

Practice Pointer

Remember that a discharge in bankruptcy relieves the debtor's personal obligation to repay a debt, *but* it does not (without some further action taken) remove the creditor's "in rem" remedies. In other words, the debtor's personal obligation to continue to make his car payments may be discharged, but if he/she stops making postpetition payments, the creditor may still get relief from the automatic stay to repossess the car.

---

47. See chapter 13 infra; Bankruptcy Rule 4004. 11 U.S.C. §707(a)(11); 11 U.S.C. §111. See chapter 13 infra; Bankruptcy Rule 4004. A personal financial management course is also required to receive a Chapter 13 discharge. 11 U.S.C. §1328(g). See chapter 17 infra.
48. 11 U.S.C. §524.
49. See chapter 21 infra.
50. 11 U.S.C. §524(a).
51. 11 U.S.C. §524(a)(3), (b).
52. 11 U.S.C. §524(f).

Before the enactment of the Bankruptcy Code, the common law of many states held that a bankrupt debtor retained the moral obligation to repay debts after receiving a bankruptcy discharge. If a debtor performed any part of the moral obligation by voluntarily repaying a portion of the debt, common law held that a new legal obligation to pay had been created by reaffirmation. Under this pre-Code law, creditors would try to convince a debtor who had received a bankruptcy discharge to "Come on, be a good guy and send in a payment." Many people who receive persistent phone calls like this tire of receiving them. Often, a payment will be made simply to stop the phone from ringing. This one act could constitute reaffirmation under existing pre-Code state law and restore the previously discharged debtor's liability. The creditor could thus negate the effects of the bankruptcy and obtain a judgment for the balance of the "reaffirmed" debt.[53] While some reaffirmations were indeed proper, all were suspect under the Act because of the abuses committed by some creditors.

The various reaffirmation provisions contained in Section 524 are intended to curb creditor abuse. Thus, Section 524(f) is essential to explain the intent of Congress in enacting the specific reaffirmation provisions into the Code. The practical effect of this provision is that a debtor may voluntarily repay a discharged debt without creating a new legal obligation. The moral obligation is free to be performed by a debtor without risk. If the discharged debtor stops paying, the creditor has no enforceable claim. A new legal obligation is created only when the Code's reaffirmation provisions are complied with. A further practical effect of Section 524(f) is that a basic principle of contract law has been altered by enactment of the Bankruptcy Code.[54]

For example, Wimpy receives a discharge. Under Bankruptcy Act practice, if Brutus could convince Wimpy to repay any part of the discharged debt, and Wimpy performed, a new legal obligation had been created free of the effects of the prior bankruptcy discharge. Wimpy would again be legally obligated to pay his debt to Brutus. Under the Bankruptcy Code, no new legal obligation is created if Wimpy voluntarily makes a payment to Brutus unless the court has properly approved a reaffirmation agreement.

No discharged debt is considered to be legally reaffirmed unless the provisions of Sections 524(c), (d), and (k) are strictly complied with.

---

53. A. Corbin, Corbin on Contracts, Chapter 9, §§222-230 (student ed. 1952), contains an excellent description of the moral obligation/reaffirmation law under common law.
54. 11 U.S.C. §524(c).

Although the provisions are lengthy, their basic elements are not difficult to comprehend. First, there must be a written reaffirmation agreement entered into prior to entry of the debtor's discharge.[55] The agreement must contain a statement that it may be rescinded by the debtor at any time prior to receiving a discharge or 60 days from when the agreement is filed with the court, whichever comes later. The agreement must comply with the provisions of Section 524(k).[56] A debtor's attorney must file a declaration or affidavit representing that the agreement is fully informed and voluntary, that the agreement does not impose an undue hardship on the debtor, and that the attorney has fully advised the debtor of the effect and consequences of the reaffirmation and any default made under it.[57] If the debtor is not represented by an attorney, the court must also find that the agreement will not impose an undue hardship on and be in the best interests of the debtor.[58]

Section 524(k) specifies the documentation, contents of the documentation, and the procedures to follow to obtain approval of a reaffirmation agreement. The Amount Reaffirmed and Annual Percentage Rate must be the most conspicuously displayed terms, along with any introductory instructions to review the documents carefully.[59] A five-part document comprises the reaffirmation agreement. Part A contains numerous preliminary disclosures, primarily with respect to credit terms, repayment terms, whether or not there is any collateral, instructions about the approval procedure, and that the debtor has 60 days from the filing of the reaffirmation with the bankruptcy court to rescind the agreement.[60] Part B is the actual reaffirmation agreement and contains signature lines for the parties.[61] Part C is a certification of the debtor's attorney, if the debtor has an attorney, that the reaffirmation agreement is voluntary and will not create an undue hardship for the debtor.[62] Part D is the Debtor's Statement in Support of Reaffirmation Agreement, which acknowledges that the agreement is voluntary, that it will not impose an undue hardship, and that entering into the agreement is in the debtor's financial interest.[63]

---

55. 11 U.S.C. §524(c)(1).
56. 11 U.S.C. §524(c)(2)(3).
57. 11 U.S.C. §524(c)(3).
58. 11 U.S.C. §524(c)(6).
59. 11 U.S.C. §524(k)(2). Annual Percentage Rate has the same meaning given it in the Federal Truth in Lending Act (TILA), 15 U.S.C. §1601 et seq.
60. 11 U.S.C. §524(k)(3); 11 U.S.C. §524(c)(4).
61. 11 U.S.C. §524(k)(4).
62. 11 U.S.C. §524(k)(5). In re Vargas, 257 B.R. 157 (Bankr. N.J. 2001), discusses counsel's obligations to clients with respect to reaffirmation agreements.
63. 11 U.S.C. §524(k)(6).

Part E is the Motion for Court Approval. This is used if the debtor is not represented by an attorney.[64]

Practice Pointer

See Form 7.9 on the forms disk for a sample reaffirmation agreement.

The court may then hold a discharge and reaffirmation hearing that, if held, the debtor is required to attend.[65] The court must find that the elements of Section 524(c) have been strictly complied with and must further instruct the debtor that a reaffirmation agreement is not required for the debtor to voluntarily repay the debt, that approval of the agreement will create a new legally enforceable obligation of the debtor.[66] To reiterate, if a debtor decides to pay $20 to Dr. Jones on a discharged debt because the debtor feels like she wants to pay the doctor, and the next month the debtor does not make a payment, Dr. Jones has no legal right to sue the debtor for any balance. There is no balance due because it has been discharged unless a reaffirmation agreement has been entered into and approved by the court. The courts are very strict about approving reaffirmation agreements and are reluctant to approve any except those concerning secured debts for the necessaries of life, such as car loans or certain purchase money security agreements. Very rarely will the court approve a reaffirmation agreement for an unsecured debt.

The case of In re Latanowich, 207 B.R. 326 (Bankr. D. Mass. 1997), illustrates the proposition that the reaffirmation requirements must be strictly complied with to be enforceable. In this case, Sears Roebuck and Co. solicited a reaffirmation agreement from a debtor. Although the debtor entered into the agreement, Sears did not file the agreement with the court, rendering it unenforceable. The court not only found the agreement to be invalid, but sanctioned Sears for attempting to enforce it and enjoined Sears from seeking to enforce any reaffirmation agreement not filed with the court in compliance with the statute. The outcome in

---

64. 11 U.S.C. §524(k)(7). If the agreement creates a presumption of undue hardship by the debtor's expenses exceeding income, in the disclosures made in Part D, then the court must hold a hearing to determine if the debtor can make the proposed payments or disapprove the reaffirmation agreement. 11 U.S.C. §524(m).
65. 11 U.S.C. §524(d); 11 U.S.C. §524(k)(7); 11 U.S.C. §521(a)(5).
66. 11 U.S.C. §524(d)(1), (2), §524(k)(7), (m).

this case contributed to the substantial changes in reaffirmation agreements enacted in Section 524(k) in the 2005 legislation.

Section 524(i) provides that creditors who willfully misapply payments received under a confirmed plan are in violation of the discharge injunction provided for by Section 524. This requires, for example, mortgage lenders to properly credit payments made to them in Chapter 13 cases. Section 524(j), on the other hand, permits creditors to communicate with debtors about postpetition payments on home mortgages without the communications constituting a violation of the discharge injunction.

The above has been a synopsis of what takes place in a typical no asset consumer Chapter 7 proceeding. Objections to a debtor's discharge and the nondischargeability of specific debts are described in greater detail in chapter 13 infra.

Summary

The process that occurs in a no asset consumer Chapter 7 bankruptcy forms a basic model of the essential core activities that occur in all bankruptcy proceedings. Initiating the proceeding and identifying the documents required to be filed have been described in detail in chapter 3 supra.

All professionals rendering services to a bankruptcy estate, such as attorneys, accountants, and appraisers, must have their employment approved by the court at the commencement of the representation. In a Chapter 7, 12, or 13, this task is normally accomplished by filing the Statement of Compensation required by Bankruptcy Rule 2016(b). In Chapter 9 or 11 proceedings, an application to be retained must be filed with and approved by the court. Additionally, a debt relief agency must also provide the various disclosures and enter into a written contract to provide services in a consumer bankruptcy case pursuant to Sections 526-528 as described in chapter 3 supra.

The fees of approved professionals rendering services to a bankruptcy estate may not be paid until the fees have been approved by the court. Court approval is obtained by filing an application for compensation, which is noticed to the creditors. A fee application brought while a case is pending is called an interim application. Generally, interim fee applications may not be brought in less than 120-day intervals. A fee application brought at the close of a proceeding or when all services have been rendered is called a *final application*.

Section 110 of the Code imposes eight requirements on bankruptcy petition preparers who prepare documents for filing by a debtor in the Bankruptcy Court. Paralegals not in the employ of an attorney are subject to this Section. Fines, damages, and injunctive relief can be sought and obtained against a bankruptcy petition preparer found violating Section 110. However, while the Section regulates the conduct of bankruptcy petition preparers, it expressly does not permit a bankruptcy petition preparer to perform services in a jurisdiction where the performance of such services will constitute the unauthorized practice of law.

When a Chapter 7 is filed, the United States Trustee will appoint an interim trustee. The interim trustee will normally become the permanent trustee, although creditors may elect a trustee. A creditors' meeting will be held within 21-40 days of the filing. In a typical consumer no asset proceeding this will usually be the only appearance required by the debtor. At the meeting of creditors, the trustee and creditors may ask questions of the debtor concerning the debtor's financial affairs. If an extended examination is required, a party in interest (such as the trustee or a creditor) may take the equivalent of a deposition of the debtor pursuant to Bankruptcy Rule 2004.

Approximately 60 to 90 days after the meeting of creditors, a debtor will normally receive a discharge. Individual debtors are required to complete a course in personal financial management as a prerequisite to receiving their discharge. The discharge relieves a debtor of all dischargeable legal obligations. Most debts are dischargeable. The discharge is the primary element of debtor relief provided for by the Bankruptcy Code. Exemptions (chapter 9 infra) and the automatic stay (chapter 12 infra) comprise the remaining elements of debtor relief.

Debtors may desire to reaffirm debts. When a debtor agrees to reaffirm a debt, the debt will not be subject to the discharge. The legal obligation to pay the debt will remain. To prevent abuse, a specific statutory procedure must be complied with for a debt to be considered legally reaffirmed.

KEY TERMS

automatic stay	final fee application
bankruptcy petition preparer	fresh start
consumer no asset bankruptcy	interim fee application
creditors' meeting	interim trustee
discharge	reaffirmation agreement
disinterested person	Rule 2004 Examination
exempt	

CHAPTER 7 CHECKLIST

7.1 COMPENSATION OF PROFESSIONALS

   7.1.1 Retention of Counsel (Sections 327, 328, 329)
1. Chapter 7, 12, or 13 debtor counsel — compliance with Bankruptcy Rule 2016(b) statement
2. In all other situations, court approval required. File:
   a. noticed motion for approval of retention,
   b. declaration of disinterest,
   c. order approving retention.

   7.1.2 Applications for Compensation (Sections 327, 330, 331; Bankruptcy Rule 2016)
1. Not more than once every 120 days
2. Noticed motion
3. Application should include
   a. summary of services
   b. itemization of time and charges

7.2 REAFFIRMATION AGREEMENTS (Section 524(c)(k))

   7.2.1 Elements
1. Written agreement prior to discharge (Section 524(c)(1))
2. Compliance with Section 524(k)
3. Affidavit of counsel that agreement is voluntary and informed (Section 524(c)(3))
4. Statement in agreement that debtor has 60 days to rescind (Section 524(c)(2))

   7.2.2 Section 524(k) Requirements

Document	Authority
1. PART "A" — Preliminary Disclosures	11 U.S.C. §524(k)(3)
2. PART "B" — Reaffirmation Agreement	11 U.S.C. §524(k)(4)
3. PART "C" — Debtor's Attorney Certification	11 U.S.C. §524(k)(5)
4. PART "D" — Debtor's Statement in Support of Reaffirmation Agreement	11 U.S.C. §524(k)(6)(A)

    5. Debtor Statement if attorney   11 U.S.C. §524(k)(6)(B)

    6. PART "E" —   11 U.S.C. §524(k)(7)
       Motion for Court Approval
       (No attorney)

    7. Court Order   11 U.S.C. §524(k)(8)

7.2.3 Hearings

1. If debtor has no attorney in connection with reaffirmation agreement 11 U.S.C. §524(d);
2. With or without an attorney if undue hardship is presumed, except where the debt is owed to a credit union pursuant to 11 U.S.C. §524(m).

7.3 BANKRUPTCY PETITION PREPARERS (Section 110)

7.3.1 Requirements

1. Must sign document including name and address of preparer (Section 110(b));
2. Provide notice that preparer may not give legal advice (Section 110(b)(2));
3. Must include preparer's Social Security number on document (Section 110(c));
4. Must furnish debtor a copy of the document on or before its being presented to debtor for signature (Section 110(d));
5. May not execute a document on behalf of a debtor or provide legal advice to a debtor (Section 110(e));
6. May not use the word *legal* or similar term in advertising and may not advertise under a "legal" category (Section 110(f));
7. May not receive or collect payment for court fees (Section 110(g));
8. Shall, at the filing of the petition, file a statement of compensation paid or promised (Section 110(h)).

7.3.2 Penalties

1. Discretionary fine of $500 (11 U.S.C. §110(k));
2. Disallowance of excessive fees (11 U.S.C. §110(h));
3. Actual damages of $2,000 or twice amount paid by debtor (11 U.S.C. §110(i));
4. Triple damages for disclosure failures (11 U.S.C. §110(k));
5. Injunction against repeated conduct (11 U.S.C. §110(j));
6. Attorneys' fees and costs (11 U.S.C. §110(i)(j)).

DISCUSSION QUESTIONS

1. When must the employment of a professional be approved by the court?

2. What is a fee application? Why might it be important to monitor professional fees in a bankruptcy proceeding?

3. Describe the basic Chapter 7 process.

4. What occurs at the creditors' meeting?

5. What is a Rule 2004 Examination and when is such an examination commonly conducted?

6. What is the effect of a discharge?

7. What is reaffirmation? What are the legal requirements of a reaffirmation agreement?

8. May a paralegal receive fees from clients for the preparation of bankruptcy petitions and schedules if not authorized by state law? What are the potential consequences of preparing bankruptcy petitions for compensation without supervision when not authorized by state law?

PRACTICE EXERCISES

Exercise 7.1
Prepare a draft Rule 2016(b) attorney compensation disclosure statement.

Exercise 7.2
Draft a letter to the Bottomlines, explaining what they can expect to occur at the 341(a) meeting of creditors, including questions that the trustee may ask.

Exercise 7.3
Draft a reaffirmation agreement on behalf of your client, Toyota Credit, to be presented to the debtors.

8

Conversion and Dismissal

A party in interest, such as the debtor, may seek to have a case converted from one Chapter to another, or dismissed. **Conversion** means, for example, that a debtor's Chapter 7 liquidation case is changed to a Chapter 11 or a Chapter 13 reorganization case or vice versa. The most common occurrence is converting a Chapter 13 case to a Chapter 7 case. A case may be converted more than once in the course of a single bankruptcy filing.[1]

A proceeding may also be dismissed upon a motion by a party in interest under appropriate circumstances such as presumed abuse of the Chapter 7 process under the needs based bankruptcy formula (see chapter 5 supra). A **dismissal** will terminate a bankruptcy proceeding and render the proceeding ineffective.

> ### Practice Pointer
> It is important to understand the distinction between a "discharge," which relieves the debtor of his/her personal liability, and a "dismissal," which returns the debtor back to his/her prepetition position and reinstates all of his/her prepetition debts and obligations.

Sections 348 and 349 of the Bankruptcy Code contain provisions that apply to the conversion or dismissal of a proceeding. In addition, each separate Chapter proceeding has a specific conversion or dismissal

---

1. See Fed. R. Bankr. P. 1019.

provision that applies only to that particular Chapter.[2] All of these provisions, however, are somewhat interrelated. The basic principles contained in them are identical, particularly where conversion rather than dismissal is the issue. In this chapter, we will focus on the generic conversion procedure applicable to all proceedings, the general effects of conversion in all proceedings, the effect of a dismissal in all proceedings, and the grounds for dismissal or conversion in Chapter 7 proceedings. The specific grounds for dismissal or conversion of Chapter 11, 12, and 13 reorganization proceedings are described in greater detail elsewhere in this text.[3]

A. CONVERSION

Generally speaking, a debtor has one opportunity to freely convert a proceeding from one Chapter to another. For example, a debtor may convert a Chapter 7 case to a case under another Chapter, unless the proceeding has been previously converted.[4] The legislative history characterizes this as a "one[-time] absolute right of conversion."[5] A debtor may convert from a Chapter 11 case to a Chapter 7 case, unless a trustee has already been appointed, the proceeding was commenced as an involuntary proceeding, or the proceeding has been previously converted from another Chapter without the debtor's request.[6] A debtor may also convert from Chapter 12 to Chapter 7,[7] or from Chapter 13 to Chapter 7.[8] A waiver of the right to convert is unenforceable.[9]

For example, Jed Clampett files a Chapter 7. One week later he discovers oil on his property. He may freely convert his Chapter 7 case to a Chapter 11 or 13 proceeding. Alternatively, Ponzi, Inc., files a Chapter 11 case. A trustee is appointed. Ponzi, Inc., now may no longer freely convert the proceeding to a Chapter 7.

---

2. 11 U.S.C. §§706, 707, 1112, 1208, 1307.
3. See chapters 23, 24, and 27 infra.
4. 11 U.S.C. §706(a).
5. H.R. Rep. No. 595, 95th Cong., 1st Sess. 380 (1977); S. Rep. No. 989, 95th Cong., 2d Sess. 94 (1978).
6. 11 U.S.C. §1112(a). See chapter 18 infra.
7. 11 U.S.C. §1208(a). See chapter 19 infra.
8. 11 U.S.C. §1307(a). See chapter 17 infra.
9. 11 U.S.C. §706(a); 11 U.S.C. §1208(a); 11 U.S.C. §1307(a).

For a debtor to convert from one Chapter proceeding to another, the debtor must also be able to be a debtor under the particular Chapter to which conversion is desired. This is consistent with Section 109.[10]

The Supreme Court has held that the right to convert from a Chapter 7 to another Chapter under the Bankruptcy Code is not entirely absolute. First, the debtor must be qualified to be a debtor under the new Chapter (see chapter 4 supra), and second, the debtor must not be acting in bad faith.[11] In the Marrama case, the debtor fraudulently transferred property to protect it from his creditors, and then he attempted to mislead the court and his creditors. When the trustee attempted to administer the asset, the debtor sought conversion of his case to a Chapter 13 to avoid having a trustee administer the fraudulently transferred property. The Court denied the debtor's right to convert.

To exercise the option to convert, a debtor typically files an ex parte application simply stating that the debtor desires to convert to a specified Chapter and that the debtor is qualified to be a debtor under the Chapter proceeding to which conversion is sought. Theoretically, a statement as simple as, "I am a Chapter 13 debtor and desire to convert to Chapter 7. I am qualified to be a debtor under Chapter 7," will suffice in most instances. A sample form is included on the forms disk that accompanies this text. Although conversion is often effectuated by the filing of an ex parte application as noted above, technically, FRBP 1017(f) requires a noticed motion. Local rules should be consulted for the acceptable procedure in a given court.

Other than the debtor's one opportunity to convert from one Chapter proceeding to another, a proceeding may only be converted by obtaining court approval after proper notice to all parties in interest. Thus, a debtor desiring to convert from Chapter 7 to Chapter 11, when the proceeding has been previously converted, must first obtain court approval. Any other party in interest, the trustee, or any of the creditors may also move before the court to convert a Chapter 7 to a Chapter 11.[12] Any party in interest may move before the court to convert a proceeding from Chapter 11 to Chapter 7,[13] or to convert a proceeding from Chapter 13 to Chapter 7, and may move to convert a Chapter 13 to a Chapter 11 or 12 prior to confirmation of a Chapter 13 plan.[14] FRBP 1017(f) implements the various applicable provisions.

---

10. See chapter 4 supra. See also 11 U.S.C. §706(d); 11 U.S.C. §1112(f); 11 U.S.C. §1208(e); 11 U.S.C. §1307(f). The trend in the case law is that the debtor must seek conversion in good faith. See, e.g., In re Copper, 314 B.R. 628 (6th Cir. BAP 2004).
11. Marrama v. Citizens Bank of Massachusetts, 549 U.S. 365 (2007).
12. 11 U.S.C. §706(b).
13. 11 U.S.C. §1112(b).
14. 11 U.S.C. §1307(c); 11 U.S.C. §1307(d).

A nondebtor may not seek conversion of a proceeding from Chapter 7 to a Chapter 12 or 13 unless the debtor consents,[15] nor may a nondebtor seek conversion of a Chapter 11 to a Chapter 12 or 13.[16] A nondebtor may not seek conversion from Chapter 12 to Chapter 7 or 13.[17] A nondebtor may also not seek conversion from Chapter 11 to Chapter 7 for those debtors who may not have an involuntary proceeding filed against them (charitable institutions, for instance),[18] nor may a nondebtor seek conversion of a Chapter 13 to a Chapter 7 if the debtor is a farmer.[19] The rationale of these various prohibitions on the ability of nondebtors to seek conversion of a proceeding from one Chapter to another is identical to the rationale described in chapter 4 supra regarding the exclusion of certain types of debtors from involuntary proceedings, and the prohibition against filing an involuntary Chapter 13.[20]

Section 348 describes the effects of conversion. For most purposes, the basic meaning of Section 348 is that if a case is converted from one Chapter to another, the proceeding is generally considered to have been filed under the converted-to Chapter as of the original petition date.[21] Although there are some exceptions, their normal effect is slight.[22] All claims, except the administrative claims of the converted proceeding, are considered to have arisen before the original filing date.[23] For example, consider a Chapter 7 case that is filed on May 28 and then converted to a Chapter 11 case on May 29. Under Section 348, the May 28 order for relief will generally be the effective date of the Chapter 11 filing. The major reason for this rule is that any other date would hopelessly complicate and confuse the many accounting features contained in the bankruptcy system. Because one function of the bankruptcy system is to reconcile the financial affairs of a debtor as of a date certain, only one date should be used, not two or more.

When a Chapter 11 or 13 is converted to a Chapter 7, the debtor or superseded trustee is responsible for filing a final report and accounting with the court. Additionally, any necessary updating that may be required to make the Statements and Schedules accurately reflect changes in the debtor's financial condition occurring between the original filing date and the conversion date should also be prepared.[24]

---

15. 11 U.S.C. §706(c).
16. 11 U.S.C. §1112(d).
17. 11 U.S.C. §§1208, 1307.
18. 11 U.S.C. §1112(c). See chapter 3 supra.
19. 11 U.S.C. §1307(f).
20. See chapter 3 supra.
21. 11 U.S.C. §348(a).
22. 11 U.S.C. §348(b), (c).
23. 11 U.S.C. §348(d).
24. Bankruptcy Rule 1019.

A table summarizing the rules on conversion looks like this:

Type of Application	Applicant	Motion Required	Notice Required	Code Section
Convert 7 to 11, 12, or 13	Debtor	Yes, FRBP 1017(f)(2); 9013	Service by debtor; conversion order served by clerk FRBP 2002(f)	706(a)
Convert 7 to 11	Any party in interest	Yes, FRBP 9014	21 days' notice by clerk FRBP 2002(a)(4)	706(b)
Convert 11 to 7	Debtor	Yes, FRBP 1017(f)(2); 9013	21 days' notice by clerk FRBP 2002(a)(4)	1112(a)
Convert 11 to 7	Any party in interest	Yes, FRBP 9014	21 days' notice by clerk FRBP 2002(a)(4)	1112(b)
Convert 11 to 7	UST	Yes, FRBP 9014	21 days' notice by clerk FRBP 2002(a)(4)	1112(e)
Convert 11 to 12 or 13	Debtor	Yes, FRBP 9014	21 days' notice by clerk FRBP 2002(a)(4)	1112(d)
Convert 13 to 7	Debtor	No, FRBP 1017(f)(3)	Conversion notice served by clerk on UST FRBP 1017(f)(3)	1307(a)
Convert 13 to 7	Any party in interest or UST	Yes, FRBP 9014	No; conversion notice served by clerk on UST FRBP 1017(f)(3)	1307(c) or 1307(e) for failure to file tax returns
Convert 13 to 11 or 12	Any party in interest or UST	Yes, FRBP 9014	21 days' notice by clerk FRBP 2002(a)(4)	1307(d)

B. DISMISSAL

A Chapter 7 case may be dismissed upon order of the court. Unlike conversion, dismissal always requires a noticed motion, except that a Chapter 13 debtor may voluntarily dismiss a Chapter 13 case by filing an ex parte application if the case has not previously been converted.[25] Additionally, Section 521(i) requires automatic dismissal of a case on the forty-sixth day after filing if a debtor has not filed all documents required by Section 521(a)(1).[26] A debtor's case may also be dismissed if he/she fails to file any tax returns that come due, or to seek an extension of the time frame, postpetition.[27] Creditors, the trustee, or the United States Trustee may seek dismissal of a Chapter 7 for cause, including unreasonable delay or failure to pay filing fees.[28] The United States Trustee may seek dismissal if a debtor fails to file Statements and Schedules in a timely manner.[29]

The court, the United States Trustee, the Chapter 7 trustee, or any party in interest may also seek a dismissal of a consumer proceeding pursuant to Section 707(b)(1) if allowing the proceeding would constitute an abuse of Chapter 7. This ground for dismissal creates a mechanism that, in appropriate circumstances, effectively forces a debtor to file a Chapter 11 or 13 if bankruptcy relief is to be obtained. Under "needs based bankruptcy," Section 707(b)(2) requires dismissal of a case where abuse is presumed pursuant to the formula described in chapter 5 supra. A motion brought pursuant to this provision must be brought within 60 days of the creditors' meeting unless this deadline is extended by the court.[30]

A proceeding may also be dismissed upon a noticed motion if the court finds that dismissal is in the best interests of creditors.[31] For example, if a sale of the debtor's assets produces sufficient revenue to pay all creditors in full and provide a dividend to the debtor, dismissal may be a cost-effective remedy, as long as the order protects the creditors' rights to ensure prompt payment of the claims. Dismissal in such a manner may save substantial time and expense, result in payment to all creditors, and remove the bankruptcy as a stigma upon the debtor. The court's ruling on a motion to dismiss on this basis is not reviewable by appeal or otherwise.[32]

Section 349 describes the effects of a dismissal. Generally, a dismissal returns all parties to their rights and liabilities as they existed prior to the filing, as if nothing had ever happened.[33]

---

25. 11 U.S.C. §1307(b).
26. 11 U.S.C. §521(a)(1). See chapter 3B supra. The provision does permit a debtor to seek one 45-day extension.
27. 11 U.S.C. §521(j).
28. 11 U.S.C. §707(a)(1)(2).
29. 11 U.S.C. §707(a)(3).
30. 11 U.S.C. §707(b)(1); FRBP 1017(e). See, e.g., In re Kornfeld, 164 F.3d 778 (2d Cir. 1999).
31. 11 U.S.C. §305(a).
32. 11 U.S.C. §305(c).
33. 11 U.S.C. §349.

A table summarizing the rules on dismissals looks like this:

Type of Application	Applicant	Motion Required	Notice Required	Code Section
Dismiss 7	Any party in interest	Yes, FRBP 9014	21 days' notice by clerk FRBP 2002(a)(4); expect for failure to pay filing fee or file schedules or for substantial abuse	707(a)
Dismiss 7 for abuse	UST or court	Yes, FRBP 9014 Within 60 days of 341 meeting FRBP 1017(e)(1)	Service by UST or court on debtor, trustee & UST FRBP 1017(e); dismissal notice served by clerk FRBP 2002(f)	707(b)
Dismiss 11	Any party in interest	Yes, FRBP 9014	21 days' notice by clerk FRBP 2002(a)(4)	1112(b)
Dismiss 13 if no prior conversion	Debtor	Yes, FRBP 1017(f)(2); 9013	Service by debtor; dismissal notice served by clerk FRBP 2002(f)	1307(b)
Dismiss 13 for failure to file tax return	Any party in interest or UST	Yes, FRBP 9014	21 days' notice by clerk FRBP 2002(a)(4)	1307(e)
Dismiss for failure to file schedules (all Chapters)	UST or court	Yes, FRBP 9014	UST to serve debtor & trustee in Ch. 7 & 13 FRBP 1017(c); 21 days' notice by clerk for Ch. 11 FRBP 2002(a)(4)	707(a)(3) 1112(e) 1307(c)(9)
Dismiss for nonpayment of fees	Court for filing fees/ clerk's fees Party in interest or UST for Ch. 11 & 13	No for court Yes for party in interest FRBP 9014	Court fees— notice goes to trustee & debtor FRBP 1017(b) Ch. 11 UST quarterly fees— 21 days' notice by clerk FRBP 2002(a)(4)	707(a)(2) 1112(b)(4) 1307(c)(2)

Summary

A bankruptcy proceeding may be converted or dismissed. A conversion will switch a bankruptcy proceeding from one Chapter to another (such as from Chapter 11 to Chapter 7). A dismissal will terminate a bankruptcy proceeding and render the proceeding ineffective.

Normally, a debtor is given one opportunity to convert a proceeding from one Chapter to another. This act is accomplished by filing an Application to Convert with the court. Provided that the debtor is qualified to be a debtor in the Chapter for which conversion is sought, and that the debtor is acting in good faith, then the right to convert is absolute.

Other than the debtor's one opportunity to convert, conversion may only otherwise occur upon court order after a noticed motion. Thus, a creditor or United States Trustee seeking to convert a case must always do so by way of a noticed motion. If the proceeding has been previously converted (such as a debtor desiring to convert a second time) or if a trustee has been appointed in a Chapter 11 proceeding, without regard to any prior conversion, even the debtor must convert by way of a noticed motion.

The general effect of a conversion is that the proceeding is considered to have been filed under the converted-to Chapter as of the petition's original filing date. When a proceeding is converted, some additional reports will also be required to be filed with the court, primarily to update changes from the original filing.

Any Chapter proceeding may be dismissed for one of two reasons: for cause or when it is in the best interest of creditors. Each Chapter proceeding contains specific provisions defining the grounds for a dismissal for cause. Unreasonable delay that prejudices creditors or a failure to pay filing fees are two common reasons for dismissal for cause. A case may also be dismissed if the court finds that dismissal will be in the best interest of creditors. A consumer Chapter 7 case is subject to dismissal if allowing the proceeding would constitute an abuse of Chapter 7. The general effect of a dismissal is to essentially render the bankruptcy proceeding ineffective, as if it had never occurred.

KEY TERMS

---

conversion   dismissal

DISCUSSION QUESTIONS

1. What does it mean to convert a bankruptcy proceeding?

2. When may a debtor convert a case from one Chapter to another without a noticed motion?

3. When must a motion to convert be made?

4. What is the difference between conversion of a bankruptcy proceeding and a dismissal of a bankruptcy proceeding?

5. What sorts of conduct may be an abuse of Chapter 7 in addition to the presumption of abuse that may exist pursuant to "needs based bankruptcy"?

PRACTICE EXERCISE

Exercise 8.1
Draft a motion to convert the Bottomlines' Chapter 7 to a Chapter 13.

9

Exemptions

A. BACKGROUND

Individual debtors seek two primary goals in obtaining bankruptcy debtor relief: a discharge and the exemption of property. The achievement of these goals provides a debtor with a **fresh start** in the debtor's financial affairs. The fresh start concept is the basic foundation of congressional intent in permitting individual debtors to seek bankruptcy relief.[1]

Only individual debtors may claim **exemptions**.[2] Exemptions allow a debtor to protect property from the reach of creditors or the trustee in a bankruptcy proceeding. Property for which an exemption is claimed and allowed is not subject to administration by a trustee and is not available for liquidation to pay a dividend to creditors.[3] A debtor may keep exempt property.

The concept of exemptions for individual debtors is a relatively recent one.[4] The Bankruptcy Act did not contain independent exemptions. Exemptions existed only as provided for under the state law of the debtor's domicile or residence. This led to the development of 50 bodies of law regarding exemptions in bankruptcy proceedings.

State exemption statutes have traditionally offered more protection to owners of real property (referring to homes and other real estate) than to owners of nonreal property (sometimes referred to as personalty). The most common form of such protection is called the **homestead**

---

1. H.R. Rep. No. 595, 95th Cong., 1st Sess., 366-367 (1977); S. Rep. No. 989, 95th Cong., 2d Sess., 81 (1978).
2. 11 U.S.C. §522(b).
3. 11 U.S.C. §522(c).
4. See chapter 1 supra.

exemption. This exemption exists in spite of the practical reality that many individual debtors do not own real property. The rise of this exemption is a historical anachronism most likely rooted in sixteenth- and seventeenth-century English bankruptcy law, which gave substantial protection to real property owners by preventing bankruptcy proceedings from being initiated against them.[5]

When Congress enacted the Bankruptcy Code, it decided to create a uniform set of federal exemptions. The **federal exemptions**, when properly utilized, eliminate the inherent economic discrimination that has existed between real property owners and those people who do not own real property but who hold other forms of property, so that these personal property owners may now have an opportunity to exempt property of a value equal to that of real property owners.[6] The federal exemption scheme also seeks to bring some national consistency to the concept of exempt property. In some states, exemption statutes reflect the style of early twenty-first century living, while other states have not significantly revised their exemption statutes in the past 100 years. There are still states in which church pews may be claimed exempt.[7] There are some states in which specific types of obsolete nineteenth-century farming implements may be claimed exempt.[8] And there are still other states with even more obscure exemptions that relate only to the nineteenth-century lifestyle.[9]

Section 522(b) provides that a debtor or joint debtors may elect to exempt property from one of two allowable sets of exemptions. A debtor may elect to utilize the exemptions that exist under the state or local law where the debtor has been domiciled for at least 730 days (two years) immediately prior to the filing of the petition, or the place where the debtor resided for a majority of the 180 days preceding the 730-day period, as well as any other nonbankruptcy exemptions permitted by federal law, plus any interest in property held by the debtor immediately preceding the filing as a tenant by the entirety or joint tenant to the extent that it is exempt under nonbankruptcy law, and various individual retirement accounts and retirement funds that are exempt from federal income taxation. Or the debtor may elect to utilize the exemptions provided for under the federal exemption scheme contained in 11 U.S.C. §522(d). If the time limits prevent a debtor from claiming any exemptions, then a debtor may select the federal exemptions. BAPCPA also limits the debtor's ability to

---

5. Leventhal, The Early History of English Bankruptcy, 67 U. Pa. L. Rev. 1 (1919).
6. See discussion concerning 11 U.S.C. §522(d)(5) infra.
7. Ala. Code §6-10-5.
8. See 32 L.P.R.A. §1130(3) permitting "one cart or wagon" to be exempt.
9. See N.H. Rev. Stat. Ann. §511:2(VII) permitting exemption of "the uniform, arms and equipments of every officer and private in the militia."

claim a homestead exemption under state law to $146,450, even if the state law provides for a greater exemption, unless the property involved was acquired more than 1,215 days prior to the filing of the petition, except for property acquired during the same period from a transfer of the debtor's principal residence in the same state.[10]

> ### *Practice Pointer*
>
> If the debtor elects to use the so-called "state exemptions" available under 522(b)(3), they are entitled to:
>
> 1. state and local law exemptions:
> 2. all federal law exemptions, except those provided in 11 U.S.C. §522(d);
> 3. property interests held as a tenant by the entirety or joint tenant IF it is exempt under nonbankruptcy law; and
> 4. retirement funds to the extent they are exempt from federal taxation.

For example, Tom Joad resides in Oklahoma. His employer, Rath Grapes, transfers Tom to California. If Tom files bankruptcy in California within 730 days of moving, his allowable state exemptions would be those of Oklahoma, and his homestead exemption would be limited to $146,450. On the other hand, if Tom lived in California in the first place and is transferred from northern to southern California, then his homestead exemption would be determined solely by California law since he has only moved within the state.

Although each individual debtor may choose which set of exemptions they wish to utilize, joint debtors must each select the same set of exemptions.[11] That is, joint debtors must each elect to utilize either the applicable state exemptions or the federal exemptions provided for in Section 522(d). They are not permitted to have one spouse claim the state exemptions while the other spouse attempts to claim the federal exemptions.

---

10. 11 U.S.C. §522(b); 11 U.S.C. §522(p). The extended time periods and limitations on homestead amounts were added to the Bankruptcy Code by BAPCPA. Their intent is to discourage persons from moving to a state with high exemption limits and then declaring bankruptcy. These revisions will require the Bankruptcy Courts to become familiar with the exemption law of all jurisdictions.
11. 11 U.S.C. §522(b)(1); 11 U.S.C. §522(m).

If joint debtors cannot agree on which set to claim, or where none are claimed, the debtors are deemed to have selected the federal exemption scheme.[12] The now-prohibited practice of one debtor claiming exemptions under state law and one debtor claiming federal exemptions was known as **stacking**. However, if each debtor holds an interest in a given item of property, they may each claim an exemption in that property, effectively doubling their marital exemption.[13]

For example, John and Jane Smith wish to file a Chapter 7 proceeding. Each may select the allowable exemptions under the state law of their domicile (residence) or each may select the federal exemptions provided in 11 U.S.C. §522(d).[14] Both John and Jane will be able to claim a full set of exemptions under this election. If John and Jane forget to claim exemptions, or if they cannot agree on which set to claim, they will be deemed to have selected the federal exemptions. John, however, cannot claim exemptions under state law while Jane claims the federal exemptions.

There is, however, one provision of 11 U.S.C. §522(b) that complicates a debtor's election to claim exemptions. Section 522(b)(2) provides that debtors can claim property exempt under subsection (d) unless the state law applicable to the debtor does not so authorize. This means that Congress has provided the states an opportunity to withdraw from the federal exemption scheme of 11 U.S.C. §522(d). That is, state law may properly prevent a debtor or joint debtors from electing the federal exemptions. Thus, although the Bankruptcy Code gives a debtor an election to use state or federal exemptions, Congress has also given individual states the opportunity to "opt out" of the federal exemption scheme. In any state that has chosen to opt out of the federal exemptions, debtors are not given a choice of exemptions to elect. Debtors residing in such a state may only claim the exemptions provided for under the law of that particular state. In the above example, if Jane and John Smith resided in a state that has successfully opted out of the federal exemptions, they would not be permitted an election. They could claim the exemptions of their state of domicile or they could claim no exemptions. Thirty-three states had successfully opted out of the federal exemption scheme as of November 2010.[15] In those remaining states that have not opted out of the federal

---

12. 11 U.S.C. §522(b).
13. 11 U.S.C. §522(m).
14. The exemptions allowed under 11 U.S.C. §522(d) shall hereafter be referred to as the *federal exemptions*.
15. As of November 2010, they are: Alabama, Arizona, California, Colorado, Delaware, Florida, Georgia, Idaho, Illinois, Indiana, Iowa, Kansas, Louisiana, Maine, Maryland, Mississippi, Missouri, Montana, Nebraska, Nevada, New York, North Carolina, North Dakota, Ohio, Oklahoma, Oregon, South Carolina, South Dakota, Tennessee, Utah, Virginia, West Virginia,

exemptions, a debtor will be able to elect state or federal exemptions pursuant to 11 U.S.C. §522(b).

B.   SELECTING EXEMPTIONS

Other than the initial decision to file a bankruptcy petition in the first place, the decision to select appropriate exemptions is the most important decision to be made in the scope of a consumer no asset Chapter 7 proceeding and it is also one of the most important decisions to make in any Chapter 12, 13, or individual Chapter 11 proceeding. Advice to a debtor concerning the proper exemptions to select is a legal decision and may only be made by a licensed attorney. Counseling a potential debtor regarding the choice of exemptions constitutes the practice of law. A nonattorney rendering this advice to a potential debtor may be guilty of the unauthorized practice of law, which is a criminal violation in many states.[16] In a state that has authorized paralegals to prepare bankruptcy petitions, the provisions of Code Section 110 will apply (see section 7B supra). This principle applies regardless of the apparent simplicity involved in counseling many potential debtors regarding the proper exemptions to select. This is not a work on the exemption law of individual states. Readers are left to their own devices to ascertain the specific exemption statutes of individual states. However, many of the items permitted to be claimed exempt under federal law are commonly permitted as exemptions under relevant state law.

Generally, a debtor should elect the exemptions that will allow the most property to be claimed exempt. Occasions may arise, however, in which a debtor for noneconomic reasons will not want to elect the exemptions that will exempt the most property. In these situations, a professional must always remember that the client always makes the ultimate choice when alternatives are available. But, as a general rule, one should always recommend selection of the exemptions that will exempt the most possible property from administration by a trustee.

---

and Wyoming. William H. Brown, Lawrence R. Ahern, III & Nancy F. MacLean, Bankruptcy Exemption Manual, §4.02 (2010).

16. In re Anderson, 79 B.R. 482 (Bankr. S.D. Cal. 1987). This case has been widely followed. See, e.g., In re Reynoso, 477 F.3d 1117 (9th Cir. 2007) (concluding the use of web-based software to complete schedules constituted unauthorized practice of law); Wynns v. Adams, 426 B.R. 457 (E.D.N.Y. 2010).

The debtor's ownership of real property subject to a homestead exemption under state law will normally determine which set of exemptions will be most appropriate for a debtor to select. In this instance, counsel must make certain that the proper procedure to declare a homestead has been followed under the applicable state law or the exemption may be lost and the property subject to administration by the trustee. Generally, a homestead declaration must be recorded prior to filing any bankruptcy petition or the exemption will be subject to invalidity under the trustee's avoiding powers.[17] However, where equity in the subject real property is limited or nonexistent, a debtor owning real property subject to a potential homestead exemption may, as a practical matter, gain greater ultimate benefits by claiming the federal rather than state exemptions.

A homestead exemption will normally allow an individual debtor to claim as exempt a defined amount of **equity** in the debtor's residence. Equity is the value of an asset over and above that of any liens or encumbrances. Of course, the equity must exist for the exemption to acquire any real value. Popular misconception to the contrary, a homestead exemption is not a guarantee to the property owner. For example, the Bunkers own a home with a value of $100,000. A mortgage in the amount of $80,000 encumbers the property. The Bunkers' equity in the home is thus $20,000. In a state with a homestead exemption of $20,000 or more, all of the equity may be claimed exempt. In a state with a homestead exemption of less than $20,000, only the maximum statutory amount would be subject to the exemption. BAPCPA limits a homestead exemption to $146,450 where a debtor has moved from one state to another in the 730 days preceding the filing of the petition, as discussed at chapter 9A supra.

C.   FEDERAL EXEMPTIONS

Section 522(d) contains the substantive federal exemptions. When reference is made to the federal exemptions, the reference is normally to the exemptions contained within Section 522(d). Consumer no asset Chapter 7 debtors not owning real estate with any significant equity will usually be able to exempt more property under these provisions than under any applicable state law, where the federal exemptions are available.

---

17. See chapter 13 infra.

Bankruptcy Code Section 104(b), enacted in 1994, is designed to account for the effects of inflation on the Section 522(d) exemption amounts. Section 104(c) provides that the adjustments do not apply to cases filed before the date of a particular adjustment. For example, the previous exemption of $3,225 applicable to motor vehicles under Section 522(d)(2) applies only to cases filed before April 1, 2010, and after April 1, 2007. The new value of $3,450 applies to cases filed after April 1, 2010.

Every third April, commencing in 1998, the exemption amounts are increased to reflect changes in the published Department of Labor Consumer Price Index for all urban consumers for the most recent three-year period. The amounts are published in the Federal Register one month before they become effective. For example, if the total inflation for the period January 1, 1995, to December 31, 1997, was 10 percent, then all of the Section 522(d) amounts would be raised accordingly, rounding off to the nearest $25. For example, a $15,000 limit in Section 522(d)(1) would become $16,500. For our purposes here, the text reflects the changes effective as of April 1, 2010.

Section 522(d)(1) allows a debtor to exempt equity in the residence of the debtor, or in real property owned by the debtor and resided in by a dependent, or in a burial plot owned by the debtor, up to $21,625. Joint debtors selecting the exemptions under 522(d) can conceivably exempt up to $43,250 of equity in real property of these types.[18] To claim this exemption under federal law, it is not necessary to record a homestead or to take any action other than the procedures described below in this chapter. When claiming the federal exemptions, this exemption is automatically available.

Under Section 522(d)(2) each debtor may claim exempt $3,450 of equity in one motor vehicle.[19] Joint debtors may therefore each claim a $3,450 exemption in equity in two separate vehicles if each debtor claims one vehicle exempt. However, a debtor owning more than one vehicle may only claim one exemption because the statute limits the exemption to only one vehicle.

Section 522(d)(3) permits a debtor to exempt household goods, household furniture, wearing apparel, books, animals, musical instruments, or crops held primarily for personal or household use. In other words, this exemption permits a debtor to exempt the so-called necessities of life. The Code eliminates the image of paupers wearing barrels with suspenders. The exemption is limited to an aggregate value of $11,525, while each item claimed exempt must have a value not exceeding $550.[20]

---

18. 11 U.S.C. §522(d)(1); §522(m).
19. 11 U.S.C. §522(d)(2).
20. 11 U.S.C. §522(d)(3).

Value is determined by looking at the realistic **market value** of the particular asset claimed exempt. This applies to all exemptions. BAPCPA requires that assets be valued in the Statements and Schedules at their **replacement value**, defined as "the price a retail merchant would charge for property of that kind considering the age and condition of the property at the time value is determined."[21]

As a practical matter, the realistic market value of an asset is normally the asset's **liquidation value**, except in the case of real property. While personal property often has a depressed value in a bankruptcy, the fair market value of real property is usually affected less in the eyes of potential buyers. Liquidation value is normally the value that one would obtain in the context of a forced sale, such as a garage liquidation sale, public auction, or "going out of business" sale. This is a realistic perception, because if the same assets are liquidated by a bankruptcy trustee they will most likely be sold at a public auction to the highest bidders.[22]

The dollar limitations contained in 11 U.S.C. §522(d)(3) apply to each individual item of personal property claimed exempt. This proviso means exactly what it says: "any particular item." For example, if a debtor has an imported Chinese rosewood dining room table and eight accompanying rosewood chairs, the whole set together may be very valuable. However, "any particular item" means each individual chair and the table are all considered as separate items. A living room set meets with the identical approach: Each end table is an individual item, each chair is an individual item, and so forth. The same applies to a bedroom set. The same analysis can apply to a home entertainment system: The television monitor is an individual item, the DVD or video cassette recorder is an individual item, the video game hardware is an individual item, the turntable is an individual item, the preamp is an individual item, the tuner is an individual item, the double-cassette tape deck is an individual item, the 20-band equalizer is an individual item, the compact disc player is an individual item, each speaker is an individual item. So long as the aggregate value is not greater than $11,525, and an individual item has a value not exceeding $550, all of the debtor's personal property may be properly claimed exempt under 11 U.S.C. §522(d)(3).

As a practical matter, it is not necessary to have a potential individual debtor provide a line-by-line itemization of all personal assets. Although there are occasions when a trustee will desire such data, it is generally not

---

21. 11 U.S.C. §506(a)(2); 11 U.S.C. §522(a)(2); 11 U.S.C. §527(a)(2)(B).
22. See chapters 10 and 15 infra. In the reorganization proceedings of Chapter 11 or 13, the retail value may need to be applied. See Associated Commercial Corp. v. Rash, 520 U.S. 953 (1997), discussed in chapter 16 infra. Case law will determine how *Rash* may be affected by BAPCPA and how "replacement value" is interpreted relative to liquidation value.

a necessity. A potential individual debtor need not normally provide an itemized list of wearing apparel, such as "twelve t-shirts, six Fruit-of-the-Looms" and so forth. Local practice may vary, however, and inquiry should always be made as to local custom, local rule, or any applicable guidelines of the United States Trustee.

For particular items that may have a value of more than $550, the exemption provided for under Section 522(d)(5), described below, may be an effective remedy for claiming such assets exempt. It is, however, prudent to itemize any items that may exceed the $550 per item limit.

Any unique collections should be itemized. If a debtor has potentially valuable furnishings or wardrobe, such as the rosewood dining room set mentioned above or a fur, or a unique collection such as a collection of Happy Meal toys, or autographs of all of the original Star Trek actors, obtaining a written appraisal prior to filing is helpful in preparing the debtor's schedules and in claiming exemptions. The appraisal will also be helpful in answering any questions of the trustee or creditors in connection with the asset's value. This one act can save time and expense, in the form of attorneys' fees, should the trustee wish to object to the exemption simply because no prior appraisal has been obtained. Debtors in this possible situation should reasonably be able to afford the nominal appraisal costs. Case law may very well determine that the duties imposed upon counsel under BAPCPA, to make "reasonable inquiry" to establish an asset's value, require written appraisals of unique assets. See Bankruptcy Code §527(a)(2)(B).

Section 522(d)(4) permits the exemption of $1,450 in jewelry held for personal use of the debtor or a dependent.[23] Most wedding rings can be safely exempted under this provision. Potentially valuable items of jewelry should be appraised beforehand as described above.

Section 522(d)(5) is perhaps the most important of the federal exemptions. It is the exemption that sets the federal exemptions apart from traditional state exemptions. In common parlance, Section 522(d)(5) is called the "omnibus," "catch-all," or "wildcard" exemption. The **catch-all exemption** consists of any unused portion of the federal homestead exemption (11 U.S.C. §522(d)(1) supra), up to the amount of $10,825, plus $1,150, for a total of $11,975 in any property of any kind.[24] "Any property" means all property, with one limited exception described below. Individual items of household goods worth more than $550 a piece may be claimed exempt under this provision. Jewelry not exempt under Section 522(d)(4) may be claimed exempt under this provision.

---

23. 11 U.S.C. §522(d)(4).
24. 11 U.S.C. §522(d)(5).

Equity in a vehicle greater than $3,450 may be claimed exempt here. An otherwise nonexempt tax refund may be claimed exempt under this provision. Cash in the bank may be claimed exempt. A second vehicle owned by one debtor or a third vehicle owned by joint debtors may be claimed exempt under this provision. Anything — absolutely, positively anything — may be claimed exempt under this provision.

Property recovered for the estate by the trustee's avoiding powers may conceivably be claimed exempt under Section 522(d)(5) as long as the transfer avoided by the trustee has been involuntary on the part of the debtor. Thus, property subject to an avoidable lien may be claimed exempt. However, if the debtor voluntarily made the avoidable transfer such as a preference or a fraudulent transfer to a relative, intending to conceal the property from creditors, or if the debtor fails to disclose the transfer in the Statements and Schedules, the transaction may not be claimed exempt under Section 522(d)(5). This is the one exception to the broad meaning of the phrase "any property." For example, creditor Snidely Whiplash obtains a judicial attachment on Debtor Nell's assets immediately prior to Nell filing her Chapter 7. Because the trustee can avoid this transaction, Nell may claim the assets exempt under Section 522(d)(5) or any other allowable exemption. If the trustee does not seek to set aside the avoidable transaction, Nell may take action herself to do so. However, if Nell proffered voluntary payment to Snidely as a preference, she likely could not claim the assets so transferred as exempt.[25]

The catch-all provision of Section 522(d)(5) attempts to eliminate the economic discrimination that existed prior to enactment of the Bankruptcy Code, when the existing exemptions available under state law favored homeowners substantially more than nonhomeowners. For individuals who did not own their homes, there generally existed no exemptions in state law beyond vehicle equity and the bare necessities of life. In enacting the Bankruptcy Code, Congress has concluded that it would be fair to create an exemption for nonhomeowners to afford them the same opportunities for a fresh start in their financial affairs that exists for homeowners able to take advantage of homestead exemptions. Hence, the catch-all exemption, which allows a debtor or debtors to claim exempt

---

25. See the Legislative Notes to 11 U.S.C. §522(d). See also chapters 13-14 for a discussion of the trustee's avoiding powers. Although it may have been thought that voluntary preferences and even voluntary fraudulent transfers could be claimed exempt under §522(d)(5), recent case law has begun to disfavor use of §522(d)(5) to claim these transactions exempt. See, e.g., In re Kaba, 2007 WL 1556842 (Bankr. N.D. Tex. 2007) (preference found not to be property of the estate and thus not subject to exemption); In re Terry, 279 B.R. 240 (Bankr. W.D. Ark. 2002) (fraudulently concealed property not subject to exemption). See also 11 U.S.C. §522(g), (h), (j), which supports this view. 11 U.S.C. §522(o), added by BAPCPA, reduces the value of property by any amount attributable to fraudulent transfers.

any property in existence up to the limits of the catch-all in lieu of a homestead exemption.

A debtor claiming real property exempt under the federal homestead provision (11 U.S.C. §522(d)(1)) may claim additional property exempt under the catch-all provision if there is an available balance after accounting for the real property equity. For example, Joe Debtor owns a house with $15,000 of equity. There is an unused balance of the Section 522(d)(1) exemption available for use under Section 522(d)(5) of $5,200 plus $1,150, for a total of $6,350. This amount may be used by Joe to claim any property in existence exempt.

Section 522(d)(6) allows a debtor to exempt $2,175 of value in tools of the trade or professional implements. For example, a word processor working as an independent contractor might be able to exempt a personal computer under this provision.[26]

Unmatured life insurance contracts are exempt under Section 522(d)(7).[27] Term insurance or policies with no cash value may also be claimed exempt under this provision.

Section 522(d)(8) allows a debtor to claim as exempt cash value in an insurance policy up to $11,525.[28] A whole life insurance policy bearing a cash value may therefore be fully or partially claimed exempt under this provision. Loans or other debts owed against the policy's cash value are specifically excluded from the total cash value claimed exempt when the insurance company has a right to set off the debt owed it against the policy's cash value.[29]

Professionally prescribed health aids of a debtor or a debtor's dependent such as glasses, contact lenses, or orthopedic shoes are exempt under Section 522(d)(9). There is no dollar limitation on this exemption.[30] Social Security benefits, welfare benefits, veterans' benefits, alimony, qualified pension and profit sharing plans, and disability and unemployment benefits may all be claimed exempt under Section 522(d)(10).[31] In Rousey v. Jacoway, 544 U.S. 320 (2005), the Supreme Court held that IRA accounts may be claimed exempt within the meaning of Section 522(d)(10), resolving a conflict among the circuits. Section 522(d)(12), enacted by BAPCPA, codifies this result. See below.

---

26. 11 U.S.C. §522(d)(6).
27. 11 U.S.C. §522(d)(7).
28. 11 U.S.C. §522(d)(8).
29. 11 U.S.C. §542(d).
30. 11 U.S.C. §522(d)(9).
31. 11 U.S.C. §522(d)(10).

Under Section 522(d)(11) certain aspects of personal injury compensation may be claimed exempt. A right to receive compensation or property under a crime victim's reparation law may be claimed exempt without regard to amount.[32] Wrongful death recoveries for an individual of whom the debtor was a dependent, payment from a life insurance policy insuring the life of an individual of whom the debtor was a dependent, and compensation for lost future earnings of the debtor or of an individual of whom the debtor was or is a dependent may be claimed exempt "to the extent reasonably necessary for the support of the debtor or a dependent of the debtor."[33] The amount reasonably necessary for the support of a debtor or dependent of the debtor will be a question of fact in each individual case. Personal injury compensation may be claimed exempt up to $21,625. However, pain and suffering and actual damages are specifically not included in calculating the exemption amount.[34] For example, a debtor with a million-dollar personal injury claim may conceivably claim all the recovery exempt depending on how the recovery is based. However, as a practical matter, since this debtor may be able to pay all creditors in full and leave a substantial balance for the debtor, if there is a recovery, a debtor in this situation might seek a dismissal of the bankruptcy proceeding under Section 305(a).[35]

11 U.S.C. §522(d)(12) expressly permits retirement funds exempt from taxation pursuant to the Internal Revenue Code to be claimed exempt. This includes 401 employer plans and IRA accounts. This exemption, added by BAPCPA and intended to resolve the case law debate upon whether or not IRA accounts could be claimed exempt, is consistent with the identical exemption also permitted to debtors not claiming the federal exemptions. See chapter 9A supra.

D. UNAFFECTED CLAIMS

Exemptions, contrary to popular opinion, do not protect a debtor's exempt property from the reach of all creditors. Exemptions do not protect otherwise exempt property from properly secured liens or properly filed tax liens. Nor do exemptions protect a debtor's otherwise exempt property

---

32. 11 U.S.C. §522(d)(11)(A).
33. 11 U.S.C. §522(d)(11)(B), (C), (E).
34. 11 U.S.C. §522(d)(11)(D). As to the pain and suffering calculation, see In re Scotti, 245 B.R. 17 (Bankr. D. N.J. 2000).
35. See chapter 8 supra.

from nondischargeable taxes, nondischargeable domestic support obligations, or debts incurred by fraud in obtaining school financial aid.[36] For example, Mark Treasure has a mortgage debt and a tax lien recorded upon his home. His divorced spouse, Virginia, is owed support payments. Mark's homestead will not protect a foreclosure by the mortgage holder, a sale to the state for the nondischarged taxes, or a judicial seizure by Virginia for collection of the unpaid support.

It is not improper for a debtor to convert nonexempt to exempt property at any time prior to filing. The Legislative Notes to Section 522 specifically state that "the debtor will be permitted to convert nonexempt property into exempt property before filing a bankruptcy petition. However, the excessive conversion of nonexempt to exempt property on the eve of a bankruptcy filing can result in the denial of a debtor's discharge."[37] Thus, Midas Touch could sell a piece of nonexempt antique jewelry prior to filing, buy a new refrigerator with the proceeds, and then claim the refrigerator exempt under Section 522(d)(3) or 522(d)(5). How the 2005 legislation may affect these practices will clarify itself in the case law.

E. LIEN AVOIDANCE TO PRESERVE EXEMPTION

An *unsecured* creditor cannot ask a debtor to agree to waive exemptions or any of a debtor's rights under Section 522. Any such waiver is unenforceable.[38] A debtor may avoid a judicial lien or a nonpossessory, **nonpurchase money security interest** in consumer, personal, or household goods, tools of the trade, or professionally prescribed health aids to the extent that any such lien impairs an otherwise allowable exemption. Judicial liens attributable to domestic support obligations are not avoidable.[39] Generally, a secured creditor has a nonpurchase money security interest if

---

36. 11 U.S.C. §522(c).
37. See Historical and Revision Notes to 11 U.S.C. §522. See also In re Grand Jury Proceedings, G.S., F.S., 609 F.3d 909 (8th Cir. 2010) (transfer of hundreds of thousands of dollars in nonexempt assets prepetition suggested fraudulent intent); In re Jennings, 533 F.3d 1333 (11th Cir. 2008) (a large premature, prepetition payment on home improvements paid to take advantage of homestead exemption was held to be fraudulent and the debtor's discharge was denied); In re Stern, 345 F.3d 1036 (9th Cir. 2003) (conversion of nonexempt to exempt on eve of bankruptcy is not per se fraudulent).
38. 11 U.S.C. §522(e).
39. 11 U.S.C. §522(f)(1)(A).

the debt that created the security interest was not obtained for the purpose of purchasing the collateral subject to the security interest. Otherwise, the security interest is generally a **purchase money security interest**. For example, a debtor purchases a new living room set and obtains credit to do so. If the seller retains a security interest in the goods, it will likely be a purchase money security interest. However, if a debtor obtains a loan from the friendly neighborhood finance company for the purpose of going on vacation, any security interest the debtor grants the finance company in household furniture will be a nonpurchase money security interest. In this instance, if the debtor then files a bankruptcy petition, the latter security interest may be avoided if it impairs the debtor's ability to claim household furniture exempt.

Section 522(f)(1)(B) allows a debtor to avoid a nonpurchase money security interest to the extent that the collateral can be claimed exempt. So if all of the furniture given as collateral can be claimed exempt, the debtor can avoid the lien. Section 522(f)(4), added by BAPCPA, defines "household goods," solely for purposes of lien avoidance, as generally one TV, one VCR, plus other specifically enumerated household goods. The same provision also excludes various items, such as works of art except by relatives, from the definition of "household goods." Once the debtor's personal obligation is discharged under Section 524, the finance company may not thereafter seek payment. Because the security interest is avoided, the debtor need not worry about the finance company repossessing the furniture. Section 522(f)(3) further limits the ability to avoid a nonpurchase money security interest in tools of the trade, farm animals, or crops if the value of the collateral exceeds $5,850.

A debtor must file a noticed motion to successfully avoid a lien subject to avoidance under Section 522(f). See chapter 5A supra.[40]

F.   CLAIMING AND OBJECTING TO EXEMPTIONS

To properly claim exemptions, a debtor must file a list of exemptions with the court. If a debtor fails to do so, a dependent of the debtor may file the list.[41] A debtor's claim of exemptions is to be filed at the same time as the

---

40. Bankruptcy Rule 4003(d); Bankruptcy Rule 9013.
41. 11 U.S.C. §522(l).

Statements and Schedules, within 14 days of the date of filing.[42] The exemption schedule may be amended at any time prior to the close of the proceeding.[43]

Practice Pointer

Remember to check your local bankruptcy court rules for the fee for amending your exemption or other bankruptcy schedules.

The trustee or any creditor may object to a claim of exemption. An objection must be filed within 30 days of the conclusion of the Section 341(a) creditors' meeting or within 30 days after any amendment is filed unless the court orders otherwise. Unless an objection is made, the property claimed exempt is exempt. The party raising an objection to a claim of exemption has the burden of proving the impropriety of the exemption at any hearing held to resolve the objection.[44] An objection to a claim of exemption is filed as a noticed motion (see chapter 4A supra). A sample notice of objection is contained on the forms disk.

In Taylor v. Freeland & Kronz, the Supreme Court held that the 30-day deadline to object to a debtor's claim of exemption is to be strictly construed. In this case, a debtor claimed an exemption in the potential proceeds of an employment discrimination lawsuit against her former employer. She disclosed to the trustee at the creditors' meeting that the suit might be worth $90,000. The trustee, however, did not object to the exemption because he did not believe the claim had any value. After the debtor obtained a $110,000 settlement, the trustee sought to recover the proceeds for the estate. The Supreme Court found a fatal flaw in the trustee's failure to object to the exemption in a timely manner. "Deadlines may lead to unwelcome results, but they prompt parties to act and they produce finality."[45]

In Schwab v. Reilly, the debtor listed a value for certain assets in Schedule B and claimed the full amount exempt in Schedule C.[46] When an appraisal indicated that the value of the assets could be in excess of the debtor's claimed exemption, the trustee sought permission to auction the assets, even though the trustee did not object to the debtor's claimed

---

42.   Bankruptcy Rules 1007(c), 4003(a). See chapter 3 supra and chapter 21 infra.
43.   Bankruptcy Rule 1009(a).
44.   11 U.S.C. §522(l); Bankruptcy Rule 4003(b)(c).
45.   Taylor v. Freeland & Kronz, 503 U.S. 638 (1992).
46.   130 S. Ct. 2652 (2010).

exemptions. The lower courts denied the trustee's relief and the Supreme Court reversed. The Court concluded that the trustee had no duty to object to the exemption where the value of the property exceeded the limits of the exemption under the Code.

In *Taylor,* the debtor scheduled a litigation asset with an unknown value. She sought to claim the entire asset exempt. The trustee did not object to the exemption in a timely manner, although the exemption claim was objectionable because it exceeded the allowable dollar amount. The Court held, in this instance, that the trustee's failure to have objected to the inappropriate exemption in a timely manner allowed the debtor to retain the asset. In *Schwab*, on the other hand, the amounts claimed exempt ". . . are facially within the limits the Code prescribes and raise no warning flags that warranted an objection."

Finally, if a debtor claims an exemption in property successfully recovered by the trustee's avoiding powers, the debtor's interest can be assessed its fair share of the costs incurred in recovering the asset.[47] For example, a trustee successfully avoids the transfer of an asset worth $10,000. The amount claimed exempt is $5,000. The cost of recovery is $2,000. One thousand dollars of the costs can be charged against the exemption (the debtor's fair share). The debtor will effectively realize $4,000 through use of the exemption in this example.

Summary

Exemptions are property that an individual debtor may protect from administration by a bankruptcy estate. Exempt property is not available for liquidation to pay a dividend to creditors. A debtor may keep exempt property. Exemptions are a primary element of debtor relief.

Section 522(b) of the Code permits individuals to claim exemptions either under applicable state law, generally where the debtor has been domiciled for the 730 days preceding the filing of the petition, or under Section 522(d) of the Code. These latter exemptions are commonly known as the federal exemptions. However, states have been afforded an opportunity to withdraw from the federal exemption scheme. Approximately 33 states have done so. Pursuant to 11 U.S.C. §522(p), homestead exemptions under state law are limited to $146,450 in certain circumstances.

The decision as to which set of or specific exemptions to select is one of the more important decisions to be made in any individual bankruptcy

---

47. 11 U.S.C. §522(k).

proceeding. The federal exemption list contains common exemptions, many of which are also normally permitted under state law.

Several specific types of debt are immune from a debtor's claim of exemptions. These types of debt include consensual liens and tax liens upon the property sought to be claimed exempt, as well as domestic support obligations, and student financial aid obligations that were fraudulently obtained.

A debtor may, however, successfully avoid certain liens that may impair an allowable exemption. Judicial liens and nonpurchase money consensual liens are subject to this potential lien avoidance. A motion is normally required to avoid such a lien.

Exemptions are claimed by filing a list of exemptions with the court. This list comprises Schedule C of the schedules, Official Form 6.

A party in interest, such as a creditor or the trustee, wishing to object to a claim of exemption, must do so by way of a noticed motion. The motion must be brought within 30 days of the creditors' meeting. If an amendment to a claim of exemption is filed, any objection to the amendment must be brought within 30 days of the amendment's being filed.

KEY TERMS

catch-all exemption	market value
equity	nonpurchase money
exemptions	security interest
federal exemptions	purchase money security
fresh start	interest
homestead exemption	replacement value
liquidation value	stacking

CHAPTER 9 CHECKLIST

9.1 SUMMARY OF FEDERAL EXEMPTIONS

	Item	*Exemption Amount*	*Authority*
9.1.1	residence of debtor or dependent	$21,625	11 U.S.C. §522(d)(1)
9.1.2	motor vehicle	$3,450	11 U.S.C. §522(d)(2)

9.1.3	household goods, furniture, and wearing apparel	$550 per item up to $11,525 in aggregate	11 U.S.C. §522(d)(3)
9.1.4	personal jewelry	$1,450	11 U.S.C. §522(d)(4)
9.1.5	any property catch-all	any unused portion of (d)(1) up to $10,825 plus $1,150 ($11,975 total)	11 U.S.C. §522(d)(5)
9.1.6	tools of trade	$2,175	11 U.S.C. §522(d)(6)
9.1.7	unmatured or term insurance	asset has no value	11 U.S.C. §522(d)(7)
9.1.8	cash value of insurance	$11,525	11 U.S.C. §522(d)(8)
9.1.9	professionally prescribed health aids	no limits	11 U.S.C. §522(d)(9)
9.1.10	Social Security, welfare, veterans' benefits, alimony, disability, or unemployment	varies	11 U.S.C. §522(d)(10)
9.1.11	certain personal injury claims	varies	11 U.S.C. §522(d)(11)
9.1.12	Retirement Accounts	varies	11 U.S.C. §522(d)(12)

9.2   RECORDING A DECLARATION OF HOMESTEAD[48]

9.2.1   Complete Appropriate Declaration

9.2.2   Have Debtors Sign Before a Notary Public

9.2.3   Record at Local Recorder or as Required by Local Law

---

48. This is a general procedure. Further reference to specifically applicable state law is recommended.

DISCUSSION QUESTIONS

1. What are exemptions?

2. What is the purpose of exemptions?

3. What factors should be considered in selecting federal or state exemptions? Specific exemptions?

4. What is a homestead?

5. How does an individual debtor claim exemptions in a bankruptcy proceeding?

6. How are exemptions objected to in a bankruptcy proceeding?

7. How can a debtor avoid a lien that impairs an exemption?

PRACTICE EXERCISES

Exercise 9.1
Complete Schedule C for your clients, the Bottomlines.

Exercise 9.2
Draft a motion on behalf of the Bottomlines to avoid the lien held by the El Repo Finance Company.

10

Trustees, Examiners, and Creditors' Committees

Chapter 7 describes the general procedure for selecting and compensating trustees. This chapter focuses on the trustee's qualifications and duties. The related concepts of Chapter 11 Examiners and Official Creditors' Committees are also discussed briefly, as they exist almost exclusively in Chapter 11 cases. The role and function of the **United States Trustee** is described. The 2005 BAPCPA legislation adds ombudsmen to the mix in selected situations. These various entities collectively comprise the various fiduciaries peculiar to the bankruptcy system.

Trustees, examiners, creditors' committees, ombudsmen, and the United States Trustee are unique players in the bankruptcy system, and these entities are of equal or greater importance than the debtor and individual creditors. Without these additional players, the bankruptcy system would simply not function because there would be no effective control or oversight over a debtor or the debtor's assets. There would also be no effective personnel to effectuate a proper distribution of dividends to creditors.

A. TRUSTEES

Code Sections 321 to 325 address the issues of who may be a **trustee**, how a trustee qualifies, and how a trustee is removed. The trustee may be either an individual or a corporation authorized to serve as a trustee. Section 321 provides that a competent individual who has an office or resides in the district or in an adjacent district where the proceeding is pending may be a trustee in a Chapter 7, 12, or 13 case. A competent individual is normally a disinterested person who has not previously served as examiner in the proceeding.[1]

Practice Pointer

Remember, a "disinterested person" is a defined term under the Bankruptcy Code. It includes a person who is not a creditor, an insider, or someone who holds "an interest materially adverse to the interest of the estate." 11 U.S.C. §101(14).

A corporation that is authorized by its charter or bylaws to be a trustee and has an office in the district where the proceeding is pending may also serve as a trustee.[2] Alternatively, the United States Trustee for that judicial district may also serve as trustee in a proceeding if necessary.[3]

In the normal course of a Chapter 7 proceeding, after the debtor files the petition, the United States trustee will appoint an interim trustee from a panel of private trustees already selected by the United States Trustee's office. Once selected, the trustee "qualifies" by posting a bond. In the case of private panel trustees, described in chapter 7 supra, the trustee need take no action if the court or United States Trustee has authorized a blanket bond that the trustee has previously obtained. This bond inures to the benefit of the creditors in all Chapter 7 estates in which the particular trustee has been appointed. A nonpanel trustee or a trustee serving in a district that has not authorized a blanket bond for trustees will be required to post a bond with the court in each case that the trustee is appointed. The bond has to be posted with the court within five days of the trustee's appointment.[4] These rules apply to trustees appointed in all proceedings, voluntary and involuntary.[5]

Practice Pointer

In some jurisdictions, the United States Trustee will appoint one or more standing Chapter 13 trustees to handle all of the Chapter 13 cases filed within a particular district.

---

1. 11 U.S.C. §321(a)(1), (b); 11 U.S.C. §701(a)(1).
2. 11 U.S.C. §321(a)(2).
3. 11 U.S.C. §321(c).
4. 11 U.S.C. §322(a); Bankruptcy Rule 2010.
5. 11 U.S.C. §701; 11 U.S.C. §1104(d); 11 U.S.C. §1202(a); 11 U.S.C. §1302(a); Bankruptcy Rule 2001.

Prior to the enactment and implementation of the United States Trustee system on a national basis in 1988, the bankruptcy court had the duty to set the amount of the trustee's bond.[6] Under the United States Trustee system, the United States Trustee has now been given this responsibility.[7]

The amount of the trustee's bond is generally based upon a percentage of the estimated value of the assets subject to administration in a particular proceeding. The amount of a blanket bond is generally based on a percentage of the value of all funds on deposit by a panel trustee in all cases subject to the blanket bond. Local rule may require the bond amount to exceed 100 percent of all funds on hand to ensure maximum protection to the creditors of estates being administered by the trustee. Local rules will generally require a trustee to file a quarterly report of funds on deposit with the court or the United States Trustee. The report may result in the bond being increased or decreased.[8]

The trustee is the official legal representative for the bankruptcy estate and in such capacity may sue as a plaintiff on behalf of the estate or be sued as a defendant, representing the estate.[9]

Practice Pointer

Remember, once the debtor files for bankruptcy, all legal interests or actions that the debtor could have maintained prepetition now belong to the bankruptcy estate. Once appointed, the trustee represents the estate and may pursue those actions on behalf of the estate.

Sections 324 and 325 concern the removal of a trustee and the appointment of a successor. A trustee may always be removed for cause. For example, cause will exist to remove a trustee who absconds with estate funds. However, it is unlikely that a trustee would be removed for exercising business judgment that creditors disagree with, unless such judgment is tantamount to gross negligence or gross incompetence. The procedure for removing a trustee requires that a motion be made before the court.

---

6. See 11 U.S.C. §322(b) as it existed prior to October 27, 1986.
7. 11 U.S.C. §322(b).
8. Bankruptcy Rule 2015.
9. 11 U.S.C. §323.

If a trustee dies or resigns during the administration of a proceeding, a successor will have to be appointed.[10]

A trustee will always be appointed in Chapter 7, 12, and 13 proceedings.[11] A trustee may or may not be appointed in a Chapter 11 case.[12] Although the United States Trustee has separate duties to perform in all proceedings, the United States Trustee will not generally serve as an individual trustee in a specific proceeding unless it is necessary, required, or the United States Trustee has been directed to do so by the court. The United States Trustee is, however, considered to be a party in interest for all purposes and "may appear and be heard on any issue in any case."[13]

B.   THE UNITED STATES TRUSTEE

The United States Trustee program began as an experiment in selected districts when the Bankruptcy Code first became effective in 1979. The United States Trustee system operates as a division of the Department of Justice. In 1986, Congress decided to implement the program nationally. The 1986 Code amendments were entitled in part as the "United States Trustees . . . Act of 1986."[14]

The Office of the United States Trustee is intended to serve primarily an administrative function. Prior to enactment of the Code, Bankruptcy Judges performed many of the administrative acts that have now been delegated to the United States Trustee. This change has been initiated in an effort to redefine the Bankruptcy Judge in a more traditional judicial role. Under the Bankruptcy Act, Bankruptcy Judges were known as referees until 1974. As referees, the judges played an active role in the administration of the estate while simultaneously determining the rights of all other parties in the proceeding. This created an inherent conflict within the system. The divestiture from the Bankruptcy Judges of their former administrative duties and the consequent delegation of these duties to the United States Trustee system was intended to resolve this conflict. Now, Bankruptcy Judges remain integral to, but independent from, the day-to-day administration of individual bankruptcy proceedings.

The Office of the United States Trustee is charged with monitoring the progress of all cases, regardless of Chapter, and to act appropriately to

---

10. 11 U.S.C. §324, 325, 703; 11 U.S.C. §1105; Bankruptcy Rule 2012.
11. 11 U.S.C. §§701-703; 11 U.S.C. §1202; 11 U.S.C. §1302.
12. 11 U.S.C. §1104. See infra this chapter.
13. 11 U.S.C. §307; 28 U.S.C. §586(a)(1), (2).
14. Pub. L. No. 99-554, Title II §257(c), 100 Stat. 3114 (Oct. 27, 1986) (28 U.S.C. §§581-586).

"prevent undue delay."[15] The United States Trustee should be served with all notices required under the Code, as described in chapter 5 supra. The United States Trustee is statutorily required to ensure that all debtors pay all of the fees and file all of the required documents in connection with all proceedings filed with the Bankruptcy Court.[16] The United States Trustee also monitors applications for the retention of professionals and applications for professional compensation and is permitted to comment thereon to the Bankruptcy Court.[17] The local United States Trustee may have published guidelines to assist in this process. See a representative sample on the forms disk. The United States Trustee may also refer any matters for investigation to the United States Attorney that may constitute a bankruptcy crime.[18]

In Chapter 7 proceedings, the United States Trustee maintains and supervises a panel of trustees.[19] In everyday practice, the United States Trustee's performance of this duty includes appointing private panel Chapter 7 trustees and supervising and monitoring the private trustee's prompt administration of asset estates (see chapter 22 infra).

The 2005 BAPCPA legislation created new responsibilities for the United States Trustee. First, Bankruptcy Code Section 704(b) charges the United States Trustee to review the debtor's materials filed pursuant to Section 521 (see chapters 4 and 7 supra), and to file a statement within ten days of the meeting of creditors indicating whether or not the filing creates a presumed abuse of Chapter 7 under "needs based bankruptcy" (see chapter 5 supra).

 Practice Pointer

It is always important to confirm when the tolling period is triggered. Frequently, the statutory period begins counting from the date of the "first" scheduled meeting of creditors.

---

15. 25 U.S.C. §586(a)(3)(G).
16. 28 U.S.C. §586(a)(3)(D).
17. 28 U.S.C. §586(a)(3)(A), (H). See chapter 7 supra.
18. 28 U.S.C. §586(a)(3)(F). Bankruptcy crimes are defined in 18 U.S.C. §§151-157. Generally, bankruptcy crimes include the fraudulent concealment of assets in connection with a pending proceeding or the commission of perjury or the taking of a false oath. These crimes include penalties of fines and/or imprisonment for not more than five years. Altering, destroying, or concealing records with the intent to obstruct proper administration of the estate could also lead to additional fines and/or imprisonment of up to 20 years. 18 U.S.C. §1519.
19. 28 U.S.C. §586(a).

If abuse is presumed, then within 30 days of filing the statement, the United States trustee must file a motion to dismiss or convert or a statement setting forth the reasons why no motion is to be filed if abuse is presumed pursuant to "needs based bankruptcy." Second, Section 603 of BAPCPA requires random audits of one out of 250 cases. Under BAPCPA, the United States Trustee is directed to retain auditors and to file the audit reports with the Bankruptcy Court.[20]

Third, the United States Trustee is charged with the approval and oversight monitoring of the various nonprofit budget and credit counseling agencies providing both the prepetition credit counseling required by Section 109(h) and the postpetition personal financial management courses mandated by Sections 727(a)(11) and 1328(g) (see chapters 4 and 7 supra).

In Chapter 11 proceedings, the United States Trustee will function to a large degree as the "eyes and ears" of the court. The United States Trustee is directed to appoint and monitor Chapter 11 creditors' committees.[21] The United States Trustee has also been charged with monitoring Chapter 11 Reorganization Plans and Disclosure Statements and is permitted to comment upon them.[22] This power is also granted to the United States Trustee in connection with Chapter 12 and 13 proceedings.[23]

In everyday practice the United States Trustee's involvement in a Chapter 11 proceeding can be extensive, particularly during the first 60 days of a Chapter 11. During this period, the United States Trustee will interact with a **debtor-in-possession** in several areas.

First, the United States Trustee will generally conduct an initial conference with the estate's representatives approximately two weeks after filing. At the initial conference, the United States Trustee will generally interview the parties present to obtain an overview of the case and to instruct counsel and the parties as to any local United States Trustee guidelines and as to the various administrative duties and responsibilities of a debtor-in-possession. In a small business Chapter 11 (see chapter 24 infra), 28 U.S.C. §586(a)(7) requires the United States Trustee to conduct an initial debtor interview. (See chapter 24 infra for a description of these duties.) The forms disk contains representative samples. The United States Trustee will follow up to monitor the debtor-in-possession's compliance with the rules and guidelines.

---

20. 28 U.S.C. §586(f).
21. 11 U.S.C. §1102; 28 U.S.C. §586(a)(3)(E). See infra this chapter.
22. 28 U.S.C. §586(a)(3)(B).
23. 28 U.S.C. §586(a)(3)(C).

Second, the United States Trustee will preside at the meeting of the creditors held pursuant to 11 U.S.C. §341(a) and 11 U.S.C. §343.

Third, the United States Trustee will act to facilitate the organizing of an Official Creditors' Committee. See infra this chapter.

The United States Trustee will collect quarterly fees from a debtor-in-possession pursuant to 28 U.S.C. §586(a)(3)(D) and 28 U.S.C. §1930(a)(6) (see chapter 24 infra).

Finally, the United States Trustee may bring motions to dismiss or convert Chapter 11 proceedings pursuant to 11 U.S.C. §586(a)(8) (see chapter 23 infra).

C.   THE TRUSTEE'S DUTIES

Although there are separate provisions in each Chapter proceeding that specify the duties of a trustee appointed under a particular Chapter, the duties remain essentially the same throughout the Code. Section 704(a) contains a list of 12 items that specify the duties of a Chapter 7 trustee. Section 1302 contains a list of items that specify the duties of a Chapter 13 trustee. A number of the duties described in Section 704(a) have been incorporated into this provision. Section 1106 specifies the duties of a Chapter 11 trustee. This Section also incorporates many of the elements from Section 704(a). A similar situation pertains to the duties of a Chapter 12 trustee as contained in Section 1202.[24] However, all of the duties of a trustee may be synthesized into four essential ones that can best be remembered by use of a mnemonic device that we can refer to as the four "ATEs." That is, the essential duties of a trustee can be described as follows: investig*ate*, liquid*ate*, litig*ate*, and administr*ate*.

Investigation is the initial duty performed by any trustee. A trustee must initially determine whether or not there are assets in an estate that can be liquidated to pay a dividend to creditors of the estate. In a consumer no asset or a small business proceeding, performance of this duty may involve little more than reviewing the Statements and Schedules and questioning the debtor at the meeting of creditors. In a larger proceeding, investigation may involve a review of significant records and documents and the taking of one or more Rule 2004 Examinations

---

24. 11 U.S.C. §1302(b); 11 U.S.C. §704(a); 11 U.S.C. §1106(a); 11 U.S.C. §1202(b).

(see chapter 7 supra) before the trustee can logically proceed further in the administration of an estate.[25]

The liquidation duty is the most visible of the trustee's duties. Liquidation involves the trustee converting nonexempt assets into cash. This is always the trustee's goal in a Chapter 7 case. Liquidation can be as simple as having a private sale or a public auction of the inventory and equipment of a bankrupt business or can be as complex as selling the assets of a major business to one or more buyers in what may be complex and unrelated transactions. BAPCPA imposes the additional requirement for a trustee to make his/her best efforts to transfer the patients of a health care business to another appropriate health care business.[26]

> ### Practice Pointer
>
> The source for the funding for the bankruptcy estate depends upon the Chapter of the case. In a Chapter 7 proceeding, the liquidation of assets is the major source of the payment tendered to the estate's creditors. In a Chapter 13 proceeding, the money usually comes from monthly payments made by the debtor.

To fully liquidate an estate may require a trustee to sue third parties. Litigation is the third of the four ATEs. As the official representative of an estate, a trustee may pursue claims against third parties that would exist even if there had been no bankruptcy. For example, collecting accounts receivable that are due a debtor may require a trustee to initiate litigation. The trustee may also be able to exercise one of the avoiding powers to recover assets of the estate for the benefit of creditors.[27] Presumably, when a trustee sues, the litigation will result in the obtaining of additional cash to pay the creditors of the estate. Thus, to a certain extent, litigation is also a part of liquidation.

Finally, a trustee has to administer the assets that have been reduced to cash by liquidation or litigation. The trustee follows additional rules and procedures for distributing the cash to creditors in the form of dividends. The accomplishment of this process is the major goal of unsecured creditors affected by the bankruptcy system and forms the essence of the debt collection aspects of the Bankruptcy Code. The entire process of

---

25. 11 U.S.C. §704(a)(4); 11 U.S.C. §1106(a)(3); 11 U.S.C. §1202(b)(2); 11 U.S.C. §1302(b)(1).
26. 11 U.S.C. §704(a)(1), (12).
27. See chapters 15-17 infra.

maintaining and distributing the cash to creditors is known as the "administration of the estate." The specific details of this administrative process are described in chapter 22 infra.

BAPCPA imposed an additional administrative duty upon trustees, requiring them to provide notice to the holders of claims for domestic support obligations, informing them that they may seek support assistance from a state agency, and requiring the trustee to provide notice of the debtor's discharge and contact information to the claim holder and the state support agency when the discharge is granted.[28]

In a Chapter 12 or 13 proceeding, a trustee is not specifically directed to liquidate assets. A Chapter 12 trustee is required to ensure that the debtor commences to make timely payments under the debtor's plan.[29] A Chapter 13 trustee actually collects payments made under a Chapter 13 plan and distributes them to the creditors on a regular basis.[30]

D. DEBTOR-IN-POSSESSION

In Chapter 11 proceedings, there may or may not be an active trustee. In the reorganization process that Chapter 11 represents, there is normally no trustee. Instead, the debtor functions as a "debtor-in-possession."[31] The essence of this concept is that the debtor acts as its own trustee. Section 1107 describes the rights, powers, and duties of the Chapter 11 debtor-in-possession. These rights, powers, and duties are essentially the four ATE*s* described above. However, because the purpose of a Chapter 11 is to reorganize rather than to liquidate, it is more accurate to substitute the term *reorganize* in place of the term *liquidate*. How a debtor properly fulfills the duty to reorganize is described in chapters 24-26 infra.

E. OFFICIAL CREDITORS' COMMITTEES

A number of mechanisms have been created to provide the creditors in a Chapter 11 proceeding with the ability to oversee and monitor the

---

28. 11 U.S.C. §704(c); 11 U.S.C. §1106(c); 11 U.S.C. §1202(c); 11 U.S.C. §1302(d).
29. 11 U.S.C. §1202(b)(4). See chapter 27 infra.
30. 11 U.S.C. §1302(b)(3)(5). See chapter 23 infra.
31. 11 U.S.C. §1101(1); 11 U.S.C. §1107.

performance by a debtor-in-possession of its statutory duties. These various mechanisms include providing the creditors an opportunity to seek the appointment of a trustee or examiner and/or the formation of an **Official Creditors' Committee**.[32]

The Official Creditors' Committee is the initial monitor of a debtor-in-possession's Chapter 11 financial affairs.[33] Keep in mind that a debtor experiencing financial difficulty will generally remain in full control of its activities. To the extent that a debtor can isolate one or more of its creditors and attempt to deal with each creditor independently, this is merely an application of the ancient Roman principle of "divide and conquer." The remedy to a debtor's use of this principle is another equally ancient principle: "In unity there is strength." The Official Creditors' Committee is simply a mechanism that puts the latter principle into practice. The major purpose of the committee is to unite the unsecured creditors so they can deal with the debtor-in-possession collectively and not as individual isolated creditors. The Official Creditors' Committee is appointed by the United States Trustee from among the 20 largest unsecured creditors of a debtor-in-possession. At the initiation of a Chapter 11 proceeding, the debtor-in-possession files a list of its 20 largest unsecured creditors with the court along with all of the other documents required to be filed by a debtor upon initiating a proceeding. This list is to be filed within two days of filing a Chapter 11 petition.[34] From this list the United States Trustee will solicit creditors to serve on the committee.[35] When a sufficient number, in the United States Trustee's discretion, consent to appointment, the committee is officially appointed. The Official Creditors' Committee is a **party in interest** to the proceeding. This means that the committee may file pleadings, initiate motions, or file plans of reorganization.[36]

Section 1102(a)(3), added to the Code in 1994, permits a small business Chapter 11 debtor to request the court not to appoint an Official Creditors' Committee. (A **small business debtor** is defined in Chapter 11 as a debtor with less than $2 million of debt who elects treatment as a small business.) Upon a showing of cause, the request shall be granted. Since the concept of the creditors' committee is important to the Chapter 11 process, the case law will probably impose strict requirements on the granting of such motions.

---

32. The 2005 legislation also created ombudsmen to deal with privacy issues in the sale of customer lists, and the best interests of patients in health care bankruptcies. 11 U.S.C. §332; 11 U.S.C. §333; 11 U.S.C. §§1102-1103; 11 U.S.C. §1104. See chapter 24 infra.
33. 11 U.S.C. §§1102-1103.
34. Bankruptcy Rule 1007(d).
35. 11 U.S.C. §1102(a)(1).
36. 11 U.S.C. §1103.

The Official Creditors' Committee has authority under the Code to hire its own professionals, such as counsel and accountants.[37] The expenses of the professionals employed by the Official Creditors' Committee are the **administrative expenses** of the estate. This means that any fees incurred are payable by the estate. Because many unsecured creditors do not necessarily have a right to recover attorneys' fees from a debtor when attempting to collect debts that are due, this is a powerful tool. These professionals are treated in the manner described in chapter 7 supra. Their employment must be approved by the court, and the committee's professionals are subject to the same fee application requirements discussed in chapter 7 supra. The membership of an Official Creditors' Committee may also receive reimbursement of expenses incurred in the performance of duties for the estate, pursuant to Section 503(b)(3)(F).

Historically, creditors' committees fail to become active in many Chapter 11 proceedings, usually to the ultimate detriment of the creditors. This failure may be directly attributed to the appointed committee members simply having no one explain to them the meaning and significance of the committee and membership upon it. This has been unfortunate because in many cases where the creditors' committee organizes itself and retains professional assistance, the chances for a successful reorganization improve immeasurably. Alternatively, the committee can seek the prompt conversion of a Chapter 11 to a Chapter 7 if it appears reorganization will not succeed, thereby preserving any possible equity in the assets to pay dividends to the creditors. The committee can also assist the debtor in negotiating a feasible and confirmable plan of reorganization.[38] In an effort to increase the number of active committees, the Code has directed the United States Trustee to meet with the appointed committee promptly after its appointment so the committee can be educated as to its rights and purposes.[39] In an appropriate proceeding it may also be helpful for the debtor-in-possession to meet with a committee promptly after its appointment. This is not as incongruous as may appear at first glance to those used to thinking solely in adversarial terms. Because a successful Chapter 11 will result in payments to creditors and survival of the debtor, the best results are often achieved when the debtor and creditors find ways to work together to resolve the situation through a confirmable plan of reorganization. Input from the committee into the internal

---

37. 11 U.S.C. §1103(a).
38. 11 U.S.C. §1103(c)(3)(5).
39. 11 U.S.C. §1103(d).

reorganization of a Chapter 11 debtor's affairs can also often provide an invaluable and essential service to an estate.[40]

An Official Creditors' Committee has the right to investigate the debtor's financial affairs, consult with the debtor or trustee (if one is appointed), request the appointment of a trustee or examiner, and perhaps most important, assist in the formulation of a plan of reorganization on behalf of all unsecured creditors.[41] In the absence of the appointment of a trustee in a Chapter 11 proceeding, the court will often look to input from the committee to assist the court in making decisions that affect the estate. This is especially so where the committee has been organized and has independently investigated the debtor's financial affairs in a manner similar to that which would be conducted by a trustee.[42] In an exceptionally large proceeding, the court may approve the appointment of multiple creditors' committees. For example, there may be a committee of trade creditors and a committee of unsecured lenders.[43] On rare occasions, a creditors' committee may be appointed in a Chapter 7.[44] If a committee investigates a debtor and reasonably believes that the debtor or its insiders have committed fraud or are incompetent, the committee may seek the appointment of a trustee or examiner. Additionally, if a debtor-in-possession fails to follow the appropriate Chapter 11 operating rules (described in chapter 24 of this text), a committee, any creditor, or the United States Trustee may seek through motion a court order appointing a trustee or examiner in a Chapter 11 proceeding.[45]

F.   CHAPTER 11 TRUSTEES AND EXAMINERS

Section 1104(a) provides three grounds for the appointment of a trustee or examiner in a Chapter 11 proceeding. The first ground is for cause, including fraud, dishonesty, incompetence, or gross mismanagement. For instance, the owner of a restaurant who is found to be misreporting sales while concealing cash is committing fraud against the creditors.

---

40. 11 U.S.C. §1103(c)(1).
41. 11 U.S.C. §1103(c).
42. 11 U.S.C. §1103(c)(2).
43. 11 U.S.C. §1102(a)(2).
44. 11 U.S.C. §705.
45. 11 U.S.C. §1104(a). As to the operating rules of a Chapter 11 debtor-in-possession, see chapter 24 infra.

The insiders of a business may simply be incapable of managing it properly. They may have no concept of budget, cash flow, or overhead costs, the inevitable results of which may be to operate the business unprofitably. Simple incompetence is probably the greatest single cause of a majority of all Chapter 11 proceedings filed by operating businesses.

The second ground for granting a motion to appoint a trustee or examiner is if the appointment is found to be in the best interests of the creditors.[46] This can be a rather nebulous concept. It usually comes into play when the creditors' committee or a creditor or the United States Trustee moves for the appointment of a trustee or examiner, alleging any of the factual scenarios described above, but with insufficient proof to justify the appointment of a trustee or examiner for cause. Nevertheless, if it is clear to the court that the creditors have lost confidence in the debtor's management and that the appointment of an independent third party, a trustee, may help to restore confidence, then the appointment of a trustee or examiner may be found to be in the best interests of creditors. This situation can also arise in proceedings involving partnerships where the general partners are in constant dispute and can agree on no course of action in any matter. The impossibility of general partners' agreeing is a classic situation that justifies the appointment of a trustee in the best interests of creditors.

Third, if grounds exist to dismiss or convert the case from a Chapter 11, the court may instead appoint a trustee in the best interests of creditors.[47]

A Chapter 11 trustee is very powerful. For example, a corporate debtor not in a bankruptcy proceeding is controlled by its board of directors and officers under applicable state law. However, a Chapter 11 trustee is superior to the officers and board in the chain of command, becoming, in a word, the boss. A Chapter 11 trustee is functionally a dictator. A Chapter 11 trustee has full power and authority under the Code to retain any insider in a management position or to relieve any or all insiders of their duties. To this extent, the appointment of a Chapter 11 trustee acts to supersede the charter or bylaws of a debtor corporation. Because the debtor has submitted itself to the court's jurisdiction, the appointment of a trustee is a burden it must accept.

A Chapter 11 trustee has the duties to investigate, litigate, and administrate as described above. Administration here includes following all Chapter 11 operating rules. A Chapter 11 trustee also has a duty to file a plan of reorganization or seek conversion of the proceeding to a

---

46. 11 U.S.C. §1104(a)(2).
47. 11 U.S.C. §1104(a)(3).

Chapter 7.[48] In many cases, a trustee will retain current management. The decision to retain or relieve current management is, as a practical matter, the most important decision a Chapter 11 trustee makes. For instance, in a relatively small business the only people who really care enough about the business's survival and reorganization to operate it on a daily basis are the owners who are also insiders. If such individuals are replaced by third parties, the new operators may not necessarily be concerned about the business's ultimate survival. The owners/insiders are usually the persons with the greatest incentive to save the business despite their actions possibly being a cause of the filing.

A decision to change current management should not be made unless it is obvious that current management is either utterly incompetent, will not follow the trustee's instructions, or is demonstrably committing fraud. A Chapter 11 trustee best fulfills the role in a Chapter 11 by showing the debtor the correct path to an effective reorganization or by seeking conversion of the proceeding to a Chapter 7 if reorganization is not feasible.

Examiners are unique to Chapter 11 proceedings. Simply put, an **examiner** is someone who examines the debtor's affairs.[49] An examiner is usually appointed when a party has moved for the appointment of a trustee and the court determines that further independent investigation is required before a final decision can be made on the issue. An examiner may also be appointed to investigate a specific issue and to act as the "eyes and ears" of the court in a fact-finding capacity. An examiner is an independent third party who is usually given specific instructions by the court to investigate certain aspects of a debtor's financial affairs. An examiner may be required to investigate all matters or simply a limited aspect of a debtor's financial affairs. The examiner will prepare a report for the benefit of the court and creditors. A Chapter 11 trustee also has a duty to prepare such a report regarding the debtor's financial affairs for the benefit of the court and creditors.[50] An examiner's report may support the debtor or it may recommend the appointment of a trustee or conversion of the proceeding to a Chapter 7. The people who serve as examiners are usually the same people who are on a panel of trustees in a given district. The only qualification to serve as an examiner, however, is to be a disinterested person.

The court has discretion to expand the powers of the examiner without appointing a trustee, effectively making the examiner with expanded

---

48. 11 U.S.C. §1106(a).
49. 11 U.S.C. §1106(b).
50. 11 U.S.C. §1106(a)(3)(4).

powers a quasi-trustee.[51] This may actually help to reduce expenses and expedite the administration of a large and complex case. However, a person who has served as examiner in a proceeding may not serve as trustee in the same proceeding.[52]

G.   OMBUDSMAN

The 2005 legislation added **ombudsman** to the list of specialized entities that may perform services for a bankruptcy estate. An ombudsman may be appointed in two discrete situations. First, where an asset sale (see chapter 18) involves the sale of **personally identifiable information** (such as a customer list), then the court shall order the appointment of an ombudsman to review the seller's privacy policy and report on the potential losses or gains to consumers and the estate by the proposed sale.[53] Second, in a **health care business** bankruptcy, the court shall order an ombudsman to represent the interests of the patients where necessary and to regularly report to the court on the quality of patient care.[54]

Summary

The Bankruptcy Code has created several unique types of fiduciaries without which the bankruptcy system could not function. These fiduciaries are the trustee, United States Trustee, debtor-in-possession, Official Creditors' Committee, examiners, and ombudsmen.

The trustee is appointed by the United States Trustee. The trustee administers the bankruptcy estate. Chapter 7, 12, and 13 proceedings will always have a trustee appointed. In a Chapter 11 proceeding, a trustee may only be appointed by way of a noticed motion. The grounds for granting such a motion are cause, such as fraud or gross incompetence, or because appointment of a trustee would be in the best interest of the creditors.

---

51. 11 U.S.C. §1106(b).
52. 11 U.S.C. §321(b).
53. 11 U.S.C. §332. "Personally identifiable information" is defined at 11 U.S.C. §101 (41A) and is generally a person's private information typically maintained in a customer list.
54. 11 U.S.C. §333. "Health care business" is defined at 11 U.S.C. §101 (27A) and generally includes hospitals, hospices, long-term care facilities, and home health agencies.

The United States Trustee program is a division of the Department of Justice responsible for monitoring the administration of bankruptcy estates. The United States Trustee also appoints private trustees in separate proceedings.

The debtor-in-possession is the entity created by a debtor filing a Chapter 11 reorganization proceeding. A debtor-in-possession is essentially a debtor acting as its own trustee.

The Official Creditors' Committee is an entity created in a Chapter 11 to act on the collective behalf of unsecured creditors. The committee may retain professionals, appear as a party in interest, and propose a plan of reorganization.

An examiner is an individual appointed in a Chapter 11 proceeding to conduct an independent investigation of some or all of a debtor's financial affairs.

An ombudsman is appointed in connection with the sale of customer lists and in health care business bankruptcies to speak for the interests of the patients.

A trustee's duties can be summarized: investigate, liquidate, litigate, and administrate. A trustee's investigation may lead to the discovery of assets. The assets are then reduced to cash by either liquidation or litigation. The process of collecting, maintaining, and distributing the cash to creditors is referred to as the administration of the estate.

KEY TERMS

administrative expenses
debtor-in-possession
examiner
health care business
Official Creditors' Committee
ombudsman
party in interest

personally identifiable
 information
small business debtor
trustee
United States Trustee

DISCUSSION QUESTIONS

1. What is the basic role of a bankruptcy trustee?

2. What are a bankruptcy trustee's basic duties? What is the difference between the duties of a Chapter 7 trustee and a trustee in a reorganization proceeding (Chapter 11, 12, or 13)?

3. What is the United States Trustee? What is its function?

4. What is a debtor-in-possession? What are a debtor-in-possession's duties?

5. What is an Official Creditors' Committee? What is the committee's role? May a committee retain its own professionals?

6. What are the grounds for the appointment of a trustee in a Chapter 11 proceeding?

7. What is an examiner?

8. What is an ombudsman? When is an ombudsman appointed?

PRACTICE EXERCISE

Exercise 10.1

Draft a letter on behalf of the trustee, identifying what documents you wish the Bottomlines to bring with them to the meeting of creditors.

11

Preparing a Proceeding for a Trustee

Private panel Chapter 7 trustees are busy people. In some districts a private panel trustee may be assigned 45 or more proceedings per month. Perhaps 10 to 15 percent of these proceedings will require the trustee to do more than review the file and ask the questions at the creditors' meeting described in chapter 7 supra. If the trustee has been on a private panel for an extended period of time, the trustee will have an enormous case load. As a result, private panel trustees can be difficult to communicate with. However, there are some effective methods that can be used to promote effective communication with a trustee. Use of these methods will help to expedite efficient and prompt administration in consumer no asset proceedings and will also aid in the efficient and proper administration of small asset proceedings. In the latter type of proceeding, these methods will also increase, sometimes significantly, the recovery obtained for the payment of creditor dividends. This benefits a debtor as well as the creditors.

A.   PREFILING ACTIONS

The primary rule for properly preparing a proceeding for filing is to make the Chapter 7 trustee's job as easy as possible in order to achieve the greatest recovery and, hence, distribution. In a typical consumer no asset proceeding this will be relatively simple. In this instance all that is usually necessary is to prepare the Statements and Schedules thoroughly and clearly so that all the relevant data is easily analyzed. Chapter 29 of this text is a tutorial regarding the preparation of these documents in a clear

and efficient manner. The general rule of preparation applies in all proceedings, but in a consumer no asset case the Statements and Schedules
will constitute a majority of the effort involved. Their clarity will expedite
administration and minimize the questioning that occurs at the creditors'
meeting under Section 342. For debtors that have little or no contact with
the legal system, adequate preparation will help to minimize any trauma
associated with the bankruptcy filing.

In all consumer cases, BAPCPA imposes new requirements upon debtors, their counsel, and trustees, requiring more preparation. Counsel will
need to prove that the prepetition disclosures required by Sections 527
and 528 have been given and that there is a prepetition retainer agreement
as described in chapter 4 supra. The statement of current income will
need to comply with the needs based bankruptcy formula described in
chapter 5 supra; counsel will need to obtain all evidence of payments
received by the debtor within 60 days of the filing date; and counsel
will also need to obtain from the debtor the debtor's most recent tax
return and for the three years preceding the filing if requested, as
described in chapter 4 supra.

BAPCPA imposes the further requirement upon counsel to make "reasonable inquiry" as to the disclosures made by debtors in their Statements
and Schedules, or risk the prospect of sanctions.[1] Case law will clarify the
meaning of "reasonable inquiry," but at a minimum it is likely to include all
the information otherwise required to be filed, credit reports, values of vehicles obtained from credible Internet sources, and copies of documents of
title, among other things. All documents relied upon by the practitioner in
making the calculations appearing on the Statement of Current Monthly
Income should be retained in case they are requested by the United States
Trustee.

Even in consumer no asset proceedings a situation may be present
where it is likely the trustee will want to ask questions in addition to those
described in chapter 7 supra. Perhaps there may be some form of inheritance
as a potential asset, or a homestead. In these instances, the best thing to do is
to obtain copies of any relevant documents from the debtor prior to filing.
In any proceeding where it can be reasonably anticipated beforehand that
the trustee will want to review documents in addition to the Statements
and Schedules, it is always a good idea to have any such documents available
so they can be delivered to the trustee promptly upon request.

In a small asset Chapter 7 business proceeding (and in all larger
proceedings), effective preparation of the proceeding for the Chapter 7

---

1. 11 U.S.C. §527(a)(2)(B); 11 U.S.C. §707(b)(4). See chapters 4 and 5 supra.

trustee will require more effort. Although a larger proceeding will require more effort still, the type of effort will not vary. A typical small asset Chapter 7 liquidation, such as a small retail store or restaurant, will normally involve an inventory valued from a nominal amount to $50,000 or more and equipment of similar value. There may also be accounts receivable to collect. In small asset business proceedings, one of the most common problems of debtors or their principals (whether the debtor is an individual, a corporation, or a partnership) is payroll or other nondischargeable taxes.[2] In proceedings of this sort, the debtor's or its insiders' primary concern will be to raise sufficient cash from the estate's liquidation to be able to satisfy a maximum amount of the nondischargeable obligations.

It is important to note that when a trustee is appointed, the trustee generally learns of the appointment only by receiving a copy of the bankruptcy petition and schedules in the mail, along with a stack of perhaps 15 or 20 other proceedings. If an estate contains assets that require prompt liquidation, unless the trustee reviews the files immediately (even if just to ascertain the existence of assets), the trustee may not know that any such assets exist until the meeting of creditors.

Recall that the creditors' meeting may not occur until 40 days after the initial filing.[3] If nothing is done during this period, assets may be at a business's premises without any type of security protection. The neighborhood kids can visit the place and help clean out the premises. Rent will continue to accrue. This rent will be an administrative expense payable before any tax creditors receive dividends. Gas and electric bills may continue to accrue and they will also receive administrative priority.[4] The longer assets go unattended the greater the likelihood they will dissipate to the detriment of all. As illustrated, this dissipation can occur by improper means or simply by the accrual of administrative expenses in the normal course of business. Both methods of dissipation can be substantially avoided by recognizing the practical difficulties encountered by trustees and by taking appropriate and simple commonsense actions that will effectively minimize any unintentional dissipation of assets.

Prior to a filing, there are at least nine things that a debtor or counsel can do to properly prepare a proceeding for the trustee. The accomplishment of these tasks will expedite the liquidation at a minimum of time and expense. Because most of these tasks can be performed by the debtor, any additional time required to be spent by counsel is minimal. Generally, a debtor and counsel should take any action reasonably designed to achieve the mutually

---

2. See chapter 13 infra.
3. See chapter 7 supra.
4. See chapter 21 infra.

desirable goals of expediting liquidation at a minimum of expense. A paralegal will often participate in much of this activity. Every possible penny that can reasonably be saved or earned will only serve to increase the ultimate funds available for distribution to prepetition creditors.

First, the debtor should obtain valuations, estimates, or appraisals of any property owned by the debtor. In a typical no asset consumer case, this is usually not as much an issue. Where there is equity in the property and/or there is the existence of other unencumbered property, accurate valuations are a must.

Practice Pointer

The debtor's property tax appraisal is generally not accepted as evidence of the fair market value for the debtor's property.

Second, all documents of title pertaining to the debtor's assets should be assembled. You should be able to provide copies of the debtor's mortgage or lease as well as ownership documents of any vehicles owned by the debtor. The debtor should also seek to obtain payoff values for any mortgages or automobile loans. Having them in hand will save the trustee time and expense if issues arise later.

Third, obtain the name, address, and telephone number of the debtor's mortgage company and/or any landlords so the trustee will be able to make prompt arrangements to sell the property or to vacate the premises if necessary.

Fourth, the debtor should always be prepared to provide as detailed an itemization as possible of all personal belongings and household goods. If a valuation of these items is also included, this data will be invaluable to the trustee. This detailed information will not always be possible to have, but when it is, it should be provided to the trustee.

Fifth, the debtor should turn over to counsel the most recent copies of all records and checks of all bank accounts. Evidence of these accounts should be promptly disclosed to the trustee if it differs in any way from the debtor's schedules. Personal accounts should not be turned over unless requested by the trustee. Providing unrequested information only clutters the trustee and distracts attention from the prompt liquidation of those assets requiring it.

Sixth, the debtor should provide the trustee with any documentation of any prepetition lawsuits or claims, pursued or otherwise. If the debtor has already obtained prepetition counsel with respect to these claims, contact information should also be provided to the trustee.

> ### *Practice Pointer*
>
> Most times, the trustee will seek to retain debtor's prepetition counsel to continue to pursue a particular state law claim, such as in a personal injury matter, only this time on behalf of the bankruptcy estate.

Seventh, the debtor should have available any documentation relating to any leased equipment or vehicles.

Eighth, the debtor will need to provide proof of insurance, both homeowners and automobile insurance, in order to provide adequate assurance that the property is insured and protected.

Finally, the debtor needs to provide his/her last three state and federal tax returns. The trustee will need this data to properly administer the estate. Any tax benefits contained in the prior returns will aid in reducing any taxes that may be incurred by a bankruptcy estate.

B.   POSTFILING ACTIONS

Once a proceeding is filed, it is necessary to promptly communicate with the trustee to ensure that liquidation of the physical assets will proceed promptly. Trustees, like anyone else, cannot act if they do not know that something needs to be acted upon. There are four things that can be done promptly on filing to ensure rapid communication with a trustee. These items will help the liquidation process proceed without delay.

First, and most obvious, is for counsel to learn who the trustee will be. You cannot communicate with the trustee unless you know who the trustee is. Because the United States Trustee must promptly appoint an interim trustee, the United States Trustee's office will generally know who the interim trustee will be within 24 hours of filing.[5] Thus, if counsel contacts the United States Trustee and asks to know who the interim

---

5. 11 U.S.C. §701. See chapter 7 supra.

trustee is, prompt contact will become possible. Under the prevailing Electronic Filing System in use by the courts (see chapter 31 infra), the interim trustee is appointed immediately and the trustee's name, address, and telephone number will appear on the court docket.

The second obvious action is to pick up the telephone and call the trustee. Because trustees do not necessarily return all phone calls, it is necessary to leave a message that will alert the trustee about the existence of the asset proceeding. The basic word to leave in the message is "assets." Use of the word *assets* will normally result in the trustee responding within 24 hours. If more than 24 hours elapse without a reply from the trustee, then written correspondence is required. In a pressing matter, such as a restaurant or other debtor with perishable goods, the correspondence should be hand-delivered immediately. It is a good idea to enclose a copy of the Statements and Schedules in the correspondence. Once the trustee has been reached, the trustee will normally move into action and commence the liquidation process.

The third action is for the debtor to close all bank accounts for turnover to the trustee and either write a check to the trustee for the balance or obtain a cashier's check from the bank for the amount of the account balance. This will eliminate any further charges by the bank for maintenance of the account. Section 521(a)(2) of the Bankruptcy Code requires turnover of all records to the trustee.

Finally, the debtor or its insiders should cooperate fully with the trustee in the liquidation process. The trustee, or the trustee's representative, may want to meet the debtor at the business premises, for example. The trustee may need assistance in properly assembling accounts receivable data for collection purposes. The liquidation process will be easier and less expensive the greater the level of cooperation given the trustee by the debtor or its insiders. Section 521(a)(3) of the Bankruptcy Code requires cooperation of the debtor with the trustee.

All of the practical and commonsense actions just described, both pre- and postfiling, will be useful in expediting the physical aspects of liquidation at a minimum of expense. This will ensure that a maximum amount of cash will be raised to distribute to the creditors as dividends. Where this results in payment in full of nondischargeable taxes, the debtor or its principals will be grateful.

Summary

It is important to make the trustee's job as simple as possible. Properly preparing a case before it is filed will often be sufficient to accomplish this task.

In all proceedings, proper preparation of the Statements and Schedules is critical. Chapter 29 of this text is a tutorial on this subject. Further, whenever it can be anticipated that the trustee may request additional documentation (such as a declaration of homestead, an escrow closing statement, or bank records), the documents should be obtained from the client before the filing. Counsel must also maintain all documents required by BAPCPA together with any materials relied upon to satisfy the "reasonable inquiry" standard.

In business proceedings, there are nine simple steps that can be taken before a filing and four additional steps that can be taken immediately after a filing to rapidly commence the liquidation process, all of which will help to economize expenses while helping to maximize returns. Generally, a debtor and counsel should take any action reasonably designed to achieve the mutually desirable goals of expediting liquidation at a minimum of expense.

CHAPTER 11 CHECKLIST

11.1   PREFILING — ASSET CASE

    11.1.1   Value Assets

    11.1.2   Obtain Documents of Title (Such as Vehicle Ownership Documents) and Keys to All Vehicles

    11.1.3   Obtain Name and Address of Landlord(s)

    11.1.4   Obtain Itemized Inventory and Equipment List, with Values, If Possible

    11.1.5   Obtain Bank Records

    11.1.6   Compile Accounts Receivable Data

    11.1.7   Return Leased Equipment to Lessors

    11.1.8   Maintain Security

    11.1.9   Obtain Prior Years' Tax Returns

11.2   POSTFILING — ASSET CASE

    11.2.1   Learn Identity of Trustee

    11.2.2   Communicate with Trustee

    11.2.3   Close Bank Accounts and Obtain Cashier's Check for Trustee

    11.2.4   Encourage Insider Cooperation with Trustee

DISCUSSION QUESTIONS

1. What are the most important concerns of a debtor in a consumer no asset Chapter 7 proceeding?

2. What is a common primary concern in an asset proceeding?

3. What actions, before and after the filing of an asset case, should be taken by the debtor or counsel that can assist the trustee in maximizing a liquidation at a minimum of expense?

PRACTICE EXERCISES

Exercise 11.1

Prepare a list of documents for the Bottomlines to provide to your firm for their case file and for possible turnover to a trustee.

Exercise 11.2

The Bottomlines have a copy of their local tax bill and property assessment and do not understand why an appraisal is necessary. Draft a letter to the Bottomlines explaining the different types of property appraisals and identifying the type of appraisal that will be required by the trustee.

PART III

Bankruptcy Litigation

12

The Automatic Stay— 11 U.S.C. §362

A.   THE AUTOMATIC STAY

The final element of debtor relief is contained in Section 362 and is known as the **automatic stay**. (The other elements of debtor relief, discharge and exemptions, have been discussed in chapters 7 and 9 supra.) All readers have probably seen commercials on television or have read advertisements in newspapers that may advertise bankruptcy as follows: "Stop creditor harassment. Stop foreclosure. Stop repossession." It is the automatic stay that allows these advertisements to make such bold and brazen claims. As shall be shown, these claims are not entirely accurate.

The essence of the automatic stay is that as of the moment a bankruptcy proceeding is filed, voluntarily or involuntarily, and with or without notice of the bankruptcy filing, all creditor activity to collect debts, obtain judgments, or obtain property of a debtor to satisfy a debt must be completely stopped. The automatic stay is effective the moment a petition is filed. The debtor does not have to do anything special to initiate the automatic stay; it does not require the filing of a particular form or order. The effectiveness or applicability of the automatic stay is also not related to the entry of an order for relief.[1] It is simply triggered by the filing of the debtor's petition.

Once a proceeding has been commenced, creditors can take no further action to affect the assets or rights of the estate or debtor except in compliance with Section 362. Through this provision, creditors can

---

1. 11 U.S.C. §362(a). See chapter 3 supra.

attempt to be relieved of the stay's effect and may often be successful. The stay is automatic but it is not permanent. Any implication to the contrary in any legal advertising is simply untrue.

A petition does not have to be filed within any particular time before an act is to occur to permit the automatic stay to become effective. For example, if a foreclosure sale is scheduled for 10:00 A.M. and a petition is filed at 9:59 A.M., the automatic stay prevents the foreclosure sale from occurring or from being valid if it does still go forward.

Practice Pointer

In some jurisdictions, a distinction is made between actions taken in violation of the automatic stay that are considered to be "void" or merely "voidable."

However, if the bankruptcy filing occurs at 10:01 A.M., after the fore-closure sale, the automatic stay will not affect the foreclosure because it was not in effect when the foreclosure occurred.[2]

Practice Pointer

The bankruptcy filing may, however, still have an impact upon the debtor's state law redemption remedies.

The automatic stay is, as its name suggests, "automatically" effective with or without notice that the bankruptcy petition has been filed.[3] Nevertheless, it is certainly better practice to provide a creditor with notice that a petition has been filed, even if only by telephone. The best approach is to transmit by facsimile or electronic means (e.g., e-mail) a file stamped copy

---

2. In re Sands, 328 B.R. 614 (Bankr. N.D.N.Y. 2005) illustrates the point. Debtor's counsel began filing the case electronically at 10:49 A.M. The foreclosure sale took place at 11:00 A.M. The bankruptcy filing was not completed until 12:05 P.M. Since the filing did not take place until after the foreclosure sale, the foreclosure sale was valid.
3. There is no requirement anywhere in the Code or Rules that requires prior notice of a filing to make the automatic stay effective. However, sanctions against a creditor without notice who violates the stay are likely to be minimal.

of the first two pages of the petition to any specific creditor, or the creditor's attorney, to whom you want to provide immediate notice of the filing. This includes, for example, a creditor threatening to repossess a car, a creditor conducting an imminent foreclosure, or a utility company attempting to terminate the debtor's service for nonpayment.

B. ACTIVITY SUBJECT TO THE AUTOMATIC STAY

Section 362(a) itemizes the types of creditor activity that are affected by imposition of the automatic stay. Section 362(a)(1) prohibits the commencement or continuation of any judicial, administrative, or other proceeding against the debtor that was or could have been commenced before the filing of the petition to recover a prepetition claim.[4] In practical terms, this means, for example, that the ABC Collection Company cannot file a lawsuit against the debtor once a petition has been filed, and the XYZ Collection Agency cannot execute on the judgment that it obtained before the petition was filed. Nor can the LMN Collection Company proceed with its motion for summary judgment in a case that was pending when the petition was filed, and the QRS Collection Agency cannot obtain a default judgment on its prepetition claim. All legal actions initiated against the debtor are stopped.

Section 362(a)(2) prohibits the enforcement of any prepetition judgment against the debtor or property of the estate.[5] Thus a collection agency cannot execute upon its judgment or take a postjudgment debtor examination to ascertain the existence of assets. Recall, however, that all of this information will be disclosed in the bankruptcy, since it is contained in the Statements and Schedules.

Practice Pointer

Remember also, in an adversarial context, the creditor may still make use of a 2004 examination and other discovery means.

---

4. 11 U.S.C. §362(a)(1).
5. 11 U.S.C. §362(a)(2). As to property of the estate, see chapter 14 infra.

Section 362(a)(3) stays any act to obtain possession of property of the estate or any act to exercise control over property of the estate.[6] This means that either by judicial process or otherwise, creditors cannot show up at the debtor's home or business and start repossessing unpaid-for merchandise. Thus, the automatic stay suspends any future attachments against the debtor or the estate. This also means that creditors cannot proceed outside of the bankruptcy system to seek the appointment of a receiver or other custodian to take control of a debtor's business or property.

Section 362(a)(4) stays any act to create, perfect, or enforce a lien against property of the estate.[7] This means that a creditor that has not perfected a security interest in collateral before the petition is filed can no longer do so; a creditor with an unperfected lien can no longer perfect it. There is one limited exception to this, which will be discussed in connection with Section 362(b)(3) below. A secured creditor is also stayed, under this subsection, from repossessing or foreclosing upon a perfected security interest, absent any other provision in Section 362.

Section 362(a)(5) stays any act to create, perfect, or enforce against property of the debtor any lien that secures a claim that arose before commencement of the case. This subsection extends the protections of Section 362(a)(4) to property of the debtor as opposed to property of the estate.[8] Thus, the exempt property of a debtor is also subject to the protections of the automatic stay.

Section 362(a)(6) stays any act to collect, assess, or recover a claim that arose before the filing of the petition.[9] This subsection includes within it the judicial activity referred to in Section 362(a)(1) and Section 362(a)(2) but also broadly extends the stay to any other form of creditor collection activity. Phone calls from a creditor seeking payment are stayed pursuant to this provision. A collection agency or other creditor also cannot continue to send the debtor collection notices in the mail. In short, this subsection prevents creditor harassment.

Section 362(a)(7) stays the making of setoffs without first obtaining relief from the automatic stay.[10] A setoff is the common law right of a creditor to balance mutual debts with a debtor. For example, Murat owes Ney $10 while Ney owes Murat $5. Ney can set off his debt to Murat and thus only have to collect $5 from Murat for both debts to be

---

6. 11 U.S.C. §362(a)(3).
7. 11 U.S.C. §362(a)(4).
8. 11 U.S.C. §362(a)(5).
9. 11 U.S.C. §362(a)(6).
10. 11 U.S.C. §362(a)(7).

satisfied. Or Murat can offer Ney $5, set off the $5 Ney owes Murat, and both debts are extinguished.

Section 362(a)(8) stays the commencement or continuation of a proceeding before the United States Tax Court concerning the debtor.[11] This Section is unusual because it does not stay an act against the debtor, but a proceeding concerning the debtor. This means that if the debtor has initiated an action in the Tax Court, the action will still be stayed. The reason for this is that Section 505 of the Bankruptcy Code permits the Bankruptcy Court to determine tax issues in a bankruptcy proceeding.[12]

As is apparent from a review of the foregoing, only actions against the debtor or property of the estate or debtor are stayed. Actions by the debtor to collect debts or property from third parties are not. Creditors are not normally stayed from enforcing a debt against a nonbankruptcy debtor, guarantor, cosigner, or statutorily liable party (such as principal liability for payroll taxes).

Practice Pointer

To determine whether an action was initiated by the debtor (usually in the context of an appeal), courts will often look to see who commenced the first action, not the current appeal. In other words, the debtor's appeal of an action originally filed against him will still be stayed.

C. ACTIVITY NOT SUBJECT TO THE AUTOMATIC STAY

Even though the automatic stay is a basic debtor relief protection of the bankruptcy system and even though it unquestionably applies to a very broad range of activities, there are also a number of actions that are not subject to the automatic stay. Actions that are not subject to the stay can proceed or continue without regard to the existence of the bankruptcy. These actions are the subject of Section 362(b). Many of these actions do

---

11. 11 U.S.C. §362(a)(8).
12. 11 U.S.C. §505. See chapter 21 infra.

not typically arise in consumer bankruptcy cases. The text focuses on the exceptions most likely to arise in a consumer bankruptcy practice.

The commencement or continuation of a criminal action or proceeding against the debtor is not stayed.[13] A debtor cannot avoid a murder trial by filing a bankruptcy petition. The reason for this exception to the automatic stay is obvious.

Practice Pointer

Courts often resort to state law to address the question of what is considered to be a "criminal" action. For example, certain traffic violations may be considered to be quasi-criminal and Section 362(b)(1) may or may not apply.

After the enactment of the Bankruptcy Code, an issue arose in those states where creditors could instigate criminal prosecutions against bad check writers. Was the prosecution an act to collect a debt and subject to the stay pursuant to 11 U.S.C. §362(a)(6) or was it a criminal prosecution and therefore not subject to the stay pursuant to 11 U.S.C. §362(b)(1)? The reported cases went both ways. Some Bankruptcy Courts held such prosecutions to be mere collection devices and therefore stayed, while other courts found them to be excepted criminal prosecutions.

In Kelly v. Robinson, the Supreme Court ruled that a criminal sentence to make restitution to creditors whose debts are subject to discharge in a bankruptcy proceeding is enforceable and therefore collection does not violate the automatic stay. The facts in this case were that in November 1980, Carolyn Robinson pleaded guilty to larceny based on her wrongful receipt of $9,932.95 in welfare benefits from the State of Connecticut. She was placed on probation, one condition of which was the payment of $100 per month in restitution. In February 1981, Robinson filed a Chapter 7 bankruptcy. She listed the creditor in her schedules. The creditor did not oppose the dischargeability of the debt and Robinson received her discharge in May 1981. Subsequently, when the creditor sought to collect the debt, Robinson sought an order from the Bankruptcy Court that the debt, and hence the restitution order, had been discharged. The Supreme Court disagreed. Because criminal sentences and restitution orders were not dischargeable under either the Bankruptcy Act or the Bankruptcy Code,

---

13. 11 U.S.C. §362(b)(1).

the Court reasoned, collection of the restitution order is not subject to the automatic stay. In addition, a further rationale to support this position is that society's interest in the criminal justice system outweighs its interest in the bankruptcy system.[14]

Section 362(b)(2) excepts from operation of the automatic stay the collection of "domestic support obligations" from property that is not property of the estate. The commencement or continuation of a paternity suit or the commencement or continuation of an action for domestic support obligations is also excepted from the automatic stay. Custody disputes, domestic violence matters and the divorce case itself, except to the extent it affects property of the estate (see chapter 13 infra) are not subject to the automatic stay.[15] As described in chapter 12 infra, domestic support obligations are not normally dischargeable.

The collection of these nondischargeable debts other than from property of the estate does not violate the automatic stay. Property of the estate is described in greater detail in chapter 13 infra, but in a Chapter 7 case, property of the estate does not include a debtor's postpetition wages.[16] One practical effect of Section 362(b)(2) is that a creditor with a prepetition claim for domestic support obligations is not barred from proceeding in the proper forum to obtain any necessary orders to permit collection of domestic support obligations from a Chapter 7 or 11 debtor's wages. Because exemptions are also ineffective against these claims, Chapter 7 or 11 is essentially ineffective against them.[17] Thus, unless Mr. Smith files a Chapter 13, Mrs. Smith will retain many of her rights to collect alimony, support, or maintenance due, without regard to Mr. Smith's Chapter 7 petition.

 Practice Pointer

Note that a domestic support obligation is nondischargeable in Chapter 7, 11, and 13 proceedings.

---

14. Kelly v. Robinson, 479 U.S. 36 (1986). This holding was excluded from Chapter 13 proceedings in Pennsylvania Dept. of Public Welfare v. Davenport, 495 U.S. 552 (1990). However, this ruling was overruled by Congress in 1991 when it enacted 11 U.S.C. §1328(a)(3), which makes criminal restitution orders not dischargeable in Chapter 13 proceedings.

15. 11 U.S.C. §362(b)(2).

16. 11 U.S.C. §541(a)(6). See chapter 14 infra. This is not the case in a Chapter 11 or 13 proceeding, where a debtor's postpetition earnings are considered property of the estate. 11 U.S.C. §1115; 11 U.S.C. §1306(a)(2). See chapters 14, 23, and 24 infra.

17. 11 U.S.C. §522(c). See chapter 9 supra.

Section 362(b)(3) is a limited exception to the effect of the automatic stay regarding acts to perfect or to maintain or continue the perfection of an interest in property described in connection with Section 362(a)(4) above. Essentially, a secured creditor that has a nonbankruptcy law right to perfect an interest in property (such as by recording a Uniform Commercial Code (UCC) security interest in personal property by recording a mortgage or deed of trust upon real estate) within a statutory period of time may do so within the allowed time period or within 30 days of the underlying transaction otherwise subject to the automatic stay.[18] This situation will arise most commonly in secured transactions subject to the UCC. Generally, the UCC permits creditors in certain secured transactions grace periods to perfect security interests by properly filing any required documents with a County Recorder or Secretary of State for a particular state.[19] Thus, if a debtor files a bankruptcy proceeding within this time period, this exception to the automatic stay provides that it will not be violated if the creditor perfects its security interest within the nonbankruptcy statutory period or 30 days from the date of the bankruptcy filing. For example, if Sammy Connifer buys a new car on Thursday and files a Chapter 7 on Friday, as long as the bank perfects its lien upon the vehicle within any underlying statutory period, the act of perfection will not be a violation of the automatic stay under Section 362(b)(3). This provision may also permit the perfection of a state law mechanic's lien without such perfection being considered a violation of the automatic stay.

There is substantial case law in existence on this latter point. It is beyond the scope or purpose of this basic text to analyze this case law in detail. A creditor in this situation should carefully review the status of the case law on this point before proceeding so that no unintended violation of the stay is committed.

Section 362(b)(4) excepts from the stay the commencement or continuation of an action or proceeding by a governmental unit to enforce its police or regulatory power.[20] The rationale for this exception is identical to the exception for criminal actions or proceedings. For example, the EPA may still enjoin Polluters Inc. from violating the Environmental Protection Act. A zoning commission may still find a debtor in violation of zoning laws for having a restaurant in the middle of a residential neighborhood. These actions are not subject to the automatic stay.

Section 362(b)(4) also permits enforcement of any orders resulting from the enforcement of a governmental unit's police or regulatory

---

18. 11 U.S.C. §362(b)(3).
19. The time period for perfection may vary from state to state pursuant to UCC §9-301(1).
20. 11 U.S.C. §362(b)(4).

powers other than the collection of a money judgment.[21] For instance, if the EPA issues an order against Polluters Inc. to pay a fine and clean up the mess, the monetary portion of the order is subject to the automatic stay, but the cleanup order is not.[22]

Section 362(b)(9) provides that the issuance to the debtor of a notice of tax deficiency will not violate the automatic stay.[23] Although the Historical and Revision Notes explain that this provision is associated with a debtor's right to have the Bankruptcy Court or Tax Court determine the amount of the tax, a practical reason for this exception to the automatic stay is that the IRS computers are not designed to factor in the bankruptcy filing of a taxpayer. Despite the law and even manual adjustments to the program, the IRS computers often still function incorrectly and send out notices. So Congress simply made the issuance of a tax deficiency an exception to the automatic stay to preclude taxing entities' being accused of violating the stay by issuing notices of deficiency. Section 362(b)(9) includes audits, demands for returns, and the assessment and issuance of a demand to pay a tax as additional exceptions to the automatic stay.

Practice Pointer

Note that a debtor's failure to file both pre- and postpetition tax returns may lead to dismissal of the bankruptcy case.

Section 362(b)(19) permits the withholding of payment from a debtor's postpetition wages for the repayment of loans from retirement plans that are qualified as such pursuant to the Internal Revenue Code, such as 401(k) plans or loans from IRA accounts.

A number of provisions designed to curb the abuse of serial bankruptcy filings were added to the Code by BAPCPA. A **serial bankruptcy** filing takes place when a debtor files successive bankruptcies in an effort to delay creditor action, typically foreclosure of a home, eviction, or repossession. Each time a debtor files, the automatic stay stops the creditor and forces the creditor to seek relief from the stay. The debtor will then usually

---

21. 11 U.S.C. §362(b)(4). The enforcement aspect of Section 362(b)(4) was contained in Section 362(b)(5) prior to 1994. In 1994, the two provisions were merged into the present form.

22. Midlantic Natl. Bank v. New Jersey Dept. of Envtl. Protection, 474 U.S. 494 (1986).

23. 11 U.S.C. §362(b)(9).

allow the case to be dismissed and then refile again just prior to the next scheduled foreclosure sale. In actual practice, it has not been uncommon to see debtors filing three or more consecutive bankruptcies and to potentially delay a foreclosure for over a year.

Section 362(b)(20) is the first provision affecting serial bankruptcy filings. This provision excepts from the automatic stay actions to enforce liens against property for two years after the entry of an order by the court in a prior bankruptcy case that the prior filing was part of a scheme to delay, hinder, and defraud creditors involving multiple bankruptcy filings or a transfer of an interest in the property not consented to by the secured creditor. This sort of scheme is also now a separate and independent ground for seeking relief from the automatic stay pursuant to 11 U.S.C. §362(d)(4). A debtor can seek to have the stay imposed in the subsequent case by filing a motion showing changed circumstances or good cause.[24]

Section 362(b)(21) excepts from the stay the enforcement of liens or security interests against real property if the debtor is not eligible to file because a bankruptcy has been filed within 180 days of dismissal of a prior case in violation of §109(g) (see chapter 4 supra), or if the bankruptcy court entered an order in a prior bankruptcy case prohibiting the debtor from being a debtor in another bankruptcy case.

Section 362(b)(22) permits an eviction to proceed if the landlord obtained a judgment for possession of residential property prior to the filing of the bankruptcy. Section 362(l) defers this for 30 days to provide the debtor an opportunity to cure and deposit all past due rent. To trigger this relief, the debtor must deposit with the bankruptcy court any rent that accrued during the 30-day period and also certify that nonbankruptcy law (meaning usually state law) allows for such a cure. Section 362(b)(23) permits evictions based upon endangerment to property or person or upon the use of illegal drugs, provided that the procedures of Section 362(m) are complied with.

Section 362(b)(26) permits the setoff of prepetition tax refunds against prepetition tax claims. For example, if a debtor is owed a tax refund for 2009, owes taxes for 2008, and files Chapter 7 in 2010, the Internal Revenue Service may use the 2009 refund and apply it to the 2008 tax liability without violating the automatic stay pursuant to this provision.

---

24. 11 U.S.C. §362(b)(20); 11 U.S.C. §362(d)(4). See chapter 12E infra. As to the transfer of an interest in property to defraud creditors, this is designed to prevent a person from transferring a partial interest in real property to a third person for the primary purpose of having the third person file a bankruptcy to gain the benefits of the automatic stay for the property.

D. DURATION OF THE AUTOMATIC STAY

The automatic stay, despite popular opinion and legal advertisements to the contrary, is not perpetual. The automatic stay may terminate by operation of law, it may be relieved on a motion by a creditor, it may effectively merge into the permanent injunction created by a debtor's discharge, or it may not exist at all in serial filing cases.[25] Section 362(c) concerns the duration of the automatic stay. Generally, the automatic stay remains in effect with regard to property of the estate until such time as the property is no longer property of the estate.[26] One way in which property might no longer be property of the estate would be if the trustee "abandons" it as burdensome.[27] Another way in which property will no longer be property of the estate is when the trustee files a Report of No Distribution in a no asset proceeding. This report effectively acts to abandon previously unadministered assets.

Practice Pointer

When a trustee "abandons" property, the property is not lost in the traditional sense. Rather, the estate relinquishes its interest and the property returns to the debtor, along with any prepetition interests (i.e., mortgages) attached to it.

Any other acts affected by the automatic stay continue until the earliest of the time a proceeding is closed, the time a proceeding is dismissed, or, if a proceeding is an individual Chapter 7 or any Chapter 9, 11, 12, or 13, the time a discharge is granted or denied.[28] In practice, the earliest of these various dates in a Chapter 7 is usually when the discharge is granted or denied, which, as described in chapter 7 supra, normally occurs about 90 days after the proceeding is filed. In a Chapter 11, a discharge is not received until a plan of reorganization is confirmed, except when the debtor is an individual.[29] In Chapters 12 and 13, and in an individual Chapter 11, a discharge is not granted until the debtor's plan has been

---

25. 11 U.S.C. §362(c), (d); 11 U.S.C. §524(a). See chapter 7 supra.
26. 11 U.S.C. §362(c)(1).
27. 11 U.S.C. §554. See chapter 20 infra.
28. 11 U.S.C. §362(c)(2).
29. 11 U.S.C. §1141(d). See chapter 18 infra.

fully performed, which in a Chapter 13 is three to five years.[30] Thus, in non-Chapter 7 proceedings, events other than receipt of a discharge will often be the earlier of the possible dates upon which the automatic stay terminates.

BAPCPA adds two additional situations in which the stay is terminated by operation of law. Each situation is designed to curb serial filings, except when a debtor can demonstrate that the debtor is proceeding in good faith. Section 362(c)(3) terminates the stay 30 days after a filing in an individual debtor case where the debtor had a case pending within the preceding year that was dismissed, except for a case refiled under a reorganization chapter if the dismissal was under Section 707(b), discussed in chapter 4 supra.[31] A party in interest, presumably the debtor in this situation, may file a motion to extend the stay if it can be demonstrated that the current petition has been filed in good faith. There is a presumption that the case is not in good faith if there have been two or more cases filed by the debtor within one year; or a prior case within one year was dismissed for failure to file required documents; or the debtor failed to make adequate protection payments; or the debtor defaulted in performing a confirmed plan; or the debtor's financial or personal affairs are unchanged from the most recent previous case; or the previous case was dismissed after a creditor moved for or obtained relief from the automatic stay (see infra this chapter). Section 362(c)(4) provides that the stay does not go into effect at all, despite the debtor's bankruptcy filing, for an individual debtor who has filed two or more cases within the preceding year that were dismissed, except for a case refiled under a reorganization chapter if the dismissal was under Section 707(b), discussed in chapter 5 supra. A party in interest (presumably an affected creditor) can seek an application for an order that no stay is in effect, often referred to as a "comfort order." A party in interest, presumably the debtor, may file a motion seeking to impose the stay in a manner identical to that set forth in Section 362(c)(3).

For example, Homer and Marge Simpson file Chapter 7. They fail to file schedules, and their case is dismissed. One month later they file a second Chapter 7. Pursuant to Section 362(c)(3), the automatic stay will terminate as to their secured and leasehold creditors 30 days after the second filing unless the Simpsons successfully move before the bankruptcy court to extend the stay. If their second case is dismissed and they

---

30. 11 U.S.C. §1141(d); 11 U.S.C. §1228(a); 11 U.S.C. §1328(a). See chapters 23, 26, and 27 infra.
31. There is some question in the case law regarding the extent to which the automatic stay is terminated. Section 362(c)(3) states that the stay terminates "with respect to the debtor." The question arises whether this also extends to property of the estate.

want to file a third, pursuant to Section 362(c)(4), the stay will not go into effect at all unless the Simpsons successfully move before the court to impose the stay. In this latter situation, the creditors may obtain an ex parte order stating that there is no stay in effect.

Although the automatic stay terminates when a debtor receives a discharge, creditors are not suddenly free to once again collect prepetition debts. Recall that the discharge is a permanent injunction with respect to all debts that are discharged.[32] In addition, exempt property is not liable for prepetition debts.[33] Technically, therefore, the automatic stay merges into the permanent injunction that results from the discharge order. Many people have an erroneous perception that the automatic stay is eternal. It is not. Rather, the automatic stay merges into a debtor's discharge. The discharge acts as an injunction against the collection of all discharged debts. This is a more accurate representation of what occurs as a result of the discharge.

BAPCPA adds an additional situation in which the stay is terminated by operation of law. Pursuant to Section 362(h), if a debtor fails to timely file a Statement of Intention and begins performance with respect to secured or leased personal property (see chapter 4 supra and chapter 21 infra), the property ceases to be property of the estate (see chapter 13 infra), which effectively terminates the stay.

E. OBTAINING RELIEF FROM THE AUTOMATIC STAY

A creditor may seek a court order, in appropriate circumstances, granting it "relief" from the automatic stay. In other words, the creditor is allowed to pursue its nonbankruptcy (state law) remedies notwithstanding the debtor's bankruptcy filing. This procedure is a noticed motion commonly known as a **motion for relief from the automatic stay**. A majority of bankruptcy litigation involves such motions. Relief from the automatic stay may take the form of annulling, conditioning, terminating, or modifying the stay.[34] The Code describes four grounds for a party to seek relief from the automatic stay. They include: (1) "for cause," including a lack of adequate protection regarding the creditor's interest in the debtor's

---

32. 11 U.S.C. §524(a). See chapter 7 supra.
33. 11 U.S.C. §522(c). See chapter 9 supra.
34. 11 U.S.C. §362(d). Bankruptcy Rule 4001(a)(1).

property; (2) with regard to acts against property of the estate (such as repossessions or foreclosures), if the debtor does not have any equity in the property and the property is not necessary for an effective reorganization; (3) with respect to a single asset real estate case, where the debtor fails within 90 days after the order for relief to file a plan that has a reasonable possibility of being confirmed within a reasonable time, or the debtor commences monthly payments to all consensual secured lenders at the contract rate of interest; or (4) real property that is part of a scheme to delay, hinder and defraud creditors involving multiple bankruptcy filings or a transfer of an interest in the property not consented to by the secured creditors.[35]

Attempting to obtain relief from the automatic stay for cause introduces the concept of **adequate protection**. This concept is utilized frequently throughout the Bankruptcy Code. Adequate protection is defined in Section 361. In its essence, adequate protection simply means maintaining the status quo for an affected creditor during the pendency of the stay, to prevent the erosion of the creditor's interest in the property. Generally, only secured creditors will benefit from this provision. The most common form of adequate protection is requiring the trustee or debtor to continue to make periodic postpetition payments on a debt subject to a secured claim.[36] Because the payments will act to minimize any increase in the creditor's claim occasioned by the stay, the payments will inhibit the erosion of the creditor's interest in the property. Providing additional or replacement collateral is also an acceptable method of providing adequate protection.[37] Finally, any other method that will serve the underlying purpose of preserving the value of the creditor's claim will also constitute adequate protection, except that a secured creditor cannot be given an administrative claim.[38] To do so would violate the distributive scheme of the Bankruptcy Code.[39]

For instance, if Chapter 7 debtors Jack and Jill Smith want to keep their home or vehicle, adequate protection simply means continuing to make their normal scheduled payments to the secured creditor. If the Smiths are already in default (a common occurrence), adequate protection will also require the ultimate curing of the default. Although Chapter 13 may provide a better remedy for the Smiths than Chapter 7 if they wish to save their

---

35. 11 U.S.C. §362(d)(1), (2), (3), (4).
36. 11 U.S.C. §361(1). These payments can be limited to interest on the secured portion of a debtor's debt. See United Savings Assn. of Texas v. Timbers of Inwood Forest Assocs., 484 U.S. 365 (1988). See also chapter 21 infra.
37. 11 U.S.C. §361(2). Also see chapter 21 infra.
38. 11 U.S.C. §361(3).
39. See chapters 21 and 22 infra.

MOTIONS FOR RELIEF FROM STAY
(11 U.S.C. §362)

Creditor files motions
and pleadings as per
Checklist 12.3

Prior notice (Consult local rules)

```
┌─────────────────────┐
│   OPPOSITION —      │
│ TRUSTEE, DEBTORS,   │
│ PARTY IN INTEREST   │
└─────────────────────┘
```

Court Options (11 U.S.C. §362(d))
  1. Grant motion:
     a) for cause, including lack of
         adequate protection;
     b) no equity;
     c) property not necessary for
         an effective reorganization
     d) single asset real estate
     e) multiple bankruptcy scheme
  2. Deny motion
  3. Schedule a final hearing within
     30 days (11 U.S.C. §362(e)(1)).
  4. Stay terminates 30 days after
     motion filed in individual case
     unless parties agree or court
     orders otherwise
     (11 U.S.C. §362(e)(2)).

```
┌─────────────────────┐
│    PRELIMINARY      │
│     HEARING         │
│  11 U.S.C. §362(c)  │
└─────────────────────┘
```

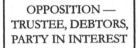

```
┌─────────────────────┐
│   FINAL HEARING     │
│  11 U.S.C. §362(c)  │
└─────────────────────┘
```

home or car from foreclosure or repossession, any default will ultimately have to be cured. Typically, the ability to make current payments will permit the court to grant the Smiths some additional time to sell or refinance their home or car, thereby at least attempting to preserve any equity the Smiths may have in the home or car through any exemptions they have claimed.

Cause for obtaining relief from the automatic stay is not limited to lack of adequate protection. Recall that a Code section's use of the term "including" does not limit the statute's applicability to only those items specifically mentioned.[40] A common cause for relief from the stay, other than lack of adequate protection, arises in the case of a personal injury claimant where the debtor is a defendant. Many personal injury defendants have insurance coverage. The insurance company will normally pay the claim up to the policy limits. It is traditional to grant relief from the stay to a creditor who can look to an insurance policy for recovery. The claimant may then proceed with litigation of the claim as long as the creditor agrees that it will not seek to enforce any judgment beyond the limits of the debtor's insurance coverage. Other creditors are not prejudiced because they have no right to payment of the claim covered by insurance. The trustee does not have any rights to collect the creditor's claim. The claim will only be paid to the one affected creditor, not to all of the estate's creditors.

Practice Pointer

The money provided by the insurance coverage in this context is not "property of the estate," and therefore is not subject to administration by the trustee and is not part of the pool of funds gathered for the estate's general unsecured creditors.

The second ground for obtaining relief from the automatic stay, lack of equity in property, is the most frequent ground utilized by creditors seeking relief from the automatic stay. Simply put, a secured creditor will be entitled to some form of relief from the automatic stay if the debtor has no equity in the property. The example of a debtor with real estate subject to foreclosure illustrates the most common scenario. The methodology of

---

40. 11 U.S.C. §102(3). See chapter 4 supra.

the example, however, applies to any motion for relief from the automatic stay based on lack of equity.

Assume that debtor M. Krebs owns a home worth $100,000. Assume that a first trust deed or mortgage debt exists encumbering the home in the amount of $75,000. Assume further that there are past due payments owed on the trust deed or to the mortgage holder of $10,000. This means that the lender is actually owed $85,000 (including principal, interest, and relevant late fees and charges). Next, the estimated costs of selling the property should be taken into account. This includes an estimate of commissions and closing costs, usually 8 to 10 percent of the selling price for a parcel of residential real property. In the example, then, 10 percent of the sales price would be $10,000. The amount of any equity in the property is determined simply by subtracting the value of all liens, encumbrances, and the estimated costs of sale from the gross value of the property. Any remainder represents equity in the property. In the example, there would thus be $5,000 of realizable equity in M. Krebs's home. If the debtor has claimed this equity as exempt pursuant to Section 522(d), there are no grounds for relief from the automatic stay because the debtor has protected equity in the property. So even if a sale of the property would provide no dividend to the unsecured creditors, if there is some equity available for the debtor to realize, the debtor may be able to maintain the automatic stay in effect.[41]

Generally, where the debtor's equity is less than 10 percent of the property's value, the courts are normally hesitant to maintain the stay for any length of time without requiring the debtor to provide some additional form of adequate protection as described above. The reason for this is that the value given is really only an estimate. If the actual sales price turns out to be lower than the estimate, the secured creditor's interest in the property may be impaired. Remember the concept of adequate protection exists for the benefit of the creditor with an interest in the property, not for the benefit of the debtor.

Thus, in the situation where the equity is marginal, the court may not be inclined to grant relief from the stay, but will likely require the making of adequate protection payments as a condition of the automatic stay remaining in effect. The court will also probably set a deadline for the debtor to obtain a sale or refinancing of the property that will result in the cure of any prefiling arrearages. This deadline may be two months, three months, or six months, or as otherwise set by the court. The court has

---

41. 11 U.S.C. §362(d)(2).

discretion in structuring relief from automatic stay orders to try to do equity to the rights of both the creditor and the debtor.

Generally, if there is no equity in the property, the stay will be terminated. If the equity is marginal, as in the example, the stay may be maintained for a limited period of time conditioned upon the making of adequate protection payments. As the equity cushion increases above 10 percent of the property's estimated value, the court will become less inclined to require adequate protection payments or to set a deadline for the sale or refinance of the asset. Where there may be substantial equity for the unsecured creditors beyond any homestead exemption for the debtor, the court may decline to grant any relief, limited or otherwise, from the automatic stay. Such a denial of relief in this latter instance will normally be without prejudice to the creditor to renew its motion at a later date.

In a Chapter 7 case, because the proceeding is a liquidation, the property will never be necessary for an effective reorganization and this will not normally be an issue in a motion for relief from the automatic stay. The necessity of the property to an effective reorganization does, however, become a critical issue in reorganization proceedings under Chapter 11, 12, or 13.[42] The principles illustrated above will also apply in these situations, but the intrinsic value of the asset to the debtor's business must also be taken into account. For instance, a print shop cannot do business without a printing press. Even if there is no equity in the press itself, because it is essential to the ability of the business to reorganize, relief from the stay may not necessarily be granted except after a period of time, so that all interested parties can ascertain whether the debtor has any realistic ability to reorganize. The courts must be creative in framing appropriate orders to protect the interests of all parties in these circumstances. On the one hand, the printing business in the example must effectively liquidate if the stay is terminated. On the other hand, the secured creditor is entitled to adequate protection of its interest in the property while the stay remains in effect.

Section 362(d)(4) permits relief from the stay to be granted if the court finds that the bankruptcy filing was part of a scheme to delay, hinder, or defraud creditors involving a transfer of an interest in real estate not consented to by a secured creditor or without court approval, or multiple bankruptcy filings affecting the real property. For example, Harry Potter files an individual Chapter 7 case to stop the foreclosure of his home by Gringotts Bank. The Bank obtains relief from the stay in Harry's case, and

---

42. 11 U.S.C. §362(d)(2)(B).

just prior to the next scheduled foreclosure date, Harry's wife Ginny files Chapter 7 for the sole purpose of gaining the benefit of the automatic stay. Bank may obtain relief from the stay on the ground that Ginny's filing was part of a scheme to defraud the Bank involving multiple filings affecting Harry and Ginny's home. If Harry, alternatively, transfers a 10 percent interest in the real property to his best friend Ron, who then files bankruptcy to help prevent the home's foreclosure, Bank may seek relief from the stay on the ground that Harry's transfer to Ron was for the sole purpose of delaying Bank's foreclosure on the home.

In consumer cases, preparation of the motion documents, either in support of or in opposition to the motion, is relatively simple. Sample forms are contained on the forms disk accompanying this text. This is a form of litigation and should be approached in a manner identical to any other litigation in the legal system.[43]

Section 362(e) deals with the length of time that the stay remains in effect once a motion for relief from the automatic stay is filed. This subsection effectively requires that a motion for relief from the automatic stay be resolved on an expedited basis.

First, the automatic stay terminates 30 days after a motion for relief is filed unless the court orders otherwise during the 30-day period.[44]

If a hearing is requested, the court will hold it within this 30-day period. This hearing is known as a preliminary hearing, but it may be considered a final hearing if the court so determines. The court will usually not accept oral testimony at a preliminary hearing. It will review any declarations submitted by the parties instead. If the court determines that it needs to hear further evidence, a final hearing will be scheduled. The final hearing must take place within 30 days of the preliminary hearing.[45]

Even if there is a preliminary hearing, the automatic stay will still terminate 30 days after the motion is filed unless the court maintains the automatic stay in effect pending the final hearing.[46] Often the court cannot schedule a final hearing within 30 days of the preliminary hearing, and the final hearing will take place more than 30 days after the motion is filed. When a debtor or trustee is in this situation, it is imperative to obtain an order from the court unequivocally maintaining the automatic stay in effect until the date of the final hearing. Unless this is done, the stay will be terminated pursuant to Section 362(e). The three different time periods

---

43. Bankruptcy Rule 4001(a)(1).
44. 11 U.S.C. §362(e)(1).
45. 11 U.S.C. §362(e)(1).
46. 11 U.S.C. §362(e)(1).

explicit or implicit within Section 362(e) are sometimes referred to as the "30/30/30 rule."

 ### *Practice Pointer*

The "30/30/30 Rule":

- 30 days after a request for relief the stay will terminate;
- a preliminary hearing must be held within 30 days of the motion;
- a final hearing, if necessary, must be held within 30 days of the preliminary hearing.

Section 362(e)(2) applies in individual cases and terminates the stay 60 days after a motion for relief from stay is filed unless the court renders a final decision within the 60-day period, the parties agree otherwise, or the court orders otherwise. For example, if the court denies the motion, the stay will remain in effect because the court has reached a final decision. If the parties reach an agreement to keep the stay in effect and reduce the agreement to an order approved by the court, the statutory requirement will have been satisfied. In an emergency, where irreparable harm may occur, it is possible to obtain ex parte relief from the automatic stay without a formal hearing.[47] This is extraordinary relief and as a result should not be taken lightly.

In any motion for relief from the automatic stay, the party bringing the motion bears the burden of proof on the issue of equity, while a party opposing the motion bears the burden of proof on all other issues.[48] Finally, a party willfully violating the automatic stay can be sanctioned by the court. Sanctions may include actual damages, costs including attorneys' fees, and, in appropriate circumstances, punitive damages.[49]

---

47. 11 U.S.C. §362(f); Bankruptcy Rule 4001(a)(3).
48. 11 U.S.C. §362(g).
49. 11 U.S.C. §362(k).

Summary

The automatic stay is one of the three fundamental features of the debtor relief provided for by the Bankruptcy Code, the other two being the discharge and the debtor's exemptions, discussed respectively in chapters 7 and 9 supra. The automatic stay is the subject of Section 362 of the Bankruptcy Code. The automatic stay is a statutory bar to collection activity by creditors after a bankruptcy petition has been filed. A summary of the most common actions subject or not subject to the automatic stay are contained in the checklist following this summary.

The automatic stay is not permanent. Pursuant to 11 U.S.C. §362(c), the stay will terminate upon the earlier of the time that the case is closed or dismissed, or, in an individual proceeding, when the debtor has received a discharge and the property is no longer property of the estate, or when the debtor has engaged in serial filings. In individual proceedings, the latter circumstances will normally trigger termination of the automatic stay. However, the effects of the automatic stay will merge into the permanent injunction contained in the debtor's discharge.

A creditor may bring a motion for relief from the automatic stay pursuant to 11 U.S.C. §362(d). Normally, secured creditors are the greatest beneficiaries of this provision. A sample motion is included on the forms disk accompanying this text. Relief from the automatic stay may be brought on one of four basic grounds: cause, including lack of adequate protection; lack of equity in the property; a single asset real estate case that fails to file a potentially confirmable plan or commence adequate protection payments within 90 days from the entry of the order for relief; or when the property has been subject to serial filings. A Bankruptcy Court may maintain the automatic stay in effect if the debtor or trustee can provide adequate protection. If adequate protection cannot be provided or if there is no equity in the property for the debtor or estate, the automatic stay will likely be relieved.

Adequate protection is described in Section 361 of the Code. Adequate protection involves various methods of protecting a secured creditor's interest in property of the debtor or estate during pendency of the automatic stay. The making of periodic payments and the providing of additional or replacement collateral are all methods of adequate protection.

A motion for relief from the automatic stay is to be given expedited treatment by the Bankruptcy Court as described in 11 U.S.C. §362(e). The automatic stay will terminate 30 days after it is filed unless the motion is opposed. If the motion is opposed, the court must hold a preliminary hearing within 30 days of the motion's filing. The automatic stay will also terminate 30 days after the motion is filed unless the court continues it in effect or unless the court requests or requires a final hearing. The final hearing must take place within 30 days of the preliminary hearing. The automatic stay will terminate 30 days after the preliminary hearing unless the court orders otherwise. In any scenario where any of these time limits will be exceeded, the party opposing the motion (debtor or trustee) must obtain a court order maintaining the automatic stay in effect until the later date. In individual cases, the stay will automatically terminate 60 days after the motion has been filed unless the parties agree or the court orders otherwise.

In any motion for relief from the automatic stay, the party bringing the motion bears the burden of proof on the issue of equity, while a party opposing the motion bears the burden of proof on all other issues.

KEY TERMS

adequate protection
automatic stay
motion for relief from the
    automatic stay

serial bankruptcy

CHAPTER 12 CHECKLIST

12.1 ACTIONS SUBJECT TO AUTOMATIC STAY   *Authority*

12.1.1	Civil Actions or Administrative Legal Proceedings	11 U.S.C. §362(a)(1)
12.1.2	Enforcement of Judgments	11 U.S.C. §362(a)(2)
12.1.3	Acts to Obtain Possession or Control of Property of the Estate	11 U.S.C. §362(a)(3)
12.1.4	Acts to Perfect Liens upon Property of the Estate	11 U.S.C. §362(a)(4)
12.1.5	Acts to Perfect Liens upon Property of the Debtor	11 U.S.C. §362(a)(5)
12.1.6	Any Act to Collect a Prepetition Claim	11 U.S.C. §362(a)(6)
12.1.7	The Making of Setoffs	11 U.S.C. §362(a)(7)

---

50. See chapter 4A supra.

3.   Points and authorities
4.   Exhibit: appraisals
5.   Any other document required by local rule

12.3.3   Motion to Impose Stay for Cause Shown
1.   Serial filings   11 U.S.C. §362(c)(3), (4)
2.   Statement of Intention   11 U.S.C. §362(h)
3.   Small Business Cases   11 U.S.C. §362 (n)
4.   Residential evictions   11 U.S.C. §362(b)(22), (l)

12.4   MOTION TIME LIMITS (11 U.S.C. §362(e))

12.4.1   Hearing Dates
1.   Preliminary hearing within 30 days of filing motion
2.   Final hearing within 30 days of preliminary hearing

12.4.2   Length of Stay (30/30/30 Rule)
1.   Terminates 30 days after motion filed, if unopposed
2.   Terminates 30 days after preliminary hearing, unless court orders otherwise
3.   Terminates 30 days after final hearing, unless court orders otherwise
4.   Terminates 60 days from filing of motion in individual cases unless the parties or court orders otherwise

DISCUSSION QUESTIONS

1.   What is the purpose of the automatic stay?

2.   What activities are subject to the automatic stay?

3.   What activities are not subject to the automatic stay?

4.   How long does the automatic stay remain in effect? What is the effect of a discharge on the automatic stay?

5.   Describe the procedure used for obtaining relief from the automatic stay.

6.   What is adequate protection? Why is a secured creditor entitled to adequate protection?

7.   Describe the situations in which a debtor may want to file a motion to impose the automatic stay. Why would a debtor want to do so?

PRACTICE EXERCISE

Exercise 12.1

Draft a relief from stay motion on behalf of Toyota Credit, to repossess the Moriah. In lieu of exhibits, prepare a list of the exhibits you believe you would need to support the motion.

13

Objections to Discharge and the Dischargeability of Individual Debts

A. DISTINGUISHING A DISCHARGE FROM THE DISCHARGEABILITY OF INDIVIDUAL DEBTS

The debtor's personal liability on most debts is relieved when the debtor receives a discharge. However, some debts are not dischargeable. These **nondischargeable debts** are described in Section 523 of the Code. Within Section 523, specific types of debts are excepted from the debtor's discharge. That is, even if the debtor receives a discharge, the bankruptcy will not relieve the debtor of personal liability on such a claim. The creditor's right to collect the debt will remain unaffected by the bankruptcy. This nondischargeability status extends only to that particular claim. In addition, a debtor's exempt property will not be exempt from some nondischargeable debts.[1]

An analogous provision to Section 523 is the objection to discharge described in Section 727 (applicable only in Chapter 7 proceedings).[2] Under Section 727, a debtor may be denied a discharge completely. That is, notwithstanding the bankruptcy filing, a denial of discharge will prevent a debtor from obtaining relief from personal liability for *any* and all debts. This is the critical distinction between Sections 523 and 727. Section 523 concerns the dischargeability of specific individual debts

---

1. 11 U.S.C. §522(c). See chapter 9 supra.
2. 11 U.S.C. §103. See chapter 2 supra.

while Section 727 is concerned with the discharge of all of the debtor's debts in their entirety. If the debtor's discharge is denied, the debtor will remain legally obligated to pay all prepetition debt.

Practice Pointer

Even if the creditor takes no action, the debtor will normally not be discharged of most debts relating to taxes, money obtained through fraud, domestic support obligations, governmental fines or penalties, and death or personal injury caused by drunk driving.

Section 523 contains 19 specific types of debt that are not dischargeable. Three of these debts require the affected creditor to initiate an adversary proceeding, commonly known as a "Complaint to Determine the Dischargeability of Debt," and to thereafter obtain a judgment that the debt is nondischargeable.[3] For any such affected debts, the creditor must file a complaint within a specific deadline or the debt will be automatically discharged when the debtor receives his/her discharge.[4]

Practice Pointer

To be considered nondischargeable, the burden is on the creditor to file an adversary complaint when the debt was obtained through a fraudulent representation, through fraud while the debtor was serving in a fiduciary capacity, through embezzlement or larceny, or as the result of willful and malicious injury.

All of the other 16 types of debts described by Section 523(a) will automatically not be dischargeable, unless successfully challenged by the debtor in an **adversary proceeding**. In these latter instances, an affected creditor will not be required to take any action for the debt to be deemed not dischargeable by operation of law. We will focus first on nondischargeable debts, which do not require a judgment of nondischargeability. Then we will analyze nondischargeable debts that require a judgment of nondischargeability by the filing of a complaint.

---

3. 11 U.S.C. §523(c); Bankruptcy Rules 4004 and 4007.
4. Bankruptcy Rule 4007.

B. DEBTS NONDISCHARGEABLE WITHOUT CREDITOR ACTION

Section 523(a)(1) provides that obligations accorded priority status under Section 507(a)(8) or gap claims incurred during the pendency of an involuntary proceeding will not be discharged.[5] These types of debts comprise most tax obligations. As a practical matter, this will commonly mean that all payroll taxes, sales taxes, and most income taxes are not dischargeable. The exceptions to this general rule are extremely limited and their analysis is beyond the scope of this basic text. The tax claims that most frequently appear in bankruptcy proceedings will be of the variety that more likely than not will be nondischargeable. As well, the debtor's right to specific exemptions will not protect otherwise exempt property from a nondischargeable tax claim.[6]

Practice Pointer

As a general rule, "exempt" property cannot be reached by any of the debtor's prepetition creditors. An exception exists, however, for most tax liens and domestic support obligations.

The second type of debt that is automatically nondischargeable is the so-called **unlisted debt**, the subject of Section 523(a)(3). Under this provision, if a debtor fails to list a creditor in the schedules so that the creditor does not receive notice of the filing, then the claim will be nondischargeable if the creditor is prevented from filing a timely proof of claim or otherwise object to dischargeability where there would have been grounds to do so. Thus, if no claims bar date is set, such as in a no asset proceeding, the claim will still be discharged because there has been no deadline set for creditors to file claims.[7]

Actual knowledge of the bankruptcy by a creditor, despite lack of notice, will also cause an unlisted debt to be discharged.[8] The rationale behind this provision is that if a creditor is prevented from receiving

---

5. 11 U.S.C. §523(a)(1). See chapter 4 supra and chapter 21 infra.
6. 11 U.S.C. §522(c). See chapter 9 supra.
7. See In re Egleston, 448 F.3d 803, 914 n.12 (5th Cir. 2006); In re Nielsen, 383 F.3d 922, 926 (9th Cir. 2004). But see Colonial Sur. Co. v. Weizman, 564 F.3d 526 (1st Cir. 2009) (an unlisted debt is not discharged).
8. 11 U.S.C. §523(a)(3)(A), (B). See Judd v. Wolfe, 78 F.3d 110 (3d Cir. 1996).

a dividend due to a lack of notice to permit filing of a claim, then the claim should not be discharged. On the other hand, if there has been no prejudice to the creditor, the discharge should be unaffected. For example, Matt Memory files a Chapter 7 and fails to list Barney's Beanery as a creditor. If the proceeding has a claims bar date set and Barney has no actual knowledge of the case so that a timely claim can be filed, the debt will be nondischargeable. In addition, if Barney would have had a claim against Matt for fraud, the unlisted claim might also be nondischargeable. Otherwise, the debt will be discharged.

As a practical matter, it may occasionally become necessary for a creditor to initiate an adversary proceeding to seek a judgment from the Bankruptcy Court that an unlisted debt is nondischargeable so that a state court judge will then believe the creditor in any subsequent action initiated to collect the debt. Conversely, the debtor may seek to initiate a complaint to determine that the debt has indeed been discharged so as to convince a state court that the debt may not be collected. A debtor may always initiate a complaint to determine the dischargeability of a debt.[9]

Practice Pointer

Moreover, there is no fee to reopen a case to determine the dischargeability of a particular debt. Fed. R. Bankr. P. 4007(b).

Similarly, if a creditor's claim is one that would be nondischargeable only if a timely complaint is filed as described above, and the creditor cannot do so due to lack of actual knowledge of the proceeding, the debt will also be nondischargeable.[10] A creditor in this position has been prejudiced because it has been deprived of the ability to file a timely complaint to determine the dischargeability of the debt.

Section 523(a)(5) addresses a third type of debt that is nondischargeable without requiring affirmative action by a creditor, and that is a debt for a domestic support obligation, unless the debt has been assigned to another entity except for collection purposes. Domestic support obligations are also accorded a priority status in the payment of claims.[11] For example, suppose a spouse who is meant to receive child support does

9. Bankruptcy Rule 4007(a).
10. 11 U.S.C. §523(a)(3)(B).
11. 11 U.S.C. §523(a)(5); 11 U.S.C. §507(a)(1). See chapter 21 infra.

not receive it and is required to go on temporary aid to needy families (TANF, formerly AFDC) so the children can eat. When the spouse obtains TANF, the spouse is normally required to assign any child support rights to the TANF agency for purposes of seeking collection from the nonpaying spouse. Once the obligation has been assigned, it becomes generally dischargeable. If the support right has not been assigned to a third entity, then the obligation remains nondischargeable and the unpaid spouse may still collect any arrears. Exemptions will not protect otherwise exempt property from a nondischargeable support obligation.[12] Debts incurred in connection with a divorce or a separation made in accordance with nonbankruptcy law or approved by a governmental unit, that are not domestic support obligations, are also nondischargeable pursuant to Section 523(a)(15). This means that separation agreements, property settlements, and decrees of equitable distribution are all automatically nondischargeable. This provision, added by BAPCPA, radically alters the former law, which held, through case law and the predecessor provision of Section 523(a)(15), that property settlement agreements and similar documents were only nondischargeable if found to be in the nature of support or, for cases filed from October 22, 1994, through the effective date of BAPCPA, October 17, 2005, if the nonfiling debtor challenged the discharge of the debt as a hardship. The ensuing discussion retains its vitality because the prior law will continue to apply to cases pending before BAPCPA's effective date.

Prior to October 22, 1994, property settlements were fully dischargeable, although whether or not an obligation was alimony, support, or otherwise was left to the sole discretion of the bankruptcy courts.[13] The courts looked to a number of factors to determine whether a domestic obligation was nondischargeable support or otherwise, including the length of the marriage, interpretation of the document, whether or not the payments were intended for dependents, and so forth.[14]

Under the Bankruptcy Reform Act of 1994, Section 523(a)(15) was added to the Code, rendering obligations for other than alimony or support nondischargeable unless the debtor could show sufficient hardship such that discharge of the debt would result in a benefit to the debtor that outweighs the detrimental consequences to a former spouse or child of the debtor. Further, debts subject to this provision were not automatically nondischargeable, but required the nonfiling spouse to affirmatively

---

12. 11 U.S.C. §522(c). See chapter 9 supra.
13. 11 U.S.C. §523(a)(5)(B) as it existed prior to October 17, 2005.
14. In re Nero, 323 B.R. 33, 36 (Bankr. D. Conn. 2005) (identifying eight factors); In re Herbert, 304 B.R. 67, 77 (Bankr. E.D.N.Y. 2004).

challenge the discharge. The 2005 amendment to this Code section makes the debt automatically nondischargeable.

For example, Tom and Kitty Katt enter into a dissolution agreement that provides that Kitty gets the house, Tom gets the car, and Tom is to pay all family bills and is to pay Kitty a monthly support allowance equal to the monthly mortgage payment on the home. If Tom had filed a Chapter 7 case under BAPCPA, all of these debts would likely have been non-dischargeable domestic support obligations. Under the prior law, in Tom's Chapter 7, the obligation to pay the family bills is probably dis-chargeable while the obligation to pay the monthly support allowance is not. Under pre-BAPCPA Section 523(a)(15), Kitty may object to the dischargeability of Tom's obligation to pay the family bills and the mort-gage. If Tom is discharged from the family bills, Kitty may remain liable to the creditors without recourse against Tom, which may also result in a bankruptcy filing by Kitty as well. Also remember that if Tom is in arrears on his support payments when he files his petition, Kitty is unaffected by the automatic stay in her ability to collect the arrears from Tom's post-petition wages.[15] Nor will Tom's claimed exemptions protect his property from Kitty's efforts to collect any arrears.[16]

 Practice Pointer

All obligations related to a divorce or separa-tion agreement need to be viewed in the con-text of both Sections 523(a)(5) and (a)(15).

The next type of debt that is automatically nondischargeable, under Section 523(a)(7), is a fine or penalty owed to a governmental unit, other than compensation for actual pecuniary loss. A penalty relating to a non-dischargeable tax will remain nondischargeable. A fine or penalty assessed more than three years before a bankruptcy filing will be dischargeable.[17] For example, Tom Toxic is fined $50,000 for the cost of a toxic waste cleanup and is penalized another $25,000 for the violation. Toxic then files a Chapter 7 proceeding. The $50,000 fine is dischargeable because it represents a fine for actual pecuniary loss. The $25,000 penalty fine is not dischargeable.

---

15. 11 U.S.C. §362(b)(2). See chapter 12 supra.
16. 11 U.S.C. §522(c); 11 U.S.C. §522(f). See chapter 9 supra.
17. 11 U.S.C. §523(a)(7). The pendency of a prior bankruptcy proceeding during this period may act to extend it. Young v. United States, 535 U.S. 43 (2002). See chapter 21 infra.

Student loans are automatically nondischargeable under Section 523(a)(8). However, for a student loan to be nondischargeable, the student loan must be made, insured, or guaranteed by a governmental unit or made under a program funded by a governmental unit or a nonprofit institution. The loan will only be dischargeable if the debtor can show that the loan's nondischargeability would impose an undue hardship upon the debtor and the debtor's dependents.[18] As a practical matter, it is the debtor who will normally file the complaint to determine the dischargeability of a student loan obligation because, as has been noted, the debtor would be seeking a determination that an otherwise nondischargeable debt is indeed dischargeable.[19]

The judicial test that has gained the widest acceptance in determining when a student loan is dischargeable on the grounds of undue hardship is known as the *Brunner* test (for Brunner v. New York State Higher Education Services Corp., 831 F.2d 395 (2d Cir. 1987)). Under this approach, a student loan may be discharged if the debtor can pass a three-part test: (1) Based on current income and expenses, the debtor cannot maintain a "minimal" standard of living for the debtor and dependents, if the educational loan is repaid as scheduled; (2) the debtor's present situation is likely to continue for a significant portion of the repayment period; and (3) the debtor has made good faith efforts to repay the educational loans.

The *Brunner* test has been adopted by the Third (In re Coco, 335 Fed. Appx. 224, 226 (2009)); Fourth (In re Spence, 541 F.3d 538, 544 (2008)); Fifth (In re Ostrom, 283 Fed. Appx. 283, 285-286 (2008)); Sixth (In re Barrett, 487 F.3d 353 (2007)); Seventh (Goulet v. Educational Credit Mgmt. Corp., 284 F.3d 773 (2002)); Ninth (In re Hedlund, 368 Fed. Appx. 819, 821 (2010)); Tenth (In re Roe, 295 Fed. Appx. 927, 929 (2008)); and Eleventh (In re Mosley, 494 F.3d 1320 (2007)) Circuits. The Eighth Circuit follows a "totality of the circumstances approach" using similar factors with an emphasis upon "fairness" and "equity" (In re Long, 322 F.3d 549 (2003)). In Tennessee Student Assistance Corp. v. Hood, 541 U.S. 440 (2004), the Supreme Court held that the sovereign immunity provided for by the Eleventh Amendment does not prevent debtors from bringing complaints to determine the dischargeability of student loan debts (see page 91, supra, at footnote 28).

For example, Justin Long obtains a guaranteed student loan to attend South Harmon Institute of Technology, graduates, and then defaults in the loan repayment. Justin majored in physical education with a specialty

---

18. 11 U.S.C. §523(a)(8). Failure to pay an invoice for unpaid tuition may be dischargeable because no loan has been made. See, e.g., In re Mehta, 310 F.3d 308 (3d Cir. 2002).
19. Bankruptcy Rule 4007(a).

in surf instruction. Justin files a Chapter 7 to discharge the loan. Justin initiates a complaint to determine the debt's dischargeability on the grounds of undue hardship, citing an inability to earn sufficient income as a surf instructor to repay the debt. Unfortunately for Justin, this will probably not act to discharge the debt. The inability to earn sufficient income from one's education will not render a student loan dischargeable. On the other hand, if Justin were involved in an accident and thereby rendered physically incapable of being a surf instructor, under the *Brunner* test, the debt might be held dischargeable only if the court could find that the injury would render him incapable of repaying the loan for a significant portion of the repayment period. The court has broad discretion in this area, but it is generally very difficult for a debtor to obtain discharge of a guaranteed student loan on the grounds of undue hardship.

A mere bank loan obtained by a student for educational purposes, but not subject to a governmental student loan insurance or guarantee program, will be discharged. For instance, Suzie English obtains a loan from the XYZ bank and uses it to go to the Zappa School of Composition. Because the loan is not insured or guaranteed, if Suzie subsequently commences a Chapter 7 proceeding, the debt will be discharged.

Section 523(a)(9) makes debts arising as a result of the debtor driving or operating a vessel or aircraft while intoxicated or under the influence of other substances nondischargeable.[20] Prior to enactment of this provision into the Code, it was a common practice for uninsured drivers who had caused damages while driving under the influence to simply file a bankruptcy to discharge any liability to the damaged or injured party. Some case law prior to 1984 held that damages caused while driving while intoxicated were willful and malicious and denied a discharge of the debt on this ground.[21] This, however, required the damaged party to initiate a complaint objecting to the debt's dischargeability. The enactment of Section 523(a)(9) obviates a party damaged in such circumstances from having to file a separate action to determine the debt's dischargeability.

Practice Pointer

Remember, the exception to discharge under Section 523(a)(9) relates to debts incurred for "death or personal injury." It does not extend to property damage.

---

20. 11 U.S.C. §523(a)(9).
21. See the discussion concerning §523(a)(6) infra in this chapter.

Section 523(a)(10) provides that any debt or debts that were or could have been listed in a prior bankruptcy proceeding where the debtor waived discharge or was denied a discharge under Section 727(a)(2)-(7) will be nondischargeable in the new proceeding.[22] Section 523(b) further provides that any debt not discharged in a proceeding under the former Bankruptcy Act will remain automatically not discharged in a proceeding filed by the same debtor under the Bankruptcy Code.[23]

Sections 523(a)(11) and (12) make automatically nondischargeable debts due to a federal depository institution where the debtor was in a fiduciary relationship with the financial institution.

Section 523(a)(13) makes nondischargeable restitution awards in criminal cases.

Section 523(a)(14) excepts from discharge debts incurred to pay federal taxes that would otherwise be nondischargeable. For example, Jack Zoran owes $1,000 in federal income taxes. He gets a cash advance on a credit card, pays the taxes, and files Chapter 7 four months later. Under Section 523(a)(14), because the taxes were not dischargeable, the cash advance becomes nondischargeable. One problem that creditors may have with this provision is the level of proof necessary to show that the loan was obtained to pay a nondischargeable tax claim. Section 523(14A), added in 2005, extends this approach to all other taxing authorities.[24]

Section 523(a)(16) makes nondischargeable any postpetition condominium or cooperative housing assessments that are incurred while the debtor or the trustee has an interest in the unit.

Section 523(a)(17) makes nondischargeable debts incurred by prisoners for court fees. Section 523(a)(18) makes nondischargeable debts owed to pension or retirement plans, such as a loan from a 401(k) plan.

Section 523(a)(19) makes nondischargeable debts arising under violations of federal or state securities laws or regulations. This provision was added to the Code by the Sarbanes-Oxley Act of 2002 (Pub. L. No. 107-204, 116 Stat. 745) in the wake of accounting scandals that occurred in well-publicized bankruptcies such as Enron Corporation and Global Crossing.

---

22. 11 U.S.C. §523(a)(10).
23. 11 U.S.C. §523(b).
24. Section 523(a)(14B) extends nondischargeability to fines and penalties imposed under federal election laws.

C.   DEBTS NONDISCHARGEABLE WITH CREDITOR ACTION

The three remaining types of debt that are nondischargeable under Section 523(a) all require the creditor to first initiate an adversary proceeding and obtain a judgment denying dischargeability of the debt in question. If no complaint is filed in a timely manner or the debtor obtains a judgment in its favor, the debt involved will be discharged.[25]

The first and most frequently utilized of these provisions is Section 523(a)(2), which concerns various forms of fraud. Under this provision, there are three forms of fraud that may not be dischargeable. The simplest of these is the form of fraud that makes nondischargeable any debt obtained by the use of a materially false written financial statement concerning the debtor or its insider upon which the creditor relies in extending credit and that the debtor has made with the intent to deceive.[26] Simply put, a debt may be held nondischargeable if the debt was incurred by use of an intentionally false written financial statement.

For example, Fred and Wilma go visit their friendly neighborhood finance company to obtain a vacation loan. In completing their financial statement, they omit a $10,000 debt owed to Wilma's parents. Subsequently, Fred and Wilma file a Chapter 7 listing the debt owed to Wilma's parents. The finance company may seek to have the vacation loan debt ruled nondischargeable based on the omission of the $10,000 debt to Wilma's parents in the original loan application.

In situations where a debtor obtains a renewal of credit or borrows additional funds from a creditor, if a new financial statement is obtained that is materially false, then it is possible that both the portion of the debt representing the new funds borrowed in reliance upon the false written financial statement, as well as the renewed previous extension of credit, will be subject to nondischargeability.[27] Previous case law had focused only on the existence of any new credit that was extended. This was known as the **fresh cash rule**.[28] Using the above example, Fred and Wilma are already indebted to the finance company when they seek the vacation loan. The finance company rewrites the loan, adding in the new funds borrowed. Because the financial statement obtained in connection with the rewritten loan is false, the original debt, as well as the additional

---

25. 11 U.S.C. §523(c).
26. 11 U.S.C. §523(a)(2)(B).
27. In re Campbell, 159 F.3d 963 (6th Cir. 1998); In re McFarland, 84 F.3d 943 (7th Cir. 1996).
28. In re Duncan, 123 B.R. 383 (C.D. Cal. 1991).

funds borrowed, will probably be nondischargeable if the creditor timely objects. The creditor's damages from the fraud in that case are beyond the additional monies borrowed.

A second form of fraud that may be nondischargeable exists where the debtor obtained money through actual fraud, false pretenses, or a false representation, other than a statement concerning the debtor's or an insider's financial condition.[29] Note that false statements concerning a debtor's financial condition are excluded from this definition. This means that any oral misrepresentation regarding the debtor's financial condition will not by itself constitute grounds for an objection to the discharge of a debt based on fraud. A false written financial statement is covered as described above.

In practice, the sort of actual fraud that often is held to be non-dischargeable is fraud so egregious that it would be an injustice to permit a debtor to be relieved from the liability. The necessary elements to prove this form of fraud nondischargeable are the traditional tort elements of fraud: that the debtor has made a knowingly false representation with intent to deceive the creditor, and that the creditor has relied on the misrepresentation and has sustained damages as a result.[30] For example, debtor Dimmesdale visits Mr. LaFata, a custom tailor recently emigrated from Italy to the United States. Mr. LaFata makes Dimmesdale a couple of custom suits, and Dimmesdale pays for them. In the process, he convinces Mr. LaFata that he is part owner of a trucking company. However, in reality and unknown to LaFata, Dimmesdale is actually a minister. After paying for the first two suits, Mr. LaFata gives debtor Dimmesdale a charge account. In the space of the next six months, Dimmesdale incurs a debt to Mr. LaFata in excess of $30,000. Meanwhile, Reverend Dimmesdale is continually complimented by his congregants about his beautiful new suits. He tells his congregants that he has met a new tailor who is a real nice guy and that he is being provided the suits for free. Because he is up on the pulpit where many people see him, it is a good promotion for the tailor. Reverend Dimmesdale then files bankruptcy, and LaFata objects to the discharge of the debt due him. The debt would be found to be nondischargeable.[31]

In Field v. Mans, 516 U.S. 59 (1995), the U.S. Supreme Court examined the form of reliance that a plaintiff must prove in a nondischarge-ability fraud claim brought under 11 U.S.C. §523(a)(2). The Court ruled

---

29. 11 U.S.C. §523(a)(2)(A).
30. In re Britton, 950 F.2d 602 (9th Cir. 1991).
31. See In re Burklow, 60 B.R. 728 (Bankr. S.D. Cal. 1986). Note that although this case was decided under the earlier "reasonable reliance" standard, the same result would still be reached under the "justifiable reliance" standard under Field v. Mans.

that a creditor need only prove that reliance was justifiable as opposed to reasonable, although "[t]he subjectiveness of justifiability cuts both ways, and reasonableness goes to the probability of actual reliance." In *Field*, Mans transferred property in violation of a due-upon transfer clause and then sought the lender's consent, which was not given. At a later date, the debtor filed for bankruptcy. Only then did the lender learn that the property had been improperly transferred, wiping out the lender's position in the collateral. The lender had never reviewed the relevant real estate records to determine whether the unconsented-to transfer had taken place. In reversing the lower courts, which had ruled in Mans's favor, and in ruling that Field's reliance upon the debtor's representations need only be justifiable, the Supreme Court rejected the notion that a lender must always investigate the veracity of a debtor's representations.

In Cohen v. De La Cruz, 523 U.S. 213 (1998), the Supreme Court extended the finding of nondischargeability to all damages resulting from the debtor's fraud. In *Cohen*, a debtor landlord had been found liable for willfully and intentionally violating a rent control ordinance. The damages awarded by the trial court included treble damages for violation of the New Jersey Consumer Fraud Act. The Supreme Court held that once it is established that specific money or property has been obtained by fraud, "any debt" arising therefrom is excepted from discharge.

In Archer v. Warner, 538 U.S. 314 (2003), the Supreme Court considered whether a settlement agreement superseded the underlying fraudulent activity. In that case, the Archers had sued the Warners for fraud in connection with the sale of a business. The parties entered into a settlement and release agreement. After performing most of the settlement agreement, the Warners filed bankruptcy. The Archers, as creditors, contended that the remaining claim was nondischargeable as a result of fraud. The Warners, as debtors, contended that the settlement agreement created an entirely new debt that was not obtained fraudulently. The Supreme Court held that the prebankruptcy settlement did not prevent the creditor from seeking a determination of dischargeability in the debtor's subsequent bankruptcy since the settlement debt "arose" from "false pretenses, a false representation or actual fraud."

The third form of fraud concerns debtors who have a problem sometimes colloquially referred to as "credit carditis." This problem is also known as the prepetition "shopping spree." The essence of the problem pertains to debtors who, on the eve of bankruptcy, purchase luxury goods on credit or make credit purchases up to maximum credit limits and then file a Chapter 7 petition, seeking to discharge their liability on the credit cards while claiming all of the goods purchased as exempt. A similar situation arises where a debtor obtains cash advances on credit cards immediately prior to filing, spends the money, and then files a Chapter 7 proceeding. In each instance, either the goods are exempt or the money is gone but the debt has been discharged.

Section 523(a)(2)(C) was enacted in an effort to help resolve this perceived abuse of the bankruptcy system by debtors. Under this provision, consumer debts owed to a single creditor totaling more than $600 for luxury goods or services incurred within 90 days prior to the filing are presumed nondischargeable. This means that if a creditor can show transactions that fall within this description, the objection to dischargeability is considered to have been proven and the burden of proof will then shift to the debtor to prove that the debt should be dischargeable. Likewise, cash advances totaling more than $875 and incurred within 70 days prior to filing are also presumed nondischargeable.[32] Thus, a debt incurred by obtaining a large cash advance in excess of this limit from an automatic teller immediately prior to filing a bankruptcy may be presumed to be nondischargeable.

This subsection defines *luxury goods or services* as goods or services not reasonably necessary to support or maintain the debtor or a dependent of the debtor. Thus, a cash advance obtained by the debtor at the racetrack is probably nondischargeable, but if the debtor can show that the money has been used to purchase food, medicine, or other necessaries, the debt may be dischargeable. Alternatively, if $600 or more is spent on a 32-inch flat screen television, the debt is probably nondischargeable, but if the money is used for summer clothes for the kids, for blue jeans and shorts and socks, the debt may be dischargeable.[33]

The second type of debt that is nondischargeable only upon the obtaining of a judgment of nondischargeability is for fraud or defalcation while acting in a fiduciary capacity, or through embezzlement or larceny. For instance, a trustee who takes trust money, goes to Tahiti, and then files a bankruptcy will find that the trust fund debt thus created is nondischargeable. A state court receiver who absconds to another state with receivership property and then files a bankruptcy will find the debt created to be nondischargeable. An employee who falsifies business

---

32. The current text reflects amounts provided for by BAPCPA, including the adjustments that became effective on April 1, 2010. For cases filed before October 17, 2005, the values were $1,225 and $750, respectively, and the time period was 60 days.

33. 11 U.S.C. §523(a)(2)(C). Section 104(b), added in 1994, accounts for the effects of inflation on these amounts at three-year intervals. The first adjustment took place in April 1998.

records while embezzling funds from the business and who then goes bankrupt will also find that this debt is nondischargeable.[34]

 Practice Pointer

There is a lot of litigation regarding the definitions used for "defalcation" and "fiduciary capacity." There are varying levels of culpability required by the courts for defalcation, although most agree that it must occur in the context of an express or a technical trust.

Finally, willful and malicious injury by the debtor to another or another's property may also be nondischargeable, but the creditor must first file a complaint in order to determine the issue.[35] In Kawaauhau v. Geiger, 523 U.S. 57 (1998), the Supreme Court held that "willful and malicious" means that the actor must act with the intent to cause injury, and "not merely [perform] a deliberate or intentional act that leads to injury," to become nondischargeable. In this case, Geiger had been found liable for medical malpractice and reckless conduct, but not for a malicious act. The Court found that gross negligence or recklessness does not satisfy the statutory standard.

Many intentional torts will not be dischargeable. However, just as in the instance of actual fraud discussed above, the willful and malicious injury has to be such that it would be an injustice to permit the debtor to be freely relieved of liability for the wrong committed. Keep in mind that issues of nondischargeability are not as concerned with the underlying issue of liability so much as they are concerned with whether, despite the bankruptcy filing, the debt created should be relieved through the bankruptcy system. Certainly though, if there is no underlying liability, then there is no debt for which to determine the dischargeability.

D. COMPLAINTS TO DETERMINE DISCHARGEABILITY OF A DEBT

Virtually all the issues previously discussed in this text that require a court decision are brought before the court through the various motion

---

34. 11 U.S.C. §523(a)(4).
35. 11 U.S.C. §523(a)(6).

procedures described in chapter 5 supra. A second way in which issues are brought before the court for its decision is known as the adversary proceeding. Many of the subjects discussed in the next several chapters are commenced by the filing of an adversary proceeding in connection with the bankruptcy proceeding (case in chief). When an issue is brought before the court in the form of a motion and is opposed, it is considered a **contested matter**. A contested matter is treated as an adversary proceeding pursuant to Federal Rule of Bankruptcy Procedure 9014.

An adversary proceeding, except for its title, assumes the form of traditional nonbankruptcy litigation. That is, an adversary proceeding is an independent lawsuit taking place in the bankruptcy proceeding. Part VII of the Federal Rules of Bankruptcy Procedure contains the pertinent procedural rules applicable to adversary proceedings. With minor variations, these rules are essentially the Federal Rules of Civil Procedure, with which all practitioners should be familiar. The discovery and trial aspects of these rules may also apply in noticed motions.[36] The practical equivalent of a trial in a contested matter is commonly known as an evidentiary hearing.

In remarking at how similar bankruptcy litigation is to other federal court litigation, at least one judge has commented: "In a routinized area, such as bankruptcy motion practice, one easily loses sight of some of such basics as the need to make out a prima facie case by competent evidence. Bankruptcy litigation is no different than any other federal litigation practice in this respect." (In re Roberts, 210 Bankr. 325 (Bankr. D. Iowa 1997))

Federal Rule of Bankruptcy Procedure 4007 contains rules regarding who may file and the time limits for initiating a **complaint to determine dischargeability of a debt**. As already noted, the debtor or any affected creditor may initiate such a complaint.[37] A debtor may desire to file a complaint to seek a judgment that a debt that would normally be considered automatically nondischargeable should in fact be discharged. For example, a debtor may file an adversary proceeding to seek a judgment that a student loan is dischargeable on the grounds of undue hardship. A complaint to determine the dischargeability of a debt that is normally considered automatically nondischargeable may be filed at any time, and a bankruptcy proceeding may be reopened to allow for this determination to be made.[38]

On the other hand, where the determination involves the type of debt that requires the creditor to initiate a complaint, the rules contain strict time limits on the initiation of such complaints. If no complaint is timely

---

36. Bankruptcy Rule 9014.
37. Bankruptcy Rule 4007(a).
38. 11 U.S.C. §350; Bankruptcy Rule 4007(b).

initiated, the debt will be discharged.[39] In a Chapter 7, 11, or 13, the complaint must be filed within 60 days of the date first set for the meeting of creditors held pursuant to Section 341.[40] In a Chapter 13, there is also a special carve-out for actions under Section 523(a)(6) where the deadline is set when the debtor applies for a discharge upon completion of a Chapter 13 plan.[41] In either situation, the time period may be extended by motion or voluntary agreement, provided that the motion or agreement is made before the expiration of the deadline set for the filing of the complaint.[42]

If a creditor objects to the discharge of a consumer debt on the grounds of fraud and if the debt is found dischargeable, the court may award costs and attorneys' fees to the debtor if the court finds that the creditor's position was not substantially justified.[43] The purpose of this provision is to deter creditors from initiating unfounded objections to dischargeability solely in order to gain an undue economic advantage over a debtor.

In Grogan v. Garner, 498 U.S. 279 (1991), the Supreme Court ruled that in complaints objecting to the dischargeability of debts, the burden of proof is by a preponderance of the evidence. This ruling reversed the law of many circuits that had required a plaintiff to prove its case by clear and convincing evidence to prevail.

In *Grogan*, the creditor had obtained a jury verdict for fraud, which was affirmed on appeal. After the debtor filed Chapter 11, the creditor filed a timely complaint objecting to the debt's dischargeability pursuant to 11 U.S.C. §523(a)(2)(A), actual fraud. The Bankruptcy Court, relying on the jury verdict, held the debt to be nondischargeable. The Eighth Circuit Court of Appeals reversed, but the Supreme Court reinstated the trial court's holding. The Court noted that the Code does not specify a burden of proof standard in dischargeability complaints. The Court also rejected the argument that the higher level of proof required by a "clear and convincing" standard is necessary to aid in a debtor's fresh start.

E.   OBJECTING TO DISCHARGE

While Section 523 affects only the dischargeability of certain specific debts, under Section 727, a debtor may have a discharge completely

---

39. 11 U.S.C. §523(c).
40. Bankruptcy Rule 4007(c).
41. Bankruptcy Rule 4007(d) (Interim).
42. Bankruptcy Rules 4007(c) and (d).
43. 11 U.S.C. §523(d).

denied. A debtor whose discharge is denied under Section 727(a) will not receive the debtor relief of legal release from any debt. Although Section 727 appears only in Chapter 7, it is also applicable in Chapter 11 proceedings, but not in Chapter 12 or 13 proceedings.[44]

Only individual debtors receive Chapter 7 discharges. Corporations and partnerships do not.[45] A Chapter 7 discharge may be obtained only once every eight years, and may not be obtained within six years of receiving a Chapter 12 or Chapter 13 discharge unless the Plan provided for payment of at least 70 percent of unsecured claims.[46]

So, if a debtor has filed a bankruptcy petition within the past eight years and has received a Chapter 7 discharge, the debtor is not entitled to a discharge in the second proceeding. A debtor may also waive a discharge if the waiver is in writing executed after the bankruptcy filing and is approved by the court.[47]

Most of the remaining provisions of Section 727(a) deny debtors a discharge due to activities that can be most succinctly described as inequitable conduct. That is, these provisions will deny a discharge if the debtor's conduct is such that it would be unjust to grant the debtor a discharge. A discharge may be denied if the debtor has concealed, transferred, or destroyed records or property of the estate with the intent to hinder, delay, or defraud creditors within one year prior to filing.[48]

A discharge may be denied if the debtor knowingly and fraudulently makes a false oath or withholds records relating to the debtor's financial condition from the trustee.[49] A discharge may be denied if the debtor refuses to obey court orders in connection with the case or fails to testify unless immunity has been granted.[50] The denial of a discharge on the grounds set forth in this paragraph may also result in criminal violations under federal law.[51]

A discharge may be denied if the debtor fails to satisfactorily explain any loss or deficiency of assets to meet the debtor's liabilities.[52] For instance, Mack MacHeath files a set of Statements and Schedules describing no assets and no prior businesses but listing claims of $10 million, and

---

44. 11 U.S.C. §103; 11 U.S.C. §1141(d)(3)(c). See chapter 2 supra and chapter 26 infra.
45. 11 U.S.C. §727(a)(1).
46. 11 U.S.C. §727(a)(8); 11 U.S.C. §727(a)(9). FRBP 4004(d) requires objections to discharge based upon these provisions to be raised by way of motion and not by way of an adversary proceeding.
47. 11 U.S.C. §727(a)(10).
48. 11 U.S.C. §727(a)(2).
49. 11 U.S.C. §727(a)(4).
50. 11 U.S.C. §727(a)(6).
51. 18 U.S.C. §152.
52. 11 U.S.C. §727(a)(5).

he fails to explain how he acquired $10 million of debt while retaining no assets and not being engaged in business. Someone does not normally acquire substantial debt without being engaged in business or retaining any assets without explanation. In this circumstance, the discharge may be denied.

A discharge may be denied to a debtor who destroys, conceals, mutilates, falsifies, or fails to keep books and records from which the debtor's financial condition may be ascertained, unless such acts are justified under the circumstances of the case.[53] For instance, most individual consumer debtors do not keep many financial records. There is no law requiring individuals to maintain checkbooks. Low-income debtors may not have earned sufficient income to require the filing of income tax returns. But most individual debtors do have some files at home with perhaps some bills, checkbook registers, and prior-year income tax returns. An individual ordinary consumer debtor cannot be expected or required to have many more records than this. Many individuals do have substantially more personal financial records in their possession, but, at a minimum, recent bills, checkbook registers, and tax returns are all that can or should be expected.

The general rule is that a debtor should be able to produce the minimum amount of records necessary or required by nonbankruptcy law to support the type of financial activity in which the debtor has been engaged prior to the bankruptcy filing.[54] Thus, if the debtor is Grandma Smith, who subsists solely on Social Security and pays all of her expenses by cash or money order, she should not be denied a discharge because she does not keep books and records. She is keeping the books and records necessary to support the activities in which she is engaged, which in this case is virtually none. However, if Grandma Smith has $10 million of debts and makes the same representations, her discharge may be denied.

On the other hand, if a debtor is engaged in business, there are certain minimum records that the debtor will be required to maintain under nonbankruptcy law. Payroll and payroll tax records are required by both federal and local law. Sales tax records and sales records will be required to be maintained where there are local sales taxes to pay. If the debtor has not maintained these records or cannot adequately justify their lack of existence, the discharge may be denied.

---

53. 11 U.S.C. §727(a)(3).

54. This test has also been restated as whatever is reasonable based on the particular circumstances. See, e.g., In re French, 499 F.3d 345, 355 (4th Cir. 2007); In re Cacioli, 463 F.2d 229, 235 (2d Cir. 2006); In re Schifano, 378 F.3d 60 (1st Cir. 2004) and whatever is necessary to ascertain the debtor's financial condition, see, e.g., In re Juzwiak, 89 F.3d 424 (7th Cir. 1996). See also In re Costello, 299 B.R. 882 (Bankr. N.D. Ill. 2003) (where the debtor's discharge was denied because his only explanation as to the unavailability of records was that mice ate them).

A discharge may be denied a debtor who has committed any of the above described acts within a year prior to filing, during the pendency of the debtor's bankruptcy proceeding, or in connection with another bankruptcy proceeding concerning an insider.[55] For example, Mack MacHeath files a Chapter 7 for his corporation, Mack's Knives, Inc. The corporation has no records whatsoever. MacHeath then files his own personal Chapter 7. His personal discharge may be denied due to his failure to have kept records for his bankrupt insider corporation.

BAPCPA added Section 727(a)(11), which requires individual debtors to complete a postpetition financial management course in order to receive a discharge. Thus, coupled with the requirement to undergo credit counseling as a prerequisite to filing a petition (see chapter 3 supra), individual bankruptcy debtors must now undergo both pre- and postpetition financial counseling, the former as a prerequisite to filing, and the latter as a prerequisite to receiving a discharge.

F.   COMPLAINTS OBJECTING TO DISCHARGE

Any creditor, the trustee, or the United States Trustee may file a **complaint to determine discharge** under Section 727(a).[56] The objection is made by filing an adversary proceeding objecting to the discharge within 60 days of the date first set for the creditors' meeting under Section 341(a) in a Chapter 7, or no later than the date first set for the confirmation hearing on the debtor's plan of reorganization in a Chapter 11 proceeding.[57] An extension of this time period can be obtained for cause if a motion for the extension is made before expiration of the time periods permitted by the rules.[58] Unless a timely complaint is filed, the debtor will receive a discharge.[59]

In Kontrick v. Ryan, 540 U.S. 443 (2004), the Supreme Court examined whether the 60-day time limit was jurisdictional or subject to waiver if not raised until after a trial on the merits. In this case, Ryan obtained a judgment against Kontrick. Kontrick intentionally concealed his assets from Ryan and admitted as much. Although Ryan filed his complaint objecting to discharge in a timely manner, he amended the complaint to add an

---

55. 11 U.S.C. §727(a)(7).
56. 11 U.S.C. §727(c).
57. Bankruptcy Rule 4004(a).
58. Bankruptcy Rule 4004(b).
59. Bankruptcy Rule 4004(c).

additional claim after expiration of the 60-day time limit. After losing at trial, Kontrick moved the court to dismiss the added claim because it had not been filed in a timely manner. Ryan contended that Kontrick's earlier failure to have raised the issue acted to waive the defense. The Supreme Court held that the 60-day time limit to file the complaint objecting to discharge is not jurisdictional and is waived if not raised until after the matter has been litigated. Although involving an objection to discharge, the scope of this holding will likely apply to complaints objecting to the dischargeability of debts subject to FRBP 4007, since the operative language in the applicable rules is identical.

A discharge may be revoked if fraudulently obtained and the fraud is not known until after the discharge has been granted, if the debtor fails to turn over property of the estate subsequent to receiving a discharge, or if the debtor fails to cooperate in a random audit (see chapter 7 supra). The trustee, a creditor, or the United States Trustee may file a complaint to revoke the discharge within one year of the original discharge date where the ground of revocation is fraud. Where the ground for revocation is a failure to turn over estate property, the same parties may initiate a complaint before the later of one year after the discharge is received or one year after the proceeding is closed.[60] Normally, the later date will be one year after the proceeding is closed.

Summary

Certain debts will not be affected by a debtor's discharge. These debts are known as nondischargeable debts. Occasionally, a debtor may be denied a discharge. When a debt is nondischargeable or a debtor is denied a discharge, the bankruptcy will not provide the debtor with legal relief from a specific debt in the former instance and from all debt in the latter.

The following debts are nondischargeable without an affected creditor being required to take any affirmative action.

Debt	*Code Section*
priority tax claims	523(a)(1)
unlisted debts	523(a)(3)
domestic support obligations	523(a)(5), (15)
certain fines and penalties	523(a)(7)
guaranteed student loans	523(a)(8)
damages from DWI conviction	523(a)(9)
debt nondischarged in prior bankruptcy	523(a)(10)
financial institution fraud	523(a)(11), (12)

---

60. 11 U.S.C. §727(d)(e).

restitution award	523(a)(13)
debts obtained to pay nondischargeable taxes, or other fines under election laws	523(a)(14), (14A), (14B)
postpetition homeowner's assessments	523(a)(16)
prisoner court costs	523(a)(17)
pension plan loans	523(a)(18)
debts arising from federal or state securities law violations	523(a)(19)

A creditor may object to the discharge of the following debts:

Debt	*Code Section*
fraud	523(a)(2)
intentional fraud	523(a)(2)(A)
false written financial statement	523(a)(2)(B)
limited prepetition credit transactions	523(a)(2)(C)
defalcation, larceny, embezzlement	523(a)(4)
willful and malicious injury	523(a)(6)

A creditor objects to the dischargeability of a debt by filing a complaint to determine the dischargeability of the debt. The creditor's object is to obtain a judgment that the debt is not dischargeable. The complaint must be filed within 60 days of the date first set for the meeting of creditors pursuant to Section 341(a) or the debt will be discharged.

A debtor may also initiate a complaint to determine dischargeability of a debt and may do so at any time. A debtor might want to initiate such a complaint to obtain a judgment that an automatically nondischargeable debt is, in fact, dischargeable.

Only individuals are entitled to a Chapter 7 discharge; corporations and partnerships are not. A Chapter 7 discharge may only be obtained once every eight years. A discharge can be denied if a debtor has engaged in various sorts of inequitable conduct, including a failure to maintain proper books and records or for concealing assets. Individual debtors will be denied a discharge if they fail to complete a postpetition financial management course.

KEY TERMS

adversary proceeding
complaint to determine discharge
complaint to determine dischargeability of a debt

contested matter
fresh cash rule
nondischargeable debts
unlisted debt

DISCUSSION QUESTIONS

1. What is the difference between an objection to a debtor's discharge and an objection to the dischargeability of a debt?

2. Why are certain debts nondischargeable without an affected creditor being required to initiate an adversary proceeding? Identify these debts.

3. What debts become nondischargeable only by a creditor commencing a complaint objecting to dischargeability of the debt?

4. What are the deadlines for initiating a complaint to determine dischargeability of a debt or an objection to the debtor's discharge?

5. Why would a debtor desire to initiate a complaint to determine dischargeability of a debt?

6. Under what circumstances can a debtor be denied a discharge?

PRACTICE EXERCISES

Exercise 13.1
Prepare a draft adversary complaint on behalf of the debtors challenging the nondischargeability of their student loan obligation.

Exercise 13.2
Prepare an objection to the debtors' discharge on behalf of the Chavez Tea Company, who was a creditor of Top O' the Mornin' and is asserting that the debtor Bretony Bottomline destroyed company records.

14

Property of the Estate and Turnover Complaints

A. PROPERTY OF THE ESTATE

The concept of **property of the estate** has been mentioned frequently but has not been previously explained in detail. Just as exemptions and discharge are fundamental to debtor relief, the concept of property of the estate is fundamental to a trustee's administration of an estate and is fundamental to the rights of creditors affected by a bankruptcy filing. Property of the estate not claimed exempt is subject to administration by a trustee by way of liquidation or abandonment of the property. With regard to secured creditors, the automatic stay protects property of the estate from foreclosure or repossession. With regard to unsecured creditors, the proceeds obtained from any liquidation of estate property by the trustee represent the funds that will ultimately be available for a distribution of dividends to the creditors. The basic mechanism for a trustee to recover property of the estate is known as a turnover complaint. Additional rights, commonly known as **avoiding powers**, have been provided to the trustee to permit the further recovery of property of the estate.[1]

Section 541 defines and describes *property of the estate*. The commencement of a proceeding creates an estate. This occurs whether the proceeding is voluntary or involuntary and irrespective of the Chapter proceeding filed.[2] The basic concept is that all property in which the

---

1. See chapters 15-17 infra with regard to the trustee's avoiding powers.
2. 11 U.S.C. §541(a).

debtor has an interest, wherever located and by whomever held, constitutes property of the estate as defined by Section 541, once the debtor files for bankruptcy relief.[3] In short, property previously considered to be assets of the debtor soon becomes synonymous with property of the estate. Even exempt property constitutes property of the estate, although such property is not available for the payment of creditor dividends.[4] The balance of Section 541 makes an effort to clarify and create specific exclusions to the rather broad definition of *estate property* provided for by the Bankruptcy Code.

Practice Pointer
Property of the estate includes any potential causes of action that the debtor may have.

In a community property jurisdiction, all interests of the debtor and the debtor's spouse in community property as of the commencement of the proceeding that is under the sole, equal, or joint management and control of the debtor or that is liable for an allowable claim against the debtor or both the debtor and the debtor's spouse constitutes property of the estate.[5] More simply put, property of the estate generally includes the community property interests of a nonfiling debtor spouse. For example, if a debtor in a community property jurisdiction files a bankruptcy proceeding but the debtor's spouse does not, all community property is still normally considered to be property of the estate.

The above rule as to community property is consistent with the treatment of community debt and the debtor's discharge. It should be recalled that community debts will normally be discharged as to the community property of both spouses.[6] It is possible to file a Chapter 7 proceeding for one spouse in a community property jurisdiction and effectively gain a discharge for both spouses as to all community debts for which any community property may be liable. However, the separate property of the nonfiling spouse will remain liable for the otherwise discharged

---

3. 11 U.S.C. §541(a)(1). See, e.g., In re Koonce, 262 B.R. 850 (Bankr. D. Nev. 2001) (lottery prize payments payable postpetition constitute property of the estate); In re Neto, 215 B.R. 939 (Bankr. D. N.J. 1997) (same).
4. See Historical and Revision Note to Section 541. See also 11 U.S.C. §522(b) and chapter 9 supra.
5. 11 U.S.C. §541(a)(2).
6. 11 U.S.C. §524(a)(3). See chapter 7 supra.

community debts and the automatic stay will be ineffective as to the non-filing spouse, who may still potentially be the subject of creditor action to collect the debts. Nevertheless, any judgment obtained against the non-filing spouse will not be enforceable against community property that has been property of the bankruptcy estate.

PROPERTY OF THE ESTATE

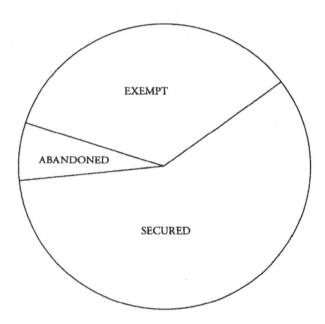

All property in which the debtor has a legal or equitable interest at the commencement of a case is property of the estate (11 U.S.C. §541(a)). During the course of the case, the trustee must "administer" all the property. The figure illustrates a typical consumer no asset Chapter 7 where all property is either collateral for one or more secured creditors (see chapter 21 infra), exempt (see chapter 9 supra), or abandoned by the trustee as burdensome or of inconsequential value to the estate (see chapter 20 infra).

Property of the estate also includes any property recovered by the trustee through use of the avoiding powers or by operation of any other Code section.[7] For instance, if the court finds that counsel has received excessive compensation under Section 329(b), any portion of the fee ordered to be refunded by counsel becomes property of the estate.

---

7. 11 U.S.C. §541(a)(3)(4).

Section 541(a)(5) concerns certain limited interests in property acquired by a debtor within 180 days after filing a bankruptcy so long as the property in question would have been property of the estate had the interest existed on the date of filing. These limited interests are property a debtor becomes entitled to receive by bequest, devise, or inheritance; property that a debtor becomes entitled to receive by way of a property settlement, agreement, or interlocutory or final divorce decree with the debtor's spouse; and property that the debtor becomes entitled to receive as a beneficiary of a life insurance policy or a death benefit plan.[8] By virtue of this subsection, Congress has expressed a policy that potential windfalls to the debtor received within 180 days of filing shall be made available to pay a dividend to the creditors. Note, however, the irony that true windfalls, such as a lottery jackpot, are not subject to this provision. Thus, a lottery jackpot won by the debtor ten days after a bankruptcy filing from a lottery ticket purchased postpetition will not be available to satisfy the claims of prepetition creditors unless the debtor desires it. Of course, if the debtor purchased the winning lottery ticket prepetition, the winnings would be property of the estate.[9] On the other hand, if the debtor's grandmother dies 175 days after the bankruptcy filing, any inheritance will be property of the bankruptcy estate.

 Practice Pointer

At least one court has determined that postpetition spousal maintenance payments received by the debtor during the 180-day period are not property of the estate. In re Wise, 346 F.3d 1239 (10th Cir. 2003).

An important clarification to the concept of property of the estate is that items that may best be called "the fruit of the tree" are also property of the estate. Proceeds, product, offspring, or rent from property of the estate will also be property of the estate.[10] More simply put, property generated from property of the estate will itself be property of the estate. For example, the proceeds earned by an operating business after a Chapter 11 filing are property of the estate. If a fruit orchard is part of an estate,

---

8. 11 U.S.C. §541(a)(5).
9. See note 3 supra.
10. 11 U.S.C. §541(a)(6).

the fruit growing on the trees is part of the estate. If the debtor owns a sheep ranch, the lambs born after the filing are property of the estate. Property produced from estate property will itself be estate property.

Earnings from personal services performed by an individual debtor after the bankruptcy filing are not included as part of the property of the estate in a Chapter 7 case. Simply put, an individual debtor's postpetition wages are not property of the estate.[11] This rule applies to self-employment earnings for personal services as well as to a wage earner's paycheck. For example, a doctor's postpetition fees earned for providing services to patients are not property of the estate in the doctor's Chapter 7 case. If the debtor is a real estate agent, a commission earned postfiling is not property of the estate. If the debtor is a movie star or professional athlete bound to a prefiling long-term contract, the fee earned for personal services rendered after the bankruptcy filing is not property of the estate.[12]

There is one major exception to the rule that postpetition earnings for personal services are not property of the estate. This exception applies in individual Chapter 11, 12, and 13 proceedings. In these Chapters, post-petition earnings *are* considered to be property of the estate.[13] The reason for this rule is that the debtor's postfiling earnings generally comprise the source of the funding behind the distributions made to the creditors in individual reorganization cases. It is logical that the source of creditor repayment itself be considered estate property.

Property of the estate does *not* include any power that the debtor may exercise solely for the benefit of another entity.[14] For example, if a debtor possesses a power of attorney exercisable for a third party, the power of attorney is not property of the estate.

Practice Pointer

When potential property of the estate is alleged to be held instead in trust, the burden is on the claimant to establish the trust relationship.

---

11. 11 U.S.C. §541(a)(6).
12. In re Tia Carrere, 64 B.R. 156 (Bankr. C.D. Cal. 1986); In re Clark, 100 B.R. 317 (E.D. La. 1989) (professional football player's postpetition salary was not property of estate).
13. 11 U.S.C. §1115; 11 U.S.C. §1207(a)(2); 11 U.S.C. §1306(a)(2). See chapters 23, 25, and 27 infra.
14. 11 U.S.C. §541(b)(1).

Any interest that a debtor may claim to have in a nonresidential lease of real property the term of which has expired prior to filing or during the proceeding is not property of the estate or ceases to be property of the estate in the latter event.[15] Thus, the landlord of an expired nonresidential lease need not seek relief from the automatic stay to be able to remove the lessee from the premises subject to the expired lease. In the first place, the landlord's action is excepted from the automatic stay. In the second place, the automatic stay is terminated as to an act against property when the property ceases to be property of the estate.[16] A nonresidential lease would normally be considered a commercial lease in a nonbankruptcy environment. BAPCPA provides additional exclusions from property of the estate, including certain educational IRA or TAP funds, some retirement funds, and property that has been pledged as collateral for a loan. This latter category comprises pawned property.[17]

Sometimes a trust or other transactional document contains **ipso facto clauses** that restrict a transfer of or purport to forfeit an interest in property upon the holder of the interest becoming insolvent or commencing a bankruptcy proceeding. These ipso facto clauses are not enforceable in a bankruptcy proceeding to defeat the holder's property interest. A debtor's interest in such a transaction will remain property of the estate.[18] For example, Thurston Howell III gives his nephew Gilligan title to an island. The deed contains language that renders Gilligan's title to the island forfeited if Gilligan becomes insolvent or files a bankruptcy proceeding. If Gilligan then files a bankruptcy, the forfeiture clause will be unenforceable. Gilligan's trustee may be able to sell the island to pay a dividend to Gilligan's creditors.

On the other hand, **spendthrift trusts** are enforceable in bankruptcy proceedings, and the principal property of a valid spendthrift trust will not be considered property of a bankruptcy estate.[19] A spendthrift trust exists when the trust instrument contains provisions restricting the transfer of a beneficial interest in the trust. Spendthrift trusts are trusts that are created to prevent creditors of the trust beneficiaries from seizing the trust's principal assets to pay the beneficiaries' debts. One form of spendthrift trust is created to preserve a family fortune from the financial indiscretions of the family members who are its beneficiaries. For example, Richie Rich has a very bad day in Las Vegas and is left with no choice but to file a Chapter 7 to attempt to discharge the legal gambling debts owed to his casino

---

15. 11 U.S.C. §541(b)(2).
16. 11 U.S.C. §362(b)(10); 11 U.S.C. §362(c). See chapter 12 supra.
17. 11 U.S.C. §541(b)(5), (6), (7), (8).
18. 11 U.S.C. §541(c)(1).
19. 11 U.S.C. §541(c)(2).

creditors. He is the beneficiary of a valid spendthrift trust. Neither the trustee nor the creditors can invade the trust principal to satisfy Richie's debts. However, the income that Richie receives from the trust for at least 180 days after filing may become property of the estate because the income is not earnings from personal services and is likely an interest from bequest, devise, or inheritance.[20]

A second form of spendthrift trust may come into existence through a qualified pension plan containing so-called spendthrift provisions. In 1992, in Patterson v. Shumate, 504 U.S. 753, the Supreme Court held that a debtor's beneficial interest in an Employment Retirement Income Security Act (ERISA) qualified pension plan is excluded from property of the estate.

Mr. Shumate was one of 400 participants in the Coleman Furniture Corporation pension plan. The plan qualified as an ERISA plan and contained spendthrift provisions. In 1984, Shumate became a Chapter 7 debtor. Shumate's trustee attempted to recover Shumate's interest in the pension plan as estate property. The district court ruled in the trustee's favor. Its decision was based on its interpretation that the phrase "applicable nonbankruptcy law" used in Section 541(c)(2) meant only state law, not federal law. The Supreme Court reversed the district court, holding that the phrase "applicable nonbankruptcy law" includes federal non-bankruptcy law such as ERISA. Accordingly, a valid spendthrift provision in an ERISA plan will exclude the debtor's beneficial interest from being considered property of the estate.

Finally, property in which the debtor holds bare legal title only is property of the estate only to the extent of the debtor's interest in it.[21] For example, if the debtor is a real estate trust deed or mortgage company servicing loans for third parties, the debtor's interest will extend only to any fees the debtor may be entitled to receive in connection with the loan servicing agreements. Any interest in the proceeds of the notes payable to nondebtor third parties would not be property of the estate.

B. TURNOVER COMPLAINTS

Having defined *property of the estate*, the next task is to describe how a trustee or debtor-in-possession acquires the property for purposes of liquidation or other administration. Recall that recovery of estate property

---

20. 11 U.S.C. §541(a)(5). See above discussion.
21. 11 U.S.C. §541(d).

for purposes of liquidation and administration is an important aspect of the trustee's duties.[22] When a bankruptcy is filed, estate property will be in one of two places: either in the possession or control of the debtor or in the possession or control of third parties. The Code provides the trustee with various rights that allow the trustee to recover all estate property for purposes of administration. Property of the estate is recoverable by a trustee through the use of a **turnover complaint** or through exercise of the trustee's various avoiding powers.

The concept of turnover is simple. Someone has property of the estate: It may be the debtor, it may be a third party, it could be anyone. If the third party refuses to voluntarily turn the property over to the trustee, the court can order the third party to turn it over. The concept is this simple. The trustee has an almost absolute right, with few exceptions, to recover property of the estate for the benefit of creditors.[23]

Practice Pointer

Courts have even required a creditor to turn over a vehicle that was lawfully repossessed prepetition.

The exceptions to this rule are quite limited. An entity without actual knowledge or notice of the bankruptcy that transfers property of the estate to an entity other than the trustee does not later have to turn the property over to the trustee.[24] For instance, XYZ, Inc., files a Chapter 7 proceeding. XYZ's customers continue to send in their payments to XYZ instead of to the trustee. Whether or not the trustee ultimately receives the payments as property of the estate, the payments are considered to have been made. An insurance company with automatic premium payment requirements may pay itself from property of the estate to the extent the payment is required to pay a premium or carry out a nonforfeiture option.[25] Any applicable setoff right may also limit a trustee's turnover rights.[26]

Attorneys or accountants in possession of the books or records of an estate can be directed to turn over such records to the trustee. Although, in limited instances, traditional privileges may be utilized to protect the

---

22. See chapter 10 supra.
23. 11 U.S.C. §542(a).
24. 11 U.S.C. §542(c).
25. 11 U.S.C. §542(d).
26. 11 U.S.C. §542(b). See chapter 17 infra.

materials from turnover, in cases involving entities other than individuals, the trustee normally becomes the holder of any applicable privilege.[27]

Special rules govern the turnover of estate property in the hands of a **custodian**.[28] In this instance, the custodian is a third party with custody of the property prior to the bankruptcy filing, such as an assignee for the benefit of creditors, or a state court receiver, or a nonbankruptcy trustee.[29] Although a custodian with knowledge of the commencement of a bankruptcy proceeding is supposed to turn over property of the estate to the bankruptcy trustee, Section 543 gives consideration to the custodian's rights.[30] The custodian may file an accounting of the custodian's activities, seek payment of any compensation that may be due, and generally be permitted to take all actions that would be required to fulfill and relieve the custodian's duties under nonbankruptcy law.[31] In an exceptional instance, the court, notwithstanding the appointment of a bankruptcy trustee, may permit the custodian to remain in possession of the property if the estate is solvent and if the custodian's continued presence would be in the best interest of the owners of the debtor.[32] For instance, perhaps the debtor owns a large apartment project and the custodian is better suited than the trustee to continue management of the property on behalf of the estate. The custodian ought to stay put. This is an instance where logic and common sense should prevail.

A turnover order is normally sought by filing an adversary proceeding known as a turnover complaint and joining as defendants those parties against whom the turnover is sought. However, a turnover proceeding may be brought before the court by way of a noticed motion rather than a complaint when the sole purpose of the motion is to seek a turnover of property held only by the debtor.[33]

Summary

The filing of a bankruptcy proceeding creates an estate. All property in which the debtor has a legal or equitable interest becomes property of the estate. Property of the estate is subject to administration by the bankruptcy

---

27. 11 U.S.C. §542(e); 11 U.S.C. §521(4); Commodity Futures Trading Commn. v. Weintraub, 471 U.S. 343 (1985).
28. 11 U.S.C. §543.
29. 11 U.S.C. §101(11). See chapter 6 supra.
30. 11 U.S.C. §543(b).
31. 11 U.S.C. §543(b)(2), (c)(2); Bankruptcy Rule 6002.
32. 11 U.S.C. §543(d).
33. Bankruptcy Rule 7001(1).

trustee for the distribution of dividends to the creditors. Property of the estate is the subject of Code Section 541.

There are a number of clarifications contained in Section 541 including or excluding certain interests as property of the estate. The following list identifies these special inclusions or exclusions:

1. Included as Property of the Estate:

Item	Statute
a. Community property	11 U.S.C. §541(a)(2)
b. Property recovered by the trustee	11 U.S.C. §541(a)(3)(4)
c. Property acquired within 180 days of filing by bequest, inheritance, or devise, domestic property settlement, life insurance proceeds	11 U.S.C. §541(a)(5)
d. Proceeds, product, or offspring from property of the estate	11 U.S.C. §541(a)(6)
e. Property subject to an ipso facto clause	11 U.S.C. §541(c)(1)

2. Excluded as Property of the Estate:

Item	Statute
a. Personal postfiling earnings of an individual Chapter 7 debtor	11 U.S.C. §541(a)(6)
b. Powers exercisable for the benefit of another (e.g., power of attorney)	11 U.S.C. §541(b)(1)
c. Interest in an expired nonresidential lease	11 U.S.C. §541(b)(2)
d. Principal assets of a spendthrift trust	11 U.S.C. §541(c)(2)
e. Property in which the debtor holds bare legal title	11 U.S.C. §541(d)

The trustee may recover property of the estate by initiating an adversary proceeding known as a turnover complaint. This right is provided the trustee by Section 542 of the Code. Where the turnover is sought from the debtor, the trustee may proceed by way of a noticed motion.

KEY TERMS

avoiding powers	**property of the estate**
custodian	**spendthrift trust**
ipso facto clause	**turnover complaint**

DISCUSSION QUESTIONS

1. What is meant by the phrase "property of the estate"?

2. Why is the general definition of estate property contained in 11 U.S.C. §541(a) intentionally broad?

3. Why are postpetition wages of a debtor not considered property of the estate in Chapter 7? Why are postpetition wages of an individual debtor included as property of the estate in Chapters 11, 12, and 13?

4. Why is the product or proceeds of estate property also considered estate property?

5. What is an ipso facto clause?

6. What is a turnover complaint?

15

Avoiding Powers — Introduction

A. FUNCTION OF THE TRUSTEE'S AVOIDING POWERS

In addition to the turnover right, the Bankruptcy Code has given the trustee rights to recover as estate property, property transferred in fraud of creditors or property distributed inequitably to the creditors during certain defined periods prior to a bankruptcy filing. Unauthorized postpetition transfers may also be recoverable. Collectively, these rights are commonly known as the trustee's avoiding powers. An **avoiding power** is the ability of a trustee to avoid certain pre- or postpetition transactions that would otherwise be valid under nonbankruptcy law. The purpose of the avoiding powers is to effectuate the Bankruptcy Code's function as a debt collection tool. This is often described as the orderly and consistent liquidation of a debtor's assets and their distribution to creditors. The successful use by a trustee of an avoiding power will recover as estate property assets that would no longer be considered property of the debtor in a nonbankruptcy environment.

The avoiding powers are designed to provide consistency and uniformity to the liquidation of bankruptcy estates and the distribution of dividends to creditors. The existence of the trustee's avoiding powers acts to prevent creditors from racing to the courthouse on the eve of a debtor's bankruptcy filing to seek unfair advantage relative to the overall creditor body. The avoiding powers also act to prohibit the enactment of conflicting nonbankruptcy nonfederal laws that might otherwise tend to defeat operation of the bankruptcy system.

The avoiding powers are contained in multiple sections of the Bankruptcy Code. The most commonly used avoiding powers are the strong arm clause, preferences, fraudulent transfers, and unauthorized postpetition transfers. The next three text chapters will focus on these avoiding powers.

B.   STRONG ARM CLAUSE

Section 544 gives the trustee various powers collectively and commonly known as the strong arm powers, or the **strong arm clause**. These are the first, most basic, of the avoiding powers. This provision existed under the Bankruptcy Act as Section 70(c).[1] Because much prior case law concerning this provision remains effective under the Code, it is a useful reference for those requiring additional research. In its essence, Section 544 transforms a trustee into a "super-creditor" as of the commencement of a bankruptcy proceeding.[2]

First, the trustee is given the power of a creditor who at the time of filing obtains a judicial lien on all of the debtor's property subject to a judicial lien, whether or not such a creditor actually exists.[3] Thus, the trustee has the status of a perfected and secured judgment creditor. This power gives the trustee priority over all other creditors who do not possess any superior lien rights upon property of the estate. This provision gives the trustee a superior right to all assets of the estate for the protection of all creditors.

Second, Section 544 gives the trustee the power of a creditor who at the time of filing has an execution of judgment returned unsatisfied, whether or not such a creditor actually exists.[4] This provision, in conjunction with the first, provides a trustee with blanket protection to avoid any other creditor's efforts to gain a superior right in estate property subsequent to the commencement of the bankruptcy proceeding.

Third, the trustee is given the status of a bona fide purchaser of real property from the debtor, whether or not such a purchaser actually exists.[5] Thus, no entity can obtain an interest superior to the trustee's

---

1. See Historical and Revision Notes to 11 U.S.C. §544.
2. It is generally accepted that a Chapter 13 debtor may utilize the trustee's strong arm powers provided for in 11 U.S.C. §§544, 545, 547, 548, and 549 to the extent provided for in 11 U.S.C. §522 (g) and (h).
3. 11 U.S.C. §544(a)(1).
4. 11 U.S.C. §544(a)(2).
5. 11 U.S.C. §544(a)(3).

in a debtor's real estate subsequent to the bankruptcy filing. For example, a debtor's transfer of real estate one day after a petition is filed is in violation of the trustee's strong arm rights.

The strong arm rights collectively place the trustee in full command of all of a debtor's assets affected by the bankruptcy proceeding. It is the trustee, through proper use of the Bankruptcy Code, who initially determines the rights of the creditors to the various assets and the proper order of distribution of any funds received from a liquidation of the assets. The trustee can of course be aided by the court in making these determinations.

C.   LIMITATIONS ON AVOIDING POWERS

Section 546 contains several limitations on the exercise of the trustee's avoiding powers. Actions on the avoiding powers must be commenced within one year of the trustee's appointment or two years after the entry of the order for relief, whichever is later, but any action must be commenced before the close or dismissal of the case.[6] This provision is essentially a statute of limitations upon the exercise of the trustee's avoiding powers.

Please note that this limitations period is measured from the entry of the order for relief or the date of the trustee's appointment, whichever is later. For example, a Chapter 11 may have been pending for 23 months prior to the trustee's appointment. Nonetheless, the trustee has one year from the date of appointment to exercise the avoiding powers. The logic of this rule is to prevent Chapter 11 debtors from filing a proceeding and then refraining from exercising an avoiding power to the detriment of all creditors. For example, John Smith fraudulently transfers real estate to his children on the eve of a Chapter 11 filing. He then files the Chapter 11 and plans to delay action for two years so that the fraudulent transfer cannot be avoided because of the Section 546 time limits. Twenty-three months later, a trustee is appointed. Unfortunately for John Smith, the trustee will have one year to commence action rather than one month.

A second limitation on the exercise of the trustee's avoiding powers concerns the limited rights of certain creditors to perfect or to continue the perfection of a security interest in property notwithstanding the commencement of a bankruptcy proceeding.[7] This is a corollary to and is

---

6. 11 U.S.C. §546(a).
7. 11 U.S.C. §546(b).

consistent with the identical exception to the automatic stay.[8] The limitation is that if nonbankruptcy law permits the perfection of an interest in property to relate back to a time prior to actual perfection, the fortuitous intervention of a bankruptcy filing will not defeat the creditor's nonbankruptcy rights to perfect the interest in accordance with nonbankruptcy law. The most common scenario that arises is the perfection of a security interest under the Uniform Commercial Code. Under the UCC a creditor normally has a ten-day statutory grace period to perfect a security interest.[9] If a bankruptcy intervenes during any applicable time period, Section 546(b) permits the creditor to complete perfection of its security interest within the statutory time period. In this event the validity and priority of the security interest will be honored in the bankruptcy proceeding. Similarly, if a state mechanic's lien law permits perfection of the lien to relate back to a prior date, then a mechanic's lien may be perfected by an affected creditor subsequent to a bankruptcy filing.

One purpose that this provision serves is to prevent a debtor from buying an asset on credit and then filing a bankruptcy before the creditor can perfect its security interest. If this could be done, then a debtor could claim the asset exempt, and the creditor would be unsecured. Such a rule would undoubtedly increase the cost of consumer credit and decrease its availability. Giving the creditor the benefit of any statutory grace period is simply fair. The Historical and Revision Notes to Section 546(b) state:

> The purpose of the subsection is to protect, in spite of the surprise intervention of a bankruptcy petition, those whom State law protects by allowing them to perfect their liens or interests as of an effective date that is earlier than the date of perfection.[10]

A third limitation on exercise of the trustee's avoiding powers concerns the rights of creditors to reclaim goods under either common law or the Uniform Commercial Code.[11] A right of reclamation is a creditor's right, in certain defined circumstances, to repossess goods previously sold to the debtor on an unsecured basis. Under this provision, a seller with a reclamation right may actually reacquire the merchandise from the buyer/debtor despite the filing of the bankruptcy if the debtor has received the goods in the ordinary course of business while insolvent within 45

---

8. 11 U.S.C. §362(b)(3). See chapter 12 supra.
9. UCC §9-301(1).
10. Historical and Revision Notes to Section 546.
11. 11 U.S.C. §546(c).

days before the bankruptcy filing, and if the seller makes written demand to reclaim the goods not later than 45 days after the debtor receives the goods or 20 days after the case is filed if the 45 days expires after commencement of the case. For example, the owner of an insolvent store buys $10,000 of inventory on Thursday and files a bankruptcy on the following Monday. If the creditor gives a written reclamation notice to the debtor within 45 days after delivery, the seller may be able to recover the goods despite the intervening bankruptcy filing. The Bankruptcy Court may deny the reclamation demand, but only if the court gives the seller an administrative claim.[12] These issues arise infrequently in consumer bankruptcy cases but are common at the beginning of many Chapter 11 proceedings.

Section 546(d) was added to the Bankruptcy Code in 1984 in reaction to a well-publicized matter that gave bankruptcy law some momentary notoriety. A grain elevator cooperative in Arkansas filed a bankruptcy. The farmers who had stored their grain in the grain elevator showed up with shotguns to reclaim their grain, and federal marshals were required to prevent the vigilante repossession. The Bankruptcy Court had held that the grain stored in the bankrupt grain elevator by the farmers was no longer their property but was property of the estate. The farmers were mere unsecured creditors.[13] Congress thought that this was an unfair predicament to put farmers in, so Section 546(d) was enacted to deal with the rights of farmers or fishermen who sell their products to a grain storage facility or fish-processing plant. Under Section 546(d), a farmer or fisherman is given the right to reclaim products from an insolvent grain storage facility or fish-processing plant if a written demand for reclamation is made within ten days after the product is delivered. The court may deny the reclamation request but must give the farmer or fisherman, like the seller of goods, an administrative claim or a lien on other assets of the estate.[14]

In stockbroker Chapter 7 proceedings, margin payments are normally not avoidable.[15] The Bankruptcy Reform Act of 1994 added a new Section 546(h) to the Code. This provision allows a trustee to return to a seller of goods any goods sold to the debtor prepetition, if such return is in the best interests of the estate. Warehouseman's liens are not avoidable by a trustee pursuant to 11 U.S.C. §546(i) enacted in 2005.

---

12. 11 U.S.C. §546(c)(2). As to administrative claims, see chapter 21 infra.
13. Missouri v. United States Bankr. Ct. for E.D. of Ark., 647 F.2d 768 (8th Cir. 1981).
14. 11 U.S.C. §546(d).
15. 11 U.S.C. §546(e), (f), (g).

D.   STATUTORY LIEN AVOIDANCE

Section 545 allows a trustee to avoid certain types of statutory liens. Recall that a **statutory lien** is a lien created by operation of law, not by court order (a judicial lien) or agreement (a consensual lien).[16] The first type of statutory lien that is avoidable is a lien that purports to become effective only upon the debtor's insolvency, the filing of a bankruptcy proceeding, or having a financial condition that fails to meet a defined standard.[17] Such statutes are the legislative equivalent of ipso facto clauses, which are disfavored by the Code.[18] The purpose of this provision is to prevent states from enacting liens that would give certain creditors priority only in the event of a debtor's bankruptcy filing.

Second, a statutory lien may be avoided if it cannot be enforced against a bona fide purchaser of the debtor's property at the commencement of the bankruptcy proceeding, whether or not such a purchaser exists except for a purchaser at a government tax lien sale.[19] For example, if a state mechanic's lien law requires recordation of the lien prior to the lien being deemed perfected, a lien recorded subsequent to a bankruptcy filing may be avoidable. Finally, statutory rent liens or liens for distress of rent are avoidable.[20]

Summary

The abilities given a trustee to avoid certain pre- or postfiling transactions that would otherwise be valid under nonbankruptcy law are known as the avoiding powers. Preferences, fraudulent transfers, and the ability to set aside unauthorized postpetition transfers are the most common avoiding powers.

The underlying purpose of the avoiding powers is often described as the orderly and consistent liquidation of a debtor's assets and their distribution to creditors. This philosophy is the foundation of the debt collection features of the bankruptcy system. The avoiding powers attempt to eliminate the effects of creditors racing to the courthouse to improve their position on the eve of a bankruptcy filing.

---

16. 11 U.S.C. §101(53). See chapter 6 supra.
17. 11 U.S.C. §545(1).
18. See chapter 14 supra.
19. 11 U.S.C. §545(2).
20. 11 U.S.C. §545(3), (4).

The initial avoiding power provides a trustee rights that make the trustee a "super-creditor" with priority to estate assets over the claims of most creditors. This permits the trustee to properly collect the assets for liquidation. This provision is known as the strong arm clause. Statutory liens, liens created by statute, will be avoidable in some situations, most notably where the lien comes into existence only if a debtor files a bankruptcy proceeding.

A trustee is given a period two years from the date of appointment to initiate an adversary proceeding to exercise an avoiding power.

Not all transactions or creditors will be subject to the avoiding powers. Limited creditors may be permitted to perfect liens in property for a limited period of time after a bankruptcy is filed. Limited unsecured creditors may also possess a right of reclamation, the right to repossess goods or crops.

KEY TERMS

avoiding power   strong arm clause
statutory lien

DISCUSSION QUESTIONS

1. What is the concept underlying the trustee's avoiding powers?

2. Why is a trustee considered a "super-creditor"?

3. When may a secured creditor perfect a claim after a bankruptcy filing?

4. How long does a trustee have to exercise the avoiding powers?

5. How are a trustee's avoiding powers exercised?

16

Avoidable Preferences — 11 U.S.C. §547

A. INTRODUCTION AND DEFINITIONS

The two most common of the trustee's avoiding powers are known as **preferences** and fraudulent transfers. Preferences permit a trustee to recover assets transferred to a creditor on the eve of the bankruptcy filing so that the assets may be distributed fairly to all creditors. The thrust of the preferential transfer provisions is to avoid payments or other prepetition transfers made to a creditor that increase the creditor's recovery at the expense of other similarly situated creditors. A secondary function of preference avoidability is to stop creditors from racing to the courthouse on the eve of bankruptcy to unfairly improve their chances of receiving payment.

A preference generally occurs when a debtor, on the eve of bankruptcy, transfers property or an interest in property to one or more creditors in full or partial satisfaction of their debt to the exclusion of all other creditors. The avoidable transfer may be voluntary or involuntary. Creditors receiving a preference have their claims wholly or partially satisfied while the remaining creditors receive nothing. Permitting a trustee to avoid these transactions and to recover property transferred for the estate so that it may be liquidated and the proceeds distributed fairly to all creditors is the goal of this avoiding power.

To illustrate, U.S. Grant owns an insolvent dry goods store. One month before filing a Chapter 7, Grant voluntarily pays in full the claims of creditors Sherman, Sheridan, and Meade. Creditors Lee, Jackson, and Longstreet receive no payments. Utilizing preference powers, Grant's Chapter 7 trustee, Lincoln, may recover the payments made to the first group of creditors so that equal dividends may ultimately be paid to all of Grant's creditors. If Lee, Jackson, and Longstreet obtain a writ of attachment, outflanking Grant with this involuntary transfer, Lincoln would also be able to avoid this transaction as a preference.

The concept of avoidable preferences does not exist outside of the bankruptcy system. When a consumer or business pays its debts in a non-bankruptcy environment, they may be paid in any order desired. For instance, in a month where cash flow is insufficient to pay all debts on a current basis, a consumer decides to postpone payment of the dentist's bill until next month. Other creditors have been "preferred" over the dentist. A debtor that is not bankrupt may normally "prefer" or pay creditors in any order desired.

Culpability or the intent of the entity receiving or giving the preference is not an issue in determining the avoidability of a preference. The only concern is the overriding philosophy of the bankruptcy system that all creditors with the same distributive priority under the Bankruptcy Code should be treated equally in the receipt of dividends. Intent or culpability is irrelevant to this consideration.

Keep in mind that the avoiding powers are also possessed by a Chapter 11 debtor-in-possession.[1] So even though a debtor-in-possession may in fact be the very entity that committed the preference in the first place, the debtor-in-possession still has an opportunity to avoid the preference for the benefit of all creditors. Section 547 of the Bankruptcy Code regulates the avoidance of preferences. The most practical way to attempt an understanding of this Section and its various subdivisions is to conceive of an avoidable preference as a cause of action or claim upon which relief may be granted. In this sense, the determination of the existence of or defenses to an avoidable preference can most easily be described in the format of a traditional lawsuit. That is, to successfully avoid a preference, there are various elements that the trustee must prove. Similarly, the party or parties against whom a preference is sought to be avoided may raise issues that in traditional litigation would be considered affirmative defenses. Actions to avoid preferences are always commenced as adversary proceedings when the trustee seeks affirmative relief.[2] The trustee is the plaintiff; the party or parties who received the preference are the defendants.

Section 547 is one of the few Bankruptcy Code sections containing definitions that are unique to it. These definitions are contained in Section

---

1. 11 U.S.C. §1107. See chapter 10 supra.
2. Bankruptcy Rule 7001.

547(a). The first of these is **inventory**: any form of personal property that a debtor uses to produce revenue. Thus, inventory for preference purposes may be raw material, finished product, merchandise on shelves, or cars available for rental.[3]

The second unique definition that is relevant primarily in business bankruptcy proceedings, and the most critical, is **new value**. *New value*, in simple and practical terms, means new consideration for the debt. **Consideration** is normally the element of exchange in any contract. New value is not created when a new obligation is substituted for an existing obligation.[4] A preference may arise by the payment of money, a transfer of property, or the granting of a security interest in property of the debtor. For example, George owes Brad $10,000. George offers Brad a lien on his pearl-handled revolver to secure repayment of the debt. To the extent that Brad is not loaning more money to George in exchange for the lien, there is no new value. The lien on the revolver will be an avoidable preference. A preference is therefore any transaction that places one creditor in a preferred position over other otherwise similar creditors, such as an unsecured creditor's becoming secured on the eve of a bankruptcy filing. Much of the preference litigation taking place before the Bankruptcy Court does not usually involve a creditor that has been paid money but rather a creditor that has received a security interest in property on the eve of bankruptcy. The definition of *new value* helps in determining whether the granting of such a security interest is or is not a transfer that may be deemed an avoidable preference.

Receivable is a third unique definition in Section 547. A *receivable* is a right to payment, whether or not such right has been earned by performance.[5] A fourth and final definition is not a definition at all but a necessary rule that helps create a consistent national scheme regarding tax preferences, because the Internal Revenue Code and each individual state have their own independent definitions concerning when a tax debt is incurred. Section 547(a)(4) provides that a tax debt is incurred on the date it is last payable without penalty, including any extensions.[6] This means that for purposes of income taxes, for example, a tax debt is incurred on April 15 for a prior year's taxes.

---

3. 11 U.S.C. §547(a)(1).
4. 11 U.S.C. §547(a)(2).
5. 11 U.S.C. §547(a)(3).
6. 11 U.S.C. §547(a)(4).

B.   ELEMENTS OF A PREFERENCE

A trustee must prove six elements to successfully avoid a preference. Each element must be proven for the trustee to prevail. Failure to prove any element will result in a failure to avoid the preference. These six elements constitute the cause of action or claim for relief.

The first element is that there must be a "transfer of an interest of the debtor in property."[7] Any sort of **transfer** of a debtor's interest in an asset may be avoidable. Recall that the Code defines *transfer* as any method that human beings may devise to convey property or an interest in it.[8] This definition of *transfer* is intentionally broad. Thus, outright payment of cash or the transfer of a physical asset, such as real estate or personal property, to a creditor by a debtor will constitute a transfer. The grant or attempted granting of a security interest in real or personal property to a creditor by a debtor will also constitute a transfer.

Practice Pointer

The Code defines a "transfer" to mean: (1) the creation of a lien; (2) retention of title; (3) foreclosure of the debtor's equity of redemption; or (4) any mode, "direct or indirect, absolute or conditional, voluntary or involuntary, of disposing of or parting with property or an interest in property."

The second element of an avoidable preference is that the transfer be "to or for the benefit of a creditor."[9] The "to a creditor" portion is fairly simple: The money, property, or security interest is transferred directly to the creditor by the debtor.

A transfer is made "for the benefit of a creditor" if it is to a creditor of a creditor. In this instance, even though the original creditor has received no direct transfer, the transfer has still been made for that creditor's benefit. For example, Huey owes Louie, and Louie owes Dewey. Louie tells Huey that if Huey pays Dewey for Louie, then Huey will no longer owe Louie, and Louie will no longer owe Dewey. Huey's payment of Louie's

---

7. 11 U.S.C. §547(b).
8. 11 U.S.C. §101(54). See chapter 6 supra.
9. 11 U.S.C. §547(b)(1).

debt to Dewey is a transfer for the benefit of a creditor, namely Louie. Huey's financial books may not show that the payment to Dewey is for Louie, but Louie's claim against Huey has still been satisfied.

The third element is that the transfer be "for or on account of an antecedent debt owed by the debtor before the transfer was made."[10] **Antecedent debt** means that the debt was incurred or existed before the transfer was made. The most common form of antecedent debt is a past-due bill. In the George and Brad example, supra, the $10,000 debt due Brad is an antecedent debt when the lien is offered by George.

 Practice Pointer

To qualify as an antecedent debt, there must be some delay between when the debt arises and when payment is made. In other words, the debt must have been incurred prior to the alleged preferential transfer, although it need not have been past due.

The fourth element of an avoidable preference is that the transfer be made "while the debtor was insolvent."[11] As noted earlier in this chapter, if the debtor is not insolvent, the order of debt repayment is of no concern to anyone. A debtor is generally **insolvent** when the debtor's liabilities exceed the debtor's assets.[12]

The fifth element is time. One of two time periods is considered in determining the existence of an avoidable preference. The first of these is the period 90 days prior to filing of a bankruptcy. An otherwise preferential transfer occurring before this time period will not constitute an avoidable preference.[13] However, when insiders are the subject of a preference action, the relevant time period is extended to one year prior to the filing of the bankruptcy petition.[14] For example, Elle Woods owes $10,000 to a grandparent for money loaned to attend law school. The grandparent is repaid from Woods's first paycheck. Woods files a bankruptcy proceeding six months later. The payment will be an avoidable preference since it was made to an insider within one year prior to filing of the petition.

---

10. 11 U.S.C. §547(b)(2).
11. 11 U.S.C. §547(b)(3).
12. 11 U.S.C. §101(32). See chapter 6 supra.
13. 11 U.S.C. §547(b)(4)(A).
14. 11 U.S.C. §547(b)(4)(B).

The sixth and final element of an avoidable preference is that the creditor must "receive more than such creditor would receive" in a Chapter 7 if the transfer had not been made.[15] Simply put, the transfer must result in the creditor having a greater percentage of its debt repaid by the transfer than the creditor would have received through a Chapter 7 dividend if the transfer had not been made. For example, a creditor receiving payment in full, when a Chapter 7 dividend would have only paid 50 percent, has received a preference payment equal to 50 percent of the debt. Similarly, a creditor that improves its position from unsecured to secured by the transfer of a security interest in property receives more than it would otherwise receive as a Chapter 7 dividend because it receives the collateral rather than a speculative right to a portion of the proceeds from a sale of the collateral.

Carefully focusing on the final element of an avoidable preference may aid in facilitating the settlement of preference disputes. In any situation where the parties can reasonably estimate the potential dividend to an affected class of creditor in a Chapter 7 proceeding, it is necessary only to calculate any excess received by the creditor and to then have the creditor return this excess to the estate and waive any further claim against the estate. The creditor will have received its dividend while the remaining creditors will have had their "fair share" returned at a minimum of expense in attorneys' fees or litigation expenses, not to mention a substantial savings in time. All this will further increase the total ultimate return to the estate's creditors, of whom the creditor receiving the preference is one.

The trustee bears the initial burden of proving the existence of each element in order for the preference to be avoided. If one element remains unproven, a preference may exist, but it will not be an avoidable preference.[16]

Under Section 547(f) a debtor is presumed insolvent during the 90 days immediately prior to the filing of the bankruptcy petition.[17] This means that the trustee does not have to affirmatively prove the debtor's insolvency when the preferential transfer occurs within 90 days prior to a bankruptcy filing. In this instance, the entity against whom the claim is brought will bear the burden of proving that the debtor was solvent during the 90-day period. As a corollary, this also means that if the subject of the avoidable preference is an insider transaction occurring more than 90 days prior to filing but within one year of the bankruptcy filing, the trustee will now have the burden of proving the debtor's insolvency during the period of time more than 90 days prior to the bankruptcy filing.

---

15. 11 U.S.C. §547(b)(5).
16. 11 U.S.C. §547(g).
17. 11 U.S.C. §547(f).

In the most common preference cases, many of the elements are generally not difficult to prove. For instance, payment of a long-overdue loan owed to a relative or payment of a long-overdue bank loan is easily identified as a transfer to a creditor on account of an antecedent debt. If the payment was made within 90 days of filing, the debtor is presumed insolvent. Because most proceedings have no assets, most avoidable preferences should generally be fully recoverable. Documents evidencing the debt, the transfer, and the transfer's timing should generally be sufficient to prove all the basic elements of an avoidable preference.

The final element of a preference, that the creditor has received more than the creditor would otherwise receive in a Chapter 7 proceeding, is also often easy to prove, as noted above. Full analysis of the ultimate effect on the creditor body can result in settlement of many preference claims asserted by a trustee. This usually requires some educated guesswork but is not overly difficult. Because the most common proceeding is a no asset Chapter 7, any creditor receiving a preference is receiving more than it otherwise would in a Chapter 7 proceeding. If a creditor owed $1,000 receives a preference of $1,000, does the creditor receive more than it otherwise would in the Chapter 7? Obviously, yes. But, the more difficult question is, how much more? For example, assume that the creditor receiving $1,000 is one of ten creditors. Assume also that the aggregate total of debts is $10,000. If $1,000 is available to distribute to creditors, the amount of dividend that each of these creditors will receive is 10 percent, because 1,000 is 10 percent of 10,000. The creditor in the example therefore received $900 more than it would in the Chapter 7. Thus, $900 is the actual amount of the avoidable preference. The creditor should be permitted to settle the dispute by returning $900 to the estate and waiving further claims against the estate.

In a large proceeding, these calculations can become complex and uncertain. Nevertheless, agreement as to an estimated amount of dividend often may lead to swift and economical settlement of avoidable preference disputes. This approach is more practical than incurring significant attorneys' fees in avoiding the preference, because the fees act to erode the ultimate dividend payable to all creditors. The suggested approach should result in greater overall distributions to the creditor body, primarily due to the reduced attorneys' fee burden.

C. AFFIRMATIVE DEFENSES

The elements of an avoidable preference thus constitute a cause of action or claim upon which relief may be granted that is unique to a bankruptcy proceeding. To complement the cause of action or claim, there also exists the functional equivalent of affirmative defenses to an avoidable preference claim. These "affirmative defenses" are described in Section 547(c) and (i) and can be easily grasped if conceived of as affirmative defenses to the avoidable preference claim. Most of these defenses exist to legitimize transactions occurring in the normal course of business, transactions that the fortuity of a bankruptcy filing should not invalidate.

The first affirmative defense is that the transfer is intended to be a **contemporaneous transfer for new value** and is in fact a substantially contemporaneous exchange.[18] That is, if there is new consideration present from both parties, the transfer will not be an avoidable preference. For example, in the usual preference transaction, a debtor in default to a creditor pays the creditor all or a portion of the debt due. The creditor does not give the debtor any new consideration in return for the payment. Recall the example earlier in this chapter of the debt owed by George to Brad. There is no new value between the parties in the example, and the payment therefore is an avoidable preference. New value generally involves an exchange of present or new consideration between the debtor and creditor. For instance, when Opie Taylor goes to the Ziffle Finance Company to refinance an existing loan and borrows an additional $500, the $500 is new value. It was not owed or previously loaned to Opie. Conversely, the preexisting loan amount would be an antecedent debt.

Practice Pointer

Some courts view "contemporaneous" as occurring within ten days of each other, while other courts look at the question on a case-by-case basis.

Substantially contemporaneous generally means an exchange taking place in the normal course of business. If a transfer is perfected within any nonbankruptcy grace periods, as described in chapter 14 supra, the transfer will normally be considered substantially contemporaneous. For example, if the bank loans a debtor money to purchase a new car but the bank fails to perfect its lien in the vehicle for one week, the transaction will still be considered substantially contemporaneous because the lien date will likely fall within any applicable nonbankruptcy grace period. The

---

18. 11 U.S.C. §547(c)(1).

reason for this flexibility is that if such a rule did not exist, it would be possible for trustees or debtors to avoid recently obtained valid liens on a debtor's assets by successfully claiming that the security interest is a preference. If this were the case, the credit industry would be in chaos and the availability of credit in American society would be reduced significantly. The statute therefore tries to reconcile this necessary fact of economic existence with the orderly distribution of assets to all creditors in the event of financial failure.

The second affirmative defense to a preference action involves an ordinary business practice, the payment of accounts payable on a regular basis. Some businesses pay them once every 30 days, or once every 40 days, or perhaps only once every 90 days, but they pay them on a regular basis. Consumers who regularly make monthly payments to their creditors are making payments in the ordinary course of business. If a creditor can show that the debt was incurred and paid in the ordinary course of the debtor's and creditor's financial affairs or according to ordinary business terms, then the transfer will not constitute an avoidable preference.[19] This provision attempts to accept the reality of the marketplace and does not attempt to alter it due to the happenstance of a bankruptcy filing.

A difficult situation arises when a debtor makes a customary monthly payment on a long-term unsecured obligation, such as the outstanding balance owed on a line of credit or unsecured promissory note obligation. Does the antecedent nature of the debt render payments made within any applicable preference period avoidable, or, because the payments are made in the ordinary course of business, are they defensible? The Supreme Court faced this issue in Union Bank v. Wolas, 502 U.S. 151 (1991).

On December 17, 1986, the debtor ZZZZ Best Co., Inc., borrowed $7 million from Union Bank. On July 8, 1987, the debtor filed a Chapter 7 petition. In the 90 days preceding the bankruptcy, the debtor paid Union Bank $100,000 in interest payments and a $2,500 loan commitment fee. The Bankruptcy Court and district courts found for the bank creditor. The Ninth Circuit reversed. Because of a conflicting ruling from the Sixth Circuit, the Supreme Court granted certiorari to review the matter.[20]

The Supreme Court held that a payment in the ordinary course will qualify for the preference exception irrespective of whether the underlying nature of the debt is long-term or short-term. Thus, the payments to the bank fell within the ordinary course of business exception.

---

19. 11 U.S.C. §547(c)(2).
20. The conflicting Sixth Circuit ruling was In re Finn, 909 F.2d 968 (1990).

The third affirmative defense to an avoidable preference is that, so long as the security interest secures new value, perfection of a security interest within 30 days of a debtor acquiring the property will not be an avoidable preference.[21] For example, Alfred Newman borrows $10,000 from the Last National Bank and gives the bank a security interest in an obsolete stereo system. If the bank perfects its security interest within 30 days, the perfection will not constitute an avoidable preference. Recall that even if Newman files a bankruptcy proceeding within the 30-day period, under Section 546 the bank might still be able to perfect its interest within the 30-day period.[22]

Practice Pointer

Perfection of the security interest in this context is governed by federal bankruptcy law and not by the individual state laws.

The fourth affirmative defense will normally arise only in proceedings involving business debtors. Essentially, a transfer will not be avoidable as a preference if, after the transfer, the creditor gives new value to the debtor that is unsecured.[23] For example, a payment in advance will not be an avoidable preference.

The fifth affirmative defense concerns a business financing arrangement commonly known as a **floating lien**. A floating lien is generally a line of credit from a bank or other financial institution secured by the inventory, equipment, or proceeds of the debtor's business. In the normal course of business, a debtor constantly sells existing inventory and replaces it with more inventory. Because the security interest attaches to the new inventory that the debtor purchases in place of the sold merchandise, the lien is said to "float." The test of this defense to avoidable preferences is identical to the test described in Section 553 involving set-offs.[24] This test is commonly referred to as the "improvement of position" test. Generally, a floating lien will not constitute a preference to the extent that the creditor does not "improve its position" in the 90 days prior to a

---

21. 11 U.S.C. §547(c)(3).
22. 11 U.S.C. §546(b). See chapter 15 supra. Recall also that the bank may perfect its interest within any applicable postfiling period as an exception to the automatic stay. 11 U.S.C. §362(b)(3). See chapter 12 supra.
23. 11 U.S.C. §547(c)(4).
24. See chapter 20 infra.

bankruptcy filing.[25] To determine whether a creditor has improved its position, the amount of the debt and the value of the collateral as of a date 90 days prior to the bankruptcy filing are compared with the amount of the debt and the value of the collateral on the date of the bankruptcy filing. To the extent that the creditor improves its secured position during the 90-day period, the improvement will be an avoidable preference, but maintenance of the creditor's position at the level held 90 days prior to the bankruptcy filing will not be.

For example, 90 days prior to filing a Chapter 11, Total Roto, Inc., owes the Bank of Plunger $200,000 secured by $100,000 in collateral. At this time, $100,000 of the debt is unsecured. On the date of filing, the debt has been decreased to $100,000 and remains secured by $100,000 of collateral. There is no longer an unsecured portion of the debt. The $100,000 in payments will be considered a preference because they have reduced the amount by which the debt exceeded the value of the security interest from $100,000 to zero. Stated another way, payments made to an undercollateralized secured creditor within 90 days of a bankruptcy filing (one year if the creditor is an insider) are preferential to the extent that the unsecured portion of the debt is decreased. The reduction of the unsecured portion of a secured claim is the portion of the debt measured. In the example, this decrease is $100,000. On the other hand, if payments of $100,000 are made during the preference period but the amount of debt and value of the collateral remain respectively at $200,000 and $100,000 on the date of filing, then the $100,000 in payments would not constitute an avoidable preference because the unsecured portion of the debt has not been reduced.

The example may be illustrated by the following diagram and formula:

	d	si	(d – si)	
1. 90 days prior*	$200,000	$100,000	$100,000	or $(d_1 - si_1)$
2. filing date	$100,000	$100,000	-0-	$> (d_2 - si_2)$

d = amount of debt; si = value at collateral; $(d - si)$ = unsecured portion of claim

* One year if insider.

To the extent that the unsecured portion of the debt is greater on the earlier date than on the later date, the difference will constitute an

---

25. 11 U.S.C. §547(c)(5).

avoidable preference. To the extent there is no change or an increase in the undersecured portion of the debt, there is no avoidable preference. In the example, the creditor has eliminated all of its unsecured debt during the preference period: The entire amount may be preferential. The same statement can be stated mathematically: If $(d_1 - si_1) > (d_2 - si_2)$, then the difference is an improvement in position and thus preferential. The first sum is a computation as of the commencement of the preference period, 90 days or one year prior to the filing, respectively. The second sum is computed as of the filing date.

This formula can be described in a third and perhaps even simpler way: A secured creditor is only considered secured up to the value of its collateral.[26] Any additional amount due the creditor is considered an unsecured debt. Thus, determine the amount of the unsecured debt due the creditor at the beginning of the preference period and compare it to the amount of the unsecured debt due the creditor on the filing. To the extent that the amount of the unsecured debt has decreased, the decrease may be an avoidable preference. On the other hand, unfortunately for the creditor, to the extent that the amount of unsecured debt increases, the creditor bears the consequences.

The fixing of a statutory lien that the trustee cannot avoid under Section 545 is also not avoidable as a preference.[27] In this context, the term "fixing" is not defined. A distinction should be drawn between a statutory lien already fixed or established and one in which the alleged transfer sets the statutory lien.[28]

Transfers made in the payment of domestic support obligations are also not avoidable as preferences.[29]

One affirmative defense to an avoidable preference applies only to consumer debtors. An individual consumer debtor may make aggregate transfers of less than $600 and the transfers will not constitute avoidable preferences.[30] This defense reflects a common occurrence in consumer situations. A potential no asset consumer debtor may have two or three creditors whom the debtor really wants to pay and not include as creditors in the bankruptcy filing. The creditors might be a credit card or medical bill, a phone bill, or perhaps a gas and electric bill. Without this defense to the trustee's avoidable preference powers, payment of all of these small debts would be avoidable. However, because an individual consumer debtor is permitted to make preferences of less than $600 in aggregate,

26. See chapter 21 infra. 11 U.S.C. §506.
27. 11 U.S.C. §547(c)(6). See also chapter 15 supra.
28. See In re Ramba, Inc., 416 F.3d 394 (5th Cir. 2005).
29. 11 U.S.C. §547(c)(7).
30. 11 U.S.C. §547(c)(8).

a consumer debtor may pay small debts that they prefer to not include in the bankruptcy filing. The only limitation is that the grand total not exceed $600.

BAPCPA added a final affirmative defense available in business bankruptcies in which the value of the transfer is less than $5,850. As a practical matter, this will eliminate many transactions that would otherwise be avoidable preferences.[31]

D. MISCELLANEOUS PROVISIONS

Section 547(d) permits a trustee to avoid a transfer to a surety furnishing a bond to dissolve a judicial lien if the underlying lien is also avoidable by the trustee.[32] For example, Snidely Whiplash attaches Nell's assets by a court order. Nell obtains a bond, giving the bond company a lien on her home to release the attachment. In Nell's subsequent Chapter 7 filing, the trustee may avoid the bonding company's lien if Snidely's judicial lien can also be avoided.

Section 547(e) clarifies the timing of when a transfer occurs for purposes of determining whether the transfer is an avoidable preference. A transfer of real property is completed when the trust deed or grant deed or other deed is recorded or when the transferee acquires an interest in property that is superior to that of a bona fide purchaser.[33] Similarly, the transfer of an interest in personal property is considered perfected when the creditor files its UCC documents, or when the creditor cannot acquire a judicial lien superior to the rights of the transferee.[34] In Barnhill v. Johnson, 503 U.S. 393 (1992), the Supreme Court ruled that a transfer by check is not complete until the check has cleared the payor's bank. In this case, the debtor delivered a check to Barnhill on November 18. The check was dated November 19 and was honored by the bank on November 20. After the debtor filed Chapter 11, it was agreed that November 20 was the ninetieth day prior to the bankruptcy filing.

In holding that the check's date of honor by the debtor's bank is the relevant date of transfer, the Supreme Court reasoned that because under

---

31. 11 U.S.C. §547(c)(9). The amount reflects the 2010 adjustments required by Section 104. See chapter 3 supra.
32. 11 U.S.C. §547(d).
33. 11 U.S.C. §547(e)(1)(A).
34. 11 U.S.C. §547(e)(1)(B).

the Uniform Commercial Code the debtor could dishonor the check until it cleared, the debtor therefore retained rights in the funds and that the transfer was not complete within the meaning of 11 U.S.C. §547(e)(1)(B).

This decision may lead to some uncertainty in practice on the part of creditors because the date that a check is honored by debtor's bank will generally be known only to the debtor because this date will appear only on the canceled check. This information will not be readily available to a creditor unless the debtor discloses it.

A second portion of Section 547(e) makes it unequivocal that creditors have at least 30 days to perfect security interests before a transfer will be considered a preference. Thus, a creditor will usually have at least 30 days to perfect a security interest, even if a bankruptcy intervenes during the 30-day period.[35]

Section 547(g) allocates the burden of proof in preference actions. The trustee bears the burden of proving the elements of an avoidable preference as itemized by Section 547(b). Conversely, the creditor or other defendant has the burden of proof regarding any of the defenses provided for in Section 547(c).[36] This rule is consistent with the prior observation that the elements of a preference constitute a traditional cause of action or claim peculiar to the bankruptcy system, while the defenses are the equivalent of affirmative defenses available to defendants in traditional nonbankruptcy litigation.

Section 547(h), added by BAPCPA, exempts from preference liability any payments made to creditors pursuant to a repayment plan created for an individual debtor by a prepetition repayment plan. This provision encourages composition agreements in individual cases. See chapter 2 supra. Section 547(i), also added by BAPCPA, creates the equivalent of another affirmative defense in preference actions. This provision provides that when the trustee can avoid a security interest preference because the transfer benefited an insider, the trustee may only recover against the insider to the extent that the transfer took place between 90 days and one year prior to the bankruptcy. For example, DePrizio guarantees the debt of DePrizio, Inc. Six months prior to filing bankruptcy, DePrizio, Inc., gives creditor Crystal a security interest in business assets to secure repayment of an overdue loan. After DePrizio, Inc., files bankruptcy, its trustee may avoid the preference only as to De Prizio, but not as to Crystal.

---

35. 11 U.S.C. §547(e)(2). See chapters 12 and 15 supra.
36. 11 U.S.C. §547(g).

Summary

A transfer of property or an interest in property to a creditor, on the eve of bankruptcy, in full or partial satisfaction of debt to the exclusion of other creditors, is a preference. A preference meeting the elements of Code Section 547 will be avoidable by a trustee. When a preference is avoided, a trustee will recover the property transferred so that it may be liquidated and the proceeds distributed fairly to all creditors. An avoidable preference is determined by the trustee initiating an adversary proceeding.

A trustee must prove six elements to prove the existence of an avoidable preference. The defendant in the adversary proceeding may be able to show the existence of one or more of several available defenses to defeat the trustee's preference claim. The elements of the claim and the potential defenses are summarized in the checklist below.

KEY TERMS

antecedent debt
consideration
**contemporaneous transfer
    for new value**
floating lien
insolvent
inventory

new value
preferences
receivable
**substantially
    contemporaneous
transfer**

CHAPTER 16 CHECKLIST

16.1   ELEMENTS OF A PREFERENCE   *Authority*
        (ALL MUST BE PROVEN)

    16.1.1   Transfer of Property or an Interest   11 U.S.C. §547(b)
                  in Property

    16.1.2   To or for the Benefit of a Creditor   11 U.S.C. §547(b)(1)

    16.1.3   On or for Account of an   11 U.S.C. §547(b)(2)
                  Antecedent or Preexisting Debt

    16.1.4   Made While the Debtor Is   11 U.S.C. §547(b)(3)
                  Insolvent

16.3 PLAINTIFF/TRUSTEE PLEADINGS

    16.3.1 Summons and Complaint

    16.3.2 Cover Sheet, as Required by Local Rule

    16.3.3 Evidence Proving Preference
        1. Checks
        2. Contracts
        3. Recorded documents
        4. Documents of title

16.4 COMMON SUBSTANTIVE CLAIM OBJECTIONS

    16.4.1 Answer

    16.4.2 Evidence Proving Defense
        1. Checks
        2. Contracts
        3. Recorded documents
        4. Documents of title

DISCUSSION QUESTIONS

1. What is the concept underlying avoidable preferences in the bankruptcy system?

2. What are the elements of an avoidable preference?

3. What affirmative defenses exist to defeat an otherwise avoidable preference?

4. What presumption exists to assist a trustee in proving the existence of an avoidable preference?

5. When is a transfer considered complete for purposes of an avoidable preference?

PRACTICE EXERCISE

Exercise 16.1

The trustee has learned that one month prior to the bankruptcy filing, Bretony Bottomline repaid a $3,000 personal loan from her sister, Jenny Spares. Prepare a draft adversary complaint on behalf of the trustee to recover this money from Jenny for the bankruptcy estate.

17

Fraudulent and Postpetition Transfers

A.   FRAUDULENT TRANSFERS

Section 548 permits a trustee to avoid a **fraudulent transfer**. In addition, many states have adopted the Uniform Fraudulent Transfer Act. This Act creates independent rights, under state law, for creditors to attempt to set aside fraudulent transfers.[1] The concept of fraudulent transfers is relatively simple. Generally, fraudulent transfers are transfers made by a debtor with actual intent to hinder, delay, or defraud creditors. A transfer without reasonable or fair consideration may also be a fraudulent transfer. The most common example of a fraudulent transfer is when a debtor transfers $10,000 to a close friend or relative to "hold on to this for me until things get a little better." The debtor then files bankruptcy expecting to "reclaim" the asset transferred when the bankruptcy is over. Similarly, when the debtor conveys a quitclaim deed to a relative for the same reason, it is also a fraudulent transfer. In each instance the critical action is that the debtor has attempted to conceal property from the creditors. These sorts of transactions have traditionally been disfavored in the law. The earliest forms of "insolvency" debt collection laws and those prevalent in the Middle Ages involved the avoidance of fraudulent transfers described in chapter 1 supra.

There are two basic ways in which a fraudulent transfer may be proven under the Bankruptcy Code. The first is to prove that the transfer was

---

1. Uniform Fraudulent Transfer Act, U.L.A. §7 (West Supp. 2007).

made with an actual intent to hinder, delay, or defraud creditors.[2] Each of the above examples probably meets this standard.

The second way to prove the existence of a fraudulent transfer is to show that the transfer has been made for less than a reasonably equivalent value in exchange and that the debtor was insolvent either prior to or as a result of the transfer.[3] For instance, if Dr. Smith sells Will Robinson a robot for $10 when the robot has been appraised for $1 million, the transfer is likely to be deemed transferred for less than a reasonably equivalent value in exchange. If a debtor transfers a boat to the debtor's best friend for $500 when the boat is worth $30,000, this transfer is likely to be deemed for less than a reasonably equivalent value in exchange. However, the "less than reasonably equivalent exchange" standard should not be interpreted necessarily to imply that the consideration should or must be at the fair market value of the asset that is subject to transfer. For example, a liquidation sale may be a "reasonably equivalent exchange."[4]

In BFP v. RTC, 511 U.S. 531 (1994), BFP contended that the price obtained at a regularly conducted foreclosure sale constituted a fraudulent transfer because the property was sold at the foreclosure sale for $433,000, whereas the alleged fair market value of the property was $725,000 at the time of foreclosure. In holding that the price obtained in a noncollusive real estate mortgage foreclosure sale, held in compliance with applicable state law, does not constitute a fraudulent transfer, Justice Scalia wrote that: ". . . the only legitimate evidence of the property's value at the time it is sold is the foreclosure sale price itself."

In addition to the transfer being for less than a reasonably equivalent value in exchange, either the transfer must have been made while the debtor is insolvent or as a result of the transfer the debtor must have been rendered insolvent or undercapitalized (without sufficient remaining assets to conduct ordinary business).[5] Thus, a transfer for less than a reasonably equivalent exchange made while a debtor is solvent or that does not render the debtor insolvent will not be considered fraudulent. A solvent multi-millionaire may transfer assets to charity on a regular basis without fear of reprisal from creditors. On the other hand, if the multi-millionaire is rendered insolvent as a result of the charitable giving, the gift becomes an avoidable fraudulent transfer. BAPCPA modified Section 548(a) to expressly render transfers made to insiders under employment contracts and not in the ordinary course of business to be fraudulent

---

2. 11 U.S.C. §548(a)(1)(A).
3. 11 U.S.C. §548(a)(1)(B).
4. In re BFP, 974 F.2d 1144 (9th Cir. 1992); *affirmed*, BFP v. RTC 511 U.S. 531 (1994).
5. 11 U.S.C. §548(a)(1)(B)(ii).

transfers where the debtor is insolvent or rendered insolvent as a result of the transfer, or if the purpose of the transfer is to hinder, delay, or defraud creditors. The purpose of this provision is to eliminate large bonuses given to corporate executives shortly prior to the corporations they manage filing for bankruptcy relief. These practices became widely publicized in cases like Enron.

Section 548(a)(2) limits the recovery by a trustee of charitable contributions considered fraudulent transfers. A charitable contribution can be a fraudulent transfer because it is a gift and is therefore made without consideration. Section 548(a)(2) provides that charitable contributions of up to 15 percent of a debtor's gross annual income for the year in which the contribution is made, or whatever is consistent with the debtor's practices in making the contribution, shall not be avoidable by the trustee. For example, a debtor earns $40,000 per year. Payment of a church tithe by the debtor of up to $6,000, 15 percent of the debtor's income, will not be avoidable as a fraudulent transfer by the debtor's bankruptcy trustee.

Practice Pointer

This safe harbor provision is not applied on a transfer-by-transfer basis but rather on the aggregate annual contribution basis.

Section 548(b) concerns a special problem relating to partnership debtors. Any transfer of partnership property or an interest therein to a general partner within one year prior to a bankruptcy filing by the partnership is avoidable by a trustee if the transfer is made when the partnership is insolvent or if the partnership has been rendered insolvent as a result of the transfer.[6] The rationale behind this provision is that a general partner is an insider of the partnership. The general partner cannot "take the money and run."

Section 548(c) contains some protection for the transferee, the entity receiving the fraudulent transfer. If the transferee obtained the transferred property for value and in good faith and if the transfer is not avoidable as a preference or other avoiding power, then the transferee is granted a lien on the transfer to the extent of any value given by the transferee.[7]

---

6. 11 U.S.C. §548(b).
7. 11 U.S.C. §548(c).

For instance, a purchaser of real estate who has a purchase set aside as a fraudulent transfer obtains a lien upon the property to the extent of the purchase price paid as long as the purchase was in good faith and not avoidable under any other avoiding power of the trustee. Thus, if the transfer is also a preference, Section 548(c) will not apply.

A transfer is deemed complete for the purpose of determining the existence of a fraudulent transfer when the transfer is perfected so that a good-faith purchaser cannot acquire an interest in the property superior to that of the transferee.[8] That is, a transfer is complete when the deed is recorded or the transferee acquires rights to the property that would be superior to those of third parties under nonbankruptcy law.

The major difference between Bankruptcy Code Section 548 and nonbankruptcy fraudulent transfer law is that under nonbankruptcy law the statute of limitations is typically longer than that provided for by Section 548.

Recall that pursuant to Section 546(a) a trustee has only two years from the date of appointment to assert the claim. Further, Section 548 limits bankruptcy fraudulent transfers to those transfers occurring within two years prior to the bankruptcy filing.[9] Nonbankruptcy fraudulent transfer statutes under state law may provide longer time periods both for commencing the action and for determining what transfers are subject to challenge. Recall further that under Section 108 a trustee may have as long as two years added to a nonbankruptcy statute of limitations.[10] Thus, a trustee may seek to avoid as a fraudulent transfer under nonbankruptcy law a transfer that would not necessarily be avoidable under the Bankruptcy Code.

An action to avoid a fraudulent transfer is always initiated by filing an adversary complaint. When initiating such a complaint, it is always a recommended practice to allege the trustee's rights under both the Bankruptcy Code and any applicable nonbankruptcy law for the reasons described in the preceding paragraph.

B.   POSTPETITION TRANSFERS

The trustee's final avoiding power permits the avoidance of certain **postpetition transfers**. Transfers of estate property taking place after the

---

8. 11 U.S.C. §548(d)(1).
9. 11 U.S.C. §548(a).
10. See chapter 4 supra.

bankruptcy is filed may be avoidable by the trustee. For instance, in an involuntary proceeding, a debtor may transfer property of the estate before an order for relief is entered. Whether or not a subsequently appointed trustee may set aside this transfer is the subject matter of Section 549. Stated another way, a debtor files a bankruptcy and transfers property of the estate to a third party after the filing but before the trustee can acquire custody of the property. Or a Chapter 11 debtor pays prepetition debt postpetition without court approval. Although these various transactions may have been avoidable as fraudulent transfers or preferences had they occurred before the bankruptcy filing, when they occur after a filing they are avoidable as improper postpetition transactions.

A trustee may avoid any postpetition transaction that has not been authorized by the Bankruptcy Court or otherwise permitted by the Bankruptcy Code.[11] Section 549(a) acts to assist the trustee in performing the duty to liquidate the property of the estate. Many sales, uses, or leases of property of an estate require prior court approval.[12] A sale of property of the estate without obtaining prior court approval is avoidable.

Transactions, for present consideration, that take place during the gap period in an involuntary proceeding are not normally avoidable.[13] This is consistent with Section 303(f), which allows the alleged debtor in an involuntary proceeding to conduct business as usual prior to the entry of an order for relief unless the court orders otherwise.[14]

Under Section 549(c), a trustee cannot avoid a postpetition transfer of real property to a bona fide purchaser unless a copy of the petition has been filed in the place where the transfer of property may be perfected to complete the transaction.[15] This provides notice to all that the property is subject to the jurisdiction of the Bankruptcy Court. As long as the property remains property of the estate, it cannot be sold without court approval. This is similar to the concept of the lis pendens in nonbankruptcy proceedings affecting title to real estate. The effect of the recording is to prevent an unauthorized transfer of the real property.

A complaint to avoid a postpetition transaction may only be commenced within the earlier of two years after the transfer or the time the bankruptcy proceeding is closed or dismissed.[16] An action to avoid a postpetition transaction is always commenced as an adversary proceeding.

---

11. 11 U.S.C. §549(a). Postpetition transactions occurring in the normal course of business in a Chapter 11 proceeding will not necessarily require prior court approval. See chapter 18 infra.
12. See chapter 18 infra.
13. 11 U.S.C. §549(b).
14. 11 U.S.C. §303(f). See chapter 3 supra.
15. 11 U.S.C. §549(c).
16. 11 U.S.C. §549(d).

C.   LIABILITY OF TRANSFEREES

Section 550 concerns the liability of the transferee of an avoided transfer: what the recipient of the avoidable preference must return or pay to the estate, what the transferee of a fraudulent transfer must return or pay to the estate, or what the transferee of an improper postpetition transaction must return or pay to the estate. This Section also concerns any rights retained by the transferees of avoided transactions.

A trustee may recover from a transferee the property transferred or the value of the property transferred.[17] The recovery may be obtained not only from the actual transferee but from a transferee of the transferee who does not acquire the property in good faith.[18] Thus, in successfully avoiding a fraudulent transfer, the trustee may recover either the real estate or payment for it from the transferee or from a transferee of the transferee who has knowledge that the transaction is fraudulent. For example, if Jethro Clampett fraudulently transfers real estate to his Granny and she then transfers the property to Miss Hathaway, the trustee can recover the value of the property from Granny or may recover the property from Miss Hathaway if Miss Hathaway had knowledge that the transfer was fraudulent. On the other hand, if Miss Hathaway has acted in good faith, the trustee may not recover from her.

Similarly, if a trustee is avoiding a preference, the recovery is limited to the property transferred or the value of the property. Thus, if a security interest in property of the estate is successfully avoided, invalidating the security interest will be the trustee's recovery. If the successfully avoided preference is a cash payment or other outright transfer of property, the trustee is entitled to a recovery of the property to the extent the transfer exceeds the Chapter 7 dividend that the transferee would otherwise receive. For example, a creditor receiving full payment where the total dividend might be 50 percent will only have to return 50 percent of the property transferred.

Regardless of how many potential entities a trustee may be entitled to recover from in a successful avoidance action (such as a transferee and then a transferee of the transferee), the trustee is only entitled to one satisfaction.[19] Thus, in the first of the above examples, the trustee could recover either the value of the property from Granny or the property itself from Miss Hathaway, but not both.

---

17. 11 U.S.C. §550(a).
18. 11 U.S.C. §550(a)(2), (b).
19. 11 U.S.C. §550(d).

If a trustee recovers property from a good-faith transferee, then the good-faith transferee is given a right to reimbursement from the estate for any improvements made to the property. Improvements are considered to be physical additions to the property, or repair or maintenance costs expended in preserving the asset, or the cost of servicing any debt existing on the property. This right to reimbursement assumes the status of a lien upon the property.[20] This rule is equitable in nature. An estate should not receive a windfall in recovering property subject to a successful avoidance action. For instance, a debtor makes an unauthorized postpetition transfer of a motor home to a prepetition creditor in repayment of a prepetition debt. The creditor is unaware of the bankruptcy filing at the time of the transfer. While the creditor has possession of the motor home, the creditor makes payments on a loan secured by the motor home, replaces the tires, insures and maintains the vehicle. Then a trustee learns of the transfer and commences an avoiding action. Because the creditor was unaware of the bankruptcy filing and has therefore presumably acted in good faith, the creditor is entitled to reimbursement for the costs of maintaining the vehicle, the new tires, insurance payments, and any payments made on the underlying loan.

Section 551 preserves for the benefit of the estate any avoided transfer. That is, any right obtained by an estate from the avoidance of a transfer is a right of the estate, not of any other creditor.[21] The practical effect of this Section is that if, for example, a trustee avoids a second priority security interest in an asset, the estate becomes, in essence, the second priority holder of an interest in the asset. Any junior lienholders of the asset do not benefit from the avoidance by improving their position in the property. Their position is unaffected. Stated another way, the estate steps into the shoes of the transferee of an avoided transfer. This is similar to an insurance company's right of subrogation in tort law.

Section 552 concerns the postpetition effect of a security interest. The applicability of this Section will normally arise only in business Chapter 11 proceedings. Recall that the **floating lien** is a common financing arrangement of a retail or manufacturing business;[22] a financing entity has given the debtor a line of credit secured by all of the debtor's existing or after-acquired physical assets. This is why the lien is called a floating lien: because it "floats" upon the proceeds and products acquired by the debtor from the original collateral. If the debtor defaults upon a loan

---

20. 11 U.S.C. §550(e).
21. 11 U.S.C. §551.
22. See chapter 16 supra in connection with 11 U.S.C. §547(c)(5).

subject to a floating lien, the financing entity may repossess all the assets subject to the lien.

Under Section 552, any property that a debtor acquires after the filing of a bankruptcy proceeding is not subject to a prepetition lien resulting from a security agreement.[23] That is, after-acquired property is not generally subject to a prepetition consensual lien, except for floating liens. Floating liens do retain their hold on postpetition property, to the extent that the afteracquired property is traceable to the collateral subject to the lien, unless the court orders otherwise. A perfected security interest in the rents and revenues of a hotel, motel, or public facility therein also extends to the postpetition rents and revenues unless the court orders otherwise.[24] For example, Chat 'N Chew Restaurant files Chapter 11 owing its secured creditor bank $100,000. Among the bank's collateral are inventory and the cash generated from sale of the inventory. As long as Chat 'N Chew uses the cash subject to the bank's lien to purchase more inventory, the bank's lien will remain intact subject to Section 552(b). On the other hand, if Chat 'N Chew sequesters the proceeds received from the sale of the inventory and uses other cash to make new purchases, the bank's lien will not extend to this new inventory not purchased from the bank's cash collateral.[25]

Section 552 should not be construed to imply that a secured creditor loses its rights upon the filing by a debtor of a bankruptcy proceeding. Quite the contrary is true. Remember that a secured creditor is entitled to adequate protection of its security interest, and a secured creditor may seek relief from the automatic stay to enforce its rights as a secured creditor.[26] Other provisions restrict a debtor's right to utilize a secured creditor's cash collateral.[27] Section 552 concerns only the effect of a prepetition security agreement on property acquired by a debtor or the estate after filing, not the validity of the security agreement itself.

D.   SETOFFS

Section 553 concerns the treatment of setoffs under the Bankruptcy Code. A **setoff** is the common law right of a creditor to balance mutual debts with

---

23. 11 U.S.C. §552(a).
24. 11 U.S.C. §552(b).
25. As to a secured creditor's rights in cash collateral, see chapter 18 infra.
26. See chapter 12 supra.
27. See chapter 18 infra.

a debtor.[28] In bookkeeping terms setoffs are also known as reconciliations. To determine a setoff, simply subtract the smaller debt from the larger. Any balance remaining due either of the parties is still owed, but the remainder of the mutual debts has been set off. For example, Harold owes Kumar $10 and Kumar owes Harold $5. To set off these debts, the debt owed from Kumar to Harold is deemed satisfied ($5) and Harold now owes Kumar $5 instead of $10.

Section 553 permits the setoff of mutual prepetition debts.[29] Court approval is theoretically required because the automatic stay applies to the making of setoffs.[30] A creditor may not use a disallowed claim to make a setoff.[31] A creditor may not utilize as a setoff a claim assigned to it by another entity within 90 days of the bankruptcy filing.[32] Nor may a creditor utilize, for purposes of setoff, a debt owed to the debtor and incurred within 90 days prior to filing for the purpose of obtaining a setoff right.[33] As is the case with preferences, the debtor is presumed insolvent 90 days prior to the bankruptcy filing.[34] These provisions effectively preclude the obtaining of a preference by setoff.

Section 553(b) is a repetition of the improvement of position test described previously in connection with avoidable preferences.[35] Essentially, the trustee may recover from a creditor who has made a setoff within 90 days prior to the bankruptcy filing the amount of the setoff to the extent that the setoff constitutes an improvement of the creditor's position in relation to other creditors. Or, more plainly, the trustee may avoid a setoff to the extent that it constitutes an avoidable preference. In this context, the setoff is the equivalent of a transfer. To the extent the transfer creates a preference, the setoff is avoidable. Simply consider a creditor's ability to make a setoff as identical to having a security interest in one of the debtor's assets, namely the debt owed to the debtor by the creditor. In this context, the same formula described in chapter 16 supra can be applied with no actual change: $(d_1 - si_1) > (d_2 - si_2)$, where d is the debt due the creditor by the debtor and s is the debt due by the creditor to the debtor. The numerals 1 and 2 pertain respectively to the dates 90 days prior to the bankruptcy filing (1) and the filing date (2). To the extent that the sum on date 2 is less than the sum on date 1, the creditor cannot make the setoff. This difference is the extent of the "improved position." As a practical

---

28. See chapter 12 supra.
29. 11 U.S.C. §553(a).
30. 11 U.S.C. §362(a)(7). See chapter 12 supra.
31. 11 U.S.C. §553(a)(1). See chapter 21 infra.
32. 11 U.S.C. §553(a)(2).
33. 11 U.S.C. §553(a)(3).
34. 11 U.S.C. §553(c).
35. See chapter 16 supra.

matter, most creditors do not bring relief from stay motions to obtain permission to make setoffs. Most debtors and trustees do not seek sanctions against creditors for doing so. Setoff issues will most commonly arise by way of noticed motions. The issue may arise in connection with relief from stay motions or in the context of claims objections, to name but two instances.

Summary

A transfer made by a debtor with intent to hinder, delay, or defraud creditors is a fraudulent transfer. A transfer without fair or reasonable consideration made while a debtor is insolvent or that renders a debtor insolvent is also fraudulent. Transfers to corporate executives not in the ordinary course of business, such as the payment of large bonuses on the eve of bankruptcy, may also be avoidable as a fraudulent transfer.

Section 548 of the Bankruptcy Code permits a trustee to avoid fraudulent transfers occurring within two years prior to the bankruptcy filing. Nonbankruptcy or state law may also permit creditors to avoid fraudulent transfers. A trustee may also be able to utilize the state law of fraudulent transfers. This may permit a trustee to avoid fraudulent transfers occurring more than two years before the bankruptcy filing. An action to avoid a fraudulent transfer is commenced by filing an adversary proceeding.

A transfer of estate property after a bankruptcy filing that is made without court approval or is not otherwise authorized by the Bankruptcy Code is an unauthorized postpetition transaction that may be avoided by the trustee. Actions to avoid postpetition transactions are initiated by filing an adversary proceeding. Avoidable postpetition transactions are the subject of Bankruptcy Code Section 549.

Section 550 determines the liability of a transferee of an avoided transfer. Conversely, Section 550 also defines the recovery that each party may receive. Generally, the trustee is entitled to either a recovery of the property or the value of the property. A good-faith transferee will be allowed a claim for reimbursement from the estate for any improvements or repairs made to the asset or maintenance costs expended in preserving the asset. This claim will assume the status of a lien upon the property.

Section 551 provides a right of subrogation to a trustee successfully avoiding an avoidable transfer. That is, the trustee takes the place of the former transferee. This preserves the status of the transferred assets in relation to the rights of all other creditors.

Section 552 defines the postpetition effect of a security interest. Normally, a prepetition lien will not attach to property acquired by an estate after filing except for floating liens.

Section 553 retains for creditors the common law right of a creditor to set off mutual debts with a debtor. However, in certain defined circumstances, a setoff will be avoidable to the extent that it constitutes the equivalent of a preference. Properly, the making of a setoff by a creditor requires obtaining relief from the automatic stay. Setoff issues will normally arise within the context of a motion.

KEY TERMS

floating lien   postpetition transfer
fraudulent transfer   setoff

DISCUSSION QUESTIONS

1. What is a fraudulent transfer?

2. How is applicable state law concerning fraudulent transfers useful to a trustee seeking to set aside a fraudulent transfer?

3. What is an improper postpetition transfer?

4. What may a trustee recover in the successful exercise of an avoiding power?

5. What is a setoff?

PRACTICE EXERCISE

Exercise 17.1
Prepare a draft adversary complaint on behalf of the trustee to recover the Santa Cruz property from the Oddborns.

PART IV

Liquidation and Claims

18

Use, Sale, or Lease
of Property

A. LIQUIDATING ESTATE ASSETS

The next five chapters describe the basic concepts regarding the liquidation and distribution of estate assets or, in the case of reorganization proceedings, the preservation of assets for the benefit of creditors. The process of liquidation, allowance and classification of claims, and ultimate distribution of dividends to creditors is the core of the Code's debt collection features.

The first subject concerns the use, sale, or lease of property of the estate. Related to this subject are the issues of an estate incurring credit or exercising or terminating the benefits or burdens of a lease or franchise type agreement.[1] Preservation of an estate's cash after its physical assets have been liquidated and how property may be abandoned by a trustee complete the liquidation provisions of the Code.[2] Collectively, these matters comprise the methods by which the property of an estate is liquidated and cash preserved for the payment of dividends to creditors through the bankruptcy system.

Section 363 concerns the use, sale, or lease of estate property. The liquidation of any asset in a bankruptcy estate is subject to this section.

---

1. 11 U.S.C. §364; 11 U.S.C. §365. See chapters 19 and 20 infra.
2. See chapter 20 infra.

B.   GENERAL RULES

The basic rule is that a trustee may use, sell, or lease property of the estate, other than in the ordinary course of business, only after notice and a hearing.[3] This means that in a Chapter 7 liquidation, *any* use, sale, or lease of estate property will require notice and a hearing because a liquidation is *not* conducted in the ordinary course of business. On the other hand, in a Chapter 11, 12, or 13 proceeding, only transactions *not* in the ordinary course of business will require prior court approval.[4] Recall that the phrase "notice and a hearing" is specifically defined in Section 102.[5] Bankruptcy Rule 6004 sets forth the procedure used to obtain court approval for a sale of estate property. The rule requires at least 21 days' prior notice of the sale and notice of a hearing date if a party objects. Only if a party objects to the sale within five days of any deadline set forth in the notice does the matter then receive treatment as a noticed motion.[6] The rule is structured in this way so that a sale or auction can go forward with certainty in most cases. In actual practice, objections to sales are rare except in the largest cases. A sale may take place by private sale or public auction. A private sale is a sale to a single buyer at an agreed-upon price. A public auction may be conducted by either a professional auctioneer or in open court where, essentially, a private sale is held subject to overbid in a court-supervised bidding procedure.[7]

The phrase **ordinary course of business** generally means normal, everyday business transactions. If a trustee is authorized to conduct the business of the debtor or if the debtor is a debtor-in-possession, normal, everyday business transactions do not require prior court approval. Transactions that are not normal, everyday transactions do require prior court approval. A practical test is to determine if the assets to be sold are capital or not. A sale involving capital assets must always have prior court approval before proceeding. If the transaction does not involve the sale of a capital asset, prior court approval will probably not be required. A **capital asset** is one that is used to operate the business, such as equipment or fixtures. A **noncapital asset** is, for example, the inventory of an operating business.

---

3. 11 U.S.C. §363(b)(1). When the asset for sale is a customer list with private data, the trustee must comply with the privacy policy of the seller. The court will order the United States Trustee to appoint an ombudsman pursuant to 11 U.S.C. §332. The ombudsman's purpose is to ensure that the privacy policy is followed. See chapter 10 supra.
4. 11 U.S.C. §363(c)(1). See infra this chapter.
5. 11 U.S.C. §102(1). See chapter 4 supra.
6. Bankruptcy Rule 6004(a). A sale of property with a value of $2,500 or less requires objection within 15 days of notice, or the sale may proceed. Bankruptcy Rule 6004(d).
7. Bankruptcy Rule 6004(f)(1).

For instance, assume that the debtor-in-possession owns a restaurant. It is not necessary for the debtor to obtain a court order every time the debtor wants to buy supplies or inventory so the restaurant can operate. It is also unnecessary to obtain a court order before serving a meal to a customer. (It is doubtful that customers would be patient enough to wait for such an order.) However, if the debtor wants to sell the restaurant, court approval will be required; a sale of the restaurant is not in the ordinary course of the restaurant's business.

Conducting normal business operations also does not require prior court approval in a Chapter 11. In a Chapter 7, because the business is being liquidated, nothing that a trustee does is in the ordinary course of business. Any sale of assets that a Chapter 7 trustee undertakes requires prior notice to creditors.

Section 721 gives a Chapter 7 trustee the opportunity to operate a business for a limited time with court approval.[8] When such approval is obtained, the Chapter 7 trustee will be able to conduct normal business operations of the debtor for the order's duration.[9] A Chapter 7 trustee may seek such approval when it is in the best interests of creditors. For instance, if the debtor's primary asset is a bakery, keeping the facility open to sell all produced inventory at full value may be a good idea. If a sale of the business is pending when the Chapter 7 is filed, the buyer may want the business to continue operations prior to court approval of the sale. In these instances, the best interest of creditors will involve a prudent business judgment by the trustee — namely, taking the course of action that will provide the maximum value to the estate.

Normally, a Chapter 7 trustee will hold a public auction of an estate's assets. A trustee may seek ex parte approval to liquidate estate assets where the liquidation must be conducted immediately if the assets are to retain any value. For example, if the estate's primary asset is a restaurant and there is unused inventory, the trustee might obtain an ex parte order to sell the inventory without delay because a 20-day notice will only result in stale eggs, lettuce, tomatoes, and milk that are not likely to fetch a worthwhile price.

Practice Pointer

In the individual debtor context, common Section 363(b) sales include the sale or auction of personalty, the sale of automobiles, and even the sale of the debtor's personal residence.

---

8. 11 U.S.C. §721.
9. 11 U.S.C. §363(c)(1).

Section 363(c)(1) is the converse of Section 363(b)(1). If the debtor is authorized to operate a business, ordinary business operations may be conducted without prior court approval.[10] The difference between the two sections is that Section 363(b)(1) requires a trustee to give notice if property is being used, sold, or leased other than in the ordinary course of business, while Section 363(c)(1) affirmatively states that a trustee or debtor-in-possession does not need to obtain prior court approval to conduct ordinary business transactions of the estate. Section 363(c)(1) makes explicit what Section 363(b)(1) only implies.

The forms disk contains a number of sample forms used in conducting bankruptcy sales. Generally, any notice should contain enough description so a creditor or party in interest can determine whether to oppose the sale. Identification of the asset or assets being sold, the buyer, and the purchase price should be adequate in a private sale. The treatment to be afforded any claim secured by the property being sold should be disclosed. In the case of a public auction or sale subject to overbid in court, the notice should additionally disclose the location of the auction or sale and any requirements to qualify as a bidder.

C.   USE OF CASH COLLATERAL

Section 363(c)(2) restricts a trustee's use of a secured creditor's **cash collateral**. *Cash collateral* is defined, for purposes of this provision, as cash or cash equivalents in which an entity other than the estate may have an interest. Cash collateral also includes hotel or motel revenues.[11] For example, a secured creditor with a security interest in accounts receivable, the proceeds of sales, or a floating lien as described in chapter 17 supra, has a security interest in cash collateral. Cash collateral issues generally do not arise in a consumer bankruptcy case.

Section 363(c)(2) prohibits a debtor from using a creditor's cash collateral unless one of two conditions can be satisfied. The first condition that permits a debtor to use cash collateral is the secured creditor's consent.[12] This is the easiest way to proceed. If consent is not obtained, prior court approval is required by filing a motion.[13] To obtain court

---

10. 11 U.S.C. §363(c)(1).
11. 11 U.S.C. §363(a).
12. 11 U.S.C. §363(c)(2)(A).
13. 11 U.S.C. §363(c)(2)(B). Bankruptcy Rule 4001(b).

approval, a debtor or trustee will be required to provide adequate protection to any affected secured creditor.[14] In practice, this typically involves negotiations between the debtor and creditor that result in an agreed-upon cash collateral order.

Obtaining the use of cash collateral is a critical issue in the early stages of a Chapter 11 proceeding. If a secured creditor does not consent to the debtor's use of the cash collateral, it can become impossible to conduct business operations because a debtor is selling products and the secured creditor is receiving the proceeds, but the day-to-day expenses have no source of repayment. It becomes difficult to meet payroll and other basic expenses in this situation. As a result, the Code directs the court to give calendar priority to a motion to use cash collateral. The motion is to be scheduled "in accordance with the needs of the debtor" and the court is to act promptly on any request to use cash collateral.[15]

It is improper to use a secured creditor's cash collateral without the secured creditor's consent or prior court order. A secured creditor whose cash collateral is used without consent will obtain a first priority administrative claim upon the assets of the estate up to the amount of any improperly used cash collateral.[16] In Chapter 11 cases involving large corporations such as U.S. Air or K-Mart, consensual cash collateral orders generally containing these priority protections are typically approved by the court as a *first-day order*.

A motion to use cash collateral bears many similarities to a motion for relief from the automatic stay. Adequate protection for a creditor in these circumstances may require more than a monthly cash payment. A debtor may have to show the court that a creditor's equity in the collateral will not be impaired. This may very well require additional or replacement collateral. The court may also be required to make a preliminary determination as to the debtor's prospects of achieving a successful reorganization. Like a motion for relief from the automatic stay, there may also be both a preliminary and final hearing in connection with a motion to use cash collateral.[17]

A debtor-in-possession or trustee is required to keep cash collateral sequestered in a separate identified bank account.[18] This means that a debtor cannot commingle a creditor's cash collateral with other estate funds that are not cash collateral, unless the use of such funds has been

---

14. 11 U.S.C. §363(c)(3); 11 U.S.C. §363(e). See chapter 12 for a discussion of adequate protection.
15. 11 U.S.C. §363(c)(3); Bankruptcy Rule 4001(b).
16. 11 U.S.C. §507(b).
17. 11 U.S.C. §363(c)(3).
18. 11 U.S.C. §363(c)(4).

permitted. Presumably, the segregation requirement acts as a further form of adequate protection to a secured creditor.

D.   EFFECT OF THE AUTOMATIC STAY

Subsection 363(d) concerns the interaction between Section 363 and Section 362, the automatic stay. If the court has entered any order modifying or relieving the stay, then any sale, use, or lease of estate property has to be consistent with any order modifying or granting relief from the stay that has already been entered.[19] This means, in practical terms, that if the court grants a creditor relief from the automatic stay to foreclose upon estate property, any sale by the trustee must occur before the foreclosure sale unless the court orders otherwise. The property must also be sold in accordance with applicable nonbankruptcy law. For example, if there is a local law requirement that there be title insurance, then the requirement must be followed.

E.   SALES FREE AND CLEAR OF LIENS

While the above provisions pay careful heed to the rights of secured creditors, Section 363(f) acts to protect an estate's rights to sell estate property over the objection of a recalcitrant or hostile secured creditor. For example, Snidely Whiplash obtains a second deed of trust or mortgage on Nell's home as security for a loan. Nell defaults and then files a Chapter 7 proceeding to prevent the foreclosure sale.[20] Nell's trustee, Dudley Doright, obtains a buyer for the property that will pay all secured claims in full, Nell's homestead, and a dividend to unsecured creditors. Snidely plans to object because if he can foreclose and resell, he will receive a big profit for himself instead of Nell and her other creditors. Snidely would prefer to obtain relief from the automatic stay and foreclose. Preventing this tactic by a secured creditor is a major underlying premise of Section 363(f). Section 363(f) is a frequently litigated provision of Section 363. It allows a trustee to sell property free and clear of liens or interests.[21]

---

19. 11 U.S.C. §363(d).
20. See chapter 12 supra.
21. 11 U.S.C. §363(f).

The essence of this provision is that the bankruptcy court may order a sale of property over the objection and free of the interest of a recalcitrant or hostile secured creditor. Use of this procedure will be effective to pass clear title to the property over the objection of any lienholders. Use of this provision requires a noticed motion. A motion to sell property free and clear of liens must be brought as a noticed motion, not by way of the abbreviated notice procedures discussed earlier in this chapter.[22]

A property may be sold free and clear of liens or interests if one of five conditions described in the provision is satisfied as to each lienholder. Each condition is exclusive. Only one condition need be found applicable to each lien for the section to be effective, although compliance with more than one condition will often be possible.

First, the sale may occur if nonbankruptcy law will permit a sale of the property free and clear of the interests or liens.[23] For instance, a property may be sold free and clear of a trust deed or mortgage interest but not sold free and clear of a public utility easement or a government lien for real property taxes. Although nonbankruptcy law will permit a sale free of the interest in the first instance, nonbankruptcy law will not generally permit a sale free of the interest in the latter two instances.

Second, if an affected creditor consents to the sale, the property may be sold free of the consenting creditor's interest.[24] If an affected creditor agrees to allow an act that it might otherwise prohibit or object to, the Bankruptcy Code will normally recognize such consent. This is simply common sense. Undisputed secured creditors who are going to be paid in full from the sale's proceeds will normally consent.

Third, if the property is being sold for an amount greater than the value of all liens owed upon it, then the sale will be permitted.[25] For example, if a house is worth $100,000 while the bank is owed $50,000 and the Whiplash Finance Company another $15,000, a sale for $100,000 will be for more than the two creditors are owed and the sale will be permitted to take place over the objection of either creditor. Because the two creditors will receive what they are entitled to — namely, payment in full of their claims — they will not be permitted to prevent the sale. It is this specific provision that most frequently prevents a recalcitrant or hostile lien creditor from wrongfully preventing liquidation of estate property. The creditor is paid its claim from the sale proceeds. In the event of a dispute, the lien will attach to the proceeds, and their distribution will

---

22. Bankruptcy Rule 6004(c). See also chapter 4 supra.
23. 11 U.S.C. §363(f)(1).
24. 11 U.S.C. §363(f)(2).
25. 11 U.S.C. §363(f)(3).

occur only upon further court order. Permitting the lien to attach to the proceeds is a form of adequate protection for the affected lienholder.[26]

Fourth, the sale will be permitted if the interest is in bona fide dispute.[27] This is unrelated to the issue of whether the property is being sold for more than the amount of the liens upon it. In this instance, the sale price might even be for less than the amount of the liens upon the property. For example, property encumbered by $65,000 of liens is being sold for $60,000. However, the trustee asserts that one lien is a preference, and the court believes that this assertion may be meritorious. Because the creditor's interest is in bona fide dispute, the sale may be permitted to take place free of the creditor's disputed interest. This provision permits a sale free of the alleged interest of a creditor who may be ultimately found to have no interest in the property. Normally, however, the court will allow the interest to attach to any available proceeds pending resolution of the dispute. The creditor is entitled to this protection.

Finally, the entity, usually the secured creditor, could be compelled to accept money rather than an interest in the property.[28] That is, if the lienholder could be ordered to receive payment in a nonbankruptcy legal proceeding in exchange for a release of the lien, the sale may be permitted.

As noted above, if at least one of the above five circumstances exists as to each lien or interest, a property may be sold free and clear of the liens or interests. Often, especially when dealing with a piece of property that may have multiple lien or interest holders upon it (such as three trust deeds or mortgages), one or more of the conditions will have to be satisfied to allow the sale to proceed. For example, a tax lien for real property taxes will require full payment (Section 363(f)(1)). A secured creditor may consent to the sale (Section 363(f)(2)). A junior disputed lien may not be paid in full (Section 363(f)(4)). In this latter instance, the lien may attach to the proceeds of sale. Many situations will arise in which compliance with multiple provisions of Section 363(f) will be necessary to permit a sale of property free and clear of all liens and interests.

F.   OTHER PROPERTY INTERESTS

Section 363(g) permits a trustee to sell property of an estate free and clear of any right of dower or curtesy. This provision applies only in those states

---

26. See legislative history to 11 U.S.C. §363(f)(3).
27. 11 U.S.C. §363(f)(4).
28. 11 U.S.C. §363(f)(5).

where dower and curtesy exist. Hence, this provision has no applicability in a community property jurisdiction. Sections 363(i) and (j) act to protect the rights of a co-owner with a dower or curtesy right by either permitting the interest holder to match the sale price of the property or requiring the trustee to pay to the interest holder any share of the proceeds to which the interest holder may be entitled.[29]

In a community property jurisdiction, a nondebtor community property interest holder in estate property may match the purchase bid of a proposed sale and thus preserve the property for the nondebtor. However, a nondebtor community property interest holder is not entitled to a separate distribution of the sale proceeds when a sale does occur. This is because all community property of a debtor constitutes property of the estate and all community debt is discharged to the extent of the community property.[30]

Section 363(h) concerns the sale of property that is subject to joint ownership interests such as joint tenancy, tenancy in common, or tenancy by the entirety. For example, a husband and wife own a home in joint tenancy. One spouse files bankruptcy and the other does not. The couple is also involved in a divorce. A property settlement agreement has been entered into, which provides that each spouse retains a joint tenancy interest in the home while one spouse retains rights to reside in the home until the children reach the age of 18. When the children reach 18, the home will be sold and the spouses will realize the value of their respective interests. The spouse not residing in the home then files a bankruptcy proceeding. The trustee determines that there is equity in the home to pay unsecured creditors a dividend and the trustee decides to sell the house. The spouse residing in the house opposes the sale. Section 363(h) allows the trustee to sell the property over the objection of the nondebtor joint or co-tenant only if four conditions can be complied with. Bankruptcy Rule 7001(3) requires the filing of an adversary proceeding to obtain approval of a sale subject to Section 363(h). In this instance, the motion procedures will be inappropriate.

The first condition that the trustee must show is that it would not be practicable to partition the property.[31] For example, it is not likely that a single family residence can be legally partitioned, such as splitting the lot in two and giving half to the filing spouse and half to the nonfiling spouse.

---

29. 11 U.S.C. §363(g), (i), (j).
30. 11 U.S.C. §363(i); 11 U.S.C. §541(a)(2); 11 U.S.C. §524(a)(3). See also chapters 7 and 14 supra.
31. 11 U.S.C. §363(h)(1).

Second, the trustee must show that a sale of only the estate's interest in the property will realize significantly less for the estate than a sale of the whole.[32] For instance, it is not likely that someone would want to purchase a half-interest in a home as a tenant in common or joint tenant with an unknown third party, particularly when the buyer might not be able to reside in the premises. A sale of the whole property is therefore likely to generate more proceeds than a sale of the debtor's interest alone.

Third, the trustee must show that the benefit to the estate of a sale of the property outweighs any detriment to the co-owners.[33] Generally, this comparison is based solely on economic factors. If the sale will provide an economic benefit to an estate's creditors and the co-owner is paid the value of the co-owner's interest in the property, there will usually be no detriment found to the nondebtor co-owner. Frankly, in the case of a nondebtor spouse with a right of occupancy, a check for the net equity in the property may have substantially less ultimate monetary value than the right to live in the premises for a fixed period of time, not to mention the potential adverse effects on a family's quality of life from being dispossessed from one residence to another.

Fourth, the trustee must show that the property is not used in the production, transmission, distribution, or sale of electric energy, natural or synthetic gas, or light and power.[34]

If the trustee demonstrates all four of the above conditions, the court may approve a sale of the property including the interest of the nondebtor co-owner. The nondebtor has a right to match the proposed purchase price and thus purchase the estate's interest in the asset.[35] If the property is sold, the trustee must distribute the net proceeds to the estate and co-owners according to their respective interests.[36] That is, the nonfiling spouse will receive payment of his or her interest in the property. For example, if a sale generates $30,000 in net proceeds to two equal co-owners, the estate will receive $15,000 for distribution to the creditors and the nondebtor co-owner will receive the remaining $15,000.

Thus, the best remedy for a nonfiling spouse who lives in a property and wants to continue to live there is to find a way to purchase the bankrupt spouse's interest in the property and pay the trustee pursuant to 11 U.S.C. §363(i). This right exists in both community property and noncommunity property jurisdictions. Although this may not be a feasible approach in some cases, it is usually the path of least resistance.

---

32. 11 U.S.C. §363(h)(2).
33. 11 U.S.C. §363(h)(3).
34. 11 U.S.C. §363(h)(4).
35. 11 U.S.C. §363(i).
36. 11 U.S.C. §363(j).

G.   MISCELLANEOUS PROVISIONS

A secured creditor, like a co-owner, may bid on a sale of the property subject to the secured claim and, if the successful bidder, may offset against the bid price the amount of the secured claim.[37]

Section 363(l) concerns ipso facto clauses.[38] Recall that a bankruptcy **ipso facto clause** is a clause in a contract or deed or other document that makes insolvency, financial condition, or a bankruptcy filing an act of default. Such clauses are generally disfavored by the Bankruptcy Code and are unenforceable.

Section 363(n) prevents collusive bidding in a bankruptcy sale.[39] For example, a group of potential bidders at a bankruptcy auction conspire together beforehand by agreeing to not bid against one another for certain assets. Each conspirator is thus assured of purchasing certain assets at a predetermined price. If the trustee discovers that this sort of activity has occurred, the trustee may avoid the sale and recover either the property or the difference between the actual price and the fair value price of the assets, including costs and attorneys' fees. Section 363(o) protects consumers to the extent that the sale of commercial paper in consumer credit transactions retains all of the protections provided for by consumer law, such as the Federal Truth in Lending Act (15 U.S.C. §1601 et seq.).

It is difficult to successfully appeal a Bankruptcy Court order approving a sale, lease, or use of property under Section 363. The primary reason for this is that unless the transaction is stayed pending appeal, the reversal or modification upon appeal will not affect the validity of the sale to a good-faith purchaser. Knowledge of the appeal's existence will not deprive the purchaser of good faith.[40] In short, unless the sale is stayed pending appeal, any appeal will likely be moot once the transaction closes. This is a strict and arbitrary provision. It exists to protect estates from frivolous appeals designed solely to delay or frustrate the effective administration of the bankruptcy system.

Federal Rule of Bankruptcy Procedure 6003(b) prohibits the sale of estate assets during the first 20 days of a case except to the extent necessary to avoid immediate and irreparable harm. For example, the sale of the perishable assets of a store would likely satisfy this standard. In any hearing under Section 363, the trustee has the burden of proof on

---

37. 11 U.S.C. §363(k).
38. 11 U.S.C. §363(l). See chapter 14 supra.
39. 11 U.S.C. §363(n).
40. 11 U.S.C. §363(m).

any issue of adequate protection. A party asserting an interest in estate property bears the burden of proof on any issue regarding the validity, priority, or extent of the interest in the property.[41]

Summary

Section 363 of the Bankruptcy Code is the basic Code provision regulating the liquidation of estate assets by the use, sale, or lease of estate property. This section, along with the material in chapters 19 through 22 infra, comprises the core of the Code's debt-collection features.

Many sales, leases, or uses of estate property will require prior Bankruptcy Court approval. Some will not. The checklist categorizes the general types of activities that will require prior court approval and those that will not. When prior court approval is necessary, notice and a hearing will also be required. Bankruptcy Rule 6004 requires prior notice of a sale. If an objection is filed, the matter is then treated as a noticed motion.

A sale requiring court approval may take place by way of either a private sale or public auction. A private sale is a sale to a specific buyer identified in advance (such as a buyer of real estate). A public auction is a sale to the highest bidder bidding at the auction. Sometimes a private sale will be subject to overbid in open court. This is a form of auction.

Where an estate's cash is part of a secured creditor's lien, the cash collateral may not be used by the estate unless the creditor consents or the court approves use of the cash collateral. A creditor with cash collateral rights is entitled to adequate protection to permit use of the cash collateral by the estate. The Code requires the Bankruptcy Court to give expedited treatment to a motion for the use of cash collateral.

Any use, sale, or lease of estate property must be consistent with any existing orders relieving or modifying the automatic stay pursuant to 11 U.S.C. §363(d).

Section 363(f) permits property of an estate to be sold free and clear of liens or interests. This provision permits the court to approve a sale over the objection or recalcitrance of lienholders. The provision contains five conditions, at least one of which must be found applicable to each lien or interest holder for the sale to be approved. The checklist summarizes these conditions.

Sections 363(g) and (i) account for the marital property interests of dower, curtesy, and community property.

---

41. 11 U.S.C. §363(p).

Section 363(h) permits a sale of property subject to co-ownership by a nondebtor only if four conditions can be shown. The three most relevant conditions are that a partition of the property is impracticable, that a sale of only the estate's interest would realize significantly less than a sale of the whole, and that any benefit to the estate outweighs any detriment to the co-owner.

KEY TERMS

capital asset   noncapital asset
cash collateral   ordinary course of
ipso facto clause   business

CHAPTER 18 CHECKLIST

		Authority
18.1	SALES REQUIRING PRIOR COURT APPROVAL	
18.1.1	Prior Court Approval Required	11 U.S.C. §363(b)(1)
1.	All Chapter 7 sales, except as in 18.1.2 ¶ 2	11 U.S.C. §363(b)(1)
2.	Sales not in the ordinary course of business	11 U.S.C. §363(b)(1)
18.1.2	Court Approval Not Required	
1.	Chapter 9, 11, 12, or 13 sales in the ordinary course of business	11 U.S.C. §363(b)(1), (c)(1)
2.	Chapter 7 sales in the ordinary course of business when a Chapter 7 trustee is authorized to operate	11 U.S.C. §363(c)(1)
18.2	SALES FREE AND CLEAR OF LIENS — CONDITIONS	
18.2.1	Nonbankruptcy Law Permits	11 U.S.C. §363(f)(1)

Authority

18.2.2	Lienholders Consent	11 U.S.C. §363(f)(2)
18.2.3	All Liens Will Be Paid in Full	11 U.S.C. §363(f)(3)
18.2.4	Lien Is in Good-Faith Dispute	11 U.S.C. §363(f)(4)
18.2.5	Lienholder Could Be Legally Compelled to Accept Money Satisfaction	11 U.S.C. §363(f)(5)

DISCUSSION QUESTIONS

1. Describe the common methods by which a bankruptcy trustee liquidates an estate's assets. When does a sale of estate property require court approval?

2. What is cash collateral? What actions must a trustee take to be authorized to use cash collateral?

3. How can property be sold over the objection of a lienholder?

4. Under what conditions may a trustee sell a nondebtor's interest in property owned as a co-tenant or joint tenant with the debtor?

5. Why is it necessary to protect private information in the sale of customer lists?

PRACTICE EXERCISES

Exercise 18.1

The Bottomlines come to you after the 341 meeting of creditors and explain that they have a way out of their bankruptcy. They have signed a contract with a real estate broker, Champion Real Estate ("If We Can't Sell Your House, No One Can!"). The broker has already found them a buyer, and they are meeting next week to sign the papers to sell their home for the value disclosed in their petition. Draft a letter to the Bottomlines explaining whether or not the sale can go forward, and if so, how.

Exercise 18.2

Prepare a motion to sell the real property that would comply with applicable procedures in your local bankruptcy court.

19

Executory Contracts and Leases

A. EXECUTORY CONTRACTS

Executory contracts are contracts for which performance remains due to some extent by both parties.[1] This is the most widely accepted definition. For example, an unexpired lease is an executory contract. The landlord has a continuing obligation to provide the premises to the tenant while the tenant has a continuing obligation to pay rent to the landlord and abide by the remaining lease provisions. Performance remains due to some extent on both sides.

Many business activities take place through executory contracts. These contracts can at times constitute the most important asset of a bankruptcy estate. A franchise agreement to operate a business is usually an executory contract. **License** agreements to operate a business or to market a product line are executory contracts. Thus, a golf shop's license to use a specific name, such as "MacDuffer," in exchange for royalty payments is an executory contract. The entity issuing the license, the **licensor** (the owner of the name "MacDuffer"), has a continuing obligation to allow the license holder to use the name and sell products with the "MacDuffer" name. The holder of the license, the **licensee**, has a continuing obligation to provide accountings to the licensor and to pay regular royalties, called license fees, to the licensor. Substantial performance remains due on both sides, and hence the transaction is an executory contract. Without the license, the

---

1. See Historical and Revision Notes to 11 U.S.C. §365. This is also known as the "Countryman" definition in honor of Professor Vernon Countryman, who described it in two articles titled Executory Contracts in Bankruptcy, 57 Minn. L. Rev. 439 (1973); 58 Minn. L. Rev. 479 (1974).

golf shop's value or ability to succeed may be seriously or fatally impaired. A Burger King restaurant franchise is an executory contract. Certainly the value of the franchise is lower if the franchisee loses the right to operate the hamburger stand as a Burger King restaurant.[2] An uncompleted contract to manufacture products or to construct a building is an executory contract.

In each of the above instances, if a trustee or debtor-in-possession is the holder of the franchise or the manufacturer of the product, the value of the franchise or value of the contract may be critical to the ability of the debtor to successfully reorganize or to provide creditors with a dividend in the event of a Chapter 7 proceeding. In this situation, the executory contract is a benefit. Assigning the executory contract to a third party or retaining the contract and continuing to perform according to its terms is a right a debtor or trustee may seek to preserve. On the other hand, if the contract is burdensome and is itself a major cause of the bankruptcy filing, the debtor or trustee may desire to abandon or reject the contract.[3]

Conversely, in each of the above instances, the nondebtor party to the contract is a creditor. This should be obvious in instances where the debtor owes payments to the nondebtor party when the bankruptcy is filed, but this is also true where any payments may be current at the filing but where future performance remains due. If monies are due or performance is not forthcoming, the creditor may seek to preserve its right to collect payment or terminate the contract. Yet recall that the automatic stay prevents collection or termination of the contract unless there is no equity in the property or the property is not necessary to an effective reorganization (not likely where the nondebtor claims are not secured by collateral).

Section 365 of the Bankruptcy Code addresses executory contracts and unexpired leases. Were it not for this provision, executory contracts and unexpired leases would be treated in a manner identical to all other property of the estate and be subject to the same rules. The reason for this special treatment is that an executory contract or unexpired lease is a specialized interest in property, which often may be sold, used, or leased. Under the executory contract or lease, the parties may have rights or interests to protect that are different from or something more than a simple right to receive payment or performance. Section 365 was created to account for the special conditions existing between the parties to an executory contract or unexpired lease.

---

2. In re Rovine Corp., 6 Bankr. 661 (W.D. Tenn. 1980).
3. As to abandonment, see chapter 20 infra.

Section 365 attempts to reconcile the competing desires of a debtor or creditor to retain or terminate an executory contract. In its essence, Section 365 treats a nondebtor party to an executory contract as the functional equivalent of a secured creditor with the contract rights constituting the creditor's security for the debtor's performance of the contract. Because the court must approve a decision to assume or reject the contract when called upon to do so, the matter bears similarities to a motion for relief from the automatic stay.

One of two actions may be taken with respect to an executory contract in a bankruptcy: a trustee or debtor-in-possession may assume or reject an executory contract or unexpired lease. In individual Chapter 7 cases, the debtor may assume a lease of personal property if it is not assumed by the trustee.[4] This is accomplished either by way of a noticed motion procedure to assume or reject the contract or by operation of the various time periods contained in Section 365.[5] The remainder of Section 365 describes the conditions and time periods under which an executory contract or unexpired lease may be assumed or rejected.

B. ASSUMING A CONTRACT

A trustee must meet certain conditions to assume an executory contract. Section 365(b) requires that every condition be complied with to permit assumption. The first condition requires the trustee to cure or provide **adequate assurance** that any existing default will be promptly cured. Nonmonetary defaults that are impossible for a trustee to cure need not be cured at the time of assumption.[6] The term *adequate assurance* has essentially the same meaning as adequate protection.[7] Thus, either six months of past-due rent must be paid, an agreement must be made with the landlord to cure the arrearage over a period of time, or the trustee must prove to the court that the default can be cured within a prompt period of time. A trustee or debtor-in-possession who wants the contract's benefits must also accept the burdens and perform under the contract.[8]

---

4. 11 U.S.C. §365(a), (p). The phrase *executory contract* will also mean *unexpired lease* for the duration of this chapter except where otherwise stated.
5. Bankruptcy Rule 6006. See chapter 5 supra and part C of this chapter infra.
6. 11 U.S.C. §365(b)(1)(A).
7. 11 U.S.C. §361. See chapter 12 supra.
8. 11 U.S.C. §365(b)(1).

Second, the trustee must provide compensation or adequate assurance that the nondebtor party will be compensated for any actual damages arising from any default. This compensation may include attorneys' fees and any costs incurred.[9]

Third, and perhaps most important, a trustee or debtor-in-possession must provide adequate assurance of future performance under the contract.[10] This may be as simple as the court's reviewing a future financial projection and concluding that the trustee will likely be able to pay the rent on time or as complex as a debtor-in-possession's being required to convince the court and the creditor that the debtor-in-possession has sufficient financial and physical resources to provide adequate assurance that performance will be rendered and the contract completed.

All of these conditions are consistent with the discussion in chapter 12 supra about adequate protection in connection with the automatic stay. Recall that adequate protection requires making payments or providing additional or replacement collateral. Curing a default and providing assurances of future performance under the term "adequate assurances" are virtually identical.[11] Further, although Section 365(b) is phrased so as to apply only to defaulted executory contracts, the Bankruptcy Courts generally require compliance with Section 365(b)(1) by a trustee or debtor-in-possession in any motion to assume an executory contract.[12]

Section 365(p) of the Bankruptcy Code permits an individual Chapter 7 debtor to assume a personal property lease if the trustee does not do so. In this event, the creditor may condition the assumption on cure of any outstanding default set by the contract. Further, a creditor contacting an individual debtor to assume a personal property lease will not violate the automatic stay. Unless the trustee assumes the lease or the debtor seeks to reaffirm the lease (see chapter 21 infra), rejection of the lease terminates the automatic stay as to the leased property. This means that the creditor may then seek repossession of its property without having to formally seek relief from the stay pursuant to the procedures described in chapter 12 supra.

A default created by an alleged *ipso facto clause* is not enforceable by the nondebtor party. Any clause in a contract placing a debtor in default solely because a bankruptcy proceeding has been filed or because the debtor may be insolvent is not enforceable. A debtor is not required to provide adequate assurances that it will not be bankrupt. Additionally,

---

9. 11 U.S.C. §365(b)(1)(B).
10. 11 U.S.C. §365(b)(1)(C).
11. See chapter 12 supra.
12. See also 11 U.S.C. §365(f)(2).

penalty rates imposed by virtue of nonmonetary defaults cannot be enforced by the nondebtor party.[13]

Subsection 365(b)(3) concerns shopping center leases and the meaning of adequate assurance of performance of a shopping center lease. A unique concern in shopping center leases is provisions regarding the tenant mix and the necessary fact that a shopping center contains multiple leases often with interrelated provisions. In these instances, adequate assurance of future performance will mean that the lease will be used for its intended purpose only and will not violate any other lease agreement concerning the shopping center.[14] A lease provision limiting a premise's use to a boutique or a provision barring other boutique tenants are examples of tenant mix provisions.

Finally, where a lease requires a lessor to provide services or amenities to a debtor, the lessor may refuse to provide the services or amenities prior to assumption unless the trustee can pay for the services.[15]

Section 365(c) further limits a trustee's ability to assume an executory contract, even if adequate assurance and a cure of any defaults can be made. First, if nonbankruptcy law excuses a party from accepting performance from an assignee of the trustee, then nonbankruptcy law will be honored unless the nondebtor party to the contract consents to the assignment.[16] That is, if a nonbankruptcy statute permits a party to a contract to prohibit assignment of an executory contract, then this statute will be honored. For example, federal law generally prohibits the assignment of a government contract unless the federal government consents. This is known as the **Anti-Assignment Act**.[17] If a trustee proposes to assume and assign a government contract to a third party, the Anti-Assignment Act will be given effect and the executory contract may not be assigned unless the federal government consents. On the other hand, an anti-assignment clause in a contract may not be an effective bar to a Section 365 assignment because the contract clause is not a statute.

If a nonresidential lease of real property has been terminated prior to the entry of an order for relief, the lease may not be assumed.[18] This is a rational rule because in this event there is nothing for a trustee to assume.

As a practical matter, from the debtor's perspective, if there is a risk that an executory contract will be terminated prior to a bankruptcy filing, the filing should take place beforehand. The automatic stay will prevent

---

13. 11 U.S.C. §365(b)(2). See discussion of ipso facto clauses generally in chapter 14 supra.
14. 11 U.S.C. §365(b)(3).
15. 11 U.S.C. §365(b)(4).
16. 11 U.S.C. §365(c)(1).
17. 41 U.S.C. §15.
18. 11 U.S.C. §365(c)(3).

the contract's termination. This rule of thumb applies to all executory contracts. In most situations, if a nondebtor party properly terminates an executory contract prior to commencement of the bankruptcy proceeding, then there is no executory contract in existence to assume. Whether or not the contract exists to assume can sometimes mean the difference between a successful or unsuccessful result for the estate and its creditors.

If an executory contract is to make a loan or other financial commitment, then the contract may not be assumed. A debtor or trustee cannot force a lender to perform a loan commitment if the borrower files a bankruptcy.[19] This does not imply that a bankruptcy estate may not obtain credit. The question of an estate obtaining credit is governed solely by Section 364, not Section 365.[20] Thus, a debtor with a prepetition loan commitment will have to proceed by Section 364 if postpetition approval of the loan is sought. This is described in chapter 20 infra.

C.   TIME LIMITS FOR ASSUMPTION

Section 365(d) concerns the time limits within which executory contracts may or must be assumed. Different rules will apply depending on the type of Chapter proceeding involved and whether the subject matter of assumption is a lease of real or personal property. Real property is further distinguished by its characterization as residential or nonresidential real property. A lease of **residential** real property most commonly exists when the debtor resides in the premises subject to the lease. A lease is **nonresidential** in virtually all other situations. This chapter's checklist summarizes these time limits.

In a Chapter 7 proceeding, if a trustee does not affirmatively act to assume or reject an executory contract or lease of real or personal property within 60 days after the order for relief is entered, then the contract or lease is deemed rejected. No court action is required to effectuate the rejection.[21] Stated another way, a Chapter 7 trustee has 60 days to assume or reject an executory contract or unexpired lease of real property or personal property. If the trustee takes no action within the 60-day period, then the contract or lease is deemed to be automatically rejected and

---

19. 11 U.S.C. §365(c)(2).
20. See chapter 20 infra.
21. 11 U.S.C. §365(d)(1); §365(d)(4).

terminated. The burden is therefore on the Chapter 7 trustee to obtain a court order if assumption is desired. A trustee who has a buyer will proceed by Section 365 to assume and assign the contract.

Practice Pointer

Generally, the debtor or the trustee may not assume a personal service contract, a contract to loan money, or a nonresidential lease that terminated prepetition.

As a practical matter, in consumer Chapter 7 proceedings, trustees do not usually act to assume residential real property leases, nor do debtors proceed to obtain court approval to assume them. Also, as a practical matter, lessors do not proceed to court on day 61 seeking to evict the debtor tenant. A lessor is generally satisfied if a tenant is continuing to pay rent. On the other hand, if the rent is in default upon the entry of an order for relief, the automatic stay may bar an eviction of the tenant debtor from the premises in some circumstances (see Chapter 12 supra). A lessor may move before the court for rejection of the lease or relief from the stay to terminate the lease. Alternatively, if the lessor waits until the sixty-first day after the entry of an order for relief, the lease will be deemed rejected and the lessor may be able to obtain a writ of possession directly from the Bankruptcy Court.

In an individual Chapter 7 case, if a trustee does not assume a lease of personal property, the debtor may assume the lease by notifying the creditor and curing the lease pursuant to the terms of the contract as set forth in Section 365(p), discussed above. This may or may not mean that an individual debtor may assume the lease more than 60 days after a filing, because the provision also provides that the automatic stay is automatically terminated if the lease is not assumed. Since Section 362(h) (see chapter 12 supra) relieves the stay with respect to personal property leases if the lease is not assumed within the "Statement of Intention" period (see chapter 21 infra), this may mean that a debtor must effectively act to assume a lease of personal property within the first 30 days of the case irrespective of the Section 365 time limits. Since Section 365(p) is an entirely new provision, this is one of the issues that the courts will have to determine. Compliance with the Statement of Intention procedure should act to satisfy this provision.

In proceedings other than a Chapter 7, such as a Chapter 11 reorganization, a trustee or debtor-in-possession may assume or reject an executory contract or lease of personal property or an unexpired residential lease at any time prior to court confirmation of a plan proposed under the particular Chapter.[22] Thus, a franchise does not terminate 60 days after filing if a debtor-in-possession does not assume the franchise prior to this date. Conversely, because there is no definite time limit to assume an executory contract in a non-Chapter 7 proceeding, any party may bring the matter before the court and request that a date certain be set for the debtor to assume or reject the contract.

A motion to assume or reject may or may not be combined with a motion for relief from the automatic stay. The latter is not necessary in this instance. In the case of a personal property lease, a motion may take the form of a motion for relief from stay, as opposed to a motion to assume or reject.

In the case of a real estate lease, a lessor will bring a motion to assume or reject the lease before the court, so that any defaults can be ordered promptly cured or the lease rejected without undue delay. A non-residential real estate lessor may take this approach when the lessor desires to act promptly after the lessee's bankruptcy filing rather than wait 120 days (see infra this chapter). Any motion will also ask the court to order appropriate adequate protection in the form of adequate assurances of future performance.

Recall that a lessor of residential real property may continue prosecution of an unlawful detainer or eviction proceeding as an exception to the automatic stay if the debtor does not pay postpetition rent on a timely basis, if the lease has already been terminated pursuant to the lease or State law, or if the debtor has filed a bankruptcy petition within the past year and failed to pay postpetition rent. See chapter 12 supra. The effect of all these provisions is to minimize the effect of bankruptcy upon landlords of residential real estate.

In the case of other forms of executory contracts, such as a manufacturing contract, a trustee or debtor-in-possession may want to bring a motion to assume the contract if the nondebtor party refuses to perform after the debtor's bankruptcy filing. This will force the nondebtor to abide by the contract's terms. A nondebtor party may wish to bring a motion to have the contract rejected if there are prepetition defaults that require cure before the contract's performance can be completed.

If a trustee or debtor-in-possession does choose to assume an executory contract, the contract's terms must be abided by, although the court may defer performance for up to 60 days.[23] A trustee or debtor-in-possession

---

22. 11 U.S.C. §365(d)(2). However, in Chapter 13, personal property lease payments must be paid current during pendency of the case. 11 U.S.C. §1326(a)(1). See chapter 23 infra.
23. 11 U.S.C. §365(d)(3).

must accept the burdens as well as the benefits in assuming an executory contract.[24]

In any Chapter proceeding, a lease of nonresidential real property must be assumed within 120 days after an order for relief is entered or the lease will be deemed rejected. A nonresidential lease that is rejected requires the trustee or debtor-in-possession to surrender the premises to the lessor and thus, conversely, entitles the lessor to obtain immediate court approval for an eviction order. The court may extend this 120-day period only upon a motion of the lessor or trustee for cause and only for 90 days, unless the lessor consents to further extensions.[25] This 120-day time limit is strictly enforced by most Bankruptcy Courts.

The 120-day rule is of critical importance where the debtor is a party to a nonresidential real property lease. If the debtor is a restaurant or retail store, a failure to properly act to assume the lease in a timely manner can result in the debtor's liquidation. When the debtor is a chain of retail stores or restaurants, there are sometimes hundreds of leases to assume or reject.

D.   MISCELLANEOUS PROVISIONS

Section 365(e) concerns *ipso facto* clauses where a trustee wants to assume an executory contract that is not otherwise in default at the time of assumption. Ipso facto clauses are unenforceable. However, if nonbankruptcy law permits termination upon bankruptcy or insolvency unless the nondebtor party consents, such nonbankruptcy law will be honored. Further, a contract to extend credit may not be enforceable postpetition. The rationale for this is the same as described in connection with Section 365(c) supra.[26]

Often when a trustee or debtor-in-possession wants to assume an executory contract, it is for the primary purpose of assigning the contract to a third party. For example, the debtor who owns the Burger King franchise desires to sell it. Section 365(f) concerns the issues that arise in the effort to assign the contract.

Section 365(f) generally permits the assignment of an executory contract.[27] However, the assignment will only be permitted if any defaults

---

24. 11 U.S.C. §365(f)(2).
25. 11 U.S.C. §365(d)(4).
26. 11 U.S.C. §365(e).
27. 11 U.S.C. §365(f)(1).

are cured, and only if the nondebtor party is provided with adequate assurance of future performance.[28] In other words, a contract must be assumed in order to be assigned. The general policy of the Bankruptcy Code is to permit the assignment of executory contracts.[29]

If an executory contract is rejected, a determination must be made as to the type of claim against the estate the nondebtor party will have. The claim can become either a prepetition unsecured claim or an administrative claim. The status of the claim will have a dramatic effect upon the distributive priority accorded to it.[30] Generally, the rejection of an executory contract is considered a breach of the contract.[31] Where a contract is rejected without ever having been assumed, rejection is considered to have occurred immediately prior to the bankruptcy filing.[32] This means that the nondebtor party will normally obtain the status of a prepetition unsecured creditor.

Practice Pointer

In the case of rejection, the nondebtor party may have rejection damages under state law. The damages for rejection of real property leases is limited under Section 502(b)(6).

On the other hand, if a trustee does assume an executory contract but then later rejects it, or if the executory contract is assumed and the proceeding is then converted to a Chapter 7, the breach is considered to have occurred at the time of rejection or, if the proceeding has been converted, immediately prior to conversion.[33] Thus, the assumption of an executory contract will have the practical effect of making any subsequent claim of the nondebtor party an administrative claim. Administrative claims have a higher distributive priority than general unsecured claims.[34]

Section 365(h)(2) concerns the rights of a nondebtor lessee where the trustee or debtor-in-possession is the lessor or seller of timeshare interests and rejects, rather than assumes, the executory contract.[35] The lessee or

---

28. 11 U.S.C. §365(f)(2).
29. See Historical and Revision Notes to Section 365(f).
30. See chapter 21 infra.
31. 11 U.S.C. §365(g); 11 U.S.C. §365(h)(1).
32. 11 U.S.C. §365(g)(1).
33. 11 U.S.C. §365(g)(2).
34. See chapter 21 infra.
35. The timeshare provision was added to the Code in 1984.

timeshare purchaser may elect either to treat the contract as terminated or to remain in possession for the term of the lease or timeshare interest.[36] In the former situation, the nondebtor's rights are limited to a claim for damages, which will likely be a general unsecured claim. In the latter instance, the nondebtor's claim is limited to a setoff against the lease or timeshare price to the extent of any actual damages sustained as a result of the trustee's rejection of the contract.[37]

E. REAL ESTATE CONTRACTS

A contract for a sale of real estate that is pending when a bankruptcy proceeding commences is an executory contract. Because the seller still has an obligation to convey title to the property and the purchaser still has an obligation to pay the price, performance remains due to some extent on both sides. Sections 365(i) and (j) concern the issues raised by this scenario. If a trustee rejects an executory contract in which the debtor is the seller, the purchaser's rights will vary depending upon whether the buyer is in possession of the real property. If the purchaser is not in possession, the purchaser is unaffected by Section 365(i) and its rights will be determined elsewhere in the Code. If the purchaser is in possession, the purchaser may elect to treat the contract as terminated or may remain in possession of the property. If the purchaser remains in possession of the property, the purchaser may complete the purchase and force the debtor or trustee to convey title. The purchase price may be offset by the amount of the purchaser's damages but the purchaser acquires no further claim.[38] To summarize, a purchaser in possession may elect either to terminate the transaction or to enforce the contract.

If the purchaser of real estate in a rejected sale of real estate treats the contract as terminated, the purchaser acquires a lien on the debtor's interest in the property to recover any part of the purchase price paid prior to rejection. A purchaser not in possession of real estate that is the subject of a rejected executory contract has a similar lien right.[39]

---

36. 11 U.S.C. §365(h)(1).
37. 11 U.S.C. §365(h)(2).
38. 11 U.S.C. §365(i).
39. 11 U.S.C. §365(j).

This lien right will make the rejected purchaser the equivalent of a secured creditor.

The assignment of an executory contract under Section 365 relieves the trustee and estate of any liability arising after the assignment.[40]

F. INTELLECTUAL PROPERTY

Section 365(n) was enacted in 1988.[41] The provisions of Section 365(n) give special treatment to executory contracts involving **intellectual property**. Patents, copyrights, and trademarks are common forms of intellectual property. Prior to enactment of these provisions, an executory contract involving intellectual property was governed by the rules described above.

The most common form of intellectual property contract is known as a license. The owner of the patent or copyright is known as the licensor. The manufacturer or publisher is known as the licensee.

If a trustee rejects an intellectual property executory contract and the debtor is the licensor, the licensee has an option to either retain its rights and keep the contract in effect or to terminate the contract. If the licensee keeps the contract in effect, performance proceeds. The only effect of the bankruptcy is that the trustee is directed to cooperate with the licensee.[42] Of course, to the extent that royalties are not exempt, they will normally constitute property of the estate.

Summary

Executory contracts are contracts for which performance remains due to some extent on both sides. Franchise or license agreements are common executory contracts. Real estate leases, whether of residential or nonresidential property, are specialized types of executory contracts. The effect of bankruptcy upon executory contracts and unexpired leases is the subject of Bankruptcy Code Section 365.

An executory contract may either be assumed or rejected by a bankruptcy estate. In an individual Chapter 7, if the trustee does not assume

---

40. 11 U.S.C. §365(k).
41. Pub. L. No. 100-56, 102 Stat. 2538 (October 18, 1988).
42. 11 U.S.C. §365(n).

a lease of personal property, the debtor may do so. At some point in time in any bankruptcy proceeding, all executory contracts will have to be assumed or rejected. In many situations, assumption will have to occur within a fixed time period, normally 60 days after the bankruptcy filing, or the contract will be deemed rejected. The checklist accompanying this chapter describes the time limits involved in the assumption of executory contracts. Assumption of an executory contract will always require a court order or be contained within the provisions of a confirmed reorganization plan.

When an estate wants to assume an executory contract, the estate must promptly cure any existing monetary defaults, compensate the nondebtor party for any actual damages, and provide adequate assurance of future performance. This latter requirement is very similar to the concept of adequate protection that has been previously discussed in connection with automatic stay and cash collateral issues in chapters 12 and 18 supra.

A trustee may not assume or assign an executory contract if a non-bankruptcy statute prohibits assignment absent the consent of the nondebtor party to the contract. Executory contracts to extend credit or make loans to a debtor may not be assumed or assigned. These transactions are more properly characterized as loans to the estate. These transactions are described in chapter 20 infra.

The effect given to a rejected executory contract differs depending upon whether the contract has been previously assumed. Claims arising from a contract rejected by operation of the time limits set forth in the Code or that are never assumed are treated as prepetition unsecured claims. When an executory contract is assumed, however, claims arising from it will thereafter receive treatment as an administrative expense and be entitled to a higher distributive priority in the event of liquidation. That is, an executory contract assumed in a Chapter 11 proceeding is treated as an administrative claim of the Chapter 11 in the event the proceeding is converted to a Chapter 7.

Section 365 contains several other features pertaining to specific types of contracts. Contracts for timeshare ownership are given special treatment in Section 365(h). Sections 365(i) and (j) regard contracts for the sale of real estate. Generally, a nondebtor buyer in possession will have greater rights to force assumption of the contract than a nondebtor buyer not in possession. Section 365(n), added to the Code in 1988, clarifies the effect of bankruptcy upon an executory contract involving intellectual property, such as patents or copyrights.

KEY TERMS

adequate assurance   licensee
Anti-Assignment Act   licensor
executory contracts   nonresidential
intellectual property   residential
license

CHAPTER 19 CHECKLIST

19.1   TIME LIMITS FOR ASSUMPTION OR REJECTION OF
       EXECUTORY CONTRACTS OR UNEXPIRED LEASES

	Chapter	Nonresidential Leases	Executory Contracts/ Residential Leases	Statute
19.1.1	7	120 days	60 days	11 U.S.C. §365(d)(1), (4)
19.1.2	9	120 days	before confirmation or prior court order after motion	11 U.S.C. §365(d)(2), (4)
19.1.3	11	120 days	before confirmation or prior court order after motion	11 U.S.C. §365(d)(2), (4)
19.1.4	12	120 days	before confirmation or prior court order after motion	11 U.S.C. §365(d)(2), (4)

				Statute
19.1.5	13	120 days	before confirmation or prior court order after motion	11 U.S.C. §365(d)(2), (4)

DISCUSSION QUESTIONS

1. What is an executory contract? Can the following be executory contracts: license agreement? royalty contract? franchise agreement? unexpired lease? pending contract for the sale of real estate? installment loan contract?

2. What is adequate assurance of performance?

3. What must a trustee or debtor-in-possession do to assume an unexpired lease or executory contract?

4. What are the time limits within which an executory contract must or may be assumed in a Chapter 7 or 13 proceeding? Residential lease?

5. What is the difference between assumption and assignment?

6. What is the effect of assumption or rejection of an executory contract or lease upon any claims of the nondebtor party to the contract?

7. What are the rights of a purchaser of an executory contract for the purchase of real estate?

20

Miscellaneous Provisions Regarding Property of the Estate

A. PRESERVATION OF CASH

The ultimate asset that a trustee will administer in any estate is cash. This is implicit in the trustee's primary duty to liquidate the assets of an estate.[1] Cash in the custody of a Chapter 11 debtor-in-possession is an estate asset. Section 345 regulates the preservation and use of cash assets in bankruptcy estates.

Section 345 illustrates the major difference between a bankruptcy and a nonbankruptcy trustee. Under nonbankruptcy law, nonbankruptcy trustees are generally permitted to invest trust funds in any prudent business manner. For example, a nonbankruptcy trustee may invest trust funds in making secured loans (secured by adequate collateral), stocks, bonds, or other investments designed to yield the greatest return at a minimum of risk. In fact, a nonbankruptcy trustee who invests trust funds only in savings accounts could possibly be held in violation of the trustee's duties to prudently maximize returns on the assets.

On the other hand, a bankruptcy trustee is not given broad discretion to invest estate assets. A bankruptcy trustee is quite restricted in the uses that may be made of an estate's cash. One fear is that because the bankruptcy system is designed to protect the assets of an estate for its creditors, no risks should be taken to cause further losses to the pool of money

---

1. See chapter 10 supra.

collected for the estate's creditors' funds. Further, giving bankruptcy trustees the discretion to invest estate funds would likely result in substantial litigation by debtors and creditors alike, constantly challenging a trustee's business judgment. Under these circumstances, no reasonable person would want to be a bankruptcy trustee. Thus, rather than creating a complex set of rules about what might or might not be a prudent investment of estate funds and permitting second guessing or Monday morning quarterbacking, the Bankruptcy Code limits a bankruptcy trustee's use of funds to deposits in a federally insured bank or savings and loan institution unless the court orders otherwise.[2]

A trustee may do one of two things with estate funds. They may be placed on deposit in an interest bearing account or they may be placed into insured certificates of deposit.[3]

In addition to being limited to investing estate funds as described, a trustee must also keep the money in approved depositories. An approved Bankruptcy Court depository is a federally insured bank or savings and loan that is willing to guarantee payment of estate funds in excess of $250,000 on deposit.[4] At all federally insured banks or savings and loan institutions, individual accounts are normally guaranteed only up to $250,000. This means that if the institution is itself declared insolvent, the insurance will only pay up to $250,000 per account. As a result, a financial institution wanting to act as a depository for bankruptcy funds must guarantee payment of deposits in excess of $250,000 per account.[5] This is a great irony of the Bankruptcy Code.

Local bankruptcy rules will often further amplify the above rules and relate them to the amount of the trustee's bond, as discussed in chapter 10 of this text. Many Bankruptcy Courts or United States Trustees will maintain lists of approved depositories for bankruptcy funds in a given area. An approved depository is one that has posted at the requisite guaranty of funds on deposit of more than $250,000.[6]

Many financial institutions are willing to comply with these provisions of the Bankruptcy Code or Rules. A major reason is that the funds are likely to be on deposit with the bank for a significantly longer time than ordinary nonbankruptcy accounts. The financial institution will thereby have use of

---

2. 11 U.S.C. §345(a).
3. 11 U.S.C. §345(a). See also the Historical and Revision Notes to Section 345(a). The notes imply that government bonds may also be appropriate investments. However, as a practical matter, the administration of most bankruptcy estates can be completed in substantially less time than the longevity rates of most government bonds. This makes them impractical as useful investments by a bankruptcy trustee.
4. 11 U.S.C. §345(b).
5. 11 U.S.C. §345(b).
6. 11 U.S.C. §345(b).

the funds for exceptional periods of time at relatively low rates of interest. As a result, the handling of bankruptcy deposits is profitable for many financial institutions, despite the above rules.

B.   UTILITY SERVICE/DISCRIMINATION

Section 366 concerns the rights of public utility companies to discontinue or to provide service to debtors or bankruptcy estates. This provision eliminates a practice that existed under the former Bankruptcy Act. Under the Bankruptcy Act, if a debtor listed a public utility company as a creditor, the public utility could promptly cut off the debtor's service. To restore service, the utility would charge the debtor an excessive deposit, the practical effect of which was to make utility debts nondischargeable. Section 366 was enacted into the Code to give a debtor protection from discrimination by a public utility.[7] Simply put, a public utility may not refuse or discontinue service because a debtor initiates a bankruptcy proceeding and lists the utility as a creditor.

The public utility may, however, request a reasonable deposit or security from the debtor or trustee to serve as adequate assurance of future performance. This phrase generally means the same as "adequate protection" in other than Chapter 11 cases. If the deposit is not made, then the utility can discontinue service. The method of determining the reasonableness of the deposit may vary from district to district. Generally speaking, amounts equal to three months of service will be considered reasonable. If either a debtor, a trustee, or a debtor-in-possession believes that the deposit request is unreasonable, the Bankruptcy Court has the authority to rule on the question of the reasonableness of the request. In Chapter 11 cases, "adequate assurance" means a cash deposit or other similar security. In larger Chapter 11 cases, a typical first-day order may limit the deposit to one month's service, while giving the utility the opportunity to object or request more. The court may not consider the lack of security prepetition or the fact that the debtor may be current to a particular utility in reviewing the reasonableness of a security deposit request. Additionally, as an exception to the rule that setoffs are subject to the automatic stay (see chapter 12 supra), a utility company of

---

7. 11 U.S.C. §366(a).

a Chapter 11 debtor may set off a prepetition security deposit against a prepetition debt without a court order.[8]

Similar to Section 366, Section 525 prevents governmental and private discrimination against debtors under the Bankruptcy Code. In addition, a government entity or business that makes government-insured or guaranteed student loans may not deny such a loan to a person who is or has been a debtor in a bankruptcy case.[9]

In FCC v. Nextwave Personal Communications, Inc., 537 U.S. 293 (2003), the Supreme Court examined Section 525(a), which prevents governmental discrimination or action against an entity that files bankruptcy owing dischargeable debts to the government. In this case, Nextwave owned a number of valuable licenses that had been issued by the FCC. When Nextwave sought Chapter 11 relief, it owed the government substantial unpaid obligations for the purchase of the licenses. When Nextwave attempted to treat the licenses as estate property, the FCC asserted that the licenses had been revoked due to the defaulted payments. The Supreme Court affirmed the ruling of the Court of Appeals, finding that by revoking the licenses for nonpayment, the FCC had violated Section 525(a): "We think that Congress meant what it said: The government is not to revoke a bankruptcy debtor's license solely because of a failure to pay his debts."

C.   ABANDONMENT

Sometimes an asset subject to administration is of no value or is burdensome to an estate. The asset may be an unfavorable executory contract, a worthless piece of equipment, or a parcel of real property with no equity. Section 554 allows a trustee to **abandon** property of the estate that is burdensome or of inconsequential value. A creditor or party in interest may move the court to compel the trustee to abandon an asset.[10] Federal Rule of Bankruptcy Procedure 6007 requires notice of the trustee's intention and contains the technical procedure for the formal abandonment of an asset. If the notice is opposed, the matter is treated as a noticed motion.[11] Local rules may add further details. An abandonment procedure

---

8. 11 U.S.C. §366(b)(c).
9. 11 U.S.C. §525.
10. 11 U.S.C. §554(a), (b).
11. 11 U.S.C. §554(c), (d); Bankruptcy Rule 5009. See chapter 22 infra.

is initiated by way of the notice procedures described in chapter 5 supra. Form 20.1 on the forms disk is a sample report of abandonment.

Practice Pointer

Abandonment simply returns the asset to its prepetition status and removes it from the bankruptcy process and the protection of the automatic stay.

The term *burdensome* generally means that the trustee cannot afford to maintain the property. The term *inconsequential value to the estate* generally means either that the property has no equity or the property has no realizable value for the creditors.

The question of what will be burdensome will vary from case to case. Burdensome may mean that a trustee will incur substantial expenses to maintain the property and has no source of money to accomplish the task. A common example is a parcel of real property with no equity. It is a waste of estate assets to incur maintenance expenses on such property. The asset will therefore be abandoned so the trustee can avoid the expense.

Practice Pointer

If the debtor's house has no equity above the mortgages on the property and the debtor's exemption, the trustee will often abandon it.

Another common example of burdensome property is the uncollected accounts receivable of a business. On paper, the amount of uncollected accounts receivable may be substantial, but after investigation, the trustee may determine that the costs of collection will exceed any likely recovery. The trustee can then abandon the assets. Perhaps a debtor lists a tort claim as an asset in the Schedules and the trustee determines, after investigation, that the claim is meritless. The trustee abandons the claim because it is burdensome or of no value to the estate. Because all property of the estate must be administered, the trustee must make this decision of whether or not to abandon certain property.

A secured creditor may sometimes be able to make use of abandonment as a potentially less expensive alternative to a motion for relief from stay since any party in interest may seek an abandonment order.[12] Recall that the automatic stay is terminated as to certain acts against property when a debtor has been discharged and the property is no longer property of the estate.[13] Thus, when a debtor is discharged, if a secured creditor obtains an abandonment of its collateral by the trustee, the automatic stay is then relieved without further action since the property is no longer property of the estate.

However, a trustee may not necessarily abandon an asset as burdensome simply because the asset is subject to an environmental cleanup order of a governmental unit. In this instance, the Supreme Court has placed the public policy of environmental concerns above that of the Bankruptcy Code.[14]

D.   OBTAINING CREDIT

Section 364 of the Bankruptcy Code concerns the subject of an estate obtaining credit during a bankruptcy proceeding. This is not as ludicrous as it may appear at first glance. To the uninitiated, the question is certain to arise as to why a debtor would want to obtain credit in a bankruptcy proceeding, or, perhaps more importantly or practically, why anyone would give credit to a trustee or a debtor-in-possession in a bankruptcy proceeding. Obtaining credit does not usually occur in a Chapter 7 proceeding except in very extraordinary circumstances. For instance, a trustee with permission to operate the debtor's business for a limited period of time under Section 721 might require credit to do so.

In a Chapter 11 proceeding, obtaining postpetition credit is often critical. Sometimes, obtaining new credit is the only way in which a Chapter 11 debtor-in-possession can acquire a realistic opportunity to survive and rehabilitate. Remember that a Chapter 11 debtor can be a very large entity. Whether the debtor-in-possession is an airline, a chain of retail stores, a chain of restaurants, or a manufacturer, the debtor will usually require some form of credit to function efficiently. Larger debtors generally have large credit lines from banks or other financial institutions. Whether or not the loans are in default at the time of filing, the debtor-in-possession will require the consent of the lender banks or financial

---

12. 11 U.S.C. §554(b). A motion to compel abandonment requires a $150 filing fee.
13. 11 U.S.C. §362(c). See chapter 12 supra.
14. Midlantic Natl. Bank v. New Jersey Dept. of Envtl. Protection, 474 U.S. 494 (1986).

institutions to continue a credit relationship, or the debtor will probably not survive for very long in the Chapter 11. Many times in Chapter 11 proceedings, the debtor finds, and the creditors will concur, that if the debtor receives an infusion of cash in the form of credit or otherwise, the debtor will gain the opportunity it needs to restore viability, which may result in a successful plan of reorganization and repayment to creditors.

Sometimes credit will come from entities that are already creditors of the estate who merely extend additional credit to the debtor in exchange for additional collateral and adequate protection. A lender may also improve its priority position by extending postpetition credit, as shall be described below. In this event, a motion to incur postpetition credit may be combined with a motion to use cash collateral under Section 363(c).[15] Sometimes the lender is an entirely new third party. Some investment banks have insolvency departments, which specialize in financing Chapter 11 or other distressed debtors.[16]

There are different forms of credit that may be incurred by a trustee or debtor-in-possession. The simplest is unsecured credit. If a trustee or debtor-in-possession is operating a business under any Chapter proceeding, the estate will incur debt in the ordinary course of business. When office supplies are ordered and billed, this is unsecured credit. Any other ordinary trade payable is unsecured debt. A debtor-in-possession or trustee operating a business may obtain unsecured credit in the ordinary course of business without prior court approval.[17] Thus, every time a restaurant in a Chapter 11 buys 100 pounds of hamburger on a 30-day invoice, a court order is not required to permit the purchase. This is a transaction in the **ordinary course of business**.

On the other hand, if an estate requires unsecured credit not in the ordinary course of business, then the estate must obtain prior court approval by a noticed motion.[18] A loan is not in the ordinary course of business when it is obtained for other than the day-to-day operations of the estate. An unsecured loan for purposes of meeting payroll is not in the ordinary course of business.[19] If prior court approval is obtained, then the debt will be accorded administrative priority for purposes of repayment.[20] If prior court approval is not obtained, then the creditor may find itself

---

15. See chapter 18 supra.
16. For example, Credit Suisse First Boston. Most major banks also have specialized departments for the type of debtor-in-possession financing seen in larger cases of the variety that are frequently filed in the Southern District of New York or the District of Delaware.
17. 11 U.S.C. §364(a).
18. 11 U.S.C. §364(b). Bankruptcy Rule 4001(c).
19. See In re Lockwood Enters., Inc., 52 Bankr. 871 (S.D.N.Y. 1985). But see In re Gloria Mfg. Corp., 65 Bankr. 341 (E.D. Va. 1985).
20. See chapter 21 infra.

subordinated to the status of a general unsecured prepetition creditor.[21] This may seem a harsh result, but the purpose of the rule is to attempt to protect the prepetition creditor body from any further erosion or impairment of their ultimate ability to receive a dividend. Allowing a creditor to obtain an administrative priority will create such an impairment. Thus, the Code requires prior court approval so a determination can be made that the incurring of new debt not in the ordinary course of business will be in the ultimate best interests of the prepetition creditors.

If a trustee or debtor-in-possession cannot obtain unsecured credit outside the ordinary course of business, it may be able to obtain the credit on a secured basis. This always requires court approval by a noticed motion.[22] The reasons for this are identical to the reasons just given for obtaining unsecured credit outside the ordinary course of business. The loan will become an administrative expense and be payable before any dividends to the prepetition creditors. Because approval of the loan may decrease the prepetition creditors' likelihood of receiving a dividend, the court has to weigh this risk against the positive effects the loan will have upon the estate's ultimate ability to successfully reorganize.

Under Subsection 364(c), the court has a number of choices to exercise in granting secured priority administrative credit. The court may give the loan priority over all other expenses of the bankruptcy, including all other administrative expenses. That is, the loan may be given priority over even the professional fees incurred in the bankruptcy. Or the court may permit the lender to obtain a security interest in any assets of the debtor not already subject to a secured interest. Or the court may give the creditor a junior lien on property that is already secured, such as a second deed of trust or mortgage upon a parcel of real estate.[23]

Sometimes when a Chapter 11 debtor-in-possession seeks to obtain approval of a secured administrative debt, all of the estate property is already subject to liens by prepetition secured creditors. In this situation, the court may also permit the incurring of secured administrative debt. The court must find, however, that the credit is not otherwise obtainable and any existing secured creditor whose position may be affected by the new debt must be given adequate protection. The trustee has the burden of proving that such adequate protection exists.[24]

---

21. In re Lockwood Enters., Inc., 52 Bankr. 871 (S.D.N.Y. 1985); In re Alafia Land Dev. Corp., 40 Bankr. 1 (M.D. Fla. 1984).
22. 11 U.S.C. §364(c). Bankruptcy Rule 4001(c).
23. 11 U.S.C. §364(c)(1), (2), (3).
24. 11 U.S.C. §364(d).

As in the case of the sale of estate property, the approval of a post-petition loan transaction is unaffected by any appeal unless the order has been stayed pending appeal.[25]

The approval of postpetition credit under Section 364 is governed by the motion procedures described in chapter 4 supra. Notice of the hearing is limited to the Official Creditors' Committee or the 20 largest unsecured creditors of the estate and any other parties the court directs. This permits a debtor to act promptly in the early stages of a proceeding.[26]

E.   HEALTH CARE BANKRUPTCIES

BAPCPA added provisions designed to account for the disposition of patient records and the transfer of patients from a closing facility in a **health care business** bankruptcy. The primary purpose of these provisions is to protect the privacy of the records and the safety of the patients. A health care business is generally any business that provides services to patients.[27] The court will appoint an ombudsman to represent the interests of patients unless the court finds that the appointment is not necessary.[28] If a trustee has insufficient funds to preserve and store patient records, Section 351 specifies the procedure to follow to make the records available to patients or to abandon the records. Section 704(12) imposes upon a Chapter 7 trustee the obligation to transfer patients to other appropriate facilities. Sections 1106 and 1107 impose a similar obligation upon a Chapter 11 debtor-in-possession.

F.   SYSTEM EXAMPLE

A major premise of the Bankruptcy Code is that it is designed to function as a self-contained system.[29] An example utilizing many of the issues raised in this and the preceding two chapters illustrates this theory. Gizmos Inc. manufactures gizmos and whatchamacallits for Engulf & Devour. Gizmos has

---

25. 11 U.S.C. §364(e).
26. Bankruptcy Rule 4001(c).
27. 11 U.S.C. §101(27A).
28. 11 U.S.C. §333. See chapter 10 supra.
29. See chapter 2 supra.

a credit line with the Yours Is Ours Bank. All assets of Gizmos are secured in favor of the bank. Gizmos falls behind in its payments to its suppliers, who cease shipping it parts to produce its products. As a result, Gizmos falls behind in its production schedule. Engulf & Devour want to terminate the contract. The bank wants to call the credit line due. Gizmos files a Chapter 11 to prevent the contract from being terminated and to prevent the bank from seizing assets due to the automatic stay (Section 362). An investor, Alex Keaton, comes forward. He agrees to loan monies to Gizmos on a superpriority secured basis and further agrees that the loan will be converted from debt to equity if Gizmos can reorganize. Gizmos then files a motion to incur superpriority secured debt under Section 364(d), a motion to assume the Engulf & Devour contract under Section 365(a), and a motion to use the bank's cash collateral under Section 363(c). Both Engulf & Devour and the bank are entitled to adequate protection as defined in Section 361. All of these provisions working together will be required to accomplish the goals sought by Gizmos and to properly protect the rights of all creditors.

Summary

Section 345 of the Bankruptcy Code restricts the investment of an estate's cash assets. Generally, cash assets must be placed on deposit in interest bearing accounts or certificates of deposit in federally insured financial institutions. An estate's funds may also be invested in government bonds, but, as a practical matter, the longevity of the bonds exceeds the effective length of most bankruptcy proceedings. A financial institution accepting the deposit of bankruptcy funds must guarantee the amount on deposit greater than the normal government limits of $250,000.

A utility may not refuse to continue or to provide service to a bankruptcy estate or debtor simply because of a bankruptcy filing. A utility may, however, request a reasonable deposit as a condition of providing future service.

A government or private entity may not discriminate against a debtor solely as a result of a bankruptcy filing.

A trustee may abandon assets that are burdensome to or of inconsequential value to the estate. All assets must be administered by the trustee before the bankruptcy proceeding may be closed. An asset is generally burdensome if the trustee cannot afford to maintain it. An asset is generally of inconsequential value to an estate if it is valueless or if the likely costs of collection would exceed any likely recovery. A secured creditor may sometimes be able to make effective use of the abandonment procedure as an alternative to a motion for relief from the automatic stay.

Section 364 regulates the obtaining of credit by a bankruptcy estate. A Chapter 7 estate will only make use of this provision if a trustee is authorized to operate a business or in extraordinary circumstances. A reorganization debtor will frequently make reference to or use of this provision.

Obtaining unsecured credit in the ordinary course of business does not require court approval. Any postpetition secured loan or loan not incurred in the ordinary course of business will always require court approval. If court approval is obtained, the loan will have priority as an administrative expense. On the other hand, if the loan is obtained without court approval, it will be relegated to the status of a prepetition unsecured claim.

An administrative secured loan may be given priority over all other expenses of the estate, including other administrative expenses. However, the court will not permit a secured loan or priority secured loan unless it can be shown that there is no other form of loan available to the debtor. In health care business bankruptcies, special provisions protect the privacy and disposition of patient records, and facilitate the safe transfer of patients from a closing facility. The court will appoint an ombudsman to represent the interests of the patients.

KEY TERMS

abandon
health care business

ordinary course of
business

DISCUSSION QUESTIONS

1. Why does the Bankruptcy Code restrict the use of an estate's cash by a trustee?

2. How must a trustee maintain a bankruptcy estate's cash assets?

3. What are the purposes of abandonment?

4. How does a trustee abandon estate property?

5. When may a secured creditor benefit from the abandonment procedure?

6. Under what circumstances may an estate incur unsecured credit without court approval?

7. Under what circumstances must an estate obtain court approval to incur credit?

8. Identify reasons why special provisions exist to protect patients and their records in health care bankruptcies.

PRACTICE EXERCISE

Exercise 20.1

The Bottomlines have received a notice from the Bankruptcy Court that the trustee has abandoned their home, and they are concerned that they will have to move. Prepare a draft of a letter to the Bottomlines explaining the impact of the trustee's abandonment of their home.

21

Claims

A. CLAIM DETERMINATION

Three of the trustee's four basic duties have been described elsewhere in this text: investigation (chapters 8, 10, 11, 12, 14), liquidation (chapters 18-20), and litigation (chapters 10, 12-18). The process of completing these duties and distributing dividends to the creditors comprises the fourth basic trustee duty: administration. This process is the least discussed and least visible of the trustee's duties unless it is being performed inefficiently, usually in terms of undue delay. Once all of the estate's assets have been liquidated, the prompt determination of "who gets what and in what order" is the goal of efficient bankruptcy administration. This chapter shall describe the general rules and procedures for determining claims — their priority. The next chapter describes the process of dividend distribution.

An easy way to comprehend the claim determination process is to compare it to a nonbankruptcy action to collect a debt. Picture the creditor as a plaintiff who wants its bill paid. The debtor is the defendant. The debtor may or may not have defenses to the claim. These same defenses may be raised in bankruptcy.[1]

A claim that is determined to be entitled to receive a dividend from the bankruptcy estate is referred to as an **allowed claim**.[2] Whether a claim is allowed or disallowed and the order in which the claim is paid should not be confused with the concept of dischargeability. These two concepts are often confused by practitioners who do not properly perceive the difference between them. Whether a claim is dischargeable has no effect

---

1. 11 U.S.C. §§502(b)(1), 558.
2. 11 U.S.C. §§502(a), 507, 724, 726, 1111, 1123, 1222, 1322.

on its allowability. A claim that is nondischargeable may be allowable, in which case the creditor will receive a dividend from the bankruptcy estate if a dividend becomes payable. This means that if a debt is nondischargeable, the creditor's receipt of a dividend will reduce the debtor's remaining nondischargeable liability. The creditor with a nondischargeable allowable claim will therefore retain two sources of recovery, the estate and the debtor. The fact that a debt is not dischargeable does not normally affect the creditor's right to receive a dividend from the estate.

> ### *Practice Pointer*
>
> Remember that a "claim" is defined as "right to payment, whether or not such right is reduced to judgment, liquidated, unliquidated, fixed, contingent, matured, unmatured, disputed, undisputed, legal, equitable, secured, or unsecured." 11 U.S.C. 101(5).

Sections 501 through 510 concern the filing and allowance of claims. Recall that all debtors, regardless of chapter, are required to file a list of creditors with their Schedules and also to state whether the claim is disputed, contingent, or unliquidated.[3] These labels place the creditors and trustee on notice as to the debtor's position regarding each claim.

B.   FILING A PROOF OF CLAIM

For a claim to be allowed and entitled to a dividend, a **proof of claim** must always be filed in a Chapter 7 case.[4] In Chapter 11, a creditor whose claim is listed as undisputed by the debtor is not required to file a claim in order for the claim to be deemed allowed. A claim scheduled as undisputed in a Chapter 11 is deemed allowed without a proof of claim having to be filed.[5] It is always wise to file a proof of claim. Even when a notice from the court or the United States Trustee recommends against filing a claim until further notice, a proof of claim should always be filed as promptly as

---

3. See chapter 7 supra; 11 U.S.C. §521(a)(1); Bankruptcy Rule 1007. See also chapter 29 infra.
4. 11 U.S.C. §502(a); Bankruptcy Rules 3002, 3003(c).
5. 11 U.S.C. §1111(a).

possible if it is known that there will most likely be a distribution of dividends. There is one very good reason for following this approach.

The original notice to creditors from the United States Trustee requesting that claims not be filed is the standard procedure in most districts. See the sample notice at Form 7.6 on the forms disk. Note how the form requests creditors not to file claims. The customary no asset notice is disseminated without regard to whether there will in fact be funds available to distribute as dividends. If a subsequent notice is distributed six or twelve months later requesting creditors to file claims, the creditors may forget to do so or may have to locate closed records before the amount of the claim can be properly calculated. On the other hand, if a claim is promptly filed at the inception of the bankruptcy, it usually takes little time to complete the proof of claim form attaching any relevant documents as exhibits. Once this is done, the creditor's right to receive a dividend from the estate is fully protected and there is nothing else to be done except to wait and see if any dividend is produced by the estate.

A creditor or a codebtor of the debtor may file their own proof of claim. The debtor or trustee may file a proof of claim for a particular creditor. This does not frequently occur in actual practice. An equity security holder may also file a proof of claim.[6] Because definite deadlines are set for the filing of proofs of claim, codebtors, the debtor, or the trustee may file a claim to preserve a creditor's rights to receive a dividend. For example, if a debtor owes substantial tax liabilities, the debtor may want to file a proof of claim on behalf of any tax creditors to ensure that the tax claims will be entitled to receive any dividend that may become payable by the estate.

Once a claim is filed, if a creditor later changes its address, the creditor must advise the court of the address change. If this is not done, the trustee will not know where to send a dividend check, and the check may be returned and the dividend possibly forfeited.[7]

In a Chapter 7 proceeding, the deadline for filing a proof of claim is 90 days after the date first set for the Section 341 creditors' meeting, except for governmental creditors, who receive a bar date of 180 days after the entry of the order for relief (normally the filing of the bankruptcy petition). This deadline is known as the **claims bar date** in all bankruptcy proceedings. There are several important exceptions to this general rule.

---

6. 11 U.S.C. §501; Bankruptcy Rule 3001.
7. 11 U.S.C. §347; Bankruptcy Rule 3009. In a Chapter 7, this forfeiture is to the United States (28 U.S.C. Chapter 129). In other proceedings the forfeiture is to the debtor or entity acquiring the debtor's assets under the plan.

Two of them affect most proceedings. The first important exception is if the United States Trustee initially notifies creditors not to file claims, as noted in the sample notice included on the forms disk. If a bar date is set at a later date, the creditors are then given 90 days' notice from the time of the later notice to file proofs of claim. The second exception permits a nondebtor party to a rejected executory contract to file a proof of claim within such time as the court may direct.[8] In a Chapter 11 proceeding, as noted above, claims listed as undisputed are deemed allowed. Other claimants must file a proof of claim within any deadline that is set by the court upon application by the debtor-in-possession and providing notice to creditors of the claims bar date.[9]

A proof of claim may be filed by using a standard form that replicates Official Bankruptcy Form 10. A sample form is included on the forms disk accompanying this text. The form will be self-explanatory once this present chapter has been completed by the reader. In addition to the form, evidence of the claim should be attached to the form, such as a promissory note, the invoice, and so forth. Evidence of a security interest, such as a recorded mortgage or UCC Financing Statement, should also be attached. This data is summarized in checklist 21.1 accompanying this chapter. The proof of claim should be served on the trustee.[10]

C.   CLAIM OBJECTIONS — PROCEDURE

Section 502 contains the basic rules for determining the allowance or disallowance of a claim. Administratively, once the claims bar date expires, the trustee will review the claims and may or may not object to them. Unless a claim is objected to, it is deemed allowed.[11] An allowed claim is entitled to receive a dividend if a distribution is to be made.

A claim is objected to by the trustee or the debtor when they file on notice to all interested parties a formal written objection to the claim. A sample notice of claim objection for use by a Chapter 7 trustee is included on the forms disk accompanying this text. A hearing on an objection to a claim requires 30 days' notice to the creditor. An opposed

---

8. Bankruptcy Rule 3002(c).
9. Bankruptcy Rule 3003(c).
10. Bankruptcy Rule 3001.
11. 11 U.S.C. §502(a).

objection will assume the status of a contested matter that will treat the objection as an adversary proceeding as described in chapter 12 supra.[12]

> ### *Practice Pointer*
>
> Although there is a deadline within which to file proofs of claim, there is no statutory deadline in the Code within which the trustee or the debtor must file an objection.

A trustee may object to a claim on either procedural or substantive grounds. There are three typical procedural grounds for objecting to claims. First, the trustee may assert that the claim was filed late (after the expiration of the claims bar date). The Supreme Court has ruled that a standard of excusable neglect may, in appropriate circumstances, obviate the harsh effects on a late-filed claim. In Pioneer Investment Services Co. v. Brunswick Associates, L.P., 507 U.S. 380 (1993), the creditors received the customary Notice to Creditors. However, the notice actually contained a claims bar date. Experienced bankruptcy counsel, assuming that the notice did not contain a claims bar date, advised the creditor that it would not be necessary to file a claim until a bar date was set. The Supreme Court set aside the rulings of the lower courts, which disallowed the creditor's late-filed claim, stating:

> We do, however, consider significant that the notice of the bar date provided by the Bankruptcy Court in this case was outside the ordinary course in bankruptcy cases. . . . [W]e conclude that the unusual form of notice employed in this case requires a finding that the neglect of respondents' counsel was, under all the circumstances, "excusable."

507 U.S. 398-399. Section 502(b)(9) of the Bankruptcy Code provides that a late-filed claim is not allowed except for priority claims (see Section 21K infra), which, pursuant to 11 U.S.C. §726(a)(1), may now be filed up to the date the trustee commences final distribution of the estate.

A second procedural claims objection is that the claim is a duplicate of a claim previously filed. It is only necessary to file a proof of claim once. The trustee must object to a duplicate claim since each claim filed must be reconciled before any distribution can occur. A third common procedural

---

12. Bankruptcy Rule 3007.

objection to a proof of claim is that the claim lacks adequate supporting documentation. Generally, a claim should contain documentation that would be sufficient to support a default judgment in a nonbankruptcy debt collection case. Nevertheless, a proof of claim properly signed and filed constitutes prima facie evidence of the claim's allowability. That is, a properly filed claim creates a presumption of the claim's validity.[13] It is then up to the trustee and the debtor to object.

D.   CLAIMS OBJECTIONS — SUBSTANCE

Substantive claims objections are more complex than procedural objections. There are two groups of substantive objections. The first is any defense the debtor would have had to the claim outside of the bankruptcy system. Any such defense is also a defense to the claim in a bankruptcy proceeding.[14] This is common sense. If a debt would be defensible outside the bankruptcy system, the fortuity of the bankruptcy should not eliminate the defense. For example, Mutt owes Jeff $10,000. However, the statute of limitations for collection has expired. If Mutt files a bankruptcy, Jeff's claim is not revived. The expiration of the statute of limitations will remain a defense to the claim in the bankruptcy.

The second group of substantive claim objections exists because of, rather than in spite of, the bankruptcy. These objections exist primarily because of the accounting peculiarities of the bankruptcy system, which attempts to account for the collective rights of all creditors. Secondarily, these objections limit certain types of claims from receiving potential windfalls as a result of the bankruptcy. These various objections are contained in Section 502(b).

A claim for unmatured interest is not allowable. That is, an unsecured creditor may only claim interest accrued up to the date of the bankruptcy filing. Postpetition interest on an unsecured claim is generally not allowable. An unsecured creditor cannot file a claim six months after a filing, adding any finance charges that have accrued between the date of the bankruptcy filing and the date the proof of claim is filed.[15] Postpetition interest on unsecured claims only becomes payable if all unsecured claims

---

13. Bankruptcy Rule 3001(f).
14. 11 U.S.C. §502(b)(1); 11 U.S.C. §558.
15. 11 U.S.C. §502(b)(2).

are paid in full and assets still remain available for distribution, as described in chapter 22 infra.

A claim for a property tax that exceeds the value of the estate's interest in the property is disallowed to the extent of the excess.[16] Do not confuse this limitation on allowability of the claim with the claim's dischargeability. The objection to a property tax claim is not related to the claim's dischargeability. A claim objection concerns the amount of a debt that will be entitled to receive a dividend from the bankruptcy estate. If the debt is also nondischargeable, the debtor will remain liable for any portion of the debt not paid by the estate.

Next, if the claimant is an insider or an attorney of the debtor, the claim will be disallowable to the extent it exceeds the reasonable value of the attorney's or insider's services. This prevents attorneys or insiders from filing excessive claims on the supposition that if a small dividend is distributed, the actual debt will be paid in full. This provision also aids a trustee in fully investigating the financial relationships between a debtor, its insiders, and attorneys.[17]

An unmatured and nondischargeable claim for alimony, support, or maintenance is not allowable.[18] For example, Mrs. Kramer is owed $1,000 in child support when Mr. Kramer files a Chapter 7. A proof of claim may be filed for the past due amount, even though the debt is nondischargeable. Any dividend will reduce the unpaid portion of the nondischargeable claim as described above. However, if Mr. Kramer continues to not pay the support after the bankruptcy filing, Mrs. Kramer may not file a claim for the additional support because it had not matured when the Chapter 7 petition was filed.

Remember that the collection of a domestic support obligation from property that is not property of the estate is excepted from the automatic stay.[19] As a result, a creditor spouse may continue to exercise all available nonbankruptcy remedies to collect nondischargeable or newly accruing domestic support obligations as long as the source of payment is not property of the estate.

Section 502(b)(6) limits a landlord's claim for future rent caused by the rejection of an unexpired real property lease. In many states, a landlord may obtain judgment against a tenant for the entire amount of rent remaining due under the term of a lease. In a multi-year commercial lease, this amount can be substantial. The Bankruptcy Code places limitations

---

16. 11 U.S.C. §502(b)(3).
17. 11 U.S.C. §502(b)(4).
18. 11 U.S.C. §502(b)(5).
19. 11 U.S.C. §362(b)(2). See chapter 12 supra.

upon the future rent that a landlord may seek in determining the amount of an allowed claim. A claim based upon a real property lease is limited to the amount of unpaid rent due on the earlier of the date prior to filing of the petition or the amount of unpaid rent due on the date the landlord regains possession of the premises. The landlord's claim for future rent is limited to the greater of one year's rent reserved under the lease or 15 percent of the total rent remaining under the lease, not to exceed three years. It is thus necessary to calculate the total rent under the lease for one year and then 15 percent of the total rent for three years. The greater of these two amounts is the maximum amount of a real property lessor's future rent claim.[20]

For example, assume that Felix's Cat Shoppe has a five-year lease. The first year's rent is $1,000 per month. The lease provides that the monthly rent will rise $500 in each subsequent year. Thus, the rent in year five will be $3,000 per month. The Shoppe stops paying rent at the end of ten months and files a Chapter 7 proceeding at the end of year one of the lease. Under Section 502(b)(6), the landlord's claim will be $20,000. The claim for unpaid rent on the date of filing is $2,000, and the second year's rent is $18,000 ($1,500 × 12). Fifteen percent of three years' rent is $10,800. (The total rent for year two is $18,000, year three, $24,000, and year four, $30,000. Fifteen percent of this total is $10,800.) One year's rent is therefore greater than 15 percent of three years' rent.

A future rent claim is determined without regard to acceleration. This means that any clause in a lease that accelerates the rent due upon termination of the lease will not serve to increase the amount of allowable claim.[21] A claim for a terminated employment contract is limited to one year's compensation dated from the earlier of the date of the petition's filing or the date when the contract is terminated, plus any compensation actually unpaid at the time of the bankruptcy filing.[22] For example, a professional track team, The Snails, files a Chapter 7. The athletes with multi-year contracts have their claims limited to one year's compensation and any compensation unpaid at the time of filing.

Sometimes, claims are filed that cannot be readily computed. For instance, a personal injury claim filed against an estate, which has not proceeded to judgment, may have an unknown value. Section 502(c) allows a trustee to have the court estimate the claim. This procedure is an expedient that allows a trustee to administer a bankruptcy estate in a

---

20. 11 U.S.C. §502(b)(6).
21. 11 U.S.C. §502(b)(6)(B).
22. 11 U.S.C. §502(b)(7).

reasonable period of time. Sometimes estimation is the only practical solution, and the Code permits this practice.[23]

Section 502(d) permits a trustee to utilize the avoiding powers as the basis for an objection to a claim. In this context, the avoiding power is used defensively as opposed to offensively. Here, the trustee does not seek an affirmative judgment but attempts to defeat a claim filed by a creditor that is the transferee of an avoidable transfer or other unreturned property of the estate.[24]

Section 502(e) concerns a creditor that files a claim for contribution or for reimbursement in some form from the debtor. For example, one of two general partners pays all the partnership debt while the other general partner files a Chapter 7. The general partner who has paid all the partnership debt files a proof of claim for contribution in the bankrupt partner's bankruptcy proceeding. The claim for contribution will be allowable only if there is no nonbankruptcy defense to the bankrupt partner's contribution.[25] Claims arising in the ordinary course of business in an involuntary proceeding are deemed prepetition claims for the purpose of allowance to the extent they arise between the commencement of the bankruptcy and the earlier of the appointment of a trustee or the entry of an order for relief.[26] A claim arising from the rejection of an executory contract is considered to have arisen immediately prior to the date of filing of the petition.[27] A claim arising from the disallowance of a setoff, of a returned avoided transfer, or avoidance of a lien under Section 522 will also be considered to have arisen immediately prior to the filing of the original petition.[28] In each of these instances, this means that the amount of the claim that will be allowed will be determined as if the claim had been incurred prepetition. However, the distributive priority accorded the claim may vary, as described infra this chapter.

A priority tax claim that does not arise or is not assessed until after the filing, but that is for a prefiling tax period, is considered to arise immediately before the bankruptcy filing. This makes the claim a prepetition priority claim as opposed to a potential administrative expense claim.[29]

---

23. 11 U.S.C. §502(c).
24. 11 U.S.C. §502(d).
25. 11 U.S.C. §502(e).
26. 11 U.S.C. §502(f). See chapter 4 supra.
27. 11 U.S.C. §502(g). See chapter 19 supra.
28. 11 U.S.C. §502(h). See chapter 9 supra.
29. 11 U.S.C. §502(i).

Section 502(j) permits the court to reconsider for cause any claim that has been disallowed. An affected creditor may bring a motion before the court to reconsider an order disallowing the claim.[30]

Section 502(k), added by BAPCPA, permits a debtor to bring a motion to reduce a consumer claim by up to 20 percent if the debtor can prove by clear and convincing evidence that the creditor unreasonably refused to negotiate, within 60 days of the bankruptcy filing, an alternative repayment schedule to repay at least 60 percent of the debt within a reasonable period. Any payment made pursuant to such a proposal is also protected from the trustee's preference powers. The purpose of these provisions is to encourage composition agreements in consumer cases (see chapter 2 supra).

E.   ADMINISTRATIVE EXPENSES

Section 503 concerns **administrative expenses**. Generally, administrative expenses are all claims incurred by an estate after an order for relief has been entered as well as any approved professional expenses incurred after commencement of the bankruptcy. Administrative expenses are normally accorded the highest distributive priority under the Bankruptcy Code except perhaps for superpriority secured claims approved by the court under Sections 364 or 507(b).[31] In a Chapter 7 proceeding, administrative expenses will normally include the trustee's fees pursuant to Section 326 and all costs the trustee incurs in administering and liquidating the estate, such as auctioneer's fees, postpetition rent, and attorneys' fees. In a Chapter 11, all expenses incurred in operating the estate's business will be administrative expenses, including postpetition taxes, rent, payroll, and accounts payable. Generally, any expense incurred by an estate after the commencement of a bankruptcy will be an administrative expense.[32] Regardless of the type of claim incurred as an administrative expense, administrative expenses are all considered to be one class of claim for purposes of ultimate distribution. If an estate cannot pay all of its administrative expenses in full, all of the administrative claims will be placed into one class and will share the estate proceeds on a pro rata

---

30. 11 U.S.C. §502(j); Bankruptcy Rule 3008.
31. See chapters 18 and 20 supra and infra this chapter. In individual bankruptcies, domestic support obligations may have priority over most administrative expenses. See infra this chapter.
32. 11 U.S.C. §503(b)(1).

basis. In this instance, administrative tax claims would share an estate's proceeds pro rata with other administrative claims.[33]

Administrative expenses also include attorneys' or professionals' fees approved by the court after notice and hearing.[34] These fees are subject to the notice and hearing requirements of Sections 330 and 331 prior to payment being made.[35] The expenses incurred by a creditor in successfully prosecuting an involuntary petition, the recovery of property of the estate or the rendition of a substantial contribution to a proceeding, including attorneys' and accountants' fees, may also be given administrative priority. Expenses incurred by members of Official Creditors' Committees in the performance of their duties are also payable as an administrative expense after court approval.[36] The theory here is that a creditor rendering a substantial benefit to an estate and to all its creditors should be rewarded by receiving reimbursement for any reasonable expenses incurred.

Section 503(c) of the Bankruptcy Code provides the court with rules and standards to guide the court with respect to the payment of bonuses to corporate executives in Chapter 11 cases.

If a lease is assumed during the course of a case, presumably a Chapter 11, and is later rejected, the landlord is entitled to an administrative claim equal to any unpaid postpetition obligations and two years of unpaid rent under the lease. The balance of any claim is computed as per Section 502(b)(6) discussed in Section 21D above.[37]

The costs of closing a health care facility and disposing of patient records are allowed administrative expenses.[38] Finally, the value of goods sold within 20 days prior to the filing in the ordinary course of business are given administrative priority.[39]

F.   FEE SHARING PROHIBITION

Section 504 prohibits fee sharing, a practice that is common in some areas of the legal profession outside of the bankruptcy system. Section 504 prohibits referral fees in bankruptcy proceedings. A professional performing

---

33. 11 U.S.C. §507(a)(1); 11 U.S.C. §726(b). See chapter 22 infra.
34. 11 U.S.C. §503(b)(2).
35. See chapter 7 supra.
36. 11 U.S.C. §503(b)(3), (4), (5).
37. 11 U.S.C. §503(b)(7).
38. 11 U.S.C. §503(b)(8). See chapter 20 supra.
39. 11 U.S.C. §503(b)(9). See chapter 15 supra.

services in a bankruptcy proceeding may not share a fee or agree to share a fee except with members of that person's own firm or a public service attorney referral program.[40] For example, if Joe Lawyer refers a bankruptcy to Mary Attorney and requests a one-third referral fee, he may not receive the referral fee. If a fee sharing agreement is made and it is discovered by the trustee, Joe Lawyer will be required to reimburse the estate with the amount of the fee paid to him as the referral fee.

G.   TAX CLAIMS DETERMINATION

Section 505 permits the Bankruptcy Court to determine previously undetermined tax claims.[41] This provision specifically states that the Bankruptcy Court has jurisdiction to rule on the validity of tax claims affecting an estate.

One activity trustees must complete in many asset estates before an estate may be closed is filing a final tax return for the estate and paying any taxes owed by the estate. However, just because a return has been filed and any taxes paid does not mean that the trustee is released from potential liability. Any prudent trustee will therefore not close an estate until the tax return filed is no longer subject to audit or redetermination. Section 505(b) attempts to solve this problem; without this provision, no prudent bankruptcy trustee would ever close an estate.

Under Section 505(b), a trustee may submit a tax return to a taxing entity, complying with any applicable regulation for the filing of tax returns by bankruptcy estates, paying any taxes that are due, and requesting that the taxing entity determine within 60 days whether it wants to examine the tax return. If the taxing entity does not request an examination or other review within 60 days, the taxing entity can no longer object to the trustee's return, and both the estate and the trustee are released from further liability. If the taxing entity does request a review or audit, the review or audit must be completed within 180 days after the return is filed or the estate and the trustee are relieved from any further liability.[42] The trustee may then conclude administration of the estate without the risk of incurring further liability for any additional or unknown taxes by the estate.

---

40. 11 U.S.C. §504.
41. 11 U.S.C. §505(a)(1).
42. 11 U.S.C. §505(a)(1).

H.   SECURED CLAIMS

The problem of determining the extent of a secured creditor's secured claim is the subject of Section 506. A **secured creditor** is a creditor with a lien upon property in which the estate has an interest. The lien may be consensual, judicial, or statutory.[43] A creditor with a right of setoff is also considered a secured creditor for purposes of this provision. The significance of the value of a secured creditor's collateral has been previously described in connection with Sections 362 and 361, relief from the automatic stay and adequate protection.[44]

The focal point of Section 506 lies in determining the value of the collateral securing a secured claim. A secured creditor will often argue that its collateral is worth less than the amount of its claim. A debtor or trustee, on the other hand, will often argue that the collateral is worth more than the amount of the secured claim upon it. A creditor who successfully argues that the value of its collateral is less than the amount of its claim may have grounds for relief from the automatic stay due to lack of equity in the property securing the claim. This may also affect the amount of any adequate protection payments ordered by the court. For example, in United Savings Association of Texas v. Timbers of Inwood Forest Associates, Ltd., 484 U.S. 365 (1988), the Supreme Court held that an **undersecured creditor**, a creditor whose collateral is worth less than the amount of its claim, is not entitled to adequate protection payments on the undersecured portion of its claim. In Timbers, the debtor owed the creditor over $4.3 million, while the value of the collateral was not more than $4.25 million. Because the value of the collateral was worth less than the amount of the debt, the creditor was undersecured. Because Section 506(b) of the Code limits the allowance of postpetition interest only up to the value of the collateral, the Supreme Court reasoned that the undersecured creditor was not entitled to interest as adequate protection.[45]

Conversely, a debtor or trustee will want to show that the value of a secured creditor's collateral is more than that suggested by the creditor, because then there may be equity in the property that may result in the automatic stay remaining in effect. If the debtor or trustee can show that the collateral has significant equity, then it is possible the court will not order interim adequate protection payments. This frequently happens in

---

43. See chapter 6 supra.
44. See chapter 12 supra.
45. United Savings Assn. of Texas v. Timbers of Inwood Forest Assocs., Ltd., 484 U.S. 365 (1988). 11 U.S.C. §506(b).

consumer proceedings involving residences. If the court feels that there is a significant **equity cushion** in the debtor's residence, the difference between the amount of the claim and the actual value of the collateral, the court may leave the automatic stay in effect indefinitely and not require any adequate protection payments. Recall the more extensive discussion of this issue in chapter 12 supra.

In Associates Commercial Corporation v. Rash, 520 U.S. 953 (1997), the Supreme Court confronted the valuation issue head on. In this case, a Chapter 13 debtor attempted to have a tractor truck valued at its wholesale value of $28,500, while the secured lender argued that the value should be the vehicle's retail value of $41,000. The creditor argued that the higher retail value should be used because the debtor was intending to retain and use the vehicle. In agreeing with the creditor, the Supreme Court adopted a replacement value approach, stating:

> The "disposition or use" of the collateral thus turns on the alternative the debtor chooses — in one case the collateral will be surrendered to the creditor, and in the other, the collateral will be retained and used by the debtor. Applying a foreclosure-value standard when the cram down option is invoked attributes no significance to the different consequences of the debtor's choice to surrender the property or retain it. A replacement-value standard, on the other hand, distinguishes retention from surrender and renders meaningful the key words "disposition or use."

520 U.S. 953, 962 (1997). BAPCPA codifies the result in *Rash* at 11 U.S.C. §506(a)(2), applicable in individual Chapter 7 and 13 cases.

Regardless of the type of lien involved, a claim is secured only to the extent of the value of the creditor's interest in the property. To this extent, the creditor must look to the collateral for satisfaction of its claim. A creditor who is undersecured, whose collateral is not worth the amount of its claim, becomes an unsecured creditor for any deficiency and is entitled to receive a dividend as an unsecured creditor for the unsecured portion of the claim. However, if the property is not disposed of in the bankruptcy, the lien "passes through bankruptcy unaffected." This was the ruling of the Supreme Court in Dewsnup v. Timm, a case in which the debtor owed the creditor $120,000, while the value of the collateral was only $39,000.[46] The debtor contended that the amount of debt that exceeded the value of the collateral should be considered discharged as an unsecured claim, thus reducing the creditor's secured obligation to $39,000. Relying on precedent established

---

46. 502 U.S. 410 (1992).

in the case law under the Bankruptcy Act, the Court disagreed with the debtor's position, stating: "[W]e are not convinced that Congress intended to depart from the pre-Code rule that liens pass through bankruptcy unaffected."[47] The secured creditor will thus bear the burden of any postbankruptcy depreciation or, conversely, gain the benefit of any postbankruptcy appreciation in the value of the collateral, up to the amount of the claim.

> ### *Practice Pointer*
> Note that secured creditors are not required to file proofs of claim but may have incentive to do so to participate in any distributions from the estate toward their unsecured deficiencies.

To the extent that the value of the collateral is greater than the amount of a secured claim, the lienholder is entitled to payment of interest, attorneys' fees, and other reasonable charges provided for under any agreement that is the source of the claim.[48] A trustee incurring expenses in preserving the collateral of a secured creditor may seek to have such costs surcharged against the secured claim.[49] A secured creditor is not required to file a proof of claim for the secured portion of its claim to be allowed.[50] The reason for this latter provision is that a secured creditor's interest in collateral is proprietary in nature.

In Chapter 13 cases, when personal property collateral is worth less than the amount of the claim, debtors have sought to **strip down** the loan and to pay the creditor the value of the collateral only. The stripped-down portion is treated as an unsecured claim. For example, Doug Frasier owns a 2004 pickup truck worth $5,000. The Bank of Ours is owed $7,000 and has the truck as collateral. In a Chapter 13 case, Doug can strip down the $2,000 unsecured portion of the debt by proposing to pay the Bank $5,000, the value of the collateral.

BAPCPA places limits on the practice of stripping down purchase money loans on motor vehicles in Chapter 13 cases. Recall that a purchase money loan is the loan obtained for the purpose of purchasing the car. Section 1325(a) effectively provides that strip-down may not take place

---

47. Id. at 417.
48. 11 U.S.C. §506(b).
49. 11 U.S.C. §506(c). Only the trustee may assert this right. Individual creditors may not. See Hartford Underwriters Ins. Co. v. Union Planters Bank, N.A., 530 U.S. 1 (2000).
50. 11 U.S.C. §506(d)(2).

where the debt was incurred to purchase a motor vehicle within 910 days preceding the bankruptcy filing, or one year preceding the bankruptcy filing for any other personal property. If the debtor files a second case within two years of the first case, then the value of the security in the second case is treated the same as in the first case. In the above example, if Doug bought the car within 910 days of his filing, Bank's secured claim would be the entire $7,000 debt. However, if Doug did not give the car as collateral to finance its purchase, then he may still be permitted to strip down the loan under BAPCPA. However, if Doug surrenders a vehicle purchased within 910 days of filing, the circuit courts have uniformly held that the secured creditor may assert any deficiency as an unsecured claim.[51]

A noticed motion to determine the value of a secured creditor's collateral will be heard by the court in a **valuation hearing**. It begins as a noticed motion and will become a contested matter if it is opposed. A valuation hearing may be sought by any party in interest and will most commonly arise in connection with a relief from stay motion or a reorganization proceeding confirmation hearing.[52]

I.   STATEMENT OF INTENTION

A debtor with consumer debt secured by estate property is required to advise secured creditors as to the debtor's intention regarding the disposition of the creditor's collateral during the bankruptcy proceeding. See 521(a)(2). This notice must be given within 30 days of filing and is known as a **Statement of Intention**. A sample form is included on the forms disk accompanying this text. Essentially, the debtor must advise each secured creditor that the debtor intends either to return the collateral, to reaffirm the obligation, or to redeem the collateral. The debtor must perform the intention within 30 days of the date first set for the meeting of creditors. If the debtor fails to reaffirm or redeem within the time period, the automatic stay is terminated by operation of law, and the property is no longer considered to be property of the estate, unless the trustee brings a motion that the property will benefit the estate.[53] The rationale behind this provision is that the notice will allow a secured creditor to determine whether a motion for relief from the

---

51. See In re Wright, 492 F.3d 829 (7th Cir. 2007); In re Long, 519 F.3d 288 (6th Cir. 2008).
52. Bankruptcy Rule 3012. See chapter 12 supra and chapters 23, 26, and 27 infra.
53. 11 U.S.C. §362(h); 11 U.S.C. §521(a)(2), (6).

automatic stay or other such relief is necessary, and allow a creditor to determine when the automatic stay is terminated by operation of law pursuant to Section 362(h).

Many secured creditors are satisfied if a debtor's intent is merely to continue making payments, and the debtor may advise the creditor of this intention in the statement.[54] Debtors should welcome the apathy of secured creditors who will accept the simple continuation of payments. The reason for this is that if a debtor continues making payments but does not formally reaffirm the debt, the creditor's only remedy upon a subsequent default would be repossession of the collateral. Any deficiency will have been discharged in the bankruptcy proceeding as an unsecured claim. Secured creditors should always insist on reaffirmation agreements as a condition of allowing a debtor to retain collateral where the debtor has recourse to a deficiency after a repossession. An approved reaffirmation agreement will preserve the creditor's deficiency rights in the event of a subsequent default.[55]

Under BAPCPA, Section 521(a)(6) limits a debtor's choice to surrender of the collateral, reaffirmation of the debt, or redemption of the collateral. However, the "fourth option" or "ride through" may still exist if a debtor otherwise complies with the statement of intention provisions but the court refuses to approve the proposed reaffirmation agreement.[56] This is a logical approach because the debtor has done everything required of the debtor. If the debtor is current and continues to make payments in this instance, the debtor should not be treated any differently than the debtor would be outside the bankruptcy system because the creditor has not been harmed.

J.   REDEMPTION

Redemption involves the right of a Chapter 7 consumer debtor to pay a secured creditor the fair market value of the collateral, thereby obtaining a release of the lien. If consumer property is exempt or abandoned, a debtor

---

54. Continuing to make installment payments as they become due is also known as the "fourth option," or "ride through," the other three options being redemption, surrender, or reaffirmation, as discussed in the text. There was a dispute among the courts on whether or not this option still exists. Compare In re Dumont, 581 F.3d 1104 (9th Cir. 2009) (no) with In re Hart, 402 B.R. 78 (Bankr. D. Del. 2009) (yes).

55. See chapter 7 supra.

56. See, e.g., In re Chim 381 B.R. 191 (Bankr. D. Md. 2008), collecting citations.

may pay to the secured creditor, in a lump sum, the amount of its secured claim. This means, in essence, paying to the secured creditor the collateral's value.[57] For example, the Nortons are Chapter 7 consumer debtors. They owe $2,000 to Cramden's Used Cars, which has a lien in a 1973 Ford Pinto as collateral. The vehicle is worth $500. If the Nortons pay Cramden a lump sum of $500 and claim the vehicle exempt, the lien will be released from the vehicle and the balance of Cramden's claim will be discharged as an unsecured debt. A valuation hearing may be held to determine the amount necessary for the debtor to pay to redeem the collateral.

K.   PRIORITY CLAIMS

Certain claims are categorized as unsecured priority claims. **Priority claims** are required to be satisfied prior to other general unsecured claims in all proceedings unless an affected creditor agrees to a lesser treatment. Priority claims are themselves prioritized in the order described in Section 507(a). Each higher-numbered class of claims described in Section 507(a) has priority over each of the lower-numbered claims. Thus, all claims under Section 507(a)(1) will be paid in full before any claims under Section 507(a)(2) and so forth. Contrary to popular belief, there are actually a number of claims that have priority over tax claims.

The first category of priority claims are claims for domestic support obligations. However, the expenses of the Chapter 7 trustee, including professional fees, shall be paid ahead of the domestic support obligations. This ensures that the trustee and the trustee's professionals will be compensated for collecting the funds that pay the domestic support obligation.[58]

The second category of priority claims includes administrative expenses under Section 503, including any filing fees incurred in connection with the bankruptcy.[59] The third category of priority claims is unsecured gap claims incurred under Section 502. Note, however, that although the claim is allowed as if it were incurred prepetition, as described supra in this chapter, the claim has a distribution priority over virtually all other unsecured claims. A **gap period claim** is a claim

---

57. 11 U.S.C. §722.
58. 11 U.S.C. §507(a)(1)(C). See chapter 13 supra.
59. 11 U.S.C. §507(a)(2).

incurred during that period of time between the filing of an involuntary petition and prior to the entry of an order for relief.[60]

The fourth category of priority claims concerns unpaid wages. Wage claims, including vacation, severance, or sick leave pay, are accorded a priority of up to $11,725 per individual for wages earned within 180 days prior to the commencement of the proceeding or the date on which the debtor's business ceased operating, whichever occurs first. Priority wage claimants include independent contractors who earned at least 75 percent of their independent contractor income from the debtor in the 12 months prior to the bankruptcy filing or cessation of the business.[61] These alternative dates account for the close of a business several months or more prior to an actual bankruptcy filing. A wage claim of greater than $11,725 becomes a general unsecured claim to the extent of any excess. For example, Wimpy is owed $12,000 from Brutus Burgers. The wages were all incurred within 180 days prior to Brutus Burgers' bankruptcy filing. Ten thousand dollars of the claim will be a priority claim under Section 507(a)(4). The remaining $1,050 will be a general unsecured claim.

Section 507(a)(5) is for unpaid contributions to an employee benefit plan, up to $11,725 per employee for unpaid contributions earned within 180 days prior to the date of the bankruptcy filing or the close of the debtor's business, whichever occurs first.[62] Any excess is treated as a general unsecured claim as described above in connection with priority wage claims.[63] The sixth priority claim concerns the unsecured claims of grain producers or fishermen for their produce or catch in the possession of a storage facility as previously described in the context of Section 546.[64] Recall that under Section 546(d) farmers or fishermen have a right to reclaim their products within ten days after delivery to an insolvent storage facility. These same creditors are also granted a priority claim of up to $5,775 per claimant.[65] Once again, similar to wage claims, to the extent the claim exceeds $5,000, the excess becomes a general unsecured claim.

The seventh category of priority claims deals with a situation that will often arise when a retail business files a bankruptcy proceeding. This situation involves consumers who have made deposits for consumer goods or services, such as furniture or appliances. The business files

---

60. 11 U.S.C. §507(a)(3). See chapter 3 supra.
61. 11 U.S.C. §507(a)(4).
62. 11 U.S.C. §507(a)(5).
63. In Howard Delivery Service, Inc. v. Zurich American Insurance Co., 547 U.S. 651 (2006), the Supreme Court held that unpaid worker's compensation premiums are not entitled to priority under this provision.
64. See chapter 15 supra.
65. 11 U.S.C. §507(a)(6).

a bankruptcy before the furniture or appliance is delivered. In such a situation, the individual consumer is given a priority claim of up to $2,600 for the goods or services not provided.[66] Once again, any excess amount of the claim will become a general unsecured claim. The eighth priority claim covers priority tax claims. Congress has determined, in enacting the Bankruptcy Code, that all of the preceding categories of priority claims will be paid in full *before* satisfaction of unsecured prepetition tax claims. Suffice it to say that the most common (income, sales, and payroll taxes) are all given priority status. Priority tax claims include income taxes incurred within three years prior to the bankruptcy filing, withholding taxes of any kind (this will include all payroll and most sales taxes), any employer taxes due on any priority wage claims, excise taxes, customs duties, and any penalties on any of the above where the penalty is compensation for actual loss.[67] Priority tax claims are those taxes that are deemed nondischargeable.[68] This is the only claim provision in the Code that relates directly to the issue of the claim's dischargeability. Section 507(a)(9) makes a commitment by a financial institution to meet minimum capital requirements to an appropriate regulatory agency as a ninth priority unsecured claim.

Section 507(a)(10) grants priority status to claims for death or personal injury resulting from the operation of a motor vehicle or vessel because the debtor was intoxicated on alcohol or drugs.

Section 507(b) provides a secured creditor a priority claim superior to all other administrative expenses where the creditor's collateral has been sold, used, or leased without consent or court approval.[69]

L.   PARTNERSHIP CLAIMS

Section 508 requires that a creditor of a partnership who receives a dividend from a nondebtor general partner may not receive further dividends from the partnership's bankruptcy proceeding in which the identical claim has been filed until all other creditors have received a distribution

---

66. 11 U.S.C. §507(a)(7).
67. 11 U.S.C. §507(a)(8). The three-year period is tolled during any period in which a prior bankruptcy is pending. Thus, where the debtor filed Chapter 7 during the three-year period, received a discharge, and then filed Chapter 13, the Supreme Court has held that the three-year period would be extended to include the time period of the first bankruptcy. Young v. U.S., 535 U.S. 43 (2002).
68. See chapter 13 supra.
69. 11 U.S.C. §507(b). See the discussion of cash collateral in chapter 18 supra.

equal to that received from the general partner.[70] For example, a creditor of The Three Musketeers receives a payment from Porthos, a general partner, equal to 50 percent of the claim. The creditor, Richelieu, may not receive a dividend from the bankruptcy estate until all the other Musketeer creditors have received payment of 50 percent of their claims. This provision is intended to facilitate the fundamental debt collection concept of bankruptcy proceedings that creditors in an equal class should share the assets of the debtor estate on an equal basis.

M.   CODEBTOR CLAIMS

Section 509 is about the claims of a codebtor of a debtor. The cosigner of a loan is a codebtor. A general partner of a partnership personally liable for the partnership debts is a codebtor. A junior lienholder that satisfies a senior lienholder is considered a codebtor for these purposes.

Generally, if a codebtor pays the debts of a debtor, then the codebtor acquires the rights of the satisfied creditor.[71] For example, if a general partner pays a partnership debt, the general partner will acquire the claim of the satisfied creditor and will essentially become that creditor. A codebtor asserting a claim in such circumstances should provide proof of payment of the claim in any proof of claim filed by the codebtor in the debtor's bankruptcy proceeding.[72] However, the codebtor will not acquire the rights of the paid creditor to the extent that the claim is disallowed or subordinated under Section 510.[73]

N.   SUBORDINATION

The final concept to be dealt with in the area of claims is that of **subordination**. A claim that is subordinated is given a lesser priority than it is otherwise entitled to under the Bankruptcy Code. A creditor may be subordinated for two reasons.

---

70. 11 U.S.C. §508.
71. 11 U.S.C. §509(a).
72. Bankruptcy Rule 3001(e).
73. 11 U.S.C. §509(b).

The first and most logical reason is if a creditor consents to subordinate itself to a lesser priority claim.[74] Frequently, in Chapter 11 proceedings, for example, creditors may request insiders to subordinate any claims to those of the noninsiders as a condition to the noninsiders' approval of a reorganization plan. In large reorganizations where there may be multiple issues of bonds, each issue typically contains consensual provisions that rank a particular bond issue in order of priority with any predecessor issues. A creditor may agree to subordination. It is a guiding principle of the Bankruptcy Code that a creditor may always agree to accept lesser treatment than the law may otherwise entitle it to.

A second common manner in which a creditor may be subordinated is under the doctrine of *equitable subordination*. A claim may be equitably subordinated by motion.[75] There are logical and equitable reasons why the claim of a creditor might be equitably subordinated. The most common reason for subordination of a claim under this theory is because the creditor involved has been guilty of "bad acts." The creditor has done something that in all fairness requires the creditor to be paid after other creditors instead of along with them.

For instance, insiders receive excessive salaries from a debtor corporation and then loan a portion of the salary back to the company, becoming among the company's largest creditors in the process. If the excessive salaries have damaged the company at the expense of the company's creditors, perhaps the insider claims should be subordinated and paid after other claims. Perhaps one factor for the company's predicament is the excessive insider payroll.

Summary

The determination of claims and the distribution of dividends to allowed claimholders is a basic function of the trustee's duty to administrate a bankruptcy estate. This and the next chapter describe this process. Sections 501 to 510 of the Bankruptcy Code govern the determination of claims against a bankruptcy estate.

A creditor, other than a secured creditor not entitled to a deficiency, must always file a proof of claim to be entitled to receive a dividend from a Chapter 7 estate. A proof of claim must be filed before the expiration of any claims bar date set by the United States Trustee or court to receive proper treatment. A late claim, other than a priority claim, is subordinated

---

74. 11 U.S.C. §510(a).
75. 11 U.S.C. §510(c).

to all other claims. As a practical matter this means no dividend in most cases. A Chapter 11 claim scheduled as undisputed by the debtor-in-possession need not file a proof of claim.

It is recommended that a creditor should always file a proof of claim. A sample proof of claim is included on the forms disk accompanying this text. A proof of claim should always attach documentary evidence verifying the claim.

A trustee or the debtor may object to a claim. A hearing on an objection to a claim requires 30-day notice. A claims objection is a noticed motion, and it is treated as a contested matter, as described in chapter 12 supra, if it is opposed. A sample notice of objection for use by a Chapter 7 trustee is included on the forms disk.

Objections to a claim may be procedural or substantive in nature. Examples of procedural objections include duplicate claims, claims not containing supporting evidence, and late-filed claims.

Substantive objections to a claim fall into two groups and are primarily the subject of Code Section 502(b). The first group includes any defense existing to the claim under nonbankruptcy law. A defense based upon expiration of an appropriate statute of limitations is an example. The second group consists of a number of objections to specific types of claims specifically provided for in the Bankruptcy Code. These various objections are outlined in the checklist accompanying this chapter.

Administrative expenses are claims incurred by a bankruptcy estate. In a typical Chapter 7, administrative expenses will consist primarily of the costs of liquidation. In a Chapter 11, all expenses incurred in operating the debtor-in-possession are administrative expenses. The professional fees of trustees, attorneys, or other professionals and the expenses of Official Creditors' Committee members are also administrative expenses.

Bankruptcy Code Section 504 prohibits referral fees in bankruptcy proceedings except to public service attorney referral programs. The recipient of a referral fee must reimburse the referral fee to the estate.

Section 505 provides the Bankruptcy Court with jurisdiction to hear and determine tax claims affecting an estate. The provision also contains a procedure providing for expedited release of a bankruptcy estate and trustee from liability for taxes due by a bankruptcy estate for which returns have been filed and all taxes paid.

Section 506 contains provisions relating to the determination of a secured claim. The provisions will also have relevance in relief from stay and adequate protection matters. A claim is generally secured only to the value of any collateral. In Chapter 13 proceedings, the value of the collateral will be the amount of the debt due for purchase money loans on motor vehicles acquired within 910 days of the bankruptcy filing, or one year prior to the filing in the case of personal property contracts. To the extent that the collateral is worth less than the claim, the deficiency is an unsecured claim. To the extent that the collateral is worth more than the claim, a secured creditor is entitled to have postpetition interest and all charges allowed under the security agreement added to the claim. The value of collateral is determined by a valuation hearing. A secured claim may also be charged with the costs incurred by the estate in maintaining or preserving the collateral. If the collateral is not disposed of in the bankruptcy, the lien will survive the bankruptcy unaffected.

A debtor is required to advise a secured creditor of consumer debt of the debtor's intent as to disposition of the creditor's collateral after the bankruptcy filing. A debtor may reaffirm the debt or return or redeem the collateral. Redemption permits an individual consumer debtor to pay a lump sum to a secured creditor equal to the value of the collateral. A valuation hearing may be necessary to determine the adequacy of the redemption amount. A valuation hearing is a noticed motion. If a debtor fails to file a Statement of Intention, or fails to perform a stated intention, within 45 days after the meeting of creditors, the automatic stay will be terminated by operation of law pursuant to Section 362(h).

Section 507 identifies priority claims. The listed claims are given priority over all other claims in the specific order set forth by Section 507(a). Priority claims are summarized in the checklist to this chapter.

Section 508 concerns the effect on partnership cases of distributions by nondebtor partners. Section 509 permits a codebtor of a debtor to acquire the claims of any claim paid by the codebtor. A payment by a nondebtor guarantor to a creditor is an example.

Section 510 allows a claim to be subordinated. When a claim is subordinated, it is accorded a lesser status than the claim is otherwise entitled to by the Bankruptcy Code. For example, an insider may subordinate its claims to that of noninsiders. A claim may be subordinated by agreement or by court order.

KEY TERMS

administrative expenses   redemption
allowed claim   secured creditor
claims bar date   Statement of Intention
equity cushion   strip down
gap period claim   subordination
priority claims   undersecured creditor
proof of claim   valuation hearing

CHAPTER 21 CHECKLIST

21.1 FILING A PROOF OF CLAIM *Authority*

    21.1.1 Deadline: By Claims Bar Date Set   Bankruptcy
            by Court or United States Trustee   Rule 3002(c)

    21.1.2 Documents
           1. Proof of claim —   Bankruptcy
              Official Form 10   Rule 3001(a)
           2. Evidence of claim (such as   Bankruptcy
              promissory note; invoice)   Rule 3001(c)
           3. Evidence of perfection of   Bankruptcy
              security interest (such as   Rule 3001(d)
              recorded mortgage or UCC
              financing statement)

21.2 OBJECTION TO PROOF OF CLAIM

    21.2.1 Objection Documents
           1. Notice of objection — 30-day   Bankruptcy
              notice required   Rule 3007
           2. Declarations, where necessary
           3. Points and authorities, where
              necessary

21.3 PROCEDURAL CLAIMS OBJECTIONS

    21.3.1 Late-Filed Claims   11 U.S.C.
                                    §502(b)(9)
                                    Bankruptcy
                                    Rules 3002,
                                    3003

    21.3.2 Duplicate Claims

    21.3.3 Claim Lacks Adequate Supporting   Bankruptcy Rule
            Documentation   3001(c),(d),(f)

21.4 SUBSTANTIVE CLAIM OBJECTIONS

    21.4.1 A Defense to the Claim Applicable   11 U.S.C.
            Under Nonbankruptcy Law   §502(b)(1)
            (Such as Statute of Limitations)

---

76. The expenses incurred by the trustee in administering assets resulting in payment of the domestic support obligations are paid first. 11 U.S.C. §507(a)(1)(C).

Authority

21.5.5 Pension Plan Contributions   11 U.S.C.
Incurred Within 180 days up to   §507(a)(5)
$11,725 per Employee

21.5.6 Farmers or Fishermen with Crops   11 U.S.C.
or Catch in Storage Facility   §507(a)(6)

21.5.7 Deposits for Consumer Goods   11 U.S.C.
or Services of Up to $2,425   §507(a)(7)

21.5.8 Most Tax Claims   11 U.S.C.
     §507(a)(8)

21.5.9 Financial Institution Minimum   11 U.S.C.
Capital   §507(a)(9)

21.5.10 Death or Personal Injury Caused by   11 U.S.C.
Substance Abuse   §507(a)(10)

21.5.11 Secured Administrative Claim   11 U.S.C. §507(b)
Where Collateral Used Without
Consent or Prior Court Order

21.6 STATEMENT OF INTENTION (11 U.S.C. §521(2))

21.6.1 Contents
1. Notice required to be given secured creditors of consumer debt, advising of intended disposition of collateral after a Chapter 7 filing
2. Methods of disposition
   a. reaffirm
   b. return collateral
   c. redeem collateral

21.6.2 Time Limits
1. Notice must be given within 30 days of filing
2. Intention must be performed within 30 days of date first set for meeting of creditors
3. Stay relieved by operation of law at end of time period (11 U.S.C. §362(h)).

DISCUSSION QUESTIONS

1. How and when should a creditor file a proof of claim in a bankruptcy proceeding?

2. How does the trustee object to a proof of claim? What are the various grounds for objection to a proof of claim that the trustee may raise?

3. What is an administrative claim?

4. How is the amount of a secured claim determined? Does a secured claim survive the bankruptcy?

5. What is the Statement of Intention procedure? What are its purposes? Should a debtor be permitted to continue payments unless the creditor objects?

6. What are the various priority unsecured claims?

7. What does it mean to subordinate a creditor's claim? How may a creditor's claim be subordinated in a bankruptcy proceeding?

PRACTICE EXERCISES

Exercise 21.1
Prepare the Bottomlines' Statement of Intention. Assume that they are going to reaffirm the debt to Toyota Credit.

Exercise 21.2
Prepare a proof of claim on behalf of any listed Bottomline creditor.

22

Administration

A.   ORDER OF DISTRIBUTION

When the assets of an estate have been fully liquidated and all allowable claims have been determined as to priority and amount, the proceeds will be distributed to the creditors. This is the ultimate goal of creditors in any bankruptcy proceeding: the receipt of a dividend. Success in any bankruptcy proceeding is based not upon the traditional adversary notions of winning or losing but upon the percentage of dividend that the unsecured creditors ultimately receive. This simple concept is the forest; everything else becomes the trees. This very basic and fundamental goal can often be overlooked or forgotten by the parties when they get mired in the seemingly infinite details of bankruptcy litigation and administration. Unlike many other areas of the law, a bankruptcy proceeding has no winners or losers in the conventional sense of these terms. A bankruptcy proceeding is considered to be most successful when all of the creditors are paid in full and the debtor still retains assets. This can happen in reorganization proceedings and even, on rare occasions, in Chapter 7 proceedings. Certainly when all of the parties receive precisely what they are entitled to, no one should be considered a loser.

The order of distribution for nonsecured creditors is specifically outlined in Section 726. Although described only in Chapter 7, these distributive provisions apply by implication in all other Chapter proceedings. This is because all reorganization plans must be consistent with the provisions of Chapter 7 and must provide unsecured creditors with at least the same treatment that they would have received in a Chapter 7 proceeding.[1]

---

1. 11 U.S.C. §§1129(a)(7), 1225(a)(4), 1325(a)(4). See chapters 23, 26, and 27 infra.

Under Section 726, the first category of claims that receives payment are priority claims, including administrative claims, so long as the priority claims are filed before the distribution is made.[2] If a Chapter 11, 12, or 13 case is converted to a Chapter 7, the Chapter 7 administrative expenses will have priority over the prior Chapter's administrative expenses and the administrative expenses of the superseded Chapter will drop into a second priority.[3] For example, if a Chapter 11 case is converted to a Chapter 7, the administrative expenses of the Chapter 7 case will have priority over the administrative expenses of the Chapter 11. Collectively, the administrative expenses will have priority over other nonsecured claims.

Next, priority claims allowed under Section 507 are paid. Each subclass of priority claim described in Section 507 must be satisfied in full before the next subclass may receive a dividend.[4]

Although not entirely accurate, the next category of claims to logically place on a list of payment priorities would be secured claims. This is not entirely accurate because a secured creditor, by virtue of its security interest, is entitled to receive its collateral or the value thereof. This may be done by the creditor obtaining relief from the automatic stay and a subsequent foreclosure or repossession of the collateral, abandonment, or return of the collateral by the debtor. Alternatively, if the trustee sells the collateral, a secured creditor is entitled to payment from the sales proceeds up to the amount of the secured claim.[5] If the secured creditor's collateral has a value of less than the amount of the allowed claim, then any deficiency becomes an unsecured claim and it is treated like any other unsecured claim.

General unsecured creditors comprise the next group entitled to receive dividends from a bankruptcy estate. Unsecured creditors who file their claims in a timely manner will receive dividends first. A claim is filed in a timely manner if it is filed before the expiration of the claims bar date, as described in chapter 21 supra.[6] Unsecured creditors filing proofs of claim after expiration of a claims bar date will have their dividends subordinated to timely-filed unsecured claims.[7] Penalties that are not compensation for actual damages or claims for punitive or exemplary damages are payable only after payment in full is provided to all other unsecured creditors.[8]

---

2. 11 U.S.C. §726(a)(1); 11 U.S.C. §507. See chapter 21 supra.
3. 11 U.S.C. §726(b).
4. 11 U.S.C. §726(b). See chapter 21 supra.
5. 11 U.S.C. §506. See chapters 18 and 21 supra.
6. 11 U.S.C. §726(a)(2); 11 U.S.C. §501; Bankruptcy Rules 3001-3003. See chapter 21 supra.
7. 11 U.S.C. §726(a)(3).
8. 11 U.S.C. §726(a)(4).

After all unsecured creditors are paid in full, any creditors subordinated under Section 510(c) will then receive dividends.

If all creditors are paid in full and there are still assets available for distribution, then the creditors are entitled to payment of postpetition interest on their claims.[9] If interest is paid and there are still assets remaining, any remainder is distributed to the debtor.[10] In the latter instance, it is said that the estate is *solvent* because its assets exceed its liabilities. The chart below sets forth the general order of distribution in the bankruptcy system. The checklist accompanying this chapter is a more complete list.

GENERAL PRIORITY OF CLAIMS

1.   Administrative (503)
2.   Priority (507)
3.   Secured (506)
4.   Unsecured (726)
5.   Subordinated (510(c))
6.   Interest (726)

Solvent   7.   Debtor (726)
Estate

When a Chapter 7 trustee knows that there will be a distribution to the creditors, the trustee will request the court or the United States Trustee to set a claims bar date. This is because, as a practical matter, a claims bar date is generally only set in a Chapter 7 case after a trustee determines that there are assets to distribute.[11] When a claims bar date is set, all creditors will receive a notice advising them to file claims prior to the claims bar date.

B.   METHOD OF DISTRIBUTION

When assets are distributed, they are distributed on a **pro rata** basis to each category or class of claim until the class has been paid in full.[12] *Pro rata* means that if there are insufficient assets to pay the claims of a

---

9. 11 U.S.C. §726(a)(5).
10. 11 U.S.C. §726(a)(6).
11. Bankruptcy Rule 3002(c)(5). See chapter 21 supra.
12. 11 U.S.C. §726(b).

class in full, then the claimants within the class are paid an equal percentage of their claims. In essence, pro rata means share and share alike. This concept is the principle underlying the trustee's avoiding powers, that creditors of the same class shall share the assets available for distribution equally. For example, if there is only enough to pay half of the unsecured claims, each claim will receive a dividend of 50 percent. If a senior class of claims is paid in full, the immediately junior class of claims will receive a dividend, and so forth until a class is reached in which only a pro rata distribution can be made, or all classes are paid in full and the debtor gets the remainder. In a typical Chapter 7 small asset case, the administrative and priority claims are often paid in full, secured creditors will obtain their collateral, and there is a pro rata distribution to unsecured creditors. Of course, secured creditors are always paid according to their rights in their secured collateral. This is the one exception to the rule of pro rata distribution.

C.   BANKRUPTCY ADMINISTRATION TIMELINE

The schematic below illustrates the *minimum* period of time it should reasonably take to administer most small asset Chapter 7 proceedings through the bankruptcy system. This minimum period is in excess of one year. Typically, the length of time it takes to fully administer an estate is longer than the minimum shown. The actions identified attempt to itemize the most important events that take place during the process, from the petition's filing to the close of the case.

The act of filing is obvious. The Section 341(a) creditors' meeting is required to take place within 40 days of the date of filing.[13] A discharge is usually received about 90 days after the Section 341(a) meeting. The discharge is to be issued forthwith after expiration of the deadline to object to the discharge, 60 days after the date first set for the meeting of creditors.[14]

In consumer debtor no asset proceedings, virtually all involvement by the debtor and counsel with the proceeding will terminate when the discharge is received or about four months after the case is filed. As a practical matter, this is the end of the bankruptcy for the debtor. But note that if there are assets in the estate, the second phase of the proceeding has just

---

13. Bankruptcy Rule 2003 requires a hearing no less than 21 days and no more than 40 days from the order for relief. See chapter 7 supra.
14. Bankruptcy Rule 4004.

begun. The trustee may be liquidating or litigating over the assets for an indefinite period of time. That is why liquidation and litigation are shown as indicated on the illustration. The length of time these functions take can vary considerably.

Event	Approximate time between events	
Filing		
	40 days	
341(a) Meeting		
	90 days	
524 Discharge		
Request for claims bar date		
	90 days	LIQUIDATION OF ASSETS AND LITIGATION
Claims bar date		
	30-60 days	
Claims docket		
	Review 30-60 days	
Claims objections		
	30-60 days	
Final report		TAX RETURNS AND CLEARANCE (60 DAYS)
Notice of intent to distribute		
	30-60 days	
Order for distribution supplemental report		
Close of Case, Bankruptcy Rule 5009	**370 days minimum**	

The next items on the timeline are the actual steps that a trustee must take to fully administer a proceeding within the bankruptcy system. First, the trustee in an asset proceeding has to request a claims bar date unless such a date was set in the original notice to creditors, which, as noted in chapter 21 supra, rarely occurs. Creditors are required to be given 90 days' notice to file claims in a Chapter 7 or 13 proceeding, except that a governmental unit may file a claim within 180 days from the filing date.[15]

When the bar date expires, the court will prepare a **claims docket** for the trustee. The *claims docket* is an itemized summary of the filed claims, including the name and address of the creditor, the general classification of the claim (secured, unsecured, priority), and the amount of the claim. This information is compiled from the proof of claims forms.

The trustee will then review the docket and inspect the filed claims where necessary. If a purpose would be served, the trustee must then bring objections to any objectionable claims and have them determined by the court.[16] A purpose is served if the objections will increase the ultimate dividends payable to creditors. A trustee is not required to bring objections that will provide no benefit to an estate. For example, let's assume that a trustee anticipates a 5 percent distribution to unsecured creditors in a proceeding. Several creditors have included postpetition interest in their claims. The amounts of included interest are less than $100. Although the postpetition interest claims are objectionable, the only result to be achieved is having $5 more to distribute (5 percent of $100), hardly worth the time and effort of a claims objection.

Creditors are given 30 days' notice of any hearing on an objection to a claim. If the objection is to the claim's substance, the court may treat the objection as a contested matter or adversary proceeding. The objection may then take an indefinite period of time to resolve because it has now entered the realm of litigation.[17]

Once all liquidation, litigation, and claims objections have been resolved, the trustee will finally know which creditors are entitled to receive a dividend. The trustee will also know what funds are available from which to pay a dividend. The trustee will then prepare and file a final report with the court and the United States Trustee.[18] When the final report is approved, the distribution will occur. The creditors will be given notice of the trustee's intent to distribute the estate and, of course, they may object to the proposed distribution. Any court hearing held to determine any such objection will result in further delay.

Federal Rule of Bankruptcy Procedure 5009 provides that if a trustee has filed a final report and certified that the estate has been fully

---

15. 11 U.S.C. §502(b)(9); Bankruptcy Rule 3002(c).
16. 11 U.S.C. §704(5).
17. Bankruptcy Rule 3007. See chapter 21 supra.
18. 11 U.S.C. §704(9); Bankruptcy Rule 2015.

administered, then there is a presumption that an estate has been fully administered.[19] The case can then be closed.

If all of the above time limits are totaled, in the smallest and simplest type of asset proceeding, the fastest administration will be approximately 12 to 15 months. In a no asset proceeding, administration is usually completed in about six months. The trustee will file a report of no assets in the matter and the proceeding will then be closed by the court in the normal course of business.

Summary

The ultimate goal of creditors in any bankruptcy proceeding is to receive a dividend. The percentage of dividend returned to the creditor body determines the success of any proceeding. Adversarial notions of winning or losing are not part of this final equation. Often, cooperation of the creditor body toward the ultimate common goal will achieve a greater return to all classes of creditors.

Dividends are distributed to claims by classes. Each class must be paid in full before the next immediate junior class receives a dividend. When there are insufficient assets to pay a class in full, the creditors within the class receive a pro rata or percentage distribution of their claims. No lesser classes will receive a dividend. When all classes are paid in full and assets remain available to return to the debtor, an estate is considered solvent. The general order of classification is: administrative, priority, secured, unsecured, subordinated, interest, and finally debtor. The checklist accompanying this chapter is a more thorough list.

It takes approximately 12 to 15 months to administer even the simplest asset estate. Estates with substantial assets or litigation, or both, can take years to fully administer. A no asset proceeding will take about six months to fully administer. The administration timeline contained in this chapter itemizes the steps taken to fully administer an estate.

KEY TERMS

claims docket   pro rata

---

19. Bankruptcy Rule 5009. See also 11 U.S.C. §350(a).

CHAPTER 22 CHECKLIST

22.1	ORDER OF CLAIMS DISTRIBUTION	*Authority*
22.1.1	Priority Secured Administrative Claims	11 U.S.C. §§503, 507(a)(1), 507(b), 726(a)(1)
22.1.2	Administrative Claims	11 U.S.C. §§503, 507(a)(1), 726(a)(1)
22.1.3	Priority Claims Authority	11 U.S.C. §§507(a)(2)-(10), 726(a)(2)
22.1.4	Secured Claims[20]	11 U.S.C. §506
22.1.5	Timely-Filed Unsecured Claims	11 U.S.C. §726(a)(2)
22.1.6	Late-Filed Unsecured Claims	11 U.S.C. §726(a)(3)
22.1.7	Fines or Penalties Not Compensation for Actual Damages; Punitive Damages	11 U.S.C. §726(a)(4)
22.1.8	Subordinated Claims	11 U.S.C. §510(c)
22.1.9	Postpetition Interest	11 U.S.C. §726(a)(5)
22.1.10	Debtor — Solvent Estate	11 U.S.C. §726(a)(6)

DISCUSSION QUESTIONS

1. What is the order of claims distribution in a bankruptcy proceeding? How does a class of claims receive a distribution when the trustee has insufficient funds to pay the class members in full?

2. What basic events must occur before a Chapter 7 bankruptcy asset estate may be closed?

---

20. This is the logical placement for secured claims in a table of this nature. However, as the text indicates, this placement is not entirely accurate, because the secured creditor has a property interest in its collateral.

PART V

Reorganization
Proceedings

23

Chapter 13: Reorganization Proceedings

A. INTRODUCTION — REORGANIZATION PROCEEDINGS

There are two basic types of proceedings available to debtors in the bankruptcy system: **liquidations** and **reorganizations**.[1] Chapter 7 is a liquidation proceeding. In a liquidation case, nonexempt assets, which may result in dividends to be distributed to the creditors, are sold, and the debtor is relieved of further personal liability by receiving a discharge.[2] In a reorganization proceeding, on the other hand, the creditors are paid over time according to a "plan" wherein the debtor attempts to repay the debt while retaining nonexempt assets and/or continuing to operate the business. Reorganization proceedings are, in their essence, no more or less than judicially approved composition agreements, the approval of which is binding upon all creditors of a debtor.[3]

The next five chapters of this text describe the most common reorganization proceedings, Chapters 13, 11, and 12. Chapter 9, applicable to municipal corporations, is rarely filed. Chapter 13 is a reorganization proceeding for individuals with regular income. Chapter 12 is a reorganization

---

1. See chapter 2 supra.
2. See chapter 7 supra.
3. See chapter 2 supra.

proceeding for family farmers or fishermen with regular income. Chapter 11 is a reorganization proceeding for all other debtors.[4]

Chapter 13 is a program for individuals (and their spouses) with regular income who have unsecured debts of less than $360,475 and secured debts of less than $1,081,400.[5] A qualified individual may attempt to repay his/her debts through a Chapter 13 plan over a period of time not to exceed five years.[6] If the plan is successfully performed, the Chapter 13 debtor will be able to retain nonexempt assets and receive a discharge.[7] Debtors typically file a Chapter 13 case to protect their homes from foreclosure or their cars from repossession because the Chapter 13 process provides them with an opportunity to cure the defaults on their secured debt in a manner that has a potentially less onerous effect on their ability to obtain new credit.

B.   SPECIAL CHAPTER 13 PROVISIONS

Chapter 13 has its own trustee system. Under Section 1302 of the Code, a judicial district may have a standing Chapter 13 trustee, one individual who will serve as the trustee for all of the Chapter 13 proceedings filed within the district, or each case may have a Chapter 13 trustee appointed in a manner similar to Chapter 7 trustees. Most districts have one or more standing trustees. The United States Trustee appoints all of the Chapter 13 trustees.[8] The major difference between a Chapter 13 trustee and a Chapter 7 trustee is that the Chapter 13 trustee is responsible for administering monthly plan payments from Chapter 13 debtors and distributing the payments to the creditors on a regular basis.[9]

Chapter 13 has the added benefit of extending the automatic stay to a codebtor of a consumer debtor who has not also filed a bankruptcy proceeding.[10] For example, if a debtor files a Chapter 13 case but the debtor's spouse does not, under Section 1301, the automatic stay will apply to the debtor and to the spouse of the nonfiling debtor. As a result, there will be instances in which only one spouse will need to file a Chapter 13 case

---

4. See chapter 4 supra.
5. 11 U.S.C. §109(e). 11 U.S.C. §104(b). This provision triannually adjusts the dollar limits contained in §109(e). The amounts shown reflect the amounts that became effective April 1, 2010. See chapter 4 supra.
6. 11 U.S.C. §1322(d).
7. 11 U.S.C. §1328(a).
8. 11 U.S.C. §1302(a).
9. 11 U.S.C. §1326(c).
10. 11 U.S.C. §1301.

because the other nonfiling spouse will still gain the benefit of the automatic stay while avoiding the burden of having filed a bankruptcy proceeding.

Chapter 13 debtors have rights and powers that are slightly different from those of Chapter 7 or Chapter 11 debtors. Unlike Chapter 7 or Chapter 11 trustees, generally, Chapter 13 trustees will not go out into the community and attempt to operate a small business owned by a Chapter 13 debtor. If a Chapter 13 debtor is engaged in business, the debtor is permitted to continue to operate the business and is given the right to use, sell, and lease property of the estate pursuant to Section 363 or to incur credit pursuant to Section 364.[11] Thus, a debtor who operates a sole proprietorship business and who satisfies the Chapter 13 filing requirements may be a Chapter 13 debtor and is permitted to continue operating the business after the filing. The income from operating the business will constitute the regular income required to perform the Chapter 13 plan.

 ### *Practice Pointer*

Remember, under Chapter 13, only "individuals," not corporations or other types of business entities, may seek relief.

Section 1306 concerns **property of the estate** in a Chapter 13 case. In Chapter 13, or Chapter 11 for an individual, unlike under Chapter 7, a debtor's postpetition earnings from services are considered to be property of the estate. The reason for this is that the regular income that is the source of the plan payments will come from the postpetition earnings received for services performed by the debtor. As a result, postpetition income is considered to be property of the estate. Because repayment is generated from the debtor's postpetition earning, a Chapter 13 debtor will normally remain in possession of all its property. Nonexempt property will not normally be turned over to the trustee's custody for liquidation.[12]

Like all other individual debtors, a Chapter 13 debtor must also comply with the requirement to file a prepetition credit counseling certificate as a prerequisite to filing the case (see chapter 4 supra). Along with the regular requirements to file a Statement of Financial Affairs, bankruptcy schedules, a statement of current income and current expenditures (Schedules I and J), and a statement of current monthly income (Official

---

11. 11 U.S.C. §§1303, 1304. See chapters 26 and 28 infra.
12. 11 U.S.C. §1306. See chapter 14 supra. 11 U.S.C. §1115. See chapter 25 infra.

Form 22C) for application of means testing to Chapter 13 (which must be filed within 15 days of filing the petition unless the court orders otherwise).[13] A Chapter 13 debtor must also file a "plan" within 15 days of filing the petition, unless the court orders otherwise.[14]

Section 1326(a) requires Chapter 13 debtors to make adequate protection payments to creditors holding security interests in personal property, and to provide evidence of the payment to the trustee. A debtor must also provide proof of any required insurance coverage to the creditor within 60 days after filing the case. Section 1308 also requires that a debtor must have filed all tax returns for the four-year period prior to the filing. The meeting of creditors may be continued for up to 120 days to permit the debtor to file the returns. Failure to file the returns can be grounds for dismissal of the case or conversion to Chapter 7 (see section C infra).

C. DISMISSAL OR CONVERSION — REORGANIZATION PROVISIONS

Section 1307 concerns the **dismissal** of a Chapter 13 case or the **conversion** of a Chapter 13 case to another proceeding.[15] Section 1112, applicable in Chapter 11 proceedings, is very similar. Accordingly, this discussion will summarize both provisions. Each section provides the grounds for a proceeding to be dismissed or converted to another Chapter under the Code. The typical situation is conversion from a Chapter 13 or 11 to a Chapter 7 proceeding — that is, from a reorganization case to a liquidation proceeding.

Consistent with the principles described in chapter 8 supra, Sections 1112 and 1307 permit a debtor one opportunity to convert a proceeding from one Chapter to another. In a Chapter 13, this right may not be waived. If a debtor wishes to convert from a Chapter 11 to a Chapter 13, the debtor must, however, meet the Chapter 13 filing qualifications. In a Chapter 11 proceeding, if the debtor is no longer a debtor-in-possession (for example, if a trustee has been appointed), or the proceeding has been commenced as an involuntary proceeding or has been previously converted, the debtor will not be able to freely convert the proceeding to another Chapter. In these circumstances, the debtor will have to obtain

---

13. 11 U.S.C. §109(h) (see chapter 4 supra). Bankruptcy Rule 1007(b)(1)(5), (c).
14. Bankruptcy Rule 3015.
15. See chapter 8 supra.

a court order to permit conversion. The ability to freely convert a proceeding from one Chapter to another takes place by filing a one-page application with the court stating that the Chapter 13 (or other reorganization) debtor is qualified to be a Chapter 7 debtor and wants to be a Chapter 7 debtor.[16]

Conversely, if a debtor has previously converted from one Chapter to another and conversion is desired for a second time, court approval will be required. A motion procedure is required to accomplish this task. The court will not permit debtors to convert from Chapter to Chapter repeatedly.

Subsections 1112(b) and 1307(c) provide a number of grounds for obtaining the dismissal or conversion of a reorganization proceeding to another Chapter for cause upon a noticed motion. Section 1112(b)(4) lists 16 examples and Section 1307(c) provides 11 examples. The common situation that arises is where a trustee or creditors seek conversion of a proceeding from a reorganization to a Chapter 7 liquidation because the reorganization has failed. Each provision uses the term *including* before listing the grounds that can result in dismissal or conversion. Recall that use of the term *including* means that the list is not exhaustive.[17] The court may find additional causes that may also constitute grounds for dismissal or conversion. However, the items identified cover the most common causes for converting a Chapter 11 or 13 to a Chapter 7 or why the proceeding should be dismissed. In a Chapter 11 case, if it is shown that a plan may be confirmed within the exclusivity periods of Section 1121 (see chapter 25 infra) or a reasonable time or if there is reasonable justification for the debtor's actions or lack thereof, the court may deny a motion to convert or dismiss. Unless the moving parties agree, a motion to convert or dismiss a Chapter 11 must be decided within 45 days of its filing.[18]

For example, the first cause under 1112(b)(4) is a continuing *loss or diminution* of the estate and the absence of a reasonable likelihood of rehabilitation.[19] This means that when a Chapter 11 estate is continuing to lose substantial amounts of money in operating under Chapter 11, or when it becomes apparent to the court and creditors that the reorganization has failed, conversion or dismissal will be in the best interest of the creditors and should occur. For example, Grandma Takeda's Instant Kosher Chicken Soup, Inc., a Chapter 11 debtor-in-possession, files operating reports that show that over an extended period of time the

---

16. 11 U.S.C. §1112(a); 11 U.S.C. §1307(a). See chapter 8 supra.
17. 11 U.S.C. §102(3). See chapter 4 supra.
18. 11 U.S.C. §1112(b)(3).
19. 11 U.S.C. §1112(b)(4)(A).

debtor is profitable. However, no plan has been proposed and the debtor intends to operate for as long as possible without filing a plan. Some debtors will take this approach because they incorrectly believe that Chapter 11 is a comfortable security blanket and it may appear possible to remain a Chapter 11 debtor indefinitely. This perception is an illusion. If the debtor persists, such behavior will return to haunt the debtor because it will ultimately constitute cause for a conversion or dismissal of the proceeding. The United States Trustee regularly files motions to dismiss or convert based on a debtor's unreasonable delay. The purpose of this Subsection is to prevent debtors from abusing the system by indefinitely postponing a resolution of their financial difficulties. In Chapter 11 cases, failure to comply with the administrative rules of Chapter 11 (see chapter 18 infra), gross mismanagement of the estate, unauthorized use of a secured claimant's cash collateral (see chapter 15 supra), failure to maintain insurance in force, failure to pay postpetition taxes or to file tax returns can all constitute cause for conversion or dismissal of the case.[20]

The first example under Section 1307(c) is an *unreasonable delay prejudicial* to the creditors of a Chapter 13 case.[21] Unreasonable delay takes place when a debtor fails to file a plan for no apparent purpose.

Both sections include a cause for conversion or dismissal of a reorganization proceeding where there is a *failure to propose a plan* within any deadline set by the court. This time period may be flexible in Chapter 11. However, as noted above, a Chapter 13 plan must be filed 14 days after a petition is filed.[22]

Another cause for dismissal or conversion of a reorganization proceeding is *failure to obtain confirmation* by the court of every plan proposed.[23] Usually, if the court denies confirmation of a first attempt at a plan, the debtor may make a second attempt to get a plan modified and/or confirmed. If the second plan cannot be confirmed, the debtor can theoretically try again and again and again. Ultimately, the creditors will tire of this. When they do, the repeated failure to obtain confirmation will constitute cause for conversion or dismissal of the reorganization proceeding.

A related cause for dismissal or conversion of a reorganization is if the *confirmation of a plan is revoked*.[24] In all reorganization proceedings, a confirmed plan may be revoked, primarily on the grounds of fraud.

---

20. 11 U.S.C. §1112(b)(4)(B), (C), (D), (F), (H), (I).
21. 11 U.S.C. §1307(c)(1).
22. 11 U.S.C. §1112(b)(4)(J); 11 U.S.C. §1307(c)(3); 11 U.S.C. §1321; Bankruptcy Rule 3015.
23. 11 U.S.C. §1307(c)(5); 11 U.S.C. §1112(b)(4)(J).
24. 11 U.S.C. §1112(b)(4)(L); 11 U.S.C. §1307(c)(7).

A confirmation's revocation may be grounds for conversion or dismissal of the proceeding.

The debtor's *inability to effectuate consummation* of a confirmed plan, or failure to commence making timely payments constitutes another cause for dismissal or conversion.[25] This means that if a plan is confirmed but performance does not commence, this failure may constitute cause for dismissal or conversion. This cause is to be distinguished from another listed cause, which permits dismissal or conversion due to a *material default with regard to a confirmed plan.*[26] In this latter event, performance has begun, but then stops or defaults.

A plan-related cause for conversion or dismissal of a reorganization proceeding occurs when the plan terminates because of some condition specified in the plan other than the completion of payments.[27] For example, the plan provides that unless an escrow closes by a date certain, the proceeding will automatically be converted to a Chapter 7. If the condition occurs, the proceeding will be converted.

Failure to pay any required court fees will also constitute cause for dismissal or conversion.[28] In a Chapter 13, the United States Trustee may seek dismissal or conversion if the debtor *fails to timely file required pleadings*, such as the Statement of Financial Affairs, Schedules, Schedule of Current Income and Expenditures, or tax returns for the four years prior to the filing of the Chapter 13 petition. In a Chapter 11, failure to provide information reasonably requested by the United States Trustee will produce a similar result.[29]

Finally, under both Chapter 11 and Chapter 13, failure to pay a post-petition domestic support obligation is grounds for dismissal or conversion.[30] When a reorganization proceeding is converted to a Chapter 7, the debtor is required to file a final report and to update the Statement of Financial Affairs and Schedule of Assets and Liabilities to account for the estate's activities during the reorganization proceeding. When a Chapter 13 is converted to another Chapter under the Bankruptcy Code, the property of the estate consists of all the property under the possession or control of the debtor on the conversion date, and the value of any secured claim shall continue to be considered fully secured unless the claim has been paid in full prior to conversion of the case.[31]

---

25. 11 U.S.C. §1112(b)(4)(M); 11 U.S.C. §1307(c)(4).
26. 11 U.S.C. §1112(b)(4)(N); 11 U.S.C. §1307(c)(6).
27. 11 U.S.C. §1112(b)(4)(O); 11 U.S.C. §1307(c)(8).
28. 11 U.S.C. §1112(b)(4)(K); 11 U.S.C. §1307(c)(2).
29. 11 U.S.C. §1112(b)(4)(H); 11 U.S.C. §1307(c)(9)(10); 11 U.S.C. §1308.
30. 11 U.S.C. §1112(b)(4)(P); 11 U.S.C. §1307(c)(11).
31. Bankruptcy Rule 1019; 11 U.S.C. §348(f).

D. CHAPTER 13 PLAN PROVISIONS

The main component of a Chapter 13 proceeding is, of course, the **plan**. Sections 1321 through 1330 contain the provisions regarding the contents of and the procedure for obtaining **confirmation** (approval), and performance of the plan. The plan is, in essence, a new contract between the debtor and all the creditors. A confirmed plan is nothing more than a composition agreement that has obtained court approval. The forms disk contains a sample Chapter 13 plan.

The filing of a Chapter 13 plan is not optional. It is a required part of the process.[32] The Federal Rules of Bankruptcy Procedure require that a Chapter 13 plan be filed within 14 days of the petition's filing. A failure to do so, as noted above, will constitute cause for dismissal or conversion.[33] A Chapter 13 debtor must file the plan promptly because the entire procedure is intended to be expeditious.

Section 1322 prescribes the contents of a Chapter 13 plan. There are **mandatory provisions** that are required to be in any plan. There are also permissive provisions that may be included in a plan.

The mandatory elements of a Chapter 13 plan are described in Section 1322(a). These provisions must be included in a Chapter 13 plan. The first mandatory provision is that the debtor must pay all of his/her future earning or a sufficient sum into the plan so that it can be performed.[34]

The second requirement is that all priority claims must be paid in full unless the holder of any such claim agrees otherwise.[35] As has been noted elsewhere in this text, a creditor may always voluntarily agree to a lesser treatment than may be mandated by the Code. For example, a priority wage claimant may agree to accept repayment as a general unsecured creditor.

The third mandatory element of a Chapter 13 plan is that if the plan classifies claims, each claimholder within a given class must be treated identically, unless a creditor agrees to a lesser treatment.[36] In other words, a debtor cannot propose to pay some unsecured creditors a 20 percent dividend and other unsecured creditors a 50 percent dividend. All of the creditors in a given class must be treated equally unless a specific creditor consents to a lesser treatment. This is consistent with the repayment philosophy of the bankruptcy system described in chapter 16 supra.

---

32. 11 U.S.C. §1321.
33. Bankruptcy Rule 3015; 11 U.S.C. §1307(c)(3).
34. 11 U.S.C. §1322(a)(1).
35. 11 U.S.C. §1322(a)(2). As to priority claims, see chapter 21 supra.
36. 11 U.S.C. §1322(a)(3).

The 2005 legislation created a fourth mandatory Chapter 13 plan provision. Section 1322(a)(4) provides that if there is a domestic support obligation owed to a governmental entity, then the plan may provide for less than full payment of this claim if the debtor pays all of his/her disposable income into the plan for a five-year period.

Section 1322(b) describes the **permissive provisions** that may be included in a Chapter 13 plan. A permissive provision is a provision that may be included in the plan but is not required to be in the plan. A permissive plan provision may also involve facts that, if present, will make inclusion of the permissive plan provision mandatory. For example, if a Chapter 13 debtor has an executory contract, it must be assumed or rejected in the plan. Section 365(p), added to the Code in 2005, requires that an executory contract be assumed prior to confirmation of a Chapter 13 plan, or be deemed rejected and the automatic stay terminated by operation of law (see chapter 15 supra).

Section 1322(b) lists 11 permissive provisions. First, a debtor may designate more than one class of unsecured claims, so long as there is no discrimination between creditors.[37] (There will not usually be more than one class of unsecured claims in a Chapter 13 case, but this is a common occurrence in Chapter 11 proceedings.[38]) For example, a Chapter 13 debtor has several claims for which there is also a codebtor who is not a debtor in the bankruptcy proceeding. These creditors could theoretically be placed into a separate class to account for the codebtor's liability.

However, a debtor may not create two classes of unsecured claims and pay one class a 10 percent dividend and the other class a 50 percent dividend. This latter activity will constitute unfair discrimination against the affected creditors receiving the lesser dividend.

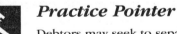

Practice Pointer

Debtors may seek to separately classify a nondischargeable debt so as to pay it in full to avoid postdischarge liability. The trend in the case law is to deny such separate classification, except in the context of public policy concerns, such as domestic support obligations.

---

37. 11 U.S.C. §1322(b)(1).
38. See chapter 25 infra.

Second, a Chapter 13 plan may modify the rights of secured creditors other than those creditors whose only security is real property that is the debtor's principal residence.[39] Stated another way, a Chapter 13 plan may seek to modify the rights of secured creditors whose collateral is other than the debtor's residence. For instance, a Chapter 13 plan may propose to reduce the amount of monthly payments and extend the loan repayment period on a secured car loan so the debtor will be able to afford to complete the contract and keep the car. However, the debtor cannot propose to modify the terms of secured home loans, except to cure any prepetition default, unless any affected secured creditors agree.

Practice Pointer

Note that this protection extends only to the debtor's "principal residence" and not to a second or vacation home.

In Nobelman v. American Savings Bank, 508 U.S. 324 (1993), the Supreme Court prohibited a practice that had been approved in some circuits, permitting the bifurcation of a secured claim into secured and unsecured portions. Under this practice, a claim secured by a lien upon a Chapter 13 debtor's residence was considered secured only up to the value of the collateral; the undersecured portion of the debt became an unsecured debt subject to a Chapter 13 discharge. For example, in *Nobelman*, supra, the debtor sought to value the creditor's residential collateral at $23,500, although the total amount of the debt was $71,335 at the time of the petition. The Supreme Court held that Section 1322(b)(2) prevents modification of the creditor's rights and thus precludes bifurcation. That is, the debtor would be required to account for the full amount of the creditor's claim ($71,335) rather than the lesser value ($23,500) of the collateral. In short, the statutory language of Section 1322(b)(2) means what it says.

BAPCPA places limits on this practice of bifurcating or "stripping down" secured claims, at least where the collateral is personal property. First, if the debtor has purchased personal property collateral within one year from the filing date, or if the claim is for a purchase money security

---

39. 11 U.S.C. §1322(b)(2). The collapse of the home mortgage market has spawned a plethora of federal legislation aimed at protecting the homeowner. Recent legislation includes the HOPE NOW Alliance, the Housing and Economic Recovery Act of 2008, Hope for Homeowners Act of 2008, Foreclosure Prevention Act of 2008, and the Streamlined Mortgage Modification Plan introduced jointly by Fannie Mae and Freddie Mac.

interest in a motor vehicle purchased within 910 days (2.5 years) prior to the filing, Section 1325(a) effectively provides that the allowed amount of the secured claim will be the amount due under the contract. Second, Section 506(a) requires that the collateral be valued at the price a retail merchant would charge for similar collateral (see chapter 21 supra). The practical effect of these provisions is to effectively eliminate the ability to bifurcate or strip down a secured claim into secured and unsecured portions, since many purchase money contracts are of short duration.

When the collateral is the debtor's home, there is a debate in the case law as to whether a claim secured by real property or a combination of real and personal property may be "stripped off" or eliminated in a Chapter 13 case. The majority view holds that if there is no value at all in the real property for the benefit of the secured claimant, then the claim is fully unsecured. The minority view holds that any secured claim secured by an interest in the debtor's home must be paid. For example, Mr. Truman owns real estate worth $50,000. He owes Dome Mortgage Company a senior mortgage of $55,000 and the Control Finance Company a junior mortgage of $10,000. Under one view, the Control debt may be stripped off because there is no value in the property to support it. Under the contrary view, the debt may not be stripped off because the collateral is Truman's home. If the debt is stripped off, it is treated as an unsecured claim and is subject to Truman's Chapter 13 discharge. See chapter 16H, supra. BAPCPA may limit this practice to the extent that the debtor must either pay the claim or receive a Chapter 13 discharge for the secured claim subject to **strip-down** or **strip-off** to be so treated. If the case is dismissed or converted to a Chapter 7, the strip-off or strip-down will not apply.[40]

A related issue concerns the debtor who seeks Chapter 13 relief to pay secured debt after receiving a Chapter 7 discharge. The Supreme Court examined this issue in Johnson v. Home State Bank, 501 U.S. 78 (1991). In this case, the Johnsons owed the bank $470,000 secured by a mortgage upon real estate. During the pendency of a state court judicial foreclosure action, the Johnsons filed a Chapter 7 case and received a discharge.

---

40. " 'Stripping off' a lien occurs when the entire lien is avoided, whereas 'stripping down' occurs when an undersecured lien is bifurcated and the unsecured portion is avoided." In re Yi, 219 B.R. 394 (E.D. Va. 1998). Every Circuit that has ruled on the debtor's ability to avoid a wholly undersecured lien has allowed it. See, e.g., In re Zimmer, 313 F.3d 1220 (9th Cir. 2002); In re Lane, 280 F.3d 663 (6th Cir. 2002); In re Pond, 252 F.3d 122 (2d Cir. 2001); In re Tanner, 217 F.3d 1357 (11th Cir. 2000); In re Bartee, 212 F.3d 277 (5th Cir. 2000); In re McDonald, 205 F.3d 606 (3d Cir. 2000). The minority view is represented by American General Finance, Inc. v. Dickerson, 229 B.R. 539 (M.D. Ga. 1999). See also In re Dickerson, 222 F.3d 924 (11th Cir. 2000) (following Tanner but stating that if it was not bound, would follow minority approach). Section 1325(a)(5)(B)(i) is the provision limiting the effect of a strip-off or strip-down in a dismissed or converted case.

The bank's right to proceed against the collateral survived the bankruptcy.[41] After obtaining relief from the stay, the bank obtained a foreclosure judgment of $200,000. The Johnsons then filed a Chapter 13 and proposed to pay the claim in five annual payments. The Supreme Court held that notwithstanding the prior Chapter 7 discharge, the bank still possessed a claim against the property, so the Johnsons could file Chapter 13 to satisfy it.

Section 1322(c) of the Code limits a debtor's ability to cure a default on an obligation secured by the debtor's principal residence by requiring the cure to be made before a foreclosure sale can be properly conducted. The provision therefore overrules Johnson v. Home State Bank because the facts of the case involved a cure of the default after the foreclosure sale had been conducted. However, Section 1322(c) also permits a Chapter 13 debtor to modify, within the plan, an obligation secured by the debtor's principal residence that becomes due during performance of the plan so long as the obligation is paid in full by the completion of the plan.

The filing of a Chapter 13 after receiving a Chapter 7 discharge is colloquially known as a "Chapter 20" and is not uncommon. In *Johnson*, supra, for example, the Johnsons did not originally qualify for Chapter 13 because the secured debt owed the bank, $470,000, exceeded the then-Chapter 13 secured debt limit of $350,000. After they received their Chapter 7 discharge and the bank obtained its foreclosure judgment, the $200,000 secured claim fell within the Chapter 13 debt limit, permitting the Johnsons to seek Chapter 13 relief.

Practice Pointer

The case law is divided on whether or not the debtor may have two simultaneous filings that effectively serve as a Chapter 20.

Third, a Chapter 13 plan may provide for the cure or waiver of any default.[42] This is precisely what most Chapter 13 plans attempt. There are five different classes of creditors that are generally paid through a Chapter 13 plan. They are administrative claims, priority claims, defaults on car loans, defaults on home loans, and general unsecured creditors. A common Chapter 13 plan will cure the defaults on the home loan or the car loan or both and pay a dividend to the unsecured creditors. The

---

41. See discussion of Dewsnup v. Timm, 502 U.S. 410 (1992), chapter 21 infra.
42. 11 U.S.C. §1322(b)(3).

major purpose in filing a Chapter 13 is commonly to protect a home or car from foreclosure or repossession rather than to satisfy unsecured debt.

A fourth permissive element that a Chapter 13 plan may include is that payments to unsecured creditors may be made at the same time as payments to secured creditors.[43] In other words, a Chapter 13 plan is not required to provide that all payments will first go to satisfy secured creditor defaults and then unsecured creditors will receive dividends. A Chapter 13 plan may allocate its payments toward secured claim defaults and unsecured creditors at the same time.

Fifth, a Chapter 13 plan frequently may provide for a cure of defaults on any claim, priority, secured, or unsecured, even though the final payment on the claim is not due until after the plan is completed.[44] For example, John Smith is three payments behind on his car loan. He files a Chapter 13 to cure the default, thereby preventing repossession. The plan proposes to repay the three payments over 12 months. There are three years of payments left under the contract. This plan will cure the default on a secured claim for which the last payment is due after the plan is performed. This is permissible and is what many debtors are seeking with a Chapter 13, a mechanism to cure existing defaults.

This same provision also requires that any current payments coming due on any underlying long-term debts must be paid during pendency of the Chapter 13.[45] Some Chapter 13 debtors form an improper impression that if the Chapter 13 plan payments are made, other ongoing payments do not have to be made. This is absolutely untrue. All that the Chapter 13 payment will do is cure any default owed prior to the filing date. A debtor still has the obligation to continue to make current payments on home or car loans and any other secured debt that comes due in the normal course. The inevitable result of a failure to maintain current payments by the debtor will be a motion for relief from stay brought by a secured creditor or a motion for dismissal or conversion.

Practice Pointer

A Chapter 13 debtor must continue to make their regular postpetition payments "outside of the plan" on any long-term secured debt if the debtor wants to keep the collateral, such as a home or car.

---

43. 11 U.S.C. §1322(b)(4).
44. 11 U.S.C. §1322(b)(5).
45. 11 U.S.C. §1322(b)(5).

Next, a Chapter 13 plan may assume or reject executory contracts or unexpired leases. Section 365(p), added by the 2005 legislation, relieves the automatic stay as to leased property if the lease is not assumed in the plan.[46] The plan may also provide for the payment of certain limited post-petition tax claims or consumer debts necessary for a debtor's performance of the plan.[47] The plan may provide for payment of a claim from property of the estate. For example, the debtor may propose to sell a nonexempt asset and to apply the proceeds toward performance of the plan.[48] The plan may provide that property of the estate will vest in the debtor upon confirmation.[49] If all claims are paid in full, and if there are nondischargeable claims, then postpetition interest becomes payable on the claims.[50] The plan may contain any other provision that is not inconsistent with the Bankruptcy Code.[51]

Section 1322(e) permits a lender to obtain interest on the cure of a default if the underlying agreement or nonbankruptcy law permits the same.

If the debtor's and the debtor's spouse's income are equal to or greater than the median national family income for a family of equal or lesser size, then the plan must be five years in duration. If the debtor's and the debtor's spouse's income are less than the median national family income for a family of equal or lesser size, then the plan must be a minimum of three years in duration, and the court may approve a plan of up to five years in length. National median family income is determined as last reported by the Census Bureau. For example, the Census Bureau provides that for a family of four filing after November 1, 2010, the median family income in California is $77,596. A family earning more than this would be required to have a five-year Chapter 13 plan. A family earning less than this would be required to have a minimum three-year Chapter 13 plan. Recall that median family income is also a threshold amount of income for application of means testing in Chapter 7 cases (see chapter 5 supra).[52]

A Chapter 13 plan may be modified at any time before confirmation. Of course, any such modification must comply with Section 1322. A debtor might discover that the plan is in error and amend it. This is

---

46. 11 U.S.C. §1322(b)(7); 11 U.S.C. §365(p)(3). See chapter 19 supra.
47. 11 U.S.C. §1322(b)(6); 11 U.S.C. §1305.
48. 11 U.S.C. §1322(b)(8).
49. 11 U.S.C. §1322(b)(9).
50. 11 U.S.C. §1322(b)(10).
51. 11 U.S.C. §1322(b)(11).
52. 11 U.S.C. §1322(d). Census Bureau national median family income data may be accessed at http://www.census.gov/hhes/www/income/statemedfaminc.html and www.justice.gov/ust.

analogous to amending a complaint before an answer is filed in traditional nonbankruptcy litigation.[53]

E. CONFIRMATION HEARINGS

Unlike Chapter 11, which is far more complex, the procedures for obtaining confirmation of a Chapter 13 plan are expedited and somewhat summary.[54] A Chapter 13 plan is confirmed at a confirmation hearing. Creditors do not have an opportunity to vote on acceptance of a Chapter 13 plan, although they may object.[55] However, unlike the creditors' meeting, the confirmation hearing is held before a judge. This entire process is very expeditious. The confirmation hearing is required to be held within 45 days of the meeting of creditors. The debtor will have filed Statements and Schedules along with a plan. Notice of the creditors' meeting and confirmation hearing will have been given to all parties in interest. A sample Chapter 13 notice to creditors is included on the forms disk.

A debtor must commence making payments under the plan within 30 days of filing the plan. If the plan has not yet been confirmed, then the debtor is supposed to tender the first plan payment to the trustee, who will then tender the payment or payments to the creditors when the plan has been confirmed. Recall that adequate protection payments to personal property secured claimants or lessors must be made until distributions under the plan begin. This acts as additional incentive to expedite the payment and confirmation process.[56] The above procedures make it relatively inexpensive and speedy for a debtor to pursue a Chapter 13 alternative as a solution for financial distress. In addition, these rapid procedures prevent debtors from abusing Chapter 13 as a haven to avoid debt repayment.

> ***Practice Pointer***
> Plan payments must commence within 30 days of filing the plan. The trustee will hold the payments until the plan is confirmed.

---

53. 11 U.S.C. §1323.
54. As to the Chapter 11 confirmation procedures, see generally chapter 18 infra.
55. 11 U.S.C. §1324.
56. 11 U.S.C. §1326(a)(3).

F.   CONFIRMATION CONDITIONS

At the confirmation hearing, the court will confirm the plan, but only if the court finds that the plan meets all the conditions of Section 1325(a). Under Section 1325(a), the court must make nine findings to approve the plan. If any of the nine items is missing, the plan cannot be confirmed.

The first finding that the court must make is that the plan complies with the provisions of Chapter 13 and the Bankruptcy Code.[57] This will not generally be a problematic issue. Second, the court must find that any filing fees required to be paid for initiating the Chapter 13 have been paid.[58] Third, the court must find that the plan has been proposed in good faith and not for any means forbidden by law.[59] For example, if the debtor is seeking to utilize Chapter 13 to accomplish an improper motive or to commit an act that would otherwise be illegal, the plan will not be confirmable.

Fourth, the court must find that unsecured creditors will receive a dividend not less than what they would have received if the proceeding were filed under Chapter 7.[60] This requirement is commonly known as the "best interests of creditors" test. For example, if there is $10,000 of nonexempt property in the debtor's Chapter 13 estate, the Chapter 13 priority and unsecured creditors must receive a total dividend of at least $10,000, because this is what they would receive in a Chapter 7. Because most Chapter 13 proceedings would be no asset Chapter 7 proceedings, this finding is rarely a problematic issue.

The fifth finding relates to secured claims. Three alternatives are provided. The existence of at least one alternative must be found as to each secured claim for the plan to be confirmed. These requirements, in their essence, comprise alternative methods of adequate protection and preservation of the secured creditor's rights during performance of the plan. First, a secured creditor may accept the plan. If a secured claimant accepts the plan, the acceptance will aid in obtaining confirmation. The remaining alternatives concern what happens if a secured claimant does not accept the plan. If the plan provides that the holder of the claim will retain its lien until the earliest of payment in full of the debt or receipt of a Chapter 13 discharge then confirmation may occur over the secured creditor's objection. The lien is also retained if the case is converted or

---

57. 11 U.S.C. §1325(a)(1).
58. 11 U.S.C. §1325(a)(2).
59. 11 U.S.C. §1325(a)(3).
60. 11 U.S.C. §1325(a)(4).

dismissed. The concept of approving a plan under these circumstances over a creditor's objection is commonly known as a **cramdown**. A creditor will not be heard to object to confirmation if the creditor will receive all that it would have received in a nonbankruptcy environment. This is the underlying principle of the cramdown concept in reorganization proceedings. Finally, a debtor may propose to surrender the collateral to the secured creditor. To summarize, as to each secured claim, the court must find that each creditor either agrees to the plan, is paid the full amount of the secured claim, or will receive the return of its collateral.[61]

BAPCPA adds three new confirmation requirements. First, that the petition has been filed in good faith. This provision will likely be used in reconciling means testing issues with Chapter 13, and in dealing with the continuing problems raised by serial bankruptcy filings (see chapter 12 supra); second, that all postpetition domestic support obligations have been paid; and third, that all postpetition tax returns have been timely filed pursuant to Section 1308.[62]

In Till v. SCS Credit Corp., 541 U.S. 465, the Supreme Court held that secured creditors, for cramdown purposes, are entitled to interest on their claims based upon the prime interest rate plus a premium for risk that can be proven by the creditor, and not on the underlying rate provided for by the contract. In this case, the debtors owed $4,894.89 to the creditor when they filed their Chapter 13. They proposed to pay the secured portion of the claim, $4,000, over installments at an interest rate of 9.5 percent, or the prime rate plus 1.5 percent. The creditor insisted upon receiving its contract rate of 21 percent. A likely effect of this ruling will make it easier for Chapter 13 creditors to reduce interest rates on collateral not secured solely by their primary residence.

G.   FEASIBILITY ANALYSIS

The final finding that the court must make to permit confirmation of a Chapter 13 plan is that the debtor will be able to make all of the payments under and comply with the plan.[63] In other words, the court must find that the plan is feasible. This determination is the most critical and problematic in a Chapter 13 case. If a plan is not feasible, the debtor will likely need to

---

61. 11 U.S.C. §1325(a)(5).
62. 11 U.S.C. §1325(a)(7), (8), and (9).
63. 11 U.S.C. §1325(a)(6).

convert to Chapter 7 if the bankruptcy system is to be of use in resolving the debtor's financial problems. Determining whether a feasible plan can be proposed will most likely decide the type of proceeding filed by the debtor in the first place. The following analysis reflects the state of the law before BAPCPA. The text will attempt to point out some of BAPCPA's effects. To determine a plan's feasibility, some calculation is required. First, determine the amount necessary to pay in full all administrative expenses and priority claims and to cure any defaults on secured debts. Second, determine the minimum amount necessary to pay unsecured creditors at least as much as they would receive in a Chapter 7. This total will be the minimum amount necessary to pay through the plan over its proposed length. Nonetheless, some courts do not generally favor zero percent or nominal unsecured dividends over objection even if the debtor's Chapter 7 would be a no asset proceeding. This is an area where local practice and custom should be ascertained.[64]

The third step used in determining the feasibility of a Chapter 13 plan is to determine the debtor's monthly budget. Schedules I and J comprise an estimated monthly family budget. This budget shows the income the family receives every month and what it will cost this family to meet its basic expenses before making its Chapter 13 plan payments. The expenses are subtracted from the income. If there is a surplus left after meeting the monthly living expenses, the surplus represents the amount available to pay into the plan on a monthly basis. If there is no surplus or if there is a deficit, the plan is not feasible. The debtor should file a Chapter 7 if the debtor wants to use the bankruptcy system.

Practice Pointer

An interesting question arises where the debtor's Section 707(b) calculation is negative but the debtor's Schedule I and J show surplus income. The courts are divided as to whether or not a dividend must be paid to unsecured creditors.

---

64. See discussion above regarding 11 U.S.C. §§1322(a), 1325(a)(5), and 1325(a)(4). Whether or not this amount must include a minimum calculated means testing payment under Section 707(b)(2), or whether or not means testing eliminates zero percent or nominal plans in Chapter 13 cases that would fall under means testing (see chapter 5 supra), are issues being explored by the courts. Compare In re Frederickson, 545 F.3d 652 (8th Cir. 2008) (commitment period is a temporal requirement even with negative disposable income) with In re Kagenveama, 541 F.3d 868 (9th Cir. 2008) (commitment period does not apply where there is no disposable income).

If the budget shows a surplus of available income with which to make plan payments, the fourth step of the feasibility calculation can be performed. Divide the total minimum amount that must be paid into the plan by the available monthly surplus.[65] The quotient will be the number of months it will take to perform the plan. If the quotient is equal to or less than 60, the plan is likely feasible. The smaller the available surplus or the closer the plan approaches to 60 months in duration, the more doubtful it will be that the plan will be found feasible by the court. Under BAPCPA, if the debtor's median family income is less than the national family median income for a family of similar size (see chapter 17D supra), then the plan may not exceed three years in duration unless the court orders otherwise, but in no event may the plan exceed five years in duration. If the debtor's median family income is equal to or greater than the national family median income for a family of similar size, then the plan must be five years in duration. If the minimum available payment would make a plan exceed five years, it is not feasible.[66] Checklist 23.2 infra summarizes the above in a formula format.

A greater understanding of the feasibility issue can be gained through use of an extended example. Robinson Crusoe files a Chapter 13. He owes $1,000 in income taxes and $600 as a priority wage claim to his servant Friday. Bank of Defoe holds a mortgage on Crusoe's island that is six payments in default, totaling $2,500. Crusoe's unsecured creditors are owed $5,000. All Crusoe's assets are exempt. Thus, Crusoe's unsecured creditors would receive no dividend in a Chapter 7. The minimum amount that Crusoe *must* pay back is therefore $4,100 (income tax, wage claim, and past-due mortgage payments).

Crusoe's Chapter 13 statement shows that he will have surplus income of $150 per month with which to make payments under the plan. Performing the final calculation, dividing $4,100 by $150, yields a result of 27.33. It will take approximately 28 months for Crusoe to pay the minimum possible Chapter 13 plan he might propose. This plan could be found feasible, but note that it does not provide any dividend to unsecured creditors. This can affect feasibility and will not permit a cramdown in the event of objections by unsecured creditors.

Under BAPCPA, Crusoe's current monthly income would need to be known. If Crusoe's income is less than the national family median income for a family of similar size, then he must propose at least a three-year

---

65. In 2010, the U.S. Supreme Court held that in calculating a Chapter 13 debtor's projected disposable income, the court may take a forward-looking approach and account for changes to the debtor's income or expenses known or virtually certain as of the date of confirmation. Hamilton v. Lanning, 130 S. Ct. 2464 (2010).

66. 11 U.S.C. §1322(d).

(36-month) plan if he wants to effectuate a cramdown. This would pay his unsecured creditors a dividend of approximately 25 percent $(36 - 27.33 = 8.67 \times \$150 = \$1,300.50)$. If Crusoe's income is equal to or greater than the national family median income for a family of similar size, then he must propose a five-year (60-month) plan to effectuate a cramdown. This would pay his unsecured creditors substantially in full $(60 - 27.33 = 32.67 \times \$150 = \$4,900.50)$. Whether or not either of these scenarios would be confirmable and subject to cramdown over the objection of unsecured creditors is the subject of 11 U.S.C. §1325(b).

H.　CRAMDOWN

Secured or unsecured creditors may object to the plan. Unlike Chapter 11, there is no voting procedure in Chapter 13. Unless a creditor objects to the plan, the creditor's acceptance is presumed. If a creditor or creditors do object to the plan, confirmation can still be obtained through a procedure commonly known as cramdown. This procedure has already been identified with regard to the secured creditors of a Chapter 13 debtor. Section 1325(b) describes the cramdown procedure when unsecured creditors object to a Chapter 13 plan.

Under Section 1325(b), there are two methods by which the debtor may effectuate a Chapter 13 cramdown upon unsecured creditors. The first method is that if the creditors are going to be paid in full, then the plan will be confirmed over their objection.[67] Creditors who will be paid in full through the plan will not be heard to object. Payment in full is, after all, the ultimate creditor goal in a bankruptcy proceeding.

 Practice Pointer
The primary effect of means testing in Chapter 13 cases is to determine whether a plan must be either three or five years long, unless creditors can be paid in full in a shorter period of time.

---

67. 11 U.S.C. §1325(b)(1)(A).

Most of the time, however, unsecured creditors will not be paid in full. In this instance, the second method of cramdown is necessary. If the unsecured creditors cannot be paid in full, a cramdown may still occur if the debtor proposes to place all disposable income into the plan for the **applicable commitment period**.[68] **Disposable income** invokes application of means testing (see chapter 5 supra). The debtor's current monthly income and expenses are determined in a manner identical to Chapter 7, except for additional deductions allowed for postpetition domestic support obligations, charitable religious contributions of up to 15 percent of gross income, and business expenses if the debtor is engaged in the operation of a business. If the debtor's current monthly income is less than the state median income for the debtor's household size, then the plan must be no less than three years in duration to effectuate a cramdown. If the debtor's current monthly income is equal to or greater than the state median income for the debtor's household size, then the plan must be of five years duration to effectuate a cramdown. When the creditors are paid in full, the plan may be less than these time periods.[69]

Thus, if Robinson Crusoe's unsecured creditors in the above example object to the plan, Crusoe must either pay them in full or propose a three- or five-year plan, depending upon his current monthly income as illustrated above. If Crusoe proposes to pay all disposable income into the plan for the appropriate three- or five-year period, the plan can be confirmed over the objection of unsecured creditors.

I. EFFECT OF CONFIRMATION AND CHAPTER 13 DISCHARGE

A confirmed Chapter 13 plan is a judicially approved composition agreement. When a Chapter 13 plan is confirmed, it acts as a new contract between the debtor and all of the creditors. All creditors are bound by a confirmed Chapter 13 plan.[70] This is the big difference between a Chapter 13 and a nonbankruptcy composition agreement. In the latter case, any objecting creditors are not bound by the agreement.

Once performance of a Chapter 13 plan has been completed, and the debtor certifies that any postpetition domestic support obligations have

---

68. 11 U.S.C. §1325(b)(1)(B).
69. 11 U.S.C. §1325(b)(2), (3), (4).
70. 11 U.S.C. §1327.

been paid, a Chapter 13 debtor becomes entitled to a Chapter 13 discharge. A Chapter 13 discharge is similar to a Chapter 7 discharge. A Chapter 13 debtor must also complete a postpetition personal financial management course identical to Chapter 7.[71]

An obligation for which final payment is due after the plan is completed is not dischargeable in Chapter 13.[72] For example, in the fifth year of a 30-year mortgage the debtor files a Chapter 13. The Chapter 13 plan cures the default and the debtor receives a discharge. The mortgage itself is not discharged because the last payment is due after the last payment under the plan. Taxes are not dischargeable to the same extent that they are not dischargeable in Chapter 7 cases (but since all priority taxes must be paid in full through the plan, this is a moot point). Domestic support obligations are not discharged by a Chapter 13. Next, student loans remain nondischargeable to the same extent that they are not dischargeable in Chapter 7 proceedings. Debts incurred fraudulently, unlisted debts, and fiduciary defalcations are not dischargeable in Chapter 13. Damages resulting from substance abuse are nondischargeable to the same extent that they are not dischargeable in Chapter 7 proceedings.[73] Criminal restitution orders or criminal fines are not dischargeable.[74] Finally, restitution orders or civil damage awards resulting from willful or malicious injury, or wrongful death, are not dischargeable.[75]

A Chapter 13 debtor who has not fully completed a plan may still apply for and receive a discharge if the court finds that a failure to complete the plan is due to circumstances for which the debtor should not justly be held accountable and if unsecured creditors have received at least the amount of dividend they would have received in a Chapter 7 proceeding.[76] A death of one of two joint debtors is such a circumstance. If the court can make such findings for a debtor that has not completed a Chapter 13 plan, the debtor will receive a discharge that is identical to a Chapter 7 discharge.[77]

Prior to the 2005 BAPCPA legislation, many debts that were not dischargeable in Chapter 7 were in fact dischargeable in Chapter 13. The theory was that since a debtor was making an effort to repay debt, the scope of the discharge should be broader. However, as the 2005 reforms evidence a strong swing of the pendulum in favor of debt collection as opposed to debtor relief, the net effect of the reforms makes Chapter 13

---

71. 11 U.S.C. §1328(a)(g).
72. 11 U.S.C. §1328(a)(1).
73. 11 U.S.C. §1328(a)(2).
74. 11 U.S.C. §1328(a)(4).
75. See chapter 12 supra.
76. 11 U.S.C. §1328(b).
77. 11 U.S.C. §1328(c).

more significant as a debt collection tool as opposed to providing honest but unfortunate debtors with a fresh start in their financial affairs. If the debtor has received a discharge in a Chapter 7, 11, or 12 filed within four years from the filing of the Chapter 13, then no debts are dischargeable. If the debtor received a Chapter 13 discharge within two years prior to the filing, then no debts are dischargeable. These provisions, added by BAPCPA, are an important departure from prior law and will seriously limit the concept of the Chapter 20 described above in chapter 23D supra.[78]

Practice Pointer

Note that the so-called "super discharge" historically provided under Chapter 13 has been greatly curtailed following the BAPCPA amendments.

A Chapter 13 discharge may be revoked if the court finds that the discharge was fraudulently obtained. Revocation must be sought within one year of the discharge's being granted.[79] Confirmation of a Chapter 13 plan that has been fraudulently obtained may also be revoked.[80]

One of three things can happen during the life of a confirmed plan. The debtor may perform and complete the plan in a timely manner. This is the goal of the system. Or the debtor may receive a windfall during the life of the plan and wish to accelerate performance. Under Section 1329, the debtor may ask the court for permission to modify the plan to accelerate its performance. Or, third, the debtor may become unable to make payments under a confirmed plan. In this instance, the debtor may ask the court to modify the plan to lower the payments or to extend the plan's duration. This is permissible as long as the modified plan still complies with the provisions of Chapter 13 and as long as final performance of the plan is still no longer than five years from the original commencement of the plan.[81] If the plan cannot be successfully modified, then conversion of the proceeding to a Chapter 7 may become necessary.

---

78. 11 U.S.C. §1328(f).
79. 11 U.S.C. §1328(e).
80. 11 U.S.C. §1330.
81. 11 U.S.C. §1329.

Summary

This and the next two text chapters describe the reorganization proceedings of Chapter 13, Chapter 11, and Chapter 12. In a reorganization proceeding, a debtor will attempt to repay debt and retain nonexempt assets or continue to operate a business. Reorganization proceedings are, in their essence, no more or less than judicially approved composition agreements.

Chapter 13 is a program for individuals with regular income who have unsecured debts of less than $360,475 and secured debts of less than $1,081,400. A qualified individual may attempt repayment of debt over a period not to exceed five years.

The Chapter 13 procedure is expedited. The checklist accompanying this chapter itemizes the important deadlines, documents to file, and the hearing dates involved in a Chapter 13 proceeding.

A trustee will always be appointed in a Chapter 13. The most important function of the Chapter 13 trustee is to collect the plan payments and distribute dividends to creditors.

A Chapter 13 plan must contain four mandatory elements. A Chapter 13 plan may contain various permissive elements. The mandatory requirements are that the plan provide for payments, that priority claims be paid in full, that all claims within a given class be treated equally, and that domestic support obligations owed to a governmental entity may only be paid less than in full if the debtor proposes a five-year plan.

The permissive elements of a Chapter 13 plan include the debtor's providing for more than one class of unsecured claims, modifying the rights of certain secured creditors, the cure or waiver of defaults, and simultaneous payments to secured and unsecured creditors.

A Chapter 13 plan is confirmed at a confirmation hearing. The court must make nine findings to confirm a plan. If one of the findings cannot be made, the plan may not be confirmed. The plan must comply with the provisions of the Bankruptcy Code. Any filing fees must be paid. The plan must be proposed in good faith. The creditors must receive a dividend not less than the dividend that they would receive in a Chapter 7 proceeding. These issues are not generally problematic. With regard to secured creditors, the court must find either that the creditor consents, the creditor will be paid the full value of its secured claim, or that any collateral will be returned to the creditor. The petition must have been filed in good faith. All postpetition domestic support obligations must be current. All postpetition tax returns must be filed.

Finally, the court must find that the plan is feasible. This requires a determination that the debtor can afford to make the plan payments. The checklist accompanying this chapter describes a simple formula to use in making this calculation.

If creditors object to a Chapter 13 plan, the plan may still be approved over their objections through use of a procedure commonly known as cramdown. A cramdown of unsecured creditors will occur in a Chapter 13 if the plan will pay the creditors in full or if all the debtor's disposable income is paid into the plan for a period of time from three to five years, depending upon whether or not the debtor's family income is less or more than the national median family income for a family of similar size. Disposable income is determined in accordance with needs based bankruptcy (see chapter 5 supra).

A Chapter 13 plan may be modified after confirmation to accelerate or reduce performance. The modified plan must still meet the confirmation requirements.

A debtor completing performance of a Chapter 13 plan, completing a financial management course, and remaining current on postpetition domestic support obligations receives a discharge. Under BAPCPA, a Chapter 13 discharge is virtually identical to a Chapter 7 discharge. Additionally, debts for which the last payment is due after performance of the plan (such as a 30-year home loan) are not dischargeable. In special circumstances, a debtor may receive a hardship discharge in Chapter 13, which has the same effect as a Chapter 7 discharge. A discharge will not issue if the debtor received a Chapter 7, 11, or 12 discharge within four years from the filing of the Chapter 13, or has received a Chapter 13 discharge in another case within two years of the filing.

Confirmation of a Chapter 13 plan may be revoked if the court finds that confirmation was fraudulently obtained.

A reorganization proceeding may be dismissed or converted to a Chapter 7 liquidation for cause. The causes identified by the Code are delineated in the checklist accompanying this chapter.

KEY TERMS

applicable commitment
  period
confirmation
conversion
cramdown
dismissal
disposable income
liquidation

mandatory provisions
permissive provisions
plan
property of the estate
reorganization
strip down
strip off

CHAPTER 23 CHECKLIST

23.1 DOCUMENTS AND DEADLINES IN CHAPTER 13

		Deadline	*Statute*
23.1.1	Petition	at filing	Bankruptcy Rule 1002
23.1.2	Credit Counseling Certificate at Filing		11 U.S.C. §109(h)
23.1.3	Statement of Financial Affairs, Schedules	14 days	Bankruptcy Rule 1007(b)(2), (c)
23.1.4	Statement of Current Monthly Income	14 days	Bankruptcy Rule 1007(b)(5), (c)
23.1.5	Chapter 13 Plan	14 days	Bankruptcy Rule 3015
23.1.6	Attorneys' Fee Statement	creditors' meeting	Bankruptcy Rule 2016
23.1.7	First Plan Payment	30 days	11 U.S.C. §1326
23.1.8	Adequate Protection Payments	30 days	11 U.S.C. §1326(a)
23.1.9	Plan Performance:		
	1. Family Income → SMFI[82]	3 years	11 U.S.C. §1322(d)
	2. Family Income SMFI[83]	5 years	11 U.S.C. §1322(d)
23.1.10	File Tax Returns for Last Four Years	creditors' meeting	11 U.S.C. §1308

---

82. "SMFI" means state family median income for a family of similar size.
83. Ibid.

23.2 CHAPTER 13 FEASIBILITY FORMULA

23.2.1 Add (A)dministrative Claims, (P)riority Claims, and (M)inimum Chapter 7 Dividend $(A + P + M)$

23.2.2 Determine Existence of Surplus or Deficit in Monthly Budget (Deficit Means Plan Is Not (B) Feasible)

23.2.3 Divide the Total Reached in 23.2.1 by Any Budget Surplus $(A + P + M) \div B$

23.2.4 If Answer Obtained in 23.2.3 Is 36 or Less, the Plan Is Likely Feasible. If Answer Obtained in 23.2.3 Is 36-60, the Plan May Be Feasible. $(A + P + M) \div (B) \leq 60$

23.2.5 Plan Must Be 3-5 Years Duration Depending upon Current Monthly Income. Add Amounts Necessary to Comply with Mandatory Length to 23.2.4.

23.3 CAUSES FOR CONVERSION OR DISMISSAL

		Statute
23.3.1	Loss or Diminution — Reorganization Unlikely	11 U.S.C. §1112(b)(4)(A)
23.3.2	Failure to Follow Operating Rules	11 U.S.C. §1112 (b)(4)(B)(C)(C) (F)(H)(I)
23.3.3	Unreasonable Delay Prejudicial to Creditors	11 U.S.C. §1307(c)(1)
23.3.4	Failure to Propose a Plan Within Court Deadlines	11 U.S.C. §§1112(b)(4)(J), 1307(c)(3)
23.3.5	Failure to Obtain Confirmation of Any Plan	11 U.S.C. §1307(c)(5)
23.3.6	Revocation of Confirmation	11 U.S.C. §§1112(b)(4)(L), 1307(c)(7)
23.3.7	Inability to Commence Plan	11 U.S.C. §§1112(b)(4)(M), 1307(c)(4)
23.3.8	Material Default in Plan	11 U.S.C. §§1112(b)(4)(N), 1307(c)(6)

Statute

23.3.9	Occurrence of a Condition Stated in Plan	11 U.S.C. §§1112(b)(4)(Q), 1307(c)(2)
23.3.10	Failure to Pay Court Fees	11 U.S.C. §§1112(b)(4)(K), 1307(c)(2)
23.3.11	Failure to File Chapter 13 Statement	11 U.S.C. §1307(c)(9), (10)
23.3.12	Failure to Pay Postpetition Domestic Support Obligations	11 U.S.C. §1307(c)(11)
23.3.13	Failure to File Tax Returns	11 U.S.C. §1308

DISCUSSION QUESTIONS

1. What is the purpose of a reorganization proceeding?

2. What are the grounds for dismissal or conversion of a reorganization proceeding?

3. What documents must a Chapter 13 debtor file with the court? What are the deadlines for filing each document? What is the effect of a failure to file a required document?

4. What is the permissible length of a Chapter 13 plan?

5. What elements must be included in a Chapter 13 plan? What elements may be included?

6. What findings must the court make to confirm a Chapter 13 plan? How is a plan's feasibility determined?

7. How does a creditor object to confirmation of a Chapter 13 plan?

8. What is meant by the term *cramdown*? How can a Chapter 13 debtor cram down a plan over the objection of an unsecured creditor?

9. How and when may a Chapter 13 plan be modified?

10. What is the effect of a Chapter 13 discharge? How, if at all, does a Chapter 13 discharge differ from a Chapter 7 discharge? What is a "hardship" discharge?

11. What is a "Chapter 20"?

PRACTICE EXERCISE

Exercise 23.1

Assuming that the debtor's case is originally filed or converted to Chapter 13, prepare a proposed Chapter 13 plan that proposes to repay any missed mortgage or car payments, along with any other debt necessary to obtain confirmation of the plan.

24

Chapter 11: Introduction and Administration

A.   INTRODUCTION TO CHAPTER 11

Chapter 11 is the most complex, time-consuming, and expensive of all bankruptcy proceedings to prosecute. Chapter 11 cases comprise less than 1 percent of all bankruptcies filed, but they consume substantial amounts of the court's time.[1] The various topics described elsewhere in this text — relief from stay motions, the assumption or rejection of executory contracts, the use or sale of property including the use of cash collateral, and the obtaining of credit by a bankruptcy estate — are all recurring issues in Chapter 11 proceedings. Each issue must be dealt with independently, but the resolution of each issue may involve one or more evidentiary hearings. Further, and most critically, the resolution of one or more of these issues may often be essential to the outcome of the case.

Chapter 11 is usually thought of as a business reorganization vehicle. It is available, however, for the use of individuals as well. Usually, it is used in the consumer context when the debtor is unable to qualify under the debt guidelines for a Chapter 13 proceeding. The focal point of this textbook is on consumer Chapter 7 and Chapter 13 cases. We will touch on Chapter 11 here only as an overview to familiarize you with the terms and concepts.

---

1. According to figures available from the United States Courts, Chapter 11 proceedings comprised 0.7 percent of all filings for the calendar year ending December 31, 2010, or 13,713 out of 1,593,081 total filings.

Often, a resolution of any or all of the above issues may be required at the inception of a Chapter 11 proceeding. For example, a manufacturing debtor-in-possession may need to obtain a cash collateral order, obtain postpetition secured credit, and assume existing manufacturing contracts within a relatively short period of time after the Chapter 11 filing. These activities will involve motions under Sections 363, 364, and 365, respectively.[2] Simultaneously, a debtor-in-possession may be required to defend motions to appoint a trustee or examiner under Section 1104 or motions for relief from stay or adequate protection under Sections 362 and 361.[3] All of these activities may occur and be determined before a debtor-in-possession can even begin to consider proposing a plan of reorganization. It is in Chapter 11 practice that the Bankruptcy Code most frequently and visibly operates as a complete system affecting all of a debtor's financial affairs. In large reorganizations typical of the Southern District of New York or the District of Delaware, any or all of those matters may be the subject of one or more **first-day orders** sought at the beginning of the case.

Like Chapter 13, the goal of a Chapter 11 proceeding is for a debtor to successfully reorganize its affairs so it may repay debt, retain assets, and remain in business. Like Chapter 13, this is accomplished by a debtor-in-possession proposing a plan of reorganization and obtaining its confirmation. Unlike Chapter 13, the Chapter 11 plan confirmation process is complex and lengthy. At least two, potentially major, court hearings are required to obtain confirmation. A further important difference is that the creditors in a Chapter 11 case are given the opportunity to vote for or against the plan. It normally takes a minimum of four to six months to obtain confirmation of a typical Chapter 11 plan.[4] Like a Chapter 13, a confirmed Chapter 11 plan is nothing more or less than a judicially approved composition agreement.

A number of actions, many of which have been described elsewhere in this text, need to be taken by a Chapter 11 debtor within 120 days of filing to ensure that all provisions of the Bankruptcy Code and Federal Rules of Bankruptcy Procedure are properly complied with in the prosecution of the Chapter 11 proceeding. In addition, because a Chapter 11 may remain pending for an indefinite period of time prior to confirmation of a plan and because the debtor acts as its own trustee as a debtor-in-possession, a number of operating rules have been created to monitor a debtor-in-possession's compliance with the Bankruptcy Code and Rules. These

---

2. See chapters 18, 19, and 20 supra.
3. See chapters 10 and 12 supra.
4. See chapter 26 infra.

operating rules are generally implemented by guidelines published by the local United States Trustee. A sample set of guidelines is contained on the forms disk accompanying this text. This chapter concerns the initial actions and ongoing operating procedures that a debtor-in-possession must follow prior to confirmation of a plan. The following two chapters will describe the procedure and requirements for proposing and obtaining confirmation of a Chapter 11 plan.

Any entity that may file under Chapter 7 is also eligible to file a Chapter 11 case.[5] Chapter 11 is intentionally designed this way. A corporation as large as Lehman Brothers or an individual debtor owing just slightly in excess of the Chapter 13 debt limits is each eligible to file a Chapter 11 proceeding.[6] Chapter 11 is thus designed to work for small debtors as well as large debtors. When a large corporation files, the filing is undoubtedly reported in the media. For example, Enron, Blockbuster Video, United Airlines, Continental Airlines, U.S. Air, and K-Mart have all been involved in widely publicized Chapter 11 cases in recent years. In remarks before the American Bankruptcy Institute, Chief Justice William H. Rehnquist stated: "Chapter 11 has become a major tool for restructuring corporate America, with broad implications for employees, retirees, business competitors, and the economy as a whole."[7]

The Bankruptcy Reform Act of 1994 created a new subcategory of Chapter 11 debtor, the **small business debtor**. A small business debtor is defined as a debtor with liquidated debts not in excess of $2,343,300 who elects treatment as a small business. A small business, however, may not be a debtor whose primary activity is owning and operating real estate.[8] A small business may have no creditor committee if the court so orders and must expedite the formulation of a reorganization plan (see chapter 10 supra and chapter 25 infra).

Chapter 11 is more than a legal program for the reorganization of a debtor. It is incorrect to think of Chapter 11 reorganization as solely a legal process. A debtor often may have one or more serious problems that may precipitate the Chapter 11 filing. Sometimes, as in the case of Texaco, the problem is related to one event, such as a large judgment that the debtor cannot satisfy without imposition of a repayment plan over the objection of the judgment creditor.

---

5. 11 U.S.C. §109. See chapter 4 supra.
6. Texaco, Inc., and a number of its subsidiaries filed a Chapter 11 proceeding in the Southern District of New York. Texaco successfully reorganized in 1988. As to individuals, see Toibb v. Radloff, 501 U.S. 157 (1991), discussed in section 4E supra.
7. Remarks of Chief Justice William H. Rehnquist, Annual Spring Meeting of the American Bankruptcy Institute, May 18, 1992.
8. 11 U.S.C. §101(51C). The amount is subject to adjustment as per 11 U.S.C. §104(b). See chapter 3 supra. The text reflects amounts in effect as of April 1, 2010.

Sometimes a debtor's problems are related to fraud, mismanagement, or the gross incompetence of its insiders. In these situations, more than a legal reorganization may be required to solve the debtor's problems. As a practical matter, the entire business may have to be internally reorganized in addition to the external reorganization represented by the plan. Internal reorganization may be as simple as teaching a debtor how to count and manage a budget over an extended period of time. This single problem is a major cause of many Chapter 11 filings. Sometimes, internal reorganization can be quite complex and involve a change of insider management, plant closings, layoffs, and so forth.

Sometimes a Chapter 11 will involve a partnership with one piece of real property that is in foreclosure. This sort of proceeding has relatively few problematic issues because all the debtor seeks is to refinance or sell the property so as to avoid the foreclosure and realize a profit. Not much may happen in the proceeding until a secured creditor moves for relief from the stay or the debtor can propose a plan.

The filing of a Chapter 11 proceeding makes the petitioner a "debtor-in-possession."[9] A debtor-in-possession is the functional equivalent of a trustee.[10] As illustrated elsewhere, the debtor-in-possession is authorized to conduct ordinary business affairs without court approval except as required by Sections 363, 364, or 365.[11]

The United States Trustee has been charged with monitoring a Chapter 11 debtor-in-possession's postpetition operations to ensure compliance with the provisions of the Bankruptcy Code and Rules.[12] Additionally, one role of the Official Creditors' Committee is to be active in monitoring the debtor's affairs during the proceeding.[13]

There are definite benefits that a debtor gains from a Chapter 11 filing. A business in serious financial condition may continue to operate without danger of immediate closure by any of its creditors. This breathing spell theoretically provides the debtor with an opportunity to attempt the successful reorganization of its financial affairs. Various Code provisions also exist to allow the debtor to restructure the repayment of its debt. However, there are also burdens that a debtor must accept along with the benefits of a Chapter 11 proceeding.

The largest burden is that the debtor will be required to comply with many new operating and/or reporting rules. The practical impact of these rules is that by filing a Chapter 11, the debtor-in-possession effectively

---

9. 11 U.S.C. §1101(1).
10. 11 U.S.C. §1107. See chapter 10 supra.
11. See chapters 18, 19, and 20 supra.
12. 28 U.S.C. §586(a)(3). See chapter 10 supra.
13. 11 U.S.C. §1103. See chapter 10 supra.

becomes an involuntary partner with its creditors. The debtor's financial affairs are no longer private. They will be subject to constant monitoring and criticism by the creditors' committee, individual creditors, or the United States Trustee.[14] All of these entities have the opportunity to intrude into and attempt to control the debtor's financial affairs in manners not normally possible in a nonbankruptcy environment.

If a debtor-in-possession fails to comply with the operating rules, the Official Creditors' Committee or the United States Trustee or any other creditor may move before the court for the appointment of a trustee or an examiner, thus removing the debtor from possession.[15] Alternatively, if the proceeding fails as a Chapter 11 or if the debtor fails to comply with the operating rules, a Chapter 11 proceeding may be converted to a Chapter 7 or dismissed pursuant to Section 1112.[16]

Practice Pointer

Failure to file operating reports may qualify as "cause" for dismissal or conversion of the case.

B. ACTIONS TO TAKE WITHIN 120 DAYS OF FILING

At the moment of filing a Chapter 11, a debtor must file the following documents with the court:

1. petition, along with payment of an $1039 filing fee;
2. a corporate resolution or partnership consent authorizing the filing;
3. a list containing the names and addresses of each creditor unless the Schedules are filed with the petition;
4. a list of the 20 largest unsecured claimants including the amount of the claims; and

---

14. See chapter 10 supra.
15. See chapter 10 supra.
16. 11 U.S.C. §1112. See chapter 23 supra for a more detailed description of §1112.

5. a corporate debtor must file Exhibit A to Voluntary Petition.
6. an individual debtor must file a credit counseling certificate (11 U.S.C. §109(h); 11 U.S.C. §521(b). See chapter 3 supra).
7. a small business debtor must file, within three days, its most recent balance sheet, statement of operations, cash-flow statement, federal income tax return or a statement under penalty of perjury as to which of the items has not been prepared or filed (11 U.S.C. §1116(1)).

Some of these time periods may be extended upon application to the court or United States Trustee.[17]

Within 15 days of filing the petition, a Chapter 11 debtor must file the following additional documents with the court:

8. a list of all equity security holders of the debtor;
9. the Statement of Financial Affairs;
10. Schedules of Assets and Liabilities; and
11. a Statement of Executory Contracts.

These time periods may be extended upon application to the court or United States Trustee.[18] The United States Trustee will conduct an informal conference known as an Initial Debtor Interview with representatives of the debtor to discuss the operating requirements and to implement compliance with the rules and guidelines applicable within a given district. In a small business case, Section 1116(2) mandates an Initial Debtor Interview. Form 10.1 is a sample of a local United States Trustee guidelines.

Within 30 days of filing, the debtor must also file an inventory, if ordered to do so by the United States Trustee, and commence to file operating reports.[19] Local rules may also supplement these basic requirements. Any applications to retain professionals, such as attorneys or accountants, must also be filed during the same initial 30-day period or within 30 days of the professional's retention.

Finally, a debtor-in-possession must act within 120 days to assume any lease of nonresidential real property or the lease is deemed rejected.[20]

---

17. 11 U.S.C. §302; Bankruptcy Rules 1002, 1004, 1006, 1007(a), (d). See chapter 4 supra.
18. Bankruptcy Rules 1007(a)(3)(4), 1007(b)(1).
19. Bankruptcy Rule 2015. As to small business debtors, 11 U.S.C. §1116 codifies these requirements.
20. 11 U.S.C. §365(d)(4). See chapter 19 supra.

C.   DEBTOR-IN-POSSESSION BANK ACCOUNTS

Local rules or United States Trustee guidelines may impose additional requirements that a Chapter 11 debtor-in-possession must perform promptly after the filing or on an ongoing basis. First, a debtor-in-possession will be required to deposit all funds in an approved depository pursuant to Section 345. Recall that an approved depository is a bank or savings and loan that guarantees bankruptcy deposits greater than $250,000.[21]

Next, local rules will require a debtor-in-possession to close its old bank accounts and open new ones. Because part of the theory behind the debtor-in-possession concept is that it is a new entity separate and distinct from the prepetition debtor, the requirement of establishing new bank accounts helps implement the theory. This requirement also serves as a useful accounting mechanism for the debtor because it closes the prepetition books and opens new ones.

Local rules or United States Trustee guidelines may require that at least three accounts be established. They are normally a general account, a payroll account, and a tax account. These new accounts will be required to identify the debtor as a debtor-in-possession. For example, it will not generally be acceptable for ABC Inc. to identify itself as such on its checks. The checks must now state "ABC Inc., Debtor-in-Possession," along with the case number. Local rules or United States Trustee guidelines should be consulted to identify the acceptable legend required in a given district.

The requirement of multiple bank accounts is designed to assist debtors in efficiently managing their cash flow, ensuring to the greatest extent possible that payroll and tax obligations will be satisfied properly and promptly and that any party in interest who desires may easily trace a debtor's cash flow during the Chapter 11. All income that a debtor receives is to be deposited into the general account. From the general account all disbursements are made to the debtor. For example, there will be disbursements from the general account into the payroll account to meet payroll. There will be disbursements from the general account into the tax account as the taxes are incurred. All other postpetition debts of the estate will be paid from the general account.

A large debtor may actually have more than three bank accounts. For example, a debtor-in-possession accumulating cash surpluses should open a savings account so the surplus funds can earn interest.

---

21. 11 U.S.C. §345. See chapter 20 supra.

In addition, any secured creditor's cash collateral will be required to be deposited into a cash collateral account before disbursement into other accounts. If use of the cash collateral is allowed, disbursements from the cash collateral account will be directed as the parties and court agree. The accompanying diagram indicates the general flow of cash through debtor-in-possession accounts.

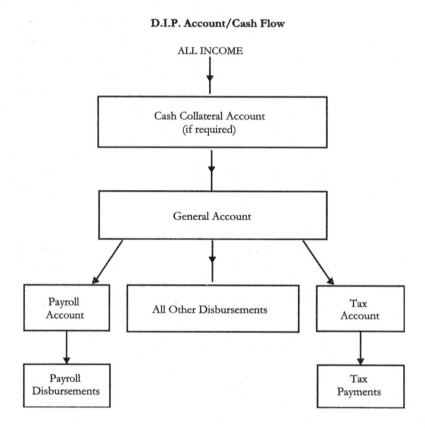

D.I.P. Account/Cash Flow

ALL INCOME

Cash Collateral Account
(if required)

General Account

Payroll Account

All Other Disbursements

Tax Account

Payroll Disbursements

Tax Payments

D.   INSIDER COMPENSATION

Local rules may require that a debtor-in-possession obtain an order from the court approving any compensation to be paid the debtor's insiders. In districts utilizing a rule of this nature, a Chapter 11 debtor will subject the salary of its insiders to the scrutiny of creditors and approval by the court. Approval of insider salaries will generally require a noticed motion.[22] The court may approve compensation on an interim basis while this process is pending. The United States Trustee normally monitors applications for insider compensation and may challenge the amount sought.

It is in the court's discretion to decide what will constitute reasonable compensation to an insider. The practitioner should be prepared to demonstrate two sets of facts to the court. First, the court should be shown what duties the insider performs for the debtor, such as the number of hours per week worked, a job description, and, if available, a comparison of salaries for similar positions in the debtor's industry. Second, the court may require disclosure of the insider's basic monthly living expenses. A budget statement similar to those used in Chapter 7 and Chapter 13 proceedings should suffice in most situations. The insider employees of a debtor-in-possession will necessarily be entitled to salaries, because it will be difficult or impossible for the debtor to reorganize if its key employees are prohibited from receiving a paycheck at least sufficient to meet basic monthly living expenses, especially in small business debtor cases. This is common sense. Once all of the foregoing acts have been accomplished, the Chapter 11 proceeding has been properly organized to function in compliance with all Federal Rules of Bankruptcy Procedure save two, a Chapter 11 debtor-in-possession has the continuing duty to file operating reports and the obligation to pay quarterly fees to the United States Trustee pursuant to 28 U.S.C. §1930(a)(6). The amount of this fee depends on the total disbursements made by the debtor-in-possession until dismissal or conversion of a case.[23] Checklist 24.3 infra is a table of United States Trustee quarterly fees.

E. OPERATING REPORTS

The most important ongoing duty of a Chapter 11 debtor-in-possession is to file operating reports. This is required by both the Code and the Rules.[24] Local rules or United States Trustee guidelines will generally

---

22. See chapter 4 supra.
23. On January 26, 1996, 28 U.S.C. §1930(a)(6), which is the operative statute for the assessment and collection of quarterly fees, was amended into its present form. Prior to this date, quarterly fees ended upon confirmation of the plan. Now collection will continue until the case is dismissed, converted, or the plan is fully performed and the case closed. Pub. L. No. 104-99, 110 Stat. 26 (1996).
24. 11 U.S.C. §308; 11 U.S.C. §1106(a)(1); 11 U.S.C. §704(8); 11 U.S.C. §1116(4); Bankruptcy Rule 2015(a)(3).

require the reports to be filed on a monthly basis. Oddly enough, there is no official form for an operating report and many local rules do not specify a particular format. Section 308 mandates the basic items to be included in operating reports in small business cases. A format approved by the United States Trustee is included on the forms disk accompanying this text.

The **operating report** serves a number of critical functions in the administration of a Chapter 11 proceeding. It is a regular report of a debtor's ongoing postpetition business operations. It will advise the creditors, Official Creditors' Committee, and the United States Trustee if the debtor is generating profits or losses during the proceeding. If the debtor is incurring debts that it is not timely paying, if any improper disbursements are being made (avoidable postpetition transactions, for example), or if any transactions have taken place without the requisite prior court approval (such as administrative loans or unauthorized use of cash collateral), this information will be disclosed in the report.[25] Undue delay in the formulation of a plan to the creditors' prejudice can be ascertained from review of a series of operating reports. Examination of the report will allow a creditor, the Official Creditors' Committee, or the United States Trustee to determine whether a proceeding should continue, be converted or dismissed, or have a trustee appointed to oversee the debtor's operations even more closely. From the results contained in operating reports, the parties will be able to evaluate the feasibility of any proposed plan that relies on operating revenues for performance.

For example, if Linus's Security Blankets, Inc., has been in a Chapter 11 for four years while accumulating cash profits sufficient to pay all claims in full, the creditors might propose their own plan or seek dismissal or conversion of the proceeding. On the other hand, if a proceeding appears interminable and a series of reports indicates that adequate profits cannot be generated to repay creditors, then the creditors may use this data to seek conversion of the proceeding to a Chapter 7. In short, the operating reports comprise an official record of a debtor-in-possession's postpetition financial activities. This record will demonstrate whether a proceeding is destined for success or failure.

Ideally, an accurate operating report will contain elements of the two basic accounting methods, cash or accrual. Each accounting method will disclose certain aspects of the debtor's postpetition financial status that may be germane to a continuation of the proceeding as a Chapter 11.

The **cash method** of accounting is the accounting method that virtually all individuals use every day of their lives. The cash method of

---

25. 11 U.S.C. §§364, 549, 363(c). See chapters 17, 18, and 20 supra.

accounting accounts for cash at the time it is received or spent. The **accrual method** of accounting, on the other hand, identifies as income any right to receive payment for goods delivered or services performed. For example, an account receivable is considered income under the accrual method of accounting, while it would not be so considered in the cash method of accounting until received. In addition, the accrual method of accounting identifies as an expense any debt that has been incurred even though it has not yet been paid. Most businesses that have inventory are required, for tax purposes, to use the accrual method of accounting on a regular basis. Manufacturing entities are also required to use the accrual method of accounting. The Schedules of Assets and Liabilities that a debtor must file in any bankruptcy proceeding are really not much more than a form of accrual basis financial statements. The accrual method describes all obligations that have been accrued but not paid by a debtor while itemizing all of a debtor's assets. This is the essence of the accrual method of accounting. The cash method of accounting identifies whether the debtor-in-possession has more or less cash on hand at the beginning or end of a reporting period as time passes. The accrual method of accounting identifies, over a period of time, whether the receivables are increasing or decreasing or if outstanding accounts payable are increasing or decreasing.

An operating report must contain an itemization of all receipts and disbursements made by a debtor-in-possession.[26] This is a cash basis representation of the debtor-in-possession's activities. Each bank account maintained by a debtor-in-possession should have its own itemized disbursement schedule included in the monthly operating report. Each disbursement must be identified. It may be sufficient in many cases simply to attach a copy of the debtor-in-possession's check register as an exhibit to the report. The check register will identify the check number, the amount, and the identity of the payee.

A debtor-in-possession should avoid making cash disbursements. If, however, cash disbursements are made, the debtor-in-possession should maintain detailed records of them. The invoices paid or payment receipts should be maintained and itemized in the report so that all transactions conducted by a debtor are accounted for. Otherwise, an examiner, a trustee, a creditor, or the United States Trustee will assume that the cash disbursement was improper.

The report should reconcile, or balance, a debtor-in-possession's bank accounts. This part of the report will disclose the amount on deposit

---

26. 11 U.S.C. §308 mandates these items in small business operating reports. See also Bankruptcy Rule 2015(2)(3).

in each account at the beginning and end of a reporting period. Each account should be identified by name, address, and account number.

The accrual portion of an operating report, where required, will iden- tify whether the debtor is or is not generally paying its postpetition debts as they become due. The debtor should disclose debts that are accrued but unpaid and the length of time such debts have been unpaid. Similarly, an aging report of accounts receivable should also be provided.

F.   REVIEWING OPERATING REPORTS

As noted above, an operating report serves as an official record of the debtor-in-possession's postpetition financial affairs. It discloses whether the reorganization is succeeding or failing. Having generally described the contents of an operating report, practical uses of them can now be further illustrated.

A compilation of data from one or more operating reports can provide admissible evidence as to positive or negative trends in a Chapter 11 pro- ceeding. First, total up all receipts for any number of months during the proceeding for which data are desired. Observe whether receipts are increasing or decreasing every month. A calculation might also be made as to the average monthly receipts. Observe the trend. Is it increasing or decreasing? If receipts are rising, the time may have arrived to propose a plan. On the other hand, if receipts are decreasing every month, it might be time to file a motion to convert, especially if the accrued but unpaid expenses are accumulating rapidly.

Second, examine the disbursements. Verify that any insider compen- sation has been approved by the court, where required, and that the amount paid does not exceed the court-approved amount. If the report discloses that an insider has suddenly received a substantial raise, this may be brought to the attention of the court. If there are substantial cash disbursements, without any verification, this should be considered evidence of improper management.

Next, review the bank account balances. If the balances at the end of each reporting period are increasing, this may be evidence that the pro- ceeding is succeeding. On the other hand, if the balance is consistently negative or is decreasing from one reporting period to the next, this may be evidence that the proceeding is failing.

The list of accrued but unpaid expenses can be very revealing. Many businesses usually pay their bills 30 to 40 days after receiving them. It is not uncommon to have an entire month of accounts payable to be accrued and unpaid at any given point in time in the normal operation of any business. This should not be considered a sign of financial difficulty. Thus, if a list of accrued but unpaid expenses is roughly equivalent to a debtor's monthly cash expenses (by reviewing a series of reports these averages can be computed), this should not be construed as a sign of failure. Sometimes, even two months of arrears do not necessarily signify danger. But once a debtor shows three months or more of unpaid post-petition debt, it is time to reconsider the continuance of the proceeding as a Chapter 11. A debtor's representative should recommend that the matter be converted to a Chapter 7. A creditor's representative may move the court for conversion or the appointment of a trustee or examiner to investigate the status of the proceeding in greater detail. Remember, all unpaid postpetition debts are administrative expenses.[27] The more of them there are, the less will be available for payment of dividends to prepetition unsecured creditors if the proceeding is converted to a Chapter 7.

In a large proceeding sometimes even one or two months of accrued and unpaid expenses can be fatal. In some situations, the delay of even a week in filing a report can result in accrual of additional substantial unpaid expenses without knowledge of the creditors. The best way to prevent this in a large proceeding is to make sure that the Official Creditors' Committee is organized promptly and demand that a debtor provide informal weekly or biweekly reports of operations to the committee. In an appropriate matter, the United States Trustee might undertake such intervention.

The burden of being a Chapter 11 debtor-in-possession is that the debtor becomes an involuntary partner with its creditors. Any effort to conceal the truth from the creditors will ultimately work to the debtor's detriment. Full cooperation and disclosure should be the norm, particularly because the most successful Chapter 11 proceedings are more a process of reconciliation between debtor and creditors than a process of continual adversarial dispute. Full compliance by a debtor-in-possession with all operating rules will only help to increase the chances for a successful outcome to the proceeding.

Summary

Chapter 11 is the most complex, time-consuming, and expensive of all bankruptcy proceedings to prosecute. Chapter 11 is available to any

---

27. See chapter 21 supra.

debtor qualified to be a Chapter 7 debtor. A major corporation or the corner store may each file Chapter 11 proceedings.

As is the case with Chapter 13, the goal of a Chapter 11 debtor-in-possession is to obtain court confirmation of a repayment plan. In Chapter 11, the plan is called a plan of reorganization. However, this is where the similarity ends. The process for obtaining confirmation of a Chapter 11 reorganization plan is complex and time-consuming. Further, a Chapter 11 debtor-in-possession is subject to substantially more administrative requirements than a Chapter 13 debtor. The checklist accompanying this chapter outlines these requirements.

The most important administrative requirement placed upon a debtor-in-possession is to file monthly operating reports with the court. The checklist accompanying this chapter outlines the critical elements of an operating report. The forms disk accompanying this text contains a sample operating report approved by the United States Trustee.

The practical effect of the Chapter 11 debtor-in-possession rules is to make the debtor an involuntary partner with its creditors. Cooperation and disclosure are required to be the norm. Full compliance by a debtor-in-possession with all operating rules will only help to increase the chance for a successful outcome to the proceeding.

KEY TERMS

accrual method   **operating report**
cash method   **small business debtor**
first-day order

Chapter 24 Checklist

24.1   CHAPTER 11 ADMINISTRATION —
       DOCUMENTS AND DEADLINES   *Authority*

    24.1.1   Deadline — At Filing
       1. Petition and $1,039 filing fee   Bankruptcy Rules
                                           1002, 1006

       2. Corporate resolution of   Bankruptcy Rule
           partnership authorization   1004
       3. List of creditors, unless   Bankruptcy Rule
           schedules filed at filing   1007(a)(1)

4. List of 20 largest unsecured claims — Bankruptcy Rule 1007(d)

5. Corporate debtor — Exhibit A to Voluntary Petition — Bankruptcy Rule Official Form 1x

6. Individual debtor credit counseling certificate — 11 U.S.C. §109(h); 11 U.S.C. §521(b)

7. Small business debtor financial statements; tax returns — 11 U.S.C. §1116(1)

24.1.2 Deadline — Within 15 Days of Filing

1. List of equity security holders — Bankruptcy Rule 1007(a)(3)

2. Statement of Financial Affairs — 11 U.S.C. §521(1), Bankruptcy Rule 1007(b)

3. Schedules of Assets and Liabilities — 11 U.S.C. §521(1), Bankruptcy Rule 1007(b)

4. Statement of Executory Contracts — Bankruptcy Rule 1007(b)

5. Debtor-in-possession bank accounts — 11 U.S.C. §345, consult local rules

6. Attorney statement of compensation — 11 U.S.C. §329, Bankruptcy Rule 2016(b)

24.1.3 Deadline — Within 30 Days of Filing

1. Applications to retain professionals — 11 U.S.C. §327, Bankruptcy Rule 2014, consult local Rules

2. Applications for insider compensation — consult local rules

3. Commence operating reports — Bankruptcy Rule 2015(a)(2), (3); 11 U.S.C. §1116(4)

4. File inventory if United States Trustee requires — Bankruptcy Rule 2015(a)(1)

Disbursements/Quarter	*Fee*
less than $15,000	$ 325
$15,000 to $75,000	$ 650
$75,000 to $150,000	$ 975
$150,000 to $225,000	$ 1,625
$225,000 to $300,000	$ 1,950
$300,000 to $1,000,000	$ 4,875
$1,000,000 to $2,000,000	$ 6,500
$2,000,000 to $3,000,000	$ 9,750
$3,000,000 to $5,000,000	$10,400
$5,000,000 to $15,000,000	$13,000
$15,000,000 to $30,000,000	$20,000
$30,000,000 and up	$30,000

DISCUSSION QUESTIONS

1. What distinguishes a Chapter 11 bankruptcy from other bankruptcy proceedings?

2. What documents must a Chapter 11 debtor file with the court? What are the deadlines for filing each document? What is the effect of a failure to file a required document?

3. What rules must a debtor-in-possession comply with regarding the administration of a Chapter 11 estate?

4. What is an operating report? Describe the major features of an operating report.

5. What is the role of the United States Trustee in the supervision of a debtor-in-possession?

PRACTICE EXERCISE

Exercise 24.1

The owner of Griffin's Quahog Convenience Store comes to you for advice regarding a possible bankruptcy filing. Your supervising attorney examines the financial data and wants to recommend a Small Business Chapter 11 filing. Prepare a memo outlining any special operating rules applicable to a Small Business Chapter 11 debtor conducting business postpetition.

25

Chapter 11: Elements of a Plan

A.   CONFIRMATION PROCESS — OVERVIEW

The process of formulating and obtaining confirmation of a Chapter 11 reorganization plan is the most complex process in the Bankruptcy Code. A Chapter 11 reorganization plan is known as a **Plan of Reorganization**. There are a number of steps that must be followed and many rules to apply to achieve confirmation. In typical situations, this process will take from four to six months. This chapter analyzes the elements of a plan. Chapter 26 infra describes the details of the confirmation process.

The goal of a Chapter 11 proceeding is to obtain confirmation of a Chapter 11 reorganization plan that will satisfy creditors while retaining assets or continuing the debtor's business. An overview of the entire process will be helpful.

The first step is to file a reorganization plan. Along with the plan, the **plan proponent** (entity filing the plan) must also file a document known as a **disclosure statement**.[1] A disclosure statement is similar to a disclosure document used in stock transactions. The purpose of a disclosure statement is to tell the creditors everything about the plan and the debtor that may affect the creditors' decision to vote for or against the plan.

Once the plan and disclosure statement have been filed, a hearing to approve the disclosure statement is held.[2] Creditors must receive at least 28 days' notice of the hearing to approve the disclosure statement.[3] This is

---

1. 11 U.S.C. §1121; Bankruptcy Rule 3016(b).
2. 11 U.S.C. §1125(b); Bankruptcy Rule 3017(a).
3. Bankruptcy Rules 2002(b), 3017(a).

an exception to the general rule contained in Federal Rule of Bankruptcy Procedure 2002, requiring 21 days' notice to creditors in most instances.[4] A small business debtor may have a disclosure statement conditionally approved and then combine the disclosure and confirmation hearings. Theoretically, this procedure will shorten the time it takes to confirm a small business Chapter 11 plan (11 U.S.C. §1125(f); see chapter 26 infra).

Once the court approves the disclosure statement as containing "adequate information," the plan proponent may solicit acceptances or rejections (votes) for or against the plan seeking creditor consensus to achieve confirmation.[5] The plan proponent must send all creditors a copy of the plan, a copy of the disclosure statement, a copy of the order approving the disclosure statement, a notice of the hearing on the confirmation of the plan, and a ballot. At least 28 days' notice of the confirmation hearing is required.[6] Creditors return their ballots to the plan proponent, who files a report with the court summarizing the results of the balloting. This balloting report, along with the original ballots, is filed before the hearing.[7] Samples of these various documents are included on the forms disk accompanying this text. The checklist for this chapter summarizes these documents. Collectively, this group of documents is called a **confirmation packet**.

Finally, the court will hold a confirmation hearing. At the confirmation hearing, the court will either confirm or deny confirmation of the plan.[8] The entire confirmation process is summarized in the nearby flowchart. The forms disk contains a sample plan and disclosure statement. Reference to them will greatly aid in illustrating the concepts introduced in the next two chapters.

B.   TIME TO FILE A PLAN

Section 1121 regulates when a plan may be filed and who may file one. Unless a trustee has been appointed, only the debtor may file a plan during the 120-day period following the entry of an order for relief.[9]

---

4. See chapter 4 supra.
5. 11 U.S.C. §1126; Bankruptcy Rule 3017(c). See chapter 26 infra.
6. Bankruptcy Rule 3017(d); 2002(b).
7. Bankruptcy Rule 3018.
8. 11 U.S.C. §1128. See chapter 26 infra.
9. 11 U.S.C. §1121(b). Recall that the order for relief is entered upon filing a voluntary petition and is the judgment sought by the petitioners in an involuntary proceeding. See chapter 3 supra.

CHAPTER 11 PLAN CONFIRMATION PROCESS

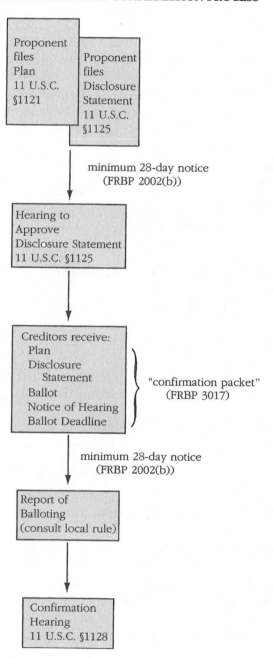

413

This **exclusivity period** is intended to provide a debtor with breathing room to permit an attempt at reorganization free from the interference that would be caused by a competing plan.

If a debtor does file a plan within the 120-day exclusivity period, the period is extended to a date 180 days from the entry of the order for relief. The reason for the extension of the exclusivity period to 180 days is to provide the debtor an opportunity to obtain confirmation of a plan without having to defend against a competing plan at the same time.[10]

 Practice Pointer

For example, Flora and Fauna, Inc., files a Chapter 11 on February 13. Flora and Fauna, Inc., has an exclusive right until June 13 (120 days) to file a plan. If a plan is filed by Flora and Fauna, Inc., during this period, whether on day 1 or day 120, the period of exclusivity is now extended to August 12 (180 days).

During this entire period of time no other party may file a plan. This time period provides Flora and Fauna, Inc., with the opportunity to reorganize its affairs without interference from competing plans of reorganization filed by creditors. On the other hand, if Flora and Fauna, Inc.'s, creditors obtain the appointment of a trustee, the exclusivity period will automatically end.

It is also possible for a debtor to obtain an extension of either of the time periods described above, pursuant to 11 U.S.C. §1121(d). However, such a request must be made within the exclusivity period. The 120-day exclusivity period may not, however, be extended to a date more than 18 months after the order for relief. The 180-day period to obtain confirmation may not, however, be extended to a date more than 20 months after the order for relief. These rules prevent debtors from obtaining indefinite extensions of exclusivity.[11]

There are three events that terminate a debtor-in-possession's period of exclusivity to file a plan. They are the appointment of a trustee, as noted above, the lapse of 120 days after the entry of an order for relief if no plan has been filed, and the lapse of 180 days after the entry of an order for relief if a plan that has been filed has not yet been confirmed.[12]

---

10. 11 U.S.C. §1121(c)(3).
11. 11 U.S.C. §1121(d).
12. 11 U.S.C. §1121(c).

Small business debtors have been provided with independent exclusivity rules in 11 U.S.C. §1121(e). For a small business, the exclusivity period is 180 days, and in all events, the plan must be filed within 300 days from the order for relief. The court may reduce the time period. The 180-day exclusivity period may be extended upon a showing that it is more likely than not that the court will confirm a plan within a reasonable period of time. Additional extensions may be granted upon a further showing of these elements. The plan must be confirmed within 45 days after the plan is filed, pursuant to 11 U.S.C. §1129(e), unless the court extends exclusivity upon the same showing described above. Failure to make this showing within the time periods is cause for dismissal or conversion pursuant to 11 U.S.C. §1112(b)(2).

Once the exclusivity period expires, any party in interest except the United States Trustee may file a reorganization plan.[13] A private trustee may file a plan, the debtor may file a plan, the Official Creditors' Committee may file a plan, or an individual creditor may file a plan. It is for this reason that the party filing a plan is known as the plan proponent. More often than not this will be the debtor.

C. PLAN CHARACTERISTICS

As a practical matter, the confirmation process takes a minimum of four to six months to complete. Because at least 28 days' notice is required to be given for each of the disclosure statement and confirmation hearings, and because a debtor must set a ballot deadline, tabulate them, and file a report with the court shortly before the confirmation hearing, it is better practice to separate the disclosure statement and confirmation hearings by at least 60 days so that ample time will exist to vote, to compile the ballots, and to file the report prior to the confirmation hearing. If this will result in the effort at confirmation exceeding the statutory 180-day exclusivity period, the court may extend the period of exclusivity for cause since the debtor is in the process of seeking confirmation of its timely-filed plan.

A confirmed Chapter 11 reorganization plan is nothing more than a judicially approved composition agreement. When confirmed, the plan constitutes a new contract between the debtor and its creditors. As a result, Chapter 11 is an area of the law where practitioners may exercise some creativity and imagination in the formulation of plans and disclosure statements.

---

13. 11 U.S.C. §1121(c); 11 U.S.C. §307.

Any reasonable and lawful method of repaying debt can conceivably form the basis of a Chapter 11 plan. The plan may consist of simple repayment to creditors over a period of time from surplus revenues in a manner similar to a Chapter 13 plan, or the plan may involve the refinancing of the debtor's business, call for a sale of the business, involve an infusion of investment capital, or may be any combination of all these ideas. The larger a proceeding the more complex the financial concepts will become, but the basic premise is that any reasonable and lawful business method for reorganizing a debtor's financial affairs that can meet with creditor acceptance is a proper foundation for a Chapter 11 plan. Thus, paradoxically, the rules can be highly flexible despite their apparent rigidity.

D.   CLASSIFICATION OF CLAIMS

Section 1122 concerns the classification of claims within a plan. All creditors must be placed within classes. All creditors in a given class must have claims that are substantially similar.[14] For example, a secured creditor and an unsecured creditor may not be included in the same class because these claims are not substantially similar. A priority tax claim may not be classified with unsecured claims. Multiple unsecured claims may be included within the same class. More than one secured claim may also be included in the same class, but it is a better and recommended practice to separately classify each secured claim. The reason for this is that different secured creditors will have different collateral or differing rights regarding the same collateral. As a result each secured claim should be separately classified.

 Practice Pointer

Claims within a class must be "substantially similar" and the plan must not unfairly discriminate against a particular claim or class of claims.

Section 1122 does not require that all creditors of the same type be placed within the same class. Thus, it is possible to divide substantially

---

14. 11 U.S.C. §1122(a).

similar claims into separate classes. For example, federal tax claims may comprise one class of claims and nonfederal tax claims another class of claims. Similarly, a business may subclassify its unsecured claims into separate classes for suppliers of goods or services, unsecured noteholders, and so on. However, claims may not be classified so as to gerrymander affirmative votes on a plan.[15]

It is specifically possible to create a **convenience class** of creditors.[16] In many Chapter 11 proceedings, there are typically a number of unsecured creditors who are owed relatively small amounts and who are only creditors because the debtor's Chapter 11 filing fortuitously took place when their monthly invoices had not been paid. These creditors are usually owed such relatively small sums that the cost of administering their claims through a plan is likely to be more costly than the claim or dividend. Accordingly, a debtor may create a class of convenience claims and give the class a treatment that would be otherwise impermissible over creditor objection. A debtor may propose that all unsecured claims of less than a fixed amount, such as $500, will be classified as the convenience class and will receive a one-time dividend in discharge of their debts. This dividend may be greater or less than that offered to other unsecured creditors. The plan may also provide that any claimant reducing its claim to qualify for convenience treatment may voluntarily elect to become a member of the convenience class.

For example, Julie's Flying Pig Buttercake Restaurant Inc. has ten unsecured creditors who are owed $100 or less each. Julie's total debt is $150,000. Because it would be uneconomical to write each small creditor a check every three months for four or five years, creation of a convenience class is permitted and its members are paid a one-time dividend on confirmation of the plan in full discharge of the claims included within the class.

In its essence then, Section 1122 merely requires that a Chapter 11 reorganization plan create classes of claims. This may be as simple as organizing the claims into classes paralleling the distribution scheme described in chapters 21 and 22 supra. Or class creation can be highly complex, involving the creation of separate classes for multiple secured creditors, multiple categories of unsecured claims, and multiple classes of shareholders or bondholders. A Chapter 11 plan for a major corporation can be quite lengthy.

It is good practice to create a separate class for each secured claim. The reason for this is that each secured claimholder usually has either different

---

15. In re Greystone III Joint Venture, 948 F.2d 134 (5th Cir. 1991).
16. 11 U.S.C. §1122(b).

collateral or different rights with respect to the same collateral than other secured creditors. To the extent that there is different collateral or different rights in the same collateral, the rights of each claimholder may be different in degree and kind.[17] As a result, classification of each secured claim into separate classes will properly account for any differences in the claims. With respect to unsecured claims, it is not uncommon to see three classes of unsecured claims within a plan in the form of a convenience class, a trade creditor class, and a class of unsecured noteholders. Insider claims sometimes form a fourth class of unsecured claim. A final class or classes will be the interests of the equity security holders, the owners of the debtor.

A reorganization plan is not created in a vacuum. Recall that one function of the Official Creditors' Committee is to negotiate a plan with the debtor so the committee can recommend acceptance to the unsecured creditors.[18] The goal is consensual agreement, a court-approved composition agreement. All parties in interest will save time and money when a debtor negotiates a suitable plan with the Official Creditors' Committee in the first place. The debtor will know what the Official Creditors' Committee will require to recommend that unsecured creditors vote for the plan. On the other hand, the Official Creditors' Committee should be realistic in recognizing just how much "blood" can be squeezed out of the "turnip." Negotiation can result in a less expensive and prompter confirmation process. Every penny saved in administrative expenses is another penny in the pockets of the unsecured creditors. Failure to attempt negotiation of a plan's terms can result in substantial time-consuming and expensive litigation at any step in the confirmation process. The time and expense consumed in litigating these issues can sometimes, ironically, make the reorganization impossible.

E.   MANDATORY PLAN PROVISIONS

Section 1123 is similar to Section 1322 in Chapter 13.[19] Like Section 1322, Section 1123 prescribes the **mandatory** and **permissive elements** of a Chapter 11 plan. The provisions of Section 1123(a) are mandatory and must be included in any Chapter 11 plan. On the other hand, the elements of Section 1123(b) are permissive.

---

17. 11 U.S.C. §506. See chapter 21 supra.
18. See chapter 10 supra.
19. See chapter 23 supra.

First, the plan must designate classes of claims and interests. The classes should be organized consistent with Section 1122, as described above. A class of interests represents the interests of the debtor's equity security holders, such as shareholders, partners, or an individual debtor.[20] Second, the plan must specify which of the classes are impaired or not impaired under the plan.[21] The concept of impairment is the subject of Section 1124 and is discussed below in this chapter.

Third, the treatment accorded to impaired claims or interests must be described.[22] This is usually the heart of any plan.

Fourth, each creditor in the same class must be treated the same, unless a particular creditor agrees to a lesser treatment.[23] In other words, in the negotiation of a plan, a creditor may agree to accept less than the Code entitles it to. This is a practical application of the principle of voluntary subordination, described in chapter 21 supra. The rules are designed for a debtor to propose a minimum performance plan that the court may be required to approve over the objections of virtually all claims by way of the Chapter 11 cramdown procedures discussed in chapter 26 infra.[24] A creditor can always voluntarily agree to a lesser treatment of its claim than the Code requires or provides.

Fifth, a plan must provide adequate means for its implementation.[25] That is, the plan must advise all parties how the plan will be performed. It is not sufficient to merely promise that creditors are going to be repaid. The plan must describe "who, what, when, where, and how" the plan will be performed. Section 1123(a)(5) provides a list of ten methods but is not all-inclusive. The list merely provides examples of methods that may be used to perform a plan. Any other reasonable and lawful method of performance devised by a plan's proponent will also be acceptable. Refinancing, sale, periodic repayments, or new investment capital are all acceptable repayment methods, as described earlier in this chapter. Combinations of some or all of these methods can be included in the plan. These are the most common methods proposed for performance of a Chapter 11 reorganization plan. The Code mandates that a method of repayment be provided for, but not what the repayment method must be.

A debtor can propose to liquidate assets as a Chapter 11 plan performance method.[26] A debtor may choose to liquidate through a Chapter 11

---

20. 11 U.S.C. §1123(a)(1).
21. 11 U.S.C. §1123(a)(2).
22. 11 U.S.C. §1123(a)(3).
23. 11 U.S.C. §1123(a)(4).
24. 11 U.S.C. §1129(b).
25. 11 U.S.C. §1123(a)(5).
26. 11 U.S.C. §1123(a)(5)(D).

rather than a Chapter 7 for a number of reasons. First, a Chapter 11 may protect the reputation of the debtor's insiders more than a Chapter 7 would. Second, a Chapter 11 debtor remains in control of the business as a debtor-in-possession, rather than a trustee's being appointed to assume control of the estate. There may be situations when this will increase the prospects for creditor dividends. Finally, the Chapter 11 process may sometimes involve less time and expense to liquidate an estate and pay creditors dividends than a Chapter 7 proceeding. For example, if the debtor is in a small specialized industry, management will likely have contacts unavailable to a Chapter 7 trustee that will aid in maximizing the price obtained from a liquidation of assets. Further, if the debtor is in a Chapter 11, the debtor does not have to deal with all the timetables described in chapter 22 supra. The debtor may sell the assets, propose a plan, obtain confirmation, and pay creditors in a fraction of the time that a Chapter 7 proceeding would take, but with exactly the same or better results.

Sixth, a plan involving a corporate debtor must provide that the corporation's charter will provide appropriate representation on its board of directors to various classes of shareholders.[27] In most proceedings, compliance with this provision will not be problematic.

Seventh, the plan must be in the interests of the creditors and equity security holders and be consistent with public policy respecting the selection of a debtor's insiders.[28] This means that the plan must identify the postconfirmation insiders of the debtor.

Finally, in Chapter 11 cases for individual debtors, the debtor must commit postpetition earnings for personal services as is necessary for performance of the plan. To aid in implementing this provision, Section 1115 makes the postpetition earnings for personal services property of the estate in a manner similar to Chapter 13.[29]

F.   PERMISSIVE PLAN PROVISIONS

Subsection 1123(b) describes the permissive elements of a Chapter 11 plan. Permissive elements are elements that may be included but are not required to be in a Chapter 11 plan. It is nevertheless recommended

---

27. 11 U.S.C. §1123(a)(6).
28. 11 U.S.C. §1123(a)(7).
29. 11 U.S.C. §1123(a)(8); 11 U.S.C. §1115; 11 U.S.C. §1306. As to Chapter 13, see chapter 23 supra.

to include these items within a plan. First, a plan may impair or leave unimpaired a class of claims or interests.[30] Impairment is described below in connection with Section 1124.

Second, a plan may provide for the assumption or rejection of any executory contracts that have not been previously assumed or rejected during the Chapter 11 proceeding.[31] As a practical matter, it is good practice to specifically provide for the assumption or rejection of all executory contracts within a reorganization plan. This may be as simple as a short paragraph assuming all executory contracts not previously assumed or rejected, or exactly the converse. This sort of simple provision appears in the sample plan included on the forms disk. Such a clause may be as complex as separately identifying and assuming or rejecting each individual executory contract. Further, it is important for the nondebtor party to an executory contract to know the debtor's intent with regard to assumption or rejection because this will affect the nondebtor party's status as a creditor in the proceeding and thus ultimately the nondebtor party's decision to vote for or against the plan.

The plan may provide for the settlement or enforcement of any claims that the estate may have.[32] In other words, the plan may act as a settlement agreement of any dispute involving the estate should the plan be confirmed. The plan may also provide for the sale of all or substantially all assets and distribution of the proceeds to claimholders.[33] This is another indication that liquidation is an acceptable method for performance of a Chapter 11 plan.

Section 1123(b)(5) prohibits modification of a security interest in real property that is the debtor's principal residence, but otherwise it permits modification of creditor rights. This provision is identical to that of Section 1322(b)(2) (see section 23D supra).

The final permissive provision of Section 1123 is that a Chapter 11 reorganization plan may contain any provision not inconsistent with the Bankruptcy Code.[34] However, when a creditor classifies claims, the classifications should follow the scheme and order described in chapters 21 and 22 supra. To act otherwise, absent the consent of any affected creditor, would not be consistent with the provisions of the Bankruptcy Code.

If the Chapter 11 debtor is an individual, the individual's exempt property may not be included in the plan unless the debtor consents.[35]

---

30. 11 U.S.C. §1123(b)(1).
31. 11 U.S.C. §1123(b)(2). See also chapter 19 supra.
32. 11 U.S.C. §1123(b)(3).
33. 11 U.S.C. §1123(b)(4).
34. 11 U.S.C. §1123(b)(6).
35. 11 U.S.C. §1123(c).

In other words, an individual debtor's exemptions are preserved in Chapter 11. If a debtor wants to voluntarily make exempt property available to perform a plan, this is acceptable. However, the creditors may not force an individual debtor to give up any claimed exemptions in a Chapter 11 plan.

Section 1123(d) permits the charging of interest upon interest if applicable nonbankruptcy law allows it.

G.   IMPAIRED CLAIMS

Section 1124 creates a distinction between impaired and unimpaired claims or interests. This concept is unique to Chapter 11. Generally, an **unimpaired claim** is a claim that is not being paid according to its pre-petition terms on the effective date of the plan. Conversely, a claim not being paid according to its terms on the effective date of the plan is an **impaired claim**. For example, when a class of unsecured claims is scheduled to be paid in full on the effective date of a plan, the class is unimpaired. The **effective date of the plan** is the date defined in the plan as the plan's commencement date. This date may be the date on which the court approves confirmation, or it may be a date on which a specific event is scheduled to occur, such as the close of an escrow in a sale or the funding of a refinancing loan. Although it is not a requirement of §1123, a plan should always define its effective date.

There is an important difference in treatment accorded to unimpaired versus impaired classes of claims. An unimpaired class of claims is deemed to have accepted a plan whether or not the class votes to accept or reject the plan.[36] This is a major reason why Section 1123 mandates that a plan designate classes of impaired claims.[37] Only impaired creditors are entitled to vote for or against confirmation of the plan.

Section 1124 describes three situations that render a class of claims unimpaired. Unless a class satisfies one of the three situations, the class will be impaired. First, a class of claims is unimpaired if the plan provides that the class will be paid in full on the effective date of the plan or that the rights of the class members will be left unaltered by the plan.[38] Simply put, an unsecured claim paid in full or according to its terms on the effective date of the plan is unimpaired. Second, if a plan proposes to continue to

---

36. 11 U.S.C. §1126(f). See chapter 26 infra.
37. 11 U.S.C. §1123(a)(3). See discussion supra.
38. 11 U.S.C. §1124(1).

pay a creditor its regular installment payments as they become due and there are no defaults, or any defaults are cured on the effective date of the plan, the creditor will be considered unimpaired.[39]

Third, a class of claims is considered unimpaired notwithstanding any contractual provision allowing a creditor to accelerate payment after a default, if the plan cures the default, reinstates the obligation according to its terms, pays to the holder of the claim any consequential damages, and does not otherwise alter the rights of the affected claimholders.[40] This is an extremely important provision because it dramatically affects the rights of debtor and creditors alike. This provision effectively allows a debtor to reinstate any defaulted obligation so long as the creditor is otherwise paid according to the underlying terms of its contract. Not only will the obligation be reinstated, but because the claim or class will be considered unimpaired, the claimant will be deemed to have accepted the plan.

For example, a debtor may reinstate a defaulted trust deed or mortgage obligation through a Chapter 11 plan even if any underlying state law reinstatement period has expired. If the formula of Section 1124(2) is followed by the debtor, the claim will be considered unimpaired and the creditor's acceptance of the plan presumed.

An unsecured obligation may also be affected by Section 1124(2). For example, Marian's Maids, Inc., owes an unsecured loan to the Bank of Nottingham. The due date of the unsecured loan is five years. Three payments are in default and the bank has accelerated the obligation. As long as the Chapter 11 reorganization plan proposes to pay the three defaulted payments and otherwise reinstate the obligation, the claim will not be impaired and will not accelerate. Because the creditor is receiving what it bargained for, it is unimpaired. In each of these situations, the creditor receives exactly what it is entitled to receive under nonbankruptcy law. A creditor receiving all it is entitled to receive is considered to consent to the identical treatment in a plan.

Summary

The process of formulating and obtaining confirmation of a Chapter 11 reorganization plan, known as a Plan of Reorganization, is the most

---

39. 11 U.S.C. §1124(2)(A)(B).
40. 11 U.S.C. §1124(2).

complex and time-consuming process in the Bankruptcy Code. The entire process will average four to six months, at a minimum.

The process involves filing a plan and a disclosure statement with the court. The disclosure statement is a history of the debtor-in-possession, an analysis of the proposed plan, and a description of the debtor's ability to perform the plan. The disclosure statement is approved by the court at a disclosure statement hearing. This hearing requires at least 28 days' notice to creditors. When the disclosure statement has been approved, the proponent of the plan may solicit the votes of those creditors entitled to vote. The results of the balloting are filed with the court. The court will hold a confirmation hearing to determine if the plan may be confirmed. The confirmation hearing also requires at least 28 days' notice to the creditors. A checklist of this process is contained in the checklist to this chapter.

A debtor-in-possession has the exclusive right to file a reorganization plan for 120 days following the entry of an order for relief. This exclusivity period can be extended to 180 days if a plan is filed during the initial 120-day period or if a motion for an extension of time is filed during the initial 120-day period. In no event can the exclusivity period extend past 20 months. The exclusivity period terminates if a trustee is appointed. A small business debtor has a 180-day exclusivity period and must have a plan filed within 300 days after the entry of the order for relief, unless the court extends the time period.

Any Chapter 11 reorganization plan must classify the claims of creditors and the interests of the equity security holders (owners of the debtor). All claims within a given class must be similar, such as administrative or priority claims. A convenience class of claims may also be created. Generally, the classification scheme should follow the priorities outlined in chapters 21 and 22 supra.

A Chapter 11 reorganization plan must contain various mandatory provisions. A Chapter 11 plan may also contain various permissive provisions. An outline of the mandatory and permissive plan provisions is contained in the checklist accompanying this chapter. The forms disk accompanying this text contains a sample reorganization plan, along with all other basic documents necessary to pursue confirmation.

One of the most important mandatory plan provisions requires designation of impaired classes of claims. Classes of claims that are impaired are entitled to vote to accept or reject the plan. Classes of claims that are unimpaired are deemed to accept the plan. Generally, a class of claims is unimpaired if it is paid in full when the plan is confirmed or if the class is paid according to the terms of the obligation as it existed before the Chapter 11 was filed.

KEY TERMS

---

confirmation packet
convenience class
disclosure statement
effective date of the plan
exclusivity period
impaired claim

mandatory elements
permissive elements
Plan of Reorganization
plan proponent
unimpaired claim

CHAPTER 25 CHECKLIST

25.1 CHAPTER 11 CONFIRMATION PROCESS

		Prior Notice Required	*Authority*
25.1.1	File a Reorganization Plan	—	11 U.S.C. §1121, Bankruptcy Rule 3016(a)
25.1.2	File a Disclosure Statement	—	11 U.S.C. §1125, Bankruptcy Rule 3016(b)
25.1.3	Disclosure Statement Hearing	28 days	11 U.S.C. §1125(b), Bankruptcy Rules 2002(b), 3017(a)
25.1.4	Voting Deadline Set	at disclosure statement hearing	Bankruptcy Rule 3017(c)
25.1.5	Confirmation Hearing	28 days	11 U.S.C. §1128, Bankruptcy Rule 2002(b)
25.1.6	Report of Balloting	prior to confirmation hearing	Bankruptcy Rule 3018, consult local rule

25.2 DOCUMENTS SUBMITTED TO CREDITORS
     FOR CONFIRMATION HEARING
     (CONFIRMATION PACKET)   *Rule*

     25.2.1 Plan or Court-Approved Summary   Bankruptcy Rule
                                                       3017(d)(1)

     25.2.2 Disclosure Statement and Order   Bankruptcy Rule
             Approving Same   3017(d)(2)

     25.2.3 Notice of the Balloting Deadline   Bankruptcy Rule
                                                       3017(d)(3)

     25.2.4 Notice of the Confirmation Hearing   Bankruptcy Rule
                                                       3017(d)

     25.2.5 Ballot — Official Form 30   Bankruptcy Rule
                                                       3018(c)

25.3 MANDATORY CHAPTER 11 PLAN
     PROVISIONS   *Statute*

     25.3.1 Designate Classes of Claims and   11 U.S.C. §§1122,
             Interests   1123(a)(1)

     25.3.2 Specify Unimpaired Classes   11 U.S.C. §1123(a)(2)

     25.3.3 Specify Treatment of Impaired Classes   11 U.S.C. §1123(a)(3)

     25.3.4 Provide Equal Treatment of Claims   11 U.S.C. §1123(a)(4)
             in a Given Class

     25.3.5 Provide Adequate Means for the   11 U.S.C. §1123(a)(5)
             Plan's Performance

     25.3.6 Corporate Charter Provision   11 U.S.C. §1123(a)(6)

     25.3.7 Disclose Postconfirmation Insiders   11 U.S.C. §1123(a)(7)

     25.3.8 Individual Debtor Earnings   11 U.S.C. §1123(a)(8);
                                                       11 U.S.C. §1115

25.4 PERMISSIVE CHAPTER 11 PLAN PROVISIONS

     25.4.1 Impair Classes   11 U.S.C. §1123(b)(1)

     25.4.2 Assume or Reject Executory Contracts   11 U.S.C. §1123(b)(2)
             Not Previously Acted Upon

     25.4.3 Provide for Settlement of Disputes   11 U.S.C. §1123(b)(3)

     25.4.4 Provide for Liquidation of Assets   11 U.S.C. §1123(b)(4)

		Statute
25.4.5	Modify Creditor Rights Unless Secured by Principal Residence	11 U.S.C. §1123(b)(5)
25.4.6	Include Any Provision Consistent with Bankruptcy Code	11 U.S.C. §1123(b)(6)

DISCUSSION QUESTIONS

1. Describe the procedure that a plan proponent must follow to obtain confirmation of a Chapter 11 reorganization plan. Identify the essential documents that must be filed with the court during the confirmation process.

2. When may a Chapter 11 reorganization plan be filed? What is the "exclusivity period"?

3. How are claims classified in a Chapter 11 reorganization plan?

4. What elements must be included in a Chapter 11 reorganization plan?

5. What elements may be included in a Chapter 11 reorganization plan?

6. What is an impaired claim? An unimpaired claim? What are the important differences between the two?

PRACTICE EXERCISES

Exercise 25.1
Assume that Griffin's Quahog Convenience Store files Chapter 11 on January 1. Your supervising attorney asks you to prepare a memo identifying the date on which exclusivity will expire.

Exercise 25.2
Mr. Griffin wants to propose a plan that favors one supplier over all others. He wants to do this because the closer supplier has offered very favorable terms. Since he won't need the other suppliers, he wants to pay them less or not at all. Prepare a draft of a letter to Mr. Griffin advising him whether or not he may propose such a plan.

26

Chapter 11: Plan Confirmation

A.   DISCLOSURE STATEMENT

Once a debtor-in-possession has formulated and filed a plan, the debtor embarks upon the confirmation process. Any proponent of a plan must follow the same process. A synopsis of this process was described at the beginning of chapter 25 supra. This chapter analyzes the process in greater detail.

When a plan is filed, it generally must be accompanied by a disclosure statement. Votes may not be solicited from creditors until the court approves the disclosure statement's contents.[1] The disclosure statement hearing is the first step in the Chapter 11 plan confirmation process. Creditors and other parties in interest are entitled to at least 28 days' notice of the hearing (an exception to the 21-day notice period generally used throughout the bankruptcy system). A small business debtor may obtain conditional approval of a disclosure statement. Votes can be solicited therefrom and the court may combine the disclosure and confirmation hearings. Theoretically, this procedure will expedite the confirmation process for a small business estate.[2]

A disclosure statement must contain information sufficient to enable a creditor or interest holder to determine whether to vote to accept or reject

---

1. 11 U.S.C. §1125(b); Bankruptcy Rule 3017(d); Bankruptcy Rule 3017.1 applies to small businesses.
2. Bankruptcy Rule 2002(b); Bankruptcy Rule 3017(a). See chapter 4 supra. 11 U.S.C. §1125(f) applies to small business debtors, as does Bankruptcy Rule 3017.1. 11 U.S.C. §105(d) gives the court discretion to combine the disclosure and confirmation hearings. This is a frequent occurrence in *prepackaged bankruptcy* cases.

the plan. The Code describes this standard as providing all parties with "adequate information."[3] The disclosure statement should be written in plain English so that anyone can understand its contents. This may be difficult, especially in complex cases, but it is not impossible.

A **disclosure statement** should follow basic journalism principles: "Who, what, where, when, why, and how." A history of the debtor should be included, identifying the causes of the Chapter 11 filing and disclosing all relevant factors that may have contributed to the debtor's financial difficulties.

The disclosure statement should summarize the debtor's progress during the Chapter 11 proceeding. A summary of the most important information from the operating reports can be helpful, particularly as a means of comparing the debtor's actual postpetition results with any relevant projections of future performance provided elsewhere in the disclosure statement. Comparing a debtor's actual Chapter 11 performance with the proposed plan will permit the plan's feasibility to be more rapidly and efficiently assessed by the court and creditors.

The disclosure statement should contain an easily understood summary of the plan. The summary should describe the practical effect of the plan rather than its technical terms. For example, a disclosure statement for Bonehead Burgers states: "Class 7 creditors will receive dividends equaling 50 percent of the total allowed claims in monthly installments not exceeding 48 months." Without reference to other parts of the plan or disclosure statement this is a confusing statement. The statement would be better stated in the disclosure statement as: "Unsecured creditors will receive payments equal to 50 percent of their claims in monthly payments over four years." In larger cases, a chart summarizing the plan's treatment by class is very helpful. A disclosure statement should contain a description of how the plan will be performed. For example, if the plan involves a sale of assets or refinancing, describe the essential terms of the sale or refinancing. In a workout situation where claimants will be paid dividends over a period of time from the debtor's surplus revenues, the disclosure statement should contain a **pro forma**. A *pro forma* is a financial projection of revenues and profits that a debtor expects to generate over the life of the plan. Any pro forma should be based upon actual past performance or be able to account in detail for variations from past performance. For instance, it would be imprudent for a debtor that has been in a Chapter 11 proceeding for two years posting annual sales increases of 10 percent to suddenly project annual increases of 25 percent in a plan pro forma without any discussion of the reasons for the increased sales.

---

3. 11 U.S.C. §1125(a)(1).

The disclosure statement should compare the plan to the likely results if the case were a Chapter 7 proceeding. This is commonly known as a **liquidation analysis**. The reason for this is that one finding that the court must make to confirm the plan is that creditors will receive at least at least as much as they would receive in a Chapter 7 proceeding.[4] The relevant facts should be shown in the disclosure statement so creditors will be able to utilize the liquidation analysis in determining whether to vote to accept or reject the plan.

The disclosure statement should describe the balloting procedure for voting on the plan and how parties in interest may file objections to the plan's confirmation. Some courts also require a description of the cramdown procedures which may permit court approval of the plan over the creditors' objection.

BAPCPA requires a disclosure statement to include a discussion of the potential material federal tax consequences of a Chapter 11 plan. Presumably, this includes a statement that there are no tax consequences to the plan.

A disclosure statement may contain other items as well. The foregoing covers only the basic elements. Any factor relating to the required confirmation findings of Section 1129 that may be problematic should be discussed in the disclosure statement. A brief summary of the important items that should be included in a disclosure statement appears in the checklist accompanying this chapter. In small business cases, the court may find and order that the plan provides adequate disclosure. BAPCPA further authorizes the formulation of a standard form disclosure statement to be used in all small business cases. The purpose of developing a standard form is to meet the needs of creditors, the courts, and the United States Trustee in eliciting adequate information while at the same time providing economy and simplicity for small business debtors.[5]

Chapter 11 disclosure statements are somewhat similar to registration statements, quarterly reports, or other types of financial reports required by federal or state securities laws. Chapter 11 disclosure statements are specifically exempt from federal or state securities laws regulating the adequacy of such documents. Nevertheless, any governmental official or agency charged with the administration of securities laws may be heard by the Bankruptcy Court on the adequacy of a Chapter 11 disclosure statement. Such an entity does not have a right of appeal or review from

---

4. 11 U.S.C. §1129(a)(7). See infra this chapter.
5. See In re Scioto Valley Mortg. Co., 88 Bankr. 168 (S.D. Ohio 1988). This case includes a detailed list of items that should be included in any Chapter 11 disclosure statement. 11 U.S.C. §1125(f) authorizes the standard form in small business cases, or permits a finding that no disclosure statement will be required where the plan itself provides adequate information.

the Bankruptcy Court's decision. Parties engaged in seeking approval of a Chapter 11 plan are thus given a "safe harbor" from federal or state securities disclosure laws in connection with the confirmation process.[6]

B.   PLAN CONFIRMATION PACKET

When the court approves the disclosure statement, the plan proponent must next send all parties in interest a notice of the confirmation hearing, the plan, the disclosure statement, a ballot, and a notice of the deadline to file ballots.[7] All impaired classes of claims or interests are given the opportunity to vote for or against the plan.[8] The results of the voting are compiled into a report, which is filed with the court prior to the confirmation hearing.[9] Section 1126 contains the provisions governing acceptance of the plan and the balloting procedures. In large reorganizations common to the Southern District of New York or the District of Delaware, plan proponents will typically file a separate motion to approve solicitation and balloting procedures.

C.   VOTING RULES

A class of claims accepts a plan if, among those voting, a majority of creditors in number and two-thirds in dollar amount vote to accept the plan.[10] This is a dual requirement. If less than a majority of creditors in number or less than two-thirds in dollar amount among those voting vote to accept a plan, then the class has rejected the plan and a cramdown procedure will be necessary to confirm the plan over rejection by one or more classes.[11] To determine class acceptance, total the number of voting creditors in a class and the amount of their claims. For example, 12 creditors collectively owed $12,000 vote on a plan. The class accepts the plan if 7 creditors owed $8,000 or more vote to accept. If only 6 vote for acceptance, the class will have rejected the plan (less than a majority). If less than $8,000 in total

---

6. 11 U.S.C. §1125(c), (d), (e); 11 U.S.C. §1145.
7. Bankruptcy Rule 3017(d).
8. 11 U.S.C. §1126(a); Bankruptcy Rules 3017(c), 3017.1(a); Bankruptcy Rule 3018(a).
9. Bankruptcy Rule 3018.
10. 11 U.S.C. §1126(a), (c).
11. 11 U.S.C. §1129(b). See this chapter infra for discussion of cramdown.

dollar amount votes to accept, the class will have rejected the plan, even if 11 creditors voted to accept the plan (less than two-thirds in amount). If only 3 creditors in a class vote, but all votes are to accept, then the class has voted for the plan since a majority in number and two-thirds in dollar amount of those voting have voted for the plan. A majority in number and two-thirds in dollar amount are required for class acceptance of a plan.

A class of interests, such as shareholders, accepts a plan if two-thirds in dollar amount of the class of interests accepts the plan.[12] A class of interests accepts a plan if two-thirds of the ownership percentage voting votes acceptance. The raw number of voters is not relevant in this instance. This would not be an accurate measure of acceptance by a class of shareholders in a corporation or partnership. One entity may own 50 percent of all shares. The only relevant element here is the percentage of shares voted.

The Bankruptcy Code contemplates that an unsuccessful attempt at a composition agreement may lead to a Chapter 11 filing. This is the subject of Section 1126(b). For example, Metternich Consulting, Inc., attempts a composition agreement before a Chapter 11 filing. If Metternich follows procedures similar to the Chapter 11 confirmation process, presenting the equivalent of a disclosure statement, plan, and ballot to the creditors in a manner consistent with the Chapter 11 plan process, then any acceptances to the composition obtained from creditors prior to the Chapter 11 filing may be acceptable as proper ballots.[13] If the debtor can show to the court that the composition process was treated in a manner similar to a Chapter 11 proceeding, then prepetition acceptances to the composition can be used as acceptances to an identical Chapter 11 plan. This recognizes the fact that debtors attempting to negotiate composition agreements with their creditors are still subject to any legal action taken by nonconsenting creditors, thus sometimes forcing the Chapter 11 filing. Section 1126(b) creates a mechanism that allows and encourages composition agreements by giving them the potential to be confirmable as Chapter 11 plans. An effort at a composition agreement that nonetheless ends up in Bankruptcy Court is often referred to as a **prepackaged bankruptcy**.

For example, National Wagonworks attempts to negotiate a composition agreement with its creditors. The proposed agreement and its accompanying "disclosure statement" are identical to a Chapter 11 plan and disclosure statement. Enough creditors consent to the plan to make it confirmable as a Chapter 11 plan. One creditor, Hupmobile Inc., does not consent and seeks to enforce a writ of execution to seize the assets of

---

12. 11 U.S.C. §1126(d).
13. 11 U.S.C. §1126(b).

National Wagonworks. Seizure of assets would make performance of the composition impossible. Because a nonbankruptcy composition agreement cannot be legally enforced against a nonconsenting creditor, National Wagonworks must file a Chapter 11 if it is to prevent the seizure by Hupmobile so the plan can proceed. Section 1126(b) will permit the prompt confirmation of the composition as a Chapter 11 plan that will also bind Hupmobile over its objection. This is a further illustration of the fundamental principle that a reorganization plan is no more or less than a court-approved composition agreement.

A vote obtained in bad faith or that has been solicited in violation of the Chapter 11 rules may be disallowed. In a prepackaged bankruptcy, a vote solicited before the filing of a petition is not in bad faith if solicited in compliance with applicable nonbankruptcy law. It is better practice, however, to mirror the Bankruptcy Code requirements as closely as possible.[14]

A class of unimpaired claims is conclusively presumed to have accepted a plan.[15] Thus, if a debtor proposes to pay all creditors in full on the effective date of the plan, all creditors are unimpaired. The votes of creditors will not be a problematic issue at the confirmation hearing. Conversely, a class that will receive nothing under the plan is deemed to have rejected it.[16]

D.   MODIFICATION OF THE PLAN

A plan may be modified at any time before confirmation, as long as the disclosure statement requirements are complied with.[17] After confirmation, modification may be sought for reasons similar to the reasons for seeking modification of a Chapter 13 plan.[18] A debtor may acquire the ability to accelerate a plan's performance, or, conversely, the payments may have to be reduced or the performance period extended. A plan proponent may bring a motion before the court to modify a plan. The court will not permit modification of a confirmed plan if the plan has been

---

14. 11 U.S.C. §1126(e), (g). Additionally, in a prepackaged bankruptcy, 11 U.S.C. §341(e) provides that the meeting of creditors may not be held if excused by the court upon a showing of cause.
15. 11 U.S.C. §1126(f).
16. 11 U.S.C. §1126(g).
17. 11 U.S.C. §1127(a).
18. 11 U.S.C. §1127(b). See chapter 23 supra.

substantially consummated, except in cases involving individuals.[19] Generally, this means the taking of an irrevocable act in performance of a plan, such as closing an escrow for a sale of the business, completing a refinancing, or repaying a substantial percentage of a promised dividend.[20] A postconfirmation motion to modify a plan must also comply with Section 1125 and provide adequate disclosure. Creditors may modify a prior ballot (that is, change their votes) due to a modified plan.[21]

E.   BALLOTING REPORT

After the balloting is complete and the Rule 3018 report is filed with the court, the confirmation hearing takes place.[22] At the confirmation hearing the court will determine whether the requirements for confirmation have been complied with. The standards for confirmation are contained in Section 1129. This is perhaps the most complex and most litigated provision of Chapter 11.

F.   CONFIRMATION CONDITIONS

At the confirmation hearing, the court will confirm the plan only if it finds that the plan meets each and every requirement of Section 1129(a). This general principle is identical to that of Section 1325 in Chapter 13, as described in chapter 23 supra. Under Section 1129(a), the court must make 16 findings. If an element has not been complied with, the plan may not be confirmed. Many of the required findings will not be problematic in most proceedings.

First, the court must find that the plan complies with all provisions of the Bankruptcy Code.[23] A plan following the guidelines described in chapter 25 supra will likely be compliant. Second, the proponent of the plan

---

19. 11 U.S.C. §1127(b); 11 U.S.C. §1101(2); 11 U.S.C. §1127(e).
20. 11 U.S.C. §1101(2).
21. 11 U.S.C. §1127(c), (d).
22. 11 U.S.C. §1128. A Chapter 11 confirmation hearing is treated as a noticed motion. Bankruptcy Rules 3020, 9014.
23. 11 U.S.C. §1129(a)(1).

must comply with all applicable provisions of the Bankruptcy Code.[24] This means that the proponent of the plan must be an entity that may file a plan pursuant to Section 1121. Third, the plan must be proposed in good faith and not by any means forbidden by law.[25] A plan designed to accomplish an improper motive or that would be illegal under applicable nonbankruptcy law is probably not a plan proposed in good faith. Fourth, the reasonableness of any fees to be paid to an issuer of securities or for acquiring property under the plan must be approved by the court.[26] Fifth, the court must approve the debtor's postconfirmation management. This will include disclosing all insiders to be employed by the debtor during the life of the plan, including their approximate duties, compensation, and manner of election. In this connection, the court must also find that continuation of such individuals in the employ of the debtor is in the interests of the creditors, equity security holders, and public policy.[27] Sixth, if the debtor's rates are subject to governmental regulation, the Bankruptcy Court must find that any applicable regulatory agency has approved any rate changes provided for in the Chapter 11 plan.[28] Because most debtors do not fall into this category, this provision will rarely apply. Disputes regarding any of the six preceding confirmation requirements arise infrequently.

Seventh, the court must find that as to each impaired class of claims, the individual claimholders have either accepted the plan or will be receiving, on the effective date of the plan, an amount not less than the class would receive in the event the debtor were liquidated under Chapter 7.[29] This is known as the "best interests of creditors" test. Unless an impaired class will receive dividends at least equal to a hypothetical Chapter 7 dividend to be paid on the effective date of the plan, the plan cannot be confirmed because it is not in the best interests of creditors. This is why a comparison of the Chapter 11 plan to the results that would be achieved if the proceeding were a Chapter 7 (liquidation analysis) should be included in the disclosure statement. Further, the hypothetical Chapter 7 dividend is the minimum amount that an objecting creditor within a given accepting class must receive for the plan to be confirmable. The mere fact that creditors are assured a minimum dividend, however, does not act to approve the plan over rejection of the plan by a class. Approval of a plan

---

24. 11 U.S.C. §1129(a)(2).
25. 11 U.S.C. §1129(a)(3).
26. 11 U.S.C. §1129(a)(4).
27. 11 U.S.C. §1129(a)(5).
28. 11 U.S.C. §1129(a)(6).
29. 11 U.S.C. §1129(a)(7)(A).

over class rejection requires use of the Chapter 11 cramdown procedures.[30]

For example, Brutus is an unsecured creditor of Wimpy. Wimpy proposes a Chapter 11 plan that will pay unsecured creditors less than they would receive in a Chapter 7 proceeding. Out of sympathy, the unsecured creditors accept the plan as a class. Brutus objects on the ground that he is not receiving a dividend greater than he would receive in a Chapter 7. The plan is not confirmable over Brutus's objection, despite overall acceptance by the class.

Eighth, the court must find that each class has either accepted the plan or is unimpaired.[31] Because unimpaired classes are conclusively presumed to have accepted a plan, their votes are unnecessary and the plan can be confirmed even if they object. A creditor receiving payment in full or the performance it would be entitled to under nonbankruptcy law will not be heard to object to the plan's confirmation. A class accepts a plan in accordance with the voting rules described above.

If an impaired class of claims or interests does not accept a plan, the plan will only be confirmable if the debtor can successfully comply with the Chapter 11 cramdown provisions.[32] For example, the plan of Green Acres, Inc., proposes to pay a secured claimholder by returning acreage to the creditor equal to the value of the claim, while Green Acres, Inc., will keep the rest. The secured creditor rejects the plan. Because the creditor is allegedly receiving what it would receive in a Chapter 7, the plan complies with Section 1129(a)(7). However, because the creditor has not accepted the plan and is not unimpaired, the plan cannot be confirmed absent a successful cramdown.

 Practice Pointer

The court will be sensitive to claims of artificial impairment, i.e., when a class is designated solely to satisfy the requirement of one impaired class accepting the plan.

Ninth, the court must find that the plan will pay all administrative expenses in full on the effective date of the plan as well as all other nontax

---

30. See infra this chapter.

31. 11 U.S.C. §1129(a)(8).

32. 11 U.S.C. §1129(b)(1). See infra this chapter.

priority claims in cash on the effective date of the plan, unless any affected class of priority claim agrees to deferred payments.[33] For example, the priority wage claimants of the Poughkeepsie Polos, a professional polo team, do not agree to receive payment of their priority wage claims on a future date. The Polos must either pay the priority wage claims in full on the effective date of the plan or the plan cannot be confirmed.

Priority tax claims may be paid over a period not exceeding five years from the date of the Order for Relief, so long as all penalties and interest are paid over the period. Secured tax claims may also be paid on this basis.[34] Alternatively, a debtor that can afford to do so and pays an unsecured priority tax claim in full on the effective date of the plan will only need to satisfy the amount of the claim as it existed on the original Chapter 11 filing date. This approach, when feasible, can save payment of substantial penalties and interest. The Supreme Court has held that a plan proponent may, in appropriate circumstances, allocate the application of dividends to tax claims. For example, the plan proponent may propose to allocate a tax dividend first to any portion of the claim to which a nondebtor may also be liable. This may aid such individuals in avoiding personal liability for the taxes.[35]

Tenth, the court must find that at least one impaired noninsider class has accepted the plan.[36] Thus, if a plan contains only one impaired class and the class rejects the plan, the plan may not be confirmed. In this instance, cramdown will not provide the debtor with a remedy because only class rejections under the eighth finding described above may be overcome by a cramdown.[37] Although one class of rejecting impaired claims may be subject to a cramdown, if it is the *only* impaired class, the plan will not be confirmable. Or, stated in another way, there must be at least two impaired classes in a plan, one of which accepts the plan, before the court can consider application of the cramdown provisions to the rejecting impaired class or classes.

Eleventh, the court must find that the reorganization is not likely to be followed by further reorganization or liquidation unless the plan so provides.[38] This is commonly known as a **feasibility requirement**. This determination will involve careful analysis of any pro forma or other financial data presented in the disclosure statement to determine the

---

33. 11 U.S.C. §1129(a)(9)(A), (B).
34. 11 U.S.C. §1129(a)(9)(C). See also 11 U.S.C. §511, added by BAPCPA, codifying the rate of interest to pay on tax claims.
35. United States v. Energy Resources Co., 495 U.S. 545 (1990).
36. 11 U.S.C. §1129(a)(10).
37. 11 U.S.C. §1129(b)(1). Only Section 1129(a)(8) may be overridden by a cramdown procedure by the specific terms of the statute.
38. 11 U.S.C. §1129(a)(11).

likelihood of the debtor successfully performing the promises contained in the plan. This may also involve a determination of the likelihood of a proposed sale or refinancing occurring within a specified period of time. The formula described in chapter 23 supra for analyzing Chapter 13 plans will also apply in Chapter 11 proceedings, albeit on a more complex level.

Practice Pointer

A feasibility analysis must consider whether the plan has reasonable probability of success. There are no guarantees, and a potential for failure alone will not be enough to upset confirmation.

Twelfth, the court must find that any fees due the court will be paid in full on the effective date of the plan.[39] Thirteenth, plans involving certain types of employee retirement or benefit plans must comply with the provisions of Section 1114. This provision is not likely to be problematic in most cases.[40]

BAPCPA imposes three new confirmation conditions. First, in a Chapter 11 case for an individual, all postpetition domestic support obligations must be current at the time of confirmation. Second, also applicable in Chapter 11 cases for individuals, if the holder of an unsecured claim objects, then the debtor must submit all disposable income for a five-year period into the plan unless all creditors can be paid in full sooner. Third, applicable in all cases, all transfers of property are to be made in accordance with local law.[41]

G. CHAPTER 11 CRAMDOWN

When there is an impaired class of claims that has not accepted the plan, the Chapter 11 cramdown procedure is available as long as at least one other impaired class has accepted the plan. Similar to Chapter 13, when a plan is successfully "crammed down," a Chapter 11 plan may be approved

---

39. 11 U.S.C. §1129(a)(12).
40. 11 U.S.C. §1114; 11 U.S.C. §1129(a)(13).
41. 11 U.S.C. §1129(a)(14), (15), (16).

over the dissenting class or classes. Any good Chapter 11 plan will be constructed so as to be able to achieve a successful cramdown upon dissenting classes. Ultimately, the ability to achieve a successful cramdown is the acid test of a Chapter 11 plan. Cramdown litigation is among the most intense in the bankruptcy system.

Cramdown battles can be expensive and time-consuming. As a result, and ironically, they can be counterproductive to the reorganization's successful outcome. The costs of the litigation will increase administrative expenses. This increase may itself affect plan feasibility. If a cramdown dispute occurs over a lengthy period of time, the underlying facts and circumstances can change. These changes may also impact a plan's feasibility. Although cramdown disputes are unavoidable in many instances, the parties should always endeavor to resolve the dispute through negotiation and not litigation, lest the "victor" be left standing alone in the rubble of the debtor.

For the court to proceed with a cramdown, it must first find that all other elements of Section 1129(a) have been complied with except for Section 1129(a)(8). The plan must comply with all other provisions of Section 1129(a) except plan acceptance by one or more impaired classes to permit confirmation by cramdown to proceed. For a cramdown attempt to succeed, the court must find that the plan does not discriminate unfairly and that the plan is fair and equitable with regard to each class of rejecting impaired claims or interests the plan seeks to cram down.[42] The issue of unfair discrimination is often raised but is rarely found. More frequently, it is the "fair and equitable" standard that creates dispute. Fortunately, Section 1129(b)(2) defines the meaning of "fair and equitable" depending upon whether the class of claim to be crammed down is secured, unsecured, or is a class of interest holders.

A plan may be confirmed over rejection by a class of secured claims in one of three ways. First, the plan may be confirmed over rejection by the class if the secured class retains the collateral and will, in addition, receive payments equal to the allowed amount of the secured claim over the life of the plan.[43] Second, a Chapter 11 plan may be confirmed over the objection of a class of secured claims if the collateral is to be sold free and clear of liens and the claim is to be paid in full from the proceeds.[44] Third, a plan may be approved over the objection of a class of secured claims if the debtor provides the claimant with the "indubitable equivalent" of its claims.[45] This final method means that if a class of secured claims is given property

---

42. 11 U.S.C. §1129(b)(1).
43. 11 U.S.C. §1129(b)(2)(A)(i).
44. 11 U.S.C. §1129(b)(2)(A)(ii).
45. 11 U.S.C. §1129(b)(2)(A)(iii).

or cash equal to the full value of the secured claim, the plan may be approved over objection by the class. A substantial body of case law has developed in this area, the analysis of which is beyond the scope of this text. Suffice it to say that as a practical matter many courts view payment in full in cash as the only form of indubitable equivalent for payment of a secured creditor's claim. Any other proposal is likely to result in substantial and expensive litigation.

In summary, the concept of cramdown regarding a class of secured claims is simple. If the class is going to be paid the full value of its claims in some manner, which may include a return of its collateral, the plan will generally be confirmable over the claimant's objection. This is the common thread contained in each of the three methodologies to cram down a class of secured claims in Chapter 11.

There are two ways to obtain confirmation over rejection of a plan by a class of unsecured claims. The first method is very simple. If the plan proposes to pay an affected unsecured class in full on either the effective date of the plan or over time, the plan will be confirmable.[46] Once again, a class that will receive all that it is entitled to will not be heard to complain. Second, if a class of unsecured claims is not going to be paid in full, the court must find that no junior class of claims or interests will retain any interest in any property of the estate.[47] This is commonly known as the **absolute priority rule**. In its essence, this rule means that if the shareholders are proposing to retain an interest in a reorganized debtor, they will not be able to do so unless any rejecting class of unsecured claims is paid in full.

A complex issue arises when an operating business proposes to pay its unsecured claimants an amount equal to or greater than the class would receive in a Chapter 7 proceeding, but where the interest holders will be retaining an interest in the reorganized debtor. Some cases have permitted this practice, holding that the debtor has in essence "repurchased" the value of the business from the creditors.[48] Other cases do not permit this practice and require payment in full to a rejecting impaired class if any junior class retains any interest in the debtor.[49] Still other cases have adopted a rule that permits a junior class to retain an interest if present and substantial consideration is paid into the plan for the retention of such interest. This is known as the "infusion of new capital" exception to the absolute priority rule.[50] In 1988, the United States Supreme Court held that performance of services by an insider to a reorganized debtor

---

46. 11 U.S.C. §1129(b)(2)(B)(i).
47. 11 U.S.C. §1129(b)(2)(B)(ii). See also the Historical and Revision Notes to this subsection.
48. In re Star City Rebuilders, Inc., 62 Bankr. 983 (W.D. Va. 1986).
49. In re Genesee Cement, Inc., 31 Bankr. 442 (E.D. Mich. 1983).
50. Case v. Los Angeles Lumber Prods., 308 U.S. 106 (1939).

(known as sweat equity) will not constitute "new capital" that will permit confirmation by way of cramdown. The Supreme Court in this decision even questioned the continued viability of the "infusion of new capital" rule referred to above.[51]

In Bank of America v. 203 North La Salle Street Partnership, 526 U.S. 434 (1999), the Supreme Court expressly declined to rule definitively on the existence of the new value exception to the absolute priority rule, but did rule that it is insufficient to offer shares in a reorganized debtor solely to the old equity interests. In *La Salle*, the debtor was a limited partnership that owned 15 floors of a high-rise building in Chicago's Loop. The bank was owed approximately $93 million, of which $38.5 million was considered to be unsecured. *La Salle*'s plan proposed to pay the bank the full value of its secured claim but a dividend of only about 16 percent on its unsecured claim and a discharge as to the balance. The source of funding for the plan was to be a $6.125 million infusion of new capital into the partnership. However, only old partners could become partners in the reorganized debtor. As the largest unsecured creditor, the bank objected to the plan, initiating the cramdown dispute. The Supreme Court found on these facts: "[A]ssuming a new value corollary, that plans providing junior interest holders with exclusive opportunities free from competition and without benefit of market valuation fall within the prohibition of §1129(b)(2)(B)(ii)." (526 U.S. 434, 458).

BAPCPA creates a statutory exception to the absolute priority rule applicable in individual Chapter 11 cases. If an individual Chapter 11 debtor commits all disposable income into the plan for at least five years, then the plan is subject to cramdown over the objection of unsecured creditors. This makes an individual Chapter 11 consistent with the similar requirement applicable in Chapter 13 cases, to the extent that the requirement is equivalent to a five-year applicable commitment period.[52]

 Practice Pointer

Whether and to what extent a new value exception exists to the absolute priority rule is the subject of dispute in the case law.

---

51. Norwest Bank Worthin v. Ahlers, 484 U.S. 999 (1988). A debate has raged in the case law ever since. It is beyond the scope of this text to more completely analyze this issue. Readers facing a problem in this area should familiarize themselves with the most recent decisions from their area.

52. 11 U.S.C. §1129(b)(2)(B)(ii). 11 U.S.C. §1129(a)(15), discussed above. See chapter 23 supra.

A plan may be confirmed over the objection of a class of interest holders in two circumstances. First, if the affected interest holders are paid any redemption prices to which they may be entitled, the plan may be confirmed over their objection. Second, if no junior interest holder retains any interest in the estate, the plan may be confirmed over rejection by a dissenting class.[53] In essence, the same principles apply to the cramdown of an affected class of interest holders that apply to the cramdown of unsecured claims — payment in full of the interest's value or application of the absolute priority rule to interest holders. Obviously, this provision will only be problematic in a proceeding involving multiple classes of shareholders that will receive dividends; it is not problematic in most common situations.

There may only be one confirmed plan in existence at any given time. If the court is faced with two competing plans, each of which has been accepted by the creditors, the court shall consider the preference of the creditors and interest holders in determining which plan to confirm.[54]

H. EFFECT OF CONFIRMATION AND CHAPTER 11 DISCHARGE

A confirmed Chapter 11 plan acts as a new contract between the debtor and all of its creditors.[55] Thus, any creditor violating the plan will be in breach of this new contract. Confirmation also revests the debtor with all of the property of the estate free and clear of all liens and interests except as provided for by the plan.[56] Confirmation of a plan also acts to discharge all debts that arose before the date of confirmation except as provided in the plan.[57]

A Chapter 11 discharge is virtually identical to a Chapter 7 discharge except that all Chapter 11 debtors receive a discharge, including corporate and partnership debtors. Debts that are nondischargeable under Section 523 are, however, also nondischargeable under a Chapter 11.[58] A discharge under Chapter 11 is the only way in which a corporation or partnership may receive a discharge under the Bankruptcy Code.

---

53. 11 U.S.C. §1129(b)(2)(C).
54. 11 U.S.C. §1129(c).
55. 11 U.S.C. §1141(a).
56. 11 U.S.C. §1141(b)(c).
57. 11 U.S.C. §1141(d)(1).
58. 11 U.S.C. §1141(d)(2).

In certain instances, a Chapter 11 debtor will not be entitled to a discharge under Chapter 11. A debtor liquidating its assets through a Chapter 11 plan that does not plan to continue in business and would not be entitled to a Chapter 7 discharge if the proceeding were a Chapter 7 will not be discharged by the confirmation of a Chapter 11 plan.[59] Thus, a corporate or partnership debtor with a liquidating Chapter 11 plan will not receive a discharge from an unpaid obligation because a corporation or partnership is not entitled to a Chapter 7 discharge.[60] On the other hand, if the debtor is an individual and liquidates all non-exempt assets to pay creditors a dividend through a Chapter 11 plan, the individual will be entitled to a discharge because an individual may receive a Chapter 7 discharge. An individual Chapter 11 debtor does not receive a discharge until all payments under the plan have been completed.[61] A confirmed plan may be revoked by motion made within 180 days after confirmation if the confirmation has been fraudulently obtained.[62]

As a final bit of practical advice, when a plan proposes to pay creditors over a period of time, the creditors should insist upon provisions in the plan requiring regular postconfirmation reports of plan performance. In this manner the creditors will know if the plan is being performed or if action should be taken to enforce the debtor's compliance with the plan up to and including revocation of confirmation and conversion of the proceeding to a Chapter 7.

Summary

A basic outline of the Chapter 11 plan confirmation process, as to both documents and deadlines, has already been provided in chapter 25 supra. This chapter explores this process in more detail.

The first step in the process is to file a reorganization plan (Plan of Reorganization) and a disclosure statement with the court. The disclosure statement is a history of the debtor and an analysis of the debtor's reorganization plan. The basic contents of a disclosure statement are outlined in the checklist accompanying this chapter.

Before creditors may be given an opportunity to vote for or against the plan, the court must approve the contents of the disclosure statement at a

---

59. 11 U.S.C. §1141(d)(3).
60. 11 U.S.C. §727(a)(1). See chapter 13 supra regarding entitlement to a Chapter 7 discharge.
61. 11 U.S.C. §1141(d)(5).
62. 11 U.S.C. §1144.

disclosure statement hearing. This hearing requires 28 days' notice to creditors. The court will approve the disclosure statement and authorize the plan proponent to solicit ballots to the creditor body if the disclosure statement is found to contain "adequate information" to enable creditors to make an informed decision when voting on the plan. In an electing small business case, the court may conditionally approve a disclosure statement and combine the disclosure and confirmation hearings.

Section 1126 of the Bankruptcy Code regulates the voting on a Chapter 11 plan. Each impaired class of creditors or interest holders is permitted to vote. A class of claims accepts a plan if a majority in number and two-thirds in dollar amount of those class members voting approve the plan. A class of interest holders accepts a plan if two-thirds in amount or percentage of those class members voting approve the plan. Special provisions permit the court, in some circumstances, to consider ballots obtained by the plan proponent in connection with a prefiling composition agreement (sometimes known as a "prepackaged bankruptcy"). A vote found to have been obtained in bad faith may be disallowed. An unimpaired class is conclusively deemed to accept the plan. Conversely, an impaired class that will receive no dividend is presumed to have rejected the plan. The results of the balloting are filed with the court in a report prepared pursuant to Federal Rule of Bankruptcy Procedure 3018.

The final step in the Chapter 11 confirmation process is the confirmation hearing held pursuant to Bankruptcy Code Section 1128. This hearing also requires 28 days' notice to creditors. The ballots are sent to creditors with a notice of the confirmation hearing along with the other documents described in checklist 25.2 in chapter 25 supra.

At the confirmation hearing, the court must make 16 findings to confirm a plan. These 16 findings are contained in Section 1129(a) and are outlined in the checklist accompanying this chapter. Many of these findings will not be problematic in most cases. Issues of feasibility and cramdown are commonly the most problematic.

The analysis performed to determine a Chapter 11 plan's feasibility is similar to that described in connection with a Chapter 13 plan, particularly where a Chapter 11 plan offers to make payments to creditors over a period of time from the surplus revenues of an operating business. If the plan involves a different methodology, such as a sale of assets or refinancing loan, the court, in ruling upon the plan's feasibility, will need to determine the debtor's ability to conclude any sale or refinancing.

The issue of a Chapter 11 cramdown will only arise if an impaired class rejects the plan and the court can make all other required confirmation findings. For a plan to prevail in a Chapter 11 cramdown, the court must find that the plan is "fair and equitable" and does not "discriminate unfairly" against a rejecting class. Whether a plan is "fair and equitable" as to a rejecting class will vary depending upon the rejecting class's status as secured, unsecured, or equity security holders. The common thread among these provisions is that if the class is being paid in full or if no junior classes will receive a dividend, then a cramdown may succeed and the plan can be confirmed over the objection of a dissenting class. In an individual Chapter 11 case, the plan is also subject to cramdown if the debtor pays all disposable income into the plan for at least five years. The checklist accompanying this chapter outlines the various cramdown provisions of Bankruptcy Code Section 1129(b)(2). This provision is one of the most complex in the Bankruptcy Code.

As in Chapter 13, a Chapter 11 plan may be modified before or after confirmation. In addition, confirmation can be revoked if it has been fraudulently obtained.

Confirmation of a Chapter 11 plan results in a discharge of the debtor pursuant to Bankruptcy Code Section 1141. Corporations and partnerships may obtain a Chapter 11 discharge. This is the only way in which a partnership or corporation may receive a discharge in the bankruptcy system.

KEY TERMS

absolute priority rule	prepackaged bankruptcy
disclosure statement	pro forma
feasibility requirement	substantially
liquidation analysis	consummated

CHAPTER 26 CHECKLIST

Authority

26.2.9   The Following Are Paid on the
         Effective Date of the Plan,
         Unless Claimant Otherwise Agrees

   1.   Administrative claims   11 U.S.C.
                                           §1129(a)(9)(A)

   2.   Nontax priority claims   11 U.S.C.
                                           §1129(a)(9)(B)

   3.   Priority tax claims may be   11 U.S.C.
        paid over five years from   §1129(a)(9)(C)
        date of the order for relief

26.2.10 At Least One Impaired Class   11 U.S.C.
         Accepts   §1129(a)(10)

26.2.11 The Plan Is Feasible   11 U.S.C.
                                           §1129(a)(11)

26.2.12 All Court and United States   11 U.S.C.
         Trustee Fees Are Paid   §1129(a)(12)

26.2.13 Employee Benefits Preserved   11 U.S.C.
                                           §1129(a)(13)

26.2.14 Postpetition Domestic Support   11 U.S.C.
         Obligations Current   §1129(a)(14)

26.2.15 Five-Year Plan for Individual   11 U.S.C.
         Debtors   §1129(a)(15)

26.2.16 All Transfers of Property   11 U.S.C.
         in Accordance with   §1129(a)(16)
         Local Law

26.3 CHAPTER 11 CRAMDOWN OUTLINE

26.3.1   May Only Occur If All Findings   11 U.S.C. §1129(b)(1)
         in 26.2 Except 26.2.8 Can Be
         Made by the Court

26.3.2   The Plan Is Fair and Equitable   11 U.S.C. §1129(b)(1)
         and Does Not Unfairly
         Discriminate Against a Rejecting
         Class

26.3.3   A Plan Is Fair and Equitable to a
Class of Secured Claims If

1.	The class retains liens and is paid the full amount of secured claim over the life of the plan	11 U.S.C. §1129(b)(2)(A)(i)
2.	The claim is paid in full by sale,	11 U.S.C. §1129(b)(2)(A)(ii)
3.	The claim receives "indubitable equivalent"	11 U.S.C. §1129(b)(2)(A)(iii)

26.3.4   A Plan Is Fair and Equitable to a
Class of Unsecured Claims If Either

1.	The class will be paid in full over the life of the plan, or	11 U.S.C. §1129(b)(2)(B)(i)
2.	No junior class will retain an interest in the estate	11 U.S.C. §1129(b)(2)(B)(ii)

26.3.5   A Plan Is Fair and Equitable to a
Class of Interest Holders if Either

1.	The interests are retained or paid in full, or	11 U.S.C. §1129(b)(2)(C)(i)
2.	No junior class will retain an interest in the estate	11 U.S.C. §1129(b)(2)(C)(ii)

DISCUSSION QUESTIONS

1. What is a disclosure statement? What is its purpose? What essential information should be included in a disclosure statement?

2. Which creditors may vote to accept or reject a Chapter 11 reorganization plan?

3. When is a class of creditors conclusively presumed to have accepted a plan? To have rejected a plan?

4. How does a class of claims accept a plan? How does a class of interests accept a plan?

5. What findings must the court make to confirm a Chapter 11 reorganization plan?

6. How may a plan proponent obtain a cramdown of a Chapter 11 reorganization plan?

7. How may a Chapter 11 plan be modified?

8. What is the scope of a Chapter 11 discharge?

PRACTICE EXERCISE

Exercise 26.1

Griffin's operates successfully for five months in Chapter 11. Mr. Griffin prepares financial projections, based on the operating results, indicating that a repayment plan can be proposed. Your firm prepares a plan and disclosure statement. The day before you are ready to file the documents, Mr. Griffin advises you that last month his energy expenses increased 25 percent, and all other costs are increasing prices so fast, "it's hard to keep the labels right." Advise Mr. Griffin about the potential consequences of submitting inaccurate financial data in a disclosure statement.

27

Chapter 12:
Reorganization
Proceedings

A.   PURPOSES OF CHAPTER 12

Throughout the 1980s, family farmers were faced with serious economic problems. Many farmers were forced to seek voluntary protection under the Bankruptcy Code to obtain debt relief and protect their family farms. (Recall that a farmer may not be the subject of an involuntary proceeding.)[1] The Bankruptcy Code of 1978, as enacted, did not contain sufficient protection for the unique economic predicament of family farmers. This resulted primarily from the recognition that a family farmer is simultaneously a wage earner and the operator of an increasingly sophisticated business.

Prior to the enactment of Chapter 12, a fundamental problem faced by many farmers seeking bankruptcy relief was the choice of proceeding. Many family farmers cannot afford the costs of a Chapter 11 proceeding. The expeditious and relatively inexpensive procedures of Chapter 13 are more consistent with an economically pressed farmer's budget. However, because many farmers owe more than $1,081,400 in secured debt, they do not qualify to file a Chapter 13.[2] As a result, farmers have had no alternative but to seek the more complex and expensive Chapter 11 proceeding if a family farm is to be preserved.

---

1. 11 U.S.C. §303(a). See chapter 3 supra.
2. 11 U.S.C. §109(c). See chapters 4 and 23 supra.

However, once a farmer becomes a Chapter 11 debtor-in-possession, the farmer's frustrations are just beginning. A secured creditor can move for relief from the automatic stay on the grounds that there is no equity in the property. The debtor-in-possession farmer can defend by asserting that the property is necessary for an effective reorganization. The court invariably orders adequate protection payments to maintain the automatic stay in effect. If the debtor cannot afford the payments, then the stay will be relieved and the undesired foreclosure becomes inevitable.[3]

The problem was even more severe when a bank or cooperative had a lien on crop proceeds. Such a lien can prevent the family from receiving even the necessities of life due to the lienholder's rights in cash collateral, as described in chapter 18 supra.

To counteract each of the above problems, Congress enacted Chapter 12 in 1986 on a temporary basis. BAPCPA makes Chapter 12 permanent. Additionally, the legislation expands the scope of Chapter 12 to a family fisherman.

Chapter 12 is essentially a hybrid of Chapters 11 and 13. There are provisions in Chapter 12 that are virtually identical to the corresponding provisions in the other reorganization proceedings. There are also a few provisions unique to Chapter 12. Chapter 12 seeks to provide a family farmer with the benefits of a Chapter 13, the flexibility and control of a Chapter 11, and a partial abrogation of the sometimes harsh effects of the "adequate protection" requirement in the special circumstances of a family farm. In short, Chapter 12 gives a beleaguered family farmer a fighting chance to resolve economic problems and retain the family farm.

B. WHO MAY FILE CHAPTER 12

Only a **family farmer** with regular income may be a Chapter 12 debtor.[4] A family farmer with regular income is a family farmer who can afford to make payments under a Chapter 12 plan.[5] Not all family farmers are farmers or families. The term *family farmer* is defined in 11 U.S.C. §101(18). When the Chapter 12 debtor is an individual or individual and spouse, the debtor will qualify for Chapter 12 relief if four conditions are met. First,

---

3. 11 U.S.C. §362. See chapter 12 supra.
4. 11 U.S.C. §109(f).
5. 11 U.S.C. §101(19).

the proposed debtor must be engaged in a "farming operation." The Code does not define this term but, fortunately, an ample body of case law defining farms has developed from interpretation of the earlier Bankruptcy Act provisions preventing the filing of involuntary bankruptcies against farmers. Generally, a farming operation is one in which primarily crops or herds are raised for purposes of ultimate sale. Hence, a gold mine with a small garden will not be a farming operation. A sheep ranch that discovers gold on the property will likely still qualify as a farming operation.

Second, the proposed debtor's total debt must not exceed $3,792,650. Third, no less than 50 percent of the undisputed liquidated debt must arise from the farming operation, exclusive of the debtor's residence unless it is also the farm. Finally, more than 50 percent of the proposed debtor's and the debtor's spouse's gross income for the year preceding the filing, or each of the second and third years preceding the filing, must be derived from the farming operation.[6] For example, Perry Mason, who visits his farm on weekends but earns only 10 percent of his income from the farm, will not qualify as a family farmer.

A corporation or partnership may also qualify for Chapter 12 relief. There are six requirements for qualification. First, the entity must be a farming operation as described above. Second, more than 50 percent of the stock or equity must belong to members of the same family. Thus, where the Hatfields and McCoys are equal partners, the partnership may not qualify because no single family owns a majority of the stock.

Third, more than 80 percent of the assets must relate to the farming operation. Fourth, the total debt may not exceed $3,792,650. Fifth, at least 50 percent of the total undisputed liquidated debt must be related to the farming operation, exclusive of a dwelling house that is not related to the farm. Finally, if the debtor is a corporation, it must be privately held.[7] If all these requirements are satisfied, Green Acres, Inc., may file a Chapter 12 proceeding.

A **family fisherman** is an individual whose debts do not exceed $1,757,475 and 80 percent of which are related to commercial fishing operations, excluding debt on the debtor's personal residence, and from which more than 50 percent of the debtor's income in the year preceding the filing has been earned. A corporation may also qualify as a family fisherman if more than 50 percent of the stock is held by family

---

6. 11 U.S.C. §101(18)(A). The dollar amounts are subject to adjustment for inflation pursuant to 11 U.S.C. §104(b). The amount shown applies to cases filed on or after April 1, 2010.
7. 11 U.S.C. §101(18)(B). The dollar amounts are subject to adjustment for inflation pursuant to 11 U.S.C. §104(b). The amount shown is the amount effective as of April 1, 2010.

members, debts do not exceed \$1,757,475, and more than 80 percent of the assets and debts are related to the fishing operation.[8]

C. COMPARISON TO CHAPTERS 11 AND 13

In examining the general provisions of Chapter 12, it becomes readily apparent that Chapter 12 is no more than a hybrid of Chapters 11 and 13. Many elements of Chapter 12 are borrowed from those proceedings, though there are a few elements that are not present in one of the other reorganization proceedings.

There are three basic similarities of Chapter 12 to Chapter 13. First, Chapter 12 imposes an automatic stay in favor of codebtors that is identical to the provision contained in Chapter 13.[9] Second, as in Chapter 13, the debtor's postpetition earnings are property of the estate.[10] Third, a Chapter 12 may be dismissed for many of the identical reasons for which a Chapter 13 may be dismissed or converted.[11] A proceeding may also be dismissed if it appears there is no reasonable likelihood of rehabilitation.[12] However, only the debtor may convert a proceeding from a Chapter 12 to a Chapter 7.[13] This is consistent with the principle that an involuntary proceeding may not be commenced against a farmer.[14]

There are two general similarities between Chapter 12 and Chapter 11. First, a Chapter 12 debtor has duties and powers that are somewhat analogous to those of a Chapter 11 debtor-in-possession.[15] This is so notwithstanding the additional fact that there is also a trustee appointed in every Chapter 12 proceeding. Second, a Chapter 12 debtor-in-possession may be removed for causes identical to the related Chapter 11 provision. A Chapter 12 debtor-in-possession may not, however, be removed from possession on the ground that removal is in the best interests of creditors.[16]

---

8. 11 U.S.C. §101(19A). This amount is also subject to triannual inflation adjustment pursuant to 11 U.S.C. §104(b).
9. 11 U.S.C. §1201; 11 U.S.C. §1301. See chapter 23 supra.
10. 11 U.S.C. §1207; 11 U.S.C. §1306. See chapter 23 supra.
11. 11 U.S.C. §1208; 11 U.S.C. §1307(a)(1)-(8). See chapter 23 supra.
12. 11 U.S.C. §1208(c)(9).
13. 11 U.S.C. §1208(a).
14. 11 U.S.C. §303(a). See chapter 3 supra.
15. 11 U.S.C. §1203; 11 U.S.C. §1107. See chapter 24 supra.
16. 11 U.S.C. §1204; 11 U.S.C. §1104(a)(1). See chapter 10 supra.

D.   UNIQUE CHAPTER 12 FEATURES

There are three general features of Chapter 12 that are unique to it. The first of these is the existence of a trustee even though the debtor is the equivalent of a debtor-in-possession.[17] A given district may have a standing Chapter 12 trustee whose duties are analogous to those of a Chapter 13 standing trustee.[18] To the extent that the trustee is not a standing trustee, the trustee's duties are somewhat the same as those of a Chapter 11 trustee with the additional duty that a Chapter 12 trustee has the responsibilities of receiving and disbursing the debtor's Chapter 12 plan payments and that the debtor commences making timely payments under a confirmed Chapter 12 plan. If the debtor owes domestic support obligations, the trustee must also provide notice to the claimholder in a manner identical to a Chapter 7 trustee.[19]

A second unique feature of Chapter 12 is a special definition of *adequate protection* applicable only in Chapter 12. Section 361, regarding adequate protection, does not apply in Chapter 12. This ameliorates the harsh results that were being meted out to farmers in Chapter 11 and Chapter 13 proceedings prior to Chapter 12's enactment. Section 1205(b) retains the traditional adequate protection methods of periodic payments and additional or replacement collateral, but adds two additional modes of adequate protection. First, customary rent in the community where the property is located may constitute adequate protection. Presumably, this sum might be less than the payments that would be required to service debt on a trust deed or mortgage secured by the debtor's real property. Second, the court has specifically been granted broad equitable discretion to formulate an adequate protection order in Chapter 12.[20] This is supposed to give a family farmer or fisherman a fighting chance.

The final unique feature of Chapter 12 permits a sale free and clear of liens if the property sold is farmland, farm equipment, or property used to carry out a commercial fishing operation. This is in addition to the five methods for obtaining approval of a sale free and clear of liens under Section 363(f).[21] For example, Ma and Pa Kettle, Chapter 12 debtors, want to sell their farm for less than the amount of all liens and encumbrances upon it. Unless the affected lienholders consent or are to be paid in full from the proceeds, the sale would not be permitted in a Chapter 11 or Chapter 7 sale

---

17. 11 U.S.C. §1202.
18. 11 U.S.C. §1202(a). See chapter 10 supra.
19. 11 U.S.C. §1202(b), (c); 11 U.S.C. §1226(c). See chapters 10 and 23 supra.
20. 11 U.S.C. §1205(b)(4).
21. 11 U.S.C. §1206; 11 U.S.C. §363(f). See chapter 18 supra.

free and clear of liens. However, because Chapter 12 specifically permits a sale free and clear of liens of farmland or farm equipment, the sale may take place over the lienholders' objections even though an affected claim will not necessarily be paid in full from the proceeds of the sale.

E. CHAPTER 12 PLANS AND DISCHARGE

With surprisingly few exceptions, the provisions of Chapter 12 relating to the contents and confirmation of a plan are virtually identical to the related provisions contained in Chapter 13. This is consistent with congressional intent to provide the speed and reduced expense of a Chapter 13 proceeding to family farmers who would otherwise be required to file more complex and expensive Chapter 11 proceedings.

A Chapter 12 plan must be filed within 90 days of commencing the proceeding unless the court extends the period upon finding an extension substantially justified.[22] This is substantially longer than the 14-day period permitted under Chapter 13 but less than the exclusivity period provided to Chapter 11 debtors. Unlike Chapter 11, however, the Chapter 12 plan filing deadline is a mandatory deadline.[23]

Section 1222 is identical to Section 1322, describing the mandatory and permissive elements of a Chapter 12 plan.[24] The one difference from Chapter 13 is that a Chapter 12 plan may modify the rights of a secured claimant secured by the debtor's principal residence. Recall that this is not permitted in Chapter 13.[25] A Chapter 12 plan is subject to the same performance limits (no longer than five years), and on the identical grounds previously described for Chapter 13 proceedings.[26] A Chapter 12 plan may be modified prior to confirmation in a manner identical to a Chapter 13 plan.[27]

A Chapter 12 confirmation hearing is to be given expedited treatment. The confirmation hearing shall be concluded no longer than 45 days after the plan is filed. A party in interest may object.[28] Except for the expedited treatment accorded the hearing date, this provision is identical to the similar provision in Chapter 13.[29] Note that no disclosure statement is required, nor do creditors vote on the plan. This is identical to Chapter 13.

---

22. 11 U.S.C. §1221.
23. See chapters 23 and 25 supra.
24. 11 U.S.C. §1222; 11 U.S.C. §1322.
25. 11 U.S.C. §1222(b)(2); 11 U.S.C. §1322(b)(2). See chapter 23 supra.
26. 11 U.S.C. §1222(c); 11 U.S.C. §1322(c). See chapter 23 supra.
27. 11 U.S.C. §1223; 11 U.S.C. §1323. See chapter 23 supra.
28. 11 U.S.C. §1224.
29. 11 U.S.C. §1324. See chapter 23 supra.

The standards for confirmation of a Chapter 12 plan are almost identical to the confirmation standards for a Chapter 13 plan.[30] The provisions for the making of Chapter 12 plan payments are essentially identical to the sister provision in Chapter 13. The standards for achieving cramdown of a Chapter 12 plan are identical to the Chapter 13 cramdown provisions. The one difference is that there is no mandatory length for a Chapter 12 plan.

Instead, the plan may be crammed down on unsecured claimants if the debtor pays all disposable surplus income into the plan for at least three years. (This is identical to Section 1325 prior to the 2005 legislation).[31] The effect of confirmation of a Chapter 12 plan is identical to the effect of confirmation in Chapter 11 and Chapter 13 proceedings. The confirmed plan has the status of a binding contract between the debtor and all creditors, those in agreement with and those opposed to the plan. Thus, as with the other reorganization proceedings, a Chapter 12 plan is no more than a judicially approved composition agreement.[32]

On the other hand, a Chapter 12 discharge is analogous to a Chapter 11 discharge and lacks the effect of a Chapter 13 discharge.[33] However, a Chapter 12 debtor may receive an early discharge under the same terms and conditions as a Chapter 13 debtor.[34] Finally, a Chapter 12 plan may be modified after confirmation under the same terms and conditions as a Chapter 13 plan.[35]

Summary

Chapter 12, commonly known as a family farmer reorganization, was enacted into the Bankruptcy Code in 1986 in an effort to provide viable bankruptcy relief to family farmers. Prior to the enactment of Chapter 12, many family farmers failed in bankruptcy reorganizations for three basic reasons. First, many family farmers could not afford the expense of a Chapter 11 proceeding. Second, many family farmers lacked the ability to provide secured creditors with proper forms of adequate protection, as described in Chapter 12 of this text. Third, many family farmers possessed debt in excess of the permissible Chapter 13 amounts. Chapter 12 has been enacted to neutralize these problems and, as a result, to provide family farmers with a viable form of bankruptcy relief. The 2005 legislation expands Chapter 12 to family fishermen.

---

30. 11 U.S.C. §1225; 11 U.S.C. §1325. See chapter 23 supra.
31. 11 U.S.C. §1225; 11 U.S.C. §1325. See chapter 23 supra.
32. 11 U.S.C. §1227; 11 U.S.C. §1141(a); 11 U.S.C. §1327(a). See chapters 23 and 26 supra.
33. 11 U.S.C. §1228; 11 U.S.C. §1141. See chapter 26 supra.
34. 11 U.S.C. §1228(b); 11 U.S.C. §1328(b). See chapter 23 supra.
35. 11 U.S.C. §1229; 11 U.S.C. §1329. See chapter 23 supra.

A family farmer may be an individual, corporation, or partnership. In the latter two instances, more than 50 percent of the ownership must belong to the same family. A qualified family farmer's debt may not exceed $3,792,650. A family fisherman may also be an individual, corporation, or partnership, in a manner similar to farmers, except that the debt limit is $1,757,475.

Chapter 12 is a hybrid of Chapters 11 and 13. The speed and brevity of the Chapter 13 confirmation process are combined with the debtor-in-possession provisions of Chapter 11.

A Chapter 12 debtor has rights similar to a Chapter 11 debtor-in-possession. However, a trustee will always be appointed in a Chapter 12. The functions of a Chapter 12 trustee are similar to those of a Chapter 13 trustee.

Additional methods of providing adequate protection to secured creditors are available to Chapter 12 debtors. Periodic payments, replacement of additional collateral, customary rent in the community, or any equitable order granted by the court may constitute adequate protection.

The elements of a Chapter 11 plan and the findings required for confirmation are identical to Chapter 13, but with three exceptions. See the checklist to chapter 23 for further description. First, a Chapter 12 plan may be filed within 90 days of filing the proceeding. Second, a Chapter 12 confirmation hearing must take place within 45 days of filing the plan. Finally, a Chapter 12 plan, unlike a Chapter 13 plan, may modify the rights of secured creditors of the debtor's residence.

KEY TERMS

family farmer   family fisherman

DISCUSSION QUESTIONS

1. Why was Chapter 12 enacted? What is a family farmer for purposes of Chapter 12?

2. What provisions of Chapter 12 are similar to those of Chapter 13?

3. What provisions of Chapter 12 are similar to those of Chapter 11?

4. What features of Chapter 12 are unique to Chapter 12 proceedings?

PART VI

Review

28

Introduction to Courts and Jurisdiction

A.   BANKRUPTCY AND FEDERAL JUDGES

Article III of the United States Constitution creates the federal court system and **federal judges**.[1] Federal judges are distinguishable from other judicial officers by the constitutional requirement that federal judges be provided with two basic protections to ensure their independence: lifetime tenure during good behavior and that their salary shall not be subject to reduction during their term of office.[2]

The 1978 legislation that enacted the "Bankruptcy Code" gave the newly created Bankruptcy Judges jurisdiction to deal with any matter whatsoever having any relationship to a bankruptcy estate.[3] This was, in essence, a grant of full plenary jurisdiction to Bankruptcy Judges. This broad grant of jurisdiction made Bankruptcy Judges equivalent to full-time federal judges except that their jurisdiction was limited to matters involving bankruptcy proceedings. However, the Bankruptcy Judges created by the 1978 Bankruptcy Reform Act were not given the lifetime tenure or the salary protection of full federal judges. Instead, Bankruptcy Judges were given 14-year terms and their salary could be subject to reduction while in office. Rather than serving as Article III judges, the Bankruptcy Judges were created by Congress pursuant to article 1, section 8, of the Constitution, which gives Congress the right to enact bankruptcy laws.[4]

---

1. U.S. Const. art. III.
2. U.S. Const. art. III, §1.
3. 28 U.S.C. §1471, Pub. L. No. 95-598, 92 Stat. 2549 (1978).
4. U.S. Const. art. I, §8.

461

In 1982, in the case of Northern Pipeline Construction v. Marathon Pipeline Company, the Supreme Court reviewed the constitutionality of the Bankruptcy Court system enacted with the Code.[5] In this case, the debtor, Northern Pipeline Construction, filed an adversary proceeding in the Bankruptcy Court to collect an account receivable due from Marathon Pipeline on a turnover theory pursuant to Section 542. In state court, this action would have been a simple debt collection suit not based upon a preference or a fraudulent conveyance or any other subject even remotely involving the Bankruptcy Code. Marathon Pipeline argued that the Bankruptcy Courts were unconstitutional because Bankruptcy Judges were not given the protections provided federal judges under article III of the Constitution and therefore they had no jurisdiction to rule upon matters unrelated to the Bankruptcy Code. In its opinion, the Supreme Court thoroughly analyzed these constitutional issues and ruled that the Bankruptcy Judge and Bankruptcy Court system enacted in 1978 was unconstitutional.

B. ACTIVITY WITHIN A BANKRUPTCY

To understand Congress's solution to the problem, it is important to review the various levels of a bankruptcy proceeding. First, there is the overall proceeding. This is the type of Chapter proceeding filed: 7, 9, 11, 12, 13, or 15. It should now be obvious that, unlike traditional litigation, a multitude of activities will take place within a bankruptcy proceeding, for the simple reason that all of a debtor's financial affairs are subject to the scrutiny and control of the court. In contrast, a traditional piece of litigation will normally examine only one event or transaction in a vacuum without regard to the parties' other financial affairs.

Within a bankruptcy proceeding, matters will be brought before a Bankruptcy Judge by one of two methods: motion or adversary proceeding. For example, a sale will generally take place by way of a motion.[6] On the other hand, an action to avoid a preference takes place by way of an adversary proceeding.[7] Adversary proceedings may also arise that will not involve application of the Bankruptcy Code. For example, the collection of an account receivable, while theoretically a turnover complaint, is

---

5. 458 U.S. 50 (1982).
6. See chapters 12 and 18 supra.
7. See chapters 12 and 16 supra.

nothing more than a simple breach of contract dispute involving no application of bankruptcy law to determine the amount due.[8]

C.   BAFJA

In 1984, Congress enacted the Bankruptcy Amendments and Federal
Judgeship Act ("BAFJA") to be consistent with the Supreme Court's direction.[9] The process thus established is summarized in the nearby flowchart.
Initially, the district courts have original and exclusive jurisdiction over
bankruptcies, but Congress may elect to make the jurisdiction nonexclusive. Congress has done this in enacting Bankruptcy Courts into law.[10]
This means that a federal district court or federal Bankruptcy Court may
hear a bankruptcy proceeding.

The nonexclusive grant of jurisdiction to the Bankruptcy Court is set
forth in 28 U.S.C. §157. Under present law, all bankruptcy proceedings
and motions or adversary proceedings occurring within them are referred
to Bankruptcy Judges, but any party in interest may request withdrawal of
the reference at any time and have the matter referred back to the district
court (the article III judge) for disposition.

 Practice Pointer
This referral is accomplished by a standing
order entered by the district courts referring
bankruptcy matters automatically to the Bankruptcy
Court.

When the reference is withdrawn, the matter may not be heard by the
Bankruptcy Court at all unless all parties in the matter consent or the
district court determines in its discretion to reserve jurisdiction with
the Bankruptcy Court. Further, any Bankruptcy Judge's rulings can be
subject to the further approval of a district judge.[11]

---

8. See chapter 14 supra.
9. Bankruptcy Amendments and Federal Judgeship Act of 1984 (BAFJA), Pub. L. No. 98-353
   (July 10, 1984).
10. 28 U.S.C. §1334.
11. 28 U.S.C. §157(a), (c), (d).

BANKRUPTCY JURISDICTION

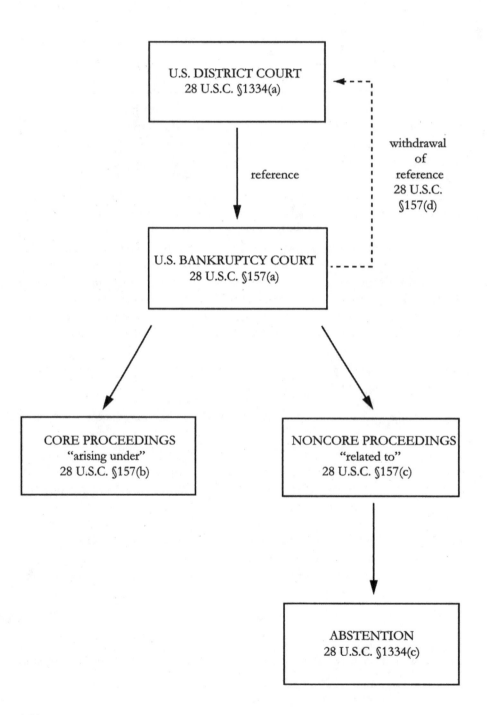

To distinguish the matters within a bankruptcy proceeding that the Bankruptcy Court may hear, Congress designated proceedings as "core" and "noncore" and relied on the phrases "arising under" or "related to" to define adversary matters within a bankruptcy proceeding.[12]

Bankruptcy Judges have jurisdiction to hear all **cases** under Title 11 and may also hear all core proceedings arising within the proceeding and matters "related to" the bankruptcy proceeding.[13]

D.   CORE AND NONCORE PROCEEDINGS

Generally, **core proceedings** "arising under" the Bankruptcy Code are those matters that arise by way of motion or adversary proceeding and involve the specific application of one or more provisions of the Bankruptcy Code for their resolution. The matters identified in 28 U.S.C. §157(b)(2) as core proceedings are items that are generally the subject matter of specific Bankruptcy Code sections. For example, objections to claims, relief from stay motions, motions to assume or reject executory contracts, objections to exemptions, objections to the dischargeability of debts or to the debtor's discharge, preferences, and other uses of the trustee's avoiding powers are all defined as *core proceedings*.[14] The resolution of these issues normally requires the application of specific Bankruptcy Code provisions.

On the other hand, a matter "related to" a bankruptcy proceeding is a matter that would arise for a debtor whether or not the particular bankruptcy proceeding exists.[15] For example, the debt collection suit filed in *Marathon Pipeline* supra is such a matter. Matters such as these are generally considered **noncore proceedings**. The Bankruptcy Court may hear noncore matters.[16] However, if a party objects to the Bankruptcy Court's hearing of a noncore matter, the Bankruptcy Court must determine whether the matter is a core or noncore proceeding. If the matter is noncore, the Bankruptcy Court must either refer the case to the district court or abstain from

---

12. 28 U.S.C. §157(b); 28 U.S.C. §1334.
13. 28 U.S.C. §157(b)(1).
14. 28 U.S.C. §157(b)(2).
15. The extent of "related to" jurisdiction has been defined as whether a lawsuit could conceivably have any impact on the bankruptcy estate without the "intervention of yet another lawsuit." In re W.R. Grace & Co., 591 F.3d 164, 172-173 (3d Cir. 2009). See also In re OCA, Inc., 551 F.3d 359 (5th Cir. 2008); In re Ryan, 276 Fed. Appx. 963, 966 (11th Cir. 2008); Valley Historic L.P. v. Bank of NY, 486 F.3d 831, 836 (4th Cir. 2007).
16. 28 U.S.C. §157(b)(1).

further hearing the matter.[17] Personal injury and wrongful death claims are specifically designated as noncore.[18] The practical effect of these provisions is to have a personal injury suit or complex commercial litigation tried in a court other than the Bankruptcy Court in appropriate circumstances.

 Practice Pointer

In a noncore matter, the Bankruptcy Court only has the authority to enter findings of fact and conclusions of law.

---

28 U.S.C. §1334(c) permits the Bankruptcy Court or district court to abstain from hearing a particular matter. If a matter is "related to" the bankruptcy proceeding but would not be heard in the federal court system absent the fact that one of the parties is a debtor in a bankruptcy proceeding, then the Bankruptcy Court or district court may abstain from hearing the matter and will defer to local jurisdiction.[19] A decision to abstain is not reviewable by appeal or otherwise.[20] For example, a trustee seeks to litigate a breach of contract suit in Bankruptcy Court. The defendant moves the court to abstain on the grounds that the claim is noncore and has no independent source of federal jurisdiction. The Bankruptcy Court agrees. This decision may not be appealed.

In Marshall v. Marshall, 547 U.S. 293 (2006), the debtor (commonly known as Anna Nicole Smith) objected to a defamation claim filed in her bankruptcy by her deceased husband's son, Pierce Marshall. In objecting to the claim, she asserted a counterclaim against Pierce, claiming that he tortiously interfered with a gift expected from her deceased husband. The Bankruptcy Court and district courts found judgment for Smith in the amount of $44.3 million. The Ninth Circuit found that matter barred from Bankruptcy Court jurisdiction by a common law exception to bankruptcy jurisdiction barring Bankruptcy Courts from hearing probate or domestic relations matters. The Supreme Court reversed the Ninth Circuit finding that the counterclaim did not seek to probate a will, contest a will, or administer the decedent's estate, and so the Bankruptcy Court had jurisdiction to hear and to rule upon the counterclaim. The claim objection was a core proceeding. The counterclaim was "related to" claim.

---

17. 28 U.S.C. §157(b)(3), (b)(4), (c), (d).
18. 28 U.S.C. §157(b)(5).
19. 28 U.S.C. §1334(c)(2).
20. 28 U.S.C. §1334(c)(2).

The various circuits within the federal judicial system have been given the power to appoint Bankruptcy Judges in each district. Bankruptcy Judges are appointed by the circuits for 14-year terms.[21]

E. REMOVAL AND APPEALS

It is possible to remove pending actions from the state court system to the Bankruptcy Court pursuant to 28 U.S.C. §1452. The procedure for removal is contained in Federal Rule of Bankruptcy Procedure 9027.[22] Many times when there is pending litigation at the time a bankruptcy proceeding is filed, the debtor or a creditor will seek to remove the litigation from state court to the Bankruptcy Court. If removal occurs and there is no objection, the Bankruptcy Court will then hear the case.

Appeals from the rulings of a Bankruptcy Court may be made to either the district court in the district where the Bankruptcy Court is located, to the Bankruptcy Appellate Panel ("BAP") of the Bankruptcy Court's particular circuit, or directly to the Court of Appeals for a given circuit.[23] A BAP may be created within a given federal judicial circuit. This panel will be comprised of three Bankruptcy Judges from districts within the circuit. The 1994 Bankruptcy Reform Act makes the establishment of BAPs mandatory unless the judicial council for a particular circuit finds insufficient resources or the likelihood that undue delay would result from establishment of a panel.[24] The BAP will hear all appeals unless the appellant elects, when filing the appeal, or the appellee elects within 30 days after service of the appeal, to have the appeal heard by the district court. In some limited instances, an appeal may be made directly to the circuit if the lower court so certifies.[25] Part 8 of the Federal Rules of Bankruptcy Procedure governs appeals. Otherwise, appeals of bankruptcy matters are similar to other federal judicial appeals, including applicability of the Federal Rules of Appellate Procedure. See the nearby flowchart.

---

21. U.S.C. §§151, 152.
22. 28 U.S.C. §1452; Bankruptcy Rule 9027.
23. 28 U.S.C. §158(a).
24. The First and Ninth Circuits have BAP panels. The Second, Third, Fourth, Fifth, Seventh, and Eleventh Circuits do not. The Sixth, Eighth, and Tenth Circuits have BAP panels for limited districts within each circuit.
25. 28 U.S.C. §158.

BANKRUPTCY APPEALS

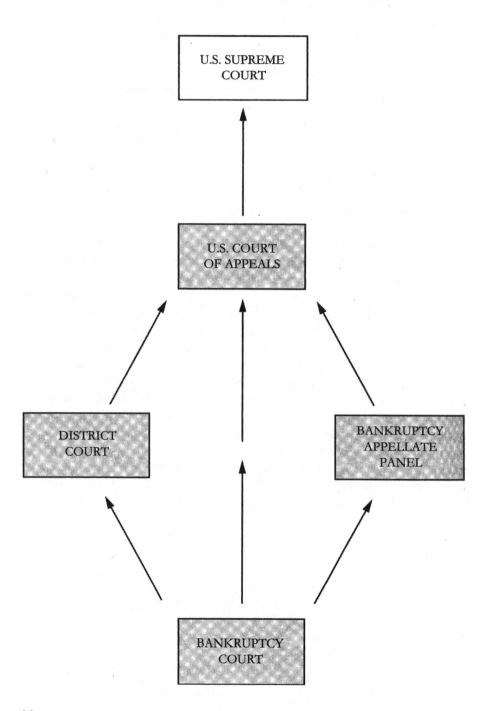

F.   JURY TRIALS

In Granfinanceria, S.A. v. Norberg, the Supreme Court explored the right to a jury trial in adversary proceedings before the Bankruptcy Court.[26] In this case, Norberg, a trustee, sued Granfinanceria to avoid fraudulent transfers. Granfinanceria requested a jury trial. The lower courts held that because suits to avoid fraudulent transfers were not triable by jury under common law and because an action to avoid a fraudulent transfer is a core proceeding, no right to a jury trial existed. The Supreme Court disagreed and reversed.

The Supreme Court held, in essence, that any action to recover money is an action at law for which a Seventh Amendment constitutional right to trial by jury exists. Notwithstanding this decision, the occurrence of a jury trial in the Bankruptcy Court is extremely rare. The 1994 Bankruptcy Reform Act permits the Bankruptcy Court to conduct jury trials if designated to do so by the district court and with the express consent of all parties.[27] Local rules should be consulted to ascertain the procedure in a particular district.

Summary

Federal law confers jurisdiction to hear bankruptcy proceedings on all federal district and Bankruptcy Courts. In some situations, a party may seek removal of a bankruptcy proceeding from a Bankruptcy Court to a federal district court. Normally, however, virtually all bankruptcy proceedings are presided over by the Bankruptcy Courts.

A Bankruptcy Court will always hear core matters. A core matter is any issue whose resolution requires specific application of a Bankruptcy Code provision. A claim objection, an action to avoid a preference, and a motion for relief from the automatic stay are examples of core proceedings.

On the other hand, a matter arising before the Bankruptcy Court that does not require application of a specific Bankruptcy Code provision for its resolution is known as a noncore matter. A party may request the Bankruptcy Court to abstain from hearing a noncore matter. A decision by the court to abstain is not reviewable by appeal or otherwise. A personal injury action is a good example of a noncore matter.

---

26. 492 U.S. 33 (1989).
27. 28 U.S.C §157(e).

KEY TERMS

cases   federal judges
core proceedings   noncore proceedings

DISCUSSION QUESTIONS

1. What is the difference between a core and noncore proceeding? Identify the following as core or noncore proceedings: motion for relief from stay; breach of contract claim; preference complaint; objection to claim of exemption; personal injury claim.

2. Describe the higher courts to which a bankruptcy ruling may be appealed.

29

Statements and Schedules Tutorial

A.   INTRODUCTION

Approximately 95 percent of all bankruptcy proceedings filed are consumer Chapter 7 or Chapter 13 proceedings. In these cases, the practitioner's most important task is to prepare the data required to be in the Statement of Financial Affairs and the Schedules of Assets and Liabilities, commonly known as the Statements and Schedules, and to complete the applicable Statement of Current Monthly Income and Means-Test Calculation. Performing these tasks well will make the debtor's visit to the bankruptcy system as smooth and uneventful as possible. Proper preparation will also minimize the trustee's effort to administer the case. In an asset proceeding, these tasks help maximize the estate's recovery because the schedules serve as an easy reference guide for the trustee as to the location and value of any assets.[1] Where the debtor's major goal is to satisfy nondischargeable tax claims, well-produced schedules will aid in achieving this result. In a practice emphasizing bankruptcy law, a paralegal will spend a significant amount of time assisting in this preparation.

It is important, when representing creditors, to carefully read the Statements and Schedules. Because these documents comprise the evidence that allows creditors or the trustee to determine the existence of assets available for liquidation and distribution, potential objections to an individual debtor's discharge, or the feasibility of a successful reorganization, understanding their contents is an important lesson to learn.

---

1. See chapter 11 supra.

This chapter is an exercise in learning to prepare and read the Statements and Schedules. This chapter also serves as a review of the Bankruptcy Code and as a final illustration of the Bankruptcy Code's functioning as a system. Chapter 30 is a tutorial about the preparation of the Statement of Current Monthly Income and Means-Test Calculation.

The first group of forms analyzed is collectively referred to as the Schedules.[2] The second form analyzed is known as the Statement of Financial Affairs.[3] These documents are used by all Chapter 7, 11, and 13 debtors.

To simplify the explanation of these forms, we will review them in the context of a statement of facts concerning two hypothetical joint debtors. Each form will then be analyzed, item by item, on the basis of the fact scenario. Chapter 30 utilizes the identical fact pattern.

Counsel's duty of reasonable investigation as set forth in Section 707(b)(4) alters the relative responsibility for the accurate preparation of the Schedules. Counsel should maintain detailed records to support the contents of the Statements, Schedules, and Statement of Current Monthly Income. The text reflects custom and practice from throughout the country and, where necessary, includes the evolving standards created by BAPCPA.

B.   KEN AND BRETONY BOTTOMLINE

Ken and Bretony Bottomline want to file Chapter 7 without delay. Circuit City is threatening to attach their computer, and Toyota Credit is threatening to repossess their Moriah SUV. Only an immediate Chapter 7 filing will prevent a loss of the car to the repossessor.

Ken and Bretony have lived at 1945 Billy Pilgrim Road in the town of Tralfamadore in the Southern District of California in San Diego County for the past two years. Prior to this, they lived at 45 Coldfish Lane in Frosty Falls, Montana.

Ken has been employed by Harrison Bergeron, Inc., for two years as a software designer. He receives an annual salary of $72,000. Bretony is currently employed as an assistant manager at the Tea Jamboree and receives a monthly salary of $1,000. She has been working at Tea Jamboree for three months. For one year before that, she was in a partnership with Kilgore Trout. The name of the partnership was Top O' the Mornin' Irish

2. Official Form 6.
3. Official Form 7.

Tea Co. Top O' the Mornin' went out of business for lack of sales, and all assets were liquidated.

The Bottomlines have three bank accounts: checking and savings accounts at the People's Bank and an IRA account at the Bank of America. The checking account has an average balance of $500. They have savings of $1,000 and a balance of $25,000 in the IRA. The Bottomlines do not have a safe deposit box.

No creditors have attached any assets of the Bottomlines as of the present time. Ken and Bretony hold no property in trust for any third party. No third party holds property in trust for them.

The following suits terminated in the past year: Symphonic Sounds v. Bottomline (judgment for plaintiff) and Dr. Laventhol v. Bottomline (judgment for plaintiff). The following suit is still pending: Williams-Sonoma v. Bottomline. Each suit is for debt collection. The Bottomlines dispute the amount due Williams-Sonoma.

Within the past six months, Bretony has transferred title to an empty lot in Santa Cruz to some old friends, Ozzie and Harriet Oddborn, for no consideration. The lot is valued at $10,000.

The Bottomlines have maintained their own personal records and have kept copies of their tax returns.

The Bottomlines have seen no attorneys in the past year other than our firm. They will be paying us a $1,500 fee for their Chapter 7 filing.

The Bottomlines owe $5,000 in income taxes to the IRS for 2009. They are not entitled to any tax refunds at the present time. They have not received any tax refunds in the past two years.

The Bottomlines do not own their own home. They owe their landlord, Billy Mountain, rent for two months at $1,200 per month. They have a month-to-month lease. They live in their home with their 15-year-old son, Ted. They have cosigned a $7,500 student loan for their 19-year-old daughter, Missy, who is an honors student at the University of Relativity where she is double-majoring in Quantum Physics and Barn Dancing. They owe Toyota Credit $9,600 secured by the 2008 Moriah. The vehicle is worth $15,000. They pay $350 per month, are two payments behind, and have 30 payments remaining. All of their furniture is secured by the El Repo Finance Company, to whom the Bottomlines owe $10,000. The furniture is worth $6,000. The debt was not incurred to purchase the furniture. They have a computer worth $1,500.

The Bottomlines have the following unsecured debts:

Circuit City	$5,000
Symphonic Sounds	3,000
Dr. Laventhol	500
MasterCard	3,000

Visa	$3,000
American Express Green Card	5,000
Macy's	3,000
Wal-Mart	1,500
Capital Ism	2,500
Bank Two	3,000
Sax Baltic Avenue	2,000
Magic Carpets	4,500

The Bottomlines have personal wardrobes collectively worth $4,000 at liquidation value. Ken also has a collection of Jerry Garcia ties worth $1,000. They each own a pair of custom WarpSpeed rollerblades, worth $400 a pair. They have no assets other than described. All assets and liabilities are jointly owned or owed. No debts are in dispute except as noted above. They will claim exemptions pursuant to 11 U.S.C. §522(d).

Ken's gross monthly income is $6,000; Bretony's gross monthly income is $1,000. They have provided us with the following approximate monthly expenses:

Rent	$1,200
Utilities (gas and electric)	175
Telephone/cell phone	150
Cable TV	75
Food	600
Clothing	100
Laundry	30
Transportation	300
Entertainment	200
Insurance —	
Auto	150
Health	200
Renter's	20
Car payment	350
Internet network fees	42

C. SCHEDULES

Official Form 6 is entitled the Schedules of Assets and Liabilities. Together, the Statement of Financial Affairs and Schedules of Assets and Liabilities are commonly known as the Statements and Schedules. Collectively, the

Schedules form an accrual basis form of a financial statement. Debts not paid are in fact accrued debts within generally accepted accounting definitions. In the Schedules, liabilities are listed according to the distribution scheme described in chapters 21 and 22 supra. Assets are segregated between real property, personal property, and other property. The debtor's claim of exemptions is also included in the Schedules. The Schedules will also disclose any executory contracts or leases, codebtors, and the debtor's monthly income and expenses.

B1 (Official Form 1) (4/10)

UNITED STATES BANKRUPTCY COURT	VOLUNTARY PETITION
Name of Debtor (if individual, enter Last, First, Middle):	Name of Joint Debtor (Spouse) (Last, First, Middle):
All Other Names used by the Debtor in the last 8 years (include married, maiden, and trade names):	All Other Names used by the Joint Debtor in the last 8 years (include married, maiden, and trade names):

Description

All names by which either debtor has been known or has conducted business during the prior eight years should be listed in the caption if any creditor would recognize the debtor only by the alias. This is important because creditors need to know all possible names that an account may be listed under for the creditor notice to have meaning. For example, a creditor of Top O' the Mornin' Irish Tea Co. may not recognize the names Ken and Bretony Bottomline. It would be acceptable to have just "Ken and Bretony Bottomline" as the caption, but it would be most accurate and informative to note Bretony's prior business name, Top O' the Mornin' (fdba). A creditor may know who Top O' the Mornin' is but not who Bretony is.

A spouse's maiden or prior married name need not be included unless any of the debts listed are in the spouse's maiden or prior married name.

If a debtor has aliases that creditors have used for billing purposes, such as a business name like Top O' the Mornin', then the name should be designated in the caption. A nickname need not be included unless it is the name creditors may use in rendering billings.

SCHEDULE A - REAL PROPERTY

DESCRIPTION AND LOCATION OF PROPERTY	NATURE OF DEBTOR'S INTEREST IN PROPERTY	HUSBAND, WIFE, JOINT OR COMMUNITY	CURRENT VALUE OF DEBTOR'S INTEREST IN PROPERTY, WITHOUT DEDUCTING ANY SECURED CLAIM OR EXEMPTION	AMOUNT OF SECURED CLAIM
None				

Description

Schedules A through C itemize all of the property of the debtors and contain their claim of exemptions. Schedule A is an itemization of real property. All ownership interests in real estate must be disclosed so that the trustee will be able to ascertain all potential property of the estate.[4] In a typical consumer proceeding where the debtors are renting, the name and address of the rental are not described in this Schedule. The lease will be disclosed in Schedule G — Executory Contracts and Unexpired Leases infra.

---

4. See chapters 11 and 14 supra.

SCHEDULE B - PERSONAL PROPERTY

TYPE OF PROPERTY	N O N E	DESCRIPTION AND LOCATION OF PROPERTY	HUSBAND, WIFE, JOINT OR COMMUNITY	CURRENT VALUE OF DEBTOR'S INTEREST IN PROPERTY, WITHOUT DEDUCTING ANY SECURED CLAIM OR EXEMPTION
1. Cash on hand.	X			
2. Checking, savings or other financial accounts, certificates of deposit, or shares in banks, savings and loan, thrift, building and loan, and homestead associations, or credit unions, brokerage houses, or cooperatives.		SAVINGS ACCOUNT - PEOPLE'S BANK PEOPLE'S BANK	J	1,000.00
		CHECKING ACCOUNT - PEOPLE'S BANK PEOPLE'S BANK	J	500.00
3. Security deposits with public utilities, telephone companies, landlords, and others.	X			
4. Household goods and furnishings, including audio, video, and computer equipment.		HOUSEHOLD GOODS - NO ITEM EXCEEDS $550 Debtor's Residence	J	6,000.00
5. Books. Pictures and other art objects, antiques, stamp, coin, record, tape, compact disc, and other collections or collectibles.		JERRY GARCIA TIE COLLECTION - NO ITEM EXCEEDS $550 IN VALUE Debtor's Residence	J	1,000.00
6. Wearing apparel.		Wearing apparel Debtor's Residence	J	5,000.00
7. Furs and jewelry.	X			
8. Firearms and sports, photographic, and other hobby equipment.		2 PAIR WARPSPEED ROLLER BLADES Debtor's Residence	J	800.00
12. Interests in IRA, ERISA, Keogh, or other pension or profit sharing plans. Give particulars.		IRA - BANK OF AMERICA BANK OF AMERICA	H	25,000.00
25. Automobiles, trucks, trailers, and other vehicles and accessories.		2008 TOYOTA MORIAH Debtor's Residence	J	15,000.00

Description

Schedule B itemizes personal property of all kinds. Only those items that most commonly appear in a consumer proceeding appear in the fact memo and in that portion of Schedule B shown. This is why the numbers are not consecutive. See form 4.3 on the forms disk for the complete Schedule B.

Cash on hand is the first item. Most debtors usually have a very small amount of cash on hand or "pocket money." "None," or "nominal," or "zero" are common responses. The location, such as "debtors' residence," should also be disclosed. Note that the form contains a column for "None." It should be used where applicable. No item should be left blank.

The next item identifies funds on deposit. Bank balances are described here. In addition, the name and address of the depository bank and the account number should also be disclosed. This information was previously disclosed in the Statement of Affairs. It will now be disclosed only in the Schedules.

Item B-4 identifies household goods, supplies, and furnishings. Simply provide the total value at liquidation prices. It is also a good idea to provide the additional legend "no item exceeds $550 in value" and to list any exceptions. This legend may affect exemptions under federal law. Recall also that "each item" specifically means each item.[5] The computer should be separately listed because it exceeds $550 in value. Note that the schedule is in error because it does not account for or disclose the value of the computer. The same description and comments apply equally to Schedules B-4 and B-6 regarding the debtors' household goods and wearing apparel. Note that there is no Schedule B-3 item described in the fact memo. The "None" column has been checked.

Item B-12 identifies any IRA or pension accounts. Item B-25 describes vehicles. It is also a good idea to note, as shown, the amount of any lien upon the vehicle. This will help the trustee easily determine the existence or lack of equity in the vehicle.

There are no other entries for the Bottomlines' Schedule B. Even so, the "None" column should be checked for all other items so there will not be a question raised as to the existence of any assets in any of the other categories.

Finally, note that all assets have been identified as being jointly owned by the Bottomlines.

---

5. See chapter 9 supra.

SCHEDULE C - PROPERTY CLAIMED AS EXEMPT

Debtor claims the exemptions to which debtor is entitled under:
(Check one box)

☐ 11 U.S.C. § 522(b)(2)

☑ 11 U.S.C. § 522(b)(3)

☐ Check if debtor claims a homestead exemption that exceeds $146,450*.

DESCRIPTION OF PROPERTY	SPECIFY LAW PROVIDING EACH EXEMPTION	VALUE OF CLAIMED EXEMPTION	CURRENT VALUE OF PROPERTY WITHOUT DEDUCTING EXEMPTION
SAVINGS ACCOUNT - PEOPLE'S BANK	C.C.P. 703.140(b)(5)	100% of FMV	1,000.00
CHECKING ACCOUNT - PEOPLE'S BANK	C.C.P. 703.140(b)(5)	100% of FMV	500.00
HOUSEHOLD GOODS - NO ITEM EXCEEDS $550	C.C.P. 703.140(b)(3)	100% of FMV	6,000.00
JERRY GARCIA TIE COLLECTION - NO ITEM EXCEEDS $550 IN VALUE	C.C.P. 703.140(b)(5)	100% of FMV	1,000.00
2 PAIR WARPSPEED ROLLER BLADES	C.C.P. 703.140(b)(5)	100% of FMV	800.00
IRA - BANK OF AMERICA	11 USC §522(b)(3)(c)	100% of FMV	25,000.00
2008 TOYOTA MORIAH	C.C.P. 703.140(b)(2)	100% of FMV	15,000.00
Wearing apparel			5,000.00

*Amount subject to adjustment on 4/1/13 and every three years thereafter with respect to cases commenced on or after the date of adjustment.

Description

Schedule C is the debtors' claim of exemptions. Each exemption should be itemized and the statute that the debtors select should be identified with particularity, whether the debtors select state exemptions or the federal exemptions, where applicable. Note the prefatory box at the top of the form. The most probable effective selection for the Bottomlines is shown.[6] Claim the maximum statutory amount exempt for each asset subject to an exemption even if there is no apparent equity in the asset. This will relieve the necessity of later making an amendment should an issue as to value arise.

Also, note that a disclosure of an asset's market value must be disclosed alongside the exemption. Recall that there is $9,600 owed on the vehicle and this lack of equity does not appear on *this* sheet although it appears in Schedules B and D, respectively. This also applies to the personal property secured to El Repo Finance Company.

---

6. It may appear that the exemption limit for household goods, furnishings, and wearing apparel of $11,525 has been exceeded, inasmuch as the value of these assets is $12,500, including the computer (11 U.S.C. §522(d)(3)). However, recall that each joint debtor may make a claim of exception, effectively doubling all the dollar amounts (11 U.S.C. §522(m)) in a state that has not opted out of the federal exemption scheme. See chapter 9 supra.

SCHEDULE D - CREDITORS HOLDING SECURED CLAIMS

State the name, mailing address, including zip code and last four digits of any account number of all entities holding claims secured by property of the debtor as of the date of filing of the petition. The complete account number of any account the debtor has with the creditor is useful to the trustee and the creditor and may be provided if the debtor chooses to do so. List creditors holding all types of secured interests such as judgment liens, garnishments, statutory liens, mortgages, deeds of trust, and other security interests.

   List creditors in alphabetical order to the extent practicable. If a minor child is a creditor, state the child's initials and the name and address of the child's parent or guardian, such as "A.B., a minor child, by John Doe, guardian." Do not disclose the child's name. See 11 U.S.C §112 and Fed. R. Bankr. P. 1007(m). If all secured creditors will not fit on this page, use the continuation sheet provided.

   If any entity other than a spouse in a joint case may be jointly liable on a claim, place an "X" in the column labeled "Codebtor," include the entity on the appropriate schedule of creditors, and complete Schedule H - Codebtors. If a joint petition is filed, state whether husband, wife, both of them, or the marital community may be liable on each claim by placing an "H," "W," "J," or "C" in the column labeled "Husband, Wife, Joint, or Community."

   If the claim is contingent, place an "X" in the column labeled "Contingent." If the claim is unliquidated, place an "X" in the column labeled "Unliquidated." If the claim is disputed, place an "X" in the column labeled "Disputed." (You may need to place an "X" in more than one of these three columns.)

   Total the columns labeled "Amount of Claim Without Deducting Value of Collateral" and "Unsecured Portion, if Any" in the boxes labeled "Total(s)" on the last sheet of the completed schedule. Report the total from the column labeled "Amount of Claim Without Deducting Value of Collateral" also on the Summary of Schedules and, if the debtor is an individual with primarily consumer debts, report the total from the column labeled "Unsecured Portion, if Any" on the Statistical Summary of Certain Liabilities and Related Data.

☐ Check this box if debtor has no creditors holding secured claims to report on this Schedule D.

CREDITOR'S NAME, MAILING ADDRESS INCLUDING ZIP CODE, AND ACCOUNT NUMBER *(See Instructions Above.)*	CODEBTOR	HUSBAND, WIFE, JOINT OR COMMUNITY	DATE CLAIM WAS INCURRED, NATURE OF LIEN, AND DESCRIPTION AND VALUE OF PROPERTY SUBJECT TO LIEN	CONTINGENT	UNLIQUIDATED	DISPUTED	AMOUNT OF CLAIM WITHOUT DEDUCTING VALUE OF COLLATERAL	UNSECURED PORTION, IF ANY
ACCOUNT NO. EL REPO FINANCE CO		J	Lien: NonPMSI in HHG Security: DEBTOR'S FURNITURE VALUE $ 5,000.00				10,000.00	5,000.00
ACCOUNT NO. TOYOTA CREDIT		J	Lien: PMSI in vehicle < 910 days Security: 2008 TOYOTA MORIAH VALUE $ 15,000.00				9,600.00	0.00
ACCOUNT NO. 			 VALUE $					

_0_   continuation sheets attached

Subtotal ➤ (Total of this page) — $ 19,600.00 | $ 5,000.00

Total ➤ (Use only on last page) — $ 19,600.00 | $ 5,000.00

(Report also on Summary of Schedules)   (If applicable, report also on Statistical Summary of Certain Liabilities and Related Data.)

Description

Schedule D itemizes all secured claims. List the creditors' names and addresses alphabetically. Also list the last four digits of any account numbers that the debtor provides. (These have not been provided in the example.) Frequently, correspondence will be received from creditors requesting account numbers. If these numbers are included in the

Schedules, it will be helpful. Describe the collateral as succinctly as possible, as shown in the example, and when the creditor acquired the security interest. List the market value of the collateral as shown. Finally, identify the amount of each secured creditor's claim. From this data, there can be estimated the existence or lack of any equity in the collateral for the benefit of the debtors or unsecured creditors. Identifying the date when a security interest was acquired will help identify the security interest as a potential preference or as a nonpurchase money lien in consumer goods that may be avoided under Section 522(f)(2).[7] (Yes, the Bottomlines may want to consider such a motion with respect to El Repo Finance Company on the facts provided.) Finally, note that the joint nature of the debts must also be disclosed.

SCHEDULE E - CREDITORS HOLDING UNSECURED PRIORITY CLAIMS

(Continuation Sheet)   Sec. 507(a)(8)

Type of Priority for Claims Listed on This Sheet

CREDITOR'S NAME, MAILING ADDRESS INCLUDING ZIP CODE, AND ACCOUNT NUMBER *(See instructions above..)*	CODEBTOR	HUSBAND, WIFE, JOINT ORCOMMUNITY	DATE CLAIM WAS INCURRED AND CONSIDERATION FOR CLAIM	CONTINGENT	UNLIQUIDATED	DISPUTED	AMOUNT OF CLAIM	AMOUNT ENTITLED TO PRIORITY	AMOUNT NOT ENTITLED TO PRIORITY, IF ANY
ACCOUNT NO. IRS		J	Consideration: TAXES				5,000.00	5,000.00	0.00

Sheet no. 1 of 1 continuation sheets attached to Schedule of Creditors Holding Priority Claims

Subtotal (Totals of this page)	$ 5,000.00	$	$
Total (Use only on last page of the completed Schedule E.) Report also on the Summary of Schedules)	$ 5,000.00		
Totals (Use only on last page of the completed Schedule E. If applicable, report also on the Statistical Summary of Certain Liabilities and Related Data.)	$	$ 5,000.00	$ 0.00

Description

Schedule E is an itemization of Section 507 priority claims, listed in the order of priority designated in Section 507(a).[8] The claim of the IRS is the only priority claim in the example. In this Schedule, as in all of the

---

7. See chapters 9 and 16 supra.
8. See chapters 21 and 22 supra.

Schedules, it is more important to place all potential creditors on the list so they receive notice. Exactness as to the amount is secondary. Often a debtor may not be certain about the exact amount due a particular creditor. When in doubt, insert the debtor's best estimate. A dischargeable debt will remain dischargeable even if an incorrect amount is listed in the Schedules but the creditor has received notice of the proceeding. However, a dischargeable debt may become nondischargeable if it is not listed in the Schedules.[9]

---

9. 11 U.S.C. §523(a)(3). See chapter 13 supra.

SCHEDULE F- CREDITORS HOLDING UNSECURED NONPRIORITY CLAIMS

State the name, mailing address, including zip code, and last four digits of any account number, of all entities holding unsecured claims without priority against the debtor or the property of the debtor, as of the date of filing of the petition. The complete account number of any account the debtor has with the creditor is useful to the trustee and the creditor and may be provided if the debtor chooses to do so. If a minor child is a creditor, state the child's initials and the name and address of the child's parent or guardian, such as "A.B., a minor child, by John Doe, guardian." Do not disclose the child's name. See 11 U.S.C. § 112 and Fed. R. Bankr. P. 1007(m). Do not include claims listed in Schedules D and E. If all creditors will not fit on this page, use the continuation sheet provided.

If any entity other than a spouse in a joint case may be jointly liable on a claim, place an "X" in the column labeled "Codebtor," include the entity on the appropriate schedule of creditors, and complete Schedule H - Codebtors. If a joint petition is filed, state whether husband, wife, both of them, or the marital community may be liable on each claim by placing an "H," "W," "J," or "C" in the column labeled "Husband, Wife, Joint, or Community."

If the claim is contingent, place an "X" in the column labeled "Contingent." If the claim is unliquidated, place an "X" in the column labeled "Unliquidated." If the claim is disputed, place an "X" in the column labeled "Disputed." (You may need to place an "X" in more than one of these three columns.)

Report the total of all claims listed on this schedule in the box labeled "Total" on the last sheet of the completed schedule. Report this total also on the Summary of Schedules and, if the debtor is an individual with primarily consumer debts, report this total also on the Statistical Summary of Certain Liabilities and Related Data.

☐ Check this box if debtor has no creditors holding unsecured claims to report on this Schedule F.

CREDITOR'S NAME, MAILING ADDRESS INCLUDING ZIP CODE, AND ACCOUNT NUMBER *(See instructions above.)*	CODEBTOR	HUSBAND, WIFE, JOINT, OR COMMUNITY	DATE CLAIM WAS INCURRED AND CONSIDERATION FOR CLAIM. IF CLAIM IS SUBJECT TO SETOFF, SO STATE.	CONTINGENT	UNLIQUIDATED	DISPUTED	AMOUNT OF CLAIM
ACCOUNT NO. AMERICAN EXPRESS GOLD		J					5,000.00
ACCOUNT NO. AMERICAN EXPRESS GREEN CARD		J					5,000.00
ACCOUNT NO. BANK TWO		J					3,000.00
ACCOUNT NO. BILLY MOUNTAIN		J					2,400.00

_3_ continuation sheets attached

Subtotal ➤ $ 15,400.00

Total ➤ $

(Use only on last page of the completed Schedule F.)
(Report also on Summary of Schedules and, if applicable, on the Statistical
Summary of Certain Liabilities and Related Data.)

SCHEDULE F- CREDITORS HOLDING UNSECURED NONPRIORITY CLAIMS
(Continuation Sheet)

CREDITOR'S NAME, MAILING ADDRESS INCLUDING ZIP CODE, AND ACCOUNT NUMBER *(See instructions above.)*	CODEBTOR	HUSBAND, WIFE, JOINT ORCOMMUNITY	DATE CLAIM WAS INCURRED AND CONSIDERATION FOR CLAIM. IF CLAIM IS SUBJECT TO SETOFF,	CONTINGENT	UNLIQUIDATED	DISPUTED	AMOUNT OF CLAIM
ACCOUNT NO. CAPITAL ISM		J					2,500.00
ACCOUNT NO. DR. LAVENTHOL		J					500.00
ACCOUNT NO. MACY'S		J					3,000.00
ACCOUNT NO. MAGIC CARPETS		J					4,500.00
ACCOUNT NO. MASTER CARD		J					3,000.00

Sheet no. 1 of 3 continuation sheets attached
to Schedule of Creditors Holding Unsecured
Nonpriority Claims

Subtotal ➤ $ 13,500.00

Total ➤ $

(Use only on last page of the completed Schedule F.)
(Report also on Summary of Schedules and, if applicable, on the
Statistical Summary of Certain Liabilities and Related Data.)

SCHEDULE F- CREDITORS HOLDING UNSECURED NONPRIORITY CLAIMS
(Continuation Sheet)

CREDITOR'S NAME, MAILING ADDRESS INCLUDING ZIP CODE, AND ACCOUNT NUMBER *(See instructions above.)*	CODEBTOR	HUSBAND, WIFE, JOINT OR COMMUNITY	DATE CLAIM WAS INCURRED AND CONSIDERATION FOR CLAIM. IF CLAIM IS SUBJECT TO SETOFF,	CONTINGENT	UNLIQUIDATED	DISPUTED	AMOUNT OF CLAIM
ACCOUNT NO. SAX BALTIC AVENUE		J					2,000.00
ACCOUNT NO. SYMPHONIC SOUNDS		J					3,000.00
ACCOUNT NO. UNIVERSITY OF RELATIVITY	X	J					7,500.00
ACCOUNT NO. VISA		J					3,000.00
ACCOUNT NO. WALMART		J					1,500.00

Sheet no. __2__ of __3__ continuation sheets attached to Schedule of Creditors Holding Unsecured Nonpriority Claims

Subtotal ➤ $ 17,000.00

Total ➤ $

(Use only on last page of the completed Schedule F.)
(Report also on Summary of Schedules and, if applicable, on the
Statistical Summary of Certain Liabilities and Related Data.)

SCHEDULE F- CREDITORS HOLDING UNSECURED NONPRIORITY CLAIMS
(Continuation Sheet)

CREDITOR'S NAME, MAILING ADDRESS INCLUDING ZIP CODE, AND ACCOUNT NUMBER *(See instructions above.)*	CODEBTOR	HUSBAND, WIFE, JOINT OR COMMUNITY	DATE CLAIM WAS INCURRED AND CONSIDERATION FOR CLAIM. IF CLAIM IS SUBJECT TO SETOFF,	CONTINGENT	UNLIQUIDATED	DISPUTED	AMOUNT OF CLAIM
ACCOUNT NO. WILLIAMS SONOMA		J					Unknown

Sheet no. _3_ of _3_ continuation sheets attached
to Schedule of Creditors Holding Unsecured
Nonpriority Claims

	Subtotal ▶	$	0.00
	Total ▶	$	45,900.00

(Use only on last page of the completed Schedule F.)
(Report also on Summary of Schedules and, if applicable, on the
Statistical Summary of Certain Liabilities and Related Data.)

Description

Schedule F is an itemization of unsecured claims or creditors. Schedule F is normally the longest Schedule to complete. As with secured claims, it is always best to list the claims alphabetically and to include the last four digits of any account numbers. There are a couple of commonly occurring errors that require further description. A careful review of the fact pattern will reveal that Billy Mountain and Williams-Sonoma are not listed on the specific list of creditors in the memo although they appear in the memo. Oftentimes, when a debtor identifies a lawsuit or overdue rent, a debtor will inadvertently omit these debts from any list of creditors provided to the practitioner. However, these creditors are also unsecured creditors and should be included in Schedule F. Omitting these debts from a creditor's list is a frequent error, but one that can affect the debtor's discharge.[10]

The middle column should be completed to identify the year in which the debts were incurred or became past due. A one-word description such as "goods" or "services" will normally be sufficient to identify the consideration. This information has not been included in the fact memo for this example. It would have to be obtained before these Schedules can be completed.

Note also the identification of all debts as joint obligations of the Bottomlines. Finally, regarding the Williams-Sonoma debt, note that it is disclosed as disputed.

---

10. 11 U.S.C. §523(a)(3). See chapter 13 supra.

SCHEDULE G - EXECUTORY CONTRACTS AND UNEXPIRED LEASES

Describe all executory contracts of any nature and all unexpired leases of real or personal property. Include any timeshare interests. State nature of debtor's interest in contract, i.e., "Purchaser," "Agent," etc. State whether debtor is the lessor or lessee of a lease. Provide the names and complete mailing addresses of all other parties to each lease or contract described. If a minor child is a party to one of the leases or contracts, state the child's initials and the name and address of the child's parent or guardian, such as "A.B., a minor child, by John Doe, guardian." Do not disclose the child's name. See 11 U.S.C. § 112 and Fed. R. Bankr. P. 1007(m).

☐   Check this box if debtor has no executory contracts or unexpired leases.

NAME AND MAILING ADDRESS, INCLUDING ZIP CODE, OF OTHER PARTIES TO LEASE OR CONTRACT.	DESCRIPTION OF CONTRACT OR LEASE AND NATURE OF DEBTOR'S INTEREST. STATE WHETHER LEASE IS FOR NONRESIDENTIAL REAL PROPERTY. STATE CONTRACT NUMBER OF ANY GOVERNMENT CONTRACT.
BILLY MOUNTAIN	MONTH TO MONTH LEASE FOR RESIDENTIAL REAL PROPERTY LOCATED AT 1945 BILLY PILGRIM ROAD

Description

Any executory contract or unexpired lease is disclosed in Schedule G. Be specific enough in describing the asset so as to help enable the trustee to determine the effect of the contract or lease as an asset or liability of the estate.[11] Also note that the nondebtor party to the contract or lease is also a creditor who needs to be scheduled appropriately on Schedules D, E, or F supra.

SCHEDULE H - CODEBTORS

Provide the information requested concerning any person or entity, other than a spouse in a joint case, that is also liable on any debts listed by debtor in the schedules of creditors. Include all guarantors and co-signers. If the debtor resides or resided in a community property state, commonwealth, or territory (including Alaska, Arizona, California, Idaho, Louisiana, Nevada, New Mexico, Puerto Rico, Texas, Washington, or Wisconsin) within the eight year period immediately preceding the commencement of the case, identify the name of the debtor's spouse and of any former spouse who resides or resided with the debtor in the community property state, commonwealth, or territory. Include all names used by the nondebtor spouse during the eight years immediately preceding the commencement of this case. If a minor child is a codebtor or a creditor, state the child's initials and the name and address of the child's parent or guardian, such as "A.B., a minor child, by John Doe, guardian." Do not disclose the child's name. See 11 U.S.C. § 112 and Fed. Bankr. P. 1007(m).

☐   Check this box if debtor has no codebtors.

NAME AND ADDRESS OF CODEBTOR	NAME AND ADDRESS OF CREDITOR
MISSY BOTTOMLINE	UNIVERSITY OF RELATIVITY

Description

The existence of any codebtor of any debt is described in Schedule H. Note also that in Schedule F, supra, unsecured claims, the column denoting the existence of a codebtor has been checked.

---

11. See chapter 19 supra.

SCHEDULE I - CURRENT INCOME OF INDIVIDUAL DEBTOR(S)

The column labeled "Spouse" must be completed in all cases filed by joint debtors and by every married debtor, whether or not a joint petition is filed, unless the spouses are separated and a joint petition is not filed. Do not state the name of any minor child. The average monthly income calculated on this form may differ from the current monthly income calculated on Form 22A, 22B, or 22C.

Debtor's Marital Status: Married	DEPENDENTS OF DEBTOR AND SPOUSE	
	RELATIONSHIP(S): SON, DAUGHTER	AGE(S): 15, 19

Employment:	DEBTOR	SPOUSE
Occupation	SOFTWARE DESIGNER	ASSISTANT MANAGER
Name of Employer	HARRISON BERGERON, INC.	TEA JAMBOREE
How long employed	2 YEARS	3 MONTHS
Address of Employer	134 PU-CPU BLVD.	6996 KARMA DR.
	GARESVILLE CA	CAMMMILE CA

INCOME: (Estimate of average or projected monthly income at time case filed)		DEBTOR		SPOUSE	
1. Monthly gross wages, salary, and commissions (Prorate if not paid monthly.)		$	6,000.00	$	1,000.00
2. Estimated monthly overtime		$	0.00	$	0.00
3. SUBTOTAL		$	6,000.00	$	1,000.00
4. LESS PAYROLL DEDUCTIONS					
a. Payroll taxes and social security		$	1,500.00	$	250.00
b. Insurance		$	300.00	$	0.00
c. Union Dues		$	0.00	$	0.00
d. Other (Specify:_____)		$	0.00	$	0.00
5. SUBTOTAL OF PAYROLL DEDUCTIONS		$	1,800.00	$	250.00
6.. TOTAL NET MONTHLY TAKE HOME PAY		$	4,200.00	$	750.00
7. Regular income from operation of business or profession or farm (Attach detailed statement)		$	0.00	$	0.00
8. Income from real property		$	0.00	$	0.00
9. Interest and dividends		$	0.00	$	0.00
10. Alimony, maintenance or support payments payable to the debtor for the debtor's use or that of dependents listed above.		$	0.00	$	0.00
11. Social security or other government assistance (Specify) _____		$	0.00	$	0.00
12. Pension or retirement income		$	0.00	$	0.00
13. Other monthly income _____		$	0.00	$	0.00
(Specify) _____		$	0.00	$	0.00
14. SUBTOTAL OF LINES 7 THROUGH 13		$	0.00	$	0.00
15. AVERAGE MONTHLY INCOME (Add amounts shown on Lines 6 and 14)		$	4,200.00	$	750.00
16. COMBINED AVERAGE MONTHLY INCOME (Combine column totals from line 15)			$ 4,950.00		

(Report also on Summary of Schedules and, if applicable, on Statistical Summary of Certain Liabilities and Related Data)

17. Describe any increase or decrease in income reasonably anticipated to occur within the year following the filing of this document:

None

Description

Schedule I discloses the existence and number of the debtors' dependents and the debtors' monthly income. Although the fact pattern does not include reference to deductions made from either Bottomline paycheck, the sample Schedule I assumes that 25 percent of their pay is deducted for taxes and additional amounts from Ken's paycheck for family medical coverage. In actual practice, a practitioner will require the exact amounts since they will be relevant for performance of the means testing calculations in the next chapter. Additionally, the information regarding dependents will aid the creditors and trustee in determining the reasonableness of the expenses disclosed in Schedule J infra.

SCHEDULE J - CURRENT EXPENDITURES OF INDIVIDUAL DEBTOR(S)

Complete this schedule by estimating the average or projected monthly expenses of the debtor and the debtor's family at time case filed. Prorate any payments made biweekly, quarterly, semi-annually, or annually to show monthly rate. The average monthly expenses calculated on this form may differ from the deductions from income allowed on Form 22A or 22C.

☐ Check this box if a joint petition is filed and debtor's spouse maintains a separate household. Complete a separate schedule of expenditures labeled "Spouse."

1. Rent or home mortgage payment (include lot rented for mobile home)		$ 1,200.00
a. Are real estate taxes included? Yes _____ No ✓		
b. Is property insurance included? Yes _____ No ✓		
2. Utilities: a. Electricity and heating fuel		$ 175.00
b. Water and sewer		$ 0.00
c. Telephone		$ 150.00
d. Other CABLE TV		$ 75.00
3. Home maintenance (repairs and upkeep)		$ 0.00
4. Food		$ 600.00
5. Clothing		$ 100.00
6. Laundry and dry cleaning		$ 30.00
7. Medical and dental expenses		$ 0.00
8. Transportation (not including car payments)		$ 200.00
9. Recreation, clubs and entertainment, newspapers, magazines, etc.		$ 200.00
10. Charitable contributions		$ 0.00
11. Insurance (not deducted from wages or included in home mortgage payments)		
a. Homeowner's or renter's		$ 20.00
b. Life		$ 0.00
c. Health		$ 0.00
d. Auto		$ 150.00
e. Other		$ 0.00
12. Taxes (not deducted from wages or included in home mortgage payments)		
(Specify)_____		$ 1,750.00
13. Installment payments: (In chapter 11, 12, and 13 cases, do not list payments to be included in the plan)		
a. Auto		$ 350.00
b. Other _____		$ 0.00
c. Other _____		$ 0.00
14. Alimony, maintenance, and support paid to others		$ 0.00
15. Payments for support of additional dependents not living at your home		$ 0.00
16. Regular expenses from operation of business, profession, or farm (attach detailed statement)		$ 0.00
17. Other _____ NETWORK FEES		$ 42.00
18. AVERAGE MONTHLY EXPENSES (Total lines 1-17. Report also on Summary of Schedules and,		$ 5,042.00
if applicable, on the Statistical Summary of Certain Liabilities and Related Data)		

19. Describe any increase or decrease in expenditures reasonably anticipated to occur within the year following the filing of this document:
    None

20. STATEMENT OF MONTHLY NET INCOME

a. Average monthly income from Line 15 of Schedule (Includes spouse income of $750.00. See Schedule I)		$ 4,950.00
b. Average monthly expenses from Line 18 above		$ 5,042.00
c. Monthly net income (a. minus b.) (Net includes Debtor/Spouse combined Amounts)		$ -92.00

Description

The debtors' typical monthly expenses are disclosed in this Schedule. As in the other Schedules illustrated, only the data contained in the fact memo has been shown. Form 4.2 on the forms disk discloses additional categories. As with all other Schedules, it is helpful to enter zero for those categories in which the debtor incurs no monthly expense. In an individual Chapter 7, the information in Schedules I and J will help permit the trustee to determine whether or not an abuse of Chapter 7 exists pursuant to means testing (see chapter 5 supra).[12] Note that in the example, the Bottomlines appear to have substantial surplus monthly income. Even if they "pass" the means test, their case could still be subject to dismissal for abuse. Their practitioner will need to ascertain if they have additional monthly expenses. In a Chapter 13, the data will help determine the feasibility of a Chapter 13 plan.[13]

D.   STATEMENT OF FINANCIAL AFFAIRS

1. Income from employment or operation of business

None
☐

State the gross amount of income the debtor has received from employment, trade, or profession, or from operation of the debtor's business, including part-time activities either as an employee or in independent trade or business, from the beginning of this calendar year to the date this case was commenced. State also the gross amounts received during the **two years** immediately preceding this calendar year. (A debtor that maintains, or has maintained, financial records on the basis of a fiscal rather than a calendar year may report fiscal year income. Identify the beginning and ending dates of the debtor's fiscal year.) If a joint petition is filed, state income for each spouse separately. (Married debtors filing under chapter 12 or chapter 13 must state income of both spouses whether or not a joint petition is filed, unless the spouses are separated and a joint petition is not filed.)

AMOUNT		SOURCE
2010(db)	$72,000.00	(H) 2010 WAGES HARRISON BERGERON, INC
2009(db)	$72,000.00	(H) 2009 WAGES HARRISON BERGERSON, INC
2008(db)		
2010(jdb)	$3,000.00	TEA JAMBOREE; TOP O' THE MORNIN TEA CO.
2009(jdb)	0.00	TOP O' THE MORNIN TEA CO.

Description

This item discloses the debtors' income for each of the past two years from employment or trade. "Preceding years" is commonly understood to mean tax years. For instance, in 2011, income for calendar years 2010 and 2009 would be described.

---

12. See chapters 5 and 7 supra. See also Forms 5.2-5.7 on the forms disk.
13. See chapter 23 supra.

2.   Income other than from employment or operation of business

None
⊠

State the amount of income received by the debtor other than from employment, trade, profession, or operation of the debtor's business during the two years immediately preceding the commencement of this case. Give particulars. If a joint petition is filed, state income for each spouse separately. (Married debtors filing under chapter 12 or chapter 13 must state income for each spouse whether or not a joint petition is filed, unless the spouses are separated and a joint petition is not filed.)

AMOUNT   SOURCE

Description

Income earned from sources other than employment should be disclosed here. Interest or dividend income and spousal or child support would be disclosed here.

None
⊠

3. Payments to creditors

Complete a. or b., as appropriate, and c.

a. Individual or joint debtor(s) with primarily consumer debts: List all payments on loans, installment purchases of goods or services, and other debts to any creditor made within 90 days immediately preceding the commencement of this case unless the aggregate value of all property that constitutes or is affected by such transfer is less than $600. Indicate with an asterisk (*) any payments that were made to a creditor on account of a domestic support obligation or as part of an alternative repayment schedule under a plan by an approved nonprofit budgeting and creditor counseling agency. (Married debtors filing under chapter 12 or chapter 13 must include payments by either or both spouses whether or not a joint petition is filed, unless the spouses are separated and a joint petition is not filed.)

NAME AND ADDRESS OF CREDITOR	DATES OF PAYMENTS	AMOUNT PAID	AMOUNT STILL OWING

None
⊠

b. Debtor whose debts are not primarily consumer debts: List each payment or other transfer to any creditor made within 90 days immediately preceding the commencement of the case unless the aggregate value of all property that constitutes or is affected by such transfer is less than $5,850*. If the debtor is an individual, indicate with an asterisk (*)any payments that were made to a creditor on account of a domestic support obligation or as part of an alternativerepayment schedule under a plan by an approved nonprofit budgeting and credit counseling agency. (Married debtors filing under chapter 12 or chapter 13 must include payments and other transfers by either or both spouses whether or not a joint petition is filed, unless the spouses are separated and a joint petition is not filed.)

*Amount subject to adjustment on 4/01/13, and every three years thereafter with respect to cases commenced on or after date of adjustment.

NAME AND ADDRESS OF CREDITOR AND RELATIONSHIP TO DEBTOR	DATES OF PAYMENTS	AMOUNT PAID	AMOUNT STILL OWING

None
⊠

c. All debtors: List all payments made within one year immediately preceding the commencement of this case to or for the benefit of creditors who are or were insiders. (Married debtors filing under chapter 12 or chapter 13 must include payments by either or both spouses whether or not a joint petition is filed, unless the spouses are separated and a joint petition is not filed.)

NAME AND ADDRESS OF CREDITOR AND RELATIONSHIP TO DEBTOR	DATES OF PAYMENTS	AMOUNT PAID	AMOUNT STILL OWING

Description

This requires debtors to disclose loan repayments made during the 90 days prior to filing or, in the case of insiders, payments made during the past year. This inquiry reveals the potential existence of preferences or sometimes a fraudulent transfer. Recall that, in a consumer proceeding, up to $600 of preferences are essentially permitted, which is why the question is concerned with payments greater than $600. In the example there are no such transfers.[14] Hence, "None" has been checked. Remember, every question should be answered, even when the answer is "None."

---

4. Suits and administrative proceedings, executions, garnishments and attachments

None   a.   List all suits and administrative proceedings to which the debtor is or was a party within one year
☐   immediately preceding the filing of this bankruptcy case. (Married debtors filing under chapter 12 or chapter 13 must include information concerning either or both spouses whether or not a joint petition is filed, unless the spouses are separated and a joint petition is not filed.)

CAPTION OF SUIT AND CASE NUMBER	NATURE OF PROCEEDING	COURT OR AGENCY AND LOCATION	STATUS OR DISPOSITION
DR. LAVENTHOL VS BOTTOMLINE 07-10001	DEBT COLLECTION	COURT OF COM. PLEAS	JUDGEMENT FOR PLAINTIFF
SYMPHONIC SOUNDS VS. BOTTOMLINE	DEBT COLLECTION	COURT OF COM. PLEAS	JUDGEMENT FOR PLAINTIFF
WILLIAMS-SONOMA VS BOTTOMLINE	DEBT COLLECTION	COURT OF COM. PLEAS	JUDGEMENT FOR PLAINTIFF

None   b.   Describe all property that has been attached, garnished or seized under any legal or equitable process
☒   within one year immediately preceding the commencement of this case. (Married debtors filing under chapter 12 or chapter 13 must include information concerning property of either or both spouses whether or not a joint petition is filed, unless the spouses are separated and a joint petition is not filed.)

NAME AND ADDRESS OF PERSON FOR WHOSE BENEFIT PROPERTY WAS SEIZED	DATE OF SEIZURE	DESCRIPTION AND VALUE OF PROPERTY

Description

Item 4 requires disclosure of all legal actions involving the debtors that have occurred during the preceding year. Item 4a asks the debtor to disclose all lawsuits pending within one year prior to the bankruptcy filing in which the debtor is a party. In the example, all suits are included in 4a. When answering this inquiry, disclose the case number and the court

---

14. See chapters 16 and 17 supra.

where the litigation is or was pending. To this extent, the example here is incomplete.

Note that this question does not ask merely for those cases in which a debtor may be the defendant. All lawsuits that are pending in which the debtor is a *party* when a bankruptcy petition is filed must be disclosed. If the debtor is or has been a plaintiff in a lawsuit, this must also be included in the response. The suit will be an asset of the estate unless it can be exempted.[15]

Also remember that a plaintiff in any lawsuit pending against the debtor is also a creditor of the debtor. Often, lawsuits pending against a debtor will be described in the Statement of Affairs but the same information will not appear on the list of creditors included in the Schedules. Remember, when a creditor is suing a debtor, the creditor must be listed on the Schedules if the debtor is to successfully seek and obtain a discharge of the obligation sued upon.[16]

Item 4b asks for the disclosure of any property that has been seized by legal process within the four months prior to the bankruptcy filing. In this example there is no such activity. If, however, a judgment creditor has a wage garnishment or some other type of judgment execution outstanding on a debtor, this action would be described here.

---

5.   Repossessions, foreclosures and returns

None
☒

List all property that has been repossessed by a creditor, sold at a foreclosure sale, transferred through a deed in lieu of foreclosure or returned to the seller, within one year immediately preceding the commencement of this case. (Married debtors filing under chapter 12 or chapter 13 must include information concerning property of either or both spouses whether or not a joint petition is filed, unless the spouses are separated and a joint petition is not filed.)

NAME AND ADDRESS OF CREDITOR OR SELLER	DATE OF REPOSESSION, FORECLOSURE SALE, TRANSFER OR RETURN	DESCRIPTION AND VALUE OF PROPERTY

Description

Any voluntary or involuntary return of or repossession of secured collateral should be identified here. These transactions could be preferential or fraudulent.[17]

---

15. See chapter 14 supra.

16. 11 U.S.C. §523(a)(3). See chapter 13 supra.

17. See chapters 16 and 17 supra.

6. **Assignments and Receiverships**

None a.   Describe any assignment of property for the benefit of creditors made within 120 days immediately
☒   preceding the commencement of this case. (Married debtors filing under chapter 12 or chapter 13 must include
         any assignment by either or both spouses whether or not a joint petition is filed, unless the spouses are separated
         and a joint petition is not filed.)

NAME AND	DATE OF ASSIGNMENT	TERMS OF
ADDRESS		ASSIGNMENT
OF ASSIGNEE		OR SETTLEMENT

None b.   List all property which has been in the hands of a custodian, receiver, or court-appointed official within
☒   one year immediately preceding the commencement of this case. (Married debtors filing under chapter 12 or
         chapter 13 must include information concerning property of either or both spouses whether or not a joint petition
         is filed, unless the spouses are separated and a joint petition is not filed.)

NAME AND	NAME AND LOCATION	DATE OF	DESCRIPTION AND
ADDRESS	OF COURT CASE TITLE	ORDER	VALUE OF PROPERTY
OF CUSTODIAN	& NUMBER		

Description

Item 6a requires a debtor to identify the existence of any third-party custodian of estate property so the estate assets may be properly turned over
to the trustee or debtor-in-possession.[18] Item 6b requires the same disclosure if the debtor has effectuated an assignment for the benefit of
creditors.[19]

7. **Gifts**

None   List all gifts or charitable contributions made within one year immediately preceding the commencement of
☒   this case, except ordinary and usual gifts to family members aggregating less than $200 in value per individual
         family member and charitable contributions aggregating less than $100 per recipient. (Married debtors filing
         under chapter 12 or chapter 13 must include gifts or contributions by either or both spouses whether or not a
         joint petition is filed, unless the spouses are separated and a joint petition is not filed.)

NAME AND	RELATIONSHIP	DATE OF	DESCRIPTION AND
ADDRESS OF	TO DEBTOR, IF ANY	GIFT	VALUE OF GIFT
PERSON OR ORGANIZATION			

Description

This item discloses evidence that may lead to the discovery of fraudulent
transfers made by the giving of extraordinary gifts.[20] As noted, any extraordinary gifts or contributions should be disclosed. In the fact memo there

---

18. See chapter 14 supra.
19. See chapter 3 supra.
20. See chapter 17 supra.

do not appear to be any, but because the information is not specifically included in the memo, this item would have to be double-checked before the document is filed.

---

8. Losses

None ☒   List all losses from fire, theft, other casualty or gambling within one year immediately preceding the commencement of this case or since the commencement of this case. (Married debtors filing under chapter 12 or chapter 13 must include losses by either or both spouses whether or not a joint petition is filed, unless the spouses are separated and a joint petition is not filed.)

DESCRIPTION AND VALUE OF PROPERTY	DESCRIPTION OF CIRCUMSTANCES, AND, IF LOSS WAS COVERED IN WHOLE OR IN PART BY INSURANCE, GIVE PARTICULARS	DATE OF LOSS

Description

This item requires disclosure of any losses sustained by the debtors from fire, theft, or gambling during the year preceding the petition's filing. The reason for this disclosure is first to ascertain the existence of "calamity" losses, which might be a cause of the bankruptcy. Second, a fire or theft loss may involve an insurance claim. If unpaid when the bankruptcy proceeding is filed, the insurance claim may be an asset of the estate.[21] In the example, this data has not been provided. It should be ascertained and completed before filing. Every item must have a completed response. "Unknown" is not a responsive answer to an inquiry that calls for a "yes" or "no" answer. If there is a "yes" response, provide all pertinent data as shown in the responses to the other items.

---

9. Payments related to debt counseling or bankruptcy

None ☐   List all payments made or property transferred by or on behalf of the debtor to any persons, including attorneys, for consultation concerning debt consolidation, relief under the bankruptcy law or preparation of a petition in bankruptcy within one year immediately preceding the commencement of this case.

NAME AND ADDRESS OF PAYEE	DATE OF PAYMENT, NAME OF PAYOR IF OTHER THAN DEBTOR	AMOUNT OF MONEY OR DESCRIPTION AND VALUE OF PROPERTY
YOUR FIRM	2010	$2,000

Description

Item 9 requires disclosure of payments to attorneys over the past year for legal services pertaining to debt relief. The purpose of these disclosures is

---

21. See chapter 14 supra.

to help ensure that the attorneys working on the case do not receive excessive compensation or are not themselves the transferee of a fraudulent transfer.[22] The fee paid in connection with the bankruptcy must be disclosed here.

---

10. Other transfers

None   a.   List all other property, other than property transferred in the ordinary course of the business or financial
☐   affairs of the debtor, transferred either absolutely or as security within two years immediately preceding the
        commencement of this case. (Married debtors filing under chapter 12 or chapter 13 must include transfers by
        either or both spouses whether or not a joint petition is filed, unless the spouses are separated and a joint petition
        is not filed.)

NAME AND ADDRESS OF TRANSFEREE, RELATIONSHIP TO DEBTOR	DATE	DESCRIBE PROPERTY TRANSFERRED AND VALUE RECEIVED
OZZIE & HARRIET ODDBORN Relationship: NONE	6 MONTHS AGO	VACANT LOT IN SANTA CRUZ NO CONSIDERATION VALUE $10,000

        b. List all property transferred by the debtor within ten years immediately preceding the commencement of this
        case to a self-settled trust or similar device of which the debtor is a beneficiary.

None
☒

NAME OF TRUST OR OTHER DEVICE	DATE(S) OF TRANSFER(S)	AMOUNT OF MONEY OR DESCRIPTION AND VALUE OF PROPERTY OR DEBTOR'S INTEREST IN PROPERTY

Description

Any transfer of property must be disclosed here unless disclosed elsewhere in the form. This evidence may lead to the discovery of fraudulent transfers or preferences made by the granting of a security interest or other transfer of property.[23] All pertinent details, including purpose, identity of transferee, value, and the date of transfer should be concisely disclosed as shown in the example. A practitioner should obtain a copy of any closing statement so it may be made promptly available to a trustee upon the trustee's request. Item 10b will rarely arise in actual practice.

---

22. See chapters 7 and 17 supra.
23. See chapters 16 and 17 supra.

11.   Closed financial accounts

None
☒   List all financial accounts and instruments held in the name of the debtor or for the benefit of the debtor which were closed, sold, or otherwise transferred within one year immediately preceding the commencement of this case. Include checking, savings, or other financial accounts, certificates of deposit, or other instruments; shares and share accounts held in banks, credit unions, pension funds, cooperatives, associations, brokerage houses and other financial institutions. (Married debtors filing under chapter 12 or chapter 13 must include information concerning accounts or instruments held by either or both spouses whether or not a joint petition is filed, unless the spouses are separated and a joint petition is not filed.)

NAME AND ADDRESS OF INSTITUTION	TYPE OF ACCOUNT, LAST FOUR DIGITS OF ACCOUNT NUMBER, AND AMOUNT OF FINAL BALANCE	AMOUNT AND DATE OF SALE OR CLOSING

Description

This item requires disclosure of all bank accounts closed by the debtor in the year prior to the filing. For any account for which disclosure must be made, itemize the name of the bank, its address, the account number, the type of account (such as checking or savings), and identify the signatories.

12.   Safe deposit boxes

None
☒   List each safe deposit or other box or depository in which the debtor has or had securities, cash, or other valuables within one year immediately preceding the commencement of this case. (Married debtors filing under chapter 12 or chapter 13 must include boxes or depositories of either or both spouses whether or not a joint petition is filed, unless the spouses are separated and a joint petition is not filed.)

NAME AND ADDRESS OF BANK OR OTHER DEPOSITORY	NAMES AND ADDRESSES OF THOSE WITH ACCESS TO BOX OR DEPOSITORY	DESCRIPTION OF CONTENTS	DATE OF TRANSFER OR SURRENDER, IF ANY

Description

If the debtors have a safe-deposit box, disclose the requested data. Otherwise, check the box "None."

13.   Setoffs

None
☒   List all setoffs made by any creditor, including a bank, against a debt or deposit of the debtor within 90 days preceding the commencement of this case. (Married debtors filing under chapter 12 or chapter 13 must include information concerning either or both spouses whether or not a joint petition is filed, unless the spouses are separated and a joint petition is not filed.)

NAME AND ADDRESS OF CREDITOR	DATE OF SETOFF	AMOUNT OF SETOFF

Description

This item requires disclosure of setoffs made during the year preceding the bankruptcy. A setoff might constitute a preference.[24]

14.   Property held for another person

None

☒

List all property owned by another person that the debtor holds or controls.

NAME AND ADDRESS OF OWNER	DESCRIPTION AND VALUE OF PROPERTY	LOCATION OF PROPERTY

Description

This item simply requests disclosure of any assets held by the debtor on behalf of a third party. In this example there is no such activity.

15.   Prior address of debtor

None

☐

If the debtor has moved within the three years immediately preceding the commencement of this case, list all premises which the debtor occupied during that period and vacated prior to the commencement of this case. If a joint petition is filed, report also any separate address of either spouse.

ADDRESS	NAME USED	DATES OF OCCUPANCY
1945 BILLY PILGRIM ROAD TRALFAMADORE CA	SAME	2009 - 2010
45 COLDFISH LANE FROSTBITE FALLS MINNESOTA	SAME	2008

Description

Item 15 requires the debtor to list all residence addresses for the three years prior to the proceeding's filing. Any earlier addresses are irrelevant. It is always easiest to read the information by listing the most current residence first and proceeding backwards chronologically. It is not usually required to recall exact addresses. An approximate address will generally

---

24. See chapters 16 and 20 supra.

suffice if the exact information cannot be recalled. Many debtors may not be able to recall all of their exact street addresses. Finally, if joint debtors have different addresses for portions of the period, the response should distinguish which debtor lived at which address and for what period.

---

16. **Spouses and Former Spouses**

None

☒

If the debtor resides or resided in a community property state, commonwealth, or territory (including Alaska, Arizona, California, Idaho, Louisiana, Nevada, New Mexico, Puerto Rico, Texas, Washington, or Wisconsin) within eight years immediately preceding the commencement of the case, identify the name of the debtor's spouse and of any former spouse who resides or resided with the debtor in the community property state.

NAME

Description

Item 16 requires the debtor to disclose the identity of any existing or former spouse if the debtor has lived in a community property jurisdiction in the six years preceding filing of the bankruptcy. The affected states are delineated on the form. The reason for this disclosure is that a present or former spouse in a community property jurisdiction could have a joint interest in estate property affecting the trustee's rights. See chapters 15 and 18 supra.

17. Environmental Sites

For the purpose of this question, the following definitions apply:

"Environmental Law" means any federal, state, or local statute or regulation regulating pollution, contamination, releases of hazardous or toxic substances, wastes or material into the air, land, soil, surface water, groundwater, or other medium, including, but not limited to, statutes or regulations regulating the cleanup of these substances, wastes, or material.

> "Site" means any location, facility, or property as defined under any Environmental Law, whether or not presently or formerly owned or operated by the debtor, including, but not limited to, disposal sites.

> "Hazardous Material" means anything defined as a hazardous waste, hazardous substance, toxic substance, hazardous material, pollutant, or contaminant or similar term under an Environmental Law

None
☒
   a.   List the name and address of every site for which the debtor has received notice in writing by a governmental unit that it may be liable or potentially liable under or in violation of an Environmental Law. Indicate the governmental unit, the date of the notice, and, if known, the Environmental Law:

SITE NAME AND ADDRESS	NAME AND ADDRESS OF GOVERNMENTAL UNIT	DATE OF NOTICE	ENVIRONMENTAL LAW

   b.   List the name and address of every site for which the debtor provided notice to a governmental unit of a release of Hazardous Material. Indicate the governmental unit to which the notice was sent and the date of the notice.

None
☒

SITE NAME AND ADDRESS	NAME AND ADDRESS OF GOVERNMENTAL UNIT	DATE OF NOTICE	ENVIRONMENTAL LAW

   c.   List all judicial or administrative proceedings, including settlements or orders, under any Environmental Law with respect to which the debtor is or was a party. Indicate the name and address of the governmental unit that is or was a party to the proceeding, and the docket number.

None
☒

NAME AND ADDRESS OF GOVERNMENTAL UNIT	DOCKET NUMBER	STATUS OR DISPOSITION

Description

This item asks the debtor to disclose any environmental issues that may affect estate property. This question is required in all cases. The purpose of this question is to bring any environmental issues to the specific attention of the trustee and creditors.

18. Nature, location and name of business

None
☐
a. If the debtor is an individual, list the names, addresses, taxpayer identification numbers, nature of the businesses, and beginning and ending dates of all businesses in which the debtor was an officer, director, partner, or managing executive of a corporation, partnership, sole proprietorship, or was self-employed in a trade, profession, or other activity either full- or part-time within six years immediately preceding the commencement of this case, or in which the debtor owned 5 percent or more of the voting or equity securities within the six years immediately preceding the commencement of this case.

If the debtor is a partnership, list the names, addresses, taxpayer identification numbers, nature of the businesses, and beginning and ending dates of all businesses in which the debtor was a partner or owned 5 percent or more of the voting or equity securities, within the six years immediately preceding the commencement of this case.

If the debtor is a corporation, list the names, addresses, taxpayer identification numbers, nature of the businesses, and beginning and ending dates of all businesses in which the debtor was a partner or owned 5 percent or more of the voting or equity securities within the six years immediately preceding the commencement of this case.

NAME	LAST FOUR DIGITS OF SOCIAL-SECURITY OR OTHER INDIVIDUAL TAXPAYER-I.D. NO. (ITIN)/ COMPLETE EIN	ADDRESS	NATURE OF BUSINESS	BEGINNING AND ENDING DATES
TOP O' THE MORNIN IRISH TEA CO.	xxxx-xx-4651	CLOSED	CLOSED - SALES PARTNERSHIP WITH KILGORE TROUT	2009 - 2010

b. Identify any business listed in response to subdivision a., above, that is "single asset real estate" as defined in 11 U.S.C. § 101.

None
☒

NAME   ADDRESS

Description

This item asks a debtor to identify any business ventures in which the debtor has been involved in the two years prior to filing. Any affirmative response should include a brief description that will explain to the trustee and creditors all pertinent facts. The most pertinent facts are the name of the business, its length of operation, how its assets were disposed of (closure, sale, or otherwise), and whether the debtor's interest retains any value. Sometimes a debtor may have been involved in more than one business over the preceding two years. Each should be described in this manner. Thoroughness here will save time at the creditors' meeting.[25] The response in the example, although only two sentences in length, provides the most critical data that the trustee and creditors initially need to know. Part "b" of the question will not apply in a consumer Chapter 7 case.

---

25. See chapters 7 and 11 supra.

19. Books, record and financial statements

None
☒
a.   List all bookkeepers and accountants who within the two years immediately preceding the filing of this bankruptcy case kept or supervised the keeping of books of account and records of the debtor.

NAME AND ADDRESS   DATES SERVICES RENDERED

None
☒
b.   List all firms or individuals who within the two years immediately preceding the filing of this bankruptcy case have audited the books of account and records, or prepared a financial statement of the debtor.

NAME   ADDRESS   DATES SERVICES RENDERED

None
☐
c.   List all firms or individuals who at the time of the commencement of this case were in possession of the books of account and records of the debtor. If any of the books of account and records are not available, explain.

NAME   ADDRESS

KEN & BRETONY BOTTOMLINE   1945 BILLY PILGRIM ROAD
                                     TRALFAMADORE CA

None
☒
d.   List all financial institutions, creditors and other parties, including mercantile and trade agencies, to whom a financial statement was issued within the two years immediately preceding the commencement of this case by the debtor.

NAME AND ADDRESS   DATE
                                                         ISSUED

Description

Recall that under Section 727, a trustee may object to a debtor's discharge for failure to keep books and records commensurate with the debtor's affairs.[26] Item 17 discloses whether the possibility of such an objection may exist in the proceeding. Further, a trustee may request to examine any such records to investigate the existence of assets, including any avoidable transactions.[27] Never leave the response to any question unanswered or blank. When this happens, the trustee will invariably ask the same question at the meeting of creditors. This can be avoided by properly responding in the first place.

Items 19 through 25 are not used unless the debtor has been engaged in business. In the example, item 21 of the form will disclose the identity of partner Kilgore Trout. Items 22 and 23, by implication only, will suggest that the business has been terminated. See Form 4.3 on the forms disk.

---

26. See chapter 13 supra.
27. See chapters 10 and 15 supra.

Summary

It is important in learning the bankruptcy system to know how to effectively prepare and read the most important documents filed at the inception of any bankruptcy proceeding, the Statement of Financial Affairs and Schedules of Assets and Liabilities. These documents are commonly known as the Statements and Schedules. Effective preparation of these documents by the paralegal will expedite an estate's administration. Knowing how to read these documents effectively will permit a creditor's representative to ascertain the potential for a dividend to the creditor or a potential objection to the debtor's discharge.

In effectively preparing the Statements and Schedules, all questions should be answered even when the answer is a simple "no" or "none." All information required to be provided should be provided in as concise a form as possible. It is good practice to identify creditors' account numbers if applicable. Although this bit of information is not required, it will greatly ease the administration of an estate.

In effectively reading the Statements and Schedules, the paralegal should focus on identifying the existence and value of nonexempt assets to determine the potential for unsecured creditors to receive a dividend.

DISCUSSION QUESTIONS

1. What purposes do the Statements and Schedules serve?

2. What are the concerns of a debtor in effective preparation of the Statements and Schedules?

3. What are the concerns of a trustee or creditor in effective review of the Statements and Schedules?

30

Means Testing
Tutorial

A. INTRODUCTION

Official Form 22, in its various versions, has become as important in individual bankruptcy proceedings as the Statements and Schedules.[1] Officially known as the Statement of Current Monthly Income and Means-Test Calculation, colloquially the form has simply become known as the Means Testing Form. As with the Statements and Schedules, a practitioner's most important task is to properly prepare the data required to be included in the form. All commercial bankruptcy software has been programmed to complete the form from data entered by the practitioner. Even more than with the Statements and Schedules, performing this task well will make a debtor's trip through the bankruptcy system as smooth and uneventful as possible. Proper preparation will minimize or eliminate inquiries from the case trustee or the United States Trustee seeking to corroborate the information disclosed in the form. Most of this is accomplished simply by maintaining all the information in the file used to complete and perform the means testing calculations.

---

1. Official Form 22A is used in Chapter 7 cases, 22B in Chapter 11 cases, and 22C in Chapter 13 cases. See chapter 5 supra.

In a practice emphasizing bankruptcy law, a paralegal will spend a significant amount of time compiling and organizing data. If the case trustee or United States Trustee requests the data, it will be at your fingertips and you will be able to respond promptly.

When a debtor's current monthly income is below the applicable state median income, then it will generally only be necessary to maintain all evidence of income for the six calendar months preceding the filing, the data necessary to perform the current monthly income calculation. When a debtor's current monthly income exceeds the applicable state median income, and a debtor is required to complete the entire form, then all additional backup information should be maintained, including evidence of a debtor's house payment, car payment, and other secured debt. This is in addition to the information required to be supplied to the trustee or United States Trustee in any case (see chapter 3 supra). However, even in a below median income case, it is good practice to compile and maintain all of the data necessary to fully complete the form. Obtaining and maintaining the necessary data likely falls within counsel's duty of reasonable investigation as set forth in Section 707(b)(4) (see chapter 5 supra).

To maintain consistency, the Bottomlines remain our debtors and all of the facts presented in chapter 29 apply here. Any additional facts are noted in this chapter. The form analyzed is the Chapter 7 version of the form, Form 22A. Since approximately 70 percent of all filings are Chapter 7 cases, the Chapter 7 version is the form most frequently used in actual practice. Although a few line items change in the Chapter 11 and Chapter 13 versions of the form, the principles for preparation and all of the information contained in the Chapter 7 form are included in the other versions of the form. For all purposes, this tutorial uses the median family income figures and allowable deductions for National Standards, local housing allowances, and transportation allowances for the period commencing November 1, 2010.

B.   CURRENT MONTHLY INCOME

In re __KEN BOTTOMLINE & BRETONY BOTTOMLINE__

          Debtor(s)

Case Number: _____

        (If known)

According to the information required to be entered on this statement (check one box as directed in Part I, III, or VI of this statement):

☐ **The presumption arises.**

☑ **The presumption does not arise.**

☐ **The presumption is temporarily inapplicable.**

CHAPTER 7 STATEMENT OF CURRENT MONTHLY INCOME AND MEANS-TEST CALCULATION

In addition to Schedules I and J, this statement must be completed by every individual chapter 7 debtor, whether or not filing jointly. Unless the exclusion in Line 1C applies, joint debtors may complete a single statement. If the exclusion in Line 1C applies, each joint filer must complete a separate statement.

	Part I. EXCLUSION FOR DISABLED VETERANS AND NON-CONSUMER DEBTORS
1A	If you are a disabled veteran described in the Veteran's Declaration in this Part I, (1) check the box at the beginning of the Veteran's Declaration, (2) check the box for "The presumption does not arise" at the top of this statement, and (3) complete the verification in Part VIII. Do not complete any of the remaining parts of this statement. ☐ **Veteran's Declaration.** By checking this box, I declare under penalty of perjury that I am a disabled veteran (as defined in 38 U.S.C. § 3741(1)) whose indebtedness occurred primarily during a period in which I was on active duty (as defined in 11 U.S.C. § 101(d)(1)) or while I was performing a homeland defense activity (as defined in 32 U.S.C. §901(1)).
1B	If your debts are not primarily consumer debts, check the box below and complete the verification in Part VIII. Do not complete any of the remaining parts of this statement. ☐ **Declaration of non-consumer debts.** By checking this box, I declare that my debts are not primarily consumer debts.

1C	**Reservists and National Guard Members; active duty or homeland defense activity**. Members of a reserve component of the Armed Forces and members of the National Guard who were called to active duty (as defined in 10 U.S.C. § 101(d)(1)) after September 11, 2001, for a period of at least 90 days, or who have performed homeland defense activity (as defined in 32 U.S.C. § 901(1)) for a period of at least 90 days, are excluded from all forms of means testing during the time of active duty or homeland defense activity and for 540 days thereafter (the "exclusion period"). If you qualify for this temporary exclusion, (1) check the appropriate boxes and complete any required information in the Declaration of Reservists and National Guard Members below, (2) check the box for "The presumption is temporarily inapplicable" at the top of this statement, and (3) complete the verification in Part VIII. **During your exclusion period you are not required to complete the balance of this form, but you must complete the form no later than 14 days after the date on which your exclusion period ends, unless the time for filing a motion raising the means test presumption expires in your case before your exclusion period ends.**
	
	☐ **Declaration of Reservists and National Guard Members.** By checking this box and making the appropriate entries below, I declare that I am eligible for a temporary exclusion from means testing because, as a member of a reserve component of the Armed Forces or the National Guard
	
	       a. ☐ I was called to active duty after September 11, 2001, for a period of at least 90 days and
	              ☐ I remain on active duty /or/
	              ☐ I was released from active duty on _____, which is less than 540 days before
	       this bankruptcy case was filed;
	           OR
	       b. ☐ I am performing homeland defense activity for a period of at least 90 days /or/
	              ☐ I performed homeland defense activity for a period of at least 90 days, terminating on
	       _____, which is less than 540 days before this bankruptcy case was filed.

	Part II. CALCULATION OF MONTHLY INCOME FOR § 707(b)(7) EXCLUSION		
2	**Marital/filing status.** Check the box that applies and complete the balance of this part of this statement as directed. a. ☐ Unmarried. **Complete only Column A ("Debtor's Income") for Lines 3-11.** b. ☐ Married, not filing jointly, with declaration of separate households. By checking this box, debtor declares under penalty of perjury: "My spouse and I are legally separated under applicable non-bankruptcy law or my spouse and I are living apart other than for the purpose of evading the requirements of § 707(b)(2)(A) of the Bankruptcy Code." **Complete only Column A ("Debtor's Income") for Lines 3-11.** c. ☐ Married, not filing jointly, without the declaration of separate households set out in Line 2.b above. **Complete both Column A ("Debtor's Income") and Column B ("Spouse's Income") for Lines 3-11.** d. ☑ Married, filing jointly. **Complete both Column A ("Debtor's Income") and Column B ("Spouse's Income") for Lines 3-11.**			
	All figures must reflect average monthly income received from all sources, derived during the six calendar months prior to filing the bankruptcy case, ending on the last day of the month before the filing. If the amount of monthly income varied during the six months, you must divide the six-month total by six, and enter the result on the appropriate line.	**Column A** **Debtor's** **Income**	**Column B** **Spouse's** **Income**	
3	**Gross wages, salary, tips, bonuses, overtime, commissions.**	$ 6,000.00	$ 500.00

4	**Income from the operation of a business, profession or farm.** Subtract Line b from Line a and enter the difference in the appropriate column(s) of Line 4. If you operate more than one business, profession or farm, enter aggregate numbers and provide details on an attachment. Do not enter a number less than zero. **Do not include any part of the business expenses entered on Line b as a deduction in Part V.**				
	a.	Gross receipts	$ 0.00		
	b.	Ordinary and necessary business expenses	$ 0.00		
	c.	Business income	Subtract Line b from Line a	$ 0.00	$ 0.00
5	**Rent and other real property income.** Subtract Line b from Line a and enter the difference in the appropriate column(s) of Line 5. Do not enter a number less than zero. **Do not include any part of the operating expenses entered on Line b as a deduction in Part V.**				
	a.	Gross receipts	$ 0.00		
	b.	Ordinary and necessary operating expenses	$ 0.00		
	c.	Rent and other real property income	Subtract Line b from Line a	$ 0.00	$ 0.00
6	**Interest, dividends and royalties.**			$ 0.00	$ 0.00
7	**Pension and retirement income.**			$ 0.00	$ 0.00
8	**Any amounts paid by another person or entity, on a regular basis, for the household expenses of the debtor or the debtor's dependents, including child support paid for that purpose.** Do not include alimony or separate maintenance payments or amounts paid by your spouse if Column B is completed.			$ 0.00	$ 0.00
9	**Unemployment compensation.** Enter the amount in the appropriate column(s) of Line 9. However, if you contend that unemployment compensation received by you or your spouse was a benefit under the Social Security Act, do not list the amount of such compensation in Column A or B, but instead state the amount in the space below: Unemployment compensation claimed to be a benefit under the Social Security Act Debtor $_____ 0.00 Spouse $_____ 0.00			$ 0.00	$ 0.00

10	**Income from all other sources.** Specify source and amount. If necessary, list additional sources on a separate page. **Do not include alimony or separate maintenance payments paid by your spouse if Column B is completed, but include all other payments of alimony or separate maintenance.** Do not include any benefits received under the Social Security Act or payments received as a victim of a war crime, crime against humanity, or as a victim of international or domestic terrorism.			
	a.	$ 0.00		
	b.	$ 0.00		
	Total and enter on Line 10		$ 0.00	$ 0.00
11	**Subtotal of Current Monthly Income for § 707(b)(7).** Add Lines 3 thru 10 in Column A, and, if Column B is completed, add Lines 3 through 10 in Column B. Enter the total(s).		$ 6,000.00	$ 500.00
12	**Total Current Monthly Income for § 707(b)(7).** If Column B has been completed, add Line 11, Column A to Line 11, Column B, and enter the total. If Column B has not been completed, enter the amount from Line 11, Column A.		$ 6,500.00	

Description

Part I of Form 22 identifies one of two applicable circumstances in which an individual debtor is excluded from means testing. If a debtor is disabled, and the indebtedness was incurred while on active duty, or if a debtor's debts are not primarily consumer debts, a debtor is not required to complete the form.[2]

Part II begins the debtor's calculation of current monthly income. Line 2 requires disclosure of the debtor's filing status. In the example, since the Bottomlines are married and filing jointly, box "d" is checked.

Line 3 requires disclosure of each joint debtor's average monthly income received from all sources in the six calendar months preceding the filing. For Ken, since he receives an annual salary and has been employed for the entire period, his average monthly pay is $6,000. However, if by reviewing all of his payment advices for the entire period, you discover that he received a bonus in one or more months, the amount of the bonus must also be factored into the calculation. This is why, among other things, it is necessary to obtain payment advices for the entire six-month period. As for Bretony, although she currently receives $1,000 per month, which is disclosed in her Schedule I (see chapter 21 supra), since she has only received the income for three months, her average monthly income over the six-month period is $500.

Lines 4 and 5 attempt to segregate gross and net income from the operation of a business or the management of income-producing real property income. If Top O' the Mornin' had been operating within six months of the Bottomline filing, then Bretony would have to complete Line 4.

---

2. 11 U.S.C. §707(b). See chapter 5 supra.

Lines 6 and 7 require disclosure of the described types of income and is self-explanatory.

Line 8 applies when a third party other than the debtor regularly contributes to the household expenses.[3] This includes monthly stipends paid by a parent, the pay earned by either child if the pay is contributed to pay household expenses, or if child support received is contributed toward household expenses, and any contributions made by any family member who is not a debtor toward the payment of household expenses. See chapter 5 supra.

Line 9 applies when either debtor has received unemployment compensation during the relevant period. There does not appear to be any in the example, but it would be prudent to inquire of Bretony as to whether she received any unemployment after the demise of Top O' the Mornin' and if so how much and for what periods. Although it is unlikely, it is prudent to ask.

Line 10 is self-explanatory. Note, however, that payments and benefits received under the Social Security Act are not included as income for purposes of determining current monthly income because receipt of such payments is excluded by the terms of the statute.[4]

Line 11 discloses the totals of lines 3 through 10 for each debtor. Line 12 aggregates the amounts. The Bottomlines' combined current monthly income is $6,500.

	Part III. APPLICATION OF § 707(b)(7) EXCLUSION	
13	**Annualized Current Monthly Income for § 707(b)(7).** Multiply the amount from Line 12 by the number 12 and enter the result.	$ 78,000.00
14	**Applicable median family income.** Enter the median family income for the applicable state and household size. (This information is available by family size at www.usdoj.gov/ust/ or from the clerk of the bankruptcy court.) a. Enter debtor's state of residence: <u>California</u> b. Enter debtor's household size: <u> 4 </u>	$ 77,596.00
15	**Application of Section 707(b)(7).** Check the applicable box and proceed as directed. ☐ **The amount on Line 13 is less than or equal to the amount on Line 14.** Check the "The presumption does not arise" box at the top of page 1 of this statement, and complete Part VIII; do not complete Parts IV, V, VI or VII. ☑ **The amount on Line 13 is more than the amount on Line 14.** Complete the remaining parts of this statement.	

---

3. 11 U.S.C. §101(10A). See chapters 5 and 6 supra.
4. Ibid.

Description

Part III compares the debtors' current monthly income to the median income of a family of similar size in the applicable state to determine whether or not the debtor needs to complete the entirety of Form 22.

Line 13 multiplies the result in Line 12 by 12. The result appears on the form.

Line 14 discloses the applicable state, the household size, and the median income figure in effect at the time of filing. In California, for the period commencing November 1, 2010, the median family income of a family of four is $77,596, the figure that appears in the form.

Line 15 reports the result from comparing the applicable median income to the debtors' annual income. If the debtors' annual income is equal to or less than the applicable median, then abuse is not presumed and the debtors need not complete the remainder of the form. If the debtors' annual income exceeds the applicable median income, then the debtors must complete the remainder of the form. In the example, the Bottomlines must complete the form as their income of $78,000 exceeds the applicable median income of $77,596.[5]

Complete Parts IV, V, VI and VII of this statement only if required. (See Line 15).

	Part IV. CALCULATION OF CURRENT MONTHLY INCOME FOR § 707(b)(2)	
16	**Enter the amount from Line 12.**	$ 6,500.00
17	**Marital adjustment.** If you checked the box at Line 2.c, enter on Line 17 the total of any income listed in Line 11, Column B that was NOT paid on a regular basis for the household expenses of the debtor or the debtor's dependents. Specify in the lines below the basis for excluding the Column B income (such as payment of the spouse's tax liability or the spouse's support of persons other than the debtor or the debtor's dependents) and the amount of income devoted to each purpose. If necessary, list additional adjustments on a separate page. If you did not check box at Line 2.c, enter zero.	
	a. $	
	b. $	
	c. $	
	Total and enter on Line 17.	$ 0.00
18	**Current monthly income for § 707(b)(2).** Subtract Line 17 from Line 16 and enter the result.	$ 6,500.00

---

5. 11 U.S.C. §707(b)(7). See chapter 5 supra.

Description

Lines 16 through 18 are used when only one spouse files a bankruptcy case. Income not regularly used to pay the household expenses of the debtor are deducted from income. For example, if Bretony is the only debtor and Ken pays child support to a former spouse on behalf of children that do not live with Ken and Bretony, the amount paid by Ken for child support would be deducted from income in Bretony's Form 22A. When there is no spouse, or when the filing is joint, as it is here, the amount inserted in Line 17 is zero.

C. DEDUCTIONS — INTERNAL REVENUE EXPENSE STANDARDS

The first group of deductions that debtors may claim from current monthly income are calculated according to Internal Revenue Service collection guidelines, excluding payments for debts. Some of these standards are national, and some are local. There are national standards for day-to-day expenses, local expenses for housing and utilities, local expenses for transportation ownership and operation, and other necessary expenses.[6] The allowable amounts are published on a regular basis. Currently applicable amounts may be found on the United States Trustee Program website: http://www.usdoj.gov/ust. Links may also be found on many local bankruptcy court websites. The forms disk includes links.

---

6. 11 U.S.C. §707(b)(2)(A)(ii)(I).

Part V. CALCULATION OF DEDUCTIONS FROM INCOME		
Subpart A: Deductions under Standards of the Internal Revenue Service (IRS)		

19A	**National Standards: food, clothing and items.** Enter in Line 19A the "Total" amount from IRS National Standards for Food, Clothing and Other Items for the applicable household size. (This information is available at www.usdoj.gov/ust/ or from the clerk of the bankruptcy court.)	$ 1,371.00

| 19B | **National Standards: health care.** Enter in Line a1 below the amount from IRS National Standards for Out-of-Pocket Health Care for persons under 65 years of age, and in Line a2 the IRS National Standards for persons 65 years of age or older. (This information is available at www.usdoj.gov/ust/ or from the clerk of the bankruptcy court.) Enter in Line b1 the number of members of your household who are under 65 years of age, and enter in Line b2 the number of members of your household who are 65 years or older. (The total number of household members must be the same as the number stated in Line 14b). Multiply line a1 by Line b1 to obtain a total amount for household members under 65, and enter the result in Line c1. Multiply Line a2 by Line b2 to obtain a total amount for household members 65 and older, and enter the result in Line c2. Add Lines c1 and c2 to obtain a total health care amount, and enter the result in Line 19B. | | |

	Household members under 65 years of age		**Household members 65 years of age or older**		
a1.	Allowance per member	60.00	a2.	Allowance per member	144.00
b1.	Number of members	4	b2.	Number of members	0
c1.	Subtotal	240.00	c2.	Subtotal	0.00

$ 240.00

20A	**Local Standards: housing and utilities; non-mortgage expenses.** Enter the amount of the IRS Housing and Utilities Standards; non-mortgage expenses for the applicable county and household size. (This information is available at www.usdoj.gov/ust/ or from the clerk of the bankruptcy court.)	$ 627.00

20B	**Local Standards: housing and utilities; mortgage/rent expense.** Enter, in Line a below, the amount of the IRS Housing and Utilities Standards; mortgage/rent expense for your county and household size (this information is available at www.usdoj.gov/ust/ or from the clerk of the bankruptcy court); enter on Line b the total of the Average Monthly Payments for any debts secured by your home, as stated in Line 42; subtract Line b from Line a and enter the result in Line 20B. **Do not enter an amount less than zero.** SAN DIEGO COUNTY		

a.	IRS Housing and Utilities Standards; mortgage/rental expense	$ 1,942.00
b.	Average Monthly Payment for any debts secured by your home, if any, as stated in Line 42	$ 0.00
c.	Net mortgage/rental expense	Subtract Line b from Line a

$ 1,942.00

21	**Local Standards: housing and utilities; adjustment.** If you contend that the process set out in Lines 20A and 20B does not accurately compute the allowance to which you are entitled under the IRS Housing and Utilities Standards, enter any additional amount to which you contend you are entitled, and state the basis for your contention in the space below:	$ 0.00

Description

Line 19A inserts the allowable amount of expenses under National Standards for food, clothing, household supplies, personal care, and miscellaneous. For a family of four as of November 1, 2010, the amount is $1,371.

Line 20A is the applicable nonmortgage expense deduction for housing. As of November 1, 2010, the allowable amount of deduction in San Diego County for a family of four is $627. Nonmortgage expenses considered in this category include utility expenses.

Line 20B is the applicable mortgage or rental expense deduction. As of November 1, 2010, the allowable amount of deduction in San Diego County for a family of four is $1,942. Because the Bottomlines rent, they do not need to complete the insert in Line 20B. If they had owned a home, the mortgage payment would be deducted from the allowance, because the amount may only be accounted for once. See chapter 5 supra. Note also, that the aggregate amount of housing deductions ($2,569) is significantly more than their actual monthly rent of $1,200, and their actual utility expenses disclosed in Schedule J in the amount of $175. Nonetheless, they are entitled to the entire allowable IRS deduction. For example, at least one court has held that military personnel living on base and having no actual housing expenses may still claim the housing deductions because this is what the statute permits.[7]

In Line 21, the debtors could disclose additional extraordinary housing or utility expenses. Any such additional expenses must be backed up by appropriate documentation, such as copies of utility bills.

22A	**Local Standards: transportation; vehicle operation/public transportation expense.** You are entitled to an expense allowance in this category regardless of whether you pay the expenses of operating a vehicle and regardless of whether you use public transportation. Check the number of vehicles for which you pay the operating expenses or for which the operating expenses are included as a contribution to your household expenses in Line 8. ☐ 0 ☑ 1 ☐ 2 or more. SAN DIEGO If you checked 0, enter on Line 22A the "Public Transportation" amount from IRS Local Standards: Transportation. If you checked 1 or 2 or more, enter on Line 22A the "Operating Costs" amount from IRS Local Standards: Transportation for the applicable number of vehicles in the applicable Metropolitan Statistical Area or Census Region. (These amounts are available at www.usdoj.gov/ust/ or from the clerk of the bankruptcy court.)	$ 274.00
22B	**Local Standards: transportation; additional public transportation expense.** If you pay the operating expenses for a vehicle and also use public transportation, and you contend that you are entitled to an additional deduction for your public transportation expenses, enter on Line 22B the "Public Transportation" amount from IRS Local Standards: Transportation. (This amount is available at www.usdoj.gov/ust/ or from the clerk of the bankruptcy court.)	$ 0.00

23	**Local Standards: transportation ownership/lease expense; Vehicle 1.** Check the number of vehicles for which you claim an ownership/lease expense. (You may not claim an ownership/lease expense for more than two vehicles.) ☑ 1 ☐ 2 or more. Enter, in Line a below, the "Ownership Costs" for "One Car" from the IRS Transportation Standards: Transportation (available at www.usdoj.gov/ust/ or from the clerk of the bankruptcy court); enter in Line b the total of the Average Monthly Payments for any debts secured by Vehicle 1, as stated in Line 42; subtract Line b from Line a and enter the result in Line 23. **Do not enter an amount less than zero.**			
	a.	IRS Transportation Standards, Ownership Costs	$ 496.00	
	b.	Average Monthly Payment for any debts secured by Vehicle 1, as stated in Line 42	$ 175.00	
	c.	Net ownership/lease expense for Vehicle 1	Subtract Line b from Line a.	$ 321.00

24	**Local Standards: transportation ownership/lease expense; Vehicle 2.** Complete this Line only if you checked the "2 or more" Box in Line 23. Enter, in Line a below, the "Ownership Costs" for "One Car" from the IRS Local Standards: Transportation (available at www.usdoj.gov/ust/ or from the clerk of the bankruptcy court); enter in Line b the total of that Average Monthly Payments for any debts secured by Vehicle 2, as stated in Line 42; subtract Line b from Line a and enter the result in Line 24. **Do not enter an amount less than zero.**			
	a.	IRS Transportation Standards, Ownership Costs	$ 496.00	
	b.	Average Monthly Payment for any debts secured by Vehicle 2, as stated in Line 42	$ 0.00	
	c.	Net ownership/lease expense for Vehicle 2	Subtract Line b from Line a.	$ 0.00

7. In re Farrar-Johnson, 353 B.R. 224 (Bankr. N.D. Ill. 2006).

Description

Line 22 permits every debtor to claim deductions for the costs of transportation or operation of a vehicle. As of November 1, 2010, the allowable operating expense deduction in San Diego County for a family with one vehicle is $274.

Line 22A allows a deduction for using public transportation if a debtor does not own a motor vehicle or if a debtor regularly uses public transportation. For example, a commuter riding the San Diego Trolley to and from work in the Southern District of California might claim a public transportation deduction.

Line 23 deducts the allowable expense for ownership of a vehicle, reduced by the average monthly payment on any debt, since the deduction is limited to the greater of the applicable deduction or the monthly payment, but not both, since to do so would count the same expense twice. See chapter 5 supra. The Bottomlines own one vehicle. The monthly payment appearing is the monthly payment as calculated by Line 42, infra. The practitioner should keep in the file a copy of the contract or a copy of a payment ticket or similar document that evidences the amount of monthly payments and the remaining payments under the contract. This will show how the average monthly debt payment was calculated. The same documentation should be maintained for any secured debt.

A more controversial issue is whether a debtor may claim a vehicle ownership deduction when a debtor owns a car free and clear. This is a very controversial issue in the case law. A majority of courts analyzing the issue permit the deduction only when the debtor is actually making car payments.[8]

---

8. In re Wilson, 383 B.R. 729 (8th Cir. B.A.P. 2008) is illustrative.

25	**Other Necessary Expenses: taxes.** Enter the total average monthly expense that you actually incur for all federal, state and local taxes, other than real estate and sales taxes, such as income taxes, self employment taxes, social security taxes, and Medicare taxes. **Do not include real estate or sales taxes.**	$ 1,750.00
26	**Other Necessary Expenses: involuntary deductions for employment.** Enter the total average monthly payroll deductions that are required for your employment, such as retirement contributions, union dues, and uniform costs. **Do not include discretionary amounts, such as voluntary 401(k) contributions.**	$ 0.00
27	**Other Necessary Expenses: life insurance.** Enter total average monthly premiums that you actually pay for term life insurance for yourself. **Do not include premiums on your dependents, for whole life or for any other form of insurance.**	$ 0.00
28	**Other Necessary Expenses: court-ordered payments.** Enter the total monthly amount that you are required to pay pursuant to court order or administrative agency, such as spousal or child support payments. **Do not include payments on past due obligations included in Line 44.**	$ 0.00
29	**Other Necessary Expenses: education for employment or for a physically or mentally challenged child.** Enter the total average monthly amount that you actually expend for education that is a condition of employment and for education that is required for a physically or mentally challenged dependent child for whom no public education providing similar services is available.	$ 0.00
30	**Other Necessary Expenses: childcare.** Enter the total average monthly amount that you actually expend on childcare—such as baby-sitting, day care, nursery and preschool. **Do not include other educational payments.**	$ 0.00
31	**Other Necessary Expenses: health care.** Enter the total average monthly amount that you actually expend on health care that is required for the health and welfare of yourself or your dependents, that is not reimbursed by insurance or paid by a health savings account, and that is in excess of the amount entered in Lin 19B. **Do not include payments for health insurance or health savings accounts listed in Line 34.**	$ 0.00
32	**Other Necessary Expenses: telecommunication services.** Enter the total average monthly amount that you actually pay for telecommunication services other than your basic home telephone and cell phone service—such as pagers, call waiting, caller id, special long distance, or internet service—to the extent necessary for your health and welfare or that of your dependents. **Do not include any amount previously deducted.**	$ 192.00
33	**Total Expenses Allowed under IRS Standards.** Enter the total of Lines 19 through 32	$ 6,717.00

Description

The next portion of Part V of the Form permits a debtor to claim deductions based upon the IRS Collection Standards for "Other Necessary Expenses." See chapter 5 supra.

Line 25 permits deductions for taxes that are withheld from pay. The average monthly amount should be computed in the same manner as current monthly income supra. This information will normally be contained on the same payment advices that are used to compute current monthly income. The amount shown is the amount shown in Schedule I of chapter 21 supra.

Line 26 allows deduction for mandatory payroll deductions. Examples include mandatory uniform expenses, union dues, and mandatory 401(k) or similar payments. Voluntary 401(k) or similar contributions, however, are not deductible. The Bottomlines do not have any deductions on this line. Every line should be completed, even if the answer is zero.

Line 27 permits deduction for term life insurance premiums for the debtors only. Premiums paid for nondebtor family members are not deductible. The Bottomlines do not have any life insurance.

Line 28 allows current court-ordered payments to be deducted. The most typical examples are child and spousal support payments. The amount here is zero.

Line 29 deducts expenses for employment-required education. For example, a nurse taking a required course to maintain her license may deduct the cost of the course. The same line permits deductions for the education of a physically or mentally challenged child who cannot obtain similar services through public education. The Bottomlines have no such expenses.

Line 30 permits childcare expenses to be deducted. The Bottomlines have no such expense.

Line 31 deducts health care expenses that are not reimbursed by insurance or a health savings account, and are in excess of the health care expense allowances at line 19B supra. There are no such expenses here.

Line 32 allows for telephone, and Internet services other than basic telephone and cell phone service to be deducted to the extent the expense is necessary for the health and welfare of the debtor and the debtor's dependents. The amount shown is an aggregate of telephone and Internet expenses shown on Schedule J in chapter 21 supra.

Line 33 is the total of lines 19-32 as shown. Note that the amount is higher than the sum of the deductions from the Bottomlines' paychecks as shown in Schedule I of chapter 21 supra, and their actual monthly expenses shown in Schedule J of chapter 21 supra.

D.   DEDUCTIONS — ADDITIONAL EXPENSE DEDUCTIONS

Section 707(b)(2) permits some additional deductions that are not included within the IRS Collection Financial Standards. Subpart B of Part V of Form 22A captures these additional expenses.

	Subpart B: Additional Expense Deductions under § 707(b) Note: Do not include any expenses that you have listed in Lines 19-32.		
34	**Health Insurance, Disability Insurance and Health Savings Account Expenses.** List the monthly expenses in the categories set out in lines a-c below that are reasonably necessary for yourself, your spouse, or your dependents. a. Health Insurance — $ 200.00 b. Disability Insurance — $ 0.00 c. Health Savings Account — $ 0.00 Total and enter on Line 34. **If you do not actually expend this total amount,** state your actual average expenditures in the space below: $ _____ 0.00		$ 200.00
35	**Continued contributions to the care of household or family members.** Enter the total average actual monthly expenses that you will continue to pay for the reasonable and necessary care and support of an elderly, chronically ill, or disabled member of your household or member of your immediate family who is unable to pay for such expenses.		$ 0.00
36	**Protection against family violence.** Enter the total average reasonably necessary monthly expenses that you actually incurred to maintain the safety of your family under the Family Violence Prevention and Services Act or other applicable federal law. The nature of these expenses is required to be kept confidential by the court.		$ 0.00
37	**Home energy costs** Enter the total average monthly amount, in excess of the allowance specified by IRS Local Standards for Housing and Utilities that you actually expend for home energy costs. **You must provide your case trustee with documentation of your actual expenses, and you must demonstrate that the additional amount claimed is reasonable and necessary.**		$ 0.00
38	**Education expenses for dependent children less than 18.** Enter the total average monthly expenses that you actually incur, not to exceed $147.92* per child, for attendance at a private or public elementary or secondary school by your dependent children less than 18 years of age. **You must provide your case trustee with documentation of your actual expenses and you must explain why the amount claimed is reasonable and necessary and not already accounted for in the IRS Standards.**		$ 0.00
39	**Additional food and clothing expense.** Enter the total average monthly amount by which your food and clothing expenses exceed the combined allowances for food and clothing (apparel and services) in the IRS National Standards, not to exceed 5% of those combined allowances. (This information is available at www.usdoj.gov/ust/ or from the clerk of the bankruptcy court.) **You must demonstrate that the additional amount claimed is reasonable and necessary.**		$ 0.00
40	**Continued charitable contributions.** Enter the amount that you will continue to contribute in the form of cash or financial instruments to a charitable organization as defined in 26 U.S.C. § 170 (c)(1)-(2)		$ 0.00
41	**Total Additional Expense Deductions under § 707(b).** Enter the total of Lines 34 through 40.	$ 200.00	

Amount subject to adjustment on 4/1/2013, and every three years thereafter with respect to cases commenced on or after the date of adjustment.

Description

Line 34 permits deduction of expenses for health insurance, disability insurance, and health savings accounts paid for the debtor or a dependent of the debtor. See chapter 5C supra. Based upon the information provided, the Bottomlines have a $200 monthly health insurance expense.

Line 35 allows debtors to deduct monies paid to support an elderly, chronically ill, or disabled family member of the debtor's household or immediate family who is unable to pay for such expenses. The Bottomlines have no such expense.

Line 36 permits deductions for expenses paid in connection with protecting the debtor's family under the Family Violence Prevention and Services Act. This is a rare deduction. The Bottomlines have no such expense.

Line 37 permits an additional utility deduction for expenses in excess of the applicable IRS allowances, provided that documentation is provided to the case trustee and the documentation justifies the additional expense. The Bottomlines do not have such an expense. Remember, every line must be completed.

Line 38 allows deduction for education expenses for children under the age of 18, not to exceed $147.92 per month, or $1,775 per year. There are no such expenses present here.

Line 39 allows deduction of an amount equal to 5 percent of the national standards for food and clothing if the debtor can produce documentation evidencing the additional expense. There are no such facts presented by the Bottomlines. If there were, observe that the national allowances would permit an additional deduction of $50 based upon the amounts in effect as of November 1, 2010.

Line 40 allows deductions for continuing charitable contributions. If the debtors found religion only upon the filing of their case, the deduction is not permissible. There are no such deductions here.

Line 41 is the total of lines 34-40.

E.   DEDUCTIONS FOR DEBT PAYMENT

Subpart C: Deductions for Debt Payment					
42	**Future payments on secured claims.** For each of your debts that is secured by an interest in property that you own, list the name of creditor, identify the property securing the debt, and state the Average Monthly Payment, and check whether the payment includes taxes or insurance. The Average Monthly Payment is the total of all amounts contractually due to each Secured Creditor in the 60 months following the filing of the bankruptcy case, divided by 60. If necessary, list additional entries on a separate page. Enter the total Average Monthly payments on Line 42.				

		Name of Creditor	Property Securing the Debt	Average Monthly Payment	Does payment include taxes or insurance?	
	a.	Toyota Credit	2008 Moriah	$ 175.00	☐ yes ☑ no	
	b.			$ 0.00	☐ yes ☑ no	
	c.			$ 0.00	☐ yes ☑ no	
				Total: Add Line a, b and c		$ 175.00

| 43 | **Other payments on secured claims.** If any of the debts listed in Line 42 are secured by your primary residence, a motor vehicle, or other property necessary for your support or the support of your dependents, you may include in your deduction 1/60th of any amount (the "cure amount") that you must pay the creditor in addition to the payments listed in Line 42, in order to maintain possession of the property. The cure amount would include any sums in default that must be paid in order to avoid repossession or foreclosure. List and total any such amounts in the following chart. If necessary, list additional entries on a separate page. | | | | |

		Name of Creditor	Property Securing the Debt	1/60th of the Cure Amount	
	a.	Toyota Credit	2008 Moriah	$ 11.66	
	b.			$ 0.00	
	c.			$ 0.00	
					$ 11.66

44	**Payments on prepetition priority claims.** Enter the total amount, divided by 60, of all priority claims, such as priority tax, child support and alimony claims, for which you were liable at the time of your bankruptcy filing. **Do not include current obligations, such as those set out in Line 28.**	$ 83.33

45	**Chapter 13 administrative expenses.** If you are eligible to file a case under Chapter 13, complete the following chart, multiply the amount in line a by the amount in line b, and enter the resulting administrative expense.		
	a.	Projected average monthly Chapter 13 plan payment.	$ 0.00
	b.	Current multiplier for your district as determined under schedules issued by the Executive Office for United States Trustees. (This information is available at www.usdoj.gov/ust/ or from the clerk of the bankruptcy court.)	x 9.2 %
	c.	Average monthly administrative expense of Chapter 13 case	Total: Multiply Lines a and b $ 0.00

46	**Total Deductions for Debt Payment.** Enter the total of Lines 42 through 45.	$ 269.99

Subpart D: Total Deductions from Income	
47	**Total of all deductions allowed under § 707(b)(2).** Enter the total of Lines 33, 41, and 46.	$ 7,186.99

Description

This portion of the form accounts for a debtor's repayment of secured debt that is contractually due, arrears on secured debt obligations, the payment of priority claims, and the hypothetical payment to a Chapter 13 trustee. The first three are formulaic as set forth in 11 U.S.C. §707(b)(2)(A)(iii). The last is set forth at 11 U.S.C. §707(b)(2)(A)(ii)(III). See chapters 5, 16, and 17 supra.

All of these obligations would have to be paid if the case were a Chapter 13 case. See chapter 17 supra.

Line 42 identifies each secured creditor, the creditor's collateral, and the average payment for the next 60 months. A copy of the debtor's vehicle finance contract, or a payment ticket for a monthly payment should provide the amount of monthly payment and the number of payments remaining. The Bottomlines' monthly payment is $350. There are 30 payments left and they are two payments behind. For line 30, multiply $350 by the remaining 30 payments. The result of $10,500 is divided by 60. The amount of $175 is placed at line 42a. Observe that this is the same amount deducted from the vehicle ownership expense at line 23. This is necessary to avoid duplicating the expense. See chapter 5D supra.

Note that no information has been provided about the payments to El Repo Finance Company. The practitioner would need to obtain the appropriate information to claim this deduction.

Line 43 deducts payments necessary to cure secured debt payments that are in arrears pursuant to an identical formula. Take the amount of the arrears and divide by 60. The answer is placed at line 43a as to Toyota Credit. Observe that the debtors are only permitted to deduct cure payments on secured debt reasonably necessary for the support of the debtor. For example, if the Bottomlines owned a personal watercraft and were behind on the payments, the cure amounts may not be a permissible expense.

Line 44 permits deductions for the repayment of priority debt. See chapter 16 supra. The Bottomlines owe $5,000 in taxes for 2009. This amount is divided by 60 and the answer is placed on line 44. If there were other priority claims, they would be totaled up and the total would be divided by 60.

Line 45 computes a hypothetical monthly payment to a Chapter 13 trustee for a hypothetical five-year Chapter 13 plan. The administrative multiplier for each district is found on the United States Trustee website: http://www.usdoj.gov/ust. The administrative multiplier for the Southern District of California as of November 1, 2010, is 9.2 percent. To make this calculation, however, requires completion of Part VI of Form 22A. See below.

Line 46 totals up lines 42 through 45.

Line 47 is the grand total of the debtor's allowable deductions.

F.   DETERMINING WHETHER THE PRESUMPTION ARISES

Part VI. DETERMINATION OF § 707(b)(2) PRESUMPTION		
48	Enter the amount from Line 18 (Current monthly income for § 707(b)(2))	$ 6,500.00
49	Enter the amount from Line 47 (Total of all deductions allowed under § 707(b)(2))	$ 7,186.99
50	**Monthly disposable income under § 707(b)(2).** Subtract Line 49 from Line 48 and enter the result.	$ -686.99
51	**60-month disposable income under § 707(b)(2).** Multiply the amount in Line 50 by the number 60 and enter the result.	$ -41,219.40
52	**Initial presumption determination.** Check the applicable box and proceed as directed. ☑ **The amount on Line 51 is less than $7,075*.** Check the box for "The presumption does not arise" at the top of page 1 of this statement, and complete the verification in Part VIII. Do not complete the remainder of Part VI. ☐ **The amount set forth on Line 51 is more than $11,725*.** Check the "Presumption arises" box at the top of page 1 of this statement, and complete the verification in Part VIII. You may also complete Part VII. Do not complete the remainder of Part VI. ☐ **The amount on Line 51 is at least $7,025*, but not more than $11,725*.** Complete the remainder of Part VI (Lines 53 through 55).	
53	Enter the amount of your total non-priority unsecured debt	$ N.A.
54	**Threshold debt payment amount.** Multiply the amount in Line 53 by the number 0.25 and enter the result.	$ N.A.
55	**Secondary presumption determination.** Check the applicable box and proceed as directed. ☐ **The amount on Line 51 is less than the amount on Line 54.** Check the box for "The presumption does not arise" at the top of page 1 of this statement, and complete the verification in Part VIII. ☐ **The amount on Line 51 is equal to or greater than the amount on Line 54.** Check the box for "The presumption arises" at the top of page 1 of this statement, and complete the verification in Part VIII. You may also complete Part VII.	

Amounts are subject to adjustment on 4/1/2013, and every three years thereafter with respect to cases commenced on or after the date of adjustment.

Part VI of Form 22A provides the final calculations that determine whether or not a debtor's case is or is not abuse presumed.

Line 48 is the current monthly income amount from line 18. Line 49 is the total of all deductions that appears on line 47. Line 50 is the result of subtracting line 49 from line 48, which for the Bottomlines is a negative amount. When the amount is negative or zero, insert 0 or the negative number in line 50. Multiply the amount in line 50 times 60 to determine how much the debtor can pay over 60 months. When the amount is negative or zero, insert 0 or the negative number in line 51.

To complete line 45, the hypothetical payment to a Chapter 13 trustee, use the amount appearing in line 50 multiplied by the administrative expense multiplier. For the Bottomlines, the amount will be zero.

Line 52 reports the results in terms of the statutory means testing formula. If the amount on line 51 is less than $7,025, then abuse is not presumed. This is the result for the Bottomlines. If the result is greater than $11,725, then abuse is presumed regardless of the percentage of debt that the Bottomlines can repay.

If the result on line 51 is at least $7,025 but less than $11,725, then abuse is presumed only if the percentage that would be repaid to unsecured creditors is at least 25 percent. This calculation is performed on lines 53 through 55. The Bottomlines' total unsecured debt, for example, is $45,900. Twenty-five percent of this amount is $11,475, an amount that triggers the presumption of abuse without regard to the percentage of debt repaid. Assume, however, that the Bottomlines' unsecured debt was only $30,000. Twenty-five percent of this amount is $7,500. If the formula determines that they can pay at least $125 per month, then abuse would be presumed.

Part VII: ADDITIONAL EXPENSE CLAIMS

56 **Other Expenses.** List and describe any monthly expenses, not otherwise stated in this form, that are required for the health and welfare of you and your family and that you contend should be an additional deduction from your current monthly income under § 707(b)(2)(A)(ii)(I). If necessary, list additional sources on a separate page. All figures should reflect your average monthly expense for each item. Total the expenses.

	Expense Description	Monthly Amount
a.		$ 0.00
b.		$ 0.00
c.		$ 0.00
	Total: Add Lines a, b and c	0.00

Part VIII: VERIFICATION

57 I declare under penalty of perjury that the information provided in this statement is true and correct. *(If this a joint case, both debtors must sign.)*

Date: 11/30/2010 Signature: /s/ KEN BOTTOMLINE
(Debtor)

Date: 11/30/2010 Signature: /s/ BRETONY BOTTOMLINE
(Joint Debtor, if any)

Part VII of Form 22A provides the opportunity for a debtor to assert additional expense claims that are required for the health and welfare of the debtor or the debtor's family. For example, joint debtors are forced for reasons beyond their control to maintain two households for employment purposes. The additional expenses may be allowable here.[9]

Observe that the Bottomlines' Form 22A results in no abuse presumed because they cannot repay their creditors pursuant to the formula. However, also observe that the result of subtracting their Schedule J expenses from their income shows surplus monthly income of $1,258 (see chapter 21 supra). "Passing" the means test only means that abuse is not presumed. The significant amount of actual surplus monthly income appearing on Schedule J renders the Bottomlines susceptible to a motion for abuse based on the totality of circumstances pursuant to 11 U.S.C. §707(b)(3). See chapter 5E supra.

9. In re Graham, 363 B.R. 844 (Bankr. S.D. Ohio 2007).

Summary

Since its introduction in late 2005, Form 22A has become ubiquitous in individual bankruptcy cases. Its proper preparation is as germane to the case as is proper preparation of the Statements and Schedules. As with the Statements and Schedules, proper preparation will minimize inquiries from the case trustee or United States Trustee and will help make a debtor's journey through the bankruptcy system as uneventful as possible.

Remembering that means testing is, ultimately, nothing more than a formula will help to keep the form and the disclosures it calls for in perspective.

Just as with the Statements and Schedules, every line on Form 22A must be completed, or the blank will result in additional questioning at the meeting of creditors and might require the filing of an amended form. Doing it right the first time will save work in the long run.

A paralegal will also want to make sure that there is sufficient detail in the file to corroborate the debtor's current monthly income, debts, and assets. Copies of the debtor's most recent pay stubs, for example, should be in the file. A copy of a bill from each creditor, including payoff amounts to secured creditors, and/or a copy of a current credit report should be obtained from the debtor. Copies of all relevant tax returns that a trustee may request should also be obtained. All the debtor's payment advices for the six months preceding the filing should also be maintained. On this last point, when the debtor's current monthly income exceeds the applicable median, the debtor will almost always be required to submit payment advices for the entire six-month period to the United States Trustee.

DISCUSSION QUESTIONS

1. What are the concerns of a debtor in effective preparation of Form 22?

2. What are the concerns of a trustee or creditor in effective review of Form 22?

31

Researching Bankruptcy Issues

A. TRADITIONAL METHODS

It is impossible for any member of the legal profession to know all of the law: There is simply too much law to know. As a result, the ability to conduct efficient, accurate, and speedy research is a fundamental skill for anyone involved in the legal profession. Knowing where to look for the answer to a question is a paramount concern. No study of the bankruptcy system can be complete without providing a useful method for researching bankruptcy issues. Fortunately, because the Bankruptcy Code is designed to be a self-contained system, an effective methodology for approaching the research of a bankruptcy issue is relatively easy to formulate. The sources described below, used in the order of their description, should produce an answer to even the most complex issue at a minimum of time and effort.

The primary source for answering all bankruptcy questions is the Bankruptcy Code itself.[1] Most basic bankruptcy questions can be answered correctly simply by finding the right Code section.

The Code is well indexed, and by following the systems approach of this text any practitioner should generally have an easy time establishing a reference point in the Code to commence researching an issue.

It is also important to note a critical difference in statutory research versus research of other sources. Each word of a statute, and often each punctuation mark, has meaning and significance. Each word must be

---

1. U.S.C., Title 11.

understood to comprehend the full meaning of any Code provision. Careful reading is thus the most useful tool in conducting effective research of this sort.

At the end of each Code section, there is text normally entitled "Historical and Revision Notes." The Historical and Revision Notes contain a capsule description of a particular Code section's legislative history, including the section's derivation from any predecessor section under the Bankruptcy Act. Leading court decisions that interpreted any predecessor Bankruptcy Act section are often referred to in these notes. The analysis discusses the rationale of the cited cases and attempts to indicate if the Code intends to follow or modify the prior law. The analysis is helpful in interpreting the meaning of a particular provision. The Historical and Revision Notes are a valuable secondary source of finding answers to bankruptcy questions. Because these notes are included in many published editions of the Bankruptcy Code, one does not need a second volume to locate them.

The Bankruptcy Code defines the collective rules regulating the collection and distribution of assets to creditors in a bankruptcy proceeding. The Code directs what may or may not be done in a bankruptcy proceeding. However, the Code often does not direct how to implement or use a Code provision within the bankruptcy system. To direct the implementation of a Code provision in the bankruptcy system, the Administrative Office of the United States Courts, in conjunction with the United States Supreme Court, has formulated the "Rules of Practice and Procedure in Bankruptcy," commonly known as the Federal Rules of Bankruptcy Procedure. The Federal Rules of Bankruptcy Procedure direct the method of doing things in a bankruptcy proceeding: What information is required in a form? What should the form look like? How is a motion filed and when? How and when is a creditor claim filed? And so forth. Many basic questions of actual practice that are not contained in the Code are answered by the Federal Rules of Bankruptcy Procedure. The rules should never be overlooked when seeking the answer to a bankruptcy question, particularly a "how to" question.[2]

Appended to the Federal Rules of Bankruptcy Procedure is a group of forms called "Official and Procedural Bankruptcy Forms." The Official Forms provide guidance as to the content and appearance of the included documents.

In addition to the Federal Rules of Bankruptcy Procedure, each Bankruptcy Court has the power to formulate its own local rules and local

---

2. 28 U.S.C. §2075. Federal Rules of Bankruptcy Procedure.

forms as long as they are not inconsistent with the Code or the Bankruptcy Rules. Many Bankruptcy Courts have devised their own local rules and local forms, and other Bankruptcy Courts have not. Local rules vary from district to district and can sometimes be the source of answering a practice or procedure question. In addition to local Bankruptcy Court rules, each federal District Court has its own local rules. These also may sometimes help in answering a procedural question. The guidelines of any applicable United States Trustee office will also prove helpful.[3]

The Bankruptcy Courts are a part of the federal court system. The Federal Rules of Civil Procedure and the Federal Rules of Evidence apply in bankruptcy proceedings.

Practice Pointer

Not all of the Federal Rules of Civil Procedure apply to a bankruptcy proceeding. The Bankruptcy Rules specifically cite which rules and which portions of those rules apply in bankruptcy cases.

There are several reporter systems that publish only bankruptcy cases. Cases decided by Bankruptcy Courts, district courts, courts of appeal, and the Supreme Court that relate solely to bankruptcy and bankruptcy-related issues are contained within these reporter systems. The largest reporter system is called the Bankruptcy Reporter and is published by West Publishing Company. Another reporter system is called Bankruptcy Court Decisions (BCD), which is published by CRR Publishing Company. Many of the cases reported in BCD are also included in the Bankruptcy Reporter, but sometimes a case will appear in one system and not in the other. It is acceptable to cite from either set of reporters when writing a brief for a Bankruptcy Court. Sometimes the BCD will release a case before it appears in the Bankruptcy Reporter and vice versa. Collier also publishes a reporter system called Collier Bankruptcy Cases. Many of these reporter systems have also been incorporated into computer research databases such as LexisNexis or Westlaw.

In addition, there are simplified methods of conducting bankruptcy research through the use of specialized treatises. The bankruptcy system has its own separate treatises. The most commonly used and cited treatise

---

3. See chapter 10 supra.

on bankruptcy is Collier on Bankruptcy.[4] Collier's is a multivolume work, organized such that a chapter number in Collier's corresponds to the same numbered Bankruptcy Code section. Thus, Chapter 521 in Collier's corresponds precisely to Section 521 of the Bankruptcy Code. If you want to find the answer to an issue involving exemptions, which is Section 522 of the Bankruptcy Code, you simply look in Chapter 522 of Collier's. There are several other major treatises, but Collier's is cited in court opinions more frequently than any other major work.[5] The publishers of Collier's also publish a major set of practice forms and guides entitled the Collier Bankruptcy Practice Guide. The Guide contains detailed practice tools and sample pleading forms, among other things.

Often a bankruptcy issue will be determined based on existing non-bankruptcy state or federal law. In these situations, one will have to make use of traditional research sources and methods outside the bankruptcy system.

The above are the primary sources of researching a bankruptcy issue, starting with the Code and continuing to the reporter systems. With this relatively small nucleus of materials reviewed in the order described in the checklist accompanying this chapter, most bankruptcy questions can be answered effectively, efficiently, and rapidly.

B. THE INTERNET

The evolution of the Internet from the mid-1990s, has transformed accessibility to both legal and factual information to assist in conducting legal research or in investigating facts. The availability of online computer research facilities such as Westlaw or LexisNexis makes legal source materials more accessible but does not necessarily make the task of finding applicable case law any easier unless the researcher knows to search under an appropriate word, phrase, or statute.

To this extent, the above methodology can also be used in computer research. First, input the precise Code section or Rule that is the subject of your inquiry. Then narrow your search by selecting an appropriate word or phrase in the universe of cases you have located by Code section. For example, assume that you need to research an issue of the effect of oral misrepresentations in dischargeability litigation (see chapter 13 supra).

---

4. Lawrence P. King, Collier on Bankruptcy (15th ed. rev. 2008) (hereafter Collier's).
5. E.g., Norton Bankruptcy Law and Practice 2d (2008).

A word search combining the phrase "oral misrepresentation" and the word "dischargeability" appearing in the same paragraph will be likely to produce a myriad of potentially relevant cases.

In addition to enhancing legal research, the Internet provides an array of bankruptcy research access tools to the fingertips of any person with online access. Many professional bankruptcy organizations have their own websites, the most notable being that for the American Bankruptcy Institute (www.abiworld.org). This site will give you daily news and report important case and legislative developments. The Federal Judiciary Home Page (www.uscourts.gov) will allow you to access any Bankruptcy Court that has created its own website. You can find your local court and place it on your Favorites menu.

 Practice Pointer

Like the individual Bankruptcy Courts, law firms and other service providers will also frequently have their own websites offering bankruptcy information and advice online. You should always be careful to verify any information you obtain that purports to have the "answer" to your bankruptcy questions.

Federal Rule of Bankruptcy Procedure 9036 authorizes local rules to permit electronic transmission of notices and documents. Many Bankruptcy Courts now require electronic filing of petitions, a practice that will become commonplace in the near future. All Bankruptcy Courts are being gradually incorporated into what is known as the Electronic Case Filing (ECF) system. Under ECF, all pleadings are filed electronically with the Bankruptcy Court online. All documents filed with a court that has adopted ECF are accessible to attorneys who enroll in the ECF system. Parties in interest may register to receive notices of all pleadings filed in a particular case, making service of process virtually instantaneous.

Use of the Internet is important to comply with the requirements of means testing (see chapter 5 supra) and the other filing requirements imposed by the 2005 legislation. With respect to means testing, the Internet is essential to remain current with the official state median family income and the various IRS expense standards applied in computing the formula. Current links necessary for means testing compliance are located at www.usdoj.gov/ust. Additionally, as counsel's duty of reasonable investigation required by Section 707(b)(4) evolves, the Internet provides rapid access to a debtor's current credit report and sites that provide valuation data for used vehicles (e.g., NADA.com). The Internet also contains websites for approved prepetition credit counselors and postpetition financial management courses required to obtain a discharge in individual cases, as described in chapters 3 and 13 supra.

CHAPTER 31 CHECKLIST

31.1   BANKRUPTCY RESEARCH CHECKLIST

     31.1.1   Bankruptcy Code

     31.1.2   Historical and Revision Notes

     31.1.3   Federal Rules of Bankruptcy Procedure

     31.1.4   Local Rules, Including United States Trustee Guidelines

     31.1.5   Federal Rules of Civil Procedure, Federal Rules of Evidence

     31.1.6   Bankruptcy Reporter Systems

     31.1.7   Bankruptcy Treatises

DISCUSSION QUESTIONS

1. What are the basic resources to utilize in researching a bankruptcy issue?

2. Describe the role that computers can play in conducting bankruptcy research.

Appendix

Noticed Motions and Ex Parte Applications

Common Ex Parte Applications

Application	*Code Section or FRBP*
Payments to trustees	§1326
Joint Administration	FRBP 1015
Debtor requested conversion	§§706(a), 1112(a), 1208(a), 1307(a)
Debtor requested dismissal	§§1208(b), 1307(b)
Extensions of time	FRBP 9006b
Rule 2004 examinations	FRBP 2004
Deferral of entry of discharge	FRBP 4004(c)
Reopening a closed case	§350(b)
Conditional approval of disclosure statement	§1125; FRBP 3017.1

Common Noticed Motions

Motion	*Code Section or FRBP*
Dismissal of Chapter 7 as abuse	§707(b)
Compensation of professionals	§§326, 330, 331; FRBP 2016
Enforcement of bankruptcy petition preparer rules	§110

Motion	*Code Section or FRBP*
Dismissal in best interests of creditors	§305
Motion to avoid lien	§522(f)
Objection to claim of exemptions	§522(c); FRBP 4003(d)
Appointment of trustee in involuntary case	§303(g); FRBP 2001
Motion for relief from the automatic stay	§362(d); FRBP 4001
Turnover from debtor	§542; FRBP 7001(1)
Sales of property of $2,500 or more and when there is no co-owner	§363; FRBP 6004
Motion to use cash collateral	§363(c)
Motion to sell property free and clear of liens	§363(f); FRBP 6004(c)
Motion to assume or reject executory contract or unexpired lease	§365; FRBP 6006
Motion to compel abandonment	§554; FRBP 6007
Objection to claim	§502; FRBP 3007
Payment of administrative expenses	§503(a)
Valuation hearing	§506
Motion to dismiss/convert	§1112, 1307
Approval of insider compensation in Chapter 11 cases	FRBP 9014(a)
Extend or reduce exclusivity	§1121
Chapter 11 confirmation hearing	§1128

Note: A noticed motion must normally be served on all creditors, the trustee, and the United States Trustee, except for motions for relief from the automatic stay, which generally require service only upon the debtor, trustee, and any other party with an interest in any property subject to the motion (such as a junior mortgage). An ex parte application is normally served only upon the trustee and the United States Trustee and any party that has requested notice. In all situations, readers should consult any applicable local rules.

Glossary

This glossary has been designed to accomplish two goals. The first is to define basic bankruptcy terms in as succinct a manner as possible. The second is to treat the glossary as a mini-index. At the end of each definition one or more numbers will appear in parentheses. The numbers correspond to the chapter or chapters of the text that contain the primary discussion of the term or phrase defined.

abandon — to remove from property of an estate assets that are burdensome or of inconsequential value to the estate. An asset with no equity or a meritless personal injury claim are common examples. Abandonment is governed by Section 554 of the Bankruptcy Code. (20)

absolute priority rule — prohibition against confirmation of a Chapter 11 reorganization plan if junior classes will receive dividends or retain interests where one or more senior classes are not paid in full and have rejected the plan. (26)

accrual accounting — an accounting method that measures all financial transactions of an entity. A debt owed is an accrued expense. An account receivable is accrued income. (24)

adequate assurance — the providing of adequate protection to a nondebtor party to an executory contract subject to Bankruptcy Code Section 365. A trustee or debtor-in-possession assuming an executory contract must provide the nondebtor party to the contract with adequate assurance of future performance. An assignee of an executory contract must also provide adequate assurance of future performance. Providing adequate assurance includes curing existing defaults and convincing the creditor and the court that future performance will be rendered by the debtor. (19)

adequate protection — a method of protecting a creditor's interest in property of the estate during pendency of the automatic stay. The making of periodic payments or the providing of additional or replacement collateral are methods of adequate protection. Section 361 statutorily defines adequate protection. (12)

administrative expenses — generally, all expenses incurred by a bankruptcy estate after a bankruptcy filing. Trustee's fees, auctioneer fees, attorneys' fees, and postpetition rent are common Chapter 7 administrative expenses. (10, 21)

adversary proceeding — a separate lawsuit filed in connection with a bankruptcy proceeding. For example, an action to set aside a preference is commenced as an adversary proceeding. A contested motion will be treated as an adversary proceeding pursuant to Federal Rule of Bankruptcy Procedure 9014. (13)

affiliate — a nondebtor entity owning or controlling 20 percent or more interest in a debtor, or a debtor entity owning or controlling 20 percent or more interest in a nondebtor entity. Section 101(2) of the Bankruptcy Code defines affiliate. (6)

"after notice and a hearing" — a phrase statutorily defined in Section 102(1) of the Bankruptcy Code. Use of this or a similar phrase in any Bankruptcy Code provision triggers the notice requirements of Section 102(1), as placed into practice by Federal Rules of Bankruptcy Procedure 2002 and 9006. Generally, 24-day notice by mail to all creditors and parties in interest is necessary to properly accomplish many bankruptcy procedures. (4)

allowed claim — a claim entitled to receive a dividend from a bankruptcy estate. (21)

antecedent debt — a debt incurred or existing before the making of a transfer. (16)

Anti-Assignment Act — a federal statute, 41 U.S.C. §15, that prohibits the assignment of a federal government contract except upon the government's consent. (19)

applicable commitment period — the required length of time for a Chapter 13 repayment plan, dependent upon whether or not the debtor's income is higher or lower than the state median family income. If equal to or higher, the period is five years. If lower, the period is three years. (23)

assignment for the benefit of creditors — the assignment of assets to a third party, in trust, to sell the assets and apply the proceeds to the payment of creditor claims. (2)

assisted person — any person whose debts are primarily consumer debts and whose nonexempt assets are less than $175,750 pursuant to 11 U.S.C. §101(3). Assisted persons are entitled to written retainer agreements and prepetition written disclosures from Debt Relief Agencies pursuant to 11 U.S.C. §§527 and 528. (3)

automatic stay — a statutory bar to the conducting of any collection activity by creditors after a bankruptcy petition has been filed. All litigation involving the debtor as a defendant is stayed. Foreclosures and repossessions are stayed. A creditor may seek relief from the stay in some situations. The automatic stay is one of the three major elements of debtor relief provided by the Bankruptcy Code and is the subject of Bankruptcy Code Section 362. (7, 12)

avoidable preference—a prepetition transfer of estate property in full or partial payment of an antecedent debt, subject to the trustee's avoiding powers. Avoidable preferences are the subject of Bankruptcy Code Section 547. (16)

avoiding powers—the ability of a trustee to set aside certain pre- or postfiling transactions that might otherwise be valid under nonbankruptcy law. Preferences, fraudulent transfers, and the ability to set aside unauthorized postpetition transfers are the most common of the trustee's avoiding powers. (14, 15)

Bankruptcy Abuse Prevention Consumer Protection Act of 2005 (BAPCPA)—"BAPCPA" is the acronym most commonly used to identify the 2005 amendments to the Bankruptcy Code. (2)

Bankruptcy Act—the name of the bankruptcy laws in effect in the United States between 1898 and September 30, 1979. (1)

bankruptcy alternatives—assignments for the benefits of creditors, bulk sales, and composition agreements. (2)

bankruptcy assistance—goods or services provided to an assisted person for the purpose of providing advice, counsel, document preparation, or court appearance in a bankruptcy proceeding. Section 101(4A) of the Bankruptcy Code defines bankruptcy assistance. (3)

Bankruptcy Code—the name of the bankruptcy laws in effect in the United States since October 1, 1979. (2)

bankruptcy petition preparer—a person other than an attorney or an attorney's employee who prepares for compensation a document for filing with the Bankruptcy Court. An unsupervised paralegal may be a bankruptcy petition preparer. Bankruptcy petition preparers are the subject of Bankruptcy Code Section 110. (7)

bankruptcy proceeding—A bankruptcy case filed pursuant to a particular Chapter of the Bankruptcy Code. Bankruptcy proceedings are Chapter 7 liquidations and the various reorganization proceedings provided for by Chapters 9, 11, 12, and 13, as well as cross-border insolvencies under Chapter 15. (2)

bankruptcy systems—the methods developed by societies to resolve the effects of financial crisis between debtors and creditors. (1)

capital asset—an asset used to operate a business, such as equipment or fixtures. (18)

cash accounting—an accounting method that measures the cash transactions (income and expenses) of an entity. (24)

cash collateral—cash, or its equivalent, in which a secured creditor may have an interest. Section 363(c) of the Bankruptcy Code restricts the use of cash collateral absent court approval. (18)

Chapter—a specific statutory division of the Bankruptcy Code. Three Chapters contain general rules applicable in all bankruptcy proceedings (1, 3, 5). The remaining six Chapters comprise the specific types of bankruptcy proceedings (7, 9, 11, 12, 13, 15). (2)

Chapter 7—a bankruptcy proceeding in which a debtor seeks to have nonexempt assets liquidated for the payment of dividends to creditors. Chapter 7 is the most common bankruptcy proceeding. (2, 3, 7)

Chapter 11—a reorganization proceeding available to any debtor qualified to be a Chapter 7 debtor. Chapter 11 is the most complex, time-consuming, and expensive of all bankruptcy proceedings. The goal of a Chapter 11 debtor-in-possession is to obtain confirmation of a reorganization plan, a judicially approved composition agreement. (1, 2, 24-26)

Chapter 13—a reorganization proceeding available for individuals with regular income whose unsecured debt is less than $360,475 and whose secured debt is less than $1,081,400. Chapter 13 is the most commonly filed reorganization proceeding. (23)

claim—a right to payment of any kind or a right to performance that may be compensated by damages. Section 101(5) of the Bankruptcy Code defines claim. (6)

claims bar date—a deadline set in a bankruptcy proceeding for creditors to file claims. A claim not filed before expiration of a claims bar date is subordinated to all timely-filed claims. (21)

claims docket—an itemized summary of creditor claims filed in a bankruptcy proceeding. (22)

collateral—an interest in property or other rights held by a secured creditor to secure repayment of a debt. For example, real property is normally collateral for a mortgage or deed of trust. (12, 21)

community claim—a claim enforceable against community property under nonbankruptcy law. Section 101(7) of the Bankruptcy Code defines community claim. (6)

Complaint to Avoid Discharge—an adversary proceeding initiated by a trustee or an interested party to entirely avoid a debtor's discharge. Time limitations are found in Fed. R. Bankr. P. 4004. (13)

Complaint to Avoid Dischargeability of a Debt—an adversary proceeding initiated by a creditor or debtor to determine the dischargeability of a specific debt pursuant to Bankruptcy Code Section 523(c). A creditor must initiate such a complaint within 60 days of the date first set for the creditors' meeting. A debtor may initiate such a complaint at any time. Time limitations are found in Fed. R. Bankr. P. 4007. (13)

composition agreement — an agreement between a debtor and multiple creditors for the repayment of debt. The various reorganization proceedings of the Bankruptcy Code (Chapters 9, 11, 12, and 13) are judicially approved composition agreements. (1, 2)

confirmation — the act of obtaining court approval of a reorganization plan in the reorganization proceedings of Chapters 9, 11, 12, or 13. A confirmed reorganization plan creates a new binding contract between the debtor and all creditors. (23)

confirmation packet — a group of documents, including a Plan of Reorganization and a Disclosure Statement, that are sent to creditors when authorized to solicit votes for or against a Chapter 11 plan. (25)

consideration — the element of exchange in any contract. (16)

consolidation — a merger, by court order, of two or more related bankruptcy proceedings. Other than a husband and wife, who may file a joint case, consolidation is the only way in which multiple debtors may have their bankruptcy proceedings administered as if they were one debtor. Consolidation is the subject of Federal Rule of Bankruptcy Procedure 1015. (3)

consumer no asset bankruptcy — a Chapter 7 bankruptcy proceeding for an individual in which there are normally no assets available for distribution to creditors. A consumer no asset bankruptcy is the most common and simplest of all bankruptcy proceedings. (7)

contemporaneous exchange — the presence of consideration in the transfer of property from a debtor to a creditor. (16)

contested matter — an opposed motion. A contested matter is treated as an adversary proceeding pursuant to Federal Rule of Bankruptcy Procedure 9014. A contested matter is resolved by way of an evidentiary hearing. (13)

convenience class — a group of unsecured claims treated as a class for administrative convenience in a Chapter 11 reorganization plan. A convenience class may receive treatment that the Bankruptcy Code would otherwise prohibit. (25)

conversion — the act of converting a bankruptcy proceeding from one Chapter to another. A typical scenario is a failed reorganization proceeding under Chapter 11 or 13 converted to a liquidation case under Chapter 7. (8, 23)

core proceeding — a matter arising before a Bankruptcy Court that involves the specific application of a Bankruptcy Code provision for its resolution. Bankruptcy Judges have jurisdiction over core proceedings, as described in 28 U.S.C. §157. For example, an action to avoid a preference is a core proceeding. (28)

cramdown—the act of obtaining confirmation of a reorganization plan over the objection of creditors. Different tests or procedures may be utilized to effectuate a cramdown on either secured or unsecured creditors. (23)

credit counseling agency—an agency approved by the United States Trustee pursuant to 11 U.S.C. §111, to provide prepetition credit counseling to consumer debtors. (3)

creditor—an entity with a claim arising before the filing of a bankruptcy petition. Section 101(10) of the Bankruptcy Code defines creditor. An entity that a debt is owed to is a creditor. (2, 6)

creditors' meeting—a mandatory hearing, held within 40 days after the entry of an order for relief in any Chapter proceeding. At the meeting of creditors, the trustee and creditors may examine the debtor regarding the assets and liabilities of the bankruptcy estate. Section 341(a) of the Bankruptcy Code mandates the meeting of creditors. (7)

current monthly income—the monthly income of a consumer debtor generally determined by the average of income received from all sources in the six months preceding the filing of a bankruptcy petition, as described in 11 U.S.C. §101(10A). Current monthly income is a key element in determining whether or not a consumer debtor is abusing Chapter 7 pursuant to needs based bankruptcy. (5, 6, 30)

custodian—a third party appointed to administer a debtor's assets in a nonbankruptcy context. A court-appointed receiver or assignee for the benefit of creditors are examples of custodians. This term distinguishes bankruptcy trustees from nonbankruptcy fiduciaries. Section 101(11) of the Bankruptcy Code defines custodian. (6, 14)

debt—a liability upon a claim. Section 101(12) of the Bankruptcy Code defines debt. (6)

debt collection—the process of collecting a debt. (1)

debt relief agency—a bankruptcy attorney or bankruptcy petition preparer and any person providing bankruptcy assistance to assisted persons for money or other valuable consideration pursuant to 11 U.S.C. §101(12A). Debt Relief Agencies are subject to written retainer and disclosure requirements of 11 U.S.C. §§527 and 528. (3)

debtor—an entity that owes a debt. The entity filing a voluntary bankruptcy proceeding or against whom an order for relief is entered in an involuntary bankruptcy is known as the debtor. Section 101(13) of the Bankruptcy Code defines debtor. (2)

debtor-in-possession—the fiduciary entity created by a debtor filing a Chapter 11 reorganization proceeding. (7, 10)

debtor relief—what an individual filing personal bankruptcy seeks: a discharge, exemptions, and the benefits of the automatic stay. (1)

disallowed claim—a claim not entitled to receive a dividend from a bankruptcy estate. (21)

discharge—legal relief from debt provided for by Section 524 of the Bankruptcy Code. The discharge is one of the three elements of debtor relief provided for in the Bankruptcy Code, the other two being exemptions and the automatic stay. In certain defined instances a debtor may not be entitled to a discharge. (1, 7)

dischargeable debt—a debt subject to a debtor's discharge. The discharge relieves a debtor from personal liability for the debt. (7, 13)

disclosure statement—a document filed in a Chapter 11 proceeding that describes a debtor-in-possession's reorganization plan, its effect upon the creditors, the ability of the plan to be performed, and a comparison of the reorganization plan's repayment proposal to the results likely to be obtained in a Chapter 7 proceeding for the same debtor. The creditors of a Chapter 11 debtor-in-possession may not vote for or against the reorganization plan until the court approves the contents of the disclosure statement at a disclosure statement hearing. (25, 26)

disinterested person—The subject of Bankruptcy Code Section 101(14). A person who is not creditor, equity security holder, or insider, or who does not have an interest materially adverse to an estate. Only disinterested persons may be employed by a bankruptcy estate or debtor-in-possession. (7, 24)

dismissal—the act of terminating a bankruptcy proceeding, the general effect of which is to restore the parties to their rights and liabilities as they existed prior to the bankruptcy filing. (8)

disposable income—all income not necessary for the maintenance or support of the debtor or a dependent of the debtor. (23)

domestic support obligation—obligations for alimony, support, or maintenance, regardless of when incurred. Section 101(14A) of the Bankruptcy Code defines domestic support obligation. (6)

due process—notice and an opportunity to be heard. (4)

effective date of the plan—a specific date upon which performance of a Chapter 11 plan begins. This date may be a specific date upon which a defined event occurs, such as an order of confirmation becoming final. (25)

Electronic Case Filing (ECF)—The name for online filing of documents with the bankruptcy court and accessibility thereto. A related system know as "Pacer" affords access to review of online court records. (31)

equity or **equity cushion** — the value in an asset over and above that of any liens or encumbrances, such as equity in a home or motor vehicle. (9, 21)

equity security holder — an entity owning an interest in a debtor. The shareholders of a corporate debtor are its equity security holders. The partners of a partnership are its equity security holders. Section 101(17) of the Bankruptcy Code defines equity security holder. (6)

estate — the debtor's property owned at the time of the bankruptcy filing. The estate is created by the filing of a bankruptcy proceeding. The estate is administered by the trustee. (14)

evidentiary hearing — a hearing held to take sworn testimony to permit a Bankruptcy Court to make a decision in a contested matter that is not a separate adversary proceeding. An evidentiary hearing is similar to a trial in a nonbankruptcy environment. A "trial" on a contested motion for relief from the automatic stay is properly called an evidentiary hearing. (12)

ex parte — an application made to the court without notice or with limited notice to limited parties. Ex parte applications are specifically permitted for various ministerial functions. In other circumstances, a legitimate extraordinary circumstance must exist for the court to consider ex parte relief. (4)

examiner — an individual appointed in a Chapter 11 proceeding to conduct an independent investigation of some or all of a debtor's financial affairs. (10)

exclusivity period — a period of time in a Chapter 11 proceeding when only the debtor-in-possession may file a reorganization plan. This period, as provided for in Section 1121 of the Bankruptcy Code, is the first 120 days from the entry of an order for relief. In small business cases, the period is 180 days. This period can be extended. The period terminates upon the appointment of a trustee. (25)

executory contract — contracts for which performance remains due to some extent on both sides. Franchise or license agreements are common executory contracts. Executory contracts are the subject of Bankruptcy Code Section 365. An executory contract may be assumed or rejected. (19)

exemptions — statutorily defined property that an individual debtor may protect from administration by a bankruptcy estate. Exempt property is not available for liquidation to pay a dividend to creditors; a debtor may keep exempt property. Exemptions are a primary element of debtor relief. (1, 9)

family farmer — a debtor meeting the filing qualifications for a Chapter 12 proceeding. A family farmer may be an individual, corporate, or partnership debtor. In the latter two instances, more than 50 percent of the ownership must belong to members of the same family. A qualified family farmer's total debt may not exceed $3,792,650. Section 101(18) of the Bankruptcy Code defines family farmer. (27)

family fisherman — a debtor meeting the qualifications for a Chapter 12 proceeding. A family fisherman may be an individual, corporate, or partnership debtor. In the latter two instances, at least 50 percent of the ownership must belong to the same family. A qualified family fisherman's total debt may not exceed $1,757,475 and at least 80 percent must be related to the fishing operation. Section 101(19A) defines family fisherman. (27)

feasibility requirement — finding that the Bankruptcy Court must make to permit confirmation of a Chapter 11 reorganization plan. (26)

federal exemptions — exemptions permitted under federal law, specifically Section 522(d) of the Bankruptcy Code. (9)

federal judges — judges appointed to the federal bench pursuant to U.S. Const., art. III, §2. (28)

Federal Rules of Bankruptcy Procedure — national rules promulgated to govern practice in all bankruptcy proceedings. (4, 31)

fiduciary — an entity that holds assets in trust for another. A bankruptcy trustee is a fiduciary. (10)

first-day order — common name of orders entered within the first day or two of a large corporate Chapter 11 filing. (24)

floating lien — a line of credit from a bank, financial institution, or other lender secured by the existing and after-acquired inventory, equipment, and proceeds of a debtor's business. (16, 17)

fraudulent transfer — a transfer made by a debtor with an intent to hinder, delay, or defraud creditors. A transfer without reasonable or fair consideration made while a debtor is insolvent or that renders a debtor insolvent will also be fraudulent. Fraudulent transfers are the subject of Bankruptcy Code Section 548. Fraudulent transfers are one of the trustee's avoiding powers. (17)

fresh cash rule — portion of a debt incurred by use of a false written financial statement. (13)

fresh start — the phrase most frequently used colloquially to describe the basic elements of debtor relief: discharge, exemptions, and the automatic stay. (7, 9)

gap claim — a claim arising during the period of time between the filing of an involuntary petition and the entry of an order for relief. (3, 21)

gap period — the common term for the period of time between the filing of an involuntary petition and the entry of an order for relief. (3, 21)

health care business — a business that provides health care services. Special rules apply for a trustee's disposition of health care business records and for the placement of patients in alternative facilities. The court will appoint an ombudsman to speak for the best interests of the patients unless the court can find that such an appointment is not necessary. Section 101(27A) of the Bankruptcy Code defines health care business. (10, 20)

homestead exemption — an exemption permitted in an individual debtor's place of residence. Section 522(d)(1) of the Bankruptcy Code provides a federal homestead exemption. State law also provides homestead exemptions. (9)

impaired claim — a claim not paid according to its terms on the effective date of a Chapter 11 plan. For example, unsecured creditors who are to be paid over an extended period of time are impaired. An impaired class of claims is entitled to vote to accept or reject a Chapter 11 reorganization plan. (25)

insider — generally, an entity in control of a debtor or a debtor's relatives. The definition of an insider will vary depending upon the debtor's identity as an individual, partnership, or corporation. Section 101(31) of the Bankruptcy Code defines insider. (6)

insolvent — an entity is generally insolvent when its liabilities exceed its assets. Section 101(32) of the Bankruptcy Code defines insolvency. (6, 16)

intellectual property — patents, copyrights, and trademarks. Section 101(35A) of the Bankruptcy Code defines intellectual property. (19)

interim trustee — the trustee appointed by the United States Trustee to administer a bankruptcy estate prior to the meeting of creditors called for by Section 341(a) of the Bankruptcy Code. The interim trustee will become the permanent trustee unless the creditors elect a different trustee at the meeting of creditors. (7)

inventory — any form of personal property that a debtor uses to produce revenue. (16)

involuntary petition — a bankruptcy proceeding initiated by one or more creditors (or general partners of a partnership) by filing a petition seeking the entry of an order for relief; a judgment that the debtor is bankrupt. Section 303 of the Bankruptcy Code governs involuntary petitions. (3)

ipso facto clause — a clause in a contract defining insolvency or a bankruptcy filing as an act of default. These clauses generally are not enforceable in bankruptcy proceedings. (14, 18)

joint case — a bankruptcy proceeding involving an individual and the individual's spouse. (3)

judicial lien—a lien arising by virtue of a court order or judgment. A judicial lien may be a prejudgment writ of attachment or a postjudgment writ of execution. Section 101(36) of the Bankruptcy Code defines judicial lien. (6)

lien—a right to property to secure repayment of a debt or the performance of an obligation. A lien may be a judicial, consensual, or statutory lien. Section 101(37) of the Bankruptcy Code defines lien. (6)

liquidation—the sale of an estate's assets to repay creditors. A Chapter 7 bankruptcy is a liquidation proceeding. A Chapter 11 plan may provide for liquidation of the estate rather than reorganization. (2, 23)

liquidation analysis—portion of a Disclosure Statement comparing a reorganization plan to the results likely to be obtained if the case were a Chapter 7. (26)

liquidation value—the value to be obtained from a forced sale of assets. (9)

mandatory provision—a provision in a reorganization plan required by the Bankruptcy Code. (23)

market value—the value of an asset, real or personal, sold in the ordinary course of business according to commercially reasonable terms. (9)

means testing—title given to formula contained in 11 U.S.C. §707(b)(2) to determine whether or not a consumer debtor is presumed to be abusing the bankruptcy system by filing a Chapter 7. Abuse is presumed when a debtor's current monthly income exceeds the state median family income and the debtor can repay unsecured creditors at least $117.08 per month over 60 months ($7,025) and a dividend of at least 25 percent or can repay unsecured creditors at least $11,725 over 60 months without regard to the percentage repaid. Where abuse is presumed, the case will be dismissed unless the debtor consents to conversion to Chapter 13. (5)

median family income—the most current figures provided by the Bureau of the Census as set forth in 11 U.S.C. §101(39A). The amount of median family income determines whether or not a debtor is subject to needs based bankruptcy analysis. (5, 6)

motion for relief from the automatic stay—a motion made by a creditor, pursuant to 11 U.S.C. §362(d), to be freed from the effect of the automatic stay. (4, 12)

new value—the providing of new consideration in a transaction between a debtor and creditor. An avoidable preference will generally not exist where a transaction occurs for new value. This definition is unique to avoidable preferences. (16)

noncapital asset — an asset not used to operate a business. For example, inventory is generally a noncapital asset. (18)

noncore proceedings — matters that are related to a bankruptcy proceeding but that do not require specific application of a Bankruptcy Code provision for the matter's resolution. (28)

nondischargeable debt — a debt not subject to a debtor's discharge; a debtor is not relieved from personal or legal liability for the affected debt. Some types of nondischargeable debts require the filing of a Complaint to Determine Dischargeability of Debt for the debt to become nondischargeable. Nondischargeable debts are described in Bankruptcy Code Section 523(a). (13)

nonpurchase money security interest — a security interest in collateral where the purpose of the loan is other than to purchase the collateral. (9)

nonresidential lease — a real property lease obtained for purposes other than to reside in the leased premises. The lease of a store is a common nonresidential real property lease. (14)

notice and a hearing — Bankruptcy Code phrase, which triggers some form of due process, such as a noticed motion, notice of intent, or ex parte application. (4)

notice of intent — the common method of providing notice to creditors, when required, to properly accomplish a bankruptcy procedure. This procedure is also sometimes known as a "notice of intended action." Generally, 24 days' notice by mail upon all creditors and parties in interest is necessary to properly accomplish many bankruptcy procedures. (4)

noticed motion — a motion brought by a party in interest seeking a ruling from the Bankruptcy Court. (4)

Official Creditors' Committee — entity created in a Chapter 11 proceeding to act on the collective behalf of unsecured creditors. (10)

ombudsman — an independent person who may be appointed to serve the best interests of patients in the bankruptcy of a health care business. An ombudsman may also be appointed to report to the court on the protection of personally identifiable information in the sale of customer lists. (10)

operating reports — a regular report of a Chapter 11 debtor-in-possession's postpetition financial activity. Local rules will normally require the filing of monthly reports. (24)

order for relief — a statutory term of art, which signifies that a debtor has obtained bankruptcy relief. (3)

ordinary course of business — generally, normal everyday business transactions. (18, 20)

party in interest — a party with a stake in the outcome of a bankruptcy proceeding. The debtor, creditors, trustee, United States Trustee, and equity security holders are all parties in interest. (10)

permissive provision — a provision in a reorganization that is not mandatory. (23)

person — any kind of entity — individual, corporate, or partnership — except a governmental unit. Section 101(41) of the Bankruptcy Code defines person for purposes of the Bankruptcy Code. (6)

personally identifiable information — information that may generally be used to contact or locate an individual, such as name and address, Social Security number, date of birth, and other similar information. Section 101(41A) of the Bankruptcy Code defines personally identifiable information. (10)

petitioning creditors — creditors initiating an involuntary petition against a debtor. (3)

plan — a Chapter 13 plan. (23)

Plan of Reorganization — common title of a Chapter 11 reorganization plan. (25)

postpetition transfer — a transfer of estate property after a bankruptcy filing that is made without court approval or is not otherwise authorized by the Bankruptcy Code. An unauthorized postpetition transaction may be avoided by a bankruptcy trustee. Postpetition transactions are the subject of Bankruptcy Code Section 549. (17)

preference — a transfer of property or an interest in property to a creditor, on the eve of bankruptcy, in full or partial satisfaction of debt to the exclusion of other creditors. A preference meeting certain defined conditions will be avoidable by a bankruptcy trustee. (16)

prepackaged bankruptcy — an effort at a composition agreement, which nonetheless ends up in Bankruptcy Court. (26)

prepetition credit counseling — counseling that a debtor must receive from a credit counseling agency as a prerequisite to seeking individual bankruptcy relief. (3)

priority claim — a claim given priority over other unsecured claims. Section 507(a) of the Bankruptcy Code describes priority claims. Tax claims and certain wage claims are common priority claims. (21)

pro forma — a financial forecast of future performance over a period of time. Pro formas are frequently used in Chapter 11 plan practice. (26)

pro rata — a distribution to creditors within a given class on a proportional basis. (22)

professional — an attorney, accountant, auctioneer, appraiser, and the like. A professional rendering services to a bankruptcy estate must be approved by the court for the services to be compensable. The fees of a professional rendering services to a bankruptcy estate are subject to court approval by way of a fee application as described in Bankruptcy Code Sections 330 and 331. (7)

proof of claim — the filing of a formal written claim by a creditor in a bankruptcy proceeding. A proof of claim must always be filed in a Chapter 7 proceeding for a claim to be entitled to receive a dividend. It is always wise to file a proof of claim on behalf of a creditor. (21)

property of the estate — property subject to administration by a bankruptcy trustee for the distribution of dividends to creditors. (14, 23)

purchase money security interest — a security interest in collateral when the purpose of the loan is to purchase the collateral. (9)

reaffirmation agreement — a debtor's agreement to remain legally liable for repayment of a debt otherwise dischargeable in a bankruptcy proceeding. For a debt to be legally reaffirmed, strict compliance with the provisions of Bankruptcy Code Section 524 is required. (7)

receivable — a right to payment, whether or not such right has been earned by performance. (16)

redemption — a right given a Chapter 7 consumer debtor to pay a lump sum to a secured creditor in an amount equal to the value of any collateral. A valuation hearing may be necessary to determine the adequacy of the redemption amount. Section 722 of the Bankruptcy Code permits redemption. (21)

regular income — income sufficient and stable enough to support performance of a Chapter 13 plan by an individual. Regular income is not limited to wages or salary. Pension, Social Security, and commission income may all constitute regular income for Chapter 13 purposes. (4)

reorganization — a bankruptcy proceeding where a debtor seeks confirmation of a plan that will repay creditors while permitting the debtor to retain assets or continue in business. The proceedings permitted by Chapters 9, 11, 12, and 13 of the Bankruptcy Code are reorganization proceedings. (2, 23)

reorganization plan — a repayment plan prepared according to the requirements of Chapter 11 of the Bankruptcy Code. (25)

residential real property — real property in which a debtor resides. (19)

Rule 2004 Examination — an extended examination of any person pursuant to Federal Rule of Bankruptcy Procedure 2004 regarding one or more aspects of a debtor's financial affairs. A Rule 2004 Examination is similar to a deposition in nonbankruptcy proceedings. (7)

sale free and clear of liens — a sale held pursuant to 11 U.S.C. §363(f). Such a sale seeks court approval to sell liened property over the objection of any lienholder. (18)

Schedules of Assets and Liabilities — a fundamental bankruptcy pleading consisting of a prioritized and itemized list of a debtor's assets (property) and liabilities (debt). (3, 29)

secured creditor — a creditor with collateral that may satisfy part or all of the creditor's allowed claim. (21)

security — commercial documents used to evidence an ownership interest in an entity, among other things. Section 101(49) of the Bankruptcy Code defines security. (6)

security agreement — an agreement creating a security interest. A security interest is a consensual lien created by agreement. Section 101(50) of the Bankruptcy Code defines security agreement. (6)

serial filing or serial bankruptcy — a debtor who files a second (or third) bankruptcy proceeding after dismissal of one or more prior proceedings. (4, 12)

setoff — the common law right of a creditor to balance mutual debts with a debtor. (17)

single asset real estate — real property that encompasses a single property or project and that generates substantially all the gross income of a debtor and on which no substantial business is conducted other than operation of the property and activities thereto, not including residential real property with three or fewer units. Single asset real estate is defined in Bankruptcy Code Section 101(51B). (6)

small business debtor — a Chapter 11 debtor with liquidated debts not in excess of $2,343,300 who elects treatment as a small business debtor, excluding a debtor whose primary activity is owning and operating real estate. Small business debtors are defined in Bankruptcy Code Section 101(51D). (10, 24)

solvent estate — an estate capable of paying all claims in full and returning assets to the debtor. (22)

spendthrift trust — a trust containing a clause precluding invasion of the trust assets to satisfy the debts of a beneficiary. (14)

stacking — individual joint debtors claiming state and federal exemptions. (9)

Statement of Financial Affairs — a fundamental bankruptcy pleading consisting of a questionnaire concerning a debtor's financial affairs. (3, 29)

Statement of Intention — a notice to be given, within 30 days after a filing, to the holders of collateral security the repayment of consumer debt. The debtor must advise any affected creditor of the debtor's intention regarding the collateral. The debtor may reaffirm the contact, redeem or return the collateral, or avoid the lien under specific defined circumstances. (21)

Statements and Schedules — common name of the Statement of Financial Affairs and Schedules of Assets and Liabilities filed by any debtor within the bankruptcy system. These pleadings will be the most important initial pleadings in any bankruptcy proceeding. (3, 29)

statutory lien — a lien created by operation of law other than a court order. A state law mechanic's lien is a statutory lien. Section 101(53) of the Bankruptcy Code defines statutory lien. (6, 15)

strip off/strip down — ability to avoid the unsecured portion of an otherwise secured debt in some circumstances in Chapter 13 cases. (21, 23)

strong arm clause — the trustee's rights as a super-creditor, which are contained in the Bankruptcy Code Section 544. (15)

subordination — the relegation of a claim to a lesser status than it is otherwise entitled to under the Bankruptcy Code. A creditor may consent to subordination or the court may order subordination for equitable reasons. Subordination is the subject of Section 510. (21)

substantially consummated — the taking of an irrevocable act in performance of a Chapter 11 plan, such as closing escrow or repaying a substantial portion of a dividend. (26)

substantially contemporaneous — an exchange taking place in the normal course of business. (16)

30/30/30 rule — time periods within which a motion for relief from the automatic stay must be resolved, as described in Bankruptcy Code Section 362(e). (12)

transfer — any means that may be devised to dispose of property or an interest in property. This is an intentionally broad definition. Section 101(54) of the Bankruptcy Code defines transfer. (6, 16)

trustee — a fiduciary appointed by the United States Trustee to administer a bankruptcy estate. (2, 10)

turnover complaint — the right of a bankruptcy trustee under 11 U.S.C. §542 to recover property of an estate in the possession of the debtor or other third party. A trustee generally obtains a turnover by filing a turnover complaint. (14)

undersecured creditor — a secured creditor whose collateral is worth less than the total amount of its allowed claim. (21)

unimpaired claim — a claim paid according to its terms on the effective date of a Chapter 11 reorganization plan. For example, if a debtor-in-possession pays all unsecured claims in full on the effective date of a plan, the claims are unimpaired. An unimpaired class of claims will be deemed to have accepted a Chapter 11 plan. (25)

United States Trustee — a division of the Department of Justice responsible for monitoring the administration of bankruptcy estates. (10)

unlisted debt — a debt not included in a debtor's schedules. (13)

valuation hearing — a hearing held, pursuant to 11 U.S.C. §506, to determine the value of a secured creditor's collateral. (21)

venue — the proper Bankruptcy Court (federal district) in which a bankruptcy proceeding should be commenced. Generally, venue is where the debtor resides or where the debtor business's primary business address or assets are located. Venue may be changed by a motion of a party in interest. (3)

voluntary petition — a bankruptcy proceeding initiated by a debtor filing a petition for relief. Most bankruptcy proceedings are voluntary. (3)

Table of Cases

Table of Statutes

Uniform Commercial Code

Miscellaneous State Statutes

Table of Federal Rules of Bankruptcy Procedure

Table of
Secondary Authorities

Report of the Commission on the Bankruptcy Laws of the United States, H.R. Doc. No. 137, 82d
    Cong., 1st Sess., pt. I, ch. 17 (1973), 15

Riesenfeld, Evolution of Modern Bankruptcy Law, 31 Minn. L. Rev. 401 (1947), 9, 11-12, 14, S.
    Rep. No. 989, 95th Cong., 2d Sess. 81 (1978), 10-11, 13, 15

S. Rep. No. 989 95th Cong., 2d Sess. 94 (1978), 126, 135

Uniform Fraudulent Transfer Act, 7A U.L.A. 7 (West Supp. 1985), 269

Wolf, Neal, The Enterprise Bankruptcy Law of the People's Republic of China, Bankruptcy Strate-
    gist Vol. 25 No. 9 (July 2008), 16

www.uscourts.gov, 20
www.census.gov, 376
www.usdoj.gov/ust, 512

Index